Creative Beading VOL. 10

The best projects from a year of *Bead&Button* magazine

KALMBACH BOOKS
WAUKESHA, WI

Kalmbach Books
21027 Crossroads Circle
Waukesha, Wisconsin 53186
www.Kalmbach.com/Books

Published in 2015
19 18 17 16 15 1 2 3 4 5

Manufactured in China

ISBN: 978-1-62700-201-1
EISBN: 978-1-62700-202-8

The material in this book has appeared previously in *Bead&Button* magazine. Bead&Button is registered as a trademark.

Editor: Erica Swanson
Book Design: Kelly Katlaps
Illustrator: Kellie Jaeger
Photographers: William Zuback, James Forbes

Publisher's Cataloging-In-Publication Data

Creative beading : the best projects from a year of Bead&Button magazine.

v. : ill.

Annual
Vol. [1] (2006)-
Description based on: vol. 7 (2012).
Latest issue consulted: vol. 7 (2012).
Material in each volume appeared in the previous year's issues of Bead&Button magazine.
Includes index.

1. Beadwork—Periodicals. 2. Beads—Periodicals. 3. Jewelry making—Periodicals. I. Kalmbach Publishing Company. II. Title: Bead&Button magazine.

TT860 .C743
745.594/2

Contents

48

54

65

72

88

94

114

136

152

163

182

202

210

218

240

249

Introduction

Welcome to *Creative Beading, Volume 10*, our annual compendium of the best projects from a year of *Bead&Button* magazine. Our contributors around the globe have been inspired by a multitude of different beads and techniques in the past year, and we've highlighted a wide range of styles in this collection of pieces.

Whether you'd like to create a beautiful, intricate necklace or everyday bracelets, earrings, and rings, the jewelry in this collection showcases many of the timeless techniques you love. Explore herringbone and peyote stitch, or branch out into new standards, such as cubic right-angle weave or soutache bead embroidery. All of the projects and techniques are presented with the complete, easy-to-follow instructions that *Bead&Button* is known for.

As in previous volumes, the projects have been grouped into three categories—single stitch projects, multi-stitch projects, and other techniques. You'll find projects in varying skill levels, from easy to more challenging, in each chapter. With more than 75 options, it's a snap to pick a project that suits your style.

So gather your beading needles and jump right into *Creative Beading, Volume 10.*

Happy beading!

Julia Gerlach
Editor, *Bead&Button*

Tools & Materials

Excellent tools and materials for making jewelry are available in bead and craft stores, through catalogs, and on the Internet. Here are the essential supplies you'll need for the projects in this book.

TOOLS

Chainnose pliers have smooth, flat inner jaws, and the tips taper to a point. Use them for gripping, bending wire, and for opening and closing loops and jump rings.

Roundnose pliers have smooth, tapered, conical jaws used to make loops. The closer to the tip you work, the smaller the loop will be.

Use the front of a **wire cutters'** blades to make a pointed cut and the back of the blades to make a flat cut. Do not use your jewelry-grade wire cutters on memory wire, which is extremely hard; use heavy-duty wire cutters, or bend the memory wire back and forth until it breaks.

Crimping pliers have two grooves in their jaws that are used to fold and roll a crimp tube into a compact shape.

Make it easier to open split rings by inserting the curved jaw of **split-ring pliers** between the wires.

Beading needles are coded by size. The higher the number, the finer the beading needle. Unlike sewing needles, the eye of a beading needle is almost as narrow as its shaft. In addition to the size of the bead, the number of times you will pass through the bead also affects the needle size that you will use; if you will pass through a bead multiple times, you need to use a thinner needle.

A **hammer** is used to harden wire or texture metal. Any hammer with a flat head will work, as long as the head is free of nicks that could mar your metal. The light ball-peen hammer shown here is one of the most commonly used hammers for jewelry making.

A **bench block** provides a hard, smooth surface on which to hammer wire and metal pieces. An anvil is similarly hard but has different surfaces, such as a tapered horn, to help form different shapes.

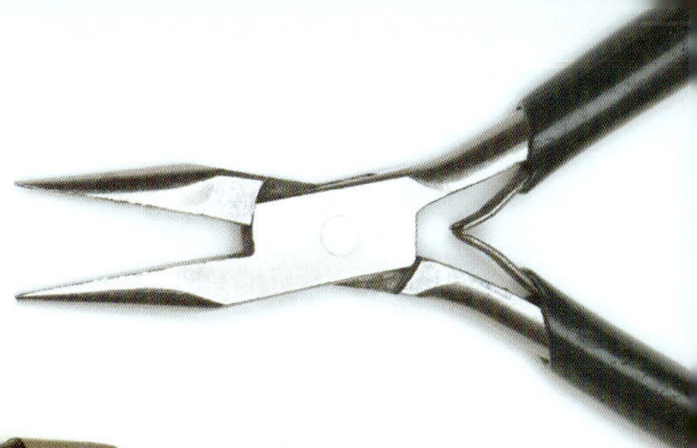

chainnose pliers

hammer

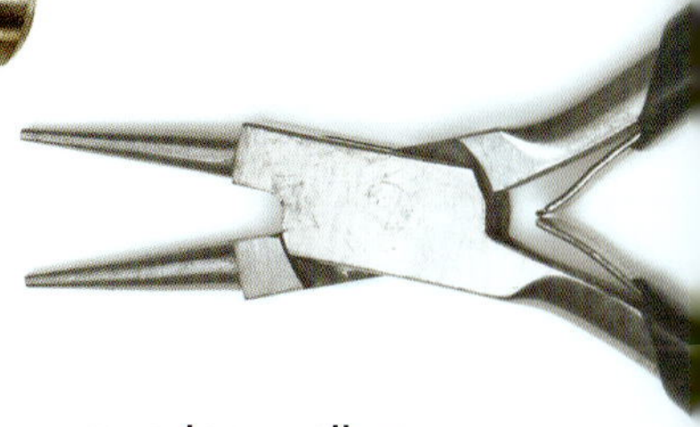

roundnose pliers

wire cutters

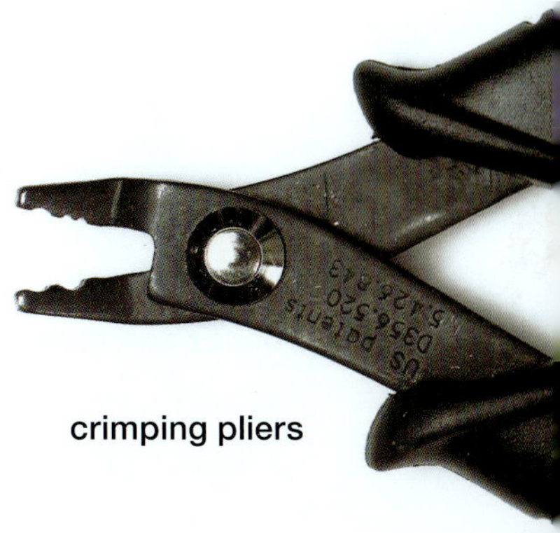

crimping pliers

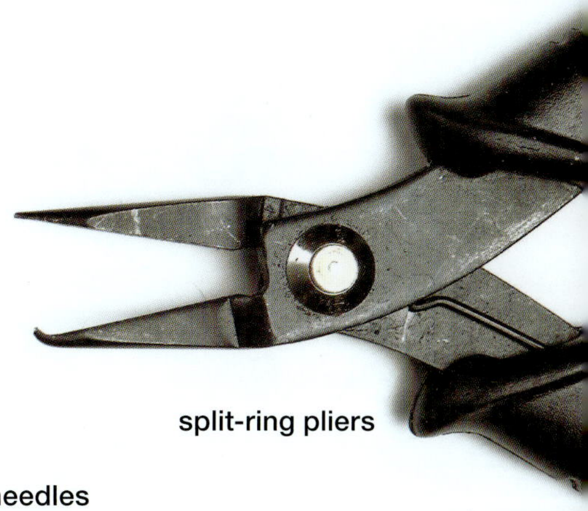

split-ring pliers

beading needles

bench block

Tools & Materials

head pin

eye pin

jump rings

split ring

crimp beads and tubes

clasps

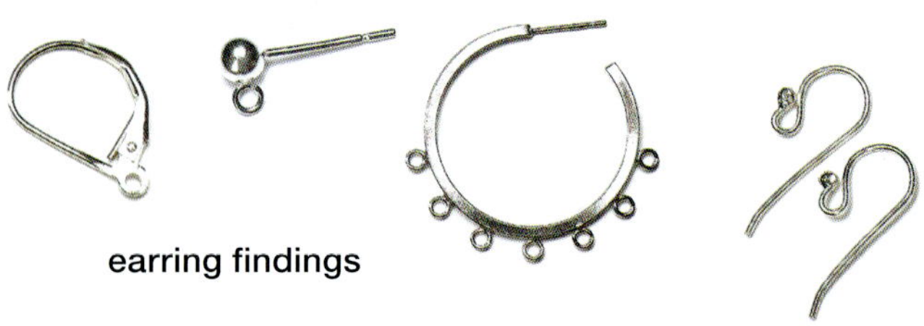
earring findings

FINDINGS

A **head pin** looks like a long, blunt, thick sewing pin. It has a flat or decorative head on one end to keep beads on. Head pins come in different diameters (gauges) and lengths.

Eye pins are just like head pins except they have a round loop on one end instead of a head. You can make your own eye pins from wire.

A **jump ring** is used to connect components. It is a small wire circle or oval that is either soldered closed or comes with a cut so it can be opened and closed.

Split rings are used like jump rings but are much more secure. They look like tiny key rings and are made of springy wire.

Crimp beads and tubes are small, large-holed, thin-walled metal beads designed to be flattened or crimped into a tight roll. Use them when stringing jewelry on flexible beading wire.

Clasps come in many sizes and shapes. Some of the most common (clockwise from the top left) are the toggle, consisting of a ring and a bar; slide, consisting of one tube that slides inside another; lobster claw, which opens when you pull on a tiny lever; S-hook, which links two soldered jump rings or split rings; and box, with a tab and a slot.

Earring findings come in a huge variety of metals and styles, including (from left to right) lever back, post, hoop, and French hook. You will almost always want a loop (or loops) on earring findings so you can attach beads.

WIRE

Wire is available in a number of materials and finishes, including brass, gold, gold-filled, gold-plated, fine silver, sterling silver, anodized niobium (chemically colored wire), and copper. Brass, copper, and craft wire are packaged in 10- to 40-yd. (9.1–37 m) spools, while gold, silver, and niobium are sold by the foot or ounce. Wire thickness is measured by gauge—the higher the gauge number, the thinner the wire. It is available in varying hardnesses (dead-soft, half-hard, and hard) and shapes (round, half-round, square, and others).

STITCHING & STRINGING MATERIALS

Selecting beading thread and cord is one of the most important decisions you'll make when planning a project. Review the descriptions below to evaluate which material is best for your design.

Threads come in many sizes and strengths. Size (diameter or thickness) is designated by a letter or number. OO and A/O are the thinnest; B, D, E, F, and FF are subsequently thicker. **Cord** is measured on a number scale; 0 corresponds in thickness to D-size thread, 1 equals E, 2 equals F, and 3 equals FF.

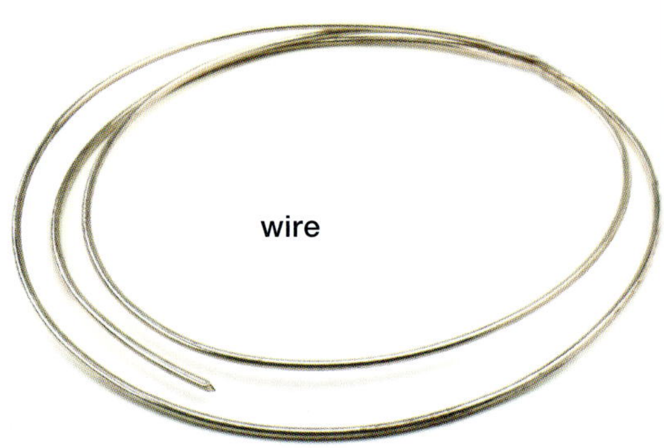
wire

Parallel filament nylon, such as Nymo or C-Lon, is made from many thin nylon fibers that are extruded and heat-set to form a single-ply thread. Parallel filament nylon is durable and easy to thread, but it can be prone to fraying and stretching. It is best used in beadweaving and bead embroidery.

Plied nylon thread, such as Silamide, is made from two or more nylon threads that are extruded, twisted together, and coated or bonded for further strength, making them strong and durable. It is more resistant to fraying than parallel filament nylon, and some brands do not stretch. It's a good material to use for twisted fringe, bead crochet, and beadwork that needs a lot of body.

Plied gel-spun polyethylene (GSP), such as Power Pro or DandyLine, is made from polyethylene fibers that have been spun into two or more threads that are braided together. It is almost unbreakable, it doesn't stretch, and it resists fraying. The thickness can make it difficult to make multiple passes through a bead. It is ideal for stitching with larger beads, such as pressed glass and crystals.

Parallel filament GSP, such as Fireline, is a single-ply thread made from spun and bonded polyethylene fibers. It's extremely strong, it doesn't stretch, and it resists fraying. However, crystals will cut through parallel filament GSP, and smoke-colored varieties can leave a black residue on hands and beads. It's most appropriate for bead stitching.

Polyester thread, such as Gutermann, is made from polyester fibers that are spun into single yarns and then twisted into plied thread. It doesn't stretch and comes in many colors, but it can become fuzzy with use. It is best for bead crochet or bead embroidery when the thread must match the fabric.

Flexible beading wire is composed of wires twisted together and covered with nylon. This wire is stronger than thread and does not stretch. The higher the number of inner strands (between 3 and 49), the more flexible and kink-resistant the wire. It is available in a variety of sizes. Use .014 and .015 for stringing most gemstones, crystals, and glass beads. Use thicker varieties, .018, .019, and .024, for heavy beads or nuggets. Use thinner wire, .010 and .012, for lightweight pieces and beads with very small holes, such as pearls. The thinnest wires can also be used for some bead-stitching projects.

flexible beading wire

nylon threads

parallel filament GSP

Tools & Materials

seed beads

SEED BEADS

cube beads

triangle beads

drop beads

A huge variety of beads is available, but the beads most commonly used in the projects in this book are **seed beads.** Seed beads come in packages, tubes, and hanks. A standard hank (a looped bundle of beads strung on thread) contains 12 20-in. (51 cm) strands, but vintage hanks are often much smaller. Tubes and packages are usually measured in grams and vary in size.

Seed beads have been manufactured in many sizes ranging from the largest, 5º (also called "E beads"), which are about 5 mm wide, to tiny size 20º or 22º, which aren't much larger than grains of sand. (The symbol º stands for "aught" or "zero." The greater the number of aughts, e.g., 22º, the smaller the bead.) Beads smaller than Japanese 15ºs have not been produced for the past 100 years, but vintage beads can be found in limited sizes and colors. The most commonly available size in the widest range of colors is 11º.

Most round seed beads are made in Japan and the Czech Republic. **Czech seed beads** are slightly irregular and rounder than **Japanese seed beads,** which are uniform in size and a bit squared off. Czech beads give a bumpier surface when woven, but they reflect light at a wider range of angles. Japanese seed beads produce a uniform surface and texture. Japanese and Czech seed beads can be used together, but a Japanese seed bead is slightly larger than the same size Czech seed bead.

Seed beads also come in sparkly cut versions. Japanese **hex-cut** or hex beads are formed with six sides. **2-** or **3-cut** Czech beads are less regular. **Charlottes** have an irregular facet cut on one side of the bead.

Japanese **cylinder beads,** otherwise known as Delicas (the Miyuki brand name), Toho Treasures (the brand name of Toho), and Toho Aikos are extremely popular for peyote stitch projects. These beads are very regular and have large holes, which are useful for stitches requiring multiple thread passes. The beads fit together almost seamlessly, producing a smooth, fabric-like surface.

Bugle beads are thin glass tubes. They can be sized by number or length, depending on where they are made. Japanese size 1 bugles are about 2 mm long, but bugles can be made even longer than 30 mm. They can be hex-cut, straight, or twisted, but the selection of colors, sizes, shapes, and finishes is limited. Seed beads also come in a variety of other shapes, including **triangles, cubes,** and **drops.**

In stitches where the beads meet each other end to end or side by side — peyote stitch, brick stitch, and square stitch — try using Japanese cylinder beads to achieve a smooth, flat surface. For a more textured surface, use Czech or round Japanese seed beads. For right-angle weave, in which groups of four or more beads form circular stitches, the rounder the seed bead, the better; otherwise you risk having gaps. Round seed beads also are better for netting and strung jewelry.

Czech seed beads

twisted bugle beads

hex-cut beads

Basics

THREAD AND KNOTS

Adding thread

To add a thread, sew into the beadwork several rows or rounds prior to the point where the last bead was added, leaving a short tail. Follow the thread path of the stitch, tying a few half-hitch knots (see "Half-hitch knot") between beads as you go, and exit where the last stitch ended. Trim the short tail.

Conditioning thread

Use beeswax or microcrystalline wax (not candle wax or paraffin) or Thread Heaven to condition nylon beading thread and Fireline. Wax smooths nylon fibers and adds tackiness that will stiffen your beadwork slightly. Thread Heaven adds a static charge that causes the thread to repel itself, so don't use it with doubled thread. Both conditioners help thread resist wear. To condition, stretch nylon thread to remove the curl (Fireline doesn't stretch). Lay the thread or Fireline on top of the conditioner, hold it in place with your thumb or finger, and pull the thread through the conditioner.

Ending thread

To end a thread, sew back through the last few rows or rounds of beadwork, following the thread path of the stitch and tying two or three half-hitch knots (see "Half-hitch knot") between beads as you go. Sew through a few beads after the last knot, and trim the thread.

Half-hitch knot

Pass the needle under the thread bridge between two beads, and pull gently until a loop forms. Cross back over the thread between the beads, sew through the loop, and pull gently to draw the knot into the beadwork.

Overhand knot

Make a loop with the thread. Pull the tail through the loop, and tighten.

Square knot

[1] Cross one end of the thread over and under the other end. Pull both ends to tighten the first half of the knot.

[2] Cross the first end of the thread over and under the other end. Pull both ends to tighten the knot.

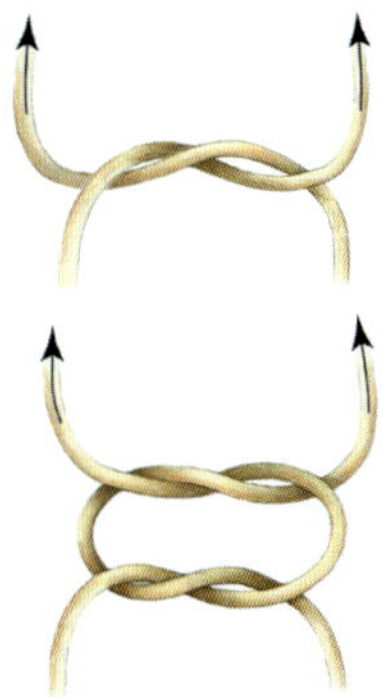

Stop bead

Use a stop bead to secure beads temporarily when you begin stitching.

Choose a bead that is different from the beads in your project. Pick up the stop bead, leaving the desired length tail. Sew through the stop bead again in the same direction, making sure you don't split the thread. If desired, sew through it one more time for added security.

Surgeon's knot

[1] Cross one end of the thread over and under the other twice. Pull both ends to tighten the first half of the knot.

[2] Cross the first end of the thread over and under the other end. Pull both ends to tighten the knot.

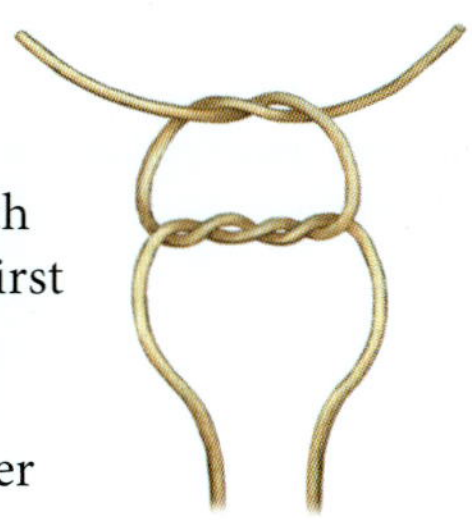

Crochet

Slip knot and chain stitch

[1] Make a slip knot: Leaving the desired length tail, make a loop in the cord, crossing the spool end over the tail. Insert the hook in the loop, yarn over, and pull the cord through the loop.

[2] Yarn over the hook, and draw through the loop. Repeat this step for the desired number of chain stitches.

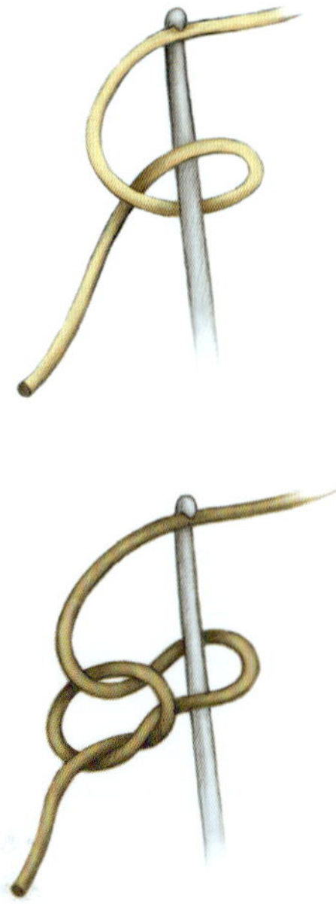

Beaded backstitch

To stitch a line of beads, come up through the fabric from the wrong side, and pick up three beads. Place the thread where the beads will go, and sew through the fabric right after the third bead. Come up between the second and third beads, and go through the third bead again. Pick up three more beads, and repeat. For a tighter stitch, pick up only one or two beads at a time.

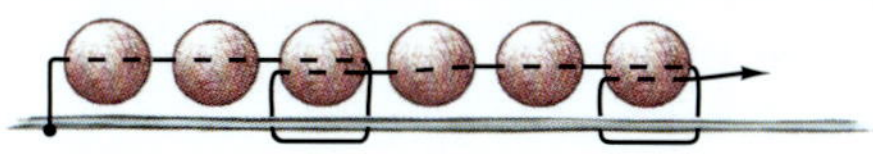

Basics

STITCHES

Brick stitch

[1] To work the typical method, which results in progressively decreasing rows, work the first row in ladder stitch (see "Ladder stitch") to the desired length, exiting the top of the last bead added.

[2] Pick up two beads, sew under the thread bridge between the second and third beads in the previous row, and sew back up through the second bead added. To secure this first stitch, sew down through the first bead and back up through the second bead.

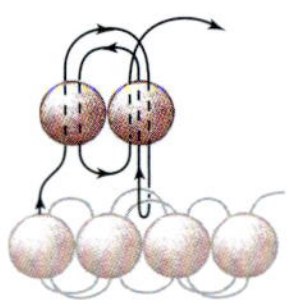

[3] For the remaining stitches in the row, pick up one bead per stitch, sew under the thread bridge between the next two beads in the previous row, and sew back up through the new bead. The last stitch in the new row will be centered above the last two beads in the previous row, and the new row will be one bead shorter than the previous row.

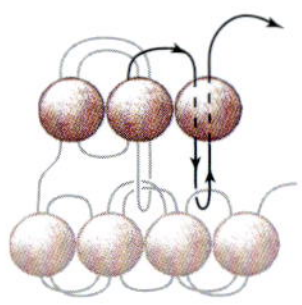

Increasing

To increase at the start of the row, repeat step 1 above, then repeat step 2, but sew under the thread bridge between the first and second beads in the previous row. To increase at the end of the row, work two stitches off of the thread bridge between the last two beads in the previous row.

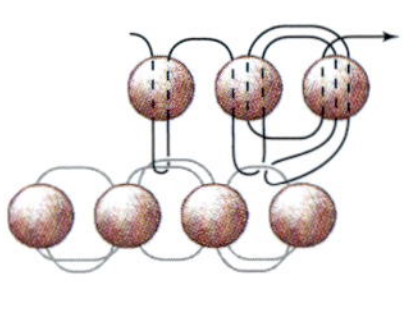

Tubular

[1] Begin with a ladder of beads, and join the ends to form a ring (see "Ladder stitch: Forming a ring"). Position the thread to exit the top of a bead.

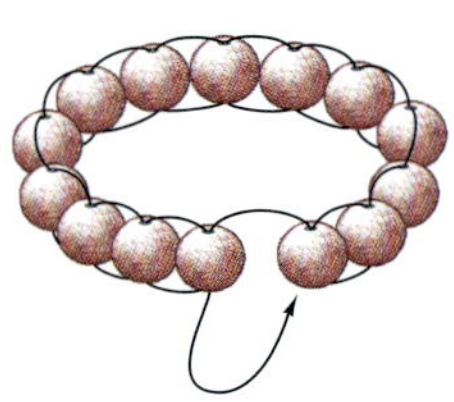

[2] Following the instructions for flat brick stitch, pick up two beads to begin the row. Stitch around the ring in brick stitch.

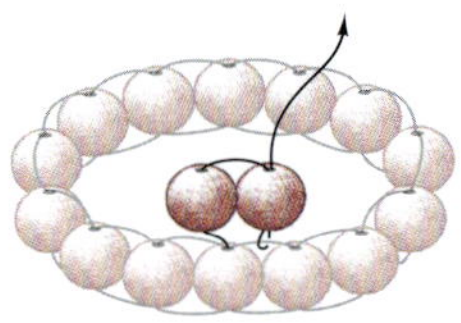

[3] Join the first and last beads of the round by sewing down through the first bead and up through the last bead.

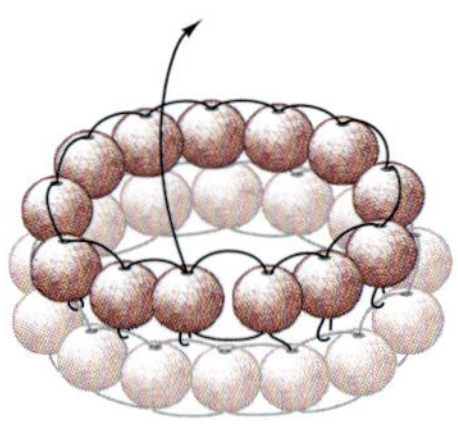

Herringbone stitch

Flat

[1] Work the first row in ladder stitch (see "Ladder stitch") to the desired length, exiting the top of an end bead in the ladder.

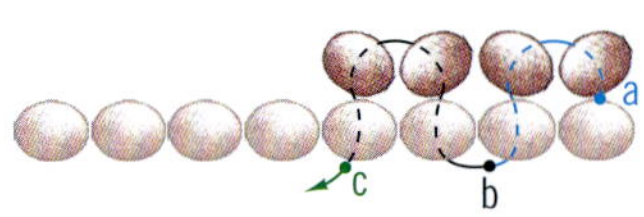

[2] Pick up two beads, and sew down through the next bead in the previous row **(a–b)**. Sew up through the following bead in the previous row, pick up two beads, and sew down through the next bead **(b–c)**. Repeat across the first row.

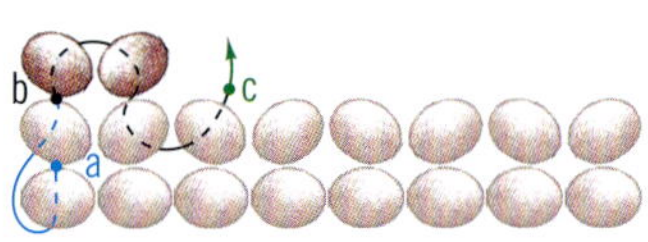

[3] To turn to start the next row, sew down through the end bead in the previous row and back through the last bead of the pair just added **(a–b)**. Pick up two beads, sew down through the next bead in the previous row, and sew up through the following bead **(b–c)**. Continue adding pairs of beads across the row.

Tubular

[1] Work a row of ladder stitch (see "Ladder stitch") to the desired length using an even number of beads. Form it into a ring to create the first round (see "Ladder stitch: Forming a ring"). Your thread should exit the top of a bead.

[2] Pick up two beads, sew down through the next bead in the previous round **(a–b)**, and sew up through the following bead. Repeat to complete the round **(b–c)**.

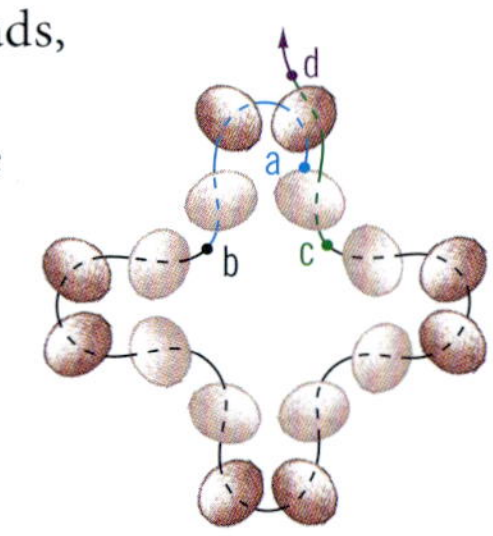

[3] You will need to step up to start the next round. Sew up through two beads — the next bead in the previous round and the first bead added in the new round **(c–d)**.

[4] Continue adding two beads per stitch. As you work, snug up the beads to form a tube, and step up at the end of each round until your rope is the desired length.

Twisted tubular

[1] Work a ladder and two rounds of tubular herringbone as explained above.

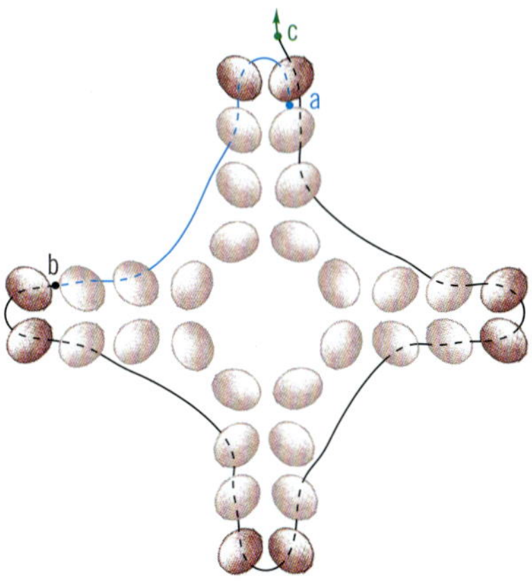

[2] To create a twist in the tube, pick up two beads, sew down through one bead in the next stack, then sew up through two beads in the following stack **(a–b)**. Repeat around, adding two beads per stitch. Step up to the next round through three beads **(b–c)**. Snug up the beads. The twist will begin to appear after the sixth round. Continue until your rope is the desired length.

Ladder stitch

Making a ladder

[1] Pick up two beads, and sew through them both again, positioning the beads side by side so that their holes are parallel **(a–b)**.

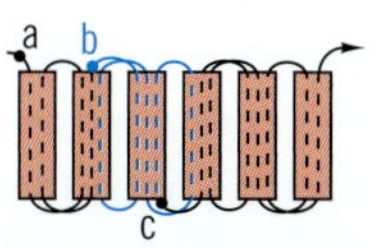

[2] Add subsequent beads by picking up one bead, sewing through the previous bead, then sewing through the new bead **(b–c)**. Continue for the desired length.

This technique produces uneven tension, which you can correct by zigzagging back through the beads in the opposite direction or by choosing the "Crossweave method" or "Alternative method."

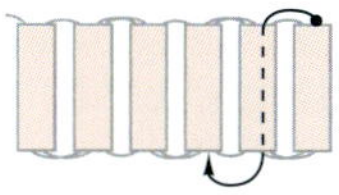

Crossweave technique

[1] Thread a needle on each end of a length of thread, and center a bead.

[2] Working in crossweave technique, pick up a bead with one needle, and cross the other needle through it **(a–b and c–d)**. Add all subsequent beads in the same manner.

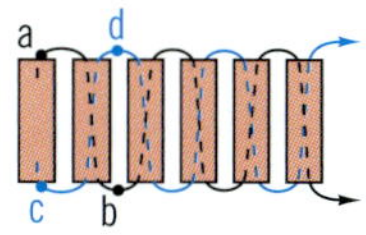

Alternative method

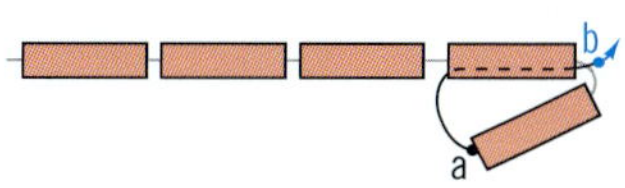

[1] Pick up all the beads you need to reach the length your project requires. Fold the last two beads so they are parallel, and sew through the second-to-last bead again in the same direction **(a–b)**.

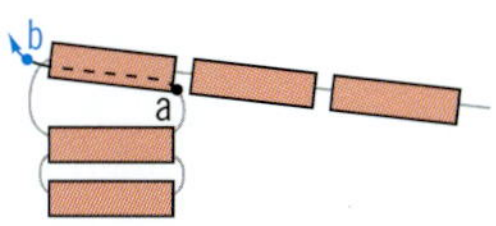

[2] Fold the next loose bead so it sits parallel to the previous bead in the ladder, and sew through the loose bead in the same direction **(a–b)**. Continue sewing back through each bead until you exit the last bead of the ladder.

Forming a ring

With your thread exiting the last bead in the ladder, sew through the first bead and then through the last bead again. If using the "Crossweave method" or "Alternative method" of ladder stitch, cross the threads from the last bead in the ladder through the first bead in the ladder.

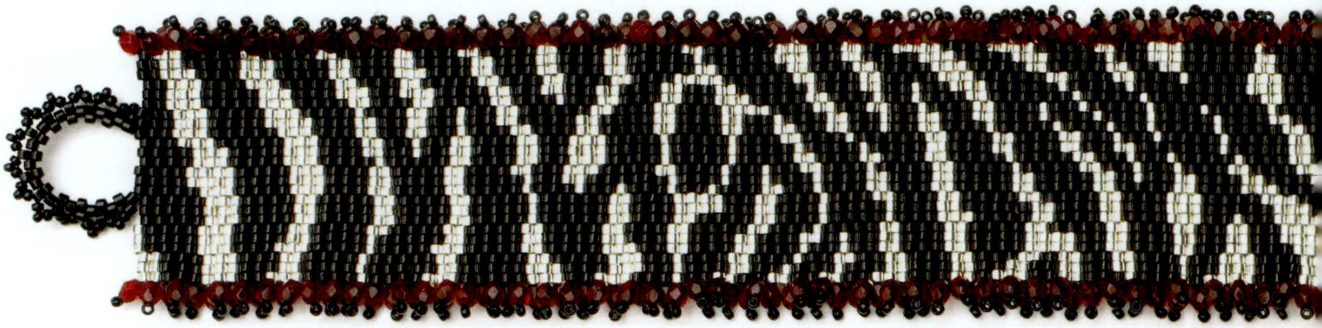

Basics

Peyote stitch

Flat even-count

[1] Pick up an even number of beads, leaving the desired length tail **(a–b)**. These beads will shift to form the first two rows as the third row is added.

[2] To begin row 3, pick up a bead, skip the last bead added in the previous step, and sew back through the next bead, working toward the tail **(b–c)**. For each stitch, pick up a bead, skip a bead in the previous row, and sew through the next bead until you reach the first bead picked up in step 1 **(c–d)**. The beads added in this row are higher than the previous rows and are referred to as "up-beads."

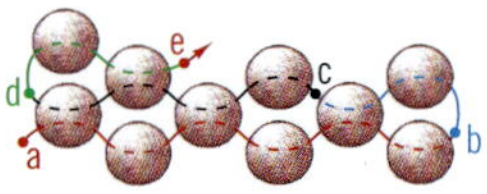

[3] For each stitch in subsequent rows, pick up a bead, and sew through the next up-bead in the previous row **(d–e)**. To count peyote stitch rows, count the total number of beads along both straight edges.

Flat odd-count

Odd-count peyote is the same as even-count peyote, except for the turn on odd-numbered rows, where the last bead of the row can't be attached in the usual way because there is no up-bead to sew through.

Work the traditional odd-row turn as follows:

[1] Begin as for flat even-count peyote, but pick up an odd number of beads. Work row 3 as in even-count, stopping before adding the last bead.

[2] Work a figure-8 turn at the end of row 3: Pick up the next-to-last bead (#7), and sew through #2, then #1 **(a–b)**. Pick up the last bead of the row (#8), and sew through #2, #3, #7, #2, #1, and #8 **(b–c)**.

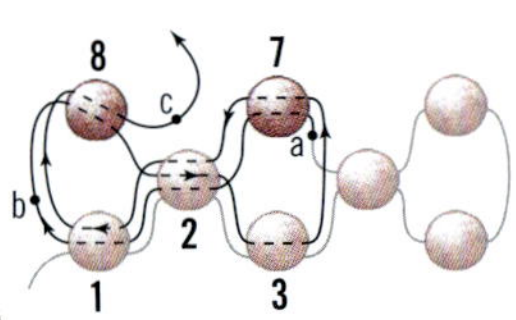

[3] In subsequent odd-numbered rows, pick up the last bead of the row, sew under the thread bridge between the last two edge beads, and sew back through the last bead added to begin the next row.

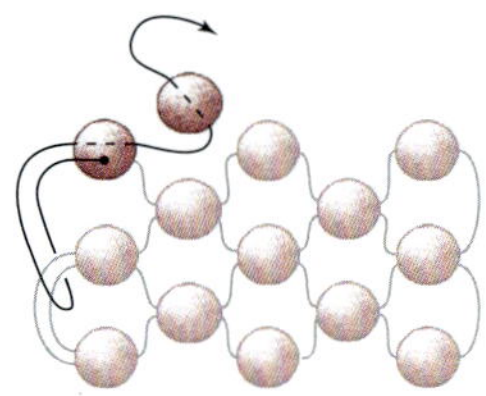

Tubular even-count

Tubular peyote stitch follows the same stitching pattern as flat peyote, but instead of sewing back and forth, you work in rounds.

[1] Start with an even number of beads tied into a ring (see "Square knot").

[2] Sew through the first bead in the ring. Pick up a bead, skip a bead in the ring, and sew through the next bead. Repeat to complete the round.

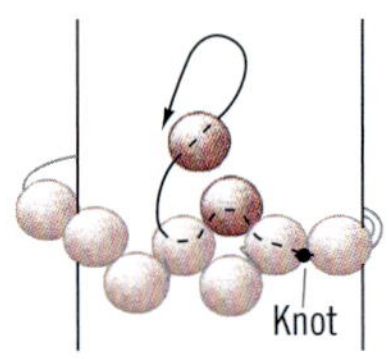

[3] To step up to start the next round, sew through the first bead added in round 3 **(a–b)**. Pick up a bead, and sew through the next bead in round 3 **(b–c)**. Repeat to complete the round.

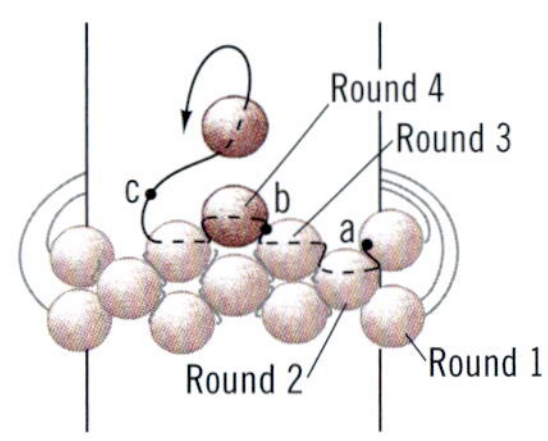

[4] Repeat step 3 to achieve the desired length, stepping up after each round.

Tubular odd-count

[1] Start with an odd number of bead tied into a ring (see "Square knot").

[2] Sew through the first bead into the ring. Pick up a bead, skip a bead in the ring, and sew though the next bead. Repeat to complete the round. At the end of the round, you will sew through the last bead in the original ring. Do not step up. Pick up a bead, and sew through the first bead in the previous round. You will be stitching in a continuous spiral.

Two-drop

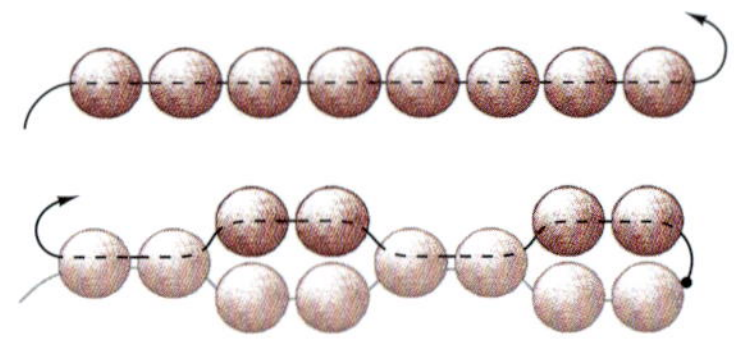

[1] Work two-drop peyote stitch the same as basic peyote, but treat pairs of beads as if they were single beads.

[2] Start with an even number of beads divisible by four. Pick up two beads (stitch 1 of row 3), skip two beads, and go through the next two beads. Repeat across the row.

Bezels

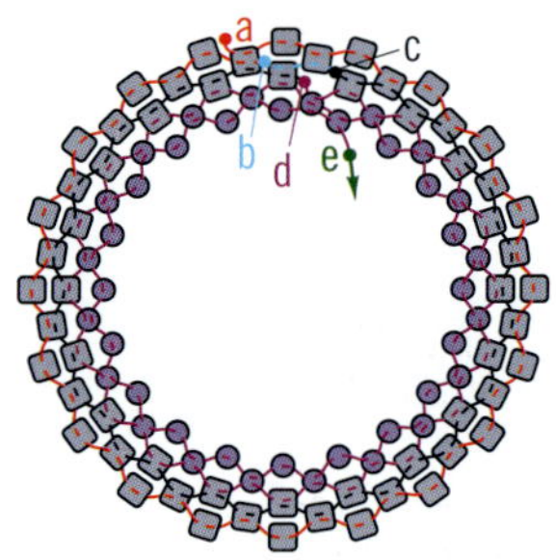

[1] Pick up enough seed beads to fit around the circumference of a rivoli or stone, and sew through the first bead again to form a ring **(a–b)**.

[2] Pick up a bead, skip the next bead in the ring, and sew through the following bead **(b–c)**. Continue working in tubular peyote stitch to complete the round, and step up through the first bead added **(c–d)**.

[3] Work the next two rounds in tubular peyote using beads one size smaller than those used in the previous rounds **(d–e)**. Keep the tension tight to decrease the size of the ring.

[4] Position the rivoli or stone in the bezel cup. Using the tail thread, repeat steps 2 and 3 to work three more rounds on the other side of the stone.

Increasing

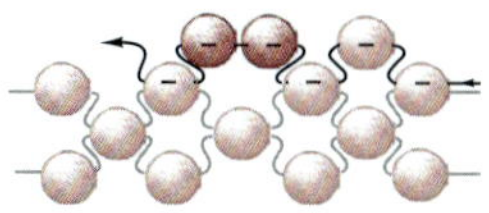

[1] At the point of increase, pick up two beads instead of one, and sew through the next bead.

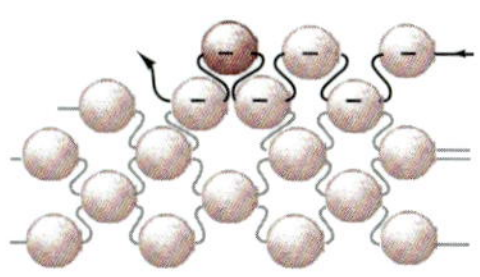

[2] When you reach the pair of beads in the next row, sew through the first bead, pick up a bead, and sew through the second bead.

Decreasing

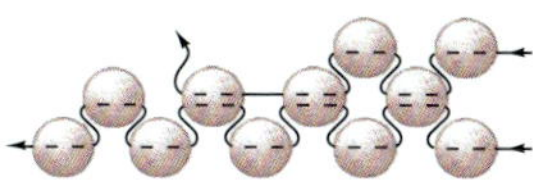

[1] At the point of decrease, sew through two up-beads in the previous row.

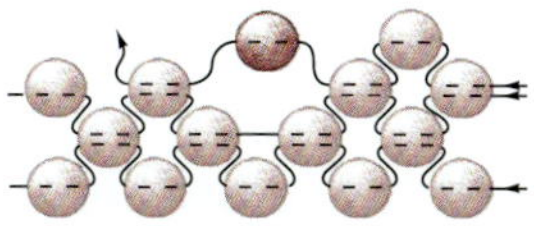

[2] In the next row, when you reach the two-bead space, pick up one bead.

Zipping up or joining

To join two sections of a flat peyote piece invisibly, match up the two pieces so the end rows fit together. "Zip up" the pieces by zigzagging through the up-beads on both ends.

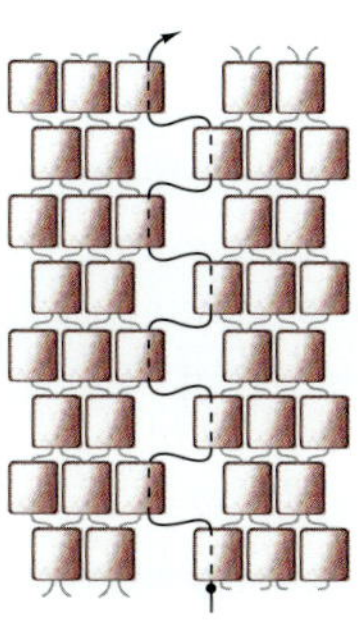

Right-angle weave

Flat strip

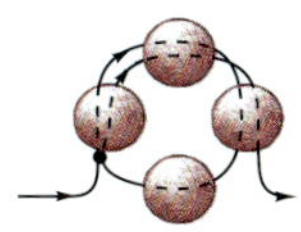

[1] To start the first row of right-angle weave, pick up four beads, and tie them into a ring (see "Square knot"). Sew through the first three beads again.

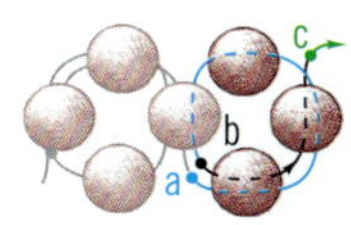

[2] Pick up three beads. Sew through the last bead in the previous stitch **(a–b)**, and continue through the first two beads picked up in this stitch **(b–c)**.

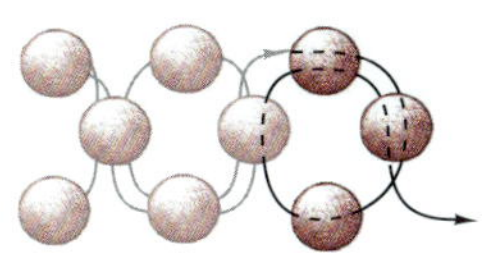

[3] Continue adding three beads per stitch until the first row is the desired length. You are stitching in a figure-8 pattern, alternating the direction of the thread path for each stitch.

Adding rows

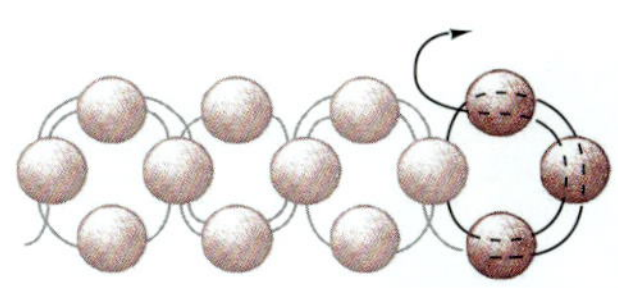

[1] To add a row, sew through the last stitch of row 1, exiting an edge bead along one side.

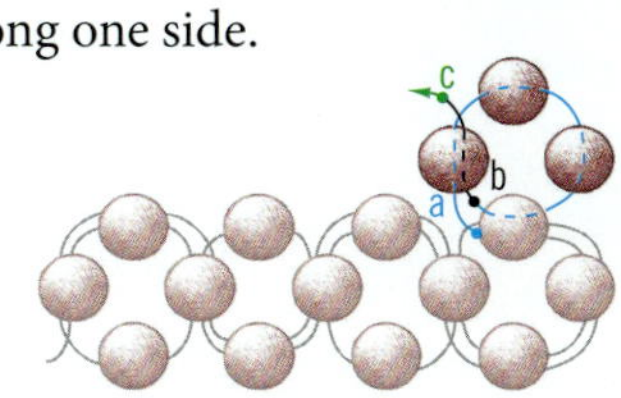

[2] Pick up three beads, and sew through the edge bead your thread exited in the previous step **(a–b)**. Continue through the first new bead **(b–c)**.

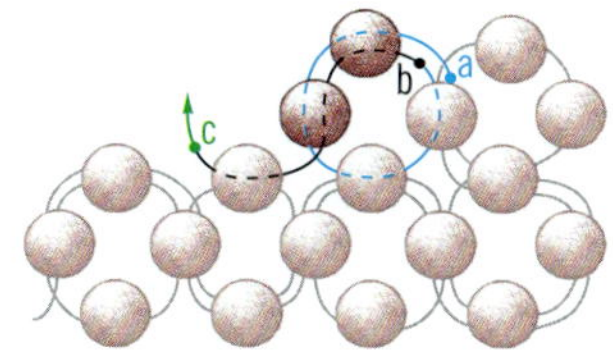

[3] Pick up two beads, and sew back through the next edge bead in the previous row and the bead your thread exited at the start of this step **(a–b)**. Continue through the two new beads and the following edge bead in the previous row **(b–c)**.

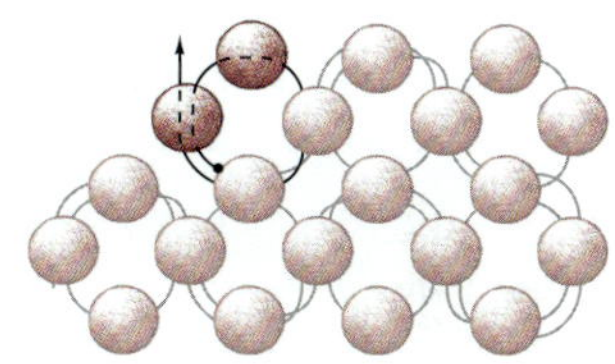

[4] Pick up two beads, and sew through the last two beads your thread exited in the previous stitch and the first new bead. Continue working a figure-8 thread path, picking up two beads per stitch for the rest of the row.

Square stitch

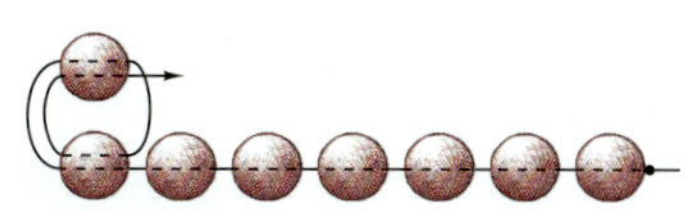

[1] String all the beads needed for the first row, then pick up the first bead of the second row. Sew through the last bead of the first row and the first bead of the second row again. Position the two beads side by side so that their holes are parallel.

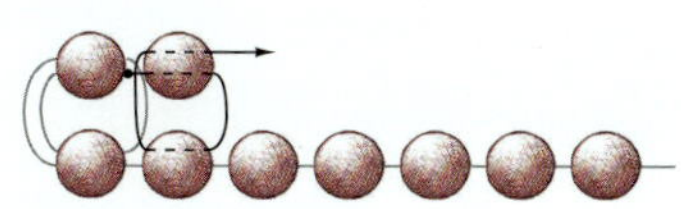

[2] Pick up the next bead of row 2, and sew through the corresponding bead in row 1 and the new bead in row 2. Repeat across the row.

Basics

STRINGING & WIREWORK

Crimping

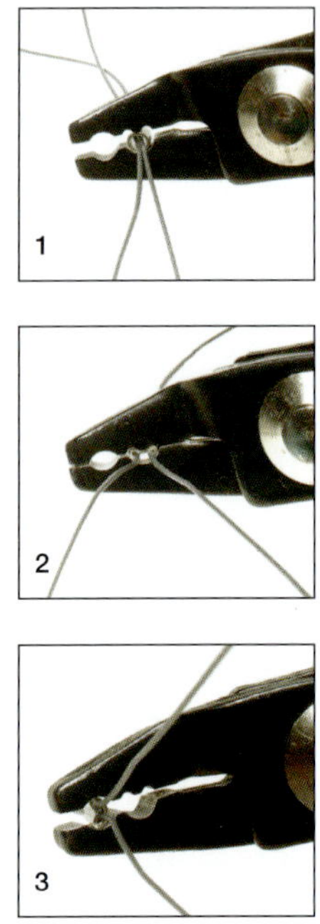

Use crimp beads to secure flexible beading wire. Slide the crimp bead into place over two strands of wire, and squeeze it firmly with chainnose pliers to flatten it. For a more finished look, use crimping pliers:

[1] Position the crimp bead in the hole that is closest to the handle of the crimping pliers.

[2] Holding the wires apart, squeeze the pliers to compress the crimp bead, making sure one wire is on each side of the dent.

[3] Place the crimp bead in the front hole of the pliers, and position it so the dent is facing the tips of the pliers. Squeeze the pliers to fold the crimp in half.

Opening and closing loops and jump rings

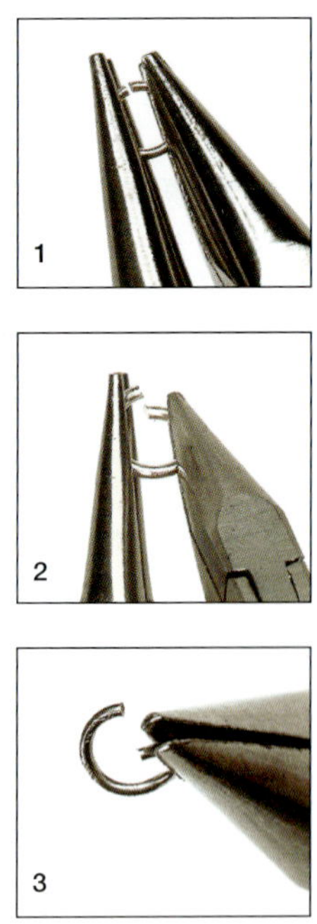

[1] Hold a loop or a jump ring with two pairs of pliers, such as chainnose, flatnose, or bentnose pliers.

[2] To open the loop or jump ring, bring the tips of one pair of pliers toward you, and push the tips of the other pair away from you.

[3] The open jump ring. Reverse the steps to close.

Plain loop

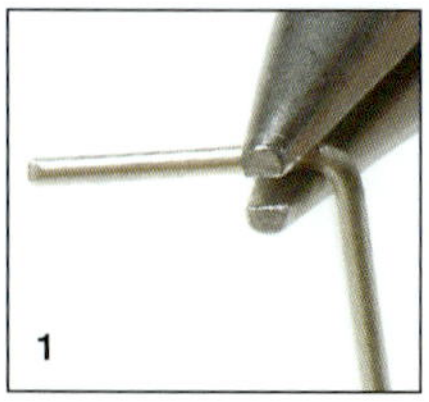

[1] Using chainnose pliers, make a right-angle bend in the wire directly above a bead or other component or at least ¼ in. (6 mm) from the end of a naked piece of wire. For a larger loop, bend the wire further in.

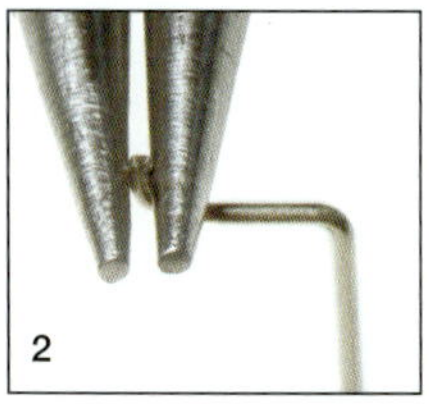

[2] Grip the end of the wire with roundnose pliers so that the wire is flush with the jaws of the pliers where they meet. The closer to the tip of the pliers that you work, the smaller the loop will be. Press downward slightly, and rotate the wire toward the bend made in step 1.

[3] Reposition the pliers in the loop to continue rotating the wire until the end of the wire touches the bend.

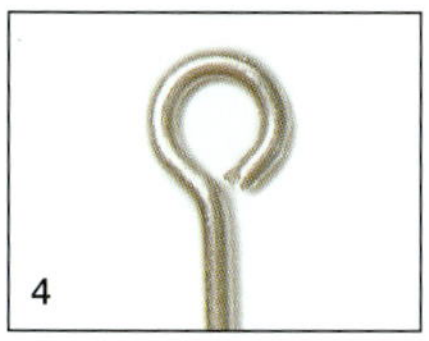

[4] The plain loop.

Wrapped loop

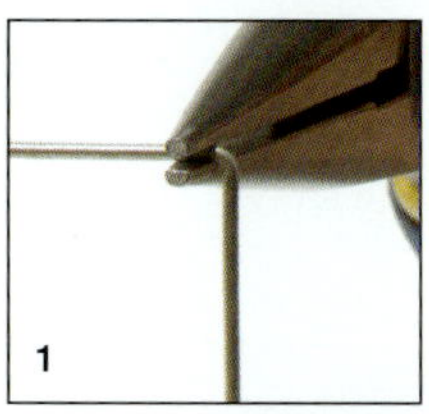

[1] Using chainnose pliers, make a right-angle bend in the wire about 2 mm above a bead or other component or at least 1¼ in. (3.2 cm) from the end of a naked piece of wire.

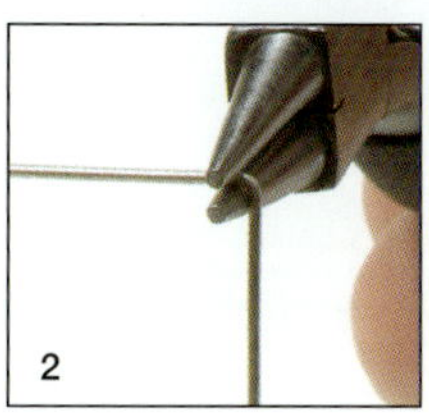

[2] Position the jaws of the roundnose pliers in the bend. The closer to the tip of the pliers that you work, the smaller the loop will be.

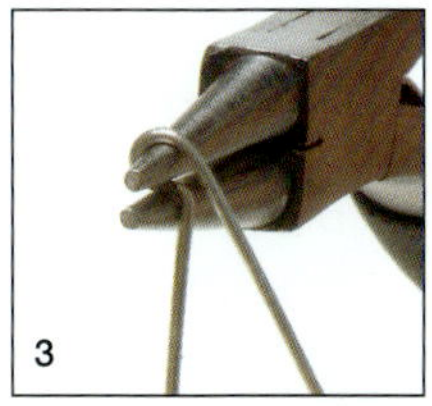

[3] Curve the short end of the wire over the top jaw of the roundnose pliers.

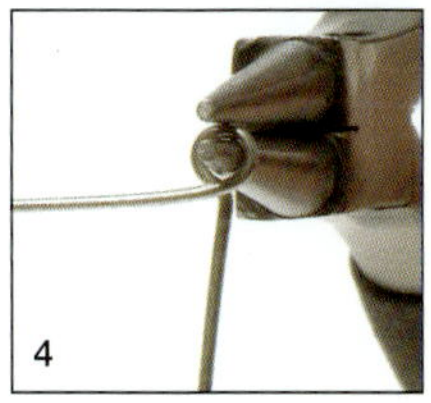

[4] Reposition the pliers so the lower jaw fits snugly in the loop. Curve the wire downward around the bottom jaw of the pliers. This is the first half of a wrapped loop.

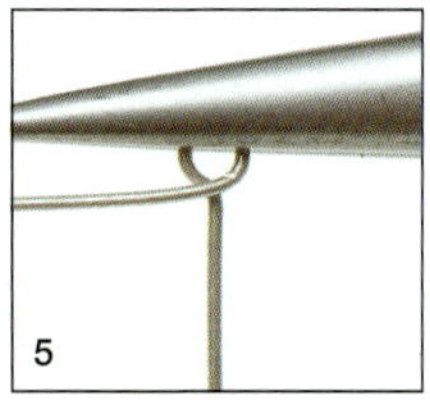

[5] To complete the wraps, grasp the top of the loop with one pair of pliers.

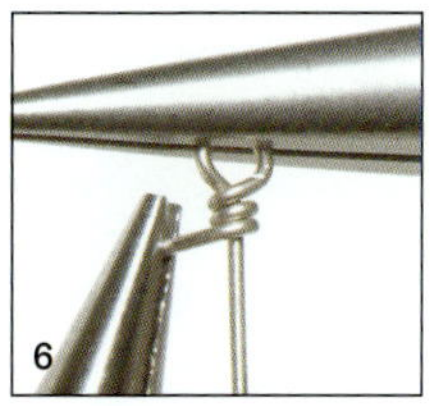

[6] With another pair of pliers, wrap the wire around the stem two or three times. Trim the excess wire, and gently press the cut end close to the wraps with chainnose pliers.

Loops, wrapped above a top-drilled bead

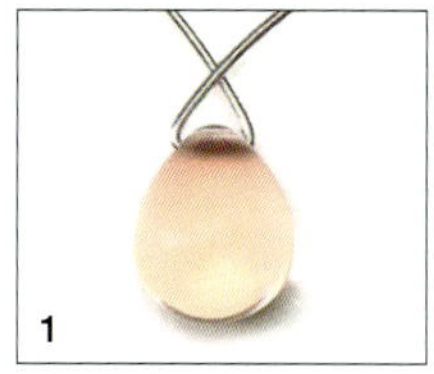

[1] Center a top-drilled bead on a 3-in. (7.6 cm) piece of wire. Bend each wire end upward, crossing them into an X above the bead.

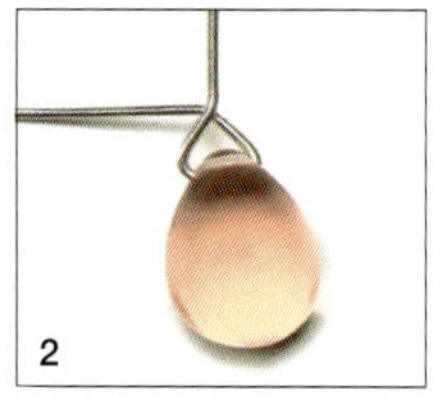

[2] Using chainnose pliers, make a small bend in each wire end so they form a right angle.

[3] Wrap the horizontal wire around the vertical wire as in a wrapped loop. Trim the excess wrapping wire.

Single-Stitch Projects

PEYOTE STITCH

Bead stud bracelet

Get in touch with your inner wild child with bead studs.

designed by **Maggie Roschyk**

If you love spike beads, get ready for the newest addition to the pressed glass bead family: bead studs. Edgy and architectural, these two-hole beads are ready for the spotlight.

stepby**step**

[1] To make an end tab: On 2 ft. (61 cm) of thread, pick up 14 2 x 4 mm peanut beads, leaving a 10-in. (25 cm) tail. Continuing with peanuts, stitch a total of eight rows in flat even-count peyote stitch (Basics). Repeat this step to make a second end tab.

[2] To make a side strip: On 2 ft. (61 cm) of thread, pick up four peanut beads, leaving a 6-in. (15 cm) tail. Continuing with peanuts, work a total of 112 rows in flat even-count peyote stitch. Repeat to make a second side strip.

[3] Line up one end of a side strip with one edge of an end tab, and zip up (Basics) the two pieces to join them **(figure 1, a–b)**. Repeat with the other side strip on the other edge of this end tab **(c–d)**. Repeat this step to connect the other end tab to the opposite end of each side strip. End this working thread only (Basics).

[4] Add 1 yd. (.9 m) of thread (Basics) at one end of the bracelet, and exit the first inside edge bead on one side of the opening. Pick up a 12 mm bead stud, and sew through the opposite inside-edge bead **(figure 2, a–b)**. Sew through the adjacent inside-edge bead, and sew back through the same hole of the bead stud and the next inside-edge bead on the other side **(b–c)**. Sew through the adjacent inside-edge bead, and follow the same process to secure the remaining hole of the bead stud within the opening **(c–d)**. Repeat this process to attach the remaining bead studs within the opening.

[5] Sew through the beadwork to exit an end edge bead. Pick up two 15º seed beads, and sew down through the next edge bead and up through the following edge bead **(e–f)**. Repeat this stitch along the entire length. Sew through the beadwork to the other edge, and embellish the entire length. End the working thread.

[6] Using a tail from an end tab, sew through the beadwork to exit a peanut that lines up with a clasp loop, and sew through the clasp loop. If desired, pick up five 15ºs to cover the thread before sewing through the following peanut. Repeat to attach the remaining clasp loops **(photo)**. Retrace the thread path a few times, and end the thread. Repeat this step at the other end of the bracelet. End any remaining threads. ●

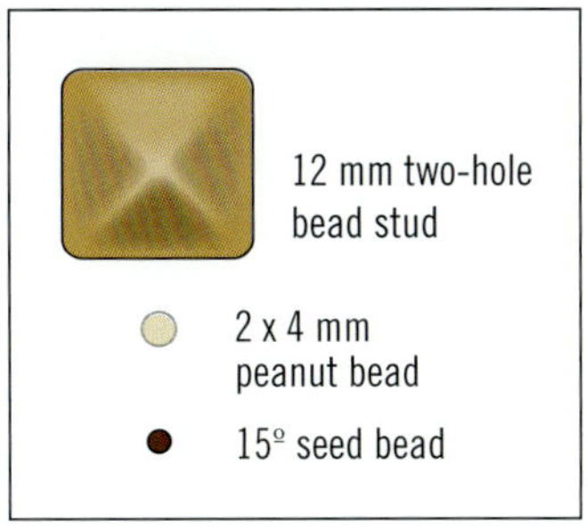

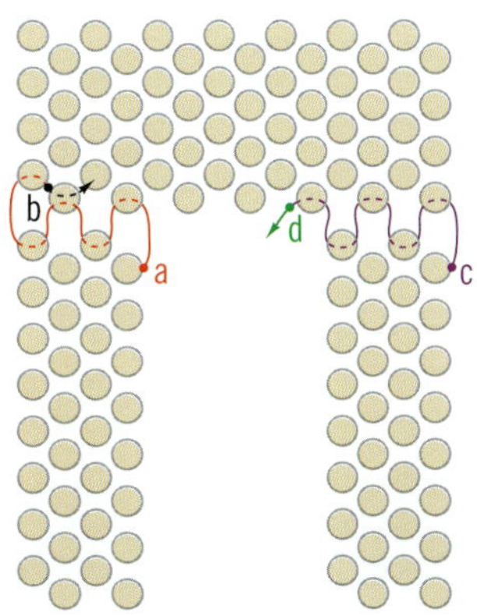

FIGURE 1

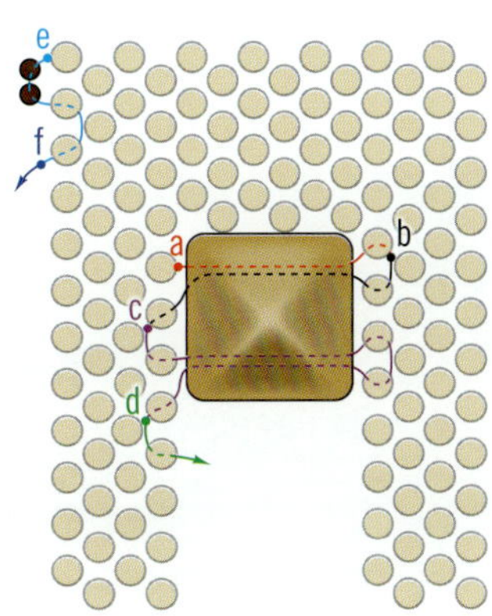

FIGURE 2

MATERIALS

bronze bracelet 6¾ in. (17.1 cm)

- **12** 12 mm two-hole bead studs (02010-15695, chalk bronze lumi)
- 20 g 2 x 4 mm peanut beads (457B, dark bronze matte)
- 1 g 15º seed beads (457C, reddish copper)
- 4-strand slide clasp
- Fireline 6 lb. test
- beading needles, #12

rose bracelet colors:

- 12 mm two-hole bead studs (23980-14415, antique bronze)
- 2 x 4 mm peanut beads (4007, old rose luster)
- 15º seed beads (Toho 459, gold-lustered dark topaz)

PEYOTE STITCH

Surfin' the waves

Make waves with this flat Cellini necklace using everything from 11º seed beads to 6ºs!

designed by **Jimmie Boatright**

MATERIALS

blue necklace 17 in. (43 cm)

- 8 g 6º Baroque pearl beads, color I (Miyuki 3951, Baroque white)
- 4–5 g 8º hex-cut seed beads, color H (Miyuki 342, berry-lined light topaz AB)
- 4–5 g 8º seed beads, color G (Miyuki 4506, transparent seafoam Picasso)
- 5 g 11º hex-cut seed beads, color F (Miyuki 462, metallic gold iris)
- 5 g 11º seed beads in each of **2** colors: D (Toho 1205, marbled opaque white/blue), E (Toho 167F, transparent rainbow frosted teal)
- 11º cylinder beads
  4–5 g color A (Miyuki DB1763, emerald-lined cobalt AB)
  2–3 g color B (Miyuki DB0322, matte metallic dark bronze)
  2–3 g color C (Miyuki DB0608, dyed silver-lined blue zircon)
- 5-strand slide clasp
- Fireline 6 lb. test
- beading needles, #10

bronze necklace colors:

- 6º seed beads, color I (Toho 223, antique bronze)
- 8º hex-cut seed beads, color H (Toho 274, teal green-lined crystal)
- 8º Japanese seed beads, color G (343A, amber/black-lined AB)
- 11º hex-cut seed beads, color F (Miyuki 462, metallic gold iris)
- 11º seed beads in **2** colors: D (Toho 221, bronze), E (Toho 1208, marbled turquoise/Ceylon grey)
- 11º cylinder beads in **3** colors: A and C (Miyuki DB0324, matte metallic rainbow), B (Miyuki DB0322, matte metallic dark bronze)

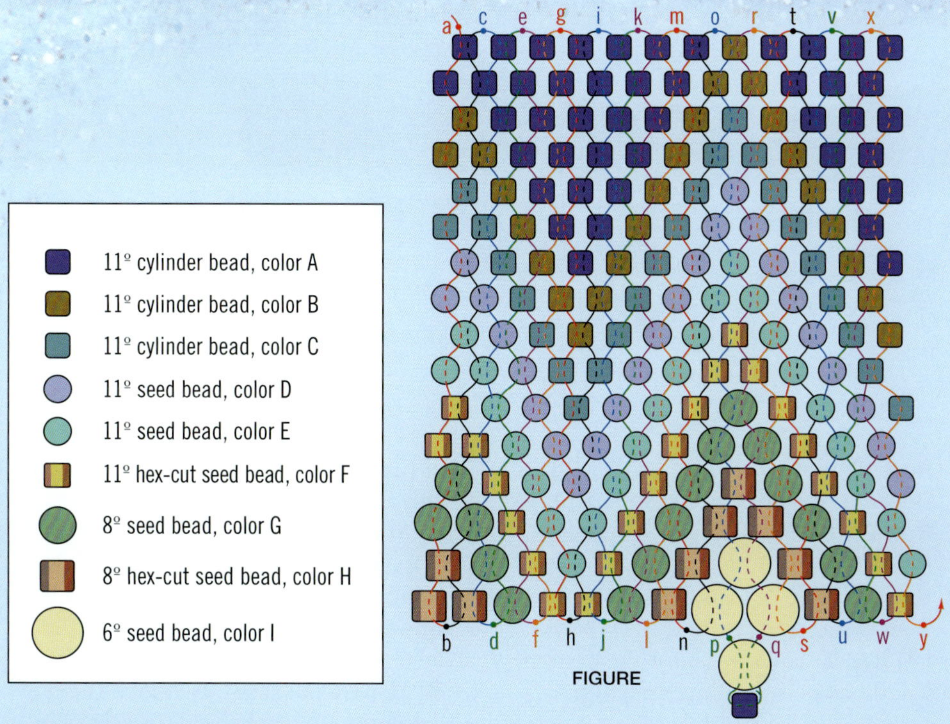

FIGURE

stepbystep

Necklace

[1] On a comfortable length of thread, attach a stop bead (Basics), leaving an 8-in. (20 cm) tail.

[2] Pick up two color A 11º cylinder beads, two color B 11º cylinder beads, two color C 11º cylinder beads, two color D 11º seed beads, two color E 11º seed beads, two color F 11º hex-cut seed beads, two color G 8º seed beads, and two color H 8º hex-cut seed beads **(figure, a–b)**. These beads will form the first two rows as the third row is added.

[3] Work in flat even-count peyote stitch (Basics) as follows, picking up one bead per stitch and referring to the **figure:**

Row 3: H, G, F, E, D, C, B, A **(b–c)**.
Row 4: A, A, B, C, D, E, F, G **(c–d)**.
Row 5: G, F, E, D, C, B, A, A **(d–e)**.

DESIGN NOTES:

- Lay out your beads in order on your work surface, and label them A–I. This will help you pick up the beads for each row, alternating between ascending and descending order.
- To make your necklace more comfortable to wear, add a few rows in the pattern at the beginning and end of the necklace so you do not start or end with a "wave." This will also help your clasp to lie flat.
- In this purple necklace, I omitted the Cs so each row is one bead shorter than the other two necklaces.

Row 6: A, A, A, B, C, D, E, F **(e–f)**.
Row 7: F, E, D, C, B, A, A, A **(f–g)**.
Row 8: A, A, A, A, B, C, D, E **(g–h)**.
Row 9: F, E, D, C, B, A, A, A **(h–i)**.
Row 10: A, A, A, B, C, D, E, F **(i–j)**.
Row 11: G, F, E, D, C, B, A, A **(j–k)**.
Row 12: A, A, B, C, D, E, F, G **(k–l)**.
Row 13: H, G, F, E, D, C, B, A **(l–m)**.
Row 14: A, B, C, D, E, F, G, H **(m–n)**.
Row 15: Color I 6º seed bead, H, G, F, E, D, C, B **(n–o)**.
Row 16: B, C, D, E, F, G, H, I **(o–p)**.
Work an increase turn: Pick up an I and an A, and sew back through the I just picked up **(p–q)**. This creates a point in the wave.
Row 17: I, H, G, F, E, D, C, B **(q–r)**.
Row 18: A, B, C, D, E, F, G, H **(r–s)**.
Row 19: H, G, F, E, D, C, B, A **(s–t)**.
Row 20: A, A, B, C, D, E, F, G **(t–u)**.
Row 21: G, F, E, D, C, B, A, A **(u–v)**.
Row 22: A, A, A, B, C, D, E, F **(v–w)**.
Row 23: F, E, D, C, B, A, A, A **(w–x)**.
Row 24: A, A, A, A, B, C, D, E **(x–y)**.

[4] Repeat rows 9–24 for the desired length necklace, ending and adding thread (Basics) as needed. You'll notice the addition of the Is creates "waves" in your beadwork. This 17-in. (43 cm) necklace has 30 waves.

Clasp

[1] Align half of the clasp along one end of the necklace. With the working thread, sew through the beadwork to exit an up-bead in the last row that corresponds with the first loop of the clasp.

[2] Sew up through the loop of the clasp, and pick up a G and an E. Sew back through the G and the loop, and continue through the next up-bead in the last row.

[3] Work as in step 2 to attach the remaining loops of the clasp. Retrace the thread path, and end the thread.

[4] Remove the stop bead from the tail, and repeat steps 1–3. ●

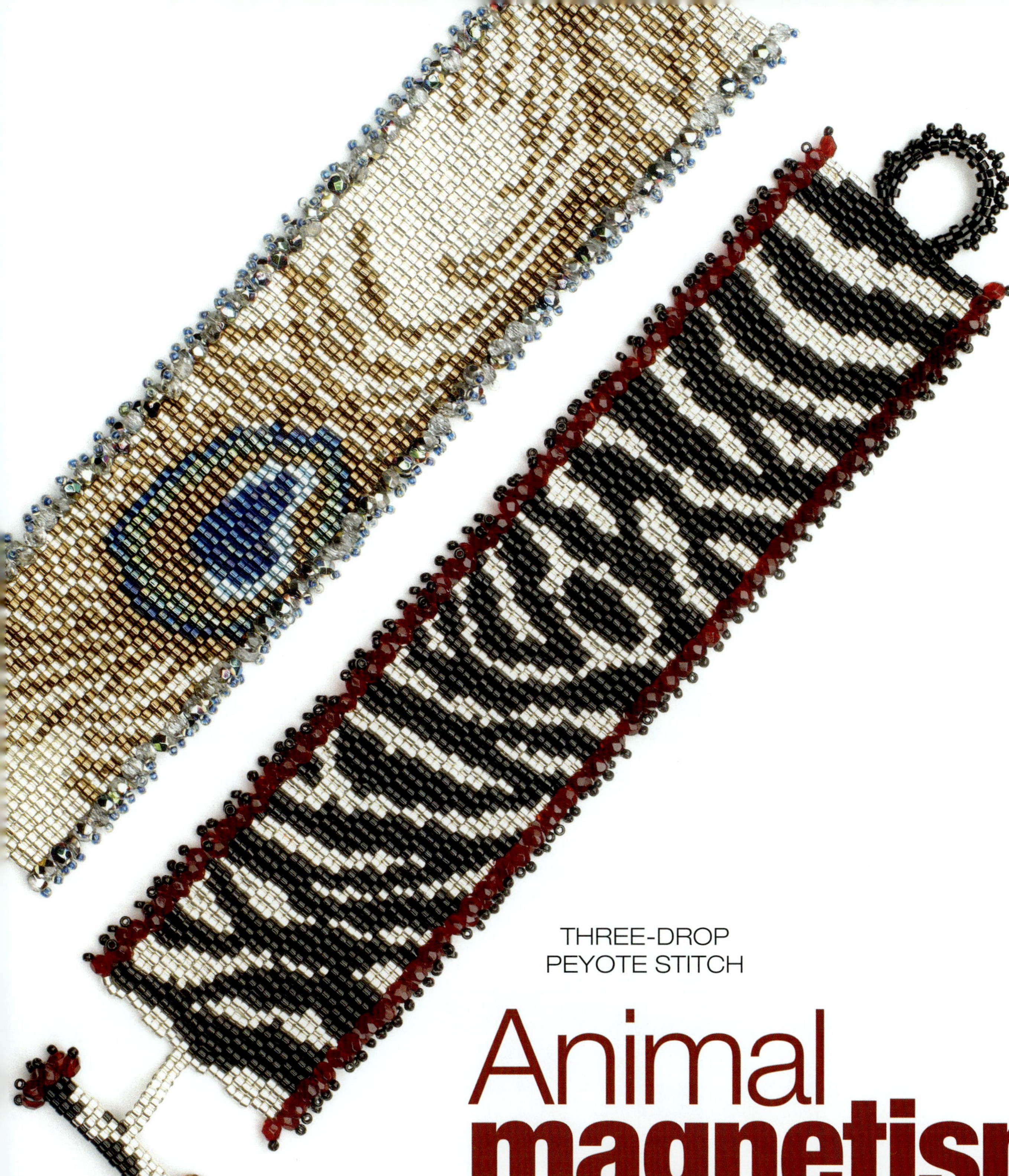

THREE-DROP PEYOTE STITCH

Animal **magnetism**

Hear the call of the wild as you stitch these gorgeous bracelets representing two favorite animal prints — zebra and peacock.

designed by **Josie Fabre**

MATERIALS

both bracelets 7 in. (18 cm)

- Fireline 4 lb. test
- beading needles, #10 or #11

zebra bracelet

- **200** 3 mm fire-polished beads (Czech, ruby red)
- 11º Miyuki Delica cylinder beads
  10 g color A (DB0010, opaque black)
  4 g color B (DB0035M, galvanized silver)
- 1 g 15º seed beads (Czech, black)

peacock bracelet

- **1** 12 mm rivoli button (Swarovski, crystal)
- **190** 3 mm fire-polished beads (Czech, crystal vitrail)
- 11º Miyuki Delica cylinder beads
  12 g color A (DB0035M, galvanized silver)
  8 g color B (DB0022, dark bronze)
  1 g color C (DB0027, metallic rainbow green/teal)
  1 g color D (DB0416, galvanized aquamarine)
  2 g color E (DB1763, rainbow eye of peacock)
- 1 g 15º seed beads (Czech, blue-lined clear)

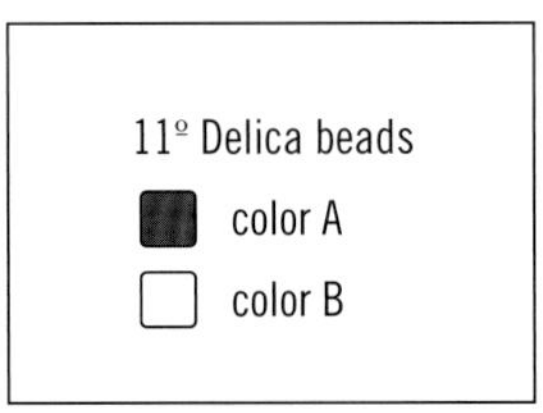

FIGURE

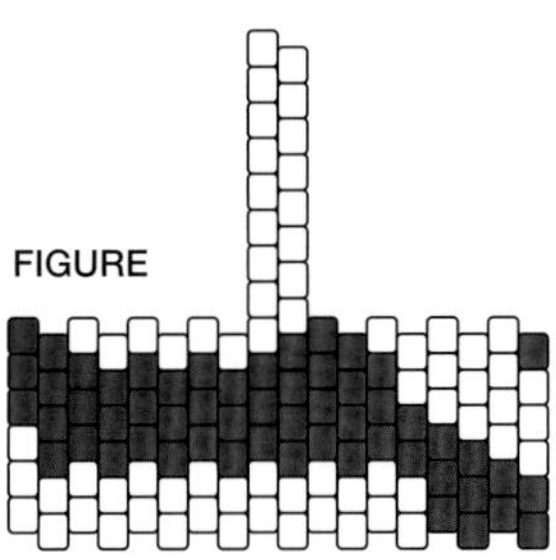

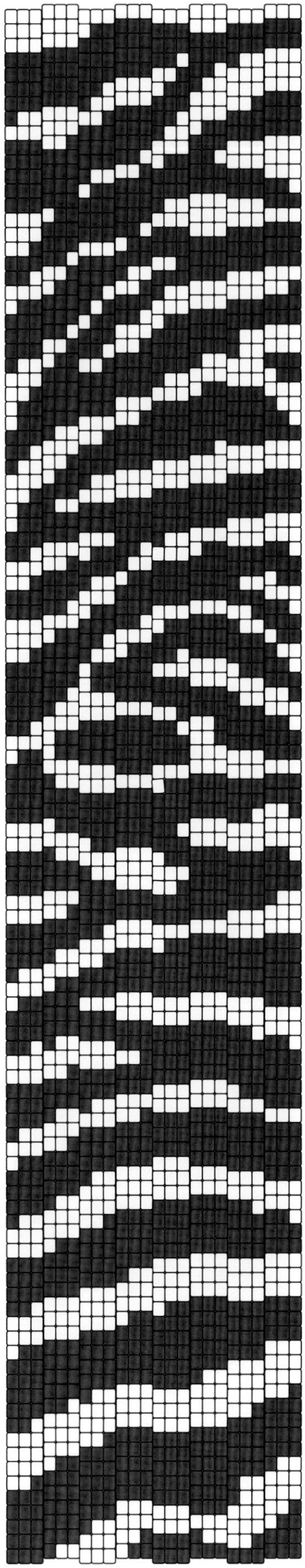

ZEBRA PATTERN

Add these two patterns to your menagerie for eye-catching, quick-to-stitch fashion!

stepby**step**

Bracelet bases

Both bracelets are worked in three-drop peyote stitch, a technique based on two-drop peyote stitch. Refer to Basics to brush up on two-drop peyote before beginning this project.

[1] On a comfortable length of thread, attach a stop bead (Basics), leaving a 6-in. (15 cm) tail. Pick up 24 11º cylinder beads for rows 1 and 2 of the desired **pattern**.

[2] Work in three-drop peyote stitch using cylinders for the desired length, minus 1 in. (2.5 cm) for the clasp. End and add thread (Basics) as needed while you stitch, and end the working thread and tail when you finish.

[3] Choose the appropriate steps below to add a clasp and edging to the base.

Zebra

Toggle bar

[1] On 1 yd. (.9 m) of thread, attach a stop bead, leaving a 6-in. (15 cm) tail.

[2] Referring to the **figure**, work in flat even-count peyote stitch (Basics) using cylinders to make a strip that is 18 beads wide and 12 rows long. Roll the strip into a tube, and zip up (Basics) the first and last rows. End the tail but not the working thread.

[3] With the thread exiting an end cylinder in the tube, pick up a 3 mm fire-polished bead and a 15º seed bead. Sew back through the 3 mm and the cylinder your thread exited at the start of this step, and sew up through the next end cylinder. Repeat this stitch around this end of the tube. Add a 3 mm and a 15º to each cylinder at the other end of the tube in the same way.

[4] Sew through the beadwork to exit a center cylinder in the bar, and work in even-count peyote stitch to create a tab that is two beads wide and 16 rows long.
[5] Stitch the end of the tab to the center cylinders at one end of the bracelet base. Retrace the thread path of the join, and end the working thread.

Toggle ring
[1] Locate the last row at the other end of the base, and notice that one side of the row begins with three up-beads. Position your beadwork so these beads are on the right. Add 20 in. (51 cm) of thread to the base, and exit the second set of three up-beads from the right with your needle pointing toward the center of the band.
[2] Pick up 26 cylinders, and sew through the next set of three up-beads with your needle pointing toward the center of the band. This forms a ring.
[3] Sew through the beadwork to exit this same set of up-beads, and work a round of peyote off of the cylinders in the ring **(photo a)**.
[4] Sew through the beadwork to exit the first up-bead added in the previous round. Pick up three 15ºs, and sew through the next up-bead. Repeat this stitch to complete the round, and end the thread.

Edging
[1] Add 1 yd. (.9 m) of thread to the base, and exit an end cylinder along one edge.
[2] Pick up a 3 mm fire-polished bead and a 15º seed bead. Sew back through the 3 mm and the cylinder your thread exited at the start of this step, and sew up through the next edge cylinder. Repeat this stitch along both edges of the base. End the thread.

Peacock

Toggle button
[1] Add 12 in. (30 cm) of thread to the base, exiting a center cylinder in the fifth row from one end. Pick up six cylinders, a 15º, a 12 mm button, a 15º, and two cylinders. Skip the last two 15ºs and two cylinders, and sew back through the next cylinder. Work two peyote stitches with one cylinder per stitch, sewing through the cylinder in the base your thread exited at the start of this step.
[2] Sew through the first cylinder picked up in step 1. Work a peyote stitch with two 15ºs, and then work a peyote stitch with one 15º. Sew through the next cylinder, 15º, button, 15º, and two cylinders. Work a peyote stitch with one 15º, and then work a peyote stitch with two 15ºs. Retrace the thread path through the button, and end the thread **(photo b)**.

Toggle ring
Work as in steps 1–4 of "Zebra: Toggle ring," but in step 2 pick up only 23 cylinders.

Edging
Work as in steps 1 and 2 of "Zebra: Edging." ●

11º Delica beads
- color A
- color B
- color C
- color D
- color E

PEACOCK PATTERN

Cute as a button bracelet

Dress up this simple peyote stitch band with sparkling crystal buttons.

designed by **Jane Danley Cruz**

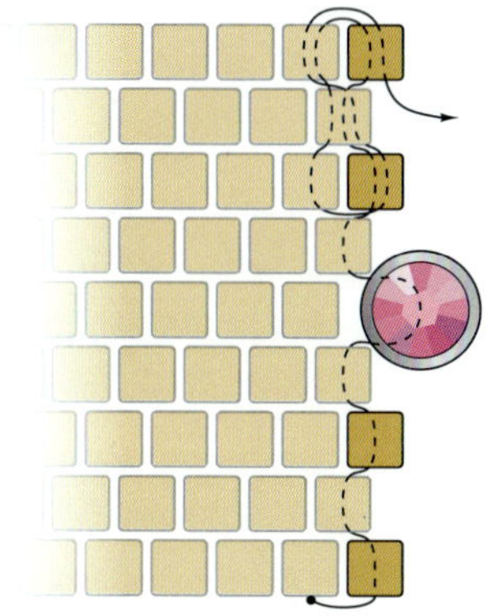
FIGURE 1

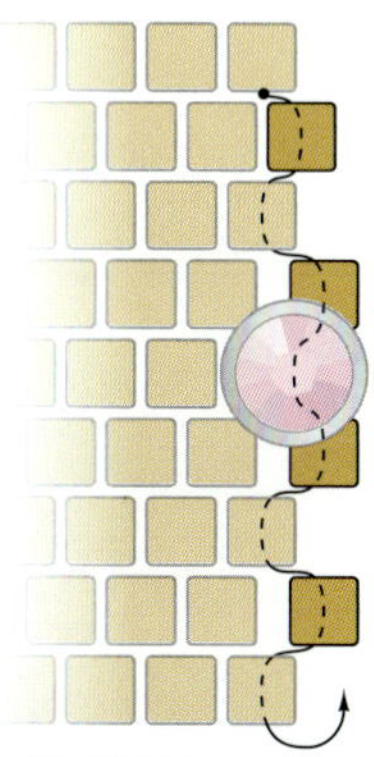
FIGURE 2

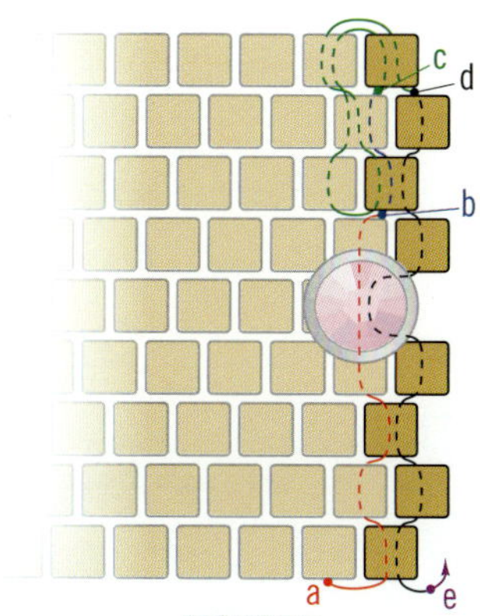

FIGURE 3

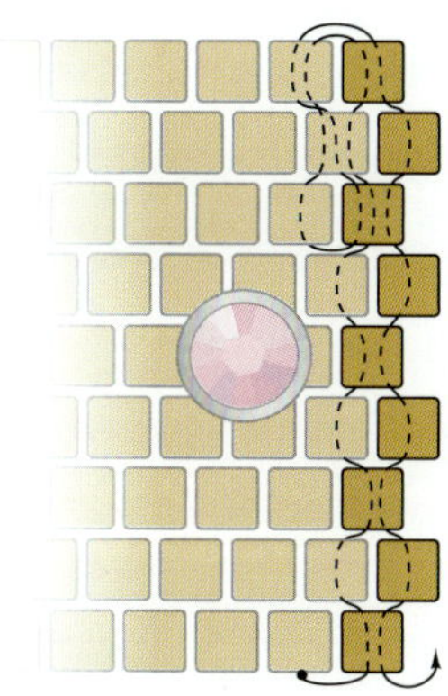
FIGURE 4

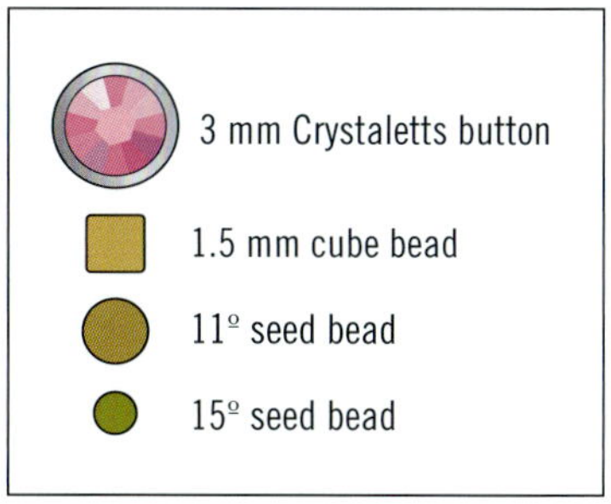

MATERIALS

bracelet 7 in. (18 cm)

- 3 mm Crystaletts buttons (www.crystaletts.com)
  41 color A (rose in black rhodium bezel)
  14 color B (aqua Bohemica in black rhodium bezel)
- 6 g 1.5 mm cube beads (Toho 1C221, bronze)
- 1 g 11º seed beads (Toho 457G, metallic golden bronze; www.beadhaven.com)
- 1 g 15º seed beads (Miyuki F460I, olivine bronze matte metallic iris; www.beyondbeadery.com)
- 2-strand slide clasp
- Fireline 6 lb. test
- beading needles, #11

stepbystep

Band

[1] On a comfortable length of thread, attach a stop bead (Basics), leaving an 8-in. (20 cm) tail. Pick up nine 1.5 mm cube beads, which will shift to form the first two rows as row 3 is added.

[2] Work the next two rows as follows:

Row 3: Work four stitches in flat odd-count peyote stitch (Basics) using cubes. Pick up the final cube of the row, and work the odd-count figure-8 turn. You are now in position to start row 4.

Row 4: Work four stitches using cubes.

[3] Work as in rows 3 and 4 until you have a total of 12 rows (you'll have six cubes along each straight edge of the band).

[4] Work the next six rows as follows, keeping your tension consistent but not tight. Note: After row 13, you may find it easier to see the stitches if you work on the back of the band so the button faces away from you.

Row 13: Work as follows **(refer to figure 1):**

- Work two stitches using cubes.
- Work a stitch using a color A 3 mm Crystaletts button.
- Work a stitch using a cube.
- Pick up a cube, and work an odd-count turn.

Row 14: Work four stitches using cubes, sewing through the button as if it were a bead **(figure 2).**

Row 15: Work in modified odd-count peyote stitch as follows:

- Work two stitches using cubes, and then sew through the button and the next up-bead in the previous row without picking up a bead **(figure 3, a–b).**
- Work a stitch using a cube **(b–c).**
- Pick up a cube, and work an odd-count turn **(c–d).**

Row 16: Work in modified odd-count peyote stitch as follows **(d–e):**

- Work a stitch using a cube.
- Pick up a cube, and sew through the button.
- Work two stitches using cubes.

Rows 17 and 18: Work in flat odd-count peyote stitch using cubes **(figure 4).**

[5] Repeat step 4 for the desired length band minus the last 12 rows and 1 in. (2.5 cm) for the clasp. End and add thread (Basics) as needed.

[6] Work 12 rows of flat odd-count peyote using cubes. Make sure the number of cubes along each edge of the band is divisible by three. Do not end the working thread or tail.

Clasp

[1] Work one stitch with a cube. Pick up an 11º seed bead, an A, an 11º, seven 15º seed beads, a loop of the clasp, and an 11º. Sew back through the A, positioning the button so it is face up on the bracelet. Pick up an 11º, and sew through the next three beads at the end of the band **(figure 5)**. Repeat this connection to attach the other loop of the clasp, and then work an odd-count turn. Retrace the thread path to reinforce the connection, and end the working thread.

[2] Remove the stop bead from the tail, and work as in step 1 to add the other half of the clasp to this end of the band. End the tail.

Edging

[1] Add 1½ yd. (1.4 m) of thread to one end of the band, and exit the second cube along one edge with the needle pointing away from the band.

[2] Pick up an 11º, three 15ºs, and an 11º. Skip the next cube along the edge of the band, sew down through the following cube, and continue up through the next cube. You have just completed one edging unit **(figure 6)**. Repeat this step for the length of the band.

[3] Sew through the beadwork to exit the second cube along the other edge, and repeat step 2.

[4] Sew through the beadwork to exit the second cube along the first edge, and sew through the first 11º in the first edging unit. Pick up an A, skip the three 15ºs, and sew down through the next 11º and the cube directly below it **(figure 7, a–b)**.

[5] Sew through the beadwork to skip the next edging unit, and exit the first 11º in the following edging unit **(b–c)**. Pick up a color B 3 mm Crystaletts button, skip the next three 15ºs, and sew down through the following 11º and the cube directly below it.

[6] Work as in step 5, but pick up an A instead of a B.

[7] Repeat step 5, alternating As and Bs, for the length of the band.

[8] Sew through the beadwork to the other edge, and repeat steps 4–7 to embellish this edge of the band. End the thread. ●

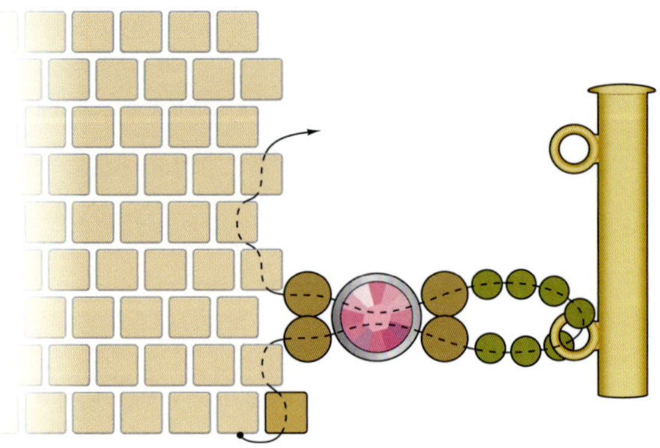

FIGURE 5

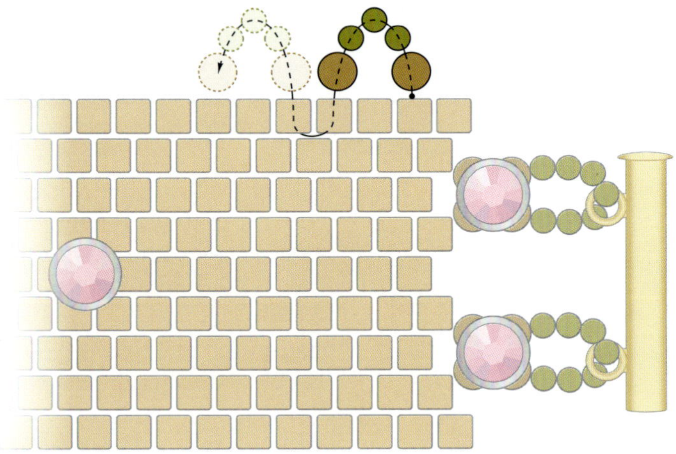

FIGURE 6

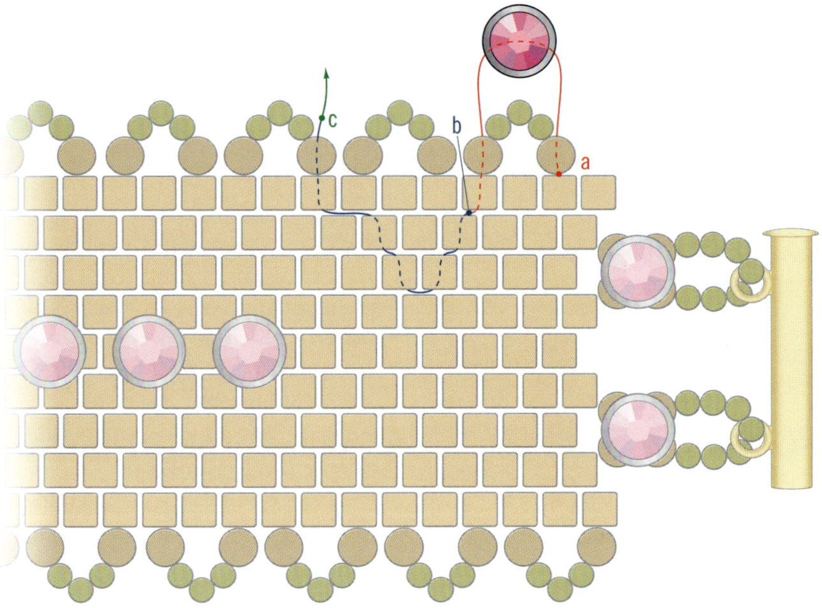

FIGURE 7

BEAD WEAVING

Coin toss pendant

The beads surrounding this pendant have a different arrangement on each side, so the piece looks great no matter which side is facing out.

designed by **Michelle McEnroe**

MATERIALS

green pendant 1½ in. (3.8 cm)

- **1** 23 mm Czech coin bead (pale green Picasso; www.stinkydogbeads.com)
- **16** 3 x 6 mm two-hole lentil beads (P65431, green opaque luster; www.bellomodo.com)
- **16** 3 x 5 mm Rulla beads (BT6303, blue turquoise bronze Picasso; www.redpandabeads.com)
- **16** 4 mm Czech druk beads, in place of pearls (BP-0191, opaque green luster; www.artbeads.com)
- 1 g 11º seed beads in each of **2** colors: A (SB1598, light matte olive over opaque light yellow; www.fusionbeads.com), B (SB1568, transparent grey; www.fusionbeads.com)
- 1 g 15º seed beads (SB3448, transparent olive green pink luster; www.fusionbeads.com)
- Fireline 6 lb. test
- beading needles, #10–12

pink pendant colors:

- 23 mm Czech coin bead (pink Picasso; www.stinkydogbeads.com)
- 3 x 6 mm two-hole lentil beads (P65491, rose gold/topaz opaque; www.bellomodo.com)
- 3 x 5 mm Rulla beads (BT6303, blue turquoise bronze Picasso; www.redpandabeads.com)
- 4 mm pearls (Swarovski, powder rose)
- 11º seed beads: A (SB2350, transparent dark red gold luster; www.fusionbeads.com), B (Toho 994, crystal transparent gold luster; www.bellomodo.com)
- 15º seed beads (SB3452, transparent reddish brown/purple luster; www.fusionbeads.com)

blue pendant colors:

- 23 mm Czech coin bead (transparent aqua blue Picasso; www.stinkydogbeads.com)
- 3 x 6 mm two-hole lentil beads (P65431, green opaque luster; www.bellomodo.com)
- 3 x 5 mm Rulla beads (SB4394, dark bronze; www.fusionbeads.com)
- 4 mm pearls (Swarovski, powder almond)
- 11º seed beads: A (Miyuki 2008, matte metallic patina iris; www.auntiesbeads.com), B (Miyuki SB2582, cocoa permanent galvanized; www.fusionbeads.com)
- 15º seed beads (Toho 82, metallic navy iris; www.artbeads.com)

a

b

c

d

stepbystep

[1] On 3 yd. (2.7 m) of thread, attach a stop bead (Basics), leaving a 6-in. (15 cm) tail.

[2] Pick up a 23 mm coin bead, and then pick up a repeating pattern of a 3 x 5 mm Rulla bead and a color A 11º seed bead seven times. Pick up a Rulla, and sew through the coin, positioning the beads around one half of the coin. Retrace the thread path, exiting the coin. Lay the beadwork on your bead mat, and position the Rullas so they stand perpendicular to the surface of your mat, with the available holes toward the top. This is to assure the proper tension and that the Rullas will lie properly for the remaining steps. Tie a half-hitch knot (Basics).

[3] Work as in step 2 to add Rullas and As around the other half of the coin, and tie a half-hitch knot.

[4] Sew through the beads around the first half of the coin, pick up an A, and continue through the beads around the remaining half. Pick up an A, and sew through the next Rulla. Do not pull the beads tight; there will be a slight gap at each end where the new As were added. Sew through the available hole of the same Rulla **(photo a)**.

[5] Pick up a 3 x 6 mm two-hole lentil bead, and sew through the available hole of the next Rulla. Repeat this stitch **(photo b)** to complete the round, and retrace the thread path using an even tension. Reposition the Rullas if necessary. Sew through the first lentil added, and continue through the available hole of the same lentil. Flip the beadwork over to the other side.

[6] Pick up a 4 mm pearl, and sew through the available hole of the next lentil. With the Rullas in the correct position, the pearls will sit on top of the Rullas. Repeat this stitch **(photo c)** to complete the round, and retrace the thread path using an even tension. Tie a half-hitch knot to hold the tension of the beads, and continue through the next pearl. Remove the stop bead, and end the tail (Basics).

[7] Pick up an A, a color B 11º seed bead, and an A, and sew through the next pearl to form a picot. Repeat this stitch **(photo d)** to complete the round. Sew through the outside hole of the next lentil, and continue through the inside hole of the same lentil.

e

f

g

h

[8] Pick up two 15º seed beads, an A, and two 15ºs. Skip the next Rulla, lentil, and Rulla, and sew through the inside hole of the following lentil. Repeat this stitch **(photo e)** to complete the round, and continue through the first two 15ºs, A, and two 15ºs added in this round.

[9] Pick up a 15º, a B, and a 15º, and sew through the next two 15ºs, A, and two 15ºs added in the previous step. Repeat this stitch **(photo f)** to complete the round, and retrace the thread path through all the beads added in this step and the previous step. Sew through the inside hole of the following lentil, and continue through the outside hole of the same lentil.

[10] Pick up a B, an A, and a B, and sew through the outside hole of the next lentil. Repeat this stitch **(photo g)** to complete the round, and continue through the next pearl. Flip the beadwork over to the other side.

[11] Pick up three 15ºs, and sew through the existing A between the adjacent Rulla beads. Pick up three 15ºs, and sew through the next pearl. Repeat these two stitches **(photo h)** to complete the round using a tight tension.

[12] Rotate the pendant so the top of the image on the coin bead is positioned at the top of the pendant. Sew through the beadwork to exit the B in the picot that is at the top of the pendant.

[13] Pick up five Bs, and sew through the B your thread is exiting to form a loop. Retrace the thread path.

[14] With your thread exiting the B in the picot, pick up a 15º, and sew through the next B in the loop. Repeat this stitch around the loop, and retrace the thread path of the loop and the join.

[15] If the beadwork still seems a little loose, sew through the pearls and the top hole of the lentils along the outside edge using a tight tension. You can also sew through the beadwork to the inside ring of beads on each side of the pendant, and retrace the thread path through the beads and the coin. End the thread. •

DESIGN NOTE:
Add a jump ring to the top of the pendant, making sure it is large enough to accommodate the necklace of your choice.

Basketweave rings

These little rings are great for using cylinder beads you already have in your stash and experimenting with different color combinations.

designed by **Nina Raizel**

stepbystep

Base rings

[1] On 2 ft. (61 cm) of thread, pick up enough color A 11º cylinder beads to fit around your finger, but make sure the number of cylinders is divisible by eight. My ring uses 48 cylinders and is approximately a size 8. Pick up 40 cylinders to make approximately a size 5 ring, and pick up 56 cylinders to make approximately a size 12 ring. Sew through all the beads again to form a ring, leaving a 6-in. (15 cm) tail, and allow some slack between the beads. These beads will shift to form rounds 1 and 2 as the next round is added.

[2] Using As, work two rounds of tubular peyote stitch (Basics) for a total of four rounds. Be sure to shape the ring into a tube rather than a flat circle. End the working thread and tail (Basics).

[3] Using 5 ft. (1.5 m) of thread, repeat steps 1 and 2, starting with the same number of As. Step up at the end of round 4 so your thread is exiting an up-bead. End the tail, but not the working thread.

Bridges

[1] To begin a bridge, pick up an A, and sew through the next up-bead along the edge **(figure 1, a–b)**.

[2] Pick up an A, and sew through the A added in the previous step **(b–c)**. Repeat this stitch to add eight more As for a total of 10 bridge beads **(c–d)**.

[3] Sew up through an up-bead along the edge of the other base ring, and sew back through the last A added in the previous step **(d–e)**.

[4] Sew through the beadwork as shown to exit an up-bead two up-beads from the bridge just created **(figure 2, a–b)**. There will be an up-bead and a down-bead between the bridges.

[5] Pick up an A, and sew through the beadwork as shown to exit the same up-bead your thread exited at the start of this step, but in the opposite direction **(b–c)**

[6] Repeat step 2 **(c–d)**.

[7] Sew through the corresponding up-bead along the edge of the other base ring, and sew back through the last A added in the previous step **(d–e)**. Sew through the beadwork as shown to exit the next up-bead from the bridge just created **(e–f)**.

[8] Repeat steps 1–7 to create a total of 12 bridges, and end the thread.

Decorative bands

[1] On 1 yd. (.9 m) of thread, pick up three color B 11º cylinder beads, leaving a 6-in. (15 cm) tail. Sew back through

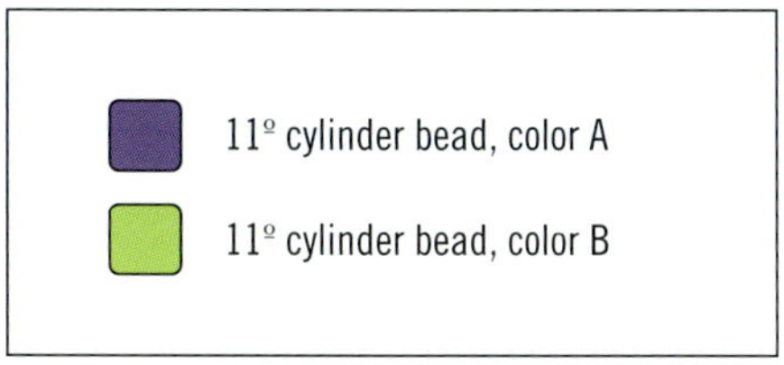

DESIGN NOTES:

- **To make a narrower ring, only add six cylinders per bridge, and omit the second decorative band.**
- **This project is a great way to use up small amounts of leftover beads.**

the first B with the needle pointing toward the tail **(figure 3, a–b)**. Position the second and third Bs to sit on top of each other, with their holes parallel.

[2] Pick up a B, and sew through the last B added **(b–c)**. Repeat this stitch to create a band that will fit around your ring.

[3] Weave the band under and over the bridges until it fits comfortably through the ring. Add or remove rows if necessary for a proper fit and to match up the ends. Zip up (Basics) the ends of the band, and end the working thread and tail.

[4] Repeat steps 1–3 for the other decorative band using color C 11º cylinder beads. ●

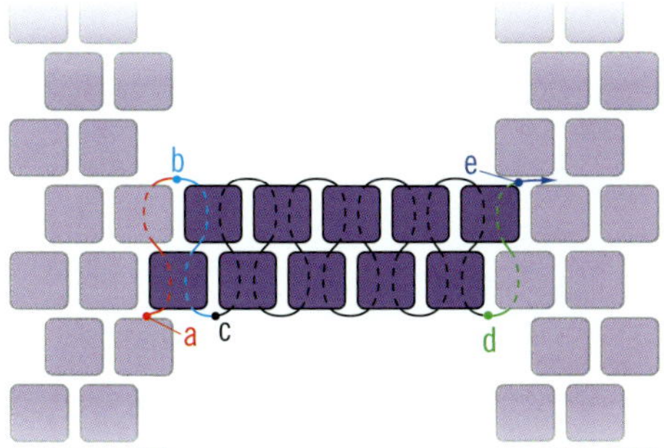

FIGURE 1

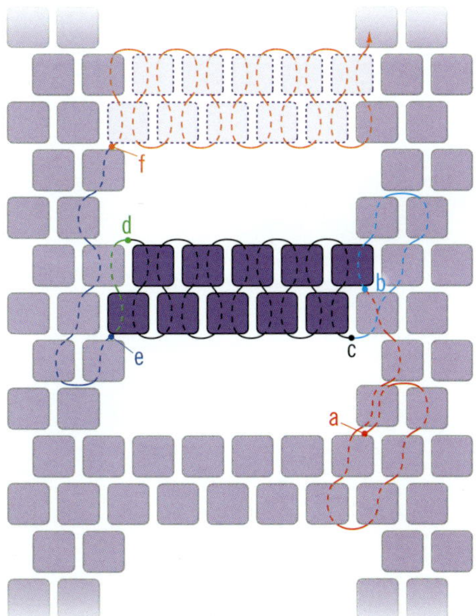

FIGURE 2

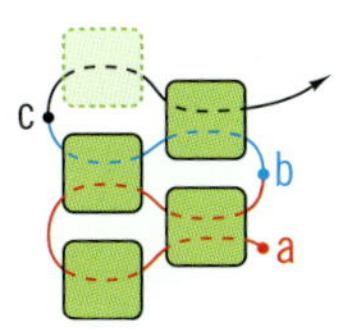

FIGURE 3

MATERIALS

blue/teal ring ½ in. (1.3 cm) wide

- 11º Miyuki Delica cylinder beads
  2 g color A (DB0005, metallic variegated blue iris)
  1 g color B (DB0149, silver-lined Capri blue)
  1 g color C (DB0413, galvanized moss green)
- Fireline 6 lb. test
- beading needles, #11 or #12

red/pink ring colors:

- 11º Miyuki Delica cylinder beads
  color A (DB1134, opaque currant)
  color B (DB1404, transparent pale green mist)
  color C (DB0082, transparent pink AB)

brown/tan ring colors:

- 11º Miyuki Delica cylinder beads
  color A (DB0380, matte metallic khaki iris)
  color B (DB052, pale peach-lined crystal AB)
  color C (DB0146, silver-lined smoky amethyst)

purple/green ring colors:

- 11º Miyuki Delica cylinder beads
  color A (DB0128, plum gold luster)
  color B (DB0604, dyed silver-lined golden olive)

HERRINGBONE STITCH

Herringbone flair

designed by **Eleanna Zegkinoglou**

Discover why herringbone stitch is always in style as you join two ropes embellished with seed beads, crystals, and pearls.

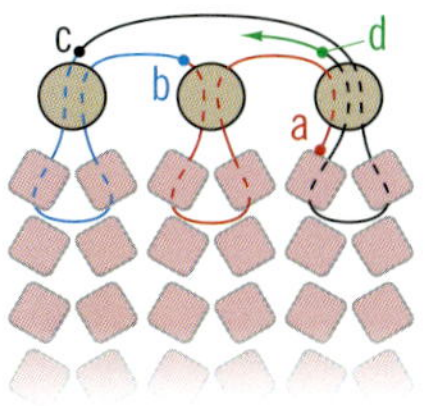

FIGURE 1

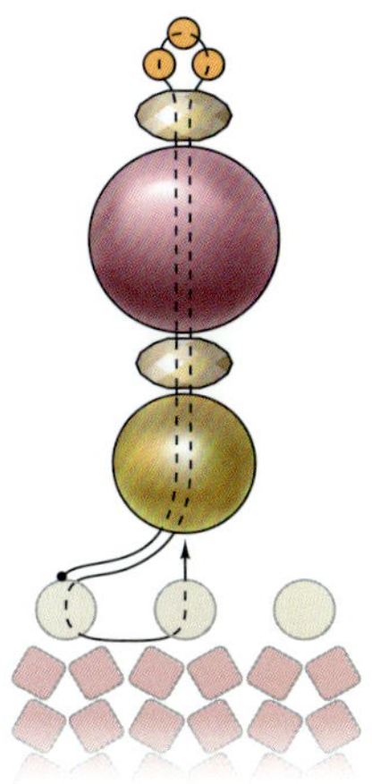

FIGURE 2

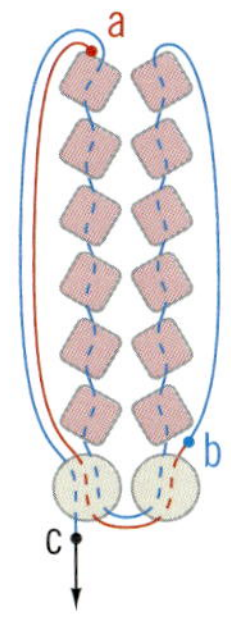

FIGURE 3

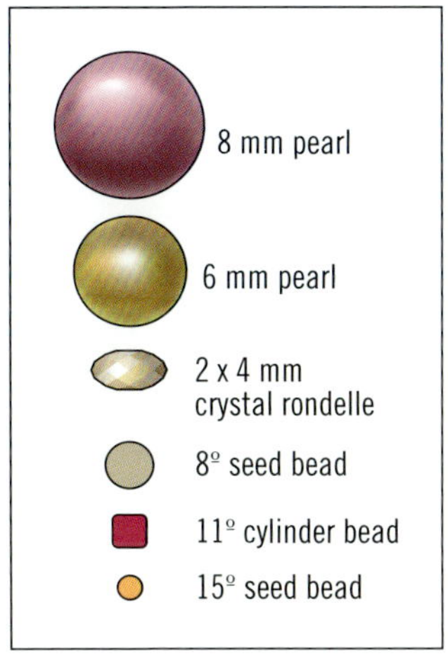

MATERIALS

necklace 17 in. (43 cm)

- **2** 8 mm crystal pearls (Swarovski, burgundy)
- **5** 6 mm crystal pearls (Swarovski, bronze)
- **9** 4 mm crystal rondelles (Swarovski #5040, crystal golden shadow)
- **16** 8º seed beads (Miyuki 4222, Duracoat pewter; www.beyondbeadery.com)
- 9 g 11º cylinder beads (Miyuki DB0611, dyed silver-lined wine; www.artbeads.com)
- 1 g 15º seed beads (Japanese 481A, apricot gold galvanized; www.beyondbeadery.com)
- lobster claw clasp (gold)
- 2–3-in. (5–7.6 cm) extender chain (gold)
- **2** 6 mm jump rings (gold)
- Fireline 6 lb. test
- beading needles, #11
- **2** pairs of pliers

stepby**step**

Ropes

[1] On a comfortable length of thread, make a six-bead ladder (Basics) using 11º cylinder beads and leaving a 2-ft. (61 cm) tail. Form the ladder into a ring (Basics). Repeat this step to make a second ring.

[2] Work in tubular herringbone stitch (Basics) using cylinders to make one 8½-in. (21.6 cm) rope and one 9-in. (23 cm) rope, ending each rope with a step up. End and add thread (Basics) as needed while you stitch, but do not end the working thread and tail when you finish.

[3] With the working thread from one of the ropes, pick up two 8º seed beads, and work a herringbone thread path to exit the second 8º **(figure 1, a–b)**. Pick up another 8º, and work a herringbone thread path to exit the new 8º **(b–c)**. Sew down through the first 8º added in this step, and work a herringbone thread path to exit the first 8º **(c–d)**. Do not end the working thread.

[4] Repeat step 3 using the tail. Do not end the tail.

[5] Work as in steps 3 and 4 for the remaining rope.

End embellishments and clasp

[1] With the working thread from one of the ropes, pick up a 6 mm pearl, a 4 mm crystal rondelle, an 8 mm pearl, a rondelle, and three 15º seed beads. Sew back through the rondelle, 8 mm, rondelle, 6 mm, and 8º your thread exited at the start of this step. Continue through the next 8º **(figure 2)**.

[2] Retrace the thread path through the beads added in the previous step, sew through the 8º your thread exited at the start of this step, and continue through the next 8º. Repeat this stitch once more to connect the last 8º to the end embellishment. End the working thread.

[3] With the tail, pick up a rondelle, a 6 mm, a rondelle, and two 8ºs. Sew back through the rondelle, 6 mm, rondelle, and 8º your thread exited at the start of this step. Continue through the next 8º.

[4] Retrace the thread path through the beads added in the previous step, sew through the 8º your thread exited at the start of this step, and continue through the next 8º. Sew through the rondelle, 6 mm, rondelle, and an 8º.

[5] Working off the two 8ºs in the end embellishment and using cylinders, make a flat strip of herringbone stitch (Basics) that's two beads wide and six rows long.

[6] Work a herringbone thread path through the 8ºs in the end embellishment, forming the herringbone strip into a loop **(figure 3, a–b)**. Sew through the cylinders on this side of the loop, the two 8ºs, the cylinders on the other side of the loop, and the following 8º **(b–c)**. Continue back through the rondelle, the 6 mm, the rondelle, and the 8º your thread exited at the end of step 4. End the tail.

[7] Open a 6 mm jump ring (Basics), and attach the lobster claw clasp to the herringbone loop.

[8] Repeat steps 1–7 for the other rope, but attach the extender chain in step 7 instead of the lobster claw clasp.

[9] On 24 in. (61 cm) of thread, pick up seven 15ºs,

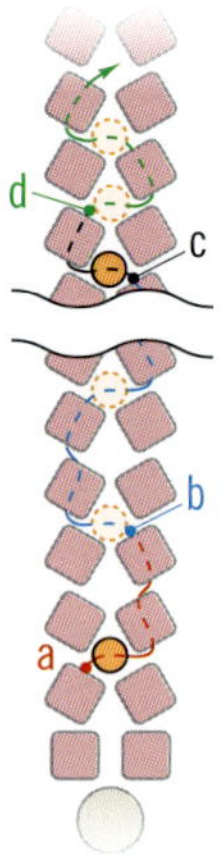

FIGURE 4

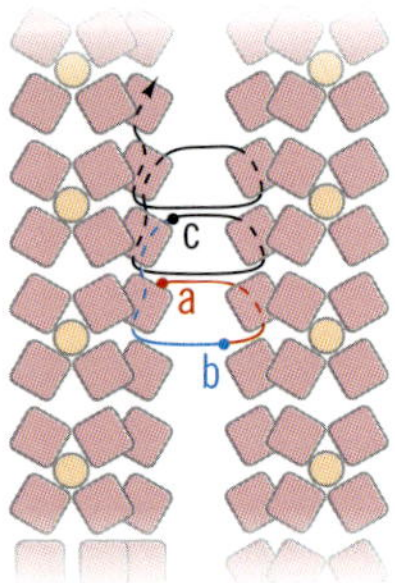

FIGURE 5

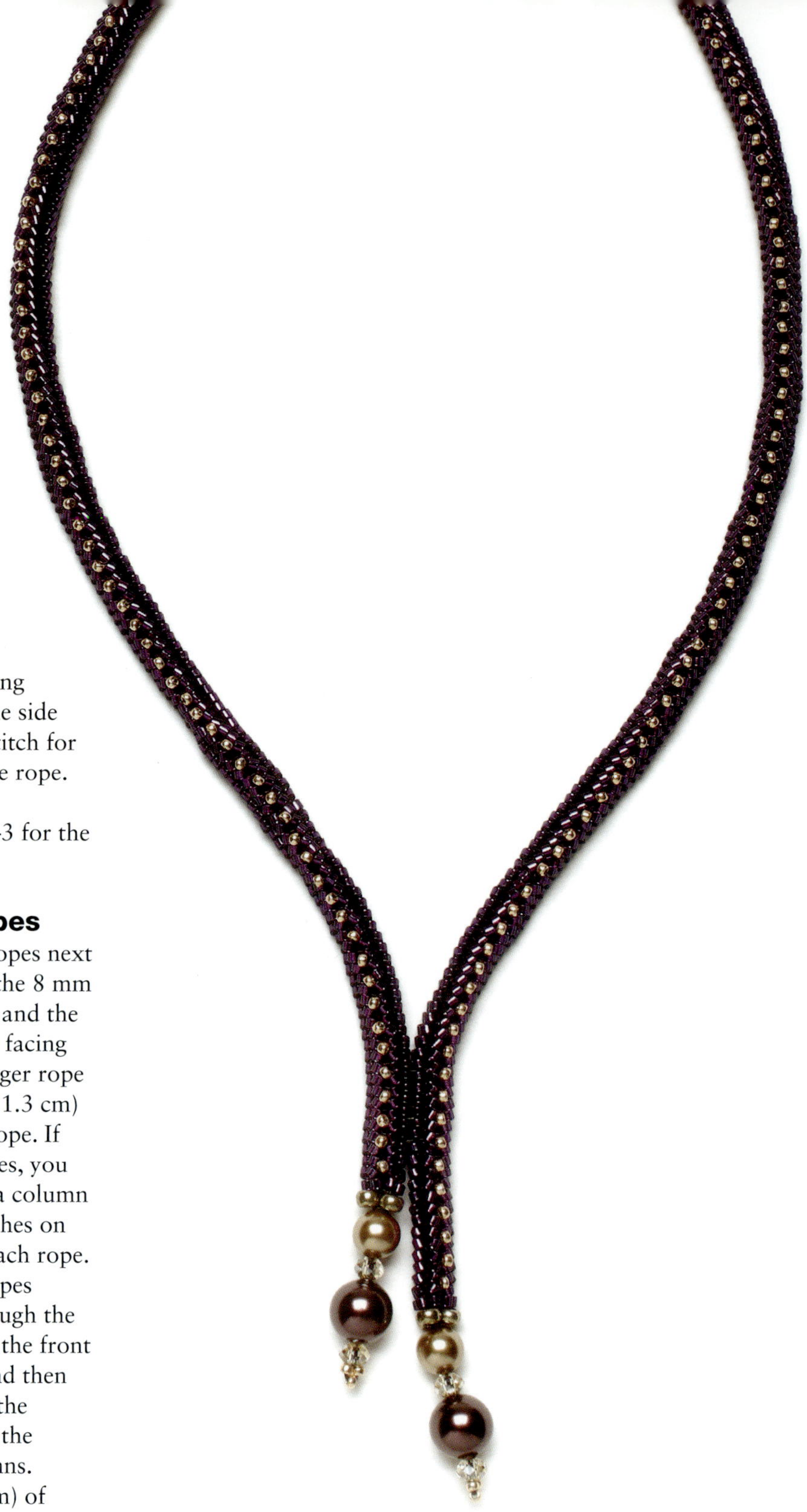

sew through the end of the chain, and sew back through the first 15º, leaving a 6-in. (15 cm) tail.

[10] Pick up a 6 mm, a rondelle, and three 15ºs. Sew back through the rondelle, the 6 mm, and the first 15º added in the previous step. Retrace the thread path through all the beads in the dangle, and end the working thread and tail.

Rope embellishment

[1] Add 1 yd. (.9 m) of thread to one rope at the end with the 8 mm pearl, and exit a cylinder in the first round of herringbone **(figure 4, point a)**.

[2] Pick up a 15º, sew through the opposite cylinder in the next herringbone stitch, and continue through the following cylinder in the same column **(a–b)**. Repeat this stitch for the length of the rope, stopping ½ in. (1.3 cm) before the end of the rope **(b–c)**. Make sure the rope does not twist and that you always embellish the same column of herringbone.

[3] To complete the rope: Pick up a 15º, and sew through the opposite cylinder in the next herringbone stitch as before, but do not continue through the following cylinder on the same side **(c–d)**. Repeat this stitch for the remainder of the rope. End the thread.

[4] Repeat steps 1–3 for the other rope.

Joining the ropes

[1] Place the two ropes next to each other with the 8 mm pearl ends together and the 15º embellishments facing up. Position the longer rope so it extends ½ in. (1.3 cm) below the shorter rope. If you look at the ropes, you will notice there is a column of herringbone stitches on the inside edge of each rope. You will join the ropes first by sewing through the cylinders that sit at the front of these columns and then by sewing through the cylinders that sit at the back of these columns.

[2] Add 2 ft. (61 cm) of thread to the indicated column on the shorter rope, and exit the fifth cylinder that sits at the front of this column with your needle pointing toward the clasp **(figure 5, point a)**. You may have to adjust the ropes slightly so that the 15º embellishments on each rope line up directly across from each other.

[3] Sew down through the corresponding cylinder in the longer rope **(a–b)**. Sew up through the cylinder your thread exited at the start of this step, and continue through the next cylinder in the same column **(b–c)**. Repeat this stitch to join a total of seven cylinders using a tight tension.

[4] Sew through the beadwork to exit the corresponding cylinder at the back of the column. Work as in step 3 to join the corresponding seven cylinders. End the thread. ●

HERRINGBONE STITCH

Herringbone bezel pendant

Stitch this quick frame for a favorite focal bead or cabochon using an easy flat herringbone technique.

designed by **Jane Danley Cruz**

MATERIALS

pendant 1¼ in. (3.2 cm)

- 22 mm focal bead by Marsha Hedrick (www.amazingporcelain.com)
- **15** 4 mm magatama beads (Miyuki 401, opaque black)
- 2 g 8º seed beads (Miyuki 401, black)
- 1 g 11º Japanese seed beads (F403, opaque bone matte; www.whimbeads.com)
- 1 g 15º seed beads (Miyuki 408, opaque red)
- **2** 6 mm jump rings
- necklace cord or chain
- WildFire beading thread
- beading needles, #10
- **2** pairs of chainnose, flatnose, and/or bentnose pliers

stepbystep

[1] On 1 yd. (.9 m) of thread and leaving a 6-in. (15 cm) tail, work in ladder stitch to make a four-bead ladder (Basics) using an 11º seed bead, an 8º seed bead, an 8º, and an 11º. Zigzag back through the beads to stabilize the ladder **(figure 1)**.

[2] Pick up an 11º and an 8º, and sew down through the next 8º in the previous row and up through the following 8º **(figure 2, a–b)**. Pick up an 8º and an 11º, and sew down through the last 11º in the previous row **(b–c)**. To turn: Pick up an 11º, and sew up through the previous 11º picked up in this step **(c–d)** to be in position for the next row.

[3] Work as in step 2 until you have a strip long enough to wrap snugly around your focal bead, ending with an even number of rows. Our strip is 30 rows long.

[4] To form the strip into a ring: Make sure the strip is not twisted. Bring the ends together, and sew through the corresponding 11º in the first row at the other end of the strip. Continue as shown in **figure 3, a–b**.

[5] Add a turn bead: Pick up an 11º, and sew through the nearest 11º in the first row **(b–c)**. Sew through the beadwork to exit a turn bead.

[6] Pick up an 11º, and sew through the next two turn beads along this edge of the bezel. Repeat this stitch to complete the round. Retrace the thread path using a firm tension, and then sew through the beadwork to exit a turn bead along the other edge of the bezel.

[7] Place the focal bead into the bezel so the back of the focal is against the beadwork. Pick up an 11º, and sew through the next turn bead along this edge. Repeat this stitch to complete the round. Retrace the thread path through the beads added in this step, and then sew through the beadwork to exit any 8º in the bezel.

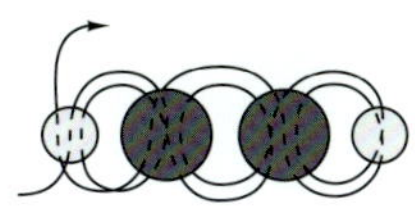

FIGURE 1

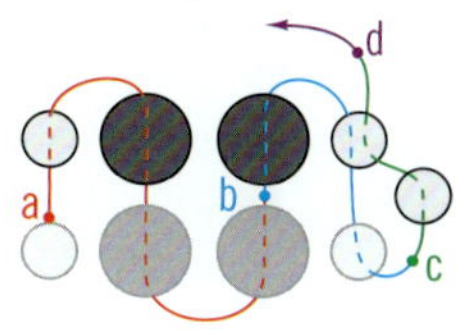

FIGURE 2

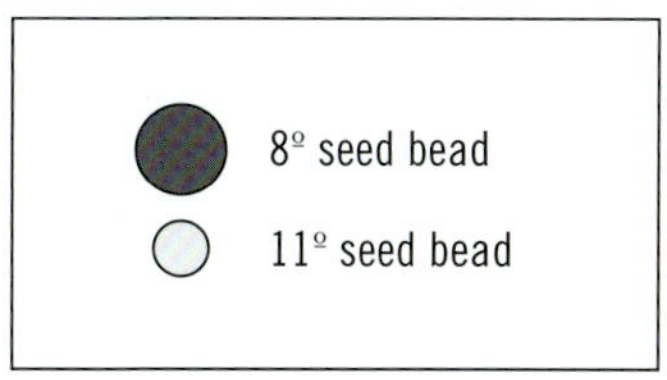

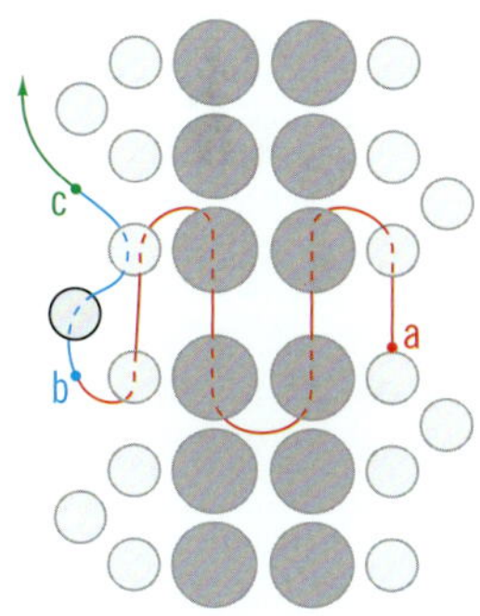

FIGURE 3

[8] Pick up a 4 mm magatama, and sew through the 8º in the next row in the opposite column. Pick up a 15º seed bead, an 11º, and a 15º, and sew through the 8º in the next row in the opposite column. Repeat these two stitches to complete the round. Sew through the beadwork to exit an 8º behind a magatama.

[9] Pick up five 15ºs, and sew through the 8º in the same direction. Retrace the thread path through the loop several times, and then sew through the next three 8ºs. Create another five-bead loop, and end the working thread and tail (Basics).

[10] Open a 6 mm jump ring (Basics), and attach a five-bead loop. Repeat for the other five-bead loop.

[11] String a necklace cord or chain through the jump rings. ●

NETTING

Totally tubular triangle beads

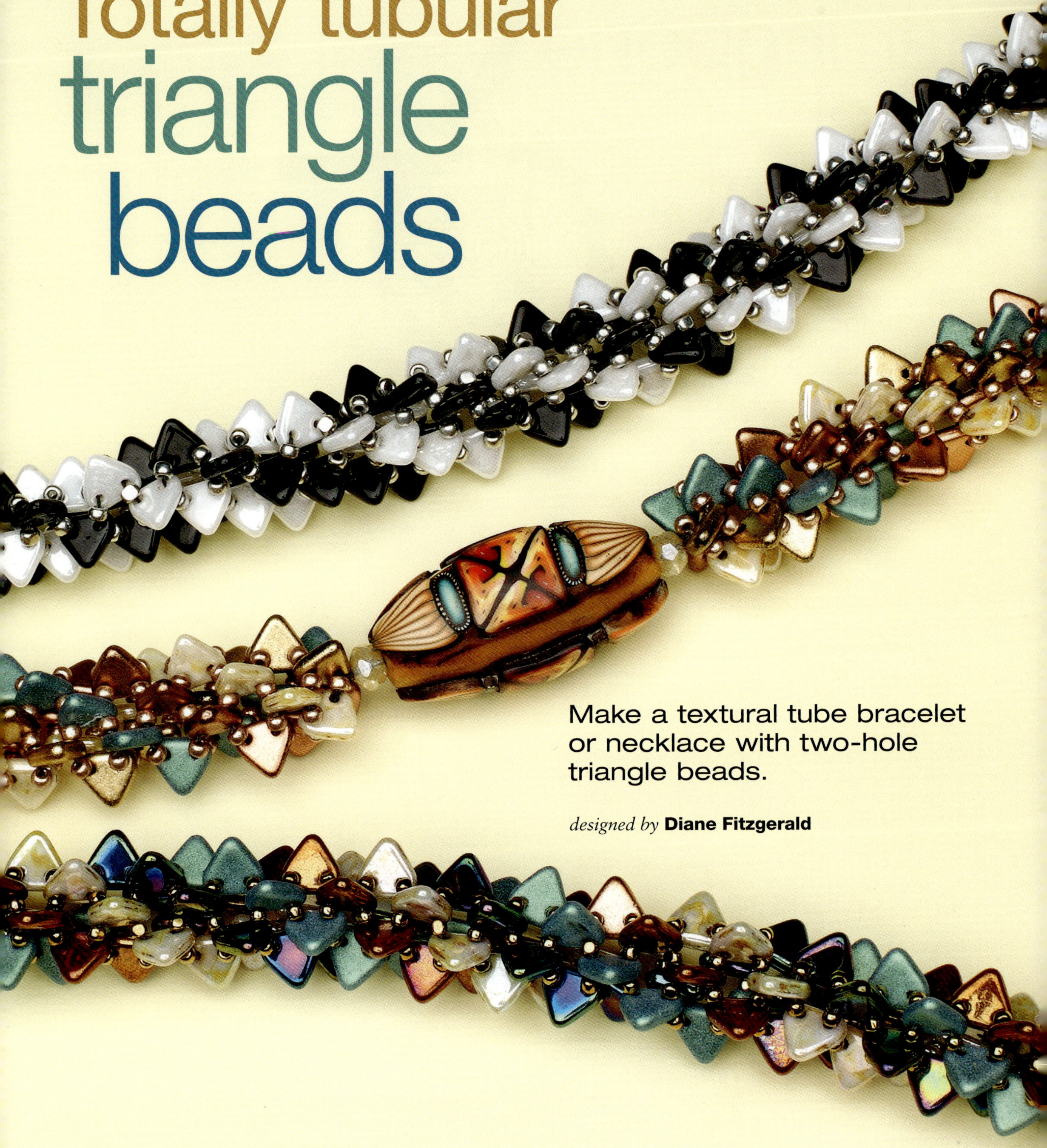

Make a textural tube bracelet or necklace with two-hole triangle beads.

designed by **Diane Fitzgerald**

stepbystep

How to pick up triangle beads: With the point of the triangle facing away from you, pick up the bead through the left hole (LH) or the right hole (RH) **(figure 1)**, per the instructions.

[1] Center a needle on 3 yd. (2.7 m) of thread. Align the ends, wax the strands so they adhere to each other, and tie an overhand knot (Basics). Trim the tails 1 mm from the knot, and melt slightly with a lighter to form a tiny ball.

[2] Pick up a repeating pattern of a 15° seed bead and a 6 mm triangle (LH) four times, picking up all four colors of triangles in A, B, C, D order **(figure 2)**.

[3] Push the beads to within 1 in. (2.5 cm) of the knot. Separate the strands between the beads and the knot, and pass the needle between the strands, creating a ring. Pick up a 15°, and sew through the D (RH) **(figure 3)**. You should now be working in a counterclockwise direction.

[4] Pick up a 15°, a D (RH), and a 15°, and sew through the open hole of the next triangle in the previous round **(figure 4)**. Repeat this stitch three times, but with each stitch pick up a triangle that is the same color as the triangle you just sewed through **(figure 5)**.

[5] Repeat step 4 for the desired length, ending and adding thread (Basics) as needed. As you work, some of the triangles may slip into the center of the tube. Be sure to adjust them so you don't miss any.

[6] To complete the tube, pick up a 15°, and sew through the remaining hole of the next triangle in the previous round. Repeat this stitch twice. Pick up one more 15°, and sew through the next triangle. There will already be a bead next to the hole of this triangle.

[7] Pick up two 8° seed beads and the toggle bar. Sew back through the 8°s and the triangle opposite the one your thread exited at the start of this step. Retrace the thread path, and end the thread.

[8] Add 8 in. (20 cm) of thread at the other end, and repeat step 7 with the toggle ring, but pick up only one 8° instead of two. ●

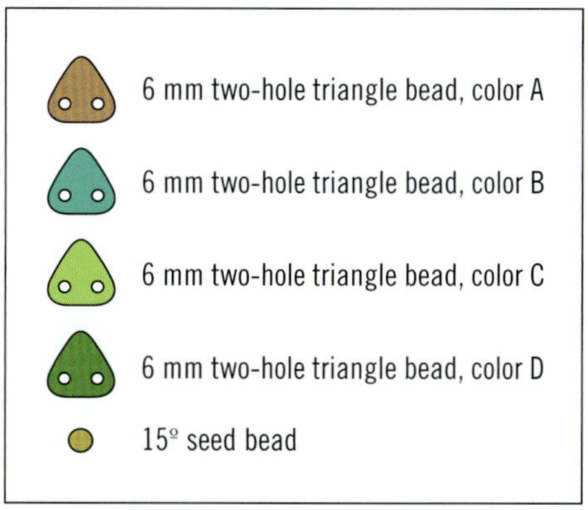

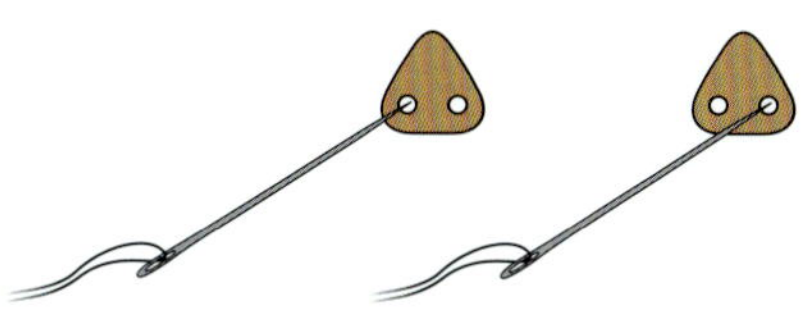

FIGURE 1

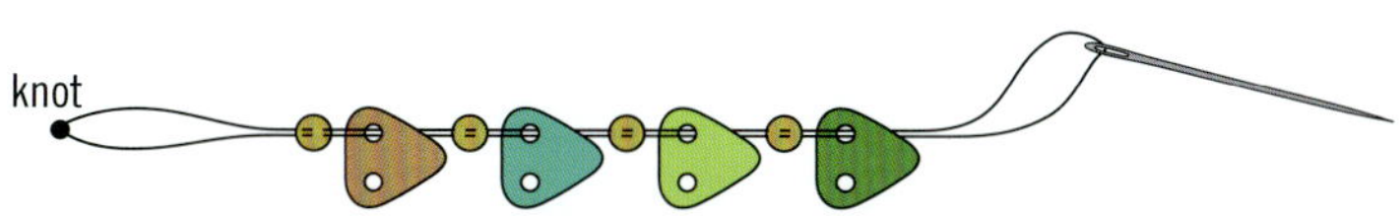

FIGURE 2

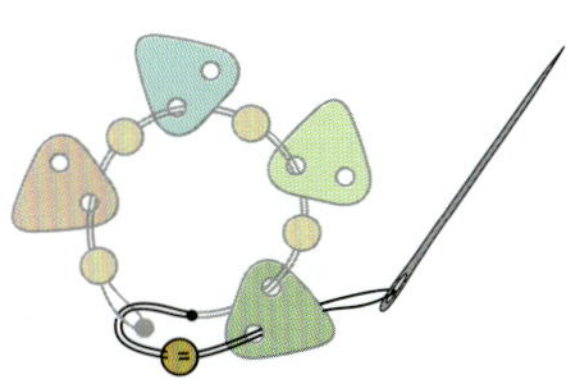

FIGURE 3

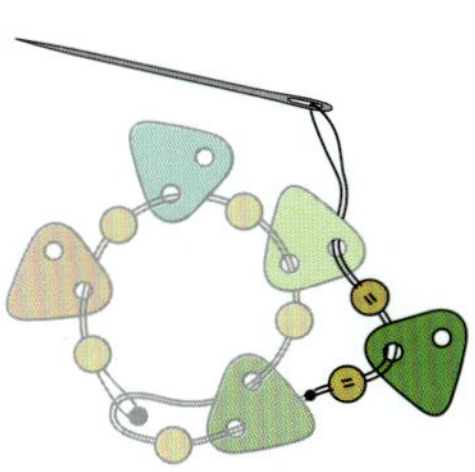

FIGURE 4

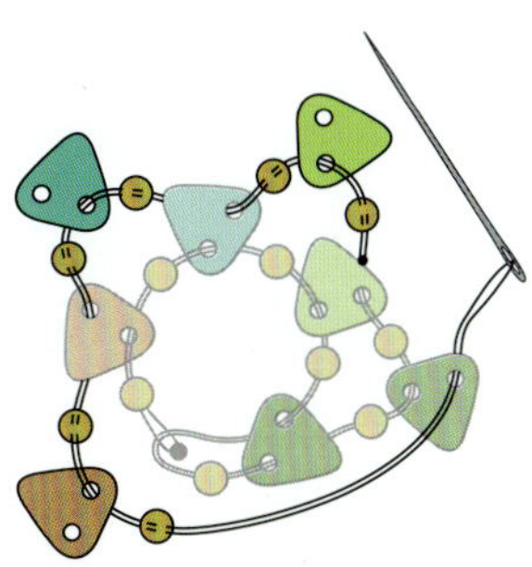

FIGURE 5

MATERIALS

copper/teal bracelet 8 in. (20 cm)

- **45–50** 6 mm CzechMates two-hole triangle beads in each of **4** colors: A (copper iris), B (teal metallic suede), C (opaque celery Picasso), D (iridescent green)
- **3** 8° seed beads (bronze)
- 8 g 15° seed beads (bronze)
- toggle clasp
- Nymo D or Fireline 6 lb. test, conditioned with microcrystalline wax
- beading needles, #10
- lighter

black/white bracelet colors:

- 6 mm two-hole triangle beads: A and C (jet), B and D (Ceylon white)
- 8° seed beads (silver)
- 11° seed beads, in place of 15°s (silver)

focal bead bracelet colors:

- polymer clay drum bead (www.klewexpressions.com)
- 6 mm two-hole triangle beads: A (vintage copper matte), B (opaque cream Picasso), C (matte metallic flax), D (teal metallic suede)
- 8° seed beads (galvanized gold)
- 11° seed beads, in place of 15°s (Miyuki 4204, champagne Duracoat)

DESIGN NOTES:

- **This technique also works well with other two-hole beads, such as half-moons, Twins, SuperDuos, and lentils, as shown above. Consider mixing two-hole bead shapes or replacing the seed beads with drops or long magatamas.**
- **To add a focal bead, stitch two equal sections of beadwork, and then use each working thread to cross through the focal bead at least twice before ending the threads.**

RIGHT-ANGLE WEAVE

Funky skunk

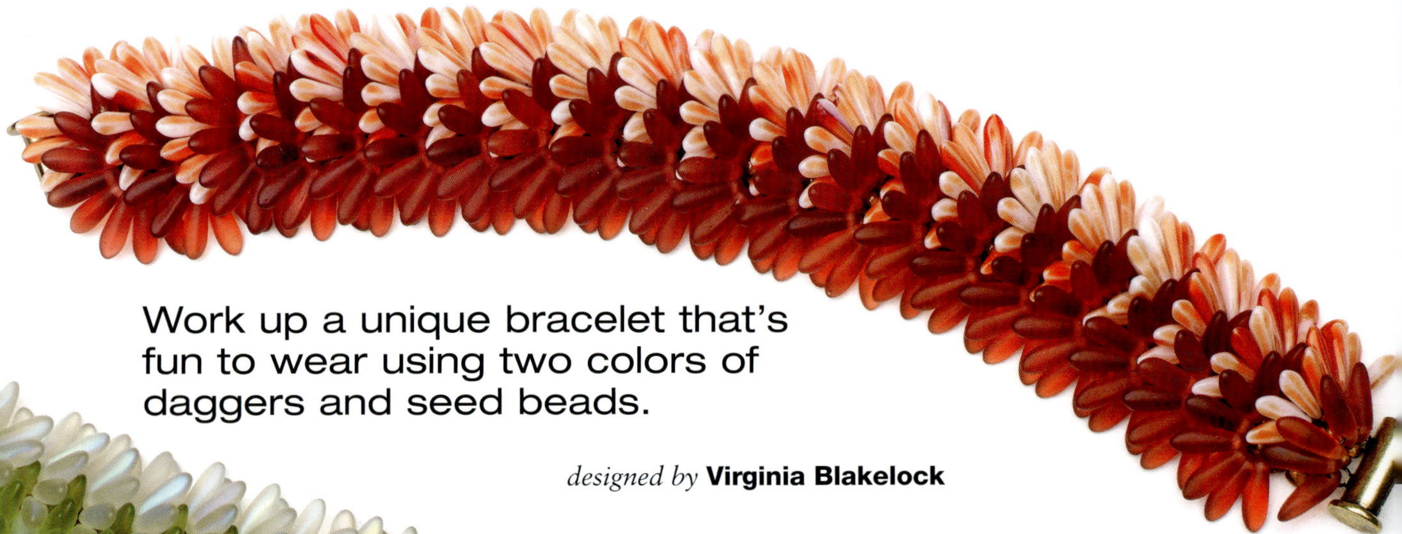

Work up a unique bracelet that's fun to wear using two colors of daggers and seed beads.

designed by **Virginia Blakelock**

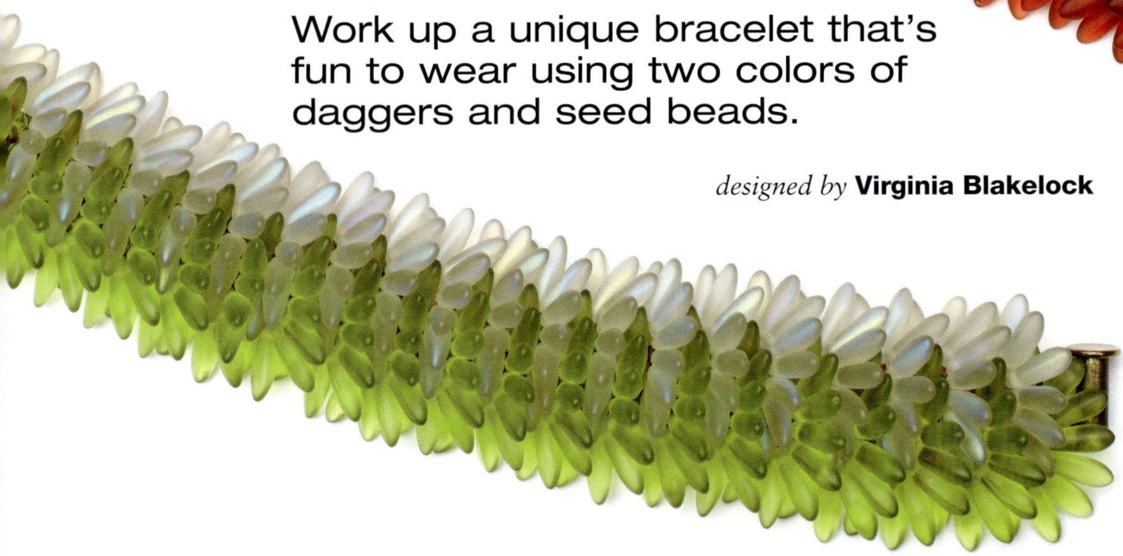

stepbystep

Base

[1] On a comfortable length of KO thread, pick up two 11º seed beads, an 8º seed bead, two 11ºs, and an 8º. Tie the beads into a ring with a square knot (Basics), leaving a 6-in. (15 cm) tail. Sew through the beads once more, exiting an 8º (figure 1, a–b).

[2] Working in modified right-angle weave (Basics), pick up two 11ºs, an 8º, and two 11ºs, and sew through the 8º your thread exited at the start of this step. Continue through the next two 11ºs and 8º (b–c).

[3] Work as in step 2, but continue through only the next two 11ºs (c–d). This completes the first row of the base.

[4] Pick up an 8º, two 11ºs, and an 8º, and sew through the two 11ºs your thread exited at the start of this step (figure 2, a–b). Continue through the beads just added (b–c) and the next two 11ºs along the edge of the previous row (c–d).

[5] Pick up an 8º and two 11ºs. Sew through the 8º from the previous stitch, the next two 11ºs along the edge of the previous row, and the 8º added in this step (d–e).

[6] Pick up two 11ºs and an 8º, and sew through the next two 11ºs along the edge of the previous row, the 8º from the previous stitch, and the two 11ºs added in this step (e–f). Flip the beadwork so your thread is exiting on the right side of the base. This completes the second row of the base.

[7] Repeat steps 4–6 for the desired length bracelet minus ¼ in. (6 mm) for the clasp. End and add thread (Basics)

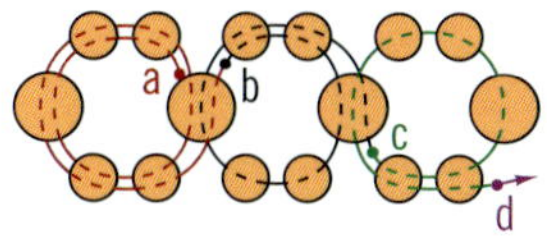

FIGURE 1

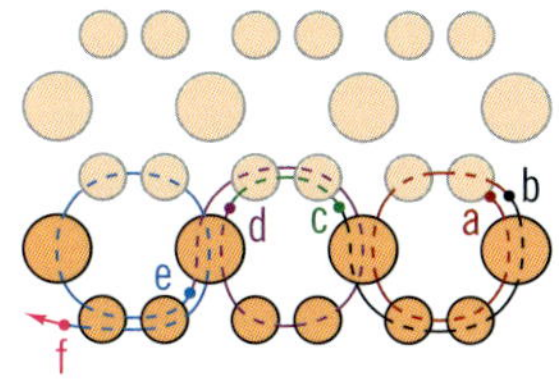

FIGURE 2

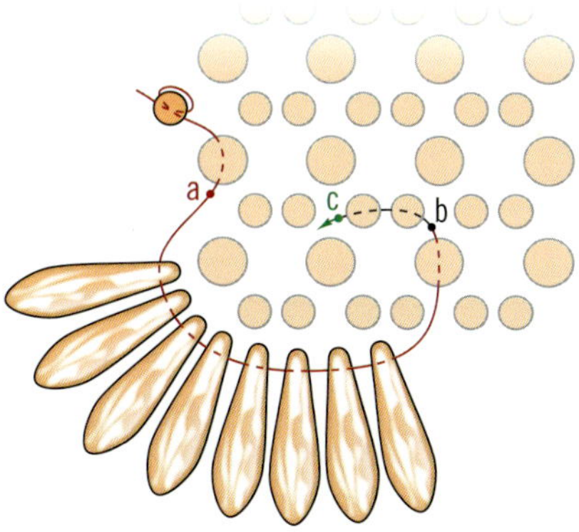

FIGURE 3

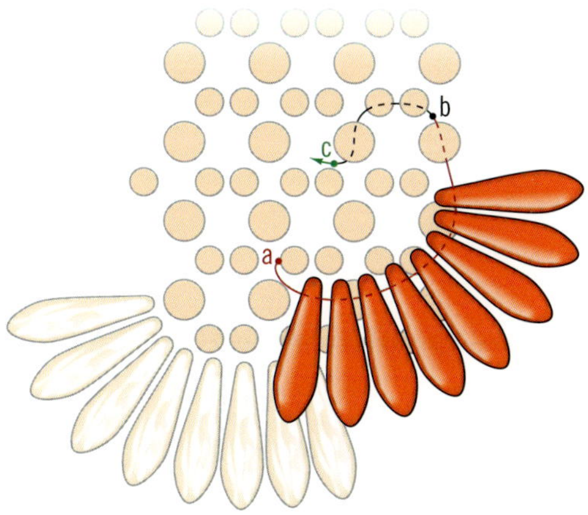

FIGURE 4

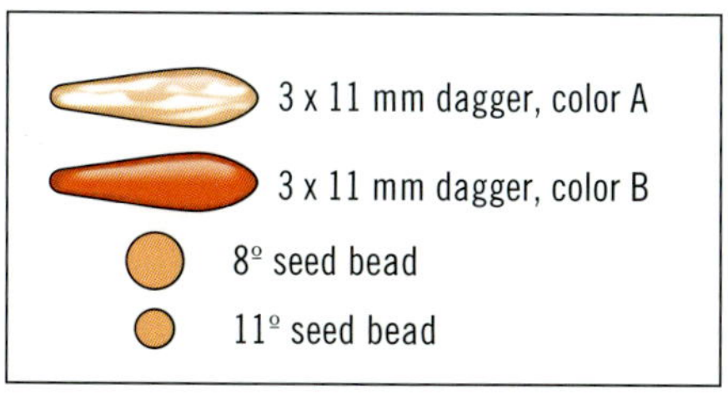

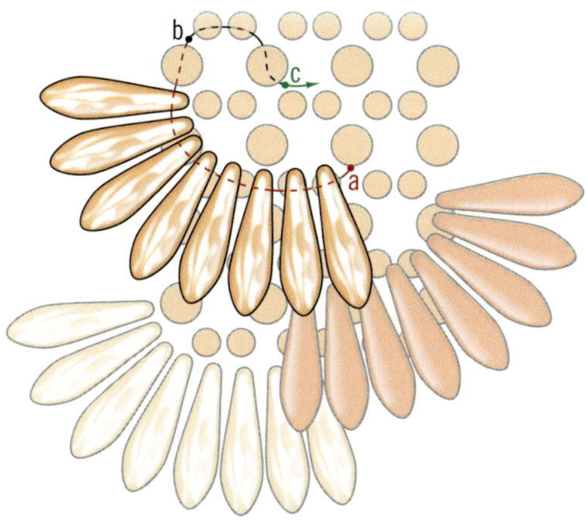

FIGURE 5

as needed, tying your half-hitch knots between the two 11ºs in the center right-angle weave stitches. When you complete the base, sew back through the beadwork at least three rows, and end the working thread and tail in the same manner.

Daggers

[1] Lay the base vertically on your work surface so that row 1 is closest to you. On 2 yd. (1.8 m) of Power Pro thread, attach a stop bead (Basics), leaving a 10-in. (25 cm) tail.

[2] Sew through the edge 8º on the left side of the base in the second row, with your needle pointing toward row 1 **(figure 3, point a)**. Pick up eight color A 11 x 3 mm daggers, and sew through the third 8º from the left side in the first row **(a–b)**. Continue through the adjacent two center 11ºs in the stitch **(b–c)**.

[3] Pick up eight color B 11 x 3 mm daggers, and sew through the edge 8º on the right side of the base in the third row **(figure 4, a–b)**. Continue through the next two 11ºs and the following 8º in the same row **(b–c)**.

[4] Pick up eight As, and sew through the edge 8º on the left side of the base in the fourth row **(figure 5, a–b)**. Continue through the next two 11ºs and the following 8º in the same row **(b–c)**.

MATERIALS

black/white bracelet 6½ in. (16.5 cm)

- 11 x 3 mm daggers in **2** colors: **165** A (D.P.5.999.10, opaque black), **160** B (D.P.5.012.11, opaque white iridescent)
- 5 g 8º seed beads (2.08.270.90, amber lined with dark brick red)
- 3 g 11º seed beads (2.11.270.90, amber lined with dark brick red)
- 2-strand tube clasp (silver)
- KO thread, size B (dark purple)
- Power Pro 20 lb. test (moss)
- beading needles, #11 milliner's

green bracelet colors:

- 11 x 3 mm daggers in **2** colors: A (D.P.5.523.03, olive transparent matte), B (D.P.5.968.06, light gray transparent matte iridescent)
- 8º seed beads (2.08.826.06, tan matte iridescent)
- 11º seed beads (2.11.826.06, tan matte iridescent)
- 2-strand tube clasp (antique bronze)
- KO thread, size B (olive)
- Power Pro 20 lb. test (moss)

orange bracelet colors:

- 11 x 3 mm daggers in **2** colors: A (D.P.5.210/012.50, red/white marbled opaque), B (D.P.5.198.03, cranberry transparent matte)
- 8º seed beads (2.08.490.90, light burnt orange lined with white)
- 11º seed beads (2.11.493.90, light olive lined with burnt orange)
- 2-strand tube clasp (antique bronze)
- WildFire (black)

Beads for this project are also available at Beadcats (email funkyskunk@beadcats.com).

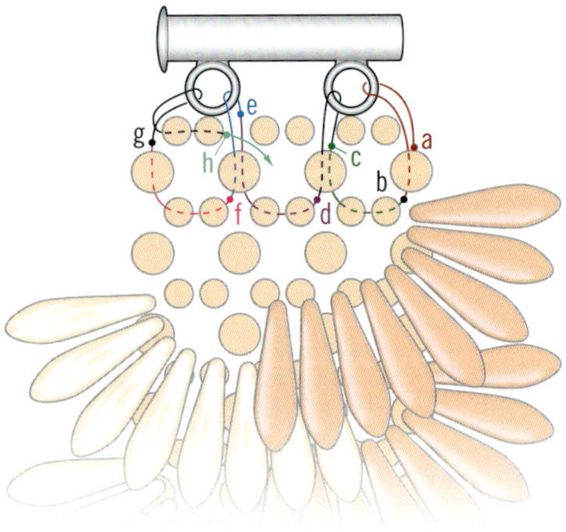

FIGURE 6

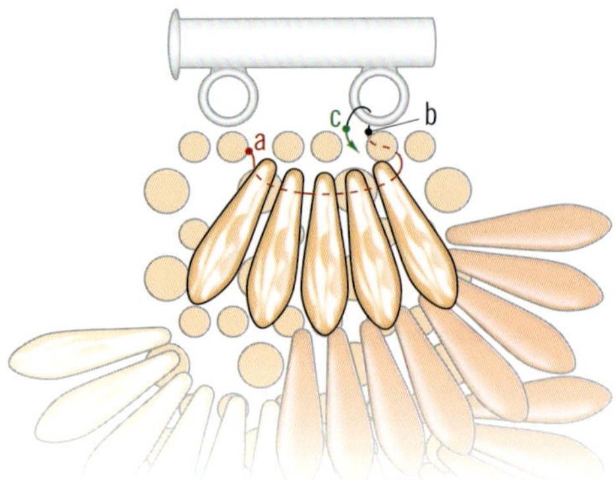

FIGURE 7

[5] Repeat steps 3 and 4 for the remainder of the base, sewing through every other edge bead for each color of dagger added. Notice that the As are added in a clockwise direction on the left side of the base and the Bs are added in a counterclockwise direction on the right side of the base. For the last repeat, sew through an 8º only. Depending on the length of your base, your last row of daggers could end with As or Bs. End and add thread as needed, making sure to tie your half-hitch knots only in the center 11ºs as before.

Clasp

[1] With the working thread exiting an end edge 8º, sew through one loop of the clasp, and sew back through the same 8º your thread is exiting **(figure 6, a–b)**. Continue through the next two 11ºs and 8º **(b–c)**.

[2] Sew through the same loop of the clasp, and continue back through the same 8º your thread is exiting **(c–d)**. Sew through the next two 11ºs and 8º **(d–e)**.

[3] Sew through the remaining loop of the clasp, and continue back through the 8º your thread is exiting **(e–f)**. Sew through the next two 11ºs and 8º **(f–g)**.

[4] Sew through the same loop of the clasp, and continue through the next two 11ºs on the end of the base **(g–h)**.

[5] Depending on which color dagger you added last, pick up five daggers of the other color, and sew through the second end 11º from the other edge as shown **(figure 7, a–b)**. Sew through the nearest loop of the clasp **(b–c)**, and retrace the thread path of the clasp connection. End the working thread.

[6] Remove the stop bead from the tail, and repeat steps 1–4 for this end of the base. End the tail. ●

DESIGN NOTES:

- **As you add each loop of daggers, it may be helpful to hold up the bracelet before tightening the loop so the daggers lie in the correct position. This way you can also make sure that the thread is not caught around previously added daggers. Then slowly snug up the loop of daggers.**
- **When adding the clasp, you may find it easier to flip the base and work from the back. Just flip it back to the front after step 4.**
- **You can substitute WildFire for the KO and Power Pro threads.**

MODIFIED RIGHT-ANGLE WEAVE

Faded denim bracelet

Use peanut beads, crystals, and seed beads to make a bracelet that's as comfortable as your favorite pair of old blue jeans.

designed by **Connie Whittaker**

MATERIALS

bracelet 7½ in. (19.1 cm)

- **42** 3 mm bicone crystals (Thunder Polish 42, white gold)
- 2 g 2 x 4 mm peanut beads (F912, matte denim)
- 2 g 8º seed beads (Toho 511F, higher metallic frosted Mediterranean blue)
- 1 g 11º seed beads (Miyuki 4207, Duracoat galvanized pink blush)
- 1 g 15º seed beads in each of **2** colors: A (Japanese 489, russet rose galvanized), B (Japanese 481A, apricot gold galvanized)
- toggle clasp
- Fireline 6 lb. test
- beading needles, #11 or #12

stepbystep

Base

[1] On a comfortable length of thread, pick up a 2 x 4 mm peanut bead, an 8º seed bead, a peanut, and an 8º. Sew through all the beads again to form a ring, leaving an 8-in. (20 cm) tail, and continue through the first peanut and 8º **(figure 1)**.

[2] Pick up a color A 15º seed bead, an 8º, and an A, and sew through the 8º your thread exited at the start of this step to form a ring. Retrace the thread path of the ring **(figure 2, a–b)**.

[3] Pick up an 11º seed bead, a color B 15º seed bead, a 3 mm bicone crystal, a B, and an 11º, and sew through the 8º added in step 2 **(b–c)**.

[4] Pick up an 11º, a B, a crystal, a B, and an 11º, and sew through the previous 8º **(c–d)**. Continue through the next 11º, B, crystal, B, 11º, and 8º **(d–e)**.

[5] Pick up a peanut, an 8º, and a peanut, and sew through the 8º your thread is exiting to form a ring. Retrace the thread path of the ring, and continue through the next peanut and 8º.

[6] Repeat steps 2–5 for the desired length bracelet, ending with step 5 and allowing ¾ in. (1.9 cm) for the clasp. End and add thread (Basics) as needed.

Clasp

[1] Pick up two 11ºs, the toggle loop, and two 11ºs, and sew through the end 8º to form a ring. Retrace the thread path of the ring several times, and end the working thread.

[2] Using the tail, repeat step 1 at the other end of the base, adding additional 11ºs if needed to allow the toggle bar to slide easily through the toggle loop. ●

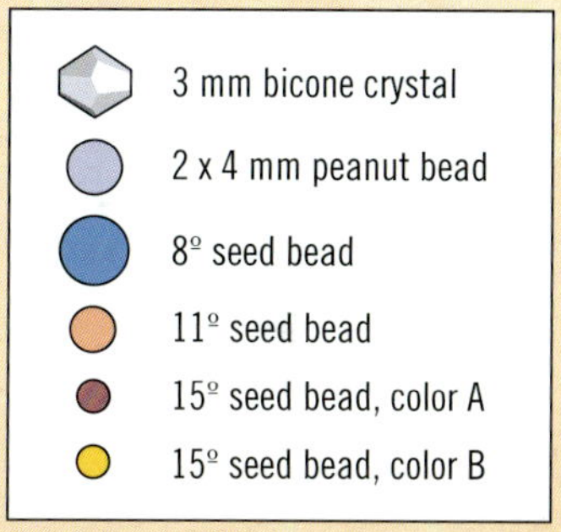

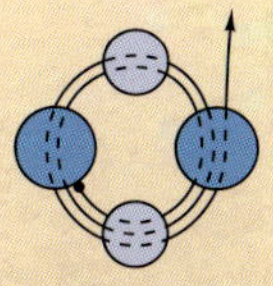

FIGURE 1

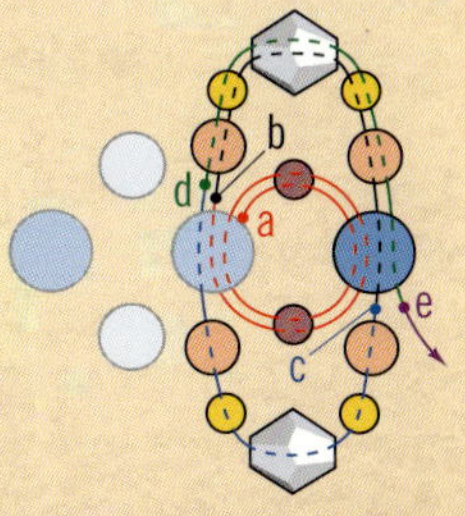

FIGURE 2

RIGHT-ANGLE WEAVE

Button-it-up bracelet

Tiny buttons add just the right amount of sparkle to a simple base.

designed by **Sharon Wagner**

stepbystep

Cuff bracelet

Wire form

Cut a 7-in. (18 cm) piece of 12-gauge electrical wire. Using nylon-jaw pliers, shape the wire into a cuff shape to fit comfortably around your wrist, leaving a 1½-in. (3.8 cm) gap between the ends. You will not be able to shape the wire after it is beaded.

Cuff base

[1] Thread an embroidery needle on a comfortable length of 10 lb. Fireline. Pick up four 8º seed beads, and tie them into a ring with a square knot (Basics), leaving a 6-in. (15 cm) tail. Retrace the thread path, and sew through the next two 8ºs.

[2] Work a flat strip of right-angle weave (Basics) using 8ºs and a tight tension until you have a total of 47 stitches, including the ring of beads from step 1. If needed, adjust the length by ½-in. (1.3 cm) increments by adding or subtracting two stitches at a time, maintaining an odd number of stitches.

[3] Add two more rows of right-angle weave (Basics), ending and adding thread (Basics) as needed. Exit the edge 8º in the last row, and place the cuff form in the center of the beadwork.

[4] To begin joining the edges of the base: Pick up an 8º, and sew through the corresponding edge 8º in the first row **(figure 1, a–b)**. Pick up an 8º, and sew through the 8º your thread exited at the start of this step **(b–c)**. Sew through the beadwork to exit the edge 8º in the next stitch of the same row **(c–d)**.

[5] Pick up an 8º, sew through the corresponding edge 8º in the opposite row, and continue through the next two 8ºs. Sew through the beadwork to exit the edge 8º in the next stitch of the opposite row.

[6] Repeat step 5 for the length of the base, forming the beadwork around the cuff form. Sew through the beadwork to exit an end 8º. Switch to the #11 beading needle.

[7] Pick up an 11º seed bead, and sew through the next end 8º. Repeat this stitch to complete the round, and step up through the first 11º added **(figure 2, a–b)**.

[8] Pick up an 11º, and sew through the next 11º added in the previous step. Repeat this stitch to complete the round, exiting the first 11º added in this round **(b–c)**. Sew through all the 11ºs added in this round **(c–d)**, and pull tight to close up the end. Make sure the beadwork covers the end of the wire. Retrace the thread path several times, and end the working thread and tail.

[9] Add 12 in. (30 cm) of thread to the other end of the base with the thread exiting an end 8º. Repeat steps 7 and 8 to close up this end of the base. End the thread.

Crystaletts embellishments

[1] Add 5 ft. (1.5 m) of 6 lb. Fireline to the base using an #11 beading needle. Holding the cuff vertically, center a row of right-angle weave along the top of the cuff, making sure the beadwork is not twisted. Counting from one end, exit the top 8º in the 13th stitch of this row **(figure 3, point a)**.

[2] Pick up an 11º, and sew through the next 8º in the same stitch. Repeat this stitch to complete the round (which will be centered above the right-angle weave stitch), and step up through the first 11º added **(a–b)**.

[3] Pick up an 11º, and sew through the next 11º added in the previous step. Repeat this stitch to complete the round, and step up through the first 11º added in this round **(b–c)**.

[4] Pick up a 3 mm Crystaletts button, and sew through the corresponding 11º on the opposite side of the round **(figure 4, a–b)**. Sew back through the button and the 11º your thread exited at the start of this step. Continue through the next 11º picked up in the previous step **(b–c)**.

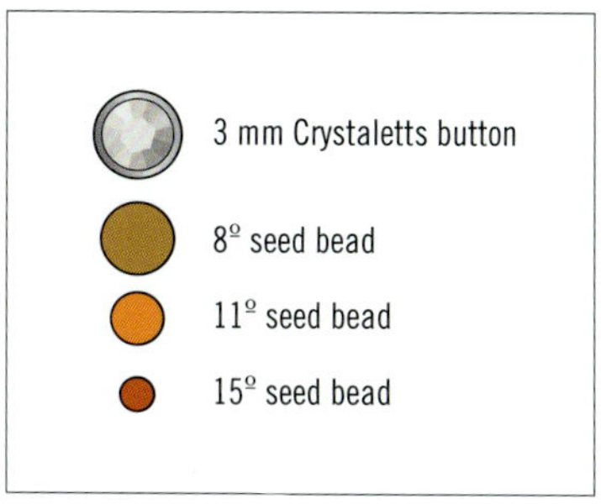

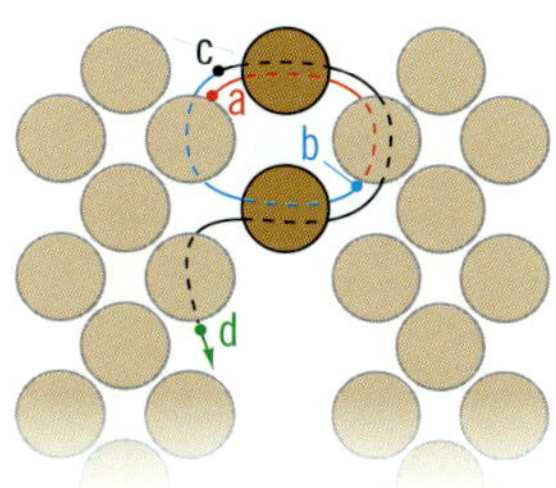

FIGURE 1

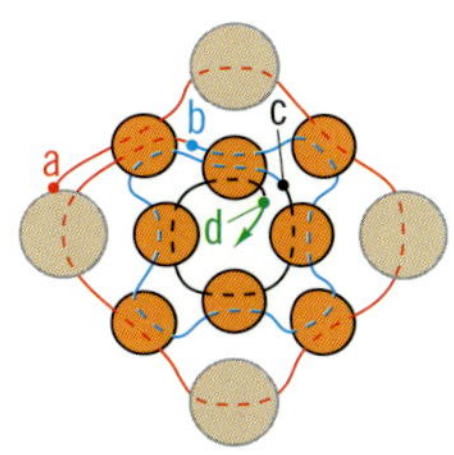

FIGURE 2

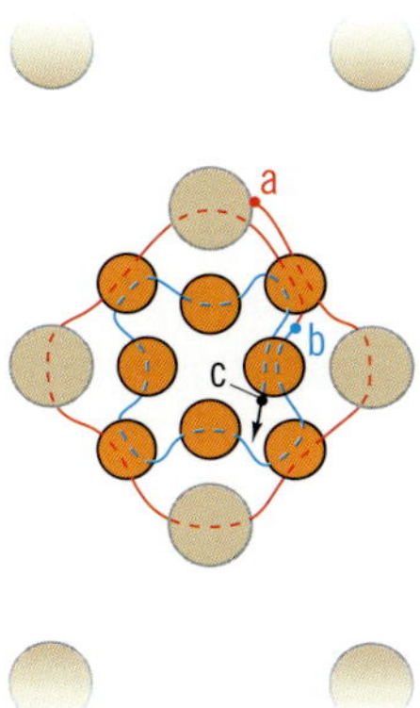

FIGURE 3

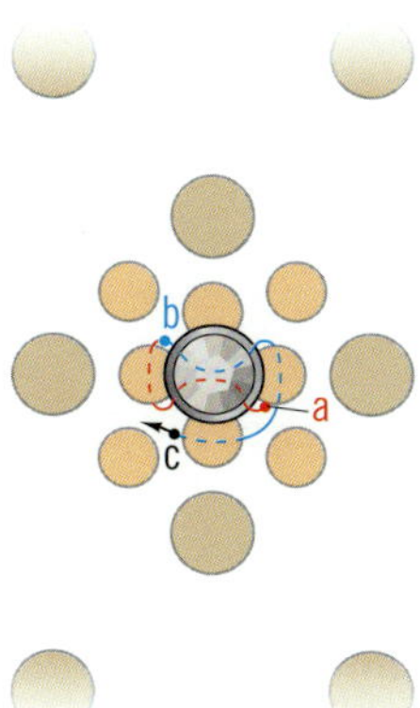

FIGURE 4

MATERIALS

all bracelets

- Fireline 6 lb. test
- Fireline 10 lb. test
- embroidery needle, #10
- beading needles, #11
- nylon-jaw pliers
- wire cutters strong enough to cut 12-gauge wire

brown cuff 3⅜ x 2¼ in. (8.6 x 5.7 cm)

- **11** 3 mm Crystaletts buttons (crystal in silver rhodium bezel; www.etsy.com/shop/yadasibeads)
- 15 g 8º seed beads (Toho 46F, matte opaque brown)
- 1 g 11º seed beads (Toho Y851, hybrid Apollo)
- 1 g 15º seed beads (Toho 222, dark bronze)
- 7 in. (18 cm) 12-gauge vinyl-coated electrical wire

gold cuff colors:

- 3 mm Crystaletts buttons (emerald in gold bezel)
- 8º seed beads (Toho P471, gold permanent galvanized)
- 11º seed beads (Toho P471, gold permanent galvanized)
- 15º seed beads (Toho P471, gold permanent galvanized)

blue bangle 2¾-in. (7 cm) diameter

- **16** 3 mm Crystaletts buttons in each of **2** colors (crystal in silver rhodium bezel and sapphire in silver rhodium bezel)
- 20 g 8º seed beads (Matsuno 399H, www.kandrasbeads.com)
- 3 g 11º seed beads (Toho 714, silver plated)
- 1 g 11º cylinder beads, in place of 15º seed beads (Miyuki DB35, galvanized silver)
- 9½ in. (24.1 cm) 12-gauge vinyl-coated electrical wire
- vinyl electrical tape

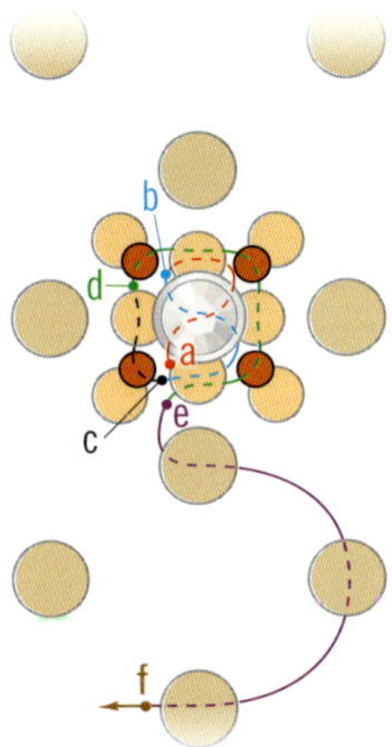

FIGURE 5

DESIGN NOTES:

- After finishing step 4 of "Cuff base," if the beadwork is not long enough to cover the wire form, work additional stitches in tubular right-angle weave (Basics). Add two rounds at a time to maintain an odd number of stitches.
- You can substitute 6 lb. Fireline for the 10 lb. Fireline if you retrace the thread path of each stitch in the right-angle weave bases.
- Noncoated 12-gauge craft wire can be used instead of electrical wire, but the beadwork of the base may shift and twist slightly. The vinyl coating helps grip the beadwork.
- You can find 12-gauge electrical wire and tape at most hardware stores or do-it-yourself home improvement centers.
- After completing step 3 of "Bangle base and embellishments," there should be an even number of stitches.

[5] Sew through the button diagonally, and continue through the corresponding 11º on the opposite side of the round (figure 5, a–b). Sew back through the button diagonally, and continue through the 11º your thread exited at the start of this step (b–c).

[6] Pick up a 15º seed bead, and sew through the next 11º added in step 3 (c–d). Repeat this stitch to complete the round, exiting the 11º from the start of this step (d–e).

[7] Sew through the center 8º directly below the 11º your thread is exiting, sewing in the opposite direction. Continue through the next two 8ºs in the following stitch (e–f).

[8] Work as in steps 2–7 to add a total of 11 button embellishments, skipping a stitch between embellishments. Make sure the base does not twist and that you are working on the same center row of right-angle weave. End the thread.

Bangle bracelet

Wire form

[1] Cut a 9½-in. (24.1 cm) piece of 12-gauge electrical wire for a 2¾-in. (7 cm) diameter bangle. Using nylon-jaw pliers, shape the wire into a bangle shape that fits comfortably around the widest part of your hand with both ends of the wire touching. You will not be able to shape the wire after it is beaded.

[2] Cut a piece of vinyl electrical tape. About 1½ in. (3.8 cm) from one end of the wire, wrap the tape around the wire at a very sharp angle. Keeping the wire ends close together, wrap the tape over the join, overlapping the tape only a small amount with each wrap so it does not add too much width to the wire. Continue wrapping about 1½ in. (3.8 cm) past the join, and trim the tape.

Bangle base and embellishments

[1] Leaving a 6-in. (15 cm) tail, work as in steps 1–3 of "Cuff base" to stitch three rows of 63 stitches each. Add or subtract two stitches at a time to adjust the length, maintaining an odd number of stitches.

[2] Join the edges of the base around the wire form as in steps 4–6 of "Cuff base."

[3] Join the ends of the base in the same manner as you joined the edges, making sure the beadwork is not twisted and the rows line up properly. End the working thread and tail.

[4] Add a comfortable length of 6 lb. Fireline to the base using an #11 needle. Work the steps for "Crystaletts embellishments," adding the buttons around the entire bangle. End the thread. ●

THREE-DROP PEYOTE STITCH

African safari

Pay homage to two fabulous creatures with animal-print bracelets that won't harm a hair on their heads!

designed by **Josie Fabre**

MATERIALS

all bracelets 7 in. (18 cm)

- Fireline 4 lb. test
- beading needles, #10 or #11

giraffe bracelet

- 11º Miyuki Delica cylinder beads
  16 g color A (DB0653, opaque pumpkin)
  8 g color B (DB0204, opaque luster light beige)

leopard bracelet

- **64** 3 mm bicone crystals (Thunder Polish, jet black)
- 11º Miyuki Delica cylinder beads
  12 g color A (DB0310, matte black)
  10 g color B (DB0353, opaque matte luster dark cream)
  3 g color C (DB0653, opaque pumpkin)
- 1 g 15º seed beads (Czech, black)

FIGURE 1

11º Delica beads

- color A, DB0653, opaque pumpkin
- color B, DB0204, opaque luster light beige

GIRAFFE PATTERN

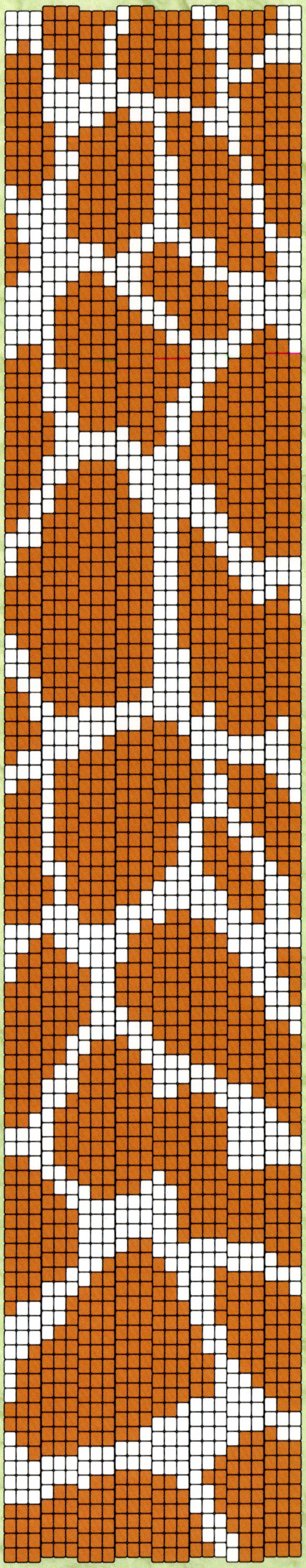

Sleek and chic, these three-drop peyote stitch bracelets work up quickly, keep a low profile, and make a huge impact.

stepby**step**

Bracelet bases

Both bracelets are worked in three-drop peyote stitch, a technique based on two-drop peyote stitch. Turn to Basics to brush up on two-drop peyote before beginning this project.

[1] On a comfortable length of thread, attach a stop bead (Basics), leaving a 6-in. (15 cm) tail. Pick up 24 11º cylinder beads for rows 1 and 2 of the desired **pattern**.

[2] Work in three-drop peyote stitch using cylinders. End and add thread (Basics) as needed while you stitch, and end the working thread and tail when you finish.

[3] Choose the appropriate steps below to add a clasp and edging to the base.

Giraffe

Toggle bar

[1] On 1 yd. (.9 m) of thread, attach a stop bead, leaving a 6-in. (15 cm) tail.

[2] Referring to **figure 1**, work in three-drop peyote stitch using cylinders to make a strip that is 18 beads wide

and 12 rows long. Roll the strip into a tube, and zip up (Basics) the first and last rows. End the tail but not the working thread.

[3] Sew through the beadwork to exit a center cylinder in the tube, and work in flat even-count peyote stitch (Basics) to create a tab that is two beads wide and 16–18 rows long.

[4] Stitch the end of the tab to the center cylinders at one end of the bracelet base. Retrace the thread path of the join, and end the working thread.

Toggle ring

[1] Locate the last row at the other end of the base, and notice that one side of the row begins with three up-beads. Position your beadwork so these beads are on the right. Add 20 in. (51 cm) of thread to the bracelet base, and exit the second set of three up-beads from the right with your needle pointing toward the center of the band.

[2] Pick up 26 cylinders, and sew through the next set of three up-beads with your needle pointing toward the center of the band. This forms a ring.

[3] Sew through the beadwork to exit this same set of up-beads, and work a round of peyote off of the cylinders in the ring (**photo**). End the thread.

Leopard

Toggle bar

[1] Referring to **figure 2**, work in flat even-count peyote stitch (Basics) to make a strip that is 18 beads wide and 12 rows long. Roll the strip into a tube, and zip up (Basics) the first and last rows. End the tail but not the working thread.

[2] With the thread exiting an end cylinder in the tube, pick up five 15º seed beads, sew down through the next end cylinder, and sew up through the following end cylinder.

[3] Pick up two 15ºs, sew down through the last 15º picked up in the previous step, and continue through the previous end cylinder in the tube. Sew up through the cylinder your thread exited at the start of this step and the first 15º picked up in this step.

[4] Pick up four 15ºs, sew down through the next end cylinder, and sew up through the following end cylinder.

[5] Repeat steps 3 and 4 once more. To complete the round, pick up a 15º, and sew down through the first 15º picked up in step 1 and the corresponding end cylinder.

[6] Sew through the beadwork to exit an end cylinder on the other end of the tube, and repeat steps 2–5.

[7] Work as in steps 3 and 4 of "Giraffe: Toggle bar."

FIGURE 2

11º Delica beads
- color A, DB0310, matte black
- color B, DB0353, opaque matte luster dark cream
- color C, DB0653, opaque pumpkin

Toggle ring

Work as in "Giraffe: Toggle ring."

Edging

[1] Add 1 yd. (.9 m) of thread to the bracelet base, and exit an end cylinder along one edge.

[2] Pick up a 15º, a 3 mm bicone crystal, and a 15º. Skip one edge cylinder, sew down through the next edge cylinder, and sew up through the following edge cylinder. Repeat this stitch along both edges of the base, and end the thread. ●

LEOPARD PATTERN

BEAD WEAVING

Flower bud necklace

Connect beaded beads made with two-hole lentils, SuperDuos, and magatamas to highlight the *Bead&Button* 20th anniversary bead (or any art bead you like).

designed by **Connie Whittaker**

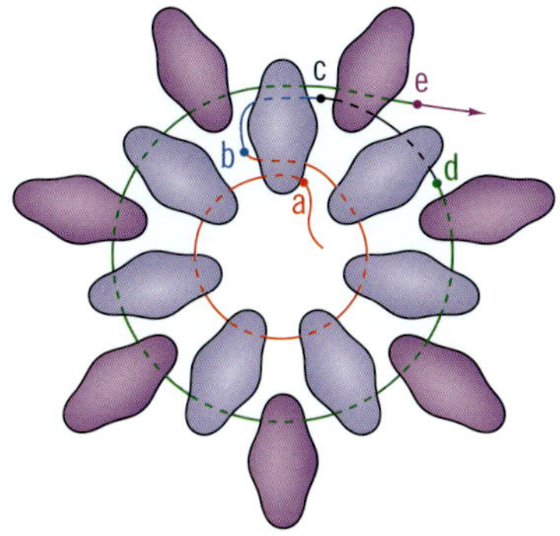

FIGURE 1

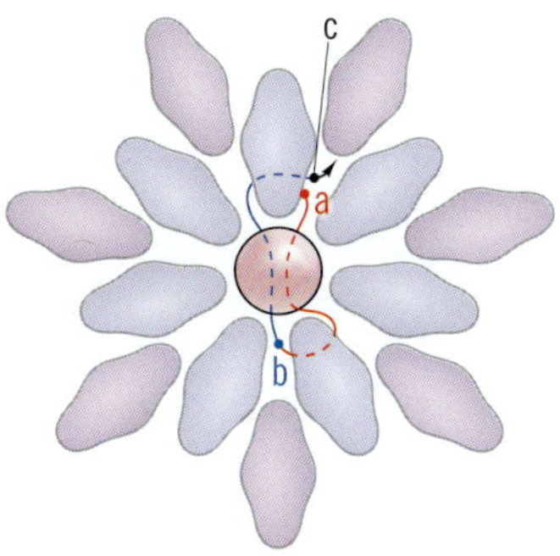

FIGURE 2

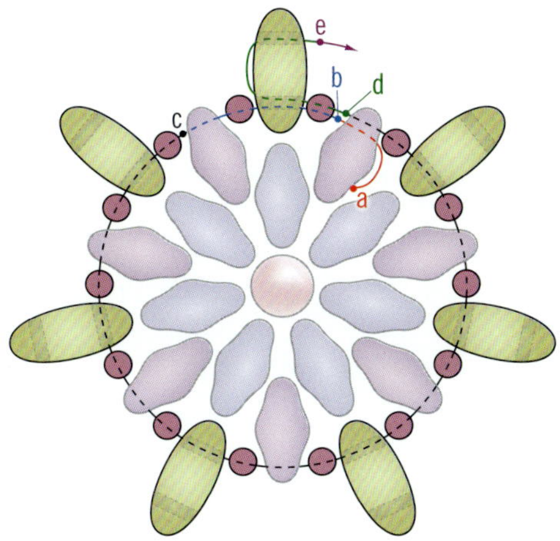

FIGURE 3

stepbystep

Beaded beads

[1] On 18 in. (46 cm) of thread, pick up seven color A 2.5 x 5 mm SuperDuo beads. Sew through all the beads again **(figure 1, a–b)** to form a ring, leaving an 8-in. (20 cm) tail, and sew through the available hole of the first A **(b–c)**.

[2] Pick up a color B 2.5 x 5 mm SuperDuo bead, and sew through the available hole of the next A **(c–d)**. Repeat this stitch to complete the round **(d–e)**. Retrace the thread path using a tight tension so the beadwork begins to cup slightly.

[3] With the tail, pick up a 3 mm pearl, skip two As, and sew through the inner hole of the next A **(figure 2, a–b)**. Sew back through the pearl and the A your thread exited at the start of this step **(b–c)**. End the working thread and tail (Basics) to complete the first half of the beaded bead.

[4] On 1 yd. (.9 m) of thread, repeat steps 1–3, but end only the tail.

[5] With the working thread, sew through the available hole of the B your thread is exiting **(figure 3, a–b)**.

[6] Pick up a 15º seed bead, a 3 x 6 mm two-hole lentil bead, and a 15º, and sew through the available hole of the next B **(b–c)**. Repeat this stitch to complete the round **(c–d)**, and retrace the thread path (not shown in the figure) using a tight tension. Sew through the next few beads to exit a lentil, and continue through the available hole of the same lentil **(d–e)**.

[7] Bring together the two halves of the beaded bead so that the 3 mm pearls are to the outside.

MATERIALS

necklace 18 in. (46 cm)

- **1** *Bead&Button* 20th anniversary bead by Lydia Muell (www.BeadAndButton.com/anniversarybead)
- **2** 6 mm crystal rondelles (Preciosa PC3005, crystal Celsian; www.fusionbeads.com)
- **16** 2 x 3 mm crystal rondelles (Chinese, wheat; www.drygulch.com)
- **24** 3 mm pearls (Swarovski, mauve)
- **70** 3 x 6 mm two-hole CzechMate lentil beads (P65431, luster opaque green)
- 9 g 2.5 x 5 mm SuperDuo beads in each of **2** colors: A (P15726, Vega on chalk; www.funkyhannahs.com), B (pastel Montana blue; www.funkyhannahs.com)
- 12 g 3 mm magatama drop beads (Toho Y185, hybrid luster opaque gold/smoky)
- 1 g 15º seed beads (Miyuki 4220, Duracoat eggplant)
- toggle clasp (brass)
- 8-in. (20 cm) chain (brass)
- **4** 6 mm jump rings (brass)
- Fireline 6 lb. test
- beading needles, #11 or #12
- **2** pairs of chainnose, flatnose, and/or bentnose pliers
- wire cutters

[8] Pick up a 15º, and sew through a B on the other half of the beaded bead. Pick up a 15º, and sew through the available hole of the next lentil **(photo a)**. Repeat this stitch to complete the round, and retrace the thread path. Your thread should be exiting a lentil.

[9] Pick up three 3 mm magatama drop beads, and sew through the corresponding hole of the next lentil **(photo b)**. Repeat this stitch to complete the round, and sew through the first two drops added.

[10] Pick up a drop, and sew through the other hole of the next lentil. Pick up a drop, and sew through the center drop from the previous round **(photo c)**. Repeat these two stitches to complete the round. End the thread.

[11] Repeat steps 1–10 to make nine more beaded beads.

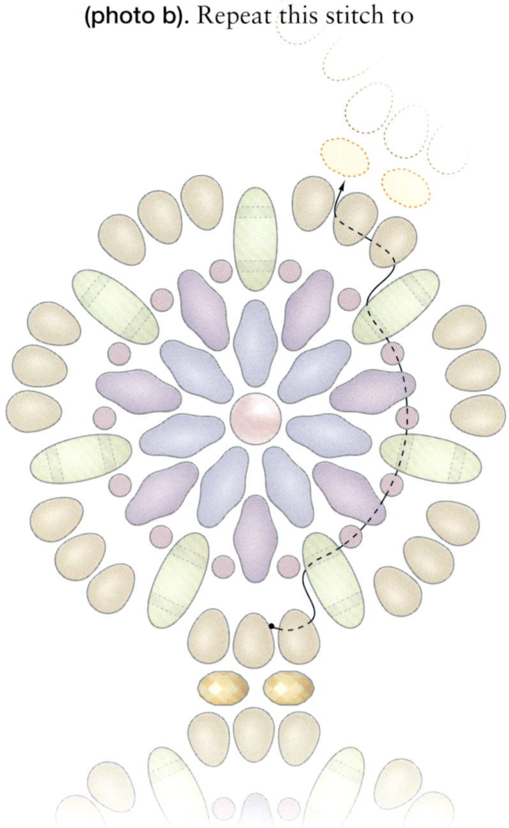

FIGURE 4

Necklace assembly

[1] Add 4 ft. (1.2 m) of thread (Basics) to a beaded bead, leaving an 18-in. (46 cm) tail. Exit a center drop along the edge.

[2] Pick up a 2 x 3 mm crystal rondelle, and sew through a center drop along the edge of another beaded bead. Pick up a rondelle, and sew through the drop your thread exited at the start of this step. Retrace the thread path several times.

[3] Sew counterclockwise through the beadwork as shown in **figure 4** to exit the center drop in the third set of drops. These drops will be slightly offset from the previous connection. This will curve the neck strap as the beaded beads are added.

[4] Repeat steps 2 and 3 to connect a total of five beaded beads.

[5] Pick up nine 15ºs, and sew through the same drop to form a loop. Retrace the thread path several times, and end the thread.

[6] Cut a 4-in. (10 cm) piece of chain. Open a 6 mm jump ring (Basics), and attach an end link of the chain to the loop of 15ºs.

[7] Open a jump ring, and attach the other end link of the chain to half of the clasp. This completes the left side of the neck strap.

[8] Work as in steps 1–7 to complete the right side of the neck strap, but sew in a clockwise direction in step 3 to make the neck strap curve in the opposite direction.

[9] With the 18-in. (46 cm) tail from the left neck strap, sew through the beadwork in a clockwise direction to exit the center drop in the third set of drops from the connection point, with the needle pointing to the outside of the neck strap. Be sure the neck strap is curving inward.

[10] Pick up a pearl, a 6 mm crystal rondelle, the anniversary bead, a 6 mm, a pearl, and a 15º, and sew back through the pearl, 6 mm, anniversary bead, and 6 mm. Pick up a pearl, and sew up through the center drop in the third set of drops from the connection point on the right neck strap, making sure that both neck straps are curving inward. Pick up a pearl, and sew through the drop your thread exited at the start of this step. Retrace the thread path several times, and end the threads. ●

BEAD WEAVING

Piggyback **bracelet**

Stack two-hole piggy beads one behind the other for a sophisticated accessory.

designed by **Jane Danley Cruz**

MATERIALS

bracelet 7½ in. (19.1 cm)

- **42** 4 x 8 mm piggy beads (black; www.ariadesignstudio.etsy.com)
- **8** 5 x 7 mm rondelles (Thunder Polish, silver)
- **42** 3 mm round beads (silver; www.firemountaingems.com)
- 1 g 11º large-hole seed beads (Toho 21F, silver-lined frosted crystal)
- 1 g 15º seed beads (Toho 558, permanent finish galvanized aluminum)
- **2** 6 mm split rings
- toggle clasp
- Wildfire or Fireline, 6 lb. test
- beading needles, #11
- split-ring pliers (optional)

stepbystep

Band

[1] On 1½ yd. (1.4 m) of thread, pick up a repeating pattern of an 11º seed bead and a 4 x 8 mm piggy bead (offset hole) six times. Tie the beads into a ring with a square knot (Basics), leaving an 8-in. (20 cm) tail. Sew through all the beads again using a firm tension, and exit a piggy bead **(figure, a–b)**.

[2] Sew through the center hole of the same piggy bead **(b–c)**, pick up a 3 mm round bead, and sew through the center hole of the next piggy bead in the ring **(c–d)**. Repeat this stitch to complete the round, and sew through the beadwork to exit the 3 mm opposite the tail **(d–e)**.
This completes one piggy bead unit.

[3] To form a connection: Pick up a 15º seed bead, an 11º, a 5 x 7 mm rondelle, an 11º, a 15º, a 3 mm, a 15º, and an 11º, and sew back through the rondelle. Pick up an 11º and a 15º, and sew through the 3 mm your thread exited at the start of this step. Continue through the next six beads to exit the opposite 3 mm **(e–f)**.

[4] Pick up a repeating pattern of a piggy bead (center hole) and a 3 mm five times, and add one more piggy bead. Sew through the 3 mm your thread exited at the start of this step, and continue through the next piggy bead.

[5] Sew through the offset hole of the same piggy bead, pick up an 11º, and sew through the offset hole of the next piggy bead. Repeat this stitch to complete the round, and snug up the beads so the 11ºs slide to the center. Sew through the beadwork to exit the 3 mm opposite the previous connection.

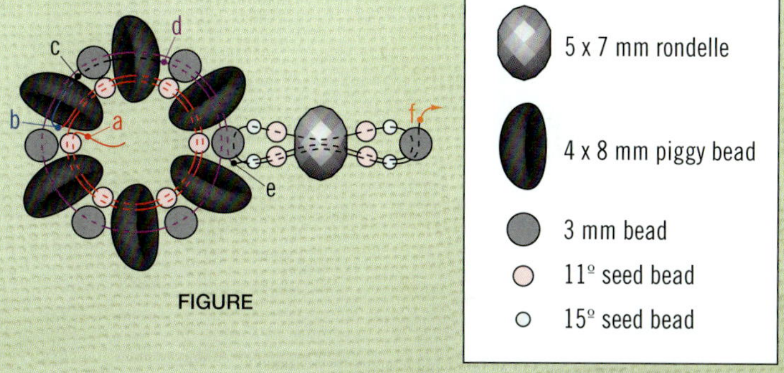

FIGURE

[6] Repeat steps 3–5 for the desired length of the bracelet minus 1 in. (2.5 cm) for the clasp. My 7½-in. (19.1 cm) bracelet has seven piggy bead units.

Clasp

[1] With the working thread exiting a 3 mm opposite the last connection, pick up a 15º, an 11º, a rondelle, an 11º, seven 15ºs, and a 6 mm split ring. Sew back through the last 11º and the rondelle. Pick up an 11º and a 15º, and sew through the 3 mm your thread exited at the start of this step. Retrace the thread path several times to reinforce, and end the working thread (Basics).

[2] Open the split ring, and attach half of the clasp.

[3] Using the tail, repeat steps 1 and 2 for the other end of the bracelet. ●

BEAD WEAVING

Coveted collar

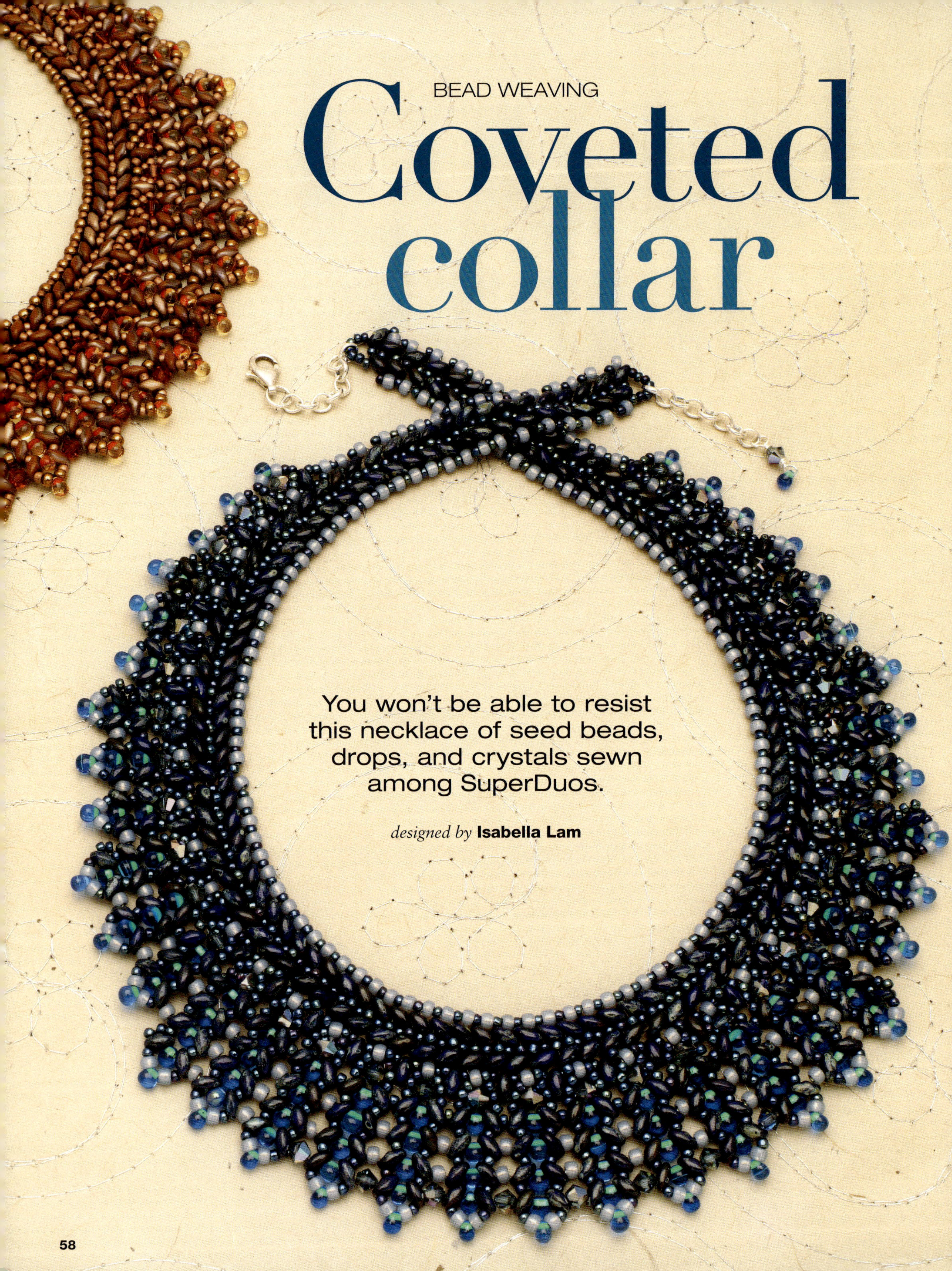

You won't be able to resist this necklace of seed beads, drops, and crystals sewn among SuperDuos.

designed by **Isabella Lam**

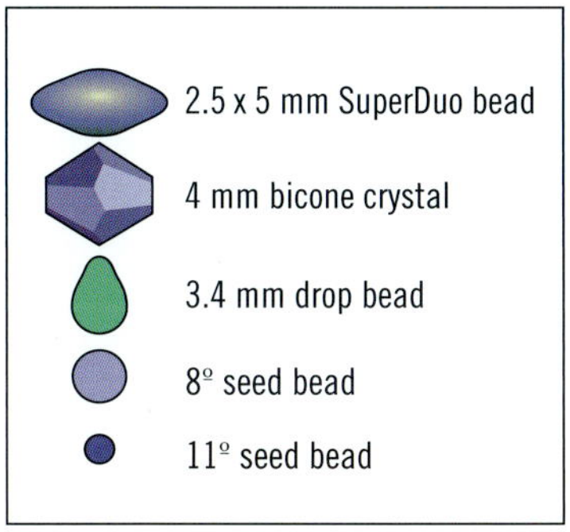

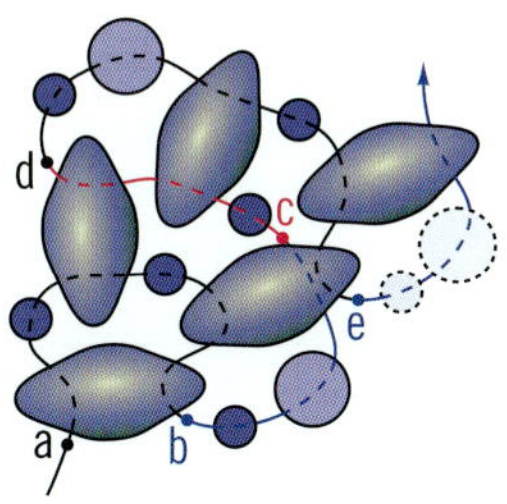

FIGURE 1

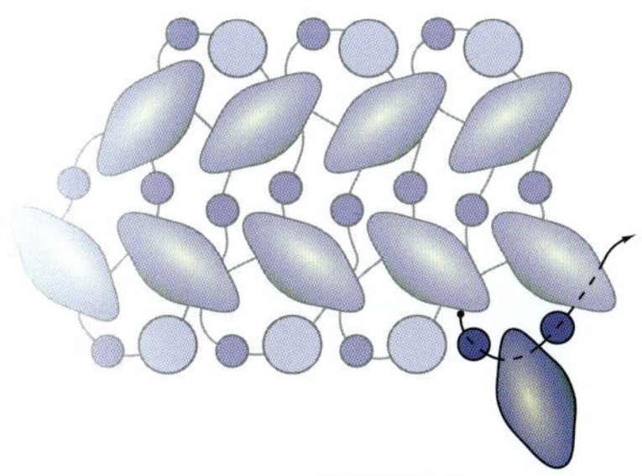

FIGURE 2

stepbystep

Band

[1] On a comfortable length of thread, attach a stop bead (Basics), leaving an 8-in. (20 cm) tail. Pick a 2.5 x 5 mm SuperDuo bead, an 11º seed bead, a SuperDuo, an 11º, and a SuperDuo, and sew through the available hole of the first SuperDuo **(figure 1, a–b)**.

[2] To make a turn: Pick up an 11º and an 8º seed bead, and sew back through the available hole of the last SuperDuo added in the previous step **(b–c)**.

[3] Pick up an 11º and a SuperDuo, and sew through the available hole of the next SuperDuo **(c–d)**.

[4] Work a turn with an 11º and an 8º. Pick up an 11º and a SuperDuo, and sew through the next SuperDuo **(d–e)**. Repeat this step until you have two parallel rows of 16 SuperDuos each.

[5] Pick up an 11º, a SuperDuo, and an 11º, and sew through the available hole of the last SuperDuo picked up in the previous step **(figure 2)**. This SuperDuo will point downward from this edge of the band, and this will become the lower edge of the necklace.

[6] Pick up an 11º and a SuperDuo, and sew through the next SuperDuo. Turn with an 11º and an 8º. Pick up an 11º and a SuperDuo, and sew through the next SuperDuo. Repeat the last two stitches two more times. Your thread will be exiting a SuperDuo along the lower edge.

[7] Repeat steps 5 and 6, ending with step 5, until you have 38 downward-pointing SuperDuos along the lower edge. End and add thread (Basics) as needed.

[8] Work a stitch with an 11º and a SuperDuo.

[9] Work as in step 4 until you have 16 SuperDuos in each row after the last downward-pointing SuperDuo along the lower edge. End the working thread but not the tail.

Lower edge

Row 1

[1] Add a comfortable length of thread to the band, and exit an edge 8º just before the first downward-pointing SuperDuo along the lower edge, with the needle pointing toward the center of the band. Pick up two 11ºs, and sew through the

MATERIALS

blue necklace 21½ in. (54.6 cm)

- 28 g 2.5 x 5 mm SuperDuo beads (Czech, opaque blue Picasso)
- **45** 4 mm bicone crystals (Swarovski, aqua green sphinx)
- 6.5 g 3.4 mm drop beads (Miyuki, silver-lined transparent Capri blue)
- 12 g 8º seed beads (Toho 2102, permanent finish silver-lined milky Montana blue)
- 28 g 11º seed beads (Toho 88, metallic cosmos)
- lobster claw clasp
- chain extender (optional)
- **2** 4 mm jump rings
- Fireline 6 lb. test
- beading needles, #10
- **2** pairs of pliers

topaz necklace colors:

- 2.5 x 5 mm SuperDuo beads (Czech, matte Apollo umber)
- 4 mm bicone crystals (Swarovski, Indian red)
- 3.4 mm drop beads (Miyuki, red-lined light topaz)
- 8º seed beads (Miyuki 457L, metallic light bronze)
- 11º seed beads (Miyuki F464D, penny copper matte metallic; www.beyondbeadery.com)

available hole of the downward-pointing SuperDuo **(figure 3, a–b)**. Pick up two 11ºs, and sew through the next edge 8º **(b–c)**. Repeat these two stitches for the rest of the downward-pointing SuperDuos, exiting the first 8º after the last SuperDuo.

[2] Continue through the next edge 11º, turn, and sew back through the previous 8º, two 11ºs, SuperDuo, and 11º **(figure 4, a–b)**.

[3] Pick up a 4 mm bicone crystal, skip the next 11º, 8º, and 11º, and sew through the following 11º **(b–c)**.

[4] Pick up two 11ºs, an 8º, a 3.4 mm drop bead, an 8º, and two 11ºs. Sew through the 11º your thread exited at the start of step 3, the 4 mm, and the 11º your thread exited at the start of this step **(c–d)**. Continue through the next SuperDuo and 11º along the lower edge of the band **(d–e)**.

[5] Repeat steps 3 and 4 twice.

[6] Pick up a 4 mm bicone crystal, skip the next 11º, 8º, and 11º, and sew through the following 11º.

[7] Pick up an 11º, a SuperDuo, a drop bead, a SuperDuo, and an 11º, and sew through the 11º your thread exited at the start of step 6, the 4 mm, and the 11º your thread exited at the start of this step **(e–f)**. This forms a SuperDuo picot. Continue through the next SuperDuo and 11º along the lower edge of the band.

[8] Repeat steps 6 and 7 until you have a total of 31 SuperDuo picots, ending and adding thread as needed.

[9] Work as in steps 3 and 4 to add three drop-bead picots.

Row 2

[1] Sew through the beadwork to exit the last 11º added in the closest SuperDuo picot in the previous row **(point g)**. Pick up two 11ºs, and sew through the available hole of the SuperDuo.

[2] Pick up an 11º, an 8º, a drop bead, an 8º, and an 11º. Sew through the available hole of the next SuperDuo to form a drop-bead picot **(g–h)**.

[3] Pick up an 11º, and sew through the available hole of the next SuperDuo **(h–i)**.

[4] Repeat steps 2 and 3 two more times.

[5] Pick up an 11º, a SuperDuo, a drop bead, a SuperDuo, and an 11º, and sew through the available hole of the next SuperDuo to form a SuperDuo picot.

[6] Pick up an 11º, and sew through the available hole of the next SuperDuo.

[7] Repeat steps 5 and 6 for a total of 25 SuperDuo picots.

[8] Repeat steps 2 and 3 twice, and then repeat step 2.

[9] Pick up two 11ºs, and sew through the 11º adjacent to the first hole of the SuperDuo your thread is exiting.

Row 3

[1] Work as in steps 1–4 of Row 2, but in step 3 pick up an 8º instead of an 11º between the SuperDuo picots.

[2] Work as in steps 5 and 6 of Row 2 for a total of 19 SuperDuo picots, but in step 6 pick up an 8º instead of an 11º between the SuperDuo picots.

[3] Work as in steps 2–4 of Row 2, but in step 3 pick up an 8º instead of an 11º between the SuperDuo picots, and in the last repeat do not add the last 8º.

[4] Work as in step 9 of Row 2.

Row 4

Work as in Row 3, but add a total of only 13 SuperDuo picots.

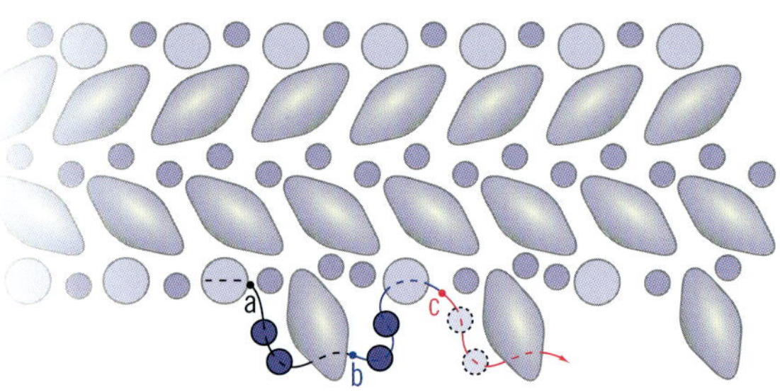

FIGURE 3

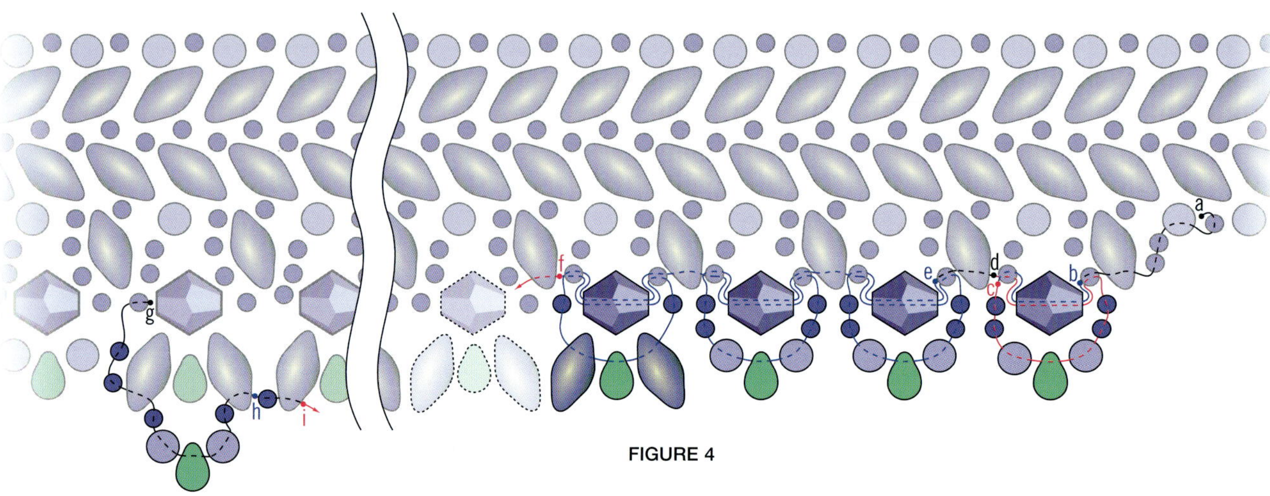

FIGURE 4

Row 5

[1] Work as in step 1 of Row 2 to be in position for the final row.

[2] Work as in steps 2 and 3 of Row 2 to add a drop-bead picot below each SuperDuo picot in Row 4, but pick up an 8º instead of an 11º after the first two drop-bead picots, a 4 mm instead of an 11º after the next eight drop-bead picots, and an 8º instead of an 11º after the final two drop-bead picots.

[3] Work as in step 9 of Row 2. End the working thread.

Clasp

[1] Add 8 in. (20 cm) of thread to the end of the band opposite the tail, and exit an end SuperDuo with the needle pointing away from the band.

[2] Pick up five 11ºs, and sew through the other end SuperDuo with the needle pointing toward the band. Sew through the beadwork to exit the SuperDuo your thread exited at the start of this step, and retrace the thread path through the five-bead loop several times. End the thread.

[3] Open a 4 mm jump ring (Basics), and attach the five-bead loop to half of the clasp.

[4] Remove the stop bead, and repeat steps 2 and 3 with the tail on the other end of the band. ●

BEAD WEAVING

Row-by-row pearls

Make a single-strand or double-decker bracelet using classic pearls, seed beads, and bicones.

designed by **Sandie Bachand**

stepbystep

Single-row bracelet

[1] On 4½ yd. (4.1 m) of thread, pick up an 8 mm pearl and nine 11° seed beads. Sew through the 8 mm again in the same direction, leaving a 1½-yd. (1.4 m) tail. This forms a loop of 11°s around one side of the pearl. Pick up nine 11°s, and sew through the 8 mm once more, forming a loop around the other side of the pearl **(figure 1)**.

[2] Sew through the first nine 11°s added in step 1 **(figure 2, a–b)**, and tie a square knot (Basics) with the working thread and tail. Pick up a 3 mm pearl, sew through the next nine 11°s, pick up a 3 mm, and sew through the following nine 11°s. Continue through the next 11 beads to exit the 3 mm opposite the tail **(b–c)**.

[3] Pick up nine 11°s, an 8 mm, and nine 11°s. Sew through the 8 mm in the same direction, forming a loop of 11°s around one side of the pearl **(figure 3)**. Position the 8 mm so the first nine 11°s trace a loop around the other side of the pearl, and then sew through the first nine 11°s to secure the loop **(figure 4, a–b)**.

[4] Pick up a 3 mm, sew through the next nine 11°s, and sew through the 3 mm from the previous pearl unit. Continue through the next 10 beads to exit the 3 mm added in this step **(b–c)**.

[5] Repeat steps 3 and 4 until you have a total of 14 8 mm pearl units.

[6] With your thread exiting the end 3 mm, pick up three 11°s and half of the clasp. Sew back through the last 11°, pick up two 11°s, and sew through the end 3 mm in the same direction **(figure 5)**. Retrace the thread path several times, and end the working thread (Basics).

[7] With the tail, sew through the first 3 mm, and repeat step 6, but do not end the thread. Sew through the next five 11°s to exit the center 11° in the loop around one side of the first 8 mm.

[8] Pick up three 15° seed beads, sew through the center 11° again, and continue through the next four 11°s, 3 mm, and five 11°s **(figure 6)**. Your thread should be exiting the center 11° in the opposite loop around the next 8 mm.

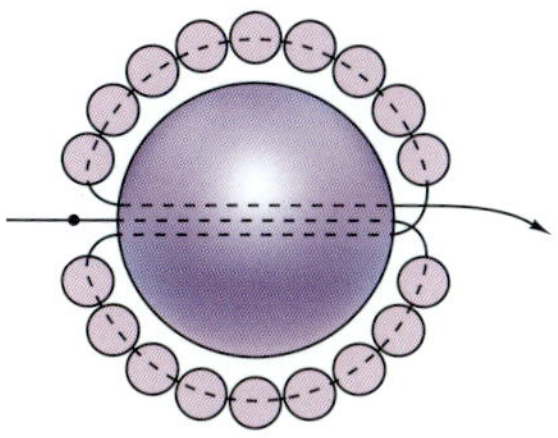

FIGURE 1

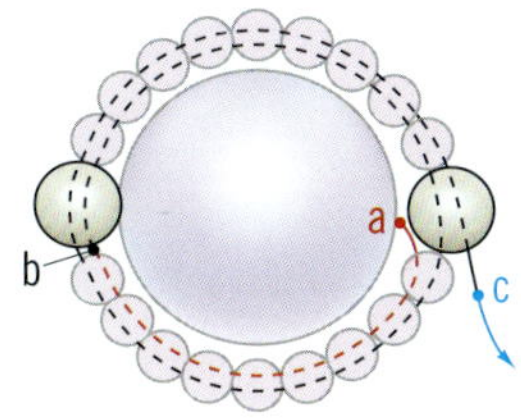

FIGURE 2

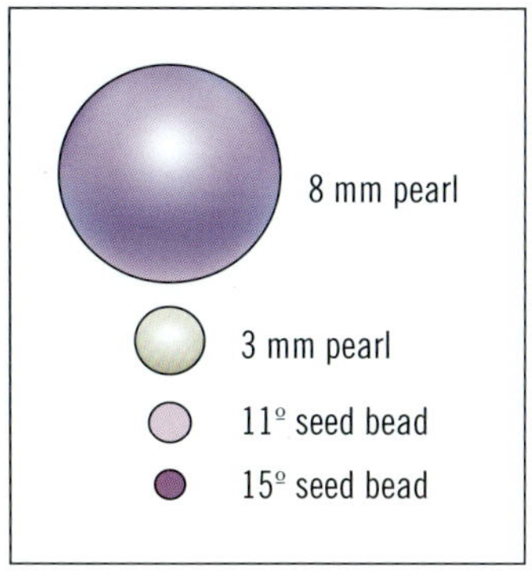

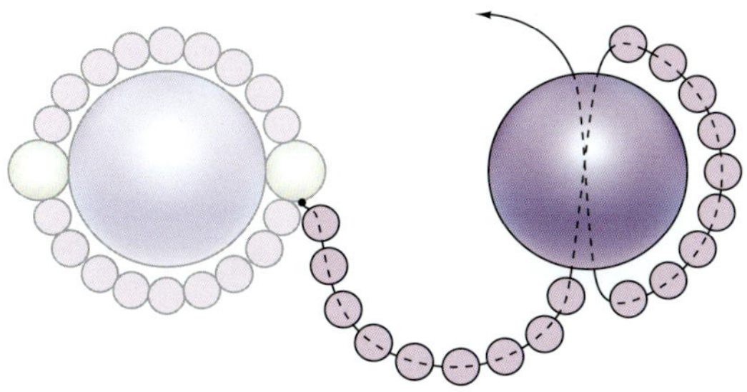

FIGURE 3

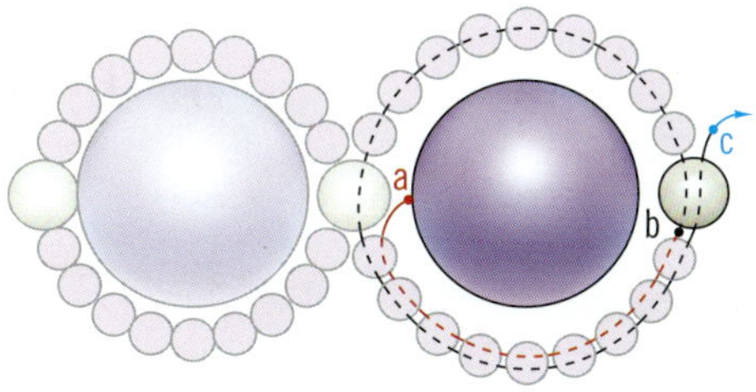

FIGURE 4

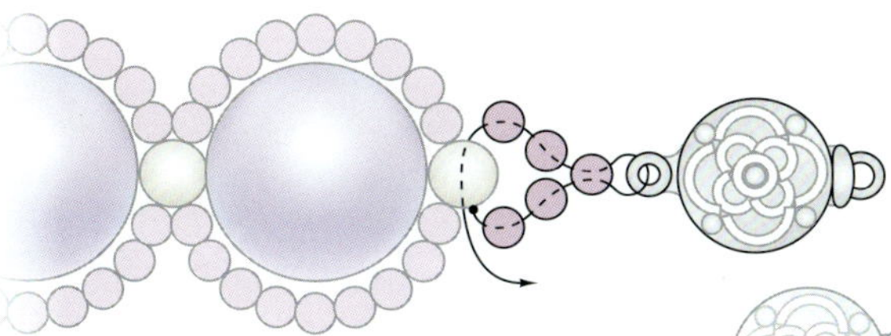

FIGURE 5

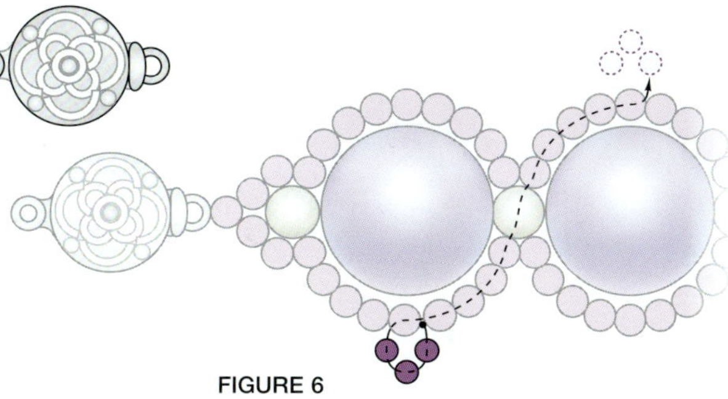

FIGURE 6

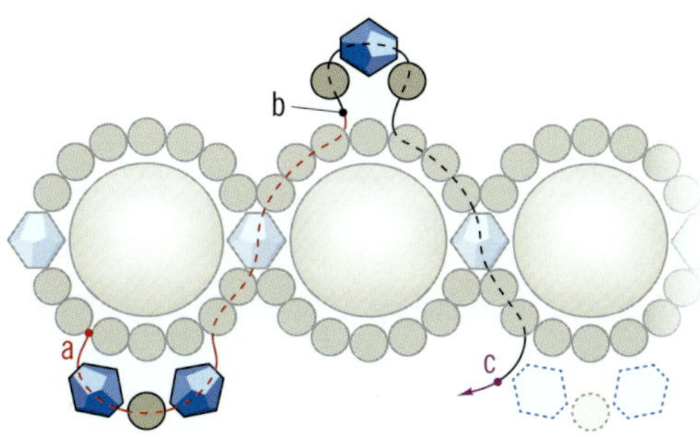

FIGURE 7

[9] Repeat step 8 for the length of the bracelet, embellishing alternating loops and exiting the end 3 mm. Sew through the next five 11ºs, and repeat step 8 to embellish the remaining loops. End the tail.

Double-row bracelet

First row

[1] Work as in steps 1–5 of "Single-row bracelet" with the following changes:

- Substitute 6 mm pearls for the 8 mms.
- Pick up or sew through only seven 11º seed beads wherever the instructions indicate nine.
- Substitute 3 mm bicone crystals for the 3 mm pearls.
- Repeat steps 3 and 4 until you have a total of 16 6 mm pearl units, but then do not end the working thread.

[2] With the tail, sew through the first 3 mm and the next two 11ºs in the loop around one side of the first 6 mm.

[3] Pick up a 3 mm, an 11º, and a 3 mm. Skip the next three 11ºs, and sew through the last two 11ºs in the loop, the next 3 mm, and the following three 11ºs **(figure 7, a–b)**. Your thread should be exiting the opposite loop around the next 6 mm.

[4] Pick up an 11º, a 3 mm, and an 11º. Skip the next 11º, and sew through the last three 11ºs in the loop, the next 3 mm, and the following two 11ºs **(b–c)**.

[5] Repeat steps 3 and 4 for the length of the bracelet, embellishing alternating loops and exiting the end 3 mm.

[6] Repeat steps 2–5 to embellish the remaining loops. Do not end the working thread or tail.

MATERIALS

all bracelets
- Fireline 6 lb. test
- beading needles, #12

purple single-row bracelet 7½ in. (19.1 cm)
- **14** 8 mm glass pearls (purple)
- **15** 3 mm glass pearls (lavender)
- 2–3 g 11º seed beads (Toho 269, silver-lined lavender)
- 1 g 15º seed beads (Miyuki 1884, dark purple)
- magnetic clasp

white/blue double-row bracelet 7 in. (18 cm)
- **32** 6 mm glass pearls (white)
- **130** 3 mm bicone crystals (Swarovski, heliotrope)
- 5–6 g 11º seed beads (Matsuno 470, silver metallic)
- 3-strand clasp

DESIGN NOTE:
Increase or decrease the bracelets by two pearl units at a time to adjust the length.

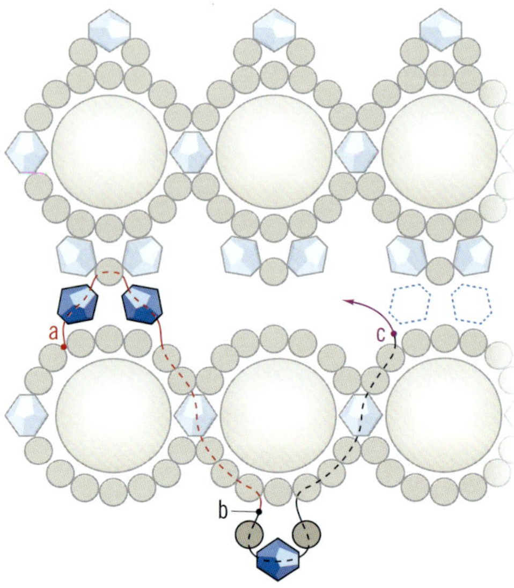

FIGURE 8

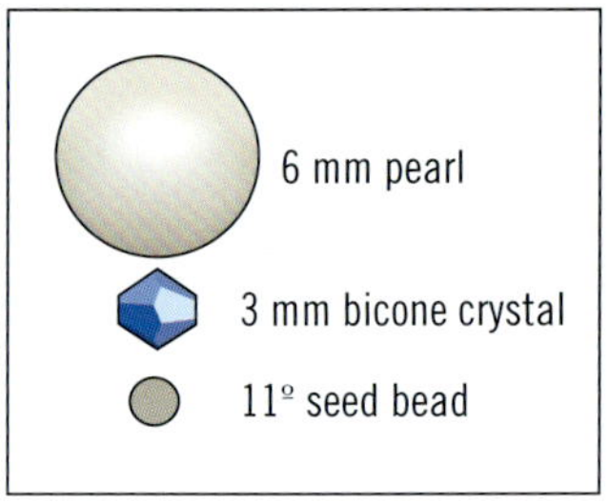

Second row and joining

[1] To begin the second row of the bracelet, work as in steps 1 and 2 of "First row." Lay the new row next to the embellished row so that the tail from the new row is pointing toward the edge of the embellished row with the 3 mm/11º/3 mm pattern.

[2] Pick up a 3 mm, sew through the 11º in the nearest 3 mm/11º/3 mm pattern on the embellished row, and pick up a 3 mm. Skip the next three 11ºs, and sew through the last two 11ºs in the loop, the next 3 mm, and the following three 11ºs (**figure 8, a–b**). Your thread should be exiting the opposite loop around the next 6 mm.

[3] Pick up an 11º, a 3 mm, and an 11º. Skip the next 11º, and sew through the last three 11ºs in the loop, the next 3 mm, and the following two 11ºs (**b–c**).

[4] Repeat steps 2 and 3 for the length of the bracelet, embellishing/joining alternating loops and exiting the end 3 mm.

[5] Sew through the next two 11ºs, and repeat steps 2–4 to embellish/join the remaining loops around the 6 mms.

Clasp

Use any of the remaining threads at either end of the bracelet to attach the clasp:

[1] With your thread exiting an end 3 mm on either row of the bracelet, work as in step 6 of "Single-row bracelet" to attach an end loop of the clasp. Sew through the next two 11ºs in the direction of the other row.

[2] Pick up three 11ºs, and sew through the center loop of the clasp. Sew back through the last 11º, pick up two 11ºs, and sew through the next two 11ºs and 3 mm on the other row of the bracelet.

[3] Work as in step 6 of "Single-row bracelet" to attach the last loop of the clasp, and end the thread.

[4] Repeat steps 1–3 to attach the clasp at the other end of the bracelet. End any remaining threads. ●

BEAD WEAVING

Scrumptious scallops

Create an elegant necklace of scallops using crystal pearls in a variety of sizes. Add crystal teardrops for movement.

designed by **Carolyn Cave**

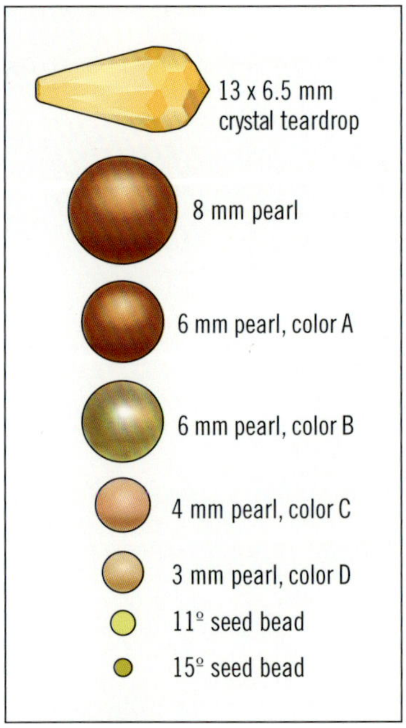

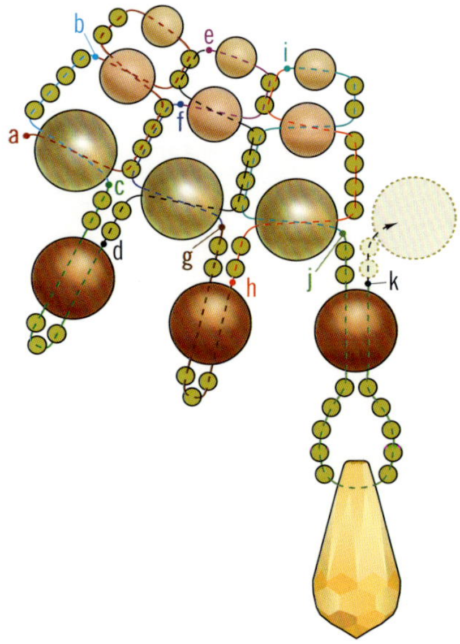

FIGURE 1

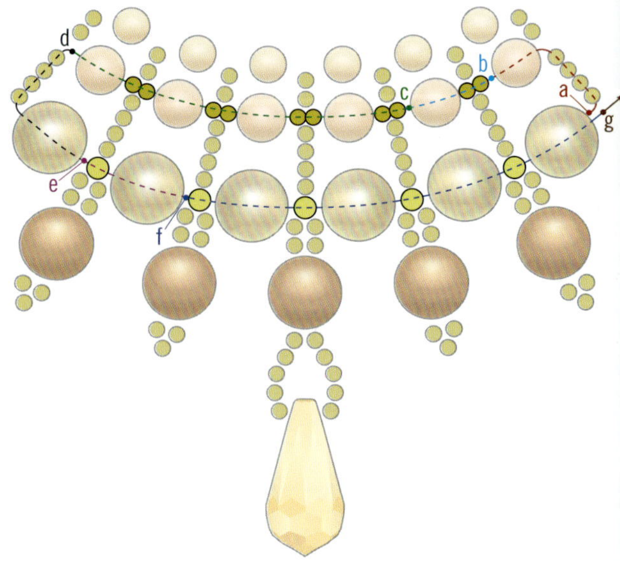

FIGURE 2

stepbystep

Necklace

[1] On a comfortable length of thread, attach a stop bead (Basics), leaving a 10-in. (25 cm) tail.

[2] Pick up a color B 6 mm pearl, four 15º seed beads, a color C 4 mm pearl, two 15ºs, a color D 3 mm pearl, and two 15ºs, and sew through the C again **(figure 1, a–b)**. Pick up four 15ºs, and sew through the B again **(b–c)**.

[3] Pick up two 15ºs, a color A 6 mm pearl, and three 15ºs, and sew back through the A, snugging up the beads **(c–d)**.

[4] Pick up two 15ºs, a B, four 15ºs, and a C, and sew through the existing two 15ºs between the C and the D added in the previous step **(d–e)**.

[5] Pick up a D and two 15ºs, and sew back through the C **(e–f)**. Sew through the following four 15ºs and B **(f–g)**.

[6] Repeat steps 3 **(g–h)**, 4 **(h–i)**, and 5 **(i–j)**.

[7] Pick up two 15ºs, an A, five 15ºs, a 13 x 6.5 mm crystal teardrop, and five 15ºs, and sew back through the A **(j–k)**.

[8] Repeat steps 4, 5, and 3, twice. Then repeat steps 4 and 5 once more.

[9] Sew through the next four 15ºs and C **(figure 2, a–b)**.

[10] Pick up two 15ºs, and sew through the next C, pulling tight **(b–c)**. Repeat this stitch four more times **(c–d)**.

[11] Sew through the next four 15ºs and B **(d–e)**. Pick up an 11º seed bead, and sew through the next B **(e–f)**. Repeat this stitch four more times **(f–g)**. Pick up a 15º, an A, and a 15º to be in position to create the next scallop.

[12] Repeat steps 2–11 to add three more scallops. End and add thread (Basics) as needed.

[13] To work the center scallop, repeat steps 2–6, and then work step 7 as follows: Pick up two 15ºs, an A, a 15º, an A, five 15ºs, a crystal teardrop, and five 15ºs, and sew back through the A, the 15º, and the A. Continue with steps 8–11.

[14] Repeat steps 2–11 four more times, ending and adding thread as needed.

Toggle ring

With the working thread, pick up a repeating pattern of a D and a 15º eight times, and sew through all the beads again except the last 15º added, forming the toggle ring. Pick up a 15º,

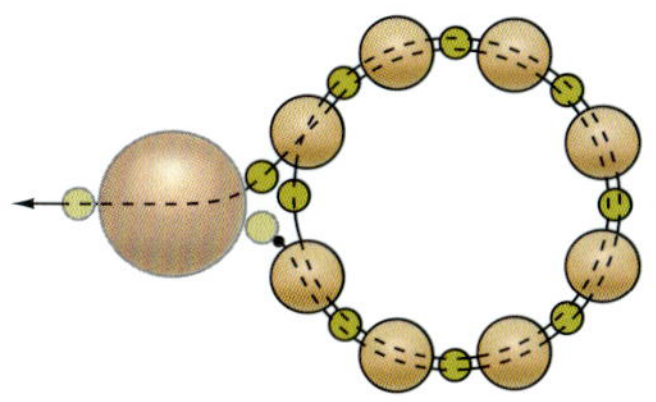

FIGURE 3

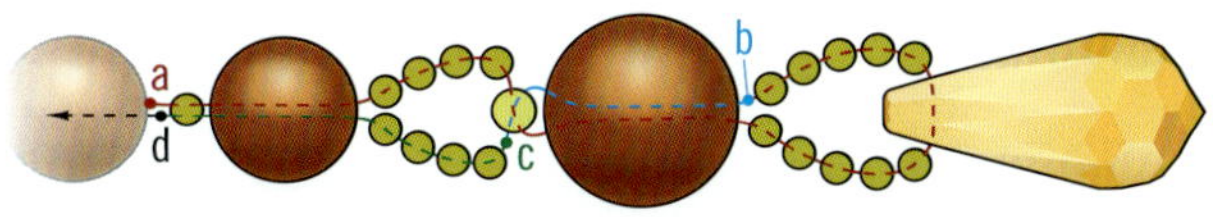

FIGURE 4

MATERIALS

bronze necklace 18 in. (46 cm)

- **10** 13 x 6.5 mm crystal teardrops (Swarovski #6000, crystal champagne; Eclectica, 262-641-0910)
- crystal pearls (Swarovski)
  1 8 mm (antique brass)
  56 6 mm, color A (antique brass)
  54 6 mm, color B (gold)
  54 4 mm, color C (light gold)
  62 3 mm, color D (cream rose light)
- 1 g 11º seed beads (Toho 22F, frosted silver-lined light topaz)
- 4 g 15º seed beads (Toho 221, bronze)
- Fireline 6 lb. test
- beading needles, #11 or #12

and sew through the last A and 15º at this end of the necklace **(figure 3)**. Do not end the thread.

Toggle bead

[1] Remove the stop bead. With the tail, pick up a 15º, an A, four 15ºs, an 11º, an 8 mm pearl, five 15ºs, a crystal teardrop, and five 15ºs **(figure 4, a–b)**. Sew back through the 8 mm, and cross through the next 11º **(b–c)**, pulling tight. Pick up four 15ºs, and sew back through the next A and 15º **(c–d)**. Sew through the beadwork, and retrace the thread path through the toggle bead. End the tail.
[2] Test the fit of the toggle bead with the toggle ring. Add or remove beads from the toggle ring if needed.
[3] With the working thread, retrace the thread path through the toggle ring, exiting the last 15º, A, and 15º in the necklace with your needle pointing toward the other end of the necklace.
[4] Sew through the Bs and 11ºs in the next scallop, and continue through the following 15º, A, and 15º. Repeat this stitch for the remainder of the necklace, and end the thread. ●

DESIGN NOTES:

- **The 8 mm pearl and 3 mm pearls used for the toggle clasp can be any of the colors from the necklace.**
- **Substitute glass pearls and Czech crystal drops for a more budget-friendly necklace.**

BEAD WEAVING

Crystal corona bracelet

Crown these unique Swarovski components with an equally unique array of beads, including metallic "squaredelles."

designed by **Sandie Bachand**

stepby**step**

Crystal units

[1] On a comfortable length of thread, pick up a 15º seed bead, a 2.5 x 5 mm Twin bead, a 15º, a 5 x 5 x 2 mm squaredelle, a 3 mm pearl, and a squaredelle. Repeat this pattern three more times, and tie the beads into a ring with a square knot (Basics), leaving a 6-in. (15 cm) tail. Sew through the first 10 beads in the ring, exiting a squaredelle. Position the Twin beads so that their available holes fall to the outside of the ring **(figure 1)**.

[2] Place an 8 x 10 mm oval sew-on stone inside the ring so that the two holes at one end of the setting are aligned with the squaredelle your thread is exiting. Working on the back side of the setting, sew through the two holes at this end of the setting and the squaredelle aligned with the hole your thread is exiting. Continue through the next 15º and Twin bead **(figure 2, a–b)**.

[3] Pick up a 15º and an 11º seed bead, and sew through the available (outer)

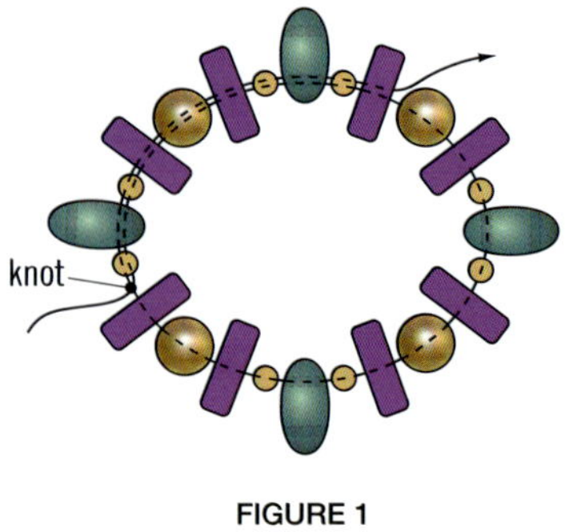

FIGURE 1

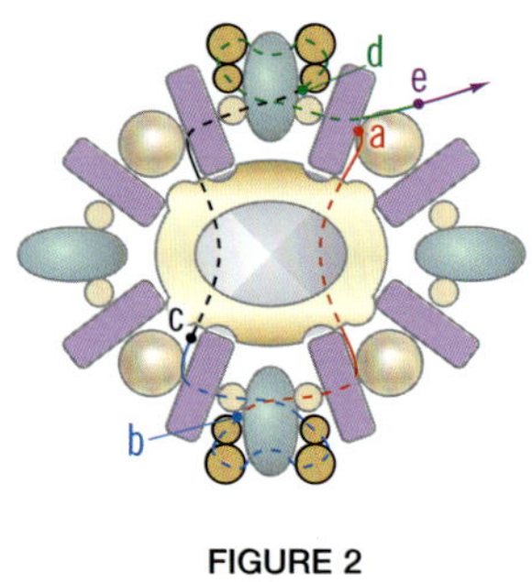

FIGURE 2

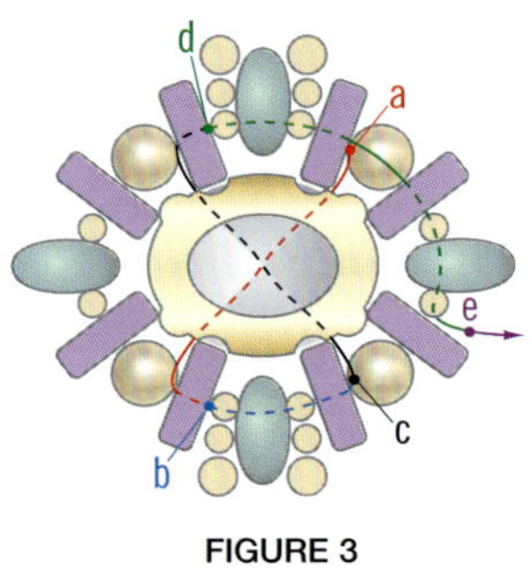

FIGURE 3

hole of the same Twin bead. Pick up an 11º and a 15º, and sew through the inner hole of the Twin bead. Continue through the next 15º and squaredelle **(b–c)**.

[4] Sew through the two holes at this end of the setting and the squaredelle aligned with the hole your thread is exiting. Continue through the next 15º and Twin bead **(c–d)**.

[5] Work as in step 3, exiting the next squaredelle **(d–e)**.

[6] Sew diagonally through the setting, and continue through the squaredelle aligned with the hole your thread is exiting **(figure 3, a–b)**. Sew through the beadwork to exit the next squaredelle **(b–c)**, sew diagonally through the setting, and continue through the squaredelle aligned with the hole your thread is exiting **(c–d)**. Sew through the beadwork to exit the 15º, unembellished Twin bead, and 15º at one end of the crystal unit **(d–e)**.

[7] Pick up two 15ºs, and sew through the outer hole of the same Twin bead. Pick up two more 15ºs, and sew through the next 15º, the inner hole of the same Twin bead, and the following 15º. Continue through the first two 15ºs added in this step, the outer hole of the Twin bead, and the following 15º **(figure 4)**.

[8] Pick up a squaredelle, a pearl, a squaredelle, a 15º, a Twin bead, and a 15º. Repeat this pattern twice more, and then pick up a squaredelle, a pearl, and a squaredelle. Sew through the three beads at the end of the previous crystal unit to form a new ring. Continue through the next seven beads, exiting a squaredelle. Position the Twin beads so that their available holes fall to the outside of the ring.

[9] Repeat steps 2–8 until you have a total of eight crystal units, but in the last repeat end with step 6. End and add thread (Basics) as needed.

Clasp

[1] Pick up a 15º and an 11º, and sew through the outer hole of the same Twin bead. Pick up an 11º and a 15º, and sew through the inner hole of the Twin bead. Continue through the first 15º and 11º added in this step, the outer hole of the Twin bead, and the following 11º.

[2] Pick up a squaredelle, a pearl, half of the clasp, a pearl, and a squaredelle, and sew through the three beads at the end of the previous crystal unit. Retrace the thread path of the clasp connection several times, and exit the first squaredelle added in this step. Pick up an 11º, and sew through the other squaredelle **(figure 5)**. Sew through the beadwork into the last crystal unit, and end the working thread.

[3] Repeat steps 1 and 2 with the tail. ●

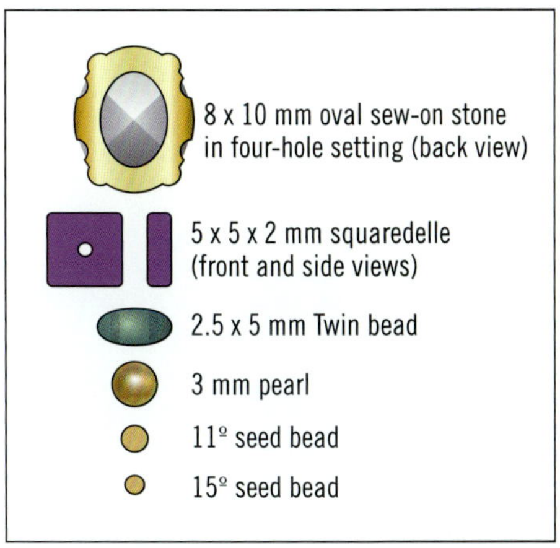

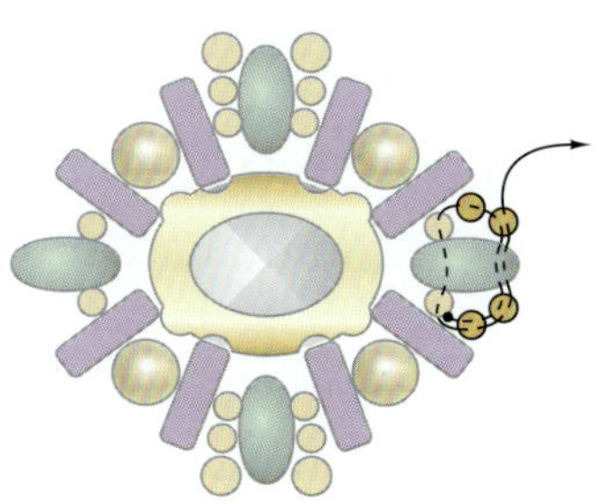

FIGURE 4

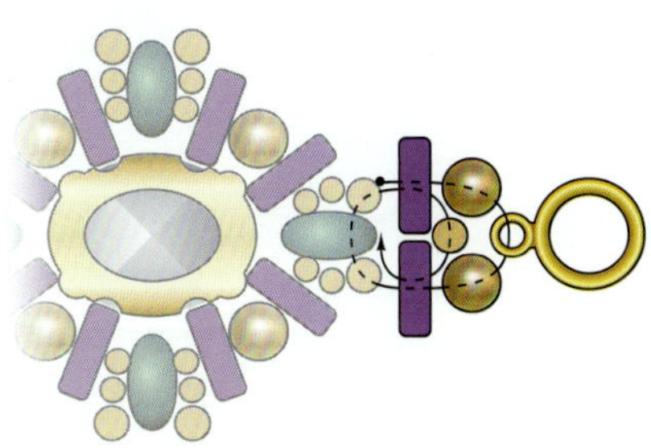

FIGURE 5

MATERIALS

bracelet 7¼ in. (18.4 cm)

- **8** 8 x 10 mm oval sew-on stones in four-hole settings (Swarovski #4100, light amethyst in silver-plated setting; www.etsy.com/shop/crystallizedmontees)*
- **68** 5 x 5 x 2 mm metallic squaredelles (magenta; Bead Gallery, www.beadgalleryca.com)
- **36** 3 mm glass pearls (gold)
- 2 g 2.5 x 5 mm Twin beads (Preciosa, terra pearl emerald)
- 1 g 11º seed beads (Toho P471, gold permanent galvanized)
- 1 g 15º seed beads (Toho P471, gold permanent galvanized)
- 10 mm Beadelle magnetic clasp (gold plated with crystal rhinestones; www.artbeads.com)
- Fireline 6 lb. test
- beading needles, #12

DESIGN NOTE:

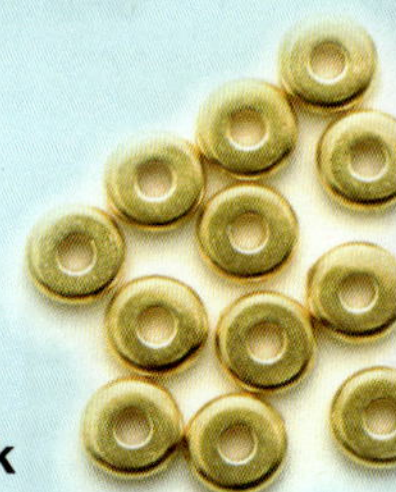

You can substitute other 5 mm flat beads or spacers for the squaredelles, as long as they measure 2 mm thick and have holes that are not too large for the 15º seed beads. For instance, the size and shape of these 5 mm heishi spacers were great, but the holes swallowed the 15ºs. Unfortunately, substituting 11ºs for the 15ºs causes the beadwork around the crystal setting to be too floppy.

BEAD WEAVING

Tila TRELLIS

Two-hole beads make this bracelet easy to stitch up while bicone crystals add a hint of sparkle.

designed by **Svetlana Chernitsky**

Tila beads and SuperDuos fit together beautifully along with an assortment of seed beads for a bracelet that has a delightful drape when worn.

stepby**step**

[1] On 3 yd. (2.7 m) of thread, attach a stop bead (Basics), leaving an 8-in. (20 cm) tail. Pick up a 5 x 5 mm Tila bead, a color A 11º seed bead, a 2.5 x 5 mm SuperDuo, an A, an 11º cylinder bead, a 3.4 mm drop bead, a cylinder, and a SuperDuo, and sew through the available hole of the first SuperDuo added. Pick up a SuperDuo, and sew through the available hole of the Tila **(figure 1, a–b)**.

[2] Pick up a color B 11º seed bead, two SuperDuos, a B, a Tila, three SuperDuos, a cylinder, a drop, and a cylinder, and sew through the available hole of the last SuperDuo added **(b–c)**.

[3] Pick up a SuperDuo, skip the next SuperDuo, and sew through the available hole of the following SuperDuo **(c–d)**.

[4] Pick up a Tila, and sew through the available hole of the next SuperDuo. Pick up a 3 mm bicone crystal, and sew through the following SuperDuo **(d–e)**.

[5] Pick up a Tila, and sew through the available hole of the next SuperDuo. Pick up a SuperDuo, and sew through the available hole of the following SuperDuo **(e–f)**.

[6] Pick up a cylinder, a drop, a cylinder, and a SuperDuo, and sew through the available hole of the next SuperDuo. Pick up a SuperDuo, and sew through the available hole of the following Tila **(f–g)**.

[7] Pick up a B, two SuperDuos, and a B, and sew through the available hole of the next Tila. Pick up a SuperDuo, and sew through the next SuperDuo. Pick up a SuperDuo, a cylinder, a drop, and a cylinder, and sew through the available hole of the last SuperDuo added.

[8] Repeat steps 3–7 for the length of the bracelet, ending with step 5. Leave approximately 1 in. (2.5 cm) for a clasp.

[9] To complete the last row: Pick up a cylinder, a drop, a cylinder, and an A, and sew through the next SuperDuo. Pick up an A, and sew through the following Tila **(figure 2, a–b)**.

[10] Pick up four Bs, and sew through the available hole of the next Tila **(b–c)**.

[11] Pick up an A, and sew through the next SuperDuo. Pick up a 15º seed bead, and sew back through the SuperDuo, the A, the Tila, and three Bs **(c–d)**.

[12] Pick up seven 15ºs, and sew through the two middle Bs to form a loop **(d–e)**. Retrace the thread path through the loop, and sew through the beadwork to reinforce the last row of beads in the bracelet. End the working thread (Basics).

[13] Remove the stop bead, and repeat steps 10–12 for this end of the bracelet.

[14] Open a 6 mm jump ring (Basics), and attach the seven-bead loop to half of the clasp. Repeat at the other end of the bracelet. ●

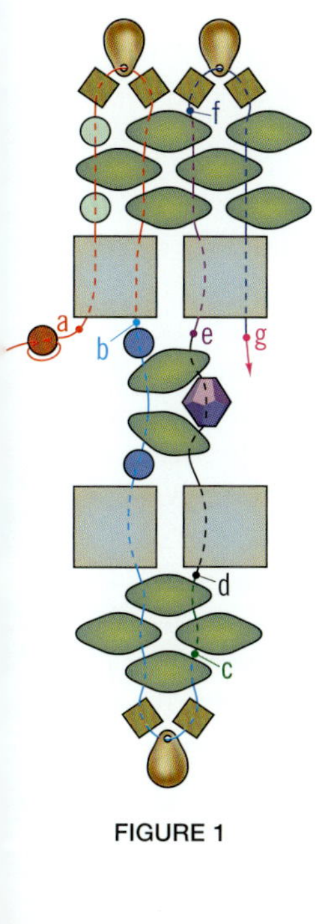

FIGURE 1

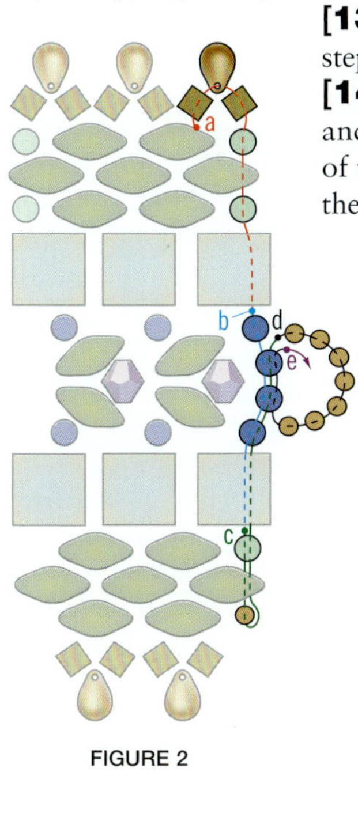

FIGURE 2

MATERIALS

grey bracelet 7 in. (18 cm)

- 5 g 5 x 5 mm Tila beads (Miyuki TL2440D, transparent dark grey luster)
- 10 g 2.5 x 5 mm SuperDuo beads (BT6303, blue turquoise bronze Picasso; www.bellomodo.com)
- **22** 3 mm bicone crystals (Swarovski, vitrail medium)
- 3 g 3.4 mm drop beads (Miyuki DP457, dark bronze)
- 11º seed beads
  6 color A (Miyuki 650, silver-lined dyed grey)
  1 g color B (Toho 82, metallic blue iris)
- 1 g 11º cylinder beads (Miyuki DB022, metallic bronze)
- 1 g 15º seed beads (Miyuki 462, metallic gold iris)
- toggle clasp (bronze)
- **2** 6 mm jump rings (bronze)
- Fireline 6 lb. test
- beading needles, #12
- **2** pairs of pliers

peach bracelet colors:

- 5 x 5 mm Tila beads (Miyuki TL596, opaque tea rose luster)
- 2.5 x 5 mm SuperDuo beads (SD-036, turquoise Picasso; www.whimbeads.com)
- 3 mm bicone crystals (Swarovski, crystal copper)
- 3 mm drop beads (Toho 222, dark bronze)
- 11º seed beads
  color A (Miyuki 2008, matte metallic patina iris; www.inmcrystal.com)
  color B (Toho 222, dark bronze)
- 11º cylinder beads (Miyuki DB131, pink luster moss green; www.redpandabeads.com)
- 15º seed beads (Miyuki 489, galvanized russet rose; www.beyondbeadery.com)

DESIGN NOTE:

For a more casual look, substitute 8º seed beads for the 3 mm bicone crystals, and 11º cylinder beads for the 3.4 mm drops.

Dreaming of diamonds

These elegant earrings look like fine jewelry yet are quick to stitch up and are easier on the wallet than real diamonds or gemstones.

designed by **Alice Kharon**

stepbystep

Earring front

[1] On 4 ft. (1.2 m) of thread, attach a stop bead (Basics), leaving a 6-in. (15 cm) tail. Pick up a 10 mm round bead, four color A 11º seed beads, a 4 mm pearl, and four As. Sew through the 10 mm again to form a loop of beads, and position the loop around one side of the 10 mm **(figure 1, a–b)**. Pick up four As, a pearl, and four As, and sew through the 10 mm again, positioning the new loop around the other side of the 10 mm **(b–c)**.
[2] Sew through the beads in the first loop. Remove the stop bead, and tie a square knot (Basics) with the working thread and tail.
[3] Pick up a pearl, and sew through the following four As, pearl, and four As. Pick up a pearl, and sew through the next four As, pearl, four As, and the first pearl added in this step **(figure 2, a–b)**.
[4] Sew through the 10 mm and the pearl directly across from the pearl your thread exited at the start of this step **(b–c)**. Sew back through the 10 mm and the pearl from the start of the step, going in the same direction **(c–d)**.
[5] Pick up four color B 11º seed beads, and sew through the next pearl, positioning the beads behind the existing As. Repeat this stitch three more times to complete the round **(figure 3)**. Retrace the thread path of the round using a tight tension.
[6] With your thread exiting a pearl, pick up a color C 4 mm bicone crystal, a pearl, and a C. Sew through the pearl your thread exited at the start of this step in the same direction to form a picot **(figure 4, a–b)**.
[7] Pick up a 15º seed bead, a color D 4 mm bicone crystal, and a 15º, and sew through the next pearl **(b–c)**.
[8] Repeat steps 6 and 7 three more times to complete the round. This completes the front of the earring.

Earring back

[1] Flip the beadwork over to the back, and sew through the next four Bs.
[2] Pick up two As, and sew through the next four Bs **(photo a)**. Repeat this stitch three more times to complete the round, and step up through the first two As added.
[3] Pick up a B, two As, and a B, and sew through the next two As added in the previous step **(photo b)**. Repeat this stitch three more times to complete the round. Do not step up at the end of the round.
[4] Pick up three or four Bs, and sew through the nearest pearl on an outside corner. Pick up three or four Bs, and sew through the two As your thread exited at the start of this step in the same direction **(photo c)**. Continue through the following B and two As.
[5] Pick up two or three Bs, and sew through the nearest

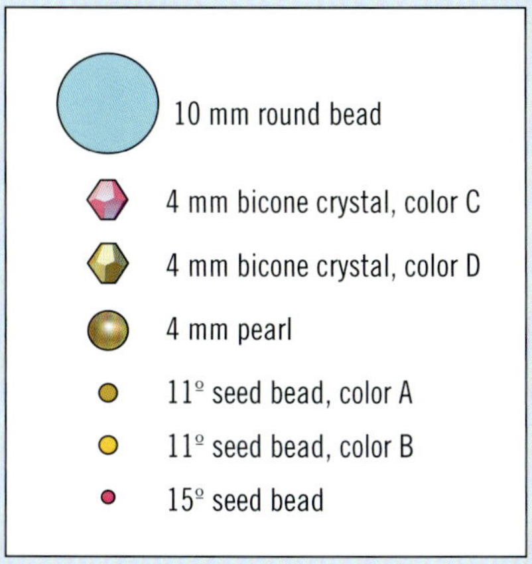

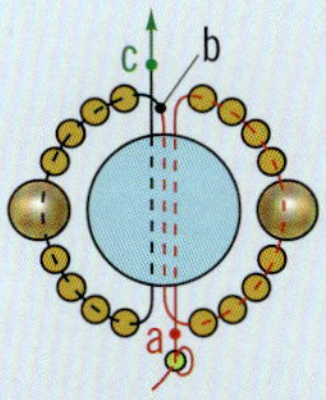

FIGURE 1

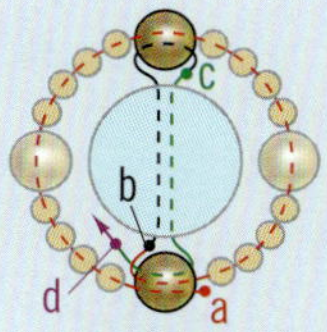

FIGURE 2

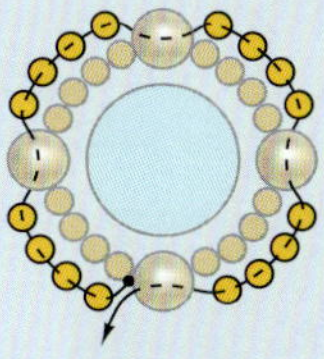
FIGURE 3

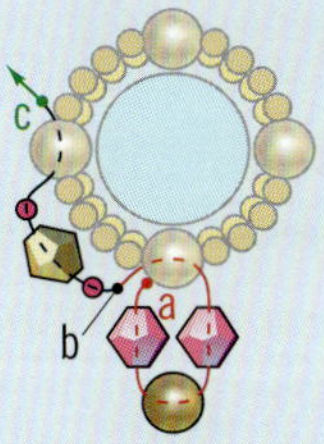

FIGURE 4

D directly above the two As your thread is exiting. Pick up two or three Bs, and sew through the two As your thread exited at the start of this step in the same direction. Continue through the next B and two As **(photo d)**.

[6] Repeat steps 4 and 5 three more times to complete the round.

[7] Sew through the beadwork to exit a corner pearl. Pick up a 15º, an A, two 15ºs, an A, and a 15º. Sew through the pearl in the same direction to form a loop, and retrace the thread path. End the working thread and tail (Basics).

[8] Open the loop of an earring finding (Basics), and attach the dangle.

[9] Make a second earring. ●

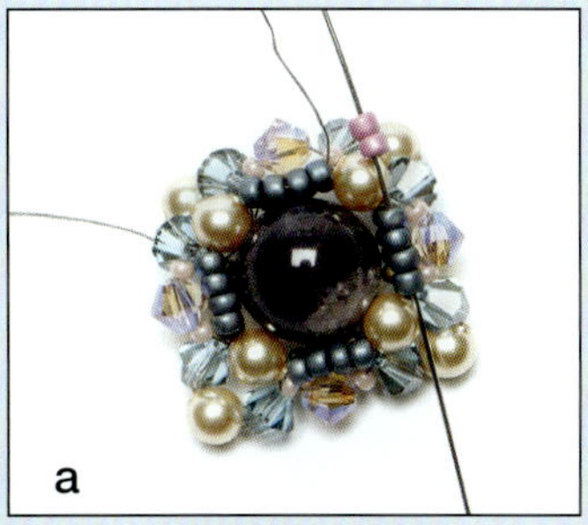
a

b

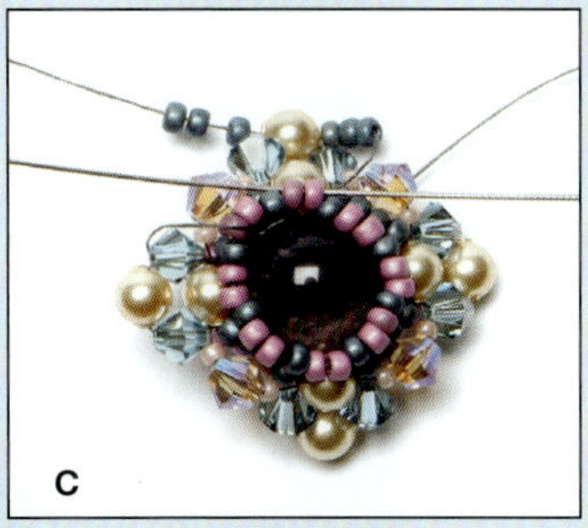
c

d

MATERIALS

fuchsia/gold earrings

1⅛ in. (2.9 cm)

- **2** 10 mm round beads (turquoise blue)
- **16** 4 mm pearls (Swarovski, copper)
- 4 mm bicone crystals (Swarovski)
  16 color C (fuchsia)
  8 color D (metallic light gold)
- 1 g 11º seed beads in each of **2** colors: A (Miyuki 457G, bronze metallic), B (Miyuki 457, gold bronze metallic)
- 1 g 15º seed beads (Miyuki 457G, bronze metallic)
- pair of earring findings
- Fireline 6 lb. test
- beading needles, #11 or #12
- **2** pairs of pliers

turquoise/grey earring colors:

- 10 mm round beads (turquoise blue)
- 4 mm pearls (Swarovski, platinum)
- 4 mm bicone crystals, color C (Swarovski, light grey opal)
- 4 mm fire-polished beads, color D (dark grey)
- 11º seed beads
  color A (Miyuki 464A, light gunmetal)
  color B (Miyuki F451D, grey mist matte metallic)
- 15º seed beads (Miyuki 464A, light gunmetal)

DESIGN NOTES:

- **In step 4 of "Earring back," two or three 10º cylinders can be substituted for the 11º seed beads.**
- **In step 5 of "Earring back," one or two 10º cylinders can be substituted for the 11º seed beads.**

Flamenco Pellets bangle

designed by **Kerrie Slade**

Stitch an easy bracelet and earrings reminiscent of a flamenco dancer's dress using linked rings of Pellet beads and contrasting seed beads.

stepbystep

First Pellet ring

[1] On 1 yd. (.9 m) of thread, pick up 12 6 x 4 mm Pellet beads, leaving a 6-in. (15 cm) tail. Sew through all the beads again to form a ring. Snug up the beads so the Pellets nestle into each other.

[2] Pick up three 11º seed beads, skip the next Pellet, and sew through the following Pellet. Repeat this stitch to complete the round **(figure 1)**. Every other Pellet in the ring will be embellished.

[3] Working in the opposite direction, pick up five 11ºs, skip the Pellet your thread is exiting, and sew through the following Pellet. Pick up five 11ºs, skip the next Pellet, and sew through the following Pellet. Repeat this stitch to complete the round, and step up through the first five 11ºs picked up in this round **(figure 2)**. The new 11ºs will loop around the outside edge of the unembellished Pellets.

[4] Working in the same direction, pick up an 11º, and sew through the next three 11ºs picked up in step 2 **(figure 3, a–b)**. Pick up an 11º, and sew through the next five 11ºs picked up in step 3 **(b–c)**. Repeat these two stitches to complete the round, and step up through the first 11º picked up in this round **(c–d)**. Retrace the thread path through all of the 11ºs, and end the working thread and tail (Basics).

Subsequent rings

[1] Work as in steps 1–4 of "First Pellet ring," but before you form the Pellets into a ring in step 1, sew through the center of the first Pellet ring so you have two linked rings **(figure 4)**.

[2] Continue to make a band of linked rings long enough to fit around your wrist, minus the clasp. Our 7½-in. (19.1 cm) bracelet has 15 rings.

Clasp

You can choose to finish your bracelet with either a ribbon or ready-made clasp following the steps below.

Ribbon option

Cut an 18-in. (46 cm) length of ribbon. Center the ribbon through the last ring on each end of the band. Place the bracelet on your wrist, and have a friend tie a bow.

Ready-made clasp option

[1] Open a 6 mm jump ring (Basics), slide it through a five-bead loop on the last ring on one end of the band, and attach half of the clasp.

[2] Repeat step 1 on the other end of the band.

Earrings

[1] Work as in steps 1–4 of "First Pellet ring," but in step 3, replace the center 11º of one of the five-bead loops with an 8º seed bead.

[2] Work as in step 1 of "Subsequent rings" to make a total of three linked rings.

[3] Open a jump ring (Basics), and attach the 8º of the first Pellet ring to the loop of an earring finding.

[4] Make a second earring. ●

MATERIALS

both projects

- Fireline 6 lb. test
- beading needles, #10 or #11

bracelet 7½ in. (19.1 cm)

- Preciosa traditional Czech beads **180** 6 x 4 mm Pellet beads (opaque red; www.kandrasbeads.com)
  10 g 11º seed beads (opaque black)
- for ribbon clasp option: 18 in. (46 cm) satin ribbon, ⅜ in. (1 cm) wide
- for ready-made clasp option: **2** 6 mm jump rings, clasp, and **2** pairs of chainnose, flatnose, and/or bentnose pliers

pair of earrings 2 in. (5 cm)

- Preciosa traditional Czech beads **72** 6 x 4 mm Pellet beads (opaque red; www.kandrasbeads.com)
  2 8º seed beads (opaque black)
  3–4 g 11º seed beads (opaque black)
- pair of post earring findings
- **2** 6 mm jump rings
- **2** pairs of chainnose, flatnose, and/or bentnose pliers

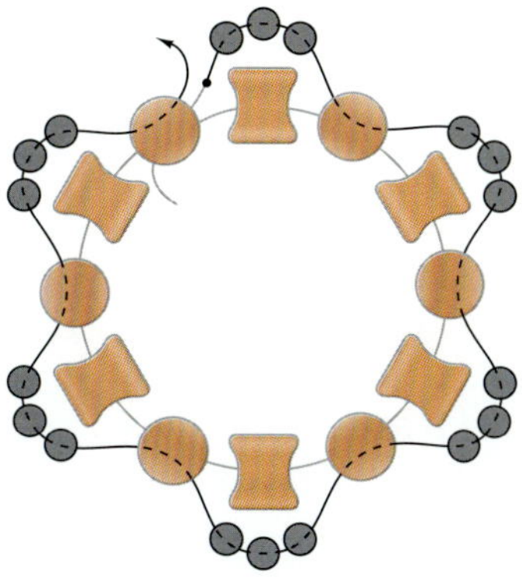

FIGURE 1

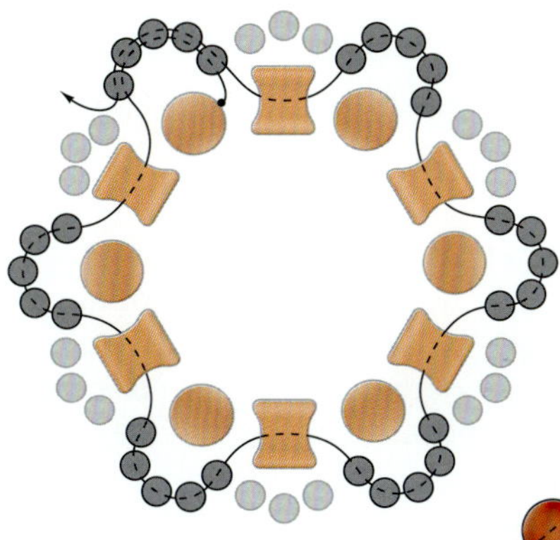

FIGURE 2

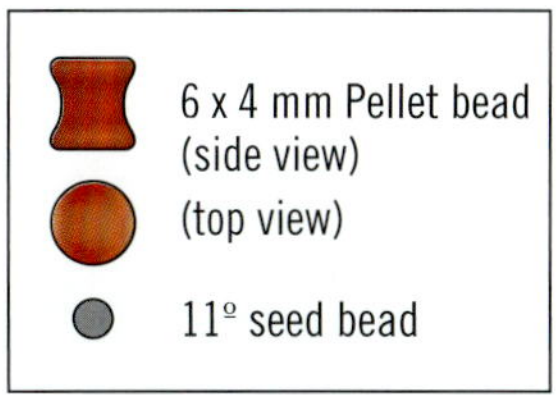

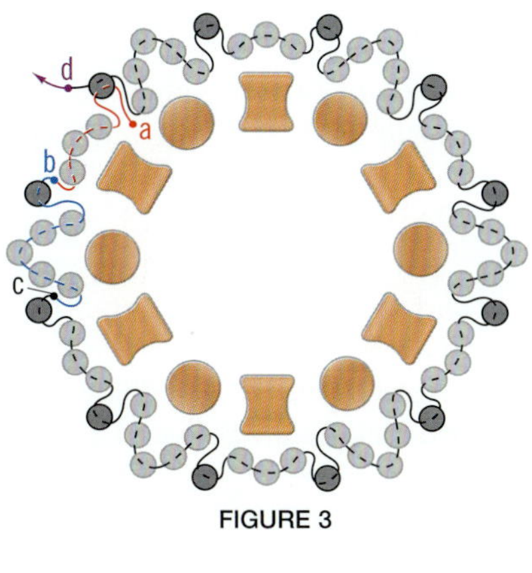

FIGURE 3

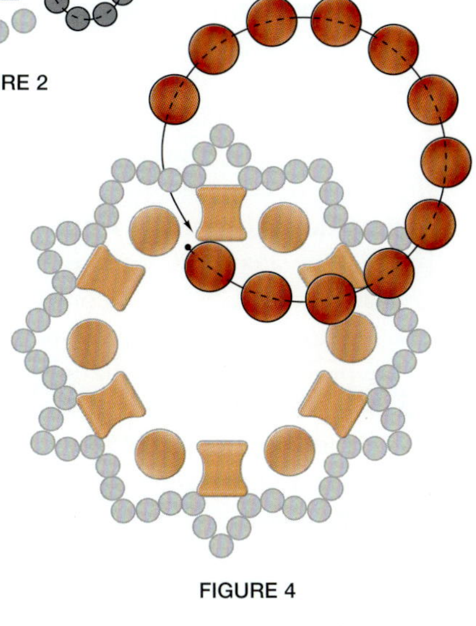

FIGURE 4

BEAD WEAVING

Shimmering snowflake earrings

Sparkling crystals and Swarovski cosmic rings light the way in these daring, dangling earrings.

designed by **Graehound**

stepbystep

Large medallion

[1] On 1½ yd. (1.4 m) of thread, pick up four color A 4 mm bicone crystals. Sew through all the beads again to form a ring, leaving a 6-in. (15 cm) tail **(figure 1, a–b)**.

[2] Pick up an 11º seed bead, and sew through the next A in the ring. Repeat this stitch to complete the round, and step up through the first 11º **(b–c)**.

[3] Pick up a color B 3 mm bicone crystal, a color C 3 mm bicone crystal, and a B, and sew through the next 11º in the previous round **(c–d)**. Repeat this stitch to complete the round. Retrace the thread path, and step up through the first B and C picked up in this round **(d–e)**.

[4] Pick up a color D 3 mm bicone crystal, an A, and a D, and sew through the C your thread exited at the start of this step in the same direction. Retrace the thread path, and sew through the next B, 11º, and B **(e–f)**.

[5] Pick up an 11º, a 15º seed bead, a 4 mm round crystal, a 15º, and an 11º, and sew through the B, 11º, and B your thread exited at the start of this step in the same direction. Retrace the thread path, and sew through the next C **(f–g)**.

[6] Repeat steps 4 and 5 three more times, and sew through the beadwork to exit an A along the outer edge of the medallion **(figure 2, point a)**.

[7] Pick up an 11º, a 15º, a color E 3 mm bicone crystal, a 15º, and an 11º, and sew through the A your thread exited at the start of this step. Retrace the thread path, and exit the E **(a–b)**.

[8] Pick up an 11º, a 15º, a B, a color F 4 mm bicone crystal, a B, a 15º, and an 11º, and sew through the E your thread

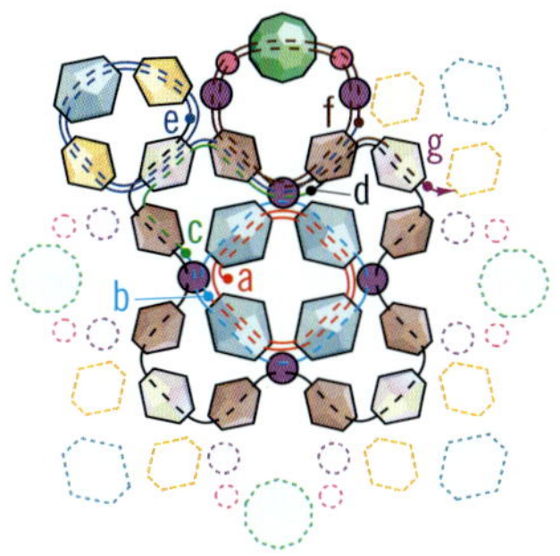

FIGURE 1

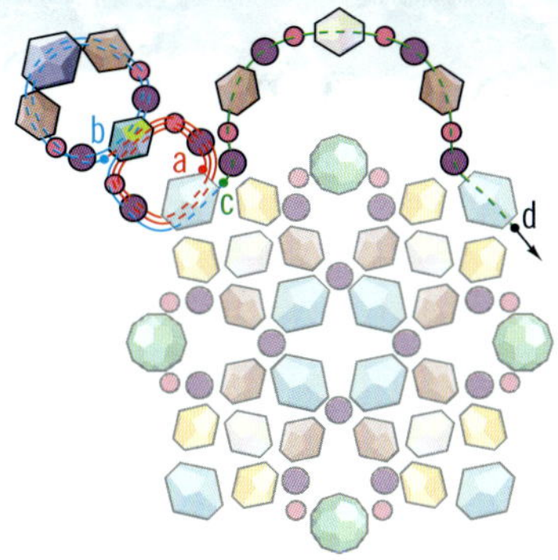

FIGURE 2

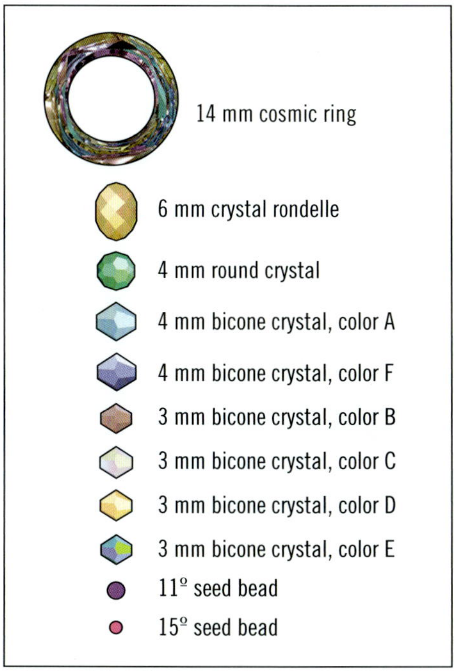

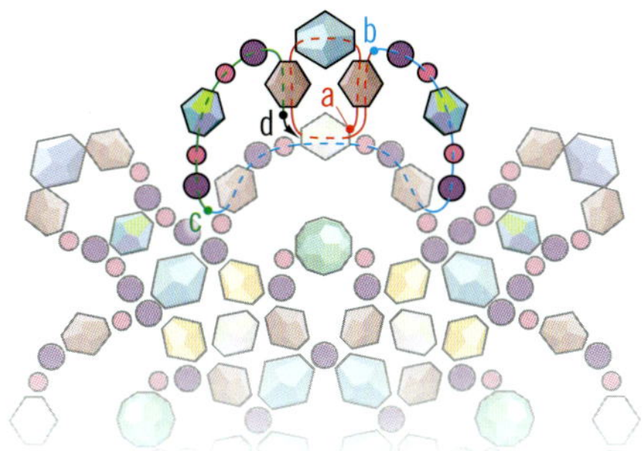

FIGURE 3

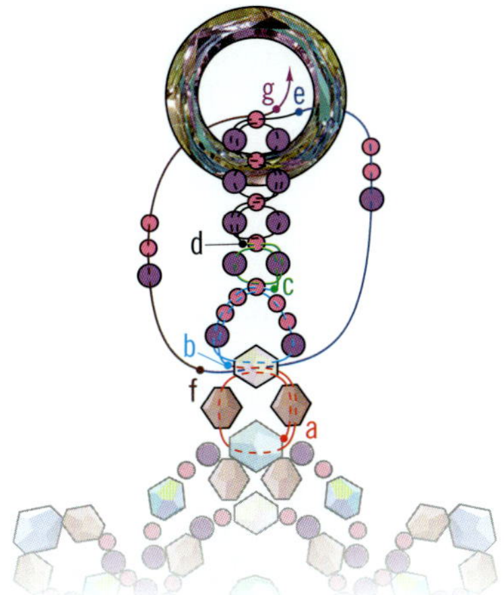

FIGURE 4

exited at the start of this step. Retrace the thread path, and sew through the beadwork to exit the same A along the outer edge of the medallion **(b–c)**.

[9] Pick up an 11º, a 15º, a B, an 11º, a 15º, a C, a 15º, an 11º, a B, a 15º, and an 11º. Sew through the next A along the outer edge of the medallion **(c–d)**.

[10] Repeat steps 7–9 three more times, and sew through the beadwork to exit an outer edge C **(figure 3, point a)**.

[11] Pick up a B, an A, and a B, and sew through the C your thread exited at the start of this step. Continue through the first B **(a–b)**.

[12] Pick up an 11º, a 15º, an E, a 15º, and an 11º, and sew through the second B added in step 9, with the needle pointing toward the B your thread exited at the start of this step. Continue through the next 11º, 15º, C, 15º, 11º, and B **(b–c)**.

[13] Pick up an 11º, a 15º, an E, a 15º, and an 11º, and sew through the second B added in step 11, with the needle pointing toward the B your thread exited at the start of this step **(c–d)**. Sew through the beadwork to exit the next available outer edge C.

[14] Repeat steps 11–13 three more times, and exit an A along the outer edge.

Cosmic ring

[1] Pick up a B, a C, and a B, and sew through the A your thread exited at the start of this step. Continue through the first B and the C just picked up **(figure 4, a–b)**. Pick up an 11º, five 15ºs, and an 11º, and sew through the C

MATERIALS

blue/purple earrings 3¾ in. (9.5 cm)

- **2** 14 mm cosmic rings (Swarovski, crystal vitrail light)
- **2** 8 mm crystal rondelles (Swarovski, indicolite)
- **2** 6 mm crystal rondelles (Swarovski, Caribbean blue opal)
- 4 mm bicone crystals (Swarovski)
  30 color A (violet AB 2X)
  12 color F (aquamarine AB 2X)
- **8** 4 mm round crystals (Swarovski, cyclamen opal)
- 3 mm bicone crystals (Swarovski)
  84 color B (Capri blue AB 2X)
  26 color C (crystal AB 2X)
  20 color D (cyclamen opal)
  32 color E (light sapphire AB 2X)
- 4 g 11º seed beads (Miyuki 91061L, galvanized rose)
- 5 g 15º seed beads (Miyuki 377J, peacock lined; www.beyondbeadery.com)
- **2** 1.5 x 5.5 mm small coiled rings (Tierra Cast; www.fusionbeads.com)
- **2** 2½-in. (6.4 cm) eye pins (sterling silver)
- Fireline 6 lb. test (crystal)
- beading needles, #12
- dowel or pen
- file
- chainnose pliers
- wire cutters

pink earrings (p. 34) colors:

- 14 mm cosmic rings (Swarovski, crystal)
- 8 mm crystal rondelles (Swarovski, crystal golden shadow)
- 6 mm crystal rondelles (Swarovski, silk)
- 4 mm bicone crystals (Swarovski)
  color A (white opal)
  color F (purple haze)
- 4 mm round crystals (Swarovski, crystal AB)
- 3 mm bicone crystals (Swarovski)
  color B (vintage rose)
  color C (crystal)
  color D (crystal golden shadow)
  color E (sand opal)
- 11º seed beads (Czech, gold-lined opalescent milk)
- 15º seed beads (Miyuki 364, color-lined fancy dusty rose)
- 5 mm daisy spacers (vermeil), in place of 1.5 x 5.5 mm small coiled rings
- 2½-in. (6.4 cm) eye pins (gold-filled)

Dazzling crystal components create light-refracting accessories.

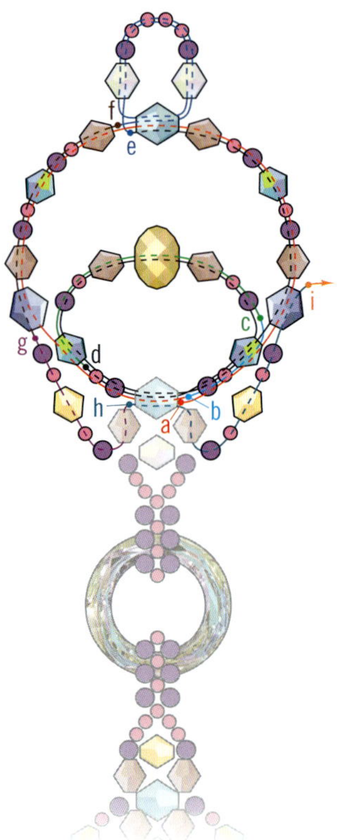

FIGURE 5

again to form a loop. Retrace the thread path through the loop, and exit the third 15º **(b–c)**.

[2] Pick up an 11º, a 15º, and an 11º, and sew through the 15º your thread exited at the start of this step. Retrace the thread path, and exit the 15º picked up in this step **(c–d)**. Repeat this step three more times to create a tab extending from the medallion **(d–e)**.

[3] Pick up two 15ºs and an 11º, insert the tab through a 14 mm cosmic ring, and sew through the C picked up in step 1 **(e–f)**. Pick up an 11º and two 15ºs, and sew through the 15º your thread exited at the start of this step **(f–g)**. Retrace the thread path several times, and end the working thread and tail (Basics).

Small medallion

[1] On 2 ft. (61 cm) of thread, pick up a B, a C, a B, and an A. Sew through the first B again to form a ring, leaving a 6-in. (15 cm) tail. Retrace the thread path, and continue through the first B and C. Pick up an 11º, five 15ºs, and an 11º, and sew through the C again to form a loop. Retrace the thread path through the loop, and exit the third 15º.

[2] Work as in steps 2 and 3 of "Cosmic ring," but do not end the threads. Position this tab on the ring opposite the large medallion. Sew through the beadwork to exit the A added in step 1 **(figure 5, point a)**.

[3] Pick up an 11º, a 15º, an E, an F, a B, an 11º, a 15º, an E, an 11º, a 15º, a B, an A, a B, a 15º, an 11º, an E, a 15º, an 11º, a B, an F, an E, a 15º, and an 11º. Sew through the A your thread exited at the start of this step to form a ring **(a–b)**. Retrace the thread path through the ring, and continue through the first 11º, 15º, and E picked up in this step **(b–c)**.

[4] Pick up an 11º, a 15º, a B, a 6 mm crystal rondelle, a B, a 15º, and an 11º, and sew through the last E added in the previous step **(c–d)**. Retrace the thread path, and continue through the ring of beads created in step 3 to exit the A at the top of the ring opposite the tab **(d–e)**.

[5] Pick up a C, an 11º, four 15ºs, an 11º, and a C, and sew through the A again to form a loop **(e–f)**. Retrace the thread path through the loop, and sew through the beadwork to exit the nearest F **(point g)** with your needle pointing toward the large medallion.

[6] Pick up an 11º, a 15º, a D, a 15º, and an 11º, and sew through the nearest B added in step 1 with the needle pointing away from the large medallion **(g–h)**.

[7] Sew through the next A and B. Pick up an 11º, a 15º, a D, a 15º, and an 11º, and sew through the F on this side of the ring **(h–i)**. End the working thread and tail.

Ear wire

[1] On an eye pin, string a C, an 8 mm crystal rondelle, a 1.5 x 5 mm coiled ring, and an A.

[2] With chainnose pliers, make a 90-degree bend in the wire above the A.

[3] Pull the wire around a dowel or a pen, bringing it toward the 90-degree bend to form an ear wire. Trim the wire if necessary.

[4] With chainnose pliers, grasp the wire approximately 3/16 in. (5 mm) from the end, and bend it slightly upward. File the end of the wire to remove any burs.

[5] Open the loop of the eye pin (Basics), and attach the loop of beads at the top of the small medallion.

[6] Make a second earring. •

DESIGN NOTES:

- **Use a firm, but not tight, tension throughout this project. If your tension is too tight, your earring will buckle.**
- **To use a premade earring finding: Make a plain loop (Basics) above the A in step 1 of "Ear wire," creating a beaded link. Work step 5, and attach the earring finding to the other loop of the link.**

MATERIALS

bracelet 7 in. (18 cm)

- **20** 6 mm crystal pearls (Swarovski, Tahitian)
- 7 g 3 x 5 mm Rulla beads (T6313, turquoise opaque Picasso; www.redpandabeads.com)
- 1 g 11º seed beads (Toho PF558, permanent finish galvanized aluminum)
- 1 g 15º seed beads (Toho 221, bronze)
- toggle clasp
- Fireline 6 lb. test
- beading needles, #11 or #12

BEAD WEAVING

Rulla wave bracelet

designed by
Connie Whittaker

For the purposes of these instructions, the Rulla beads will have a top hole (the one closest to you) and a bottom hole (the one closest to your work surface), and there will be a top and a bottom 11º seed bead that lines up with those holes.

stepbystep

[1] On a comfortable length of thread, pick up an 11º seed bead, a 6 mm pearl, an 11º, and three 3 x 5 mm Rulla beads. Sew through the first 11º and the pearl, leaving a 6-in. (15 cm) tail. Position the Rullas to the right of the pearl with their available holes in the bottom position (closest to your work surface) **(figure 1)**.

[2] Pick up an 11º, and sew through the bottom hole of the three Rullas just added. Pick up an 11º, and sew through the pearl and the first bottom 11º added in this step.

[3] Sew through the bottom hole of the first Rulla, pick up a 15º, and sew through the bottom hole of the next Rulla. Repeat this stitch once more. Sew through the next bottom 11º and the pearl **(figure 2)**.

[4] Sew through the next top 11º and the top hole of the first Rulla. Pick up a 15º seed bead, and sew through the top hole of the next Rulla. Repeat this stitch once more. Sew through the next top 11º, the pearl, and the following top 11º.

DESIGN NOTE:
For a budget-friendly option, replace the Swarovski crystal pearls with glass pearls or druks.

[5] Pick up a pearl, an 11º, and three Rullas, and sew through the previous top 11º and the pearl just added. Position the Rullas opposite the Rullas around the previous pearl with their available holes in the bottom position **(figure 3)**.

[6] Repeat steps 2–5 for the desired length of the bracelet, leaving ¾ in. (1.9 cm) for the clasp, but in step 2, after you sew through the Rullas, continue through the existing 11º. End the working thread and tail (Basics).

[7] Add 14 in. (36 cm) of thread (Basics) to one end, and exit the top 11º with the needle pointing toward the Rullas. Pick up two 15ºs, the toggle ring, and two 15ºs, and sew through the bottom 11º with your needle pointing toward the pearl. Continue through the top 11º, and retrace the thread path several times. End the thread.

[8] Repeat step 7 to attach the toggle bar at the other end, adding 15ºs if necessary to allow the toggle bar to slide through the ring.

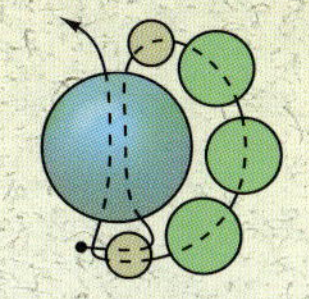

FIGURE 1

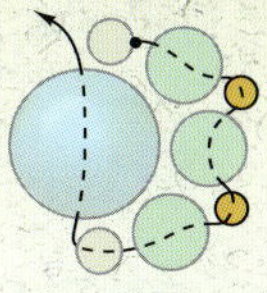

FIGURE 2

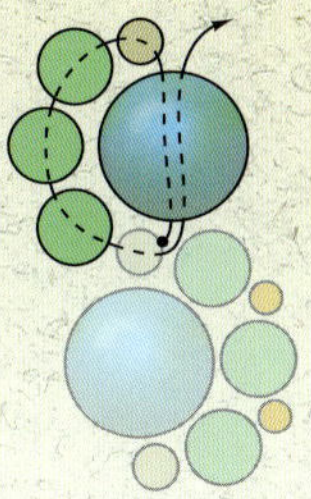

FIGURE 3

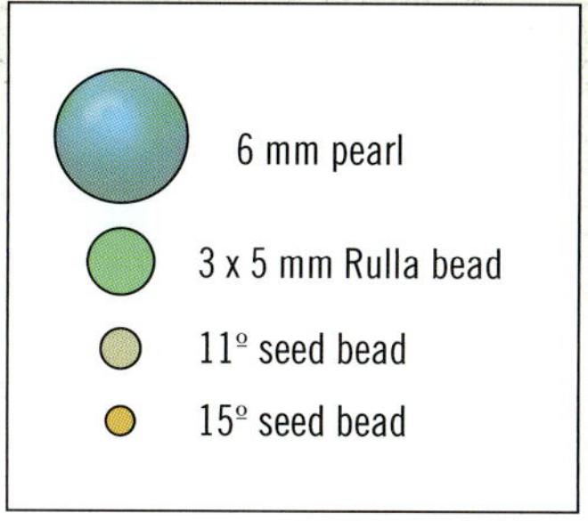

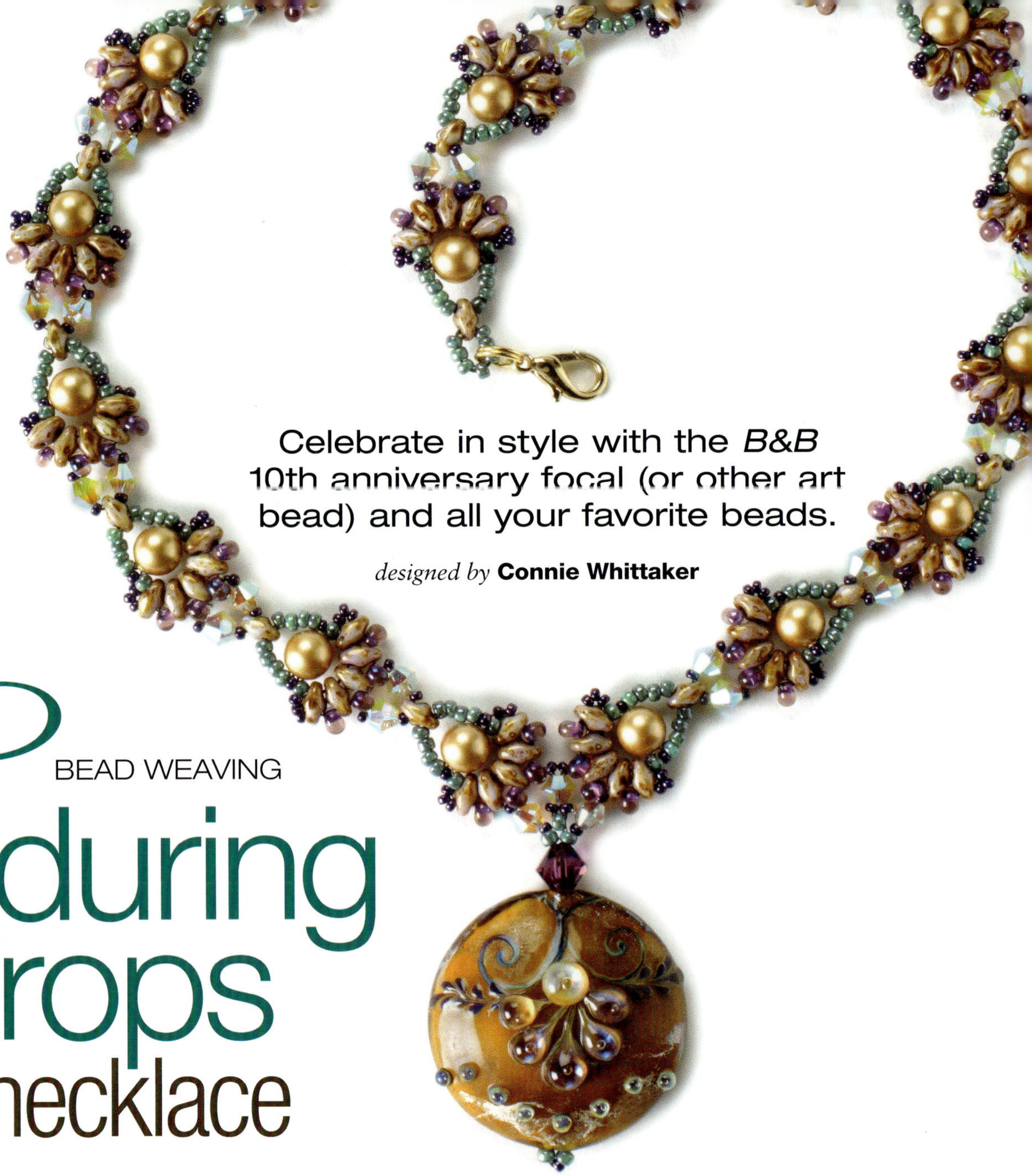

Celebrate in style with the *B&B* 10th anniversary focal (or other art bead) and all your favorite beads.

designed by **Connie Whittaker**

BEAD WEAVING

Enduring drops necklace

stepby**step**

Pearl units

[1] On 24 in. (61 cm) of thread, pick up an 11º seed bead, a 6 mm pearl, an 11º, and five 2.5 x 5 mm SuperDuo beads. Sew through all the beads again to form a ring, leaving a 6-in. (15 cm) tail **(figure 1, a–b)**.

[2] Pick up three 15º seed beads, and sew through the available hole of the SuperDuo your thread exited at the start of this step **(b–c)**.

[3] Pick up a 3 mm magatama, and sew through the available hole of the next SuperDuo **(c–d)**. Repeat this stitch three more times **(d–e)**.

[4] Pick up three 15ºs, and sew through the inner holes of the SuperDuos, the next 11º, and the pearl **(e–f)**.

[5] Pick up four 11ºs, a SuperDuo, and four 11ºs, and sew through the pearl in the same direction to form a loop **(figure 2, a–b)**. Retrace the thread path through the loop, exiting the last four 11ºs **(b–c)**.

[6] Pick up a 15º, and sew through the next 11º, the inner holes of the next five SuperDuos, and the following 11º **(c–d)**. Pick up a 15º, and sew through the next four 11ºs and SuperDuo. Continue through the available hole of the same SuperDuo **(d–e)**. End the tail (Basics) but not the working thread.

[7] Repeat steps 1–6 to make a total of 20 pearl units for a 19½-in. (49.5 cm) necklace.

Pendant attachment

[1] Position the anniversary bead so the drops in the center are on the bottom half of the bead. On 1 yd. (.9 m) of thread, sew up through the anniversary bead from the bottom, leaving a 6-in. (15 cm) tail. Pick up a 6 mm bicone crystal and three 11ºs. Sew back through the 6 mm crystal and the anniversary bead **(figure 3, a–b)**.

[2] Pick up an 11º, a 15º, and an 11º, and sew up through the anniversary bead, the 6 mm crystal, and the first 11º added in step 1 **(b–c)**.

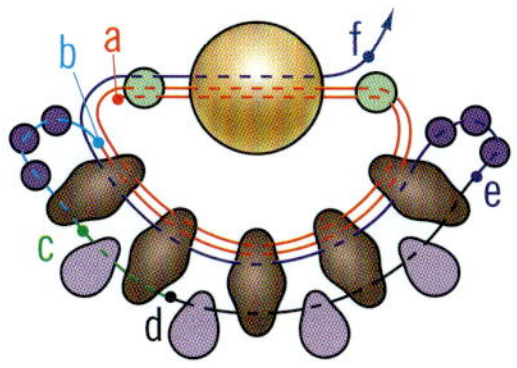

FIGURE 1

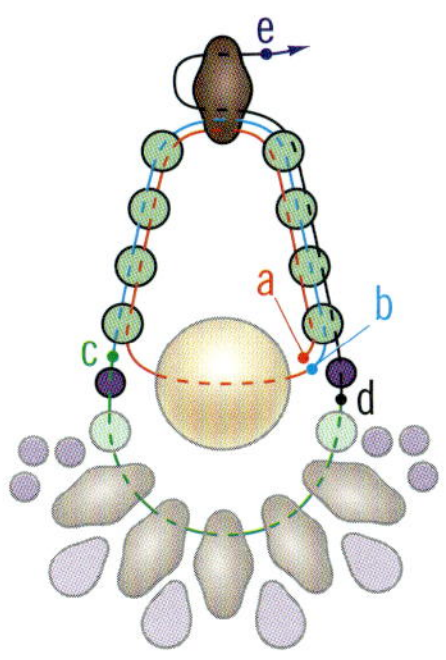

FIGURE 2

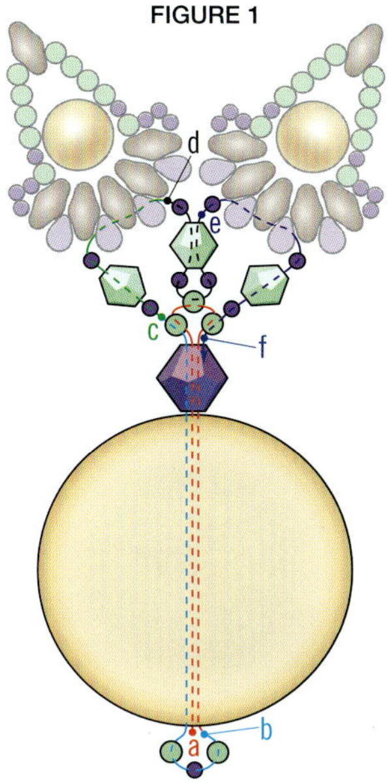

FIGURE 3

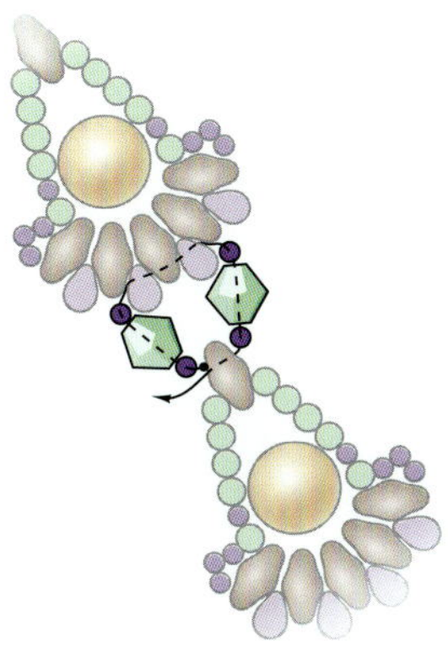

FIGURE 4

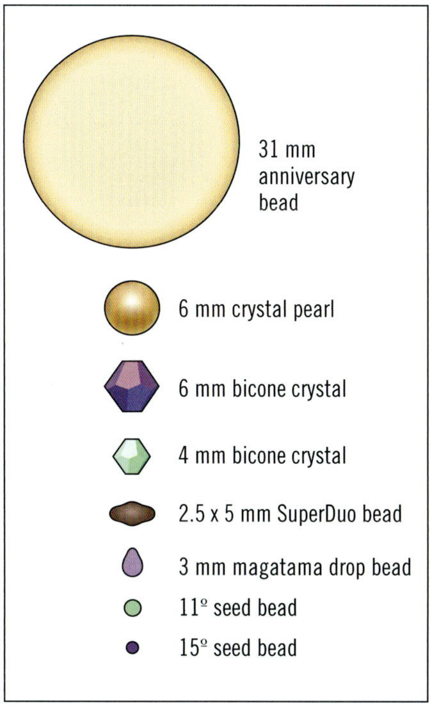

[3] Pick up a 15º, a 4 mm bicone crystal, and a 15º, and sew through the second drop along the outside edge of a pearl unit, the center SuperDuo, and the next drop **(c–d)**.

[4] Pick up a 15º, a 4 mm crystal, and a 15º, and sew through the center 11º added in step 1. Pick up a 15º, and sew back through the 4 mm crystal just added **(d–e)**.

[5] Pick up a 15º, and sew through the second drop along the outside edge of another pearl unit. Continue through the center SuperDuo and the following drop. Pick up a 15º, a 4 mm crystal, and a 15º, and sew through the third 11º added in step 1 **(e–f)**.

[6] Retrace the thread path down through the anniversary bead and seed beads at the bottom, back up through the anniversary bead and 6 mm crystal at the top, and through the connection points of the pearl units. End the working thread and tail.

Necklace assembly

[1] With the working thread from a pearl unit added in "Pendant attachment," pick up a 15º, a 4 mm crystal, and a 15º. Sew through the second drop from the outside edge of another pearl unit, the center SuperDuo, and the next drop. Pick up a 15º, a 4 mm crystal, and a 15º, and sew through the hole of the SuperDuo your thread exited at the start of this step **(figure 4)**. Retrace the thread path two more times, and end the working thread.

[2] Work as in step 1 to connect the remaining pearl units so there are 10 units on each side of the necklace. Do not end the working threads on the end pearl units.

[3] With the thread from an end pearl unit, pick up seven 11ºs and a split ring with half of the clasp attached. Sew through the SuperDuo in the same direction to form a ring. Retrace the thread path several times to reinforce, and end the thread. Repeat this step for the other side of the necklace. ●

MATERIALS

necklace 19½ in. (49.5 cm)

- 31 mm *Bead&Button* 20th anniversary commemorative bead (www.BeadAndButton.com/anniversarybead)
- **20** 6 mm crystal pearls (Swarovski, vintage gold)
- **1** 6 mm bicone crystal (Swarovski, amethyst)
- **39** 4 mm bicone crystals (Swarovski, chrysolite opal AB 2X)
- 8 g 2.5 x 5 mm SuperDuo beads (P15695, gold/smoky topaz; www.bellomodo.com)
- 4 g 3 mm magatamas or drop beads (Toho 928, purple-lined rosaline AB; www.artbeads.com)
- 2 g 11º seed beads (Toho 1207, marbled opaque turquoise blue; www.beadaholique.com)
- 1 g 15º seed beads (Miyuki 430l, dark purple opaque luster; www.beyondbeadery.com)
- clasp
- **2** 6 mm split rings
- Fireline 6 lb. test
- beading needles, #11 or #12
- split-ring pliers (optional)

DESIGN NOTE:

The split rings for the clasp may be omitted if you like.

Cubes & cradles

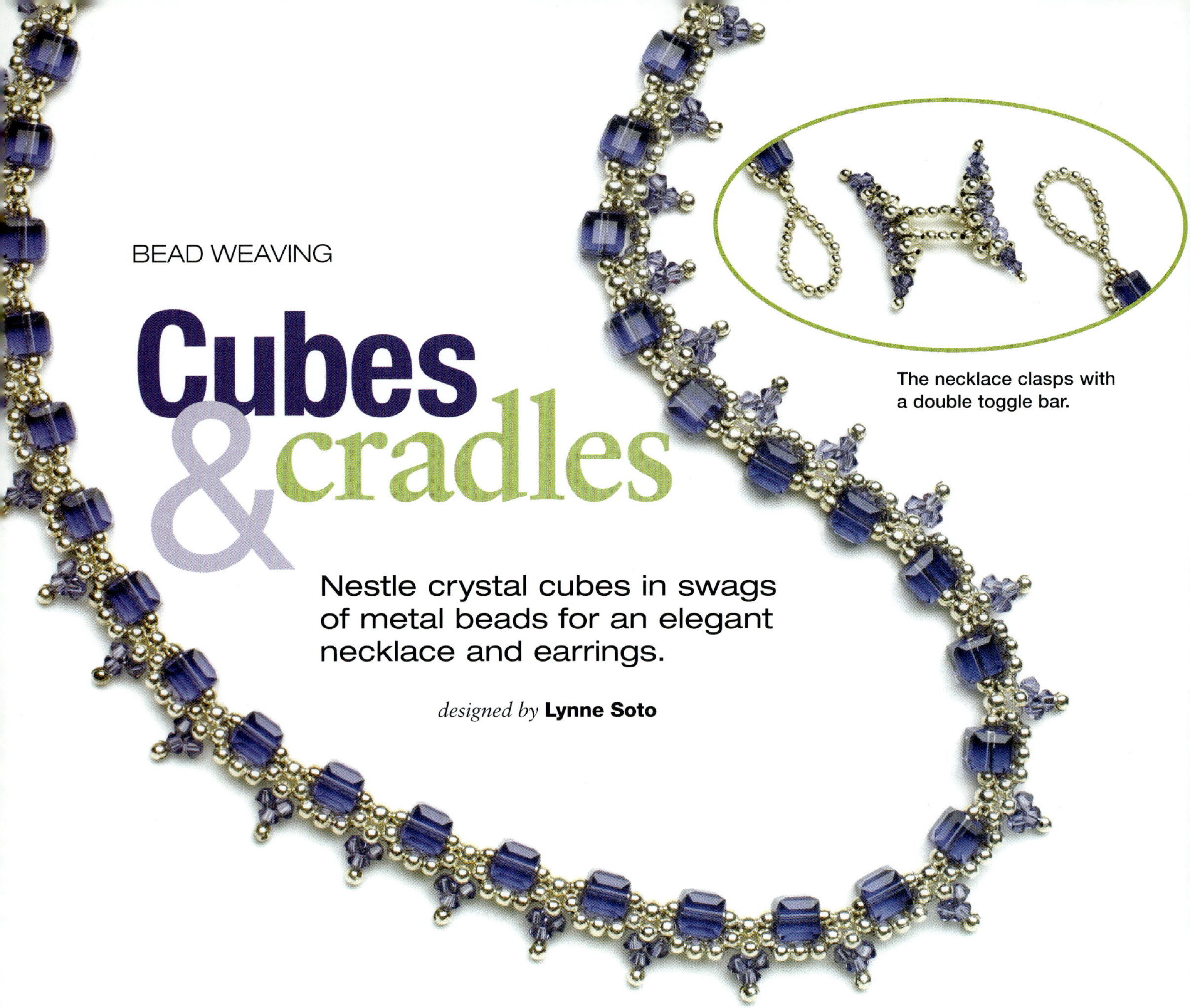

The necklace clasps with a double toggle bar.

Nestle crystal cubes in swags of metal beads for an elegant necklace and earrings.

designed by **Lynne Soto**

stepbystep

Necklace

Strand

[1] Attach a stop bead (Basics) at the center of 5 yd. (4.6 m) of thread, and wrap half of the thread around a bobbin or piece of cardboard.

[2] Pick up a 2.4 mm round bead, a 3 mm round bead, a 2.4 mm, and a 6 mm crystal cube. Repeat this pattern 34 more times.

[3] Pick up a 2.4 mm, a 3 mm round bead, and 18 2.4 mms. Sew back through the first three beads picked up in this step, and continue through the next cube, 2.4 mm, and 3 mm round bead **(figure 1, a–b)**. Snug up the beads to form a loop at this end of the strand.

[4] Pick up two 2.4 mms, two 3 mm bicone crystals, and a 2.4 mm, and sew back through the last bicone **(b–c)**. Pick up a bicone, and sew through the second 2.4 mm picked up in this step in the same direction **(c–d)**. Note: Adjust the alignment of the 2.4 mm so the bead hole is parallel to the strand. Pick up a 2.4 mm, and sew through the 3 mm round bead your thread exited at the start of this step **(d–e)**. Sew through the next four beads in the strand **(e–f)**.

[5] Repeat step 4 for the length of the strand, but on the last repeat, sew through the last five beads. End the working thread (Basics).

[6] Remove the stop bead added in step 1. Pick up 17 2.4 mms, and sew back through the first two beads added in step 2 to form a loop at this end of the strand.

[7] Pick up five 2.4 mms, and sew through the next 3 mm round bead in the strand **(figure 2)**. Repeat this step for the length of the strand. These will be called the back swags.

[8] Without picking up any beads, sew through the beads in the loop at this end of the strand, exiting the last 3 mm round bead with your needle pointing toward the other end of the strand.

[9] Pick up four 2.4 mms, skip the next 2.4 mm, cube, and 2.4 mm in the strand, and sew through the closest 2.4 mm picked up in step 4 **(figure 3, a–b)**. Sew through the adjacent 3 mm round bead and the next 2.4 mm picked up in step 4 **(b–c)**.

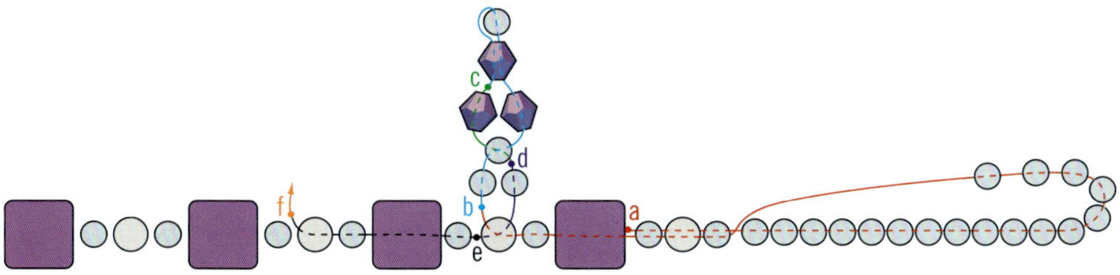

FIGURE 1

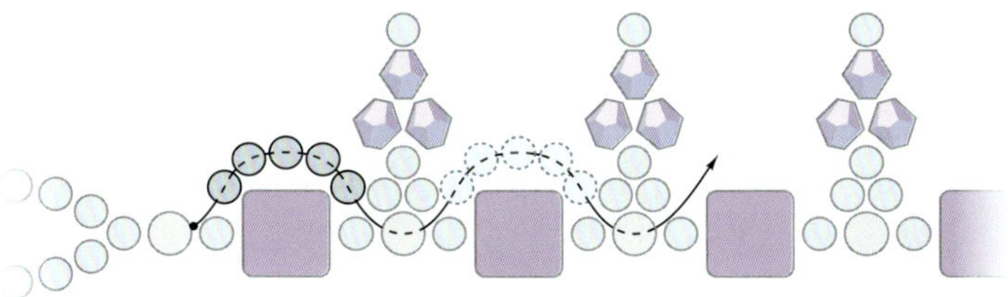

FIGURE 2

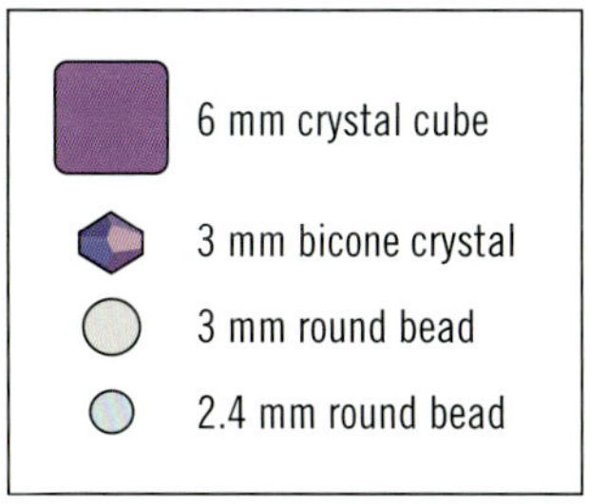

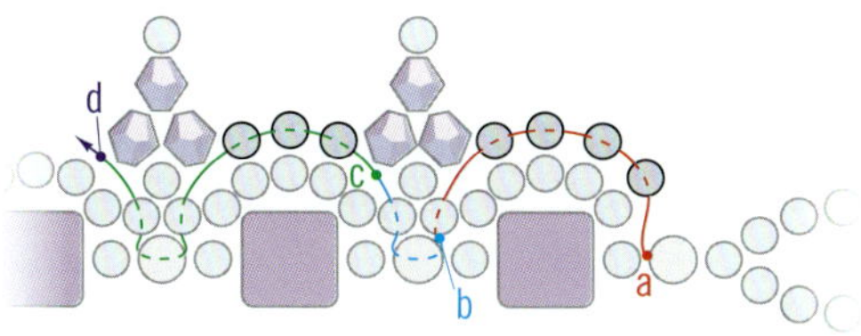

FIGURE 3

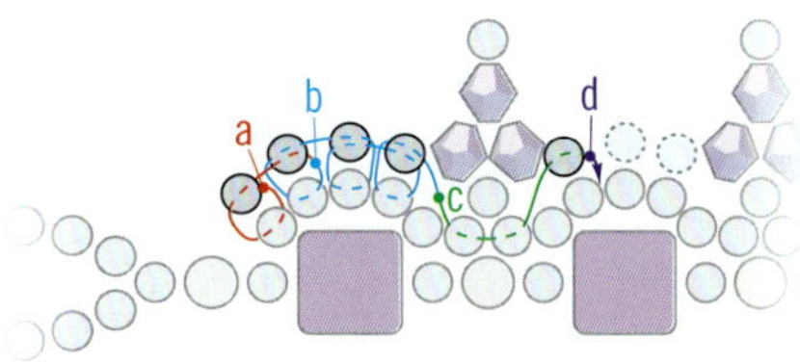

FIGURE 4

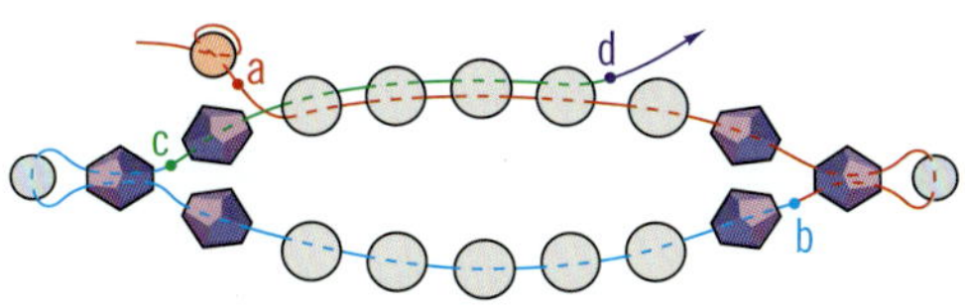

FIGURE 5

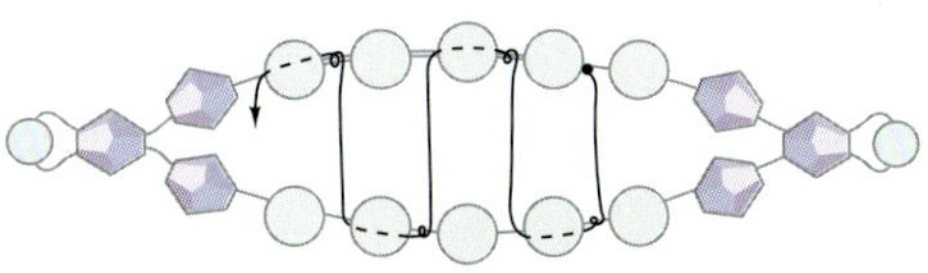

FIGURE 6

[10] Pick up three 2.4 mms, skip the next 2.4 mm, cube, and 2.4 mm in the strand, and sew through the next 2.4 mm picked up in step 4. Continue through the adjacent 3 mm round bead and the next 2.4 mm picked up in step 4 **(c–d)**. Repeat this step for the length of the strand. These will be called the front swags.

[11] Pick up four 2.4 mms, skip the next 2.4 mm, cube, and 2.4 mm in the strand, and sew through the beads in the loop at this end of the strand. Step up through the last 2.4 mm picked up in this step.

[12] Work a square stitch thread path as follows: Sew through the adjacent 2.4 mm in the back swag, the 2.4 mm your thread exited at the start of this step, and the next 2.4 mm in the front swag **(figure 4, a–b)**. Repeat this stitch three times **(b–c)**. Sew through the beadwork to exit the first 2.4 mm in the next front swag **(c–d)**. Continue working a square stitch thread path to connect the remaining front and back swags of 2.4 mms. End the thread.

Double toggle bar

[1] On 1 yd. (.9 m) of thread, attach a stop bead, leaving a 6-in. (15 cm) tail.

[2] Pick up five 3 mm round beads, two bicones, and a 2.4 mm. Sew back through the second bicone **(figure 5, a–b)**. Pick up a bicone, five 3 mm round beads, two bicones, and a 2.4 mm. Sew back through the second bicone **(b–c)**. Pick up a bicone, and sew through the first four 3 mm round beads picked up in this step **(c–d)**.

[3] Referring to **figure 6**, wrap the thread one-and-a-half times around the

MATERIALS

necklace 19½ in. (49.5 cm)

- **35** 6 mm crystal cubes (Swarovski, tanzanite)
- **122** 3 mm bicone crystals (Swarovski, tanzanite)
- **64** 3 mm silver-plated round beads (www.nmbeadandfetish.com)
- **545** 2.4 mm silver-plated round beads (www.nmbeadandfetish.com)
- Fireline 4 lb. test
- beading needles, #10
- bobbin or piece of cardboard

pair of earrings

- **2** 6 mm crystal cubes (Swarovski, tanzanite)
- **6** 3 mm bicone crystals (Swarovski, tanzanite)
- **54** 2.4 mm silver-plated round beads (www.nmbeadandfetish.com)
- pair of earring findings
- Fireline 4 lb. test
- beading needles, #10

DESIGN NOTE:

Reinforcing the swags with a square stitch thread path in step 12 of "Necklace: Strand" will prevent them from twisting around the cubes.

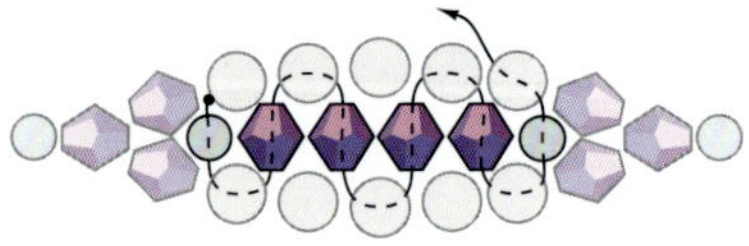

FIGURE 7

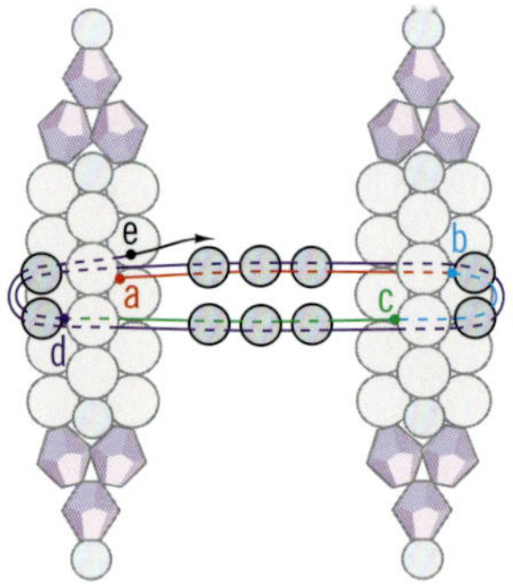

FIGURE 8

adjacent thread bridge, and sew through the next 3 mm round bead in this column. Repeat this stitch three more times, and exit an end 3 mm round bead.

[4] Pick up a 2.4 mm, and sew through the 3 mm round bead in the opposite column. Pick up a bicone, and sew through the next 3 mm round bead in the opposite column. Referring to **figure 7**, add three more bicones and a 2.4 mm.

[5] Sew through the next four edge 3 mm round beads to exit an end 3 mm. Flip the beadwork so the bicones are face down on your work surface, and repeat step 4, but replace the bicones with 3 mm round beads. This side will be referred to as the spine of the bar. Sew through the beadwork to exit the second 3 mm round bead in the spine. Do not end the working thread or tail.

[6] Repeat steps 1–5 to make a second toggle bar.

[7] With the working thread from the first toggle bar, pick up three 2.4 mms, and sew through the corresponding 3 mm round bead in the spine of the second toggle bar **(figure 8, a–b)**.

[8] Pick up two 2.4 mms, and sew through the third 3 mm round bead in the spine of the second toggle bar **(b–c)**.

[9] Pick up three 2.4 mms, and sew through the corresponding 3 mm round bead in the spine of the first toggle bar **(c–d)**.

[10] Pick up two 2.4 mms, and sew through the second 3 mm round bead in the spine **(d–e)**. Retrace the thread path through the connecting 2.4 mms.

[11] With the working thread from the second toggle bar, retrace the thread path through the connecting 2.4 mms. Remove the stop bead from each bar, and end the threads.

Earrings

[1] On 24 in. (61 cm) of thread, attach a stop bead (Basics), leaving a 6-in. (15 cm) tail.

[2] Pick up a 2.4 mm round bead, a 6 mm crystal cube, and seven 2.4 mms. Sew through the loop of an earring finding and back through the last 2.4 mm. Pick up five 2.4 mms, and sew through the first three beads picked up in this step in the same direction. Retrace the thread path through all the beads, exiting the 2.4 mm, cube, and 2.4 mm at the bottom of the earring.

[3] Pick up five 2.4 mms, and sew through the 2.4 mm, cube, and 2.4 mm at the bottom of the earring. Repeat this step to create a second swag.

[4] Work as in step 12 of "Necklace: Strand" to connect the two swags of five 2.4 mms, and then sew through the beadwork to exit the center 2.4 mm in the front swag.

[5] Work as in step 4 of "Necklace: Strand," and continue through the next two 2.4 mms and the first three beads picked up in step 2. Remove the stop bead, and end the working thread and tail (Basics).

[6] Make a second earring. ●

Bead embroidered

stamped leather cuff

designed by **Abigail Engelking**

When you think of creating stamped leather, you probably don't think of rubber stamps and bead embroidery!

a

b

c

stepbystep

Purchase a leather cuff complete with closure, or create your own following these easy steps.

Preparing the band

[1] Measure your wrist. Using a razor blade tool, a steel ruler, and a cutting mat, cut a 2-in. (5 cm) wide band of leather that is equal to the length of your wrist plus 2 in. (5 cm).

[2] Determine which side of the band is the front, and place the band on your wrist so that the ends overlap. Mark the location for the snaps with a permanent marker.

[3] Using a leather punch, make holes large enough to fit the snap shaft.

[4] Using a rawhide or rubber hammer and the mini anvil and setter that came with the snaps, assemble the snaps following the manufacturer's instructions.

Band embellishment

[1] Stamp the desired design(s) on the front of the band (photo a). Allow the ink to dry.

[2] Determine where you want the beaded embellishments to go, and use a sewing pin to pierce small holes in the band along the desired path (photo b). Space the holes to match the bead size.

[3] Tie an overhand knot (Basics) at one end of a comfortable length of thread. Tie a second overhand knot, and slide it down over the first. Sew up through the band from back to front at the desired location of the first bead embellishment. Use a variety of seed beads, drops, and charms to embellish the band as desired using beaded backstitch (Basics and photo c) and/or stop stitch (Basics). Retrace the thread path through each bead for a secure connection.

[4] End the thread on the back of the band by tying two overhand knots, one on top of the other, as you did in step 3. Apply a small dab of superglue to both the starting and ending knots, and trim the threads.

Edging

[1] With the sewing pin, pierce a line of holes along each edge of the band approximately 2 mm from the edge. The beads will sit between the holes, so space the holes accordingly. Also, make sure to leave a little extra space

d

e

DESIGN NOTES:

- **Make sure to use a solvent ink. Solvent inks contain no water and are therefore fade-resistant and waterproof.**
- **When sizing the band to your wrist, be sure to leave enough room to slide your finger between your wrist and the band to close the snap.**

to accommodate the thickness of the cord on each side of the beads.

[2] Cut a 16-in. (41 cm) piece of S-Lon cord, and tie two overhand knots at one end as before. With a thread burner or lighter, trim the tail close to the knot. String enough 4 mm round beads (or a pattern of 4 mms and accent beads, such as daggers) to create a strand the same length as the band, and attach a Bead Stopper to the end without the knot.

[3] Cut a 16-in. (41 cm) piece of cord, tie an overhand knot at one end, and thread a glover's needle or a Big-Eye needle at the other. Stitch from back to front through the first hole along one edge of the band. Align the strand of 4 mm beads along this edge.

[4] Using a couching stitch, loop the thread over the 4 mm strand between the first two beads, and sew from back to front through the next hole in the band **(photo d)**. Continue using couching stitches to secure the 4 mm strand to this edge of the band. Use a consistent tension so the couching stitches drop down slightly between the beads. The 4 mm strand will tighten up as you work, so loosen the Bead Stopper a little bit at a time to allow more slack. This will also prevent the edge from puckering and allow the finished cuff to lie flat.

[5] When you reach the last stitch, end the thread by looping back between the last two beads, and sewing under the thread bridge on the back of the band **(photo e)**. Tie a couple of half-hitch knots (Basics), and then trim the cord close to the last knot with a thread burner. Dab the knot with superglue if desired.

[6] Remove the Bead Stopper from the 4 mm strand, and tie two overhand knots on this end. Trim the cord close to the knot with a thread burner, and dab the knot with superglue if desired.

[7] Work as in steps 2–6 to embellish the other edge of the band. ●

MATERIALS

both cuffs

- 8 x 2-in. (20 x 5 cm) piece of leather or pre-cut soft leather strip, semi-polished on one side (JoAnn fabric and craft stores)*
- **2** ⅝-in. (1.6 cm) brass snaps with included mini anvil and setter (JoAnn fabric and craft stores)
- Fireline 6 lb. test
- S-Lon beading cord to match edging beads
- beading needles, #10
- glover's needle or Big-Eye needle
- Bead Stopper
- cutting mat
- leather hole punch
- permanent marker
- rawhide or rubber hammer
- razor blade tool
- sewing pin or quilter's pin
- solvent ink, such as StazOn brand (JoAnn fabric and craft stores)
- steel ruler
- superglue
- thread burner or lighter

cuff with bird design 7½ in. (19.1 cm)

- **13** 15 x 5 mm dagger beads (Czech, blood red with peacock finish)
- **73** 4 mm round beads (blue howlite)
- assorted bugle beads, drop beads, and 11º, 13º, and 15º seed beads
- rubber stamps (Stampin' up "Always" collection; www.stampinup.com)

cuff with shell design 8 in. (20 cm)

- 38 x 13 mm brass seahorse (www.thecraftstar.com/shopdetails/2180/calliopesattic)
- 5 mm round beads
  47 blue (dyed howlite)
  24 white (shell beads)
- assorted seed beads and pearls
- rubber stamps (Michaels stores)

BEAD EMBROIDERY

Rainbow bright bracelet

If you've always wanted to try bead embroidery, test the waters by using easy stop stitches to attach sequins in a rainbow of colors.

designed by **Sarah Meadows**

a

b

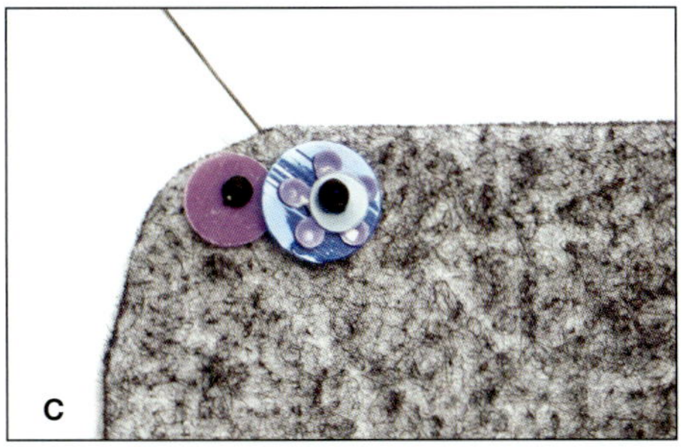

c

stepbystep

Embroidery

[1] Cut a strip of beading foundation to 1½ in. (3.8 cm) wide and the desired length of your bracelet minus about ½ in. (1.3 cm) for the button clasp. Round the corners of the strip by trimming them off. Trace the foundation onto Ultrasuede or upholstery vinyl, and cut it out.

[2] Using a ruler and a pencil or marker, divide the strip of foundation into six equal sections (one for each color of the rainbow) or as desired **(photo a)**.

[3] Tie an overhand knot (Basics) at the end of a comfortable length of thread. Sew up through the foundation near one edge. Working in stop stitch (Basics), add color A sequins to the first section as follows: Pick up a sequin and a 15º seed bead, and sew back through the sequin and the foundation **(photo b)**. Sew up through the foundation a short distance away.

[4] Work as in step 3 to add color A sequins to fill the first section, layering sequins as desired **(photo c)**. Repeat with the remaining colors in the other sections. Bead up to the very edge of the foundation, and use larger sequins at the edge to make it easier to add the brick stitch edging later on. When the working thread gets short, sew to the back of the foundation, and sew through the foundation in the same spot several times. Tie an overhand knot close to the foundation, and trim the thread. Start a new thread as in step 3.

d

Assembly and edging

[1] Place the embellished foundation on the Ultrasuede or vinyl backing. Apply E6000 or fabric glue to the back of the foundation, and glue the layers together. Allow to dry, placing a book or other heavy object on top so the bracelet dries flat.

[2] Tie an overhand knot at the end of 2 yd. (1.8 m) of thread. Sew between the foundation and the backing to exit the front of the foundation about 1 mm from the edge, hiding the knot between the two layers.

[3] Pick up two 11º seed beads, sew up through both layers about one bead's width away from where the thread is exiting, and continue up through the second bead just added **(photo d)**.

[4] Pick up an 11º, sew up through both layers about one bead's width away from where the thread is exiting, and continue through the new bead **(photo e)**. Repeat this stitch around the perimeter of the bracelet. After adding the final bead, sew down through the

MATERIALS

bracelet 7½ in. (19.1 cm)

- **700–800** 3–6 mm assorted round and flower sequins in **6** or more colors (www.ccartwright.com)
- 3 g 11º seed beads (black)
- 2 g 15º seed beads (black)
- ½-in. (1.3 cm) button with shank
- 12–15 mm rubber O-ring (www.antelopebeads.com)
- beading foundation (black or gray; http://nicolecampanella.com)
- Ultrasuede or upholstery vinyl (black)
- Fireline 6 lb. test (smoke)
- beading needles, #12
- E6000 adhesive or washable fabric glue
- pencil or marker
- ruler

DESIGN NOTE:

Add an image! Before you start adding sequins, draw a simple shape like a heart or a kitty face in the center, and work a line of beaded backstitch (Basics) around the perimeter. Fill in the shape with sequins, and then work the rest of the bracelet as described in the instructions.

first bead in the edging, through the foundation and backing, and up through the first bead again. End the working thread in the edging beads (Basics).

Clasp

[1] Add 1 ft. (30 cm) of thread in the edging beads (Basics) at one end of the bracelet, and exit the center edge bead. Pick up approximately four 11ºs, the shank of a button, and four 11ºs, and sew through the adjacent edge bead **(photo f)**. Retrace the thread path several times, and end the thread in the edging beads.

[2] Add 1 ft. (30 cm) of thread in the edging beads at the other end of the bracelet, and exit the center edge bead. Pick up approximately eight 11ºs and the rubber O-ring, and sew back through the same edge bead **(photo g)**. Retrace the thread path through the loop, and end the thread. ●

DESIGN NOTES:

Almost everything about this bracelet is budget friendly!

- **A single package of sequins costs only a couple of dollars, so you can get several styles or colors without breaking the bank.**
- **The rubber O-ring is an economical option for a clasp. But if the rubber ring doesn't appeal to you, make a simple loop of 11ºs large enough to fit around your button.**
- **Upholstery vinyl is also very budget friendly. You can find it (or another option — marine vinyl) at fabric stores. It generally comes in 56–60-in. widths, so a quarter-yard piece is enough to make a bracelet plus a lot more.**

BEAD EMBROIDERY

Tuscan sunset cuff

Highlight the warm Tuscan colors of the *Bead&Button* 20th anniversary bead in a bead-embroidered cuff.

designed by **Julia Gerlach**

stepbystep

Petal motifs

[1] On 18 in. (46 cm) of thread, pick up a 3 mm pearl and four color B 11º seed beads. Sew through the pearl and the first B again, leaving a 6-in. (15 cm) tail **(figure 1)**.

[2] Pick up a 5 x 7 mm drop and a B, sew back through the drop, and continue through the next B. Repeat twice **(figure 2)**. End the working thread and tail (Basics).

[3] Repeat steps 1 and 2 to make a total of five petal motifs.

Bead embroidery

[1] Make a bracelet template: Cut a piece of cardstock 1½ in. (3.8 cm) wide and the desired length of your bracelet plus about 1 in. (2.5 cm) for the snap closure overlap. Round the corners.

[2] Trace the template onto a 2 x 10-in. (5 x 25 cm) piece of Ultrasuede, but don't cut out the shape. Cut a 2 x 10-in. (5 x 25 cm) piece of interfacing, apply

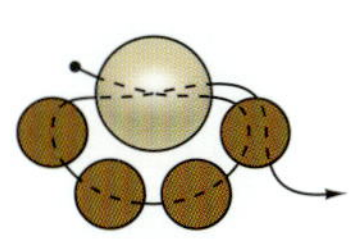

FIGURE 1

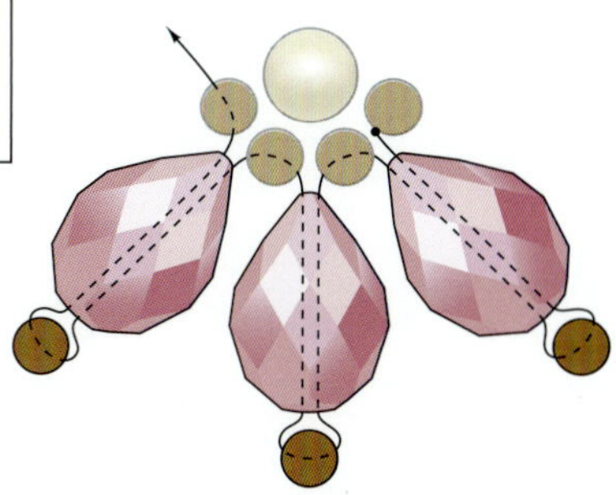

FIGURE 2

MATERIALS

bracelet 7 in. (18 cm)

- **1** *B&B* 20th anniversary bead by Lydia Muell (www.BeadAndButton.com/anniversarybead)
- **19** 5 x 7 mm faceted drop beads (Czech, topaz pink luster; www.landofodds.com)
- **4** 4 x 6 mm top-drilled drop beads (turquoise Picasso; www.landofodds.com)
- **40–50** 3 mm crystal pearls (Swarovski, light gold)
- 1 g 10º two-cut seed beads (silky gold/bronze/copper; www.evezbeadz.artfire.com)
- 11º seed beads
  4 g color A (Toho 332, gold-lustered raspberry)
  2 g color B (Czech, metallic bronze)
- 15º seed beads (Miyuki 342, berry-lined light topaz AB)
- **2** sets of 2/0 garment snaps, sew-on
- nylon beading thread
- beading needles, #12
- all-purpose glue
- Gorilla Glue two-part epoxy or double-sided tape
- cardstock
- marker
- 2 x 10 in. (5 x 25 cm) interfacing
- 4 x 10 in. (10 x 25 cm) Ultrasuede

all-purpose glue around the perimeter, and adhere it to the back of the Ultrasuede, making sure you don't get glue in the areas where you'll be beading.

[3] Apply Gorilla Glue or double-sided tape to the back of the anniversary bead, and adhere it to the center of the front of the Ultrasuede.

[4] Tie an overhand knot (Basics) at the end of 2 yd. (1.8 m) of thread, and sew up through the interfacing and Ultrasuede next to the anniversary bead. Using 10º two-cut beads, work a round of beaded backstitch (Basics and **photo a**), ending with an even number of beads. Exit near the hole of the anniversary bead.

[5] Pick up a 3 mm pearl, skip the next two-cut, and sew through the following two-cuts around the anniversary bead to exit the other end of the hole. Pick up a pearl, skip a two-cut, and sew through the following two-cuts around the other side of the anniversary bead to exit the first pearl. Sew through the anniversary bead and the opposite pearl, and then sew back through the anniversary bead, the first pearl, and a few more two-cuts (**photo b**). Sew down and up through the Ultrasuede and interfacing, exiting next to the round of two-cuts.

[6] Using color A 11º seed beads, work a round of beaded backstitch (**photo c**).

[7] Using 15º seed beads, work a round of tubular peyote stitch (Basics) off of the As, pulling snug so the 15ºs sit on top of the As (**photo d**).

[8] Sew through the beadwork to exit an outer-round A just below the center stitch on one side of the anniversary bead. Pick up a 4 x 6 mm drop bead, and sew through the next A in the round (**photo e**). Pick up a 5 x 7 mm drop and a B, sew back through the drop, and continue through the next A in the round (**photo f**). Pick up a 4 x 6 mm drop, and sew through the next A in the round (**photo g**).

[9] Pick up three Bs, skip the next A, and sew through the following three As to form a picot (**photo h**). Repeat this stitch around half of the anniversary bead. Add three more drop beads as in step 8, positioning them opposite the first set, and then continue adding picots with Bs around the other half of

j

k

l

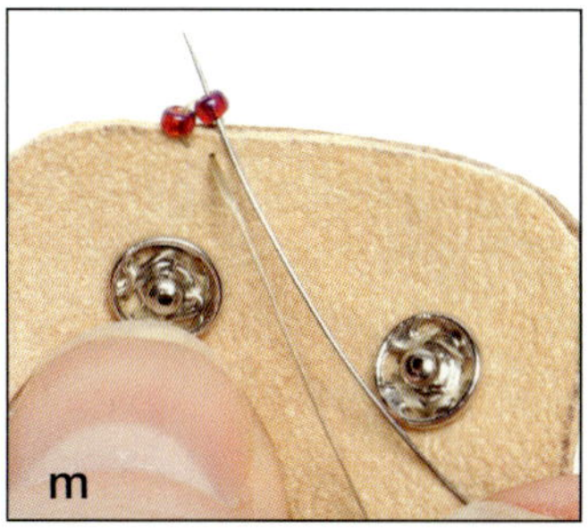

m

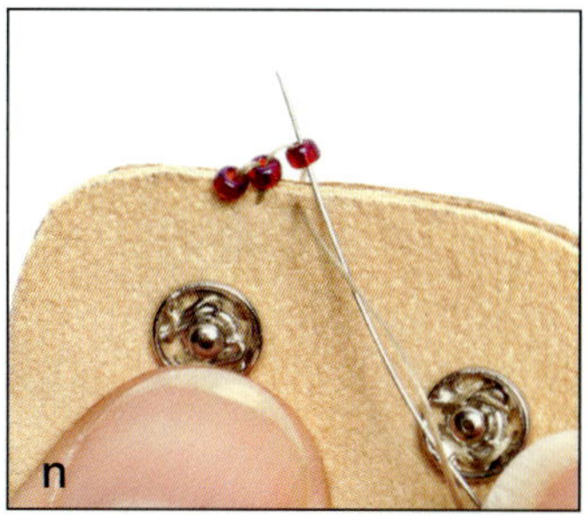

n

the anniversary bead **(photo i)**.

[10] Sew through the beadwork to exit the B at the tip of a 5 x 7 mm drop. Sew down and up through the Ultrasuede and interfacing, and continue through the B to tack it in place.

[11] Using 3 mm pearls, work in beaded backstitch to create a wavy line with two or three peaks extending from the B to about ½–¾ in. (1.3–1.9 cm) from the end of the band. The side of the band that will be on the top of the snap closure overlap will have three peaks; the side that will be on the bottom of the overlap will have two peaks. Make sure you leave enough room for the snap closure. At the end, pick up a 5 x 7 mm drop and a B, sew down and up through the Ultrasuede and interfacing, and continue through the B to tack it in place **(photo j)**. Sew back through the drop and a few pearls.

[12] Nestle a petal motif in the nearest curve, and sew down and up through the Ultrasuede and interfacing so the needle exits next to the pearl. Tack the pearl and the Bs at the tips of the drops in place using the same technique as before **(photo k)**. Repeat this step to attach a petal motif in each curve.

[13] Sew through the beadwork to exit the B at the tip of the drop on the other side of the anniversary bead. Tack it in place as in step 10, and then work as in steps 11 and 12 to embellish this side of the band. End the thread.

Assembly

[1] Cut around the bracelet shape, trace it onto a second piece of Ultrasuede, and cut out the shape.

[2] Align the two layers, and mark where the snaps should go. Half of each set will be positioned on the outer surface of the top layer, and the other half of each set will go on the inner surface of the bottom layer.

[3] Using 18 in. (46 cm) of thread, sew half of each snap set in place **(photo l)**. Repeat with the other half of each set on the other layer of Ultrasuede.

[4] Align the two layers of Ultrasuede. Tie an overhand knot at the end of a comfortable length of thread, and sew up through the top layer of Ultrasuede about 1 mm from the edge, hiding the knot between the layers. Pick up two As, and sew through both layers of Ultrasuede about one bead's width away. Sew up through the second A **(photo m)**.

[5] Pick up an A, sew through both layers of Ultrasuede, and continue up through the new A **(photo n)**. Repeat this stitch around the perimeter. End and add thread (Basics) in the edging as needed. After adding the last bead, sew down through the first edging bead and through both layers of Ultrasuede, and continue up through the first bead. End the thread in the edging. •

SOUTACHE BEAD EMBROIDERY

Oh, lolly, lolly pendant

Layer soutache "lollipops" to create a beautiful pendant that will make you proud as a peacock!

designed by **Amee K. Sweet-McNamara**

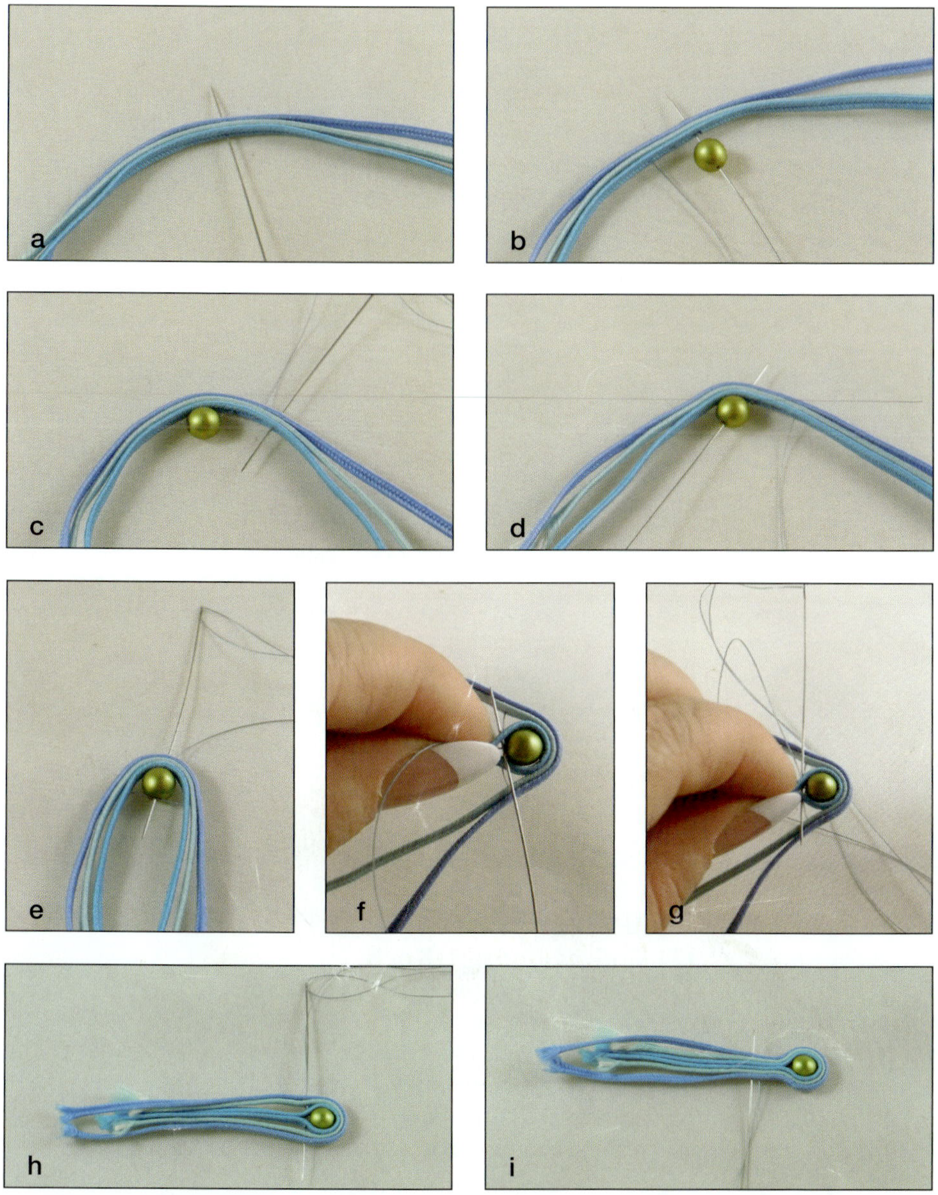

step**by**step

Lollipops

[1] Tie a double knot (Soutache Basics, p. 97) at one end of 12 in. (30 cm) of thread. Trim the tail close to the knot.

[2] Cut a 1½–2-in. (3.8–5 cm) piece of soutache braid in each of three colors, and create a stack (Soutache Basics). Locate the center of the stack, and sew through the center Vs of all three braids from bottom to top **(photo a)**.

[3] Working from right to left, make three shaping stitches (Soutache Basics).

[4] Pick up a 6 mm bead, and sew through the stack near the knot **(photo b)**.

[5] Working from left to right, make three shaping stitches **(photo c)**.

[6] Sew through the bead and the stack as shown, exiting near the knot **(photo d)**. Sew back through the stack and the bead **(photo e)**.

[7] Make a two-sided join (Soutache Basics), keeping the needle close to the bead **(photos f, g,** and **h)**. Do not use a tight tension.

[8] Retrace the thread path through all six braids two or three times, using an increasingly firmer tension each time so the braids wrap smoothly around the bead to make the lollipop shape.

[9] Make three or four stitches, moving away from the bead, for about ½ in. (1.3 cm) **(photo i)**.

[10] Tie an overhand knot (Basics) close to an outer braid, and trim the thread close to the lollipop.

MATERIALS

pendant 4 in. (10 cm) with 24-in. (61 cm) chain

- **80–90** 1½–4-in. (3.8–10 cm) scraps of ⅛-in. (3 mm) soutache braid (assorted colors)
- **1** 12–18 mm bead
- **20–30** 3–6 mm beads (assorted shapes and colors)
- 1 g 8º seed beads (assorted colors)
- 3–4 g 11º seed beads
- 1 g 15º seed beads (assorted colors)
- **2** 4–5 mm bead caps or cones
- toggle clasp
- 24 in. (61 cm) beaded chain or jewelry chain
- **2** 6 mm soldered jump rings
- nylon beading thread, such as Nymo size B (colors to match soutache braid)
- beading needles, #10 or #11
- **2** pairs of chainnose, flatnose, and/or bentnose pliers
- wire cutters
- toothpicks (optional)
- 5 x 5 in. (13 x 13 cm) Ultrasuede
- washable fabric glue, such as api brand Crafter's Pick

DESIGN NOTE:

Don't throw away those scraps of soutache braid! This layering technique is fast, easy, and a great way to use up short ends of braid as well as leftover beads from your stash. Make small shapes for support elements or large focal pieces. Make them in pairs if you want a symmetrical pendant. Just have fun with it!

j

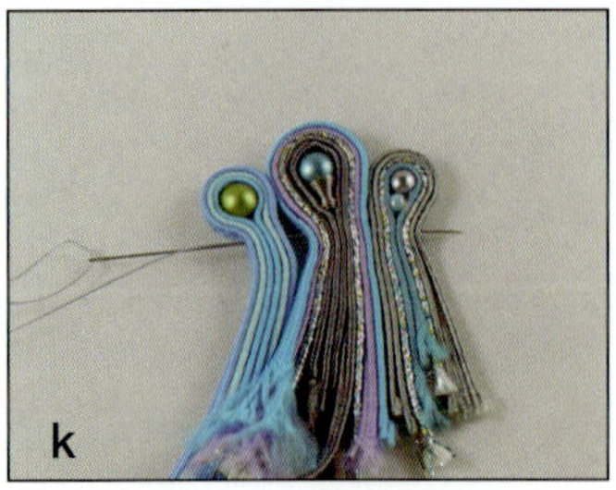
k

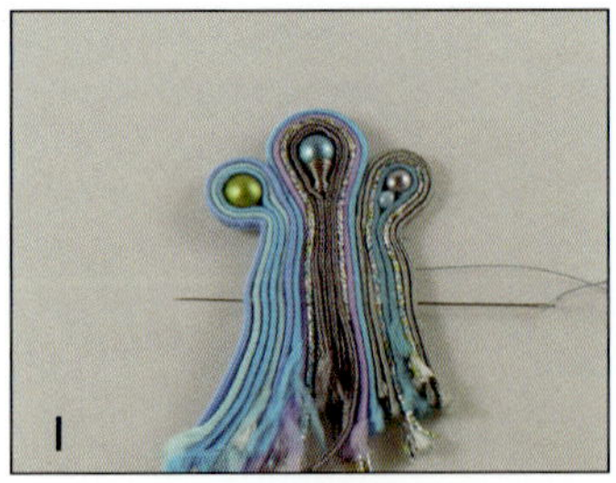
l

m

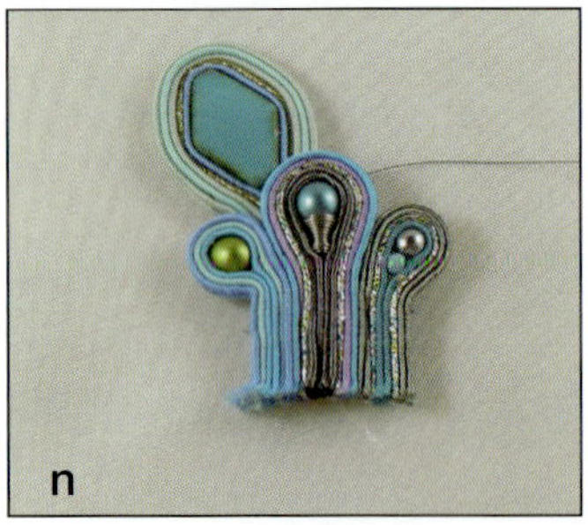
n

o

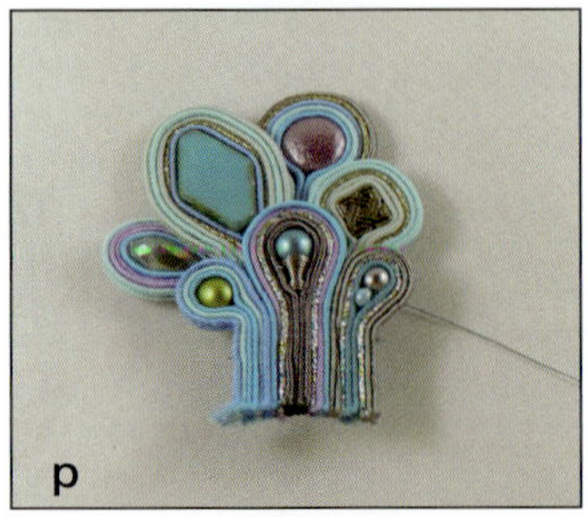
p

q

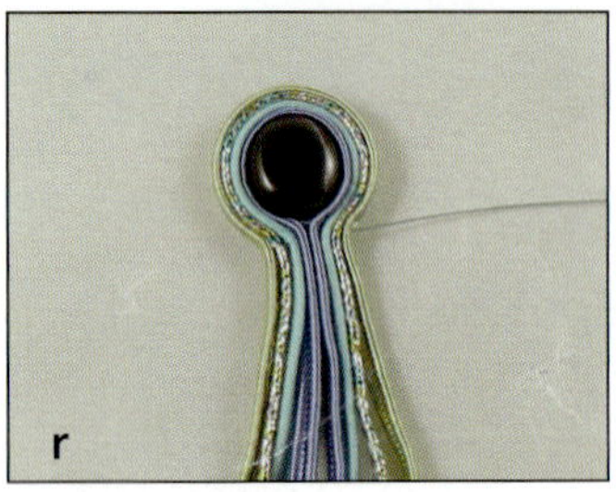
r

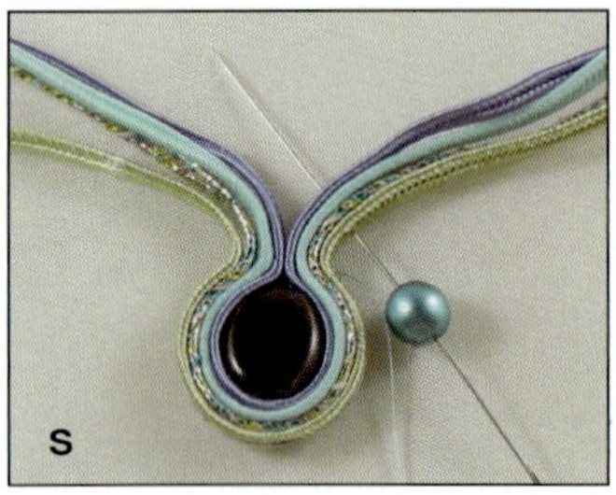
s

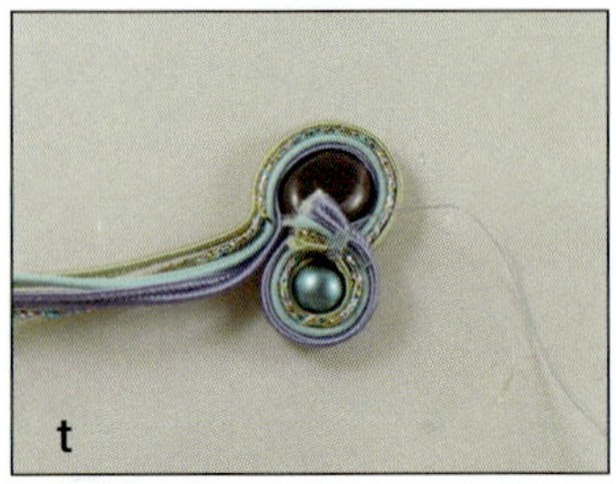
t

u

[11] Repeat steps 1–10 to create 17 or 18 lollipops. Be creative: Increase the number of braids in step 2 to create thicker stacks, use a variety of different bead shapes, include bead caps or cones, or embellish some of the lollipops with seed beads. If you use a large bead in a lollipop, you will have to increase the number of shaping stitches in steps 3 and 5.

Joining the lollipops

[1] Tie a double knot at the end of 12 in. (30 cm) of thread. Place two lollipops side by side, and sew through both lollipops at their join **(photo j)**. Retrace the thread path twice, increasing the tension slightly with each pass.

[2] Sew through a third lollipop at the join. Sew back through all three lollipops at their joins **(photo k)**. Retrace the thread path.

[3] Moving away from the beads, make three stitches through the combined stacks to join them **(photo l)**. End the thread (Soutache Basics). Trim the stacks approximately 1 in. (2.5 cm) below the beads **(photo m)**.

[4] Tie a double knot at the end of 1 yd. (.9 m) of thread. Position another lollipop behind the three-lollipop component, roughly centered between two lollipops **(photo n)**. Make three tacking stitches (Soutache Basics) to attach the new lollipop to the component.

[5] Center another lollipop behind the two remaining lollipops in the component, and work as in step 4 to tack the new lollipop in place **(photo o)**.

[6] Add the remaining lollipops, one behind the other, to form an asymmetrical but balanced "tree shape" **(photos p and q)**. End the thread.

Final shape

[1] Work as in steps 1–8 of "Lollipops" using four 4-in. (10 cm) pieces of braid and a 12–18 mm bead, and making the appropriate number of shaping stitches for the size of the bead **(photo r)**.

[2] Separate the large stack below the bead into two equal stacks. Pick up a 4–6 mm bead, and sew through the nearest four-braid stack where the hole of the bead meets the stack **(photo s)**.

[3] Make three shaping stitches, and push the ends of the stack behind your work. End the stack (Soutache Basics and **photo t**).

[4] Sew through your work to exit the other four-braid stack, and work as in steps 2 and 3 to add another 4–6 mm bead **(photo u)**.

[5] Position the finial shape over the base of the lollipop component, and tack it in place **(photo v)**. End the thread.

v

Neck strap attachment

[1] Determine where you want the two neck strap connection points to be. Working on the back of the piece, begin a new 10-in. (25 cm) thread and bury the knot (Soutache Basics) to exit the outer braid near the connection point. Sew through the middle braid at the connection point, still working on the back of the piece.

[2] Pick up a 6 mm soldered jump ring, and sew back through the same braid on

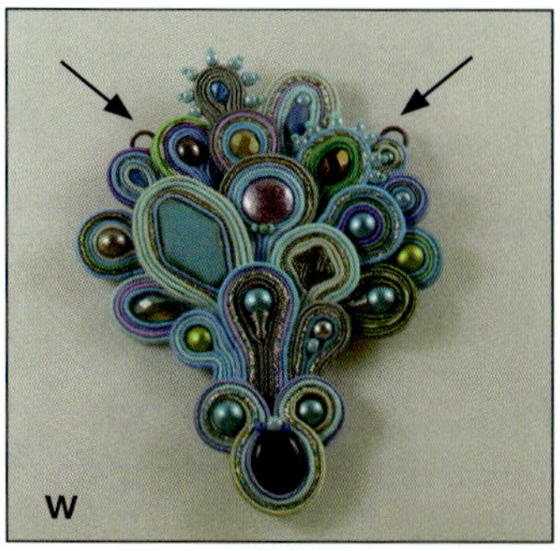

the back. Make sure the jump ring extends slightly past the edge of the piece, and secure it to the back with several small stitches.

[3] Sew through the back of the piece, and work as in steps 1 and 2 for the other connection point. End the thread **(photo w)**.

Assembly

[1] Apply a small dab of glue to the back of the piece, using a toothpick or the tip of your finger to spread the glue evenly to the edges of the work. Do not push glue between the beads. Place the piece on the wrong side of the Ultrasuede, and let dry completely **(photo x)**.

[2] Trim the Ultrasuede around the piece **(photo y)**, making sure you cannot see the outer braids from the back.

Beaded edge

[1] Begin a new 1-yd. (.9 m) thread, and bury the knot to exit an outer braid.

[2] Pick up two 11º seed beads **(photo z)**, and sew down through the outer braid so the thread exits the Ultrasuede. Sew up through the last bead added.

[3] Pick up an 11º, sew down through the braid and the Ultrasuede, and then sew back up through the 11º just added. Work in this manner around the perimeter of the piece. After adding the last bead, sew down through the first 11º, the braid, and the Ultrasuede, and then sew back up through the first 11º again. End the thread (Basics) in the edge beads.

Attaching the neck straps

[1] Cut the beaded chain into two 12-in. (30 cm) lengths.

[2] Open an end link on one piece of chain as if it were a jump ring (Basics), and attach half of the clasp. Open the other end link, and attach a soldered jump ring on the piece.

[3] Repeat step 2 for the other piece of chain, the other half of the clasp, and the other soldered jump ring. ●

Soutache Basics

Creating a stack
Lay the cut lengths of braid on your work surface with their center Vs of thread running in the same direction. Create a stack by laying one braid on top of the other, and hold the stack gently on the sides between your thumb and finger.

Shaping stitches
Sew down through the stack ¼ in. (6 mm) from the point where your thread exited. Working in the same direction, sew up 1/16 in. (2 mm) from the point where your thread exited, and then sew down ¼ in. (6 mm) from the last point. The larger stitches are along the outside of the curve, and the smaller stitches are along the inside.

Double knot
Tie one overhand knot. Tie another overhand knot, but slide it down to the first knot before pulling the thread tight.

Beginning a new thread and burying the knot
To begin a new thread, tie a double knot at one end of the new thread, and trim the tail close to the knot. To bury the knot, sew through a bead and the inside curve of the adjacent stack, or just sew through the stack.

Ending the thread
To end the thread, sew to the back of your work, and make a few small stitches in the closest braid. Tie a knot, and trim the thread.

Two-sided join
Joining is where either two portions of the same stack or two separate stacks meet, typically at the base of a bead or focal piece. To join, separate the stack of braids, and pinch together both sides of the inner braid close to the bead. Sew back and forth between both sides of the inner braid several times. Sew through the outer layers to one side of the join, sew through the join, and then sew through the outer layers to the other side of the join. Retrace the thread path several times.

Ending a stack and tacking stitches
Push the loose ends of the stack to the back of your work, and make a couple tacking stitches: Sew up from the back through all the layers. Exit the side of one braid on the front of your work. Sew down through all the layers as close as possible to the point where the thread exited, sewing through the side of the same braid. Repeat this last stitch several times to secure the end of the stack, and trim the ends ¼ in. (6 mm) from the last stitch, being careful not to trim too closely, as the braids will fray. You can whip stitch the frayed ends together on the back of the piece to keep them contained.

SOUTACHE BEAD EMBROIDERY

Serpentine soutache bracelet

designed by **Alexandra Sydorenko**

stepbystep

Cabochon component

[1] Cut a 1¼-in. (3.2 cm) square of beading foundation, and draw a diagonal line from one corner to the opposite corner.

[2] Apply a thin coat of E6000 on the back of the 22 mm square cabochon, and place it in the center of the foundation. Allow the glue to dry, and then trim the foundation, leaving a 2–3 mm border on all four sides (**photo a**).

[3] Tie a double knot (Soutache Basics, p. 101) at one end of 1 yd. (.9 m) of thread. Trim the tail close to the knot.

[4] Cut a 5½-in. (14 cm) piece of soutache braid in each of the three colors, and create a stack by laying one braid on top of the other, with color C on top, color A in the middle, and color B on the bottom. Make sure the center Vs of all three braids are pointing in the same direction.

[5] Locate the center of the stack, and sew through the center Vs of all three braids from bottom to top. Sew down through the stack about ¼ in. (6 mm) away.

[6] Lay the stack along the edge of the cabochon, with the B braid closest to the cabochon and the knot aligned with an unmarked corner of the foundation. Sew down through the foundation next to the cabochon, and then sew back up through the foundation and the stack about ¼ in. (6 mm) away. Repeat these two stitches until you are within ¼ in. (6 mm) of the next corner (**photo b**).

[7] Pick up a 4 mm bead, curve the stack around the bead in the opposite direction, and sew through the stack where it meets the hole of the bead (**photo c**). Make two or three small stitches through the stack, bring the stack around the other side of the bead, and end the stack (Soutache Basics and **photo d**).

Create ribbons of soutache braid that meander through clusters of SuperDuos and flow around a cabochon.

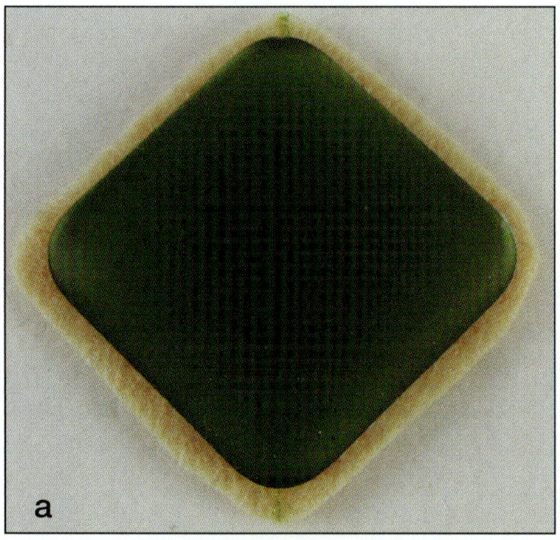

a

b

c

d

MATERIALS

green bracelet 7½ in. (19.1 cm)

- **1** 22 mm square cabochon (Luna Soft, olive)
- **80** 2.5 x 5 mm SuperDuo beads (full amber)
- **10** 4 mm fire-polished beads (magic apple; www.redpandabeads.com)
- **12** 3 mm fire-polished beads, optional (magic apple; www.redpandabeads.com)
- 1 g 8º seed beads (Miyuki 9577, dyed cream silver-lined alabaster)
- 1 g 11º seed beads (Miyuki 9577, dyed cream silver-lined alabaster)
- 1 g 15º seed beads, optional (Miyuki 3564, peach-lined transparent chartreuse AB; www.fusionbeads.com)
- **2** 3 mm daisy spacers (gold)
- toggle clasp
- ⅛-in. (3 mm) domestic soutache braid
  27 in. (69 cm) color A (rose)
  43 in. (1.1 m) color B (celery/ivy stripe)
  27 in. (69 cm) color C (celery)
- Fireline 6 lb. test
- beading needles, #12
- 1¼-in. (3.2 cm) square of beading foundation, such as Lacy's Stiff Stuff
- 3-in. (7.6 cm) square of leather or Ultrasuede backing
- E6000 adhesive
- paper
- pencil or marker
- small craft scissors

blue bracelet colors:

- 22 mm square cabochon (Luna Soft, spearmint)
- 2.5 x 5 mm SuperDuo beads (moon dust turquoise)
- 4 mm fire-polished beads (turquoise Picasso)
- 8º seed beads (Czech, green iris)
- 11º seed beads (Toho 264, inside-color rainbow crystal teal)
- 3 mm daisy spacers (silver)
- ⅛-in. (3 mm) domestic soutache braid: color A (teal), color B (beige), color C (silver)
- Nymo nylon beading thread (cream), in place of Fireline

Materials continued on p. 101

e

f

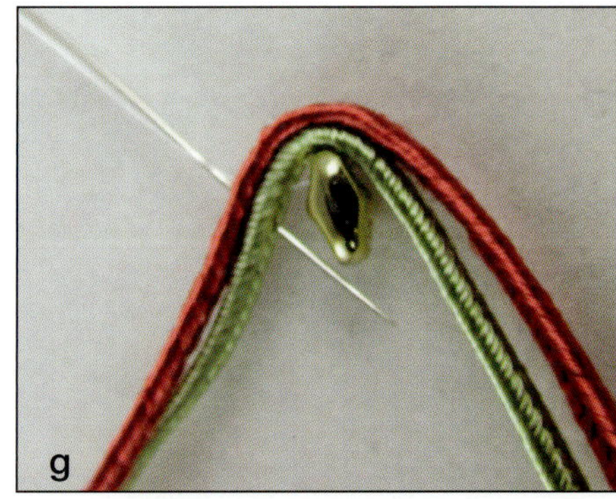
g

h

i

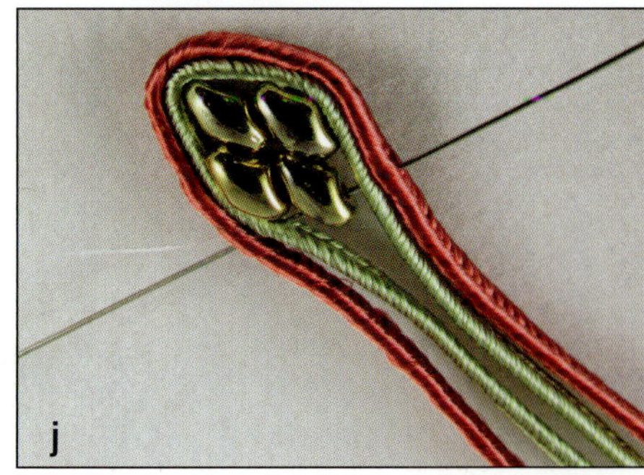
j

k

l

[8] Bring the thread across the back of the cabochon, and sew through the foundation and the stack near the knot. Work as in step 6 to secure the stack to this side of the cabochon. Then repeat step 7 to add a 4 mm bead. End the thread (Soutache Basics).

[9] Repeat steps 4–8 along the other two sides of the cabochon **(photo e)**.

Bracelet bands

Center straps

[1] Tie a double knot at one end of 1 yd. (.9 m) of thread. Trim the tail close to the knot.

[2] Cut an 8-in. (20 cm) piece of color A and color C braid. Create a two-braid stack with color A on top. Locate the center of the stack, and sew through it from bottom to top.

[3] Sew back through the stack, pick up a 2.5 x 5 mm SuperDuo bead, and sew through the stack on the other side of the SuperDuo **(photo f)**.

[4] Sew back through the stack about 1–2 mm away from where your thread exited, with the needle at an angle **(photo g)**. Pick up a SuperDuo, sew through the available hole of the existing SuperDuo, pick up a SuperDuo, and sew through the stack where it meets the hole of this last SuperDuo **(photo h)**.

[5] Sew back through the stack about 1–2 mm away from where your thread exited, with the needle at an angle. Sew through the available hole of the nearest SuperDuo, pick up a SuperDuo **(photo i)**, sew through the available hole of the next SuperDuo, and sew through the stack where it meets the hole of this SuperDuo.

[6] Sew back through the stack about 1–2 mm away from where your thread exited, with the needle at an angle. Sew through the available hole of the last SuperDuo, and sew through the other stack where it meets the hole of this SuperDuo **(photo j)**.

[7] Pinch the two stacks together after the last SuperDuo, and sew through all four braids close to the last bead **(photo k)**. Make two small stitches about 1–2 mm apart through all four braids. This completes the first SuperDuo cluster.

[8] Work as in steps 3–7 to add three more SuperDuo clusters **(photo l)**. Do not end the thread.

[9] Make a second center strap.

Side straps

[1] Tie a double knot at one end of 2 ft. (61 cm) of thread.

[2] Cut an 8-in. (20 cm) piece of color B braid, and fold it in half.

[3] Sew through one of the center straps from inside to outside near the top hole of the first SuperDuo **(photo m)**. Sew through the B braid near the fold, pick up an 8º seed bead, and sew through the other side of the B braid where it meets the hole of the bead

(photo n). Sew back through the B braid, the 8º, the B braid, and the stack of the center strap.

[4] Sew back through the stack and the B braid about one bead's width away, pick up an 8º, and sew through the B braid where it meets the hole of the bead. Sew back through the B braid, the 8º, the B braid, and the stack. Repeat this step to add a total of three 8ºs.

[5] Sew back through the stack and the B braid, pick up a SuperDuo, and sew through the B braid where it meets the hole of the SuperDuo. Continue to work as in steps 3–7 of "Center straps" to add a total of three SuperDuo clusters between the B braids, making sure to secure this side strap to the center strap **(photo o)**.

[6] Work as in step 7 of "Cabochon component" to add a 4 mm bead **(photo p)**, and end the stack.

[7] Work as in steps 1–6 to make a second side strap, and secure it to the other side of this center strap. This completes one bracelet band.

[8] Repeat steps 1–7 to secure two side straps to the other center strap, completing the other bracelet band.

Assembly

[1] Position one of the bracelet bands behind the cabochon component at one of the marked corners. With the working thread from the center strap, secure the band to the foundation with small stitches up through the foundation and back down through the band **(photo q)**.

[2] Sew through the stack above one of the 4 mm beads at the end of a side strap. Pick up an 8º, and sew through the corresponding stack in the cabochon component. Retrace the thread path, and then repeat this step to add another 8º **(photo r)**.

[3] Bring the thread across the back of the piece, and repeat step 2 for the other side strap on this bracelet band.

Materials continued from p. 99

purple bracelet colors:

- 22 mm square cabochon (Luna Soft, lilac)
- 2.5 x 5 mm SuperDuo beads (Vega on chalk; www.redpandabeads.com)
- 4 mm Czech glass pearls, in place of fire-polished beads (rose)
- 3 mm bicone crystals, in place of **2** of the 4 mm fire-polished beads (Swarovski, crystal AB)
- 8º seed beads (Miyuki 274, amethyst-lined crystal AB)
- 11º seed beads (Toho 395C, raspberry clear-lined rose; www.whimbeads.com)
- 3 mm daisy spacers (silver)
- ⅛-in. (3 mm) domestic soutache braid: color A (navy), color B (beige), color C (mauve)
- Nymo nylon beading thread (rose), in place of Fireline

SOUTACHE BASICS

Double knot
Tie one overhand knot. Tie another overhand knot, but slide it down to the first knot before pulling the thread tight.

Ending a stack
Push the loose ends of the stack to the back of your work, and fan them out so they lie as flat as possible. Sew up from the back through all the layers, and exit the side of one braid on the front of your work. Sew down through all the layers as close as possible to the point where the thread exited, sewing through the side of the same braid. Repeat this stitch several times to secure the stack, and trim the ends.

Ending the thread
To end the thread. Sew to the back of your work, and make a few small stitches in the closest braid. Tie a knot, and trim the thread close to the knot.

s

t

u

v

[4] Sew up through the band and the foundation at the marked corner of the cabochon. Pick up a 3 mm daisy spacer and an 11º seed bead, and sew back down through the spacer, the foundation, and the band (photo s).

[5] Sew up through the center band and the foundation at the base of the nearest SuperDuo cluster, pick up a 4 mm bead, and sew down through the center strap in the band (photo t). Retrace the thread path, and end the thread.

[6] Work as in steps 1–5 to assemble the other bracelet band on the opposite side of the cabochon component.

Backing

[1] Trace the outline of the cabochon component and the bracelet bands up to and including the 4 mm beads of the side straps onto a piece of paper (photo u). Cut out the shape.

[2] Trace the shape onto a leather or Ultrasuede backing, and cut it out.

[3] Apply a small amount of E6000 to the back of the piece, covering the ends of the stacks. Place the backing on the back of the piece, and allow it to dry completely.

[4] Tie a double knot at the end of 15 in. (38 cm) of thread, and sew through the edge of the foundation around the cabochon, hiding the knot between the backing and the foundation.

[5] Sew up between the two outside braids to the front of the piece. Making a 2 mm stitch, sew down between the two outside braids, the foundation, and the backing. Repeat these stitches around the entire backing. End the thread.

Clasp

[1] Tie a double knot at the end of 1 ft. (30 cm) of thread. Sew through the available end of the center strap on one side of the SuperDuo from inside to outside. Pick up a 4 mm bead, an 8º, five 11ºs, and half of the clasp. Sew back through all the beads and the stack. Retrace the thread path several times.

[2] Sew back through the beads, the clasp, and the five 11ºs. Pick up an 8º and a 4 mm, and sew through the center strap on the other side of the SuperDuo (photo v). Retrace the thread path several times, and end the thread.

[3] Repeat steps 1 and 2 at the other end of the band.

Optional embellishment

[1] Tie a double knot at the end of 2 ft. (61 cm) of thread, and sew through the stack around the cabochon near a 4 mm bead.

[2] Pick up a 3 mm fire-polished bead and a 15º seed bead, and sew back through the 3 mm and the stack.

[3] Sew back through the stack about one bead's width away, pick up an 8º and a 15º, and sew back through the 8º and the stack.

[4] Repeat steps 2 and 3 to embellish the edge of the cabochon component.

[5] Sew between the backing and the foundation to exit the opposite edge of the cabochon component, and repeat steps 2–4. ●

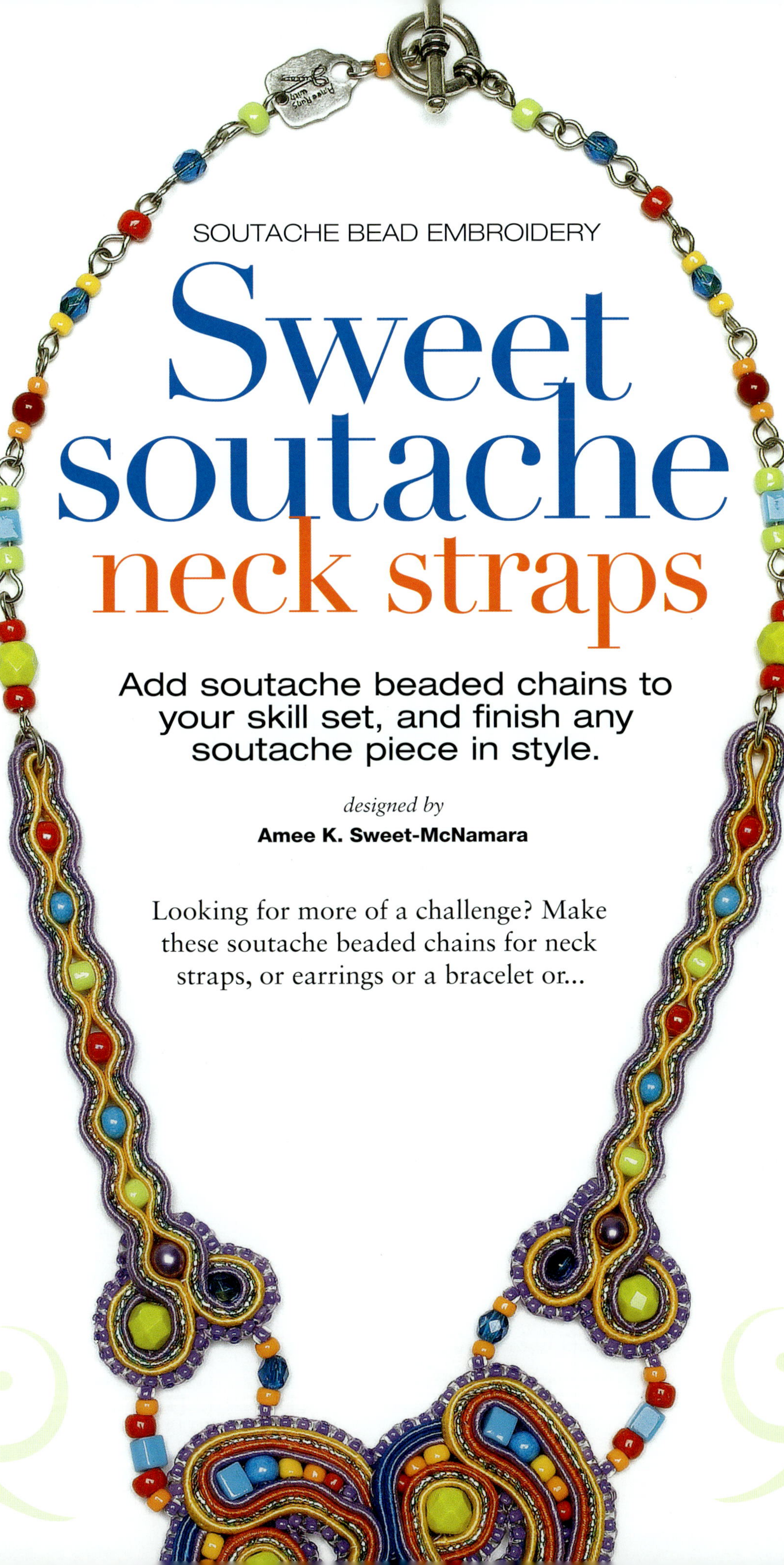

SOUTACHE BEAD EMBROIDERY

Sweet soutache neck straps

Add soutache beaded chains to your skill set, and finish any soutache piece in style.

designed by

Amee K. Sweet-McNamara

Looking for more of a challenge? Make these soutache beaded chains for neck straps, or earrings or a bracelet or...

stepbystep

Before you begin, read "Soutache Basics" on p. 97 to get acquainted with the techniques used in this project.

Soutache neck straps

Soutache chain

[1] Cut a 24-in. (60 cm) piece of soutache braid in each of the three colors.
[2] Thread the gold braid through both 6 mm jump rings **(photo a)**.
[3] Thread the rainbow metallic braid through the jump rings so it is resting on top of the gold braid, making sure the center V is pointing in the same direction as the gold braid **(photo b)**.
[4] Fold the two braids back on themselves, and push the jump rings into the fold. This will make enough room to thread the orchid braid through the jump rings. Once again, make sure the center V is pointing in the same direction as the other two braids.
[5] Keeping the braids aligned, fold the stack in half. Separate the jump rings so they are on either side of the fold **(photo c)**, and cut the stack in half at the fold so you have two 12-in. (30 cm) stacks, each with a jump ring. Set one stack aside.
[6] With the working stack, center the jump ring on the stack, and fold the stack in half over the jump ring. Make sure the orchid braid is on the outside.
[7] Tie a double knot (Soutache Basics) at one end of 1 yd. (.9 m) of thread. Trim the tail close to the knot.
[8] Sew through the left stack from inside to outside approximately 1/8 in. (3 mm) from the center fold **(photo d)**. Sew back through the left stack close to the last stitch, and continue through the right stack. Sew back through the right stack close to the last stitch, and continue through the left stack. Retrace the thread path through both stacks twice.
[9] Sew through the right stack from outside to inside close to the last stitch.
[10] Pick up a color A 6º seed bead, sew through the left stack from inside to outside, and then sew back through the left stack, the A, and the right stack **(photo e)**.
[11] To make a double-sided join:
• Join the two stacks below the bead (Soutache Basics) **(photos f and g)** to complete the first half of the double-sided join.
• Working from left to right, sew down through the join on the other side of the A, and then working from right to left, sew up through the join to the left of the A **(photo h)**. Retrace the thread path. This completes the double-sided join.
[12] Work as in steps 9–11 to add a color B 6º seed bead, a color C 6º seed bead, an A, a B, a C, and a 5 mm freshwater pearl to make a seven-bead soutache chain. Retrace the last double-sided join to secure in preparation for the three-bead cluster.

Three-bead cluster

[1] Separate the left stack from the right stack. Pick up a 6 mm round bead, wrap the left stack snugly around the 6 mm, and sew through the left stack where the bead meets the stack **(photo i)**. Sew down through the stack 1/4 in. (6 mm) to the left. Sew up 1/16 in. (2 mm) to the left of the previous stitch, and then sew down 1/4 in. (6 mm) to the left of the last stitch. This sequence of stitches will be referred to as "shaping stitches," with the larger stitches always along the outside of the curve and the smaller stitches always along the inside of the curve. End the stack (Soutache Basics).
[2] Hiding your thread on the back of your work, sew through the join after the 5 mm pearl to exit the right stack.
[3] Pick up a 4 mm round bead, wrap the right stack snugly around the 4 mm, and sew through the right stack where the bead meets the stack. Working from left to right, make four shaping stitches. End the stack, and end the thread (Soutache Basics).
[4] Make a second soutache chain, but reverse the position of the last two beads to make this three-bead cluster a mirror image of the first three-bead cluster.

Finishing

Backing

[1] Apply a small dab of glue to the back of a three-bead cluster, using a toothpick or the tip of your finger to spread the glue evenly to the edges. Place the cluster on the wrong side of a piece of Ultrasuede, and let dry completely.
[2] Trim the Ultrasuede around the cluster, making sure you cannot see the outer edge of the cluster from the back of the piece.

Beaded edge

[1] Tie a double knot at the end of 18 in. (46 cm) of thread. Beginning at an inside curve of a soutache stack surrounding a three-bead cluster, sew

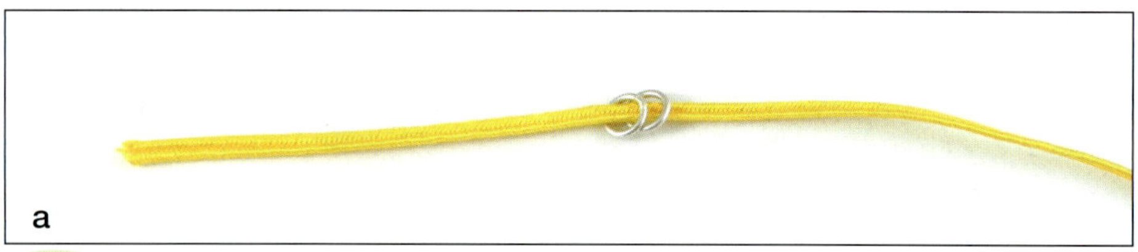
a

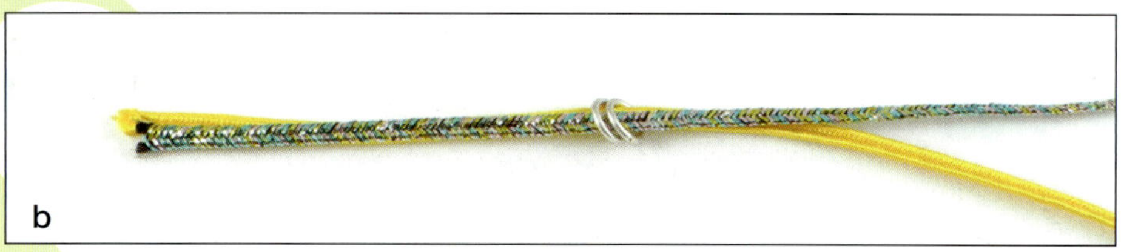
b

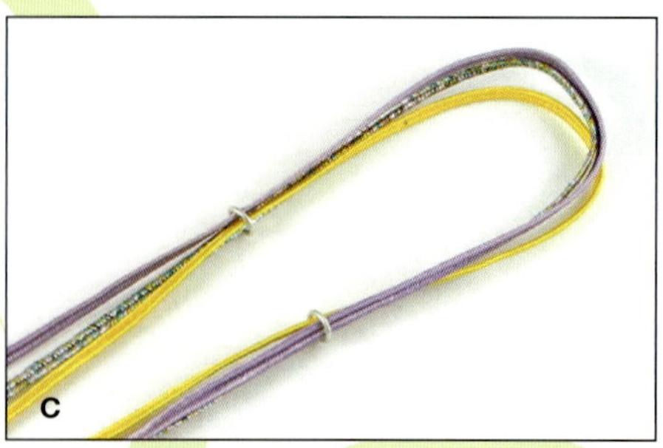
c

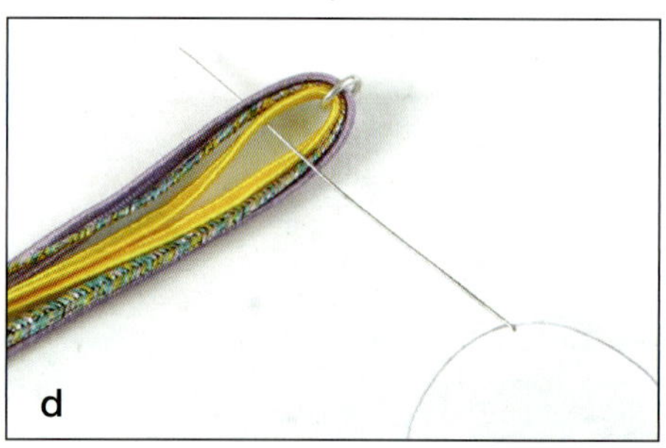
d

through the stack to the outside edge of the cluster. The knot should be buried in one of the small crevices on the front of the work.

[2] For the first stitch of the edging: Pick up two 11º seed beads, sew down through the outermost braid and the Ultrasuede, and sew back up through the second 11º just picked up.

[3] For subsequent stitches: Pick up an 11º, sew down through the outermost braid and the Ultrasuede, and then sew back up through the 11º just picked up.

[4] Work step 3 around the perimeter of the cluster. When you reach the point where the cluster meets the chain, work the edging stitches behind the chain. End the thread (Basics) in the edge beads.

[5] Repeat steps 1–4 for the three-bead cluster on the other soutache chain.

Pendant attachment

[1] Decide where you want a three-bead cluster to connect to a pendant. Tie a double knot at the end of 12 in. (30 cm) of thread, and sew through the 6 mm, the outer stack, and the edge 11º at the desired connection point around the cluster.

[2] Pick up assorted beads as desired, and sew through the corresponding edge 11º on the pendant and the soutache stack. Retrace the thread path twice to reinforce the connection.

[3] Carefully sew through the front of the pendant, keeping the thread hidden inside the soutache stacks as you go, and exit the edge 11º at the next desired connection point.

[4] Pick up assorted beads (one or two beads fewer than in step 2), and sew through the corresponding edge 11º on the three-bead cluster and soutache stack at the desired connection point. Retrace the thread path twice, and end the thread in the edge beads.

[5] Repeat steps 1–4 to attach the other three-bead cluster to the other side of the pendant.

Clasp

[1] Cut two 4½-in. (11.4 cm) pieces of chain, or make your own beaded chains: On an eye pin, string one to three beads, and make a plain loop (Basics). Repeat, attaching the new link to the previous link, until the beaded chain reaches 4½ in. (11.4 cm). Make a second beaded chain.

[2] Attach one end link of the chain to the jump ring on a soutache chain, and attach the other end link to half of the clasp. Repeat to finish the other side of the necklace. ●

MATERIALS

neck straps 8 in. (20 cm) each

- 24 in. (61 cm) ⅛-in. (3 mm) domestic soutache braid in each of **3** colors: gold, rainbow metallic, orchid
- **2** 6 mm fire-polished round beads (Czech, lime)
- **2** 5 mm freshwater pearls (lilac)
- **2** 4 mm fire-polished round beads (Czech, dark turquoise AB)
- **4** 6º seed beads in each of **3** colors: A (red), B (blueberry), C (lime)
- 1 g 11º seed beads (lilac-lined crystal clear)
- assorted beads of your choice for pendant attachment
- clasp
- 9 in. (23 cm) chain, or **12–16** 1-in. (2.5 cm) eye pins with assorted beads of your choice
- **2** 6 mm soldered jump rings
- nylon beading thread, size B (color to coordinate with soutache braids)
- beading needles, #10
- small craft scissors
- toothpicks (optional)
- washable fabric glue, such as api brand Crafter's Pick
- 2 x 2-in. (5 x 5 cm) piece of Ultrasuede (jazz blue)
- chainnose pliers and roundnose pliers (optional)
- wire cutters

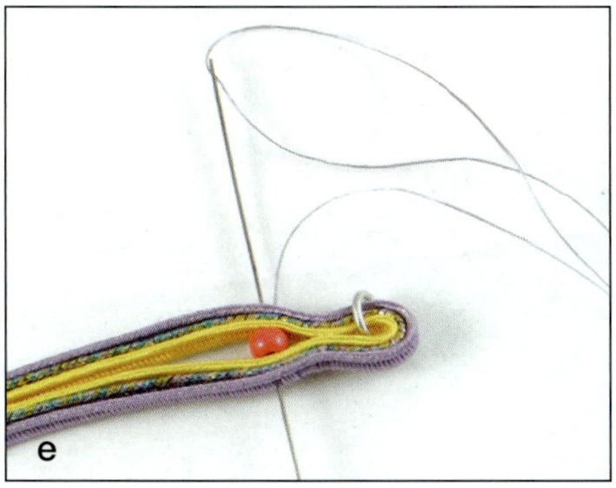
e

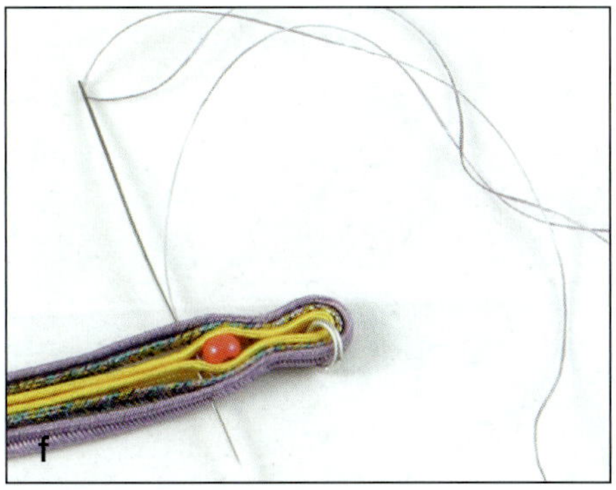
f

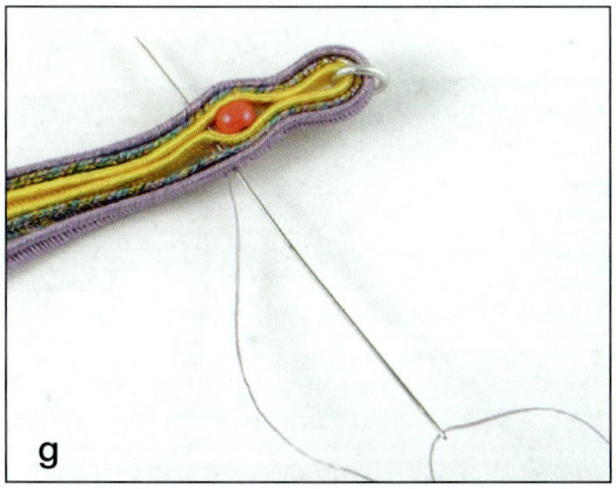
g

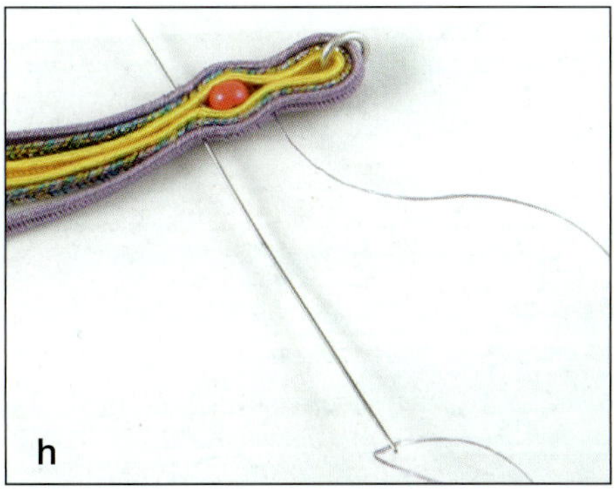
h

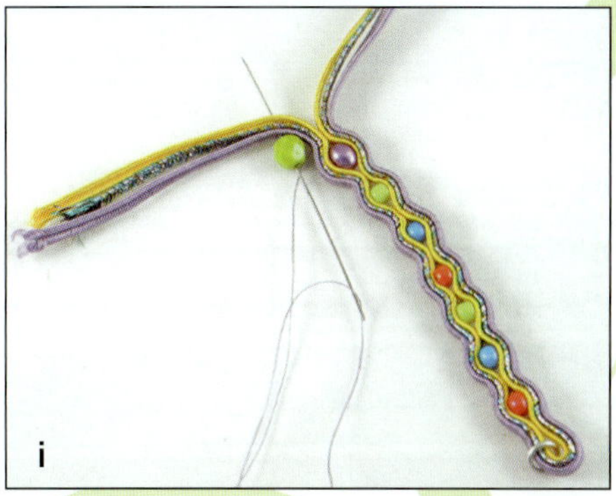
i

Bracelet loomed by Georgia Grisolia.

LOOMWORK

Serape bracelet

designed by **Lesha McPhearson**

Inspired by the traditional Mexican shawl, this loomwork bracelet is both bold and beautiful.

stepbystep

[1] Prepare the loom with 40 warp threads according to the manufacturer's instructions, or watch our how-to video — go online to www.BeadAndButton.com/videos, and search "loomwork."

[2] Tie a comfortable length of thread to the far-left warp thread, leaving a 6-in. (15 cm) tail. Tie the thread near the top of the loom if you wish to work the pattern from top to bottom, or tie the thread near the bottom of the loom to work from bottom to top. Thread the loomwork needle on this thread.

Note: The pattern makes an 8¼-in. (21 cm) bracelet. To adjust the length, consider these options:

- Stitch more or fewer rows. Four rows equals about ¼ in. (6 mm) of finished beadwork. Make sure you add or omit the same number of rows at each end to keep the pattern symmetrical. If you are making the bracelet shorter, this may mean starting a few rows in from one end.
- Instead of adding or omitting rows at the ends, make one or more of the stripes thicker or thinner.
- To shorten the bracelet without omitting rows, overlap the ends and use snaps or hook-and-eye closures instead of a slide clasp.

[3] Reading the **pattern** from left to right, pick up the appropriate 11º cylinder beads for the first row (as determined by your choice in step 2).

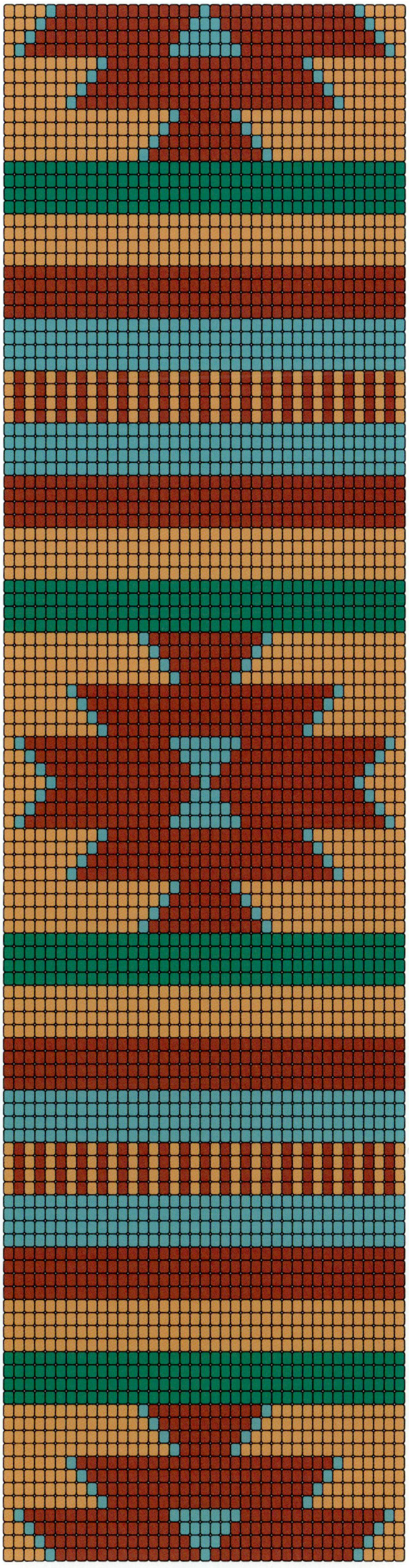

PATTERN

MATERIALS

bracelet 8¼ in. (21 cm)

- 11º Miyuki Delica cylinder beads
  - 9 g color A (DB0116, wine gold luster)
  - 4 g color B (DB0166, turquoise green opaque AB)
  - 8 g color C (DB0272, goldenrod-lined topaz AB)
  - 4 g color D (DB0273, forest green-lined topaz AB)
- 5-loop slide clasp
- beading thread
- beading needles, #12
- loomwork needle, or extra-long beading needle, #10 or #11
- bead loom

Sew behind the warp threads **(figure 1)**, use your finger to push the beads up between the warp threads **(figure 2)**, and sew back through the beads over the top of the warp threads **(figure 3)**.

[4] Work as in step 3 for the entire pattern. Using the #12 beading needle, end your thread when it gets short (Basics), and then add a new thread as in step 2, tying it on where your next row will begin.

[5] When you complete the pattern, cut the beadwork from the loom, leaving the warp threads long enough to tie off. Using the #12 beading needle, end the working thread and tails, and do the same for each warp thread.

[6] Add 10 in. (25 cm) of thread (Basics) at one end of the beadwork. Center half of the clasp on this end, so that the loops are hidden behind the beadwork. Stitch each loop to its neighboring beads, retracing the thread path of each connection. End the thread. Repeat this step for the other end of the beadwork. ●

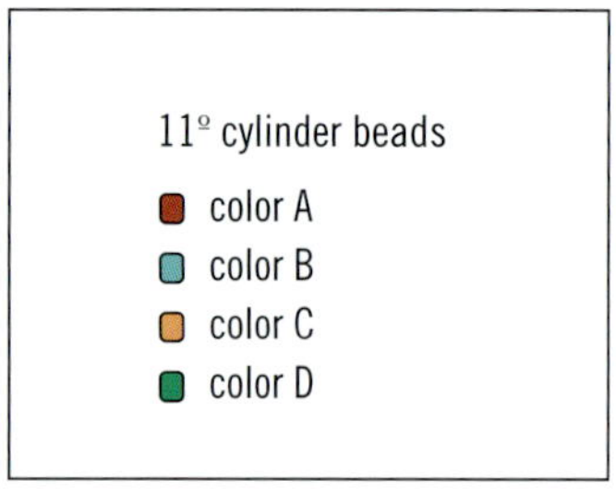

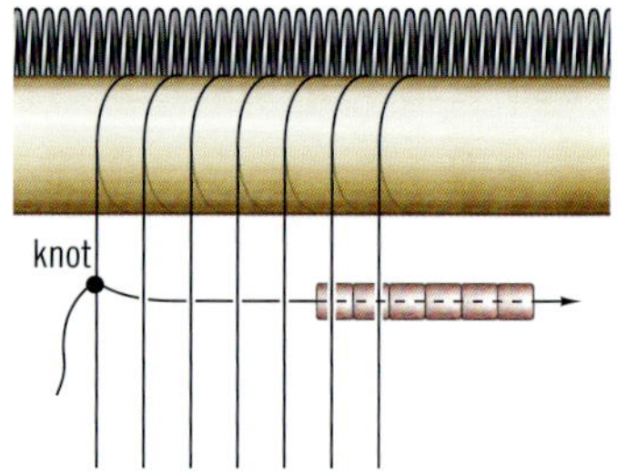

FIGURE 1

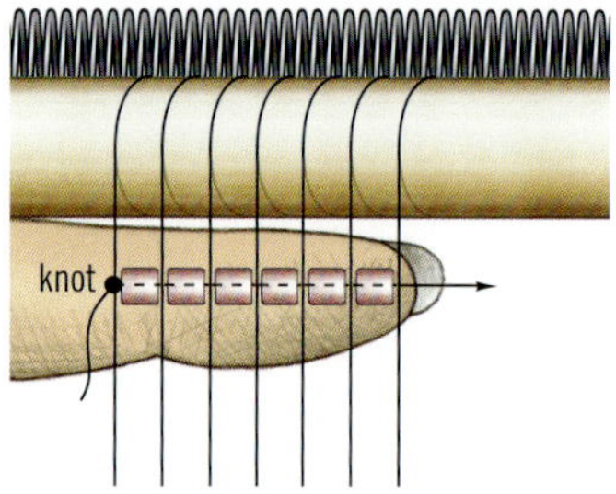

FIGURE 2

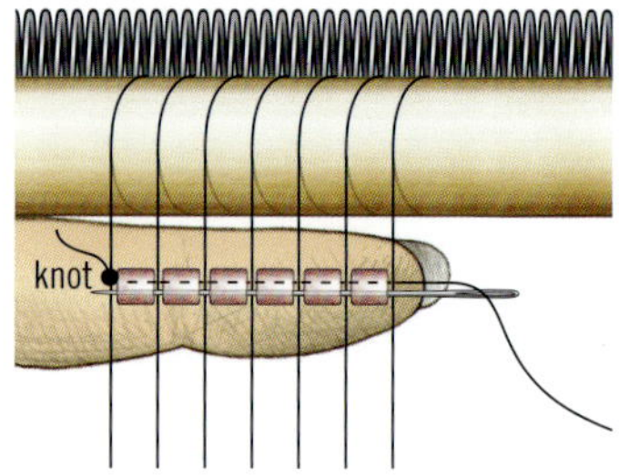

FIGURE 3

Bead crochet
Sonoko's way

Sonoko Nozue is one of the most well-known international beaders with a following of dedicated students and admirers that circles the globe.

designed by **Sonoko Nozue**
with **Jane Danley Cruz**

stepby**step**

Rather than the typical slip-stitch method that many people use, Sonoko favors single crochet, which allows more thread to show. She features the thread as a design element in both her one- and two-bead methods. Sonoko uses Fujix Tire Silk #16 thread and crystal beads for her bead crochet. You can use Tuff-Cord #1 or Amiet size 0 and seed beads, if you prefer.

One-bead method

Rope

[1] With the thread on the spool or card, string the desired number of beads using a Big Eye needle. For a 2¼-in. (5.7 cm) inside-diameter bangle, string 30 in. (76 cm) of 3 mm crystal rondelles. If desired, use a repeating pattern of four colors.

[2] Leaving a 4-in. (10 cm) tail, make a slip knot **(figure 1)**, and insert the crochet hook into it. Work a bead chain stitch: Slide a bead down to the hook, yarn over the hook **(figure 2)**, and pull the thread through the loop. Repeat to make a total of four bead chain stitches **(photo a)**.

[3] Use a bead single crochet to form the chain into a ring: Insert the hook to the left of the first bead in the chain, flipping the bead to the right of the hook **(photo b)**. Slide the next bead down to the hook, and yarn over **(photo c)**. Pull the thread through the stitch in the previous round, yarn over **(photo d)**, and pull the thread through both loops on the hook. This is the first stitch of the next round.

[4] Continue working in bead single crochet: Insert the hook to the left of the next bead in the previous round, and flip that bead to the right **(figure 3)**. Slide a bead down to the hook, yarn over **(figure 4)**, pull the thread through the stitch in the previous round, yarn over, and pull the thread through both loops on the hook. Repeat around the ring, working each stitch into the loop that attaches the next bead in the previous round.

[5] Repeat step 4 for the desired length. Cut the thread, leaving a 6-in. (15 cm) tail, and pull the thread through the last stitch.

Invisible join

[1] To bury the ending tail, thread a tapestry needle, and carefully sew into the middle

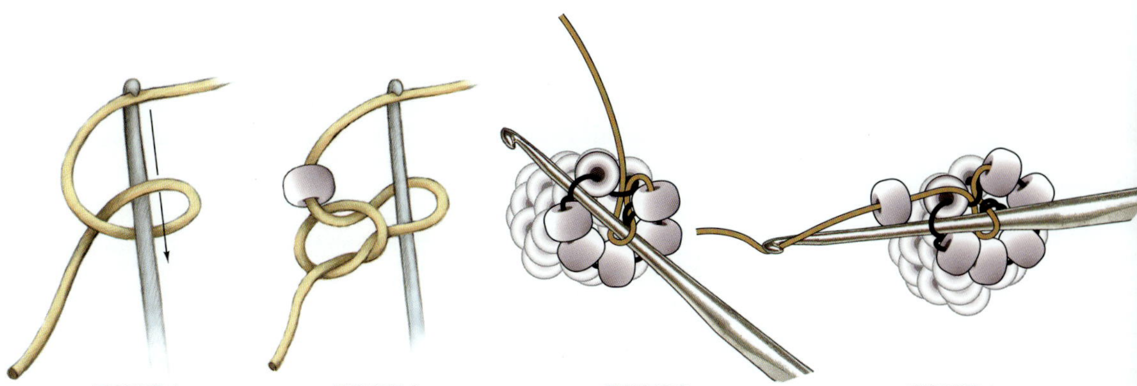

FIGURE 1 FIGURE 2 FIGURE 3 FIGURE 4

MATERIALS

bead crochet bangle

- 3 x 4 mm crystal rondelles
- 3 mm bicone crystals (optional)
- Fujix Tire silk #16 button-hole twist thread, 0.25 mm (www.jewelsinfiber.com)
- Big Eye needle
- tapestry needle
- crochet hook, 1.4 mm

DESIGN NOTE:

Sonoko used 2.5 mm Swarovski bicone crystals and 3 mm round crystals in her necklace. You can substitute Thunder Polish beads to save money and still achieve the sparkle.

a

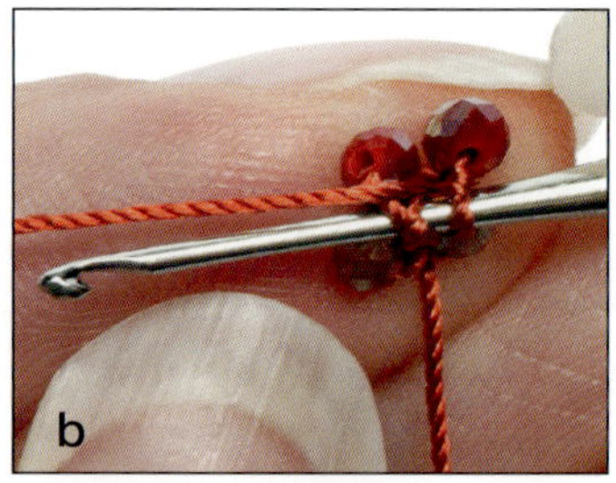
b

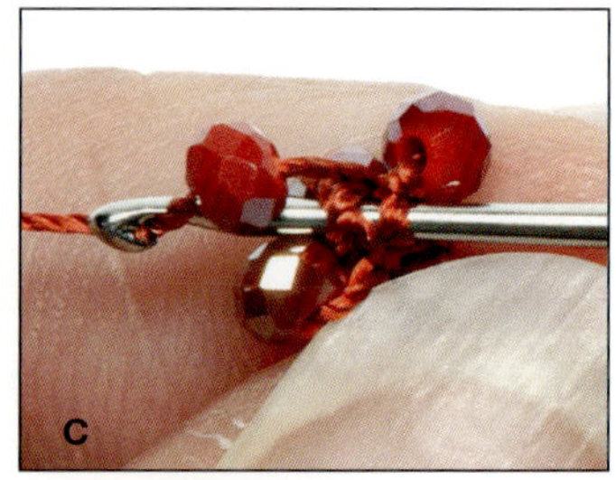
c

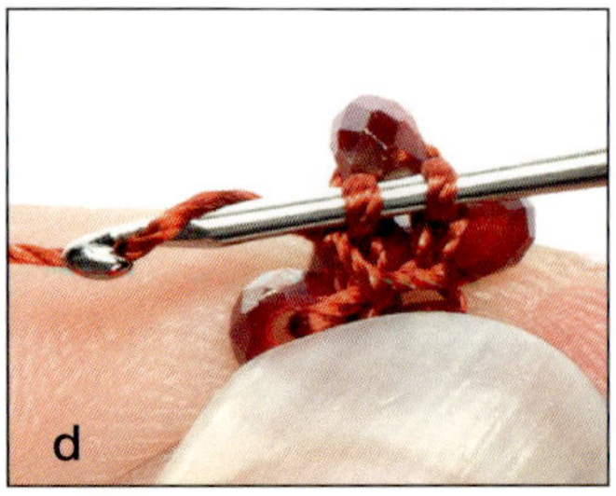
d

e

f

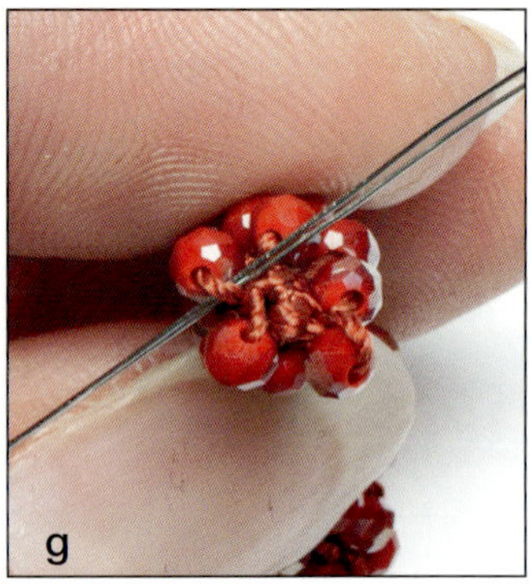
g

h

i

of the rope, exiting between two beads several rounds into the work (photo e). Sew in and out of the rope several times, crossing over the thread within the rope without sewing through any beads (photo f), and trim the thread as close to the beadwork as possible.

[2] Thread a tapestry needle on the beginning tail, which is exiting the first stitch in the first round. On each end of the rope, push the beads down and out so you can identify the beads in the first round and the beads in the last round. The beads in the last round lie sideways because they haven't been locked into place yet.

[3] Line up the ends of the rope, aligning the spiral pattern. On the tail end of the rope, sew under the loop of the first bead in the last round. Flip the bead to the right as you would if you were crocheting (photo g). If you created a pattern in your rope, this bead should be the same color as the one your thread is exiting on the other end of the rope.

[4] At the beginning of the rope, sew under the loop of the second bead in the first round, sewing toward the third bead (photo h).

[5] Cross over to the tail end again, and sew under the second bead in the final round (photo i).

[6] Continue working back and forth between the ends, flipping the beads in the final round and matching up the spiral pattern. Snug up the ends as you work. After you've flipped the last bead on the tail end, sew under the first bead at the beginning end again. End the tail as in step 1.

Two-bead method

Rope

This method creates texture and a more defined spiral look in your rope. For this variation, use 3–4 mm beads in two colors and shapes.

[1] For a 2¼-in. (5.7 cm) inside-diameter bangle, string approximately 39 in. (.99 m) of 3 mm bicone crystals and 3 x 4 mm crystal rondelles in a repeating pattern, ending with a bicone.

[2] Leaving a 4-in. (10 cm) tail, make a slip knot, and insert the crochet hook into it. Work four chain stitches without beads.

[3] To form the chain into a ring: Insert the hook into the first stitch, yarn over, and pull the thread through the loop. This stitch is a joining stitch and will not be sewn through again.

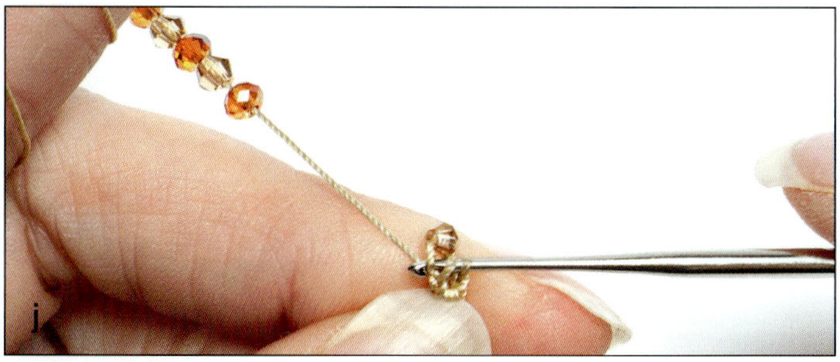

j

k

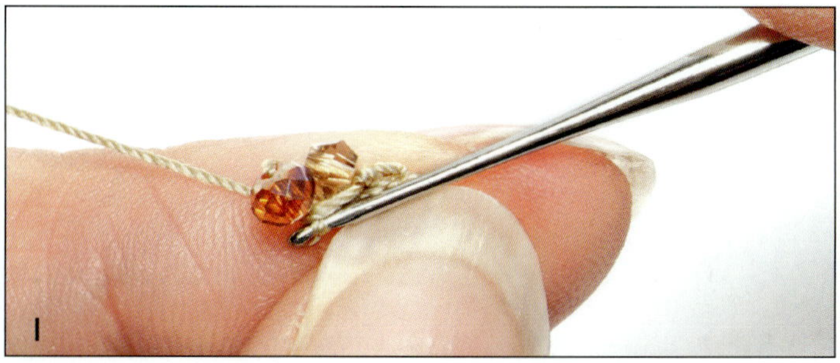

l

[4] Insert your hook into the next stitch, and work a two-bead single crochet as follows:

• Slide a bicone down to the hook, and yarn over **(photo j)**. Pull the thread through the stitch in the previous round. There will be two loops remaining on the hook. This completes one half of a two-bead single crochet stitch.

• Slide a rondelle down to the hook, yarn over **(photo k)**, and pull the thread through both loops on the hook **(photo l)**. This completes the second half of a two-bead single crochet stitch.

[5] Repeat step 4 two more times to complete the round.

[6] Work all subsequent rounds as follows:

• Insert the hook into the first half of the next stitch (this is the first stitch in the previous round with the bicone), and work as in step 4.

• Skip the second half of the previous stitch (the stitch with the rondelle).

• Repeat step 4 in the first half of each of the following two stitches.

[7] Repeat step 6 for the desired length. Cut the thread, leaving a 6-in. (15 cm) tail, and pull the thread through the last stitch.

Join

Work as in the steps for "Invisible join," but only sew under the loops of the bicones in the first and last rounds of the rope. ●

Three tips for success

1. At the beginning of each round, pull down the number of beads needed for that round to rest on the thread between your fingers and your work **(below, bottom)**. That way you are less likely to miss a stitch.

2. Choose a thread color to coordinate with your beads.

3. Control the tension by wrapping your thread around your fingers as shown **(below, top)** so it does not slide through your fingers too easily. Release the last loop around your index finger as needed to keep your tension consistent.

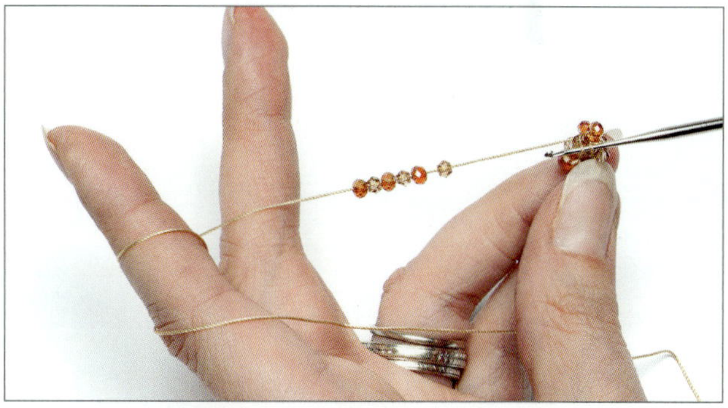

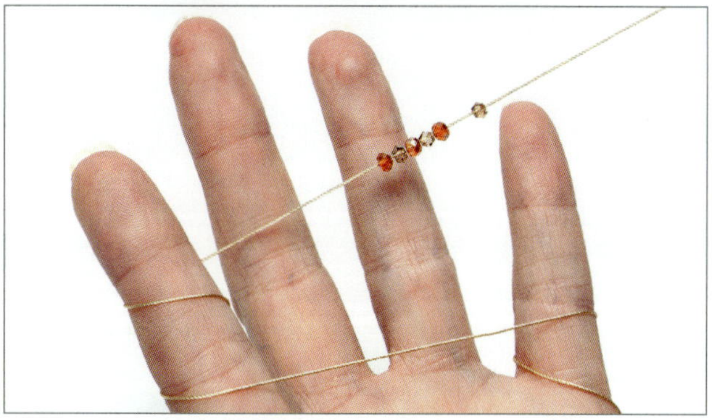

Multiple-Stitch Projects

Rizo florets necklace

Stitch up cute little beaded beads using Rizos and pearls, and then string them together for a floral look that's great for summer.

designed by

Sandie Bachand

stepbystep

Beaded beads

[1] On 4 ft. (1.2 m) of thread, pick up a 4 x 6 mm crystal rondelle and three 2.5 x 6 mm Rizo beads, and sew through all the beads again, leaving a 9-in. (23 cm) tail. Tie the working thread and tail together with a square knot (Basics), and sew through the rondelle.

[2] Pick up an 11º seed bead, three Rizos, and an 11º, and sew through the rondelle **(photo a)**.

[3] Repeat step 2 eight more times using a moderate tension for a total of nine loops with Rizos and 11ºs.

[4] On one end of the rondelle, sew through the nearest 11º with the needle pointing away from the center of the beaded bead, and continue through the next 11º with the needle pointing toward the center of the rondelle **(photo b)**. Using a moderate tension, continue sewing through each 11º with the needle pointing toward the center of the rondelle to form a ring of 11ºs **(photo c)**. You may have to adjust the 11ºs a little to get them to form a ring. Sew through all the 11ºs again.

[5] Using the tail, repeat step 4 at the other end of the rondelle, and end the tail (Basics).

[6] Using the working thread, sew through the nearest three Rizos to exit the other end of the beaded bead. Pick up a 3 mm pearl, and sew through the next three Rizos **(photo d)** back to the first end. Repeat this stitch around the beaded bead, adding 3 mm pearls on both ends. Continue this stitch to add a 3 mm pearl between the existing 3 mm pearls **(photo e)** for a total of nine 3 mm pearls on each end of the beaded bead.

[7] Sew through the ring of 3 mm pearls on one end of the beaded bead to tighten **(photo f)**. Sew through three Rizos to the other end of the beaded bead, and sew through the ring of 3 mm pearls on this end to tighten. End the working thread.

[8] Repeat steps 1–7 to make 14 more beaded beads.

Necklace

[1] Cut 2 ft. (61 cm) of beading wire. On one end, string a crimp bead and half of the clasp. Go back through the crimp bead, crimp it (Basics), and trim the excess wire. Using chainnose or crimping pliers, close a crimp cover over the crimp.

[2] String a 6 mm pearl, a beaded bead, a 6 mm, a 3.5 mm square heishi spacer, a 4 mm cube bead, and a spacer. Repeat this pattern 13 more times.

[3] String a 6 mm, a beaded bead, a 6 mm, a crimp bead, and the other half of the clasp. Go back through the crimp bead, crimp it, and add a crimp cover as before. ●

MATERIALS

necklace 17 in. (43 cm)

- **15** 4 x 6 mm crystal rondelles (jet)
- crystal pearls (Swarovski, rose gold)
  30 6 mm
  270 3 mm
- **14** 4 mm cube beads (Miyuki 1053, metallic gold)
- 32 g 2.5 x 6 mm Rizo beads (jade AB)
- 3 g 11º seed beads (Toho PF557, starlight metallic galvanized permanent finish)
- **28** 3.5 mm square heishi spacers (item 0430, gold; www.ubeaditsacramento.com)
- clasp
- **2** crimp beads
- **2** 4 mm crimp covers (gold)
- flexible beading wire, .014 (Soft Flex)
- Fireline 6 lb. test
- beading needles, #11 or #12
- chainnose pliers (optional)
- crimping pliers
- wire cutters

Top a flat floral bracelet with a trio of dimensional bezels.

designed by **Lorraine Coetzee**

Colorful blossoms bracelet

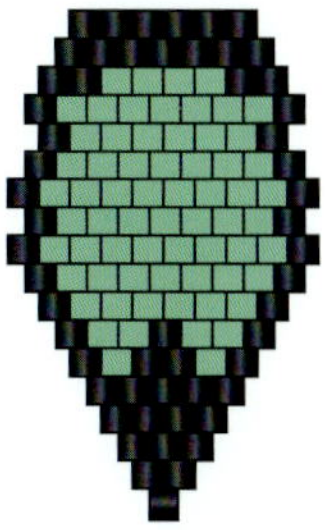

PETAL PATTERN

Create a shapely bracelet base and flower petals in brick stitch, bezel the flower centers in peyote, and then put all the parts together to create a stunning accessory!

stepby**step**

The bracelet base features a number of increases and decreases as well as negative spaces. While it can be worked in peyote stitch or brick stitch, our instructions cover brick stitch only. See "Shaping in brick stitch," p. 119, for help with increasing and decreasing.

Base

[1] Condition a comfortable length of thread (Basics). Starting at one end of the **base pattern**, leave a 6-in. (15 cm) tail, and work the first row in ladder stitch (Basics).

[2] Working in brick stitch (Basics), follow the **base pattern**, increasing, decreasing, and leaving negative space as indicated. End and add thread (Basics) as needed.

Petals

[1] Condition 1 yd. (.9 m) of thread. Starting at the wide end of the **petal pattern**, work the first row in ladder stitch, leaving a 6-in. (15 cm) tail.

- 11º cylinder bead, color A
- 11º cylinder bead, color B
- 11º cylinder bead, color C
- 11º cylinder bead, color D
- 11º cylinder bead, color E
- 11º cylinder bead, color F
- 11º cylinder bead, color G
- 15º cylinder bead

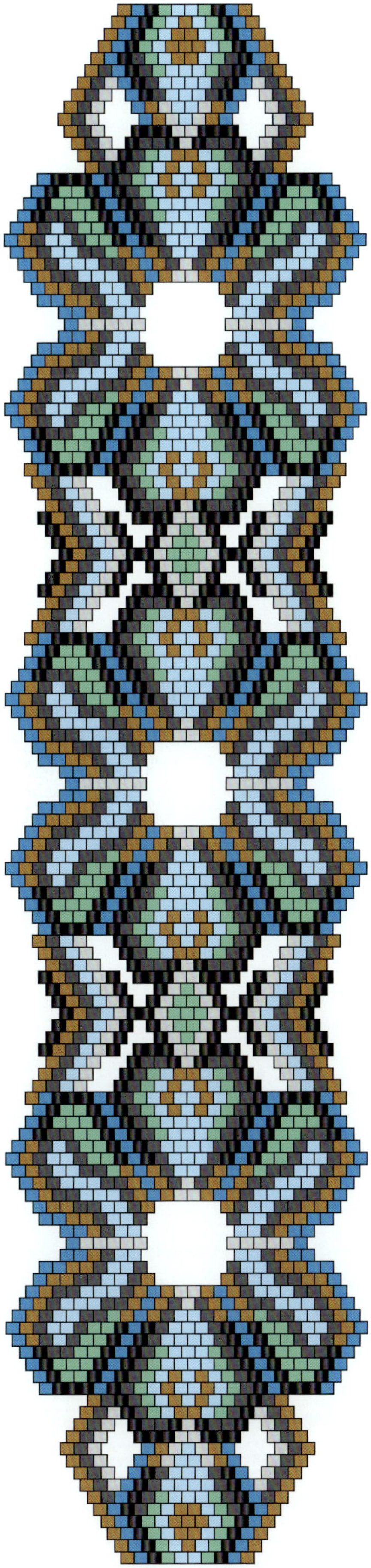

BASE PATTERN

MATERIALS

blue bracelet 7½ in. (19.1 cm)

- **3** 8 x 6 mm oval crystals (#R452, www.vintagejewelrysupplies.com)
- **11** 6 x 9 mm glass drops (black; www.landofodds.com)
- 11º Japanese cylinder beads (Miyuki Delica)
  2 g color A (DB862, matte medium blue)
  3 g color B (DB023, metallic light bronze iris)
  5 g color C (DB010, black)
  2 g color D (DB310, matte black)
  5 g color E (DB984B, lined teal aqua mix)
  3 g color F (DB985B, green/blue mix)
  1 g color G (DB035, galvanized silver)
- 1 g 15º Japanese cylinder beads (Miyuki Delica DBS041, silver-lined crystal)
- nylon beading thread conditioned with beeswax, microcrystalline wax, or Thread Heaven
- beading needles, #12

red bracelet colors:

- 8 x 6 mm pearlized glass, in place of crystals (Gutermann #1250)
- 4 x 7 mm glass drops, in place of 6 x 9 mm drops (topaz and matte topaz)
- 11º Japanese cylinder beads (Miyuki Delica)
  color A (DB601, dyed silver-lined dark burnt orange)
  color B (DB034, 24kt gold plated)
  color C (DB254, galvanized tarnished silver)
  color D (DB380, matte metallic khaki iris)
  color E (DB603, silver-lined burnt orange)
  color F (DB283A, lined amber cranberry)
  color G (DB052, peach-lined crystal AB)
- 15º seed beads, in place of 15º cylinder beads (Miyuki 457L, metallic light bronze)

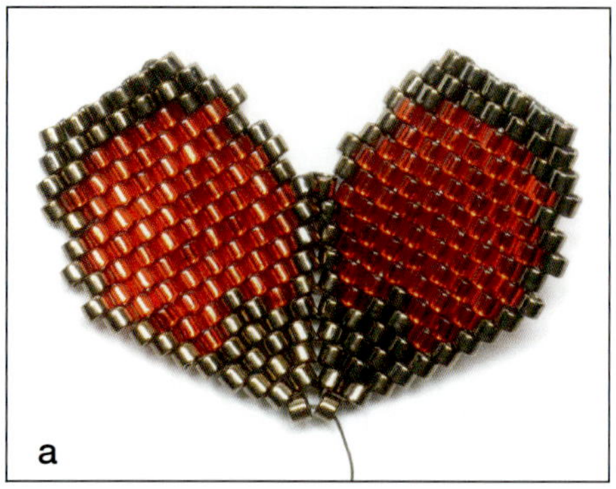

a

c

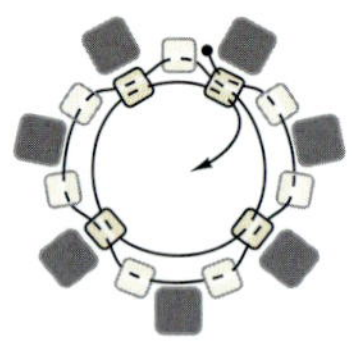

FIGURE 1

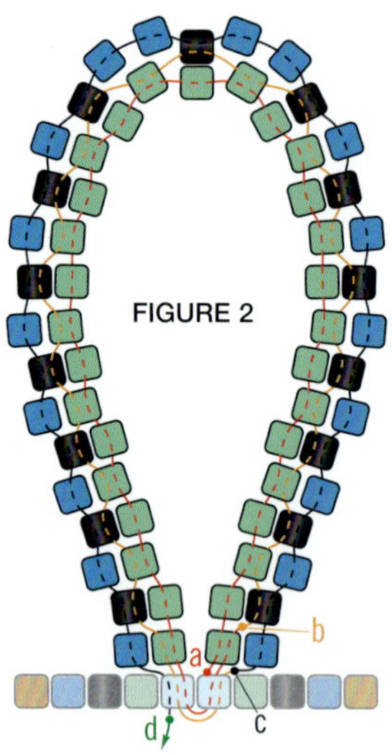

FIGURE 2

Continue in brick stitch following the petal pattern to complete the petal. End the tail but not the working thread. Make a total of five petals.

[2] Using the remaining thread on one of the petals, stitch two petals together, circling through the 10 corresponding edge beads **(photo a)**, and end the thread. Repeat to connect all five petals, ending threads as you go.

b

d

Bezeled flower centers

[1] On 1 yd. (.9 m) of thread, pick up 14 color E 11º cylinder beads. Tie the beads into a ring with a square knot (Basics), leaving a 6-in. (15 cm) tail. These beads will shift to form rounds 1 and 2 as the next round is added. Sew through the first two beads.

[2] Working in tubular peyote stitch (Basics), work one round with color C 11º cylinder beads, and step up through the first bead added in this round.

[3] Work two rounds using 15º cylinder beads. This will be the front of the bezel, so pull the beadwork snug, and test to see that the face of the 8 x 6 mm oval crystal will sit comfortably in this opening. Work additional rounds if needed. Sew through the beadwork to exit an up-bead in round 1.

[4] Work two rounds with Cs, and insert the crystal face down into the beadwork.

[5] To close up the beadwork around the back of the crystal, work two decreasing rounds of peyote stitch with 15º cylinders:

Round 1: Work one complete round.

Round 2: Work one stitch, and decrease by sewing through the next up-bead in the previous round. Repeat twice, work one more stitch, and step up through the first bead added in this round. Sew through the beads added in this round **(figure 1)**.

[6] Sew through the beadwork to exit an E in round 1. Pick up three color F 11º cylinder beads, and sew through the next

SHAPING IN BRICK STITCH

Increasing and decreasing is easy in brick stitch. Here's how!

Increase at the start of a row

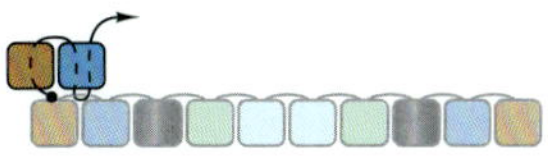

For a regular increase at the beginning of a row, work a normal first stitch, but attach it to the first thread bridge in the row below instead of the second thread bridge.

Increase at the end of a row

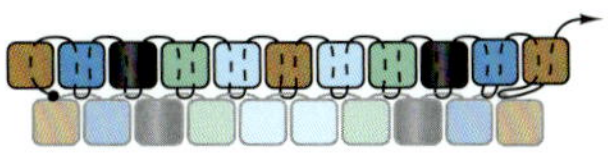

For an increase at the end of a row, work an additional stitch off the last thread bridge in the previous row.

Extended increase

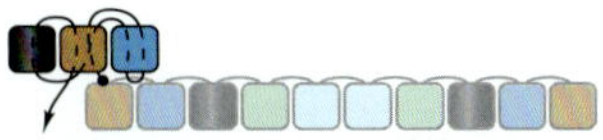

To do an extended increase at the start or end of a row, first work a regular increase, and then add one or more beads in ladder stitch.

Decrease

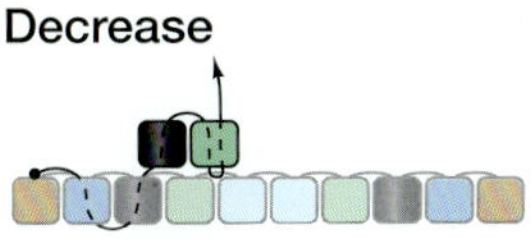

Normal brick stitch will result in naturally decreasing rows. To decrease more dramatically, simply sew through the beadwork to exit the spot where you want your decrease row to begin, and resume normal stitching.

E in the round to create a picot. Repeat to complete the round.

[7] Repeat steps 1–6 to bezel a second crystal. Repeat once more with the final crystal, but in step 6 add drops around the edge instead of picots: Pick up a 6 x 9 mm drop, and sew through the next E. Repeat to complete the round, pushing the drops so they angle up toward the face of the crystal. Don't end the working thread on this bezel.

Toggle bar

[1] On 1 yd. (.9 m) of thread, pick up 16 color A 11º cylinder beads, leaving a 6-in. (15 cm) tail. Working in flat even-count peyote stitch (Basics), work two rows each of B 11º cylinders, C 11º cylinders, and E 11º cylinders. Zip up (Basics) the end rows to form a tube.

[2] Sew through the hollow center of the tube to exit one end. Pick up three Bs, and sew back through the center of the tube to exit the other end. Repeat to make a picot at this end.

[3] Sew through the beadwork to exit a bead in the middle of the toggle bar. End the tail but not the working thread.

Assembly

[1] Using the thread remaining from the crystal embellished with drops, attach the brick stitch flower **(photo b)**, sewing through corresponding beads until the connection is secure. End the thread.

[2] Using a thread remaining from the brick stitch flower, attach it to the center opening in the base **(photo c)**, sewing through corresponding beads until the connection is secure. End the thread.

[3] Using the threads remaining from the other bezels, attach each to a remaining opening on the base.

[4] With the thread remaining from the toggle bar, pick up four Bs, and sew down through the fifth bead from one edge at one end of the base. Sew up through the sixth bead from the edge to center the toggle bar.

[5] Pick up a B, skip the last B picked up in the previous step, and sew back through the next B **(photo d)**. Work one peyote stitch with a B, and sew into the toggle bar. Retrace the thread path through the clasp connection, and end the thread.

[6] Add 1 yd. (.9 m) of thread at the other end of the base, and exit the fifth bead from one edge. Pick up 31 Es, and sew down through the sixth bead from the edge to center the loop. Sew up through the fifth bead again and the first bead picked up in this step **(figure 2, a–b)**.

[7] Work 15 peyote stitches with one C per stitch **(b–c)**.

[8] Work 16 stitches with As, picking up two As per stitch as needed along the outer curve **(c–d)**. End the thread. ●

BRICK STITCH / PEYOTE STITCH

Twin flower lariat

Stitch a textural, organic rope with floral finials and a smooth slide.

designed by **Kerrie Slade**

MATERIALS

purple necklace 32 in. (81 cm)

- **16** 6 mm Czech glass pearls (matte gold)
- 2.5 x 5 mm Twin beads
  80 g color A (Preciosa 28998, matte dark purple)
  20 color B (Preciosa 01710, matte gold)
- 2 g 10º Czech seed beads (matte gold)
- Fireline 6 lb. test
- beading needles, #10 and #12
- bobbin

gunmetal necklace colors:

- 6 mm Czech glass pearls (matte silver)
- 2.5 x 5 mm Twin beads
  color A (Preciosa 28949, gunmetal)
  color B (Preciosa 01700, matte silver)
- 10º Czech seed beads (matte silver)

stepbystep

Rope

[1] On 3½ yd. (3.2 m) of thread, center three color A 2.5 x 5 mm Twin beads, and sew through all the beads again to form a ring **(figure 1, a–b)**. Wrap the tail around a bobbin.

[2] Work a round of modified tubular brick stitch as follows, ending and adding thread (Basics) as needed:

First stitch: Pick up two As, sew under the thread bridge between the adjacent two As in the previous round, and sew up through the last A just added **(figure 2, a–b)**.

Second stitch: Pick up an A, sew under the thread bridge between the next two As in the previous round, and sew up through the A just added **(b–c)**.

Join: Sew down through the first A added in this round, and sew up through the last A added in this round **(figure 3)**.

[3] Work as in step 2 to make a rope the desired length. Do not end the working thread or tail.

Flowers

[1] Work in rounds as follows:

Round 1: Pick up an A, sew down through the next A in the rope, and sew up through the following A **(figure 4, a–b)**. Pick up an A, sew down through the previous A in the rope, and sew up through the next A in the rope **(b–c)**. Pick up an A, sew down through the next A in the rope, sew up through the following A, and then sew through the first A added in this round **(c–d)**. Sew through the available hole of this A **(d–e)**.

Round 2: Pick up two As, and sew through the available hole of the next A

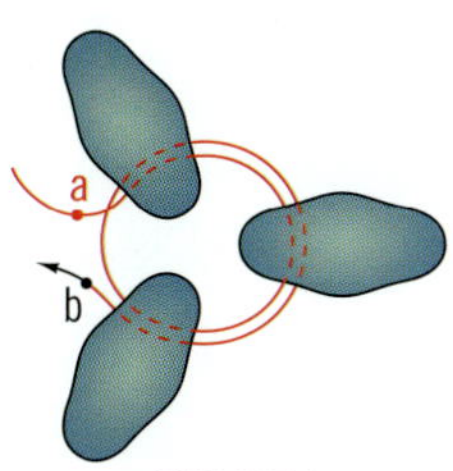

FIGURE 1

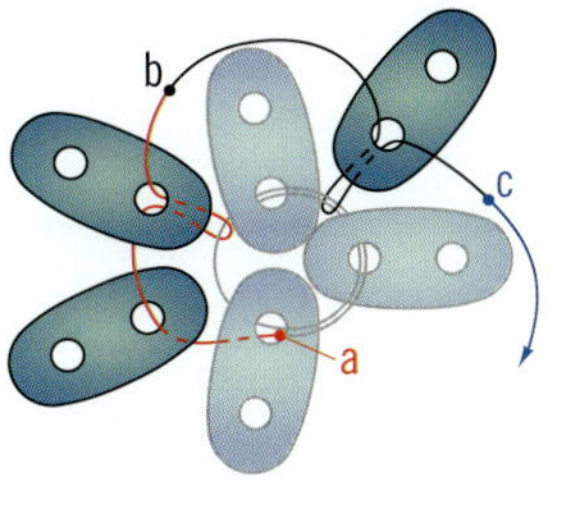

FIGURE 2

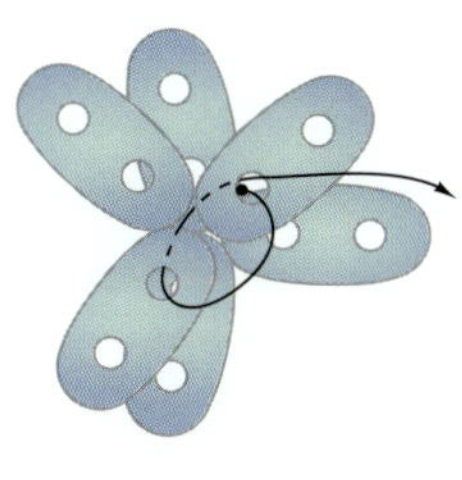

FIGURE 3

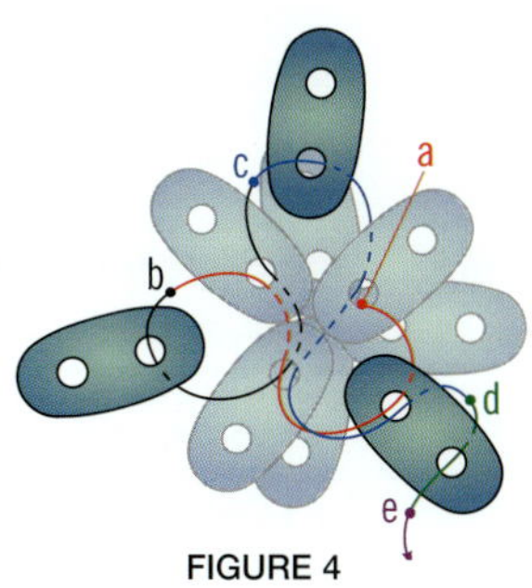

FIGURE 4

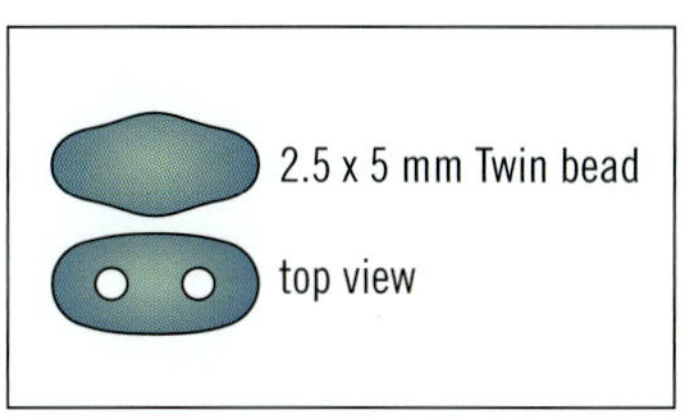

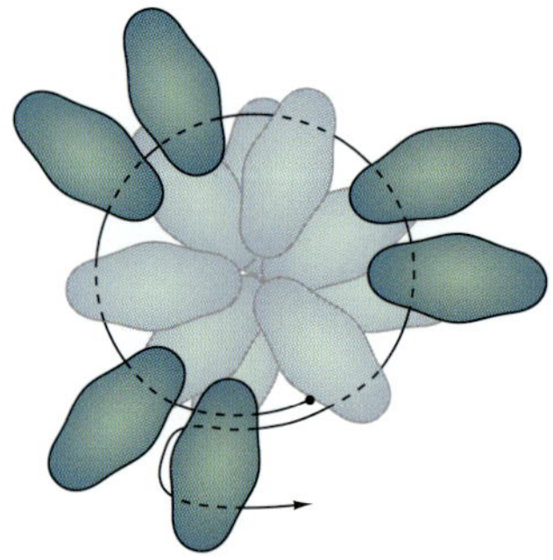

FIGURE 5

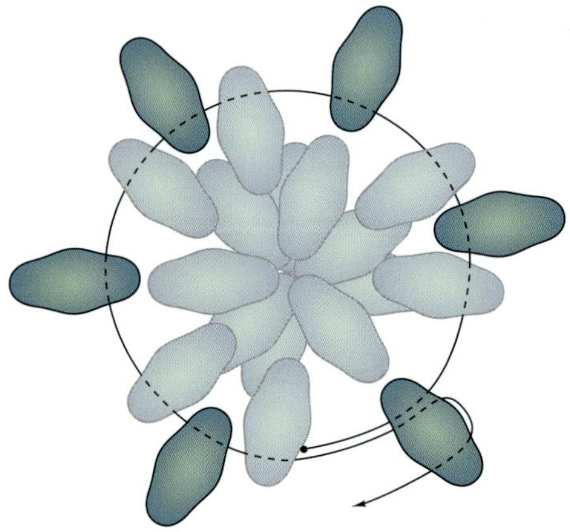

FIGURE 6

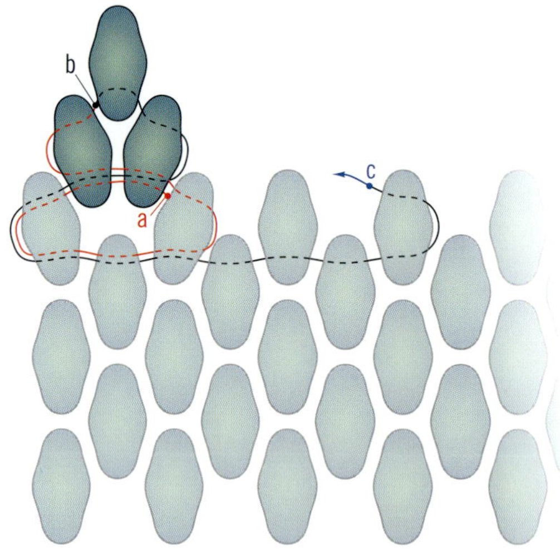

FIGURE 7

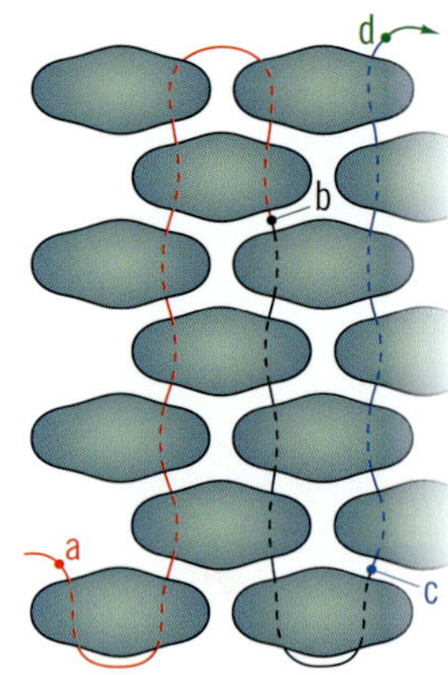

FIGURE 8

in the previous round. Repeat this stitch to complete the round. Step up through the first A added in this round, and then sew through the available hole of the same A **(figure 5)**.

Round 3: Pick up an A, and sew through the available hole of the next A in the previous round. Repeat this stitch to complete the round, adding a total of six As in this round. Step up through the first A added in this round, and then sew through the available hole of the same A **(figure 6)**.

Round 4: Pick up two As, and sew through the available hole of the next A in the previous round. Repeat this stitch to complete the round, adding a total of 12 As in this round. Step up through the first A added in this round, and then sew through the available hole of the same A.

Rounds 5–13: Pick up an A, and sew through the available hole of the next A in the previous round. Repeat this stitch to complete each round. Step up through the first A added in each round, and then sew through the available hole of the same A. Retrace the thread path through the last two rounds for stability.

[2] Pick up two As, and sew through the available hole of the next A in the previous round. Sew through the other hole of the same A, the nearest hole of the adjacent A in the previous round, the nearest hole of the A your thread exited at the start of this step, and the other hole of the same A. Sew through the two As added in this step, and sew through the available hole of the second A **(figure 7, a–b)**.

[3] Pick up an A, sew through the available hole of the first A added in the previous step, and then sew through the next nine As as shown **(b–c)**.

[4] Repeat steps 2 and 3 to add a total of six points. End the working thread.

[5] Add 8 in. (20 cm) of thread to the flower where it meets the rope, and exit the end of the rope inside the flower. Pick up eight 6 mm pearls and a 10º seed bead. Sew back through the pearls, continue through a few Twins at the end of the rope, and end the thread.

[6] Unwind the tail from the bobbin, and repeat steps 1–5 to add a flower to this end of the rope.

Beaded slide

[1] On 1½ yd. (1.4 m) of thread, pick up an A, and sew through the available hole of this A, leaving a 12-in. (30 cm) tail. Pick up seven As, skip the last two As, and sew through the available hole of the next A **(figure 8, a–b)**.

[2] Work in modified flat odd-count peyote stitch as follows: Pick up an A, and sew through the available hole of the next A. Repeat this stitch, and then pick up an A, and sew through the available hole of the same A **(b–c)**.

[3] Work three peyote stitches with one A per stitch **(c–d)**.

[4] Work as in steps 2 and 3 for a total of 20 rows. Do not end the working thread or tail.

[5] Fold the rope in half, wrap the beadwork around the two ropes, and using the tail, zip up (Basics) the ends to form a tube. End the tail.

[6] With the working thread exiting an edge A in the slide, pick up a color B 2.5 x 5 mm Twin bead and three 10ºs. Sew through the available hole of the B, sew down through the nearest hole of the next edge A, and sew up through the other hole of the same A. Repeat this stitch to complete the round. You will have a total of 10 Bs along this edge.

[7] Sew through the beadwork to exit an A along the opposite edge, and work as in step 6. End the thread. ●

PEYOTE STITCH / BEAD WEAVING

Pixie petals bracelet

Make a statement with this organic and classic cuff.

designed by **Rose Kasallis**

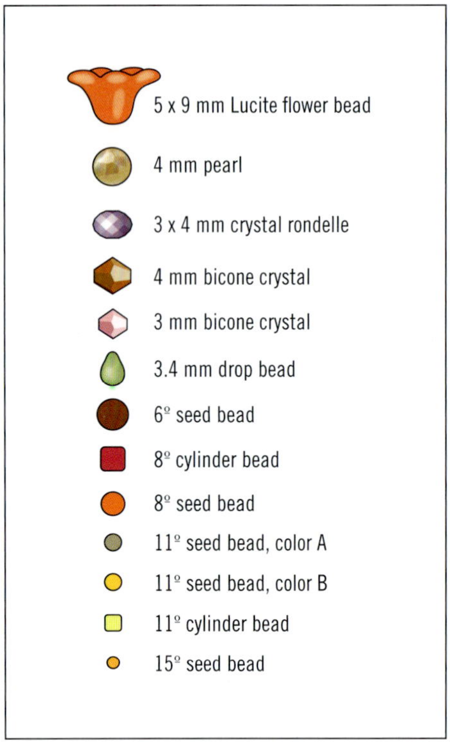

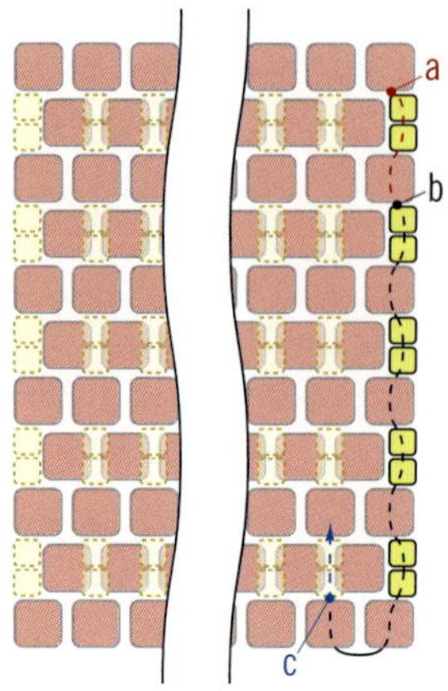

FIGURE 1

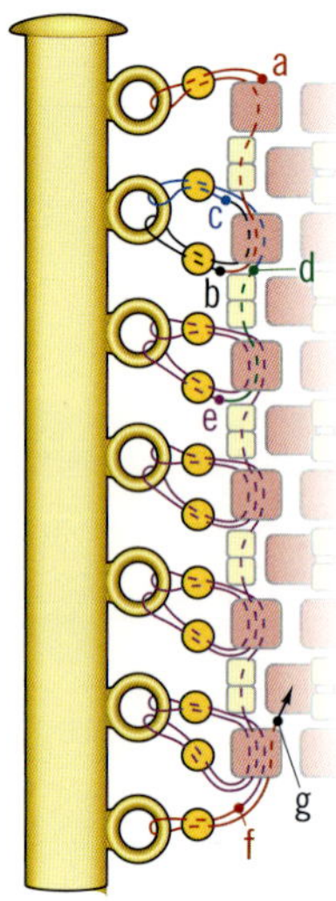

FIGURE 2

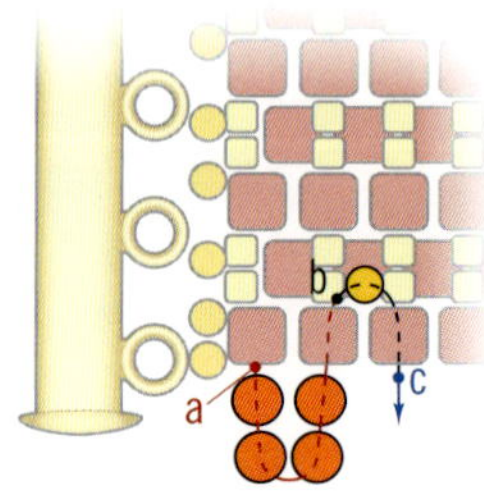

FIGURE 3

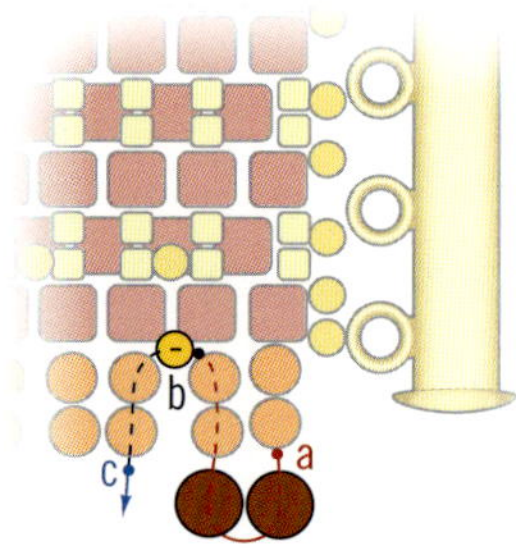

FIGURE 4

stepbystep

Bracelet base

[1] On a comfortable length of thread, attach a stop bead (Basics), leaving a 16-in. (41 cm) tail.

[2] Pick up 11 8º cylinder beads, and working in flat odd-count peyote stitch (Basics), make a band that is long enough to fit around your wrist minus ½ in. (1.3 cm) for the clasp. A 6⅜-in. (16.2 cm) finished bracelet has 50 beads along each straight edge. Add or remove rows in sets of four as needed. The last row should begin and end with an up-bead. End and add thread (Basics) as needed.

[3] With your thread exiting an edge cylinder in the last row, and with your needle pointing toward the beadwork, pick up two 11º cylinder beads, and sew through the next 8º cylinder in the row **(figure 1, a–b)**. Repeat this stitch to complete the row, and sew through the next edge cylinder **(b–c)**. Repeat the row to embellish the remainder of the base, ending and adding thread as needed.

Clasp

[1] Sew through the beadwork to exit the edge 8º cylinder in the last row with your needle pointing away from the beadwork. Make sure the embellished side of the base is facing up.

[2] Pick up a color B 11º seed bead, and sew down through the end loop of the clasp, the B just added, and the edge 8º cylinder. Continue through the next three beads **(figure 2, a–b)**.

[3] Pick up a B, sew down through the next loop of the clasp and the B just added, and sew back through the 8º cylinder in the opposite direction **(b–c)**. Pick up a B, sew down through the same loop of the clasp and the B just added, and sew through the same 8º cylinder in the original direction **(c–d)**. Continue through the next three beads **(d–e)**.

[4] Work as in step 3 to attach the next four loops of the clasp **(e–f)**. Work as in step 2 to attach the last loop of the clasp with your thread exiting the edge 8º cylinder bead in the last row **(f–g)**. Do not end the working thread.

[5] Remove the stop bead from the tail, and repeat steps 1–4 to attach the other half of the clasp. End the tail.

Edge embellishment

[1] Sew through the beadwork to exit the same edge 8º cylinder in the last row with your needle pointing away from the beadwork. Work in modified herringbone stitch as follows: Pick up four 8º seed beads, and sew through the next edge 8º cylinder **(figure 3, a–b)**. Pick up a B, and sew through the following edge 8º cylinder **(b–c)**. Repeat these two stitches for the length of the base. Sew through the beadwork to exit the last two 8º seed beads added with your needle pointing away from the beadwork.

[2] Pick up two 6º seed beads, and sew through the next two 8º seed beads **(figure 4, a–b)**. Pick up a B, and sew through the following two 8º seed beads

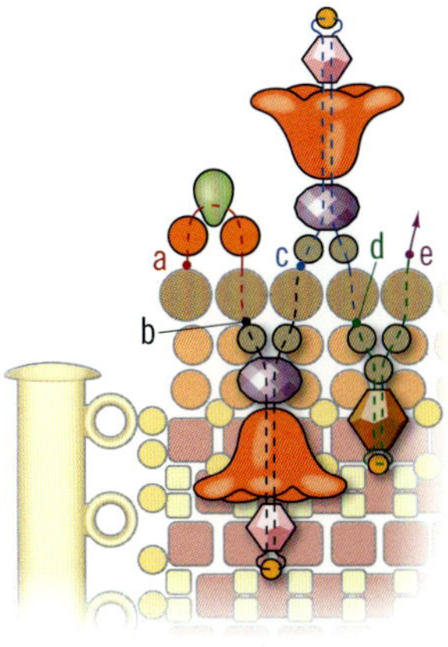

FIGURE 5

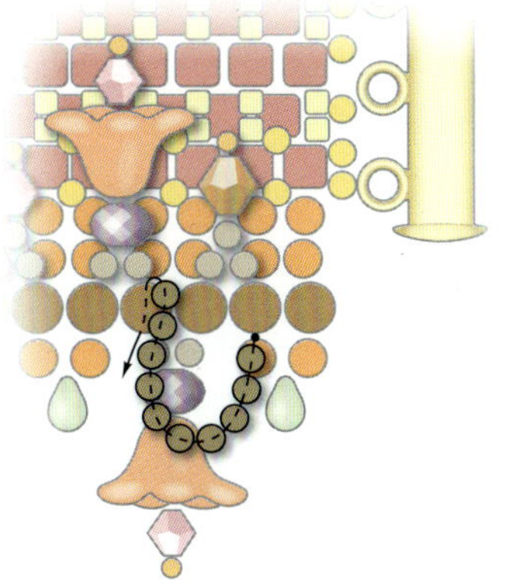

FIGURE 6

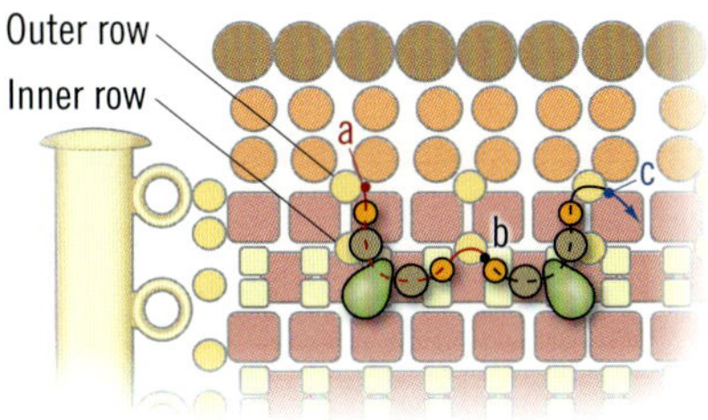

FIGURE 7

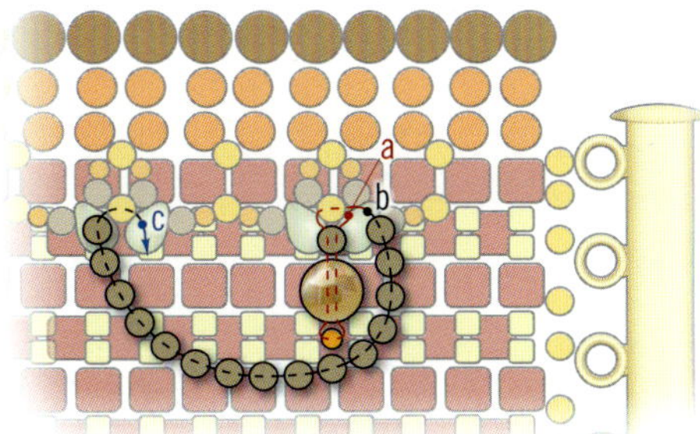

FIGURE 8

(b–c). Repeat these two stitches for the length of the base, positioning the first 6º added in each set toward the back of the base and the second 6º added in each set toward the front.

[3] Sew through the beadwork to exit the edge 8º cylinder in the last row on the other edge of the base. Work as in steps 1 and 2 to embellish this edge. When positioning the 6ºs, make sure they mirror the first edge. End and add thread as needed.

[4] Sew through the beadwork to exit the last 6º added on this edge of the base.

Flower embellishment

[1] Making sure the 6ºs stay in the same angled positions as before, pick up an 8º seed bead, a 3.4 mm drop bead, and an 8º seed bead, and sew through the next 6º **(figure 5, a–b)**. These beads will lie toward the outside of the base.

[2] Pick a color A 11º seed bead, a 3 x 4 mm crystal rondelle, a 5 x 9 mm Lucite flower bead, a 3 mm bicone crystal, and a 15º seed bead. Sew back through the bicone, flower, and rondelle. Pick up an A, and sew through the next 6º **(b–c)**, pulling tight. These beads will lie toward the center of the base.

[3] Pick up an A, a rondelle, a flower, a 3 mm bicone, and a 15º, and sew back through the bicone, flower, and rondelle. Pick up an A, and sew through the next 6º **(c–d)**, pulling tight. These beads will lie toward the outside of the base.

[4] Pick up two As, a 4 mm bicone crystal, and a 15º, and sew back through the bicone and the following A. Pick up an A, and sew through the next 6º **(d–e)**, pulling tight. These beads will lie toward the center of the base.

[5] Repeat steps 1–4 for the length of the base, ending and adding thread as needed. End the working thread when you complete this edge.

[6] Add a comfortable length of thread to the other edge of the base, and exit the first 6º on the same end you started with for the first edge. Your needle should be pointing away from the beadwork. Repeat steps 1–5 for this edge of the base, but do not end the working thread.

MATERIALS

bracelet 2¼ x 6⅜ in. (5.7 x 16.2 cm)

- **67** 5 x 9 mm Lucite five-petal flower beads (a mix of cranberry, light pink, and watermelon; www.fusionbeads.com)
- **36** 4 mm crystal pearls (Swarovski, bronze)
- **67** 3 x 4 mm crystal rondelles (Chinese, light amethyst AB; www.ubeaditsacramento.com)
- bicone crystals (Swarovski)
  34 4 mm (topaz AB 2X)
  67 3 mm (vintage rose and Ceylon topaz AB 2X)
- 6 g 3.4 mm drop beads (Miyuki 2035, matte khaki iris; www.redpandabeads.com)
- 11 g 6º seed beads (Miyuki 409F, matte brown; www.auracrystals.com)
- 8 g 8º seed beads (Miyuki 409F, matte brown; www.auracrystals.com)
- 14 g 8º cylinder beads (Miyuki DB122, transparent rainbow golden brown; www.artbeads.com)
- 11º seed beads
  4 g color A (Toho 281, gray-lined topaz AB; www.artbeads.com)
  9 g color B (Miyuki 462, gold iris; www.auntiesbeads.com)
- 3 g 11º cylinder beads (Miyuki DB907, sparkling light bronze-lined crystal; www.beadaholique.com)
- 2 g 15º seed beads (Miyuki 462, gold iris; www.auracrystals.com)
- 7-strand slide clasp
- Fireline 6 or 8 lb. test
- beading needles, #11 or #12

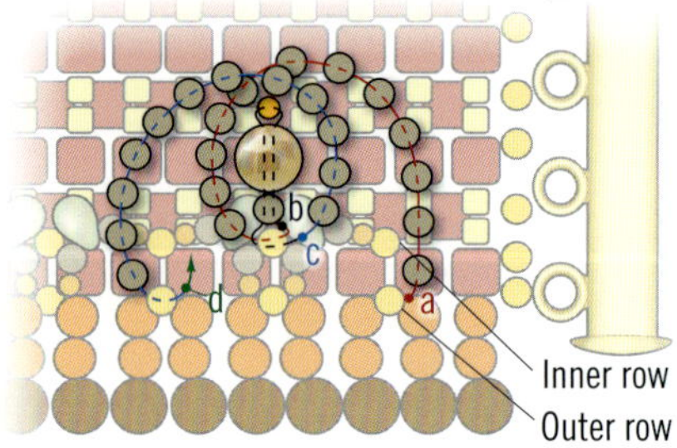

FIGURE 9

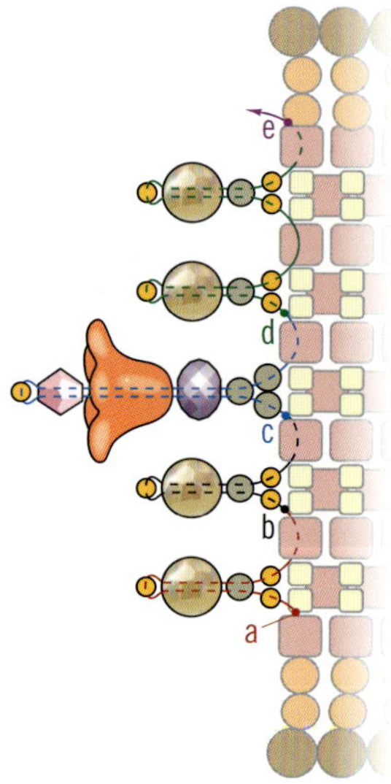

FIGURE 10

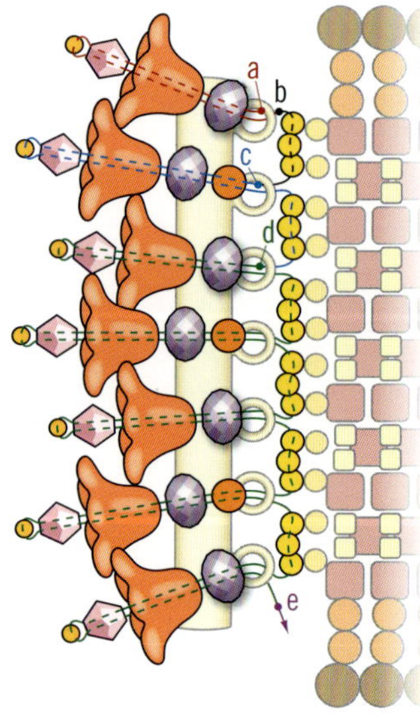

FIGURE 11

Outside edge loops

For the outside edge loops, work with the 6ºs that are angled toward the front of the base and skip the 6ºs angled toward the back.

[1] Sew through the beadwork to exit the end 6º that is positioned toward the front of the base with your needle pointing away from the beadwork.

[2] Pick up 10 As, and sew through the next 6º that is positioned toward the front of the base, sewing in the direction shown **(figure 6)**. Repeat this stitch for the length of the base, and end the working thread.

[3] Add 1 yd. (.9 m) of thread to the other edge of the base, and exit the 6º that is positioned toward the front of the base on the same end you started with for the first edge. Your needle should be pointing away from the beadwork. Repeat step 2 for this edge of the base, making sure the loops mirror the first edge, and end the working thread.

Top edge embellishment

For the purposes of these instructions, the front of the base will have a top and a bottom edge. The edge you just completed will be the top edge, and you will start this embellishment at the left corner of the top edge. The embellishment will lie on top of the base but under the previous flower embellishment. For clarity, the flower embellishment is not shown in the figures.

Along the top edge of the base are two parallel "rows" of Bs from previous embellishments, an inner row and an outer row (see **figure 7**).

[1] Add a comfortable length of thread to the base, and exit the leftmost B in the outer row with your needle pointing away from the clasp **(figure 7, point a)**.

[2] Pick up a 15º, an A, a drop, an A, and a 15º, skip an inner-row B, and sew through the next inner-row B **(a–b)**. Pick up a 15º, an A, a drop, an A, and a 15º, skip an outer-row B, and sew through the next outer-row B **(b–c)**. Repeat these two stitches for the length of the base. After the last stitch, your thread should exit the rightmost B in the inner row.

[3] Sew through the beadwork to exit the previous inner-row B with your needle pointing toward the clasp on this end **(figure 8, point a)**.

[4] Pick up an A, a 4 mm pearl, and a 15º, and sew back through the pearl and the A. Continue through the B your thread exited at the start of this step, sewing in the same direction **(a–b)**.

[5] Pick up 15 As, skip an inner-row B, and sew through the next inner-row B **(b–c)** with the needle pointing toward the clasp on this end.

[6] Repeat steps 4 and 5 for the length of the base. Notice the Bs you are sewing through do not have stitches in them from step 2. End and add thread as needed, but do not end the working thread when you complete the edge.

Bottom edge embellishment

The other edge of the base will be the bottom edge, and you will start this embellishment at the left corner of the bottom edge. The embellishment will lie on top of the base but above the previous flower embellishment. For clarity, the flower embellishment is not shown in the figures.

Once again, there are two parallel "rows" of Bs from previous embellishments, an inner row and an outer row.

[1] Sew through the beadwork to exit the leftmost B in the outer row with your needle pointing away from the clasp on this end.

[2] Repeat step 2 of "Top edge embellishment."

[3] Sew through the beadwork to exit the rightmost B in the outer row with your needle pointing toward the clasp on this end **(figure 9, point a)**.

[4] Pick up 12 As, skip an inner-row B, and sew through the next inner-row B **(a–b)** with your needle pointing toward the clasp on this end.

[5] Pick up an A, a 4 mm pearl, and a 15º, and sew back through the pearl and the A. Continue through the B your thread exited at the start of this step, sewing in the same direction **(b–c)**.

[6] Pick up 12 As, skip an outer-row B, and sew through the next outer-row B with your needle pointing toward the clasp on this end **(c–d)**.

[7] Repeat steps 4–6 for the length of the base. Notice the Bs you are sewing through do not have stitches in them from step 2. End and add thread as needed, but do not end the working thread when you complete the edge.

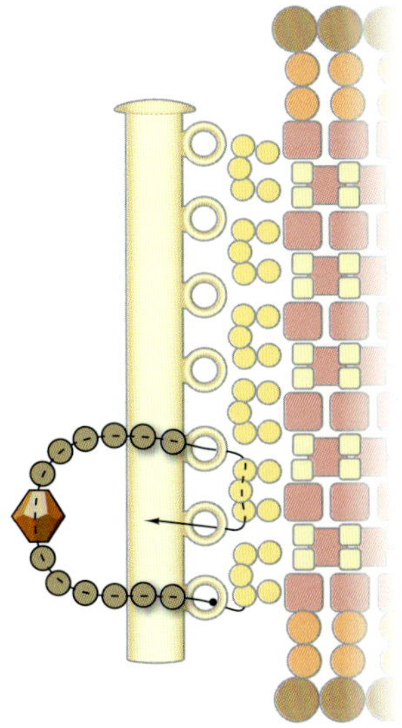

FIGURE 12

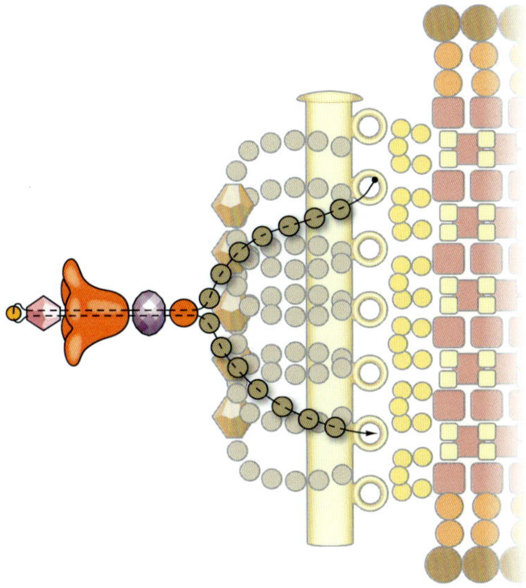

FIGURE 13

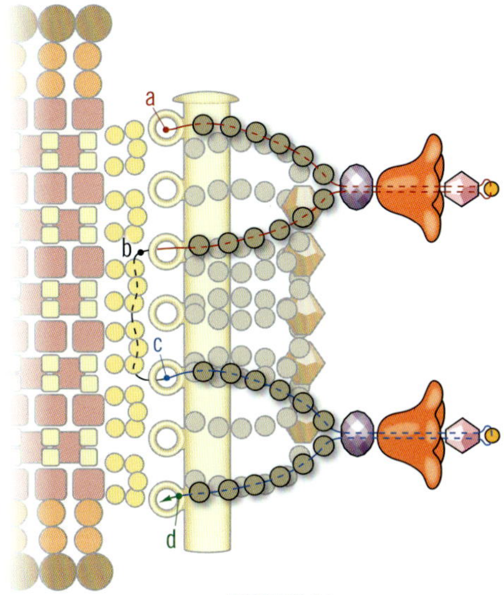

FIGURE 14

Clasp embellishments

For clarity, previous embellishments are not shown in the figures. End and add thread as needed.

Embellishment #1

[1] Sew through the beadwork to exit the edge 8° cylinder in the last row with your needle pointing toward the beadwork **(figure 10, point a)**.

[2] Pick up a 15°, an A, a pearl, and a 15°, and sew back through the pearl and the A. Pick up a 15°, and sew through the next 8° cylinder in the row **(a–b)**. Repeat this step once more **(b–c)**.

[3] Pick up two As, a rondelle, a flower, a 3 mm bicone, and a 15°, and sew back through the bicone, flower, rondelle, and A. Pick up an A, and sew through the next 8° cylinder **(c–d)**.

[4] Repeat step 2 **(d–e)**, and sew up through the end loop of the clasp. These embellishments will not be shown in the remaining figures.

Embellishment #2

[1] Pick up a rondelle, a flower, a 3 mm bicone, and a 15°, and sew back through the first three beads just added and the clasp loop **(figure 11, a–b)**. Pick up three Bs, and sew up through the next clasp loop **(b–c)**.

[2] Pick up an 8° seed bead, a rondelle, a flower, a 3 mm bicone, and a 15°, and sew back through the first four beads just added and the clasp loop. Pick up three Bs, and sew up through the next clasp loop **(c–d)**.

[3] Repeat steps 1 and 2 twice, and then repeat step 1 once more **(d–e)**. Sew through the beadwork to exit up through the end clasp loop. These embellishments will not be shown in the remaining figures.

Embellishment #3

The following embellishment will lie on top of the clasp loops but under the previous embellishments.

[1] Pick up six As, a 4 mm bicone, and six As. Skip a clasp loop, and sew down through the next clasp loop. Continue through the adjacent three Bs on the back of the clasp, sewing toward the skipped clasp loop. Sew up through the skipped clasp loop and between the beaded loop just added and the flower embellishment **(figure 12)**.

[2] Work as in step 1 to add four more beaded loops.

Embellishment #4

With your thread exiting the second clasp loop from the end, pick up seven As, an 8° seed bead, a rondelle, a flower, a 3 mm bicone, and a 15°. Sew back through the bicone, flower, rondelle, and 8°. Pick up seven As, skip three clasp loops, and sew down through the next clasp loop **(figure 13)**. Retrace the thread path through the embellishment to reinforce. End the working thread.

Other end

[1] Add 4 ft. (1.2 m) of thread to the other end of the base, and work "Embellishments #1, #2, and #3."

[2] Sew through the beadwork to exit up through the end clasp loop.

[3] Pick up six As, a rondelle, a flower, a 3 mm bicone, and a 15°. Sew back through the bicone, flower, and rondelle. Pick up six As, skip a clasp loop, and sew down through the next clasp loop **(figure 14, a–b)**.

[4] Sew through the beadwork to exit the fifth clasp loop from the end **(b–c)**, and repeat step 3 **(c–d)**. Retrace the thread path through this embellishment to reinforce. End the thread. ●

DESIGN NOTE:

If desired, you can substitute 3 x 8 mm star-shaped glass flower beads for the Lucite flowers. When adding the star-shaped flowers, replace the 3 mm crystal and 15° seed bead with just an 11° seed bead. Star-shaped glass flowers can be found at www.beadhaven.com or www.fusionbeads.com.

PEYOTE STITCH / LADDER STITCH

Double diamond delights

designed by **Phyllis Dintenfass**

This design was inspired by Coptic crosses The Coptic cross is a widely used symbol in the Coptic, Ethiopian, and Eretrian churches.

a

b

c

d

stepbystep

Small diamond

[1] On 1 yd. (.9 m) of thread, pick up a repeating pattern of three color A 11º seed beads and nine color B 11º cylinder beads four times. Sew through the first three As to form a ring, leaving a 6-in. (15 cm) tail. The Bs in the ring will shift to form the first two rounds as round 3 is added. The As will form the corners.

[2] Work round 3 as follows: Working in tubular peyote stitch (Basics), pick up a B, skip the next B, and sew through the following B. Work four more peyote stitches, and then sew through the next two As without picking up any beads **(photo a)**. Repeat these stitches to complete the round, and step up through the first B on the inside of the ring.

[3] Rounds 4–6 are decrease rounds worked on the inside of the ring.

Round 4: Work four peyote stitches using Bs. Pick up an A, skip the next three As, and sew through the following B in the previous round. Pull tight so the center A in round 1 pops out and forms a corner **(photo b)**. Repeat these stitches to complete the round, and step up through the first B added in this round. The beadwork should now resemble a square.

Round 5: Work three peyote stitches using Bs. Pick up an A, skip the A in the previous round, and sew through the following B, keeping a tight tension **(photo c)**. Repeat these stitches to complete the round, and step up through the first B added in this round.

Round 6: Work two peyote stitches using Bs. Pick up a B, an A, and a B, skip the A in the previous round, and sew through the following B **(photo d)**. Repeat these stitches to complete the round, and step up through the first B added in this round. The beads added in the corners of this round will not lie flat.

[4] The remaining rounds are increase rounds.

Round 7: Work two peyote stitches using Bs, and then sew through the following A and B in the corner without picking up any beads. For the next three sides, work three peyote stitches using Bs, and then

MATERIALS

blue pendant 1⅞ x 2⅛ in. (4.8 x 5.4 cm)

- 2 g 8º seed beads, color C (Czech 105, opaque grey; www.shipwreckbeads.com)
- 3 g 10º cylinder beads, color D (Miyuki DBM0002, dark blue metallic iris; www.beyondbeadery.com)
- 1 g 11º seed beads, color A (Toho F451D, grey mist matte metallic; www.beyondbeadery.com)
- 1 g 11º cylinder beads, color B (Miyuki DB0002, dark blue metallic iris)
- Nymo D or Fireline 6 lb. test
- beading needles, #11 or #12

black/white pendant colors:

- 8º seed beads, color C (Miyuki 592, antique ivory pearl Ceylon; www.auntiesbeads.com)
- 10º cylinder beads, color D (Miyuki DBM310, matte black; www.beyondbeadery.com)
- 11º seed beads, color A (Miyuki 592, antique ivory pearl Ceylon; www.auntiesbeads.com)
- 11º cylinder beads, color B (Miyuki DB310, opaque matte black)

raspberry pendant colors:

- 8º seed beads, color C (Miyuki 452, metallic dark blue iris)
- 10º cylinder beads, color D (Miyuki DBM0012, raspberry metallic; www.beyondbeadery.com)
- 11º seed beads, color A (Miyuki 460, metallic dark raspberry)
- 11º cylinder beads, color B (Miyuki DB254, bronze luster; www.whimbeads.com)

pair of earrings

- 1 g 11º seed beads, color A (Toho F451D, grey mist matte metallic; www.beyondbeadery.com)
- 1 g 11º cylinder beads, color B (Miyuki DBM0002, dark blue metallic iris)
- pair of earring findings
- Nymo D or Fireline 6 lb. test
- beading needles, #11 or #12

DESIGN NOTE:
When connecting the diamonds, you can also start with 1½ yd. (1.4 m) of thread; then instead of ending the thread at each corner, sew through the beadwork to the next corner.

sew through the following A and B in the next corner without adding any beads. Work one peyote stitch using a B to complete the first side, and step up.
Round 8: Work two peyote stitches using Bs, sewing through the existing corner A of round 6 for the second stitch. For each of the next three sides, work four peyote stitches using Bs, sewing through the corner A of round 6 for the fourth stitch. Work two peyote stitches on the first side using Bs, and step up. Sew through the next two Bs to exit the last up-bead on this side.
Round 9: Pick up three As, sew through the first B on the next side, and work three peyote stitches using As. Repeat these stitches to complete the round, and end the working thread and tail (Basics).

Large diamond

[1] On 4 ft. (1.2 m) of thread, pick up a repeating pattern of three color C 8º seed beads and 15 color D 10º cylinder beads four times. Sew through the first three Cs, leaving a 6-in. (15 cm) tail.
[2] The rounds of the large diamond are worked in the same manner as the small diamond.
Round 3: Work eight peyote stitches using Ds, sewing through the corner Cs. Repeat these stitches to complete the round, and step up.
Round 4: On the inside of the ring, work seven peyote stitches using Ds, and pick up a C at the corner. Repeat these stitches to complete the round, and step up.
Round 5: Work six peyote stitches using Ds, and then pick up a C at the corner. Repeat these stitches to complete the round, and step up.
Round 6: Work five peyote stitches using Ds, and then pick up a D, a C, and a D in the corner. Repeat these stitches to complete the round using a tight tension, and step up.
Round 7: Work five peyote stitches using Ds on the first side, and sew through the next C and D in the corner. For the remaining sides, work six peyote stitches using Ds, and sew through the C and D in the corners. Work one more peyote stitch using a D on the first side, and step up.
Round 8: Work five peyote stitches using Ds, sewing through the corner C for the last stitch. For the remaining sides, work seven peyote stitches using Ds, sewing through the corner C for the last stitch. Work two more peyote stitches on the first side using Ds, and step up.
Round 9: Work three peyote stitches using Ds, and then work one stitch using a C. Sew through the C in the corner, and continue through the next D. For the remaining sides, work one peyote stitch using a C, four stitches using Ds, and one stitch using a C. Sew through the corner C, and continue through the next D. To complete the first side, work one peyote stitch using a C and one stitch using a D, and step up. End the working thread and tail.

Connecting the diamonds

The front of each diamond will curve outward, and the back will be flat.
[1] With the back of the large diamond facing up, add 14 in. (36 cm) of thread (Basics) to the beadwork with the needle exiting the C on the inside corner **(photo e)**.
[2] Pick up a B, and sew through the C your thread exited at the start of this step. Retrace the thread path twice, and exit the B.

g

[3] Place the small diamond in the center of the large one with the back facing up. Sew through the center A in a corner of the small diamond **(photo f)**, and then sew through the B again. Retrace the thread path twice, and end the thread.
[4] Repeat steps 1–3 for the remaining corners, but for the last corner add 1 yd. (.9 m) of thread, and do not end the working thread.

Bail

[1] Sew through the beadwork to exit the center C in an outer corner of the large diamond. Work in ladder stitch (Basics) using Cs to make a six-bead ladder, retracing the thread path after each bead is added **(photo g)**.
[2] With your thread exiting the last bead in the ladder, fold the ladder toward the back of the beadwork. Sew through the center C in the corner of the large diamond, and continue through the last C in the ladder again. Retrace the join several times, and exit the corner C.
[3] Pick up a D, and sew through the next C in the ladder. Pick up a D, and sew through the corner C **(photo h)**. Retrace the thread path, and then continue through the next D and C. Repeat these stitches to add Ds along the remainder of the ladder, and end the thread. String the pendant as desired.

Earrings

[1] Work steps 1–4 of "Small diamond," but do not end the working thread.
[2] With the back side of the diamond facing up, sew through the beadwork to exit the nearest up-bead next to the corner As. Pick up three Bs, three As, four Bs, an A, the loop of an earring

h

finding, an A, and four Bs, and sew back through the three As to form a loop. Pick up three Bs, and sew through the nearest up-bead on the other side of the corner As **(photo i)**. Retrace the thread path twice, and end the thread.
[3] Make another earring. ●

i

PEYOTE STITCH / BEAD WEAVING

Edgy elegance

Edge a simple peyote stitch band with cup chain and seed beads for a little bracelet that really rocks.

designed by **Judy Henegar**

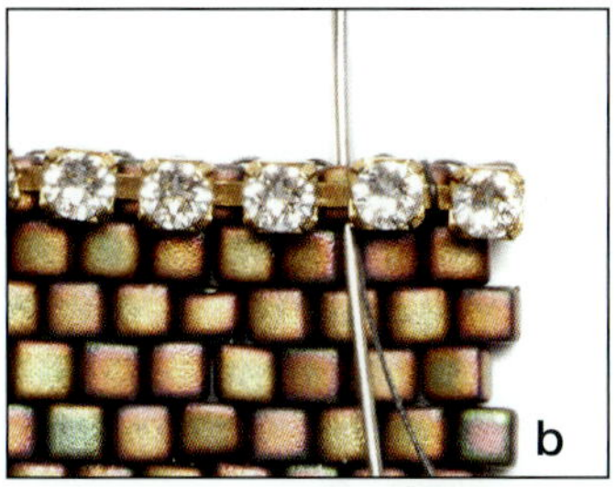

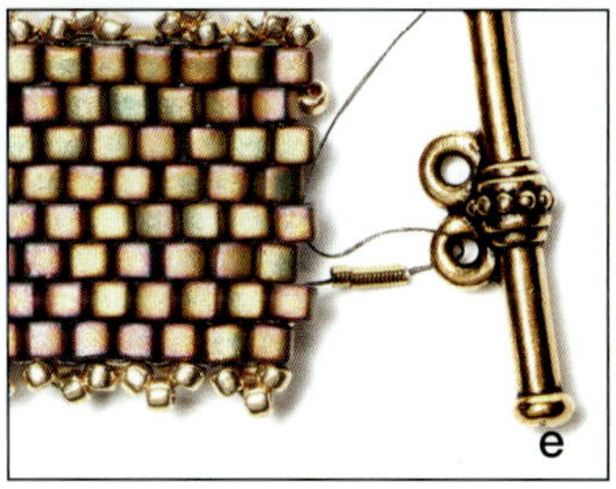

MATERIALS

white bracelet 6½ in. (16.5 cm)

- 7–8 g 1.8 mm cube beads (Miyuki 420, Ceylon white)
- 2 g 15º seed beads (Miyuki 464E, galvanized silver)
- 12–16 in. (30–41 cm) PP14 cup chain (Swarovski, crystal)
- 2-strand clasp
- **4** 4 mm pieces of French wire
- Fireline 6 lb. test
- beading needles, #11
- wire cutters

blue bracelet colors:

- 1.8 mm cube beads (Miyuki 148FR, aqua matte)
- 15º seed beads (Miyuki 464E, galvanized silver)
- PP14 cup chain (Swarovski, crystal AB)

beige bracelet colors:

- 1.5 mm cube beads (Toho 856F, hybrid frost light beige Apollo)
- 15º seed beads (Miyuki 577, candlelight opal gilt lined)
- PP14 cup chain (Swarovski, crystal AB)

stepbystep

Band

On a comfortable length of thread, attach a stop bead (Basics), leaving a 6-in. (15 cm) tail. Pick up eight 1.8 mm cube beads, and work in flat even-count peyote stitch (Basics) to create the desired length band minus ½ in. (1.3 cm) for the clasp. End and add thread (Basics) as needed.

Cup chain edging

[1] Sew through the beadwork to exit the second edge cube from the end of the band with your needle pointing away from the band. Place the cup chain on top of the band along this edge. Your thread should be aligned with the metal tab between the first and second cups in the chain. Sew across the metal tab, and sew through the cube in the same direction **(photo a)**.

[2] Sew through the next cube, sew across the metal tab between the nearest two cups in the chain, and sew through the cube in the same direction **(photo b)**. Repeat this stitch for the length of the edge, tacking the cup chain to the band using an even but not tight tension and stretching the cup chain to its fullest extent. If at any point your thread exits a cube in the middle of a cup, sew through the beadwork to exit the cube aligned with the metal tab between the next two cups in the chain.

[3] Trim the excess cup chain. Count the number of cups in the cup chain you just tacked down, and then trim the second piece of cup chain to the same number of cups. Our 6½-in. (16.5 cm) bracelet has 58 cups in each chain.

[4] Sew through the beadwork to exit the corresponding cube along the opposite edge. Remove the stop bead, and end the tail. With the working thread, repeat steps 1 and 2 to tack the cup chain to the top of the band along this edge. End the working thread.

Seed bead edging

[1] Add a comfortable length of thread to one end of the band, and exit the first edge cube with your needle pointing away from the band.

[2] Pick up three 15º seed beads, and sew through the next edge cube **(photo c)**. Pick up three 15ºs, and sew through the previous edge cube **(photo d)**. Continue through the first three 15ºs picked up in this step, the next cube, and the following cube so that your needle is pointing away from the band.

[3] Repeat step 2 to embellish this edge of the band. Sew through the beadwork to exit the first cube along the other edge of the band, and work as in step 2 along this edge. End the thread.

Clasp

[1] Add 16 in. (41 cm) of thread to one end of the bracelet, and working on the back of the band, exit the first up-bead in the end row with the needle pointing toward the opposite edge.

[2] Pick up a 4 mm length of French wire and a loop of the clasp, and sew through the following up-bead **(photo e)**. Sew through the beadwork to exit the next up-bead. Pick up a 4 mm length of French wire and the other loop of the clasp, and sew through the following up-bead. Retrace the thread path of the clasp connection.

[3] Flip the band to the front, and sew through the beadwork to exit the first up-bead in the end row with the needle pointing toward the opposite edge. Pick up five 15ºs, and sew through the up-bead in the same direction. Sew through the beadwork to exit the next up-bead in the end row, and repeat this stitch. Continue to work in this manner to add a loop of beads around each up-bead in the end row. End the thread.

[4] Repeat steps 1–3 on the other end of the bracelet. ●

DESIGN NOTE:
This project works with 1.5 mm cubes as well as 1.8 mm cubes.

EARN YOUR STRIPES

Learn to create a set of striped beaded beads in three graduated sizes to take advantage of inexpensive wooden bead sets sold in craft stores.

designed by **Anna Elizabeth Draeger**

There are many ways to make beaded beads, but covering existing beads allows you to focus on design rather than worry about structure.

When making these beaded beads, it is best to begin with bead counts that are evenly divisible by four. That's because as you work subsequent rounds, you'll reduce the number of beads per round by half, and then by half again. For example, if you have a starting round of 40 beads, as you begin to work in peyote stitch, your subsequent rounds will drop to 20 beads per round. Then as you get to the decrease rounds, you'll end up working with 10 beads per round.

I find it is best to begin at the center or equator of the bead and work my way out to the ends, alternating sides as I go. This helps keep the beadwork centered on the bead and maintains even tension within the stitches.

stepbystep

Large beaded bead

[1] On 2 yd. (1.8 m) of thread, center 40 11º cylinder beads, and tie them into a ring with a square knot (Basics). These beads will shift to form the first two rounds as you work the next round. Test that the ring of beads fits around the equator of a 16 mm wooden bead. It should be slightly snug to slightly loose.

[2] With one end of the thread, stitch a round of tubular peyote stitch (Basics) using cylinders, and step up through the first bead added in this round. Slip the beadwork around the equator of the wooden bead. If desired, first wrap the equator with a strip of double-sided tape to keep the beadwork in place.

[3] On each side of the equator, work as follows. Alternate sides as you go to keep your tension even:

- One round of 11º cylinders
- Two rounds of color A 15º seed beads
- Two rounds of color B 15º seed beads
- Two rounds of color C 15º seed beads

As you work the rounds of 15ºs, take advantage of the size variations between the beads and select the largest As, average-sized Bs, and smallest Cs.

[4] On each side of the bead, work a round of modified netting to decrease the number of stitches in the round: Pick up five Bs, skip the next C in the previous round, sew through the following C in the round, and sew back through the last B just picked up **(figure 1, a–b)**.

[5] Pick up four Bs, skip the next C in the previous round, sew through the following C in the round, and sew back through the last B picked up **(b–c)**. Repeat this stitch until there is one stitch remaining in the round **(c–d)**.

[6] To complete the round, pick up three Bs, and sew down through the first B picked up in the first stitch of this round. Sew through the corresponding C in the previous round, and sew back through the first three Bs added in the first stitch of this round **(d–e)**.

[7] Pick up an A, and sew through the middle B in the next stitch. Repeat to complete the round, and step up through the first A added in this round **(figure 2, a–b)**.

[8] For the final round, pick up an A, and sew through the next A in the previous round. Repeat to complete the round **(b–c)**, and end the threads (Basics).

Medium beaded bead

Work as in "Large beaded bead" with the following changes:

- In step 1, begin with 1½ yd. (1.4 m) of thread, and use 36 11º cylinders and a 12 mm wooden bead.
- In step 3, omit the first round of cylinders on each side, and then work two rounds with A 15ºs and two rounds with B 15ºs. Do not work two rounds with C 15ºs.
- In steps 4–6, work the round of modified netting with C 15ºs.
- Work step 7 using As.
- In the final round, pick up an A, and sew through the next two As in the previous round. Repeat three times, and then work one more regular peyote stitch.

Note: Because the number of beads in the original ring was not evenly divisible by four, the decrease doesn't work out perfectly. However, since the decrease is at the end of the bead, it is not noticeable without close inspection.

Retrace the thread path through the final round to draw the work in tight around the opening of the bead. End the threads.

Small beaded bead

Work as in "Large beaded bead" with the following changes:

- In step 1, begin with 1 yd. (.9 m) of thread, and use 28 11º cylinders and a 10 mm wooden bead.
- In step 3, skip the first round of cylinders on each side, and then work one round with A 15ºs and two rounds with B 15ºs. Do not work two rounds with C 15ºs.
- In steps 4–6, work the round of modified netting with C 15ºs.
- Work as in step 7 for the final round. Retrace the thread path through the last round, and end the threads.

■	11º cylinder bead
●	15º seed bead, color A
●	15º seed bead, color B
○	15º seed bead, color C

MATERIALS

one beaded bead

- wooden bead (16 mm, 12 mm, or 10 mm)
- 1 g 11º cylinder beads
- 1 g 15º seed beads in each of **3** colors: A, B, C
- double-sided tape (optional)
- Fireline 6 lb. test
- beading needles, #12

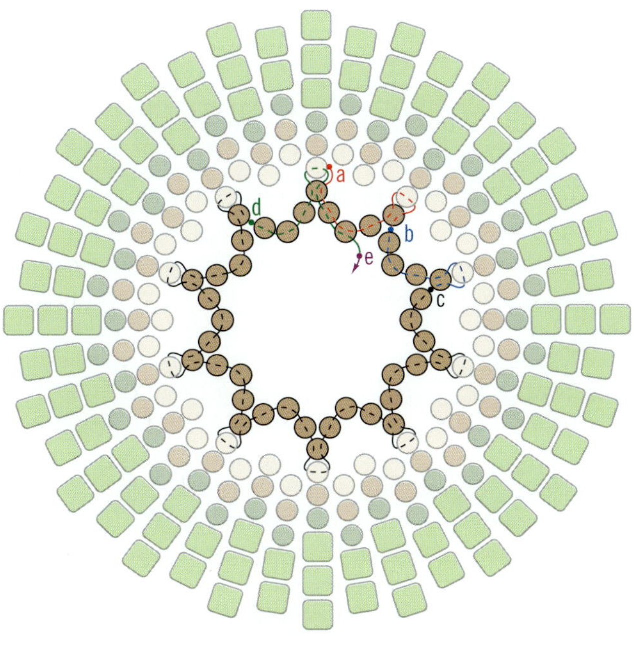

FIGURE 1

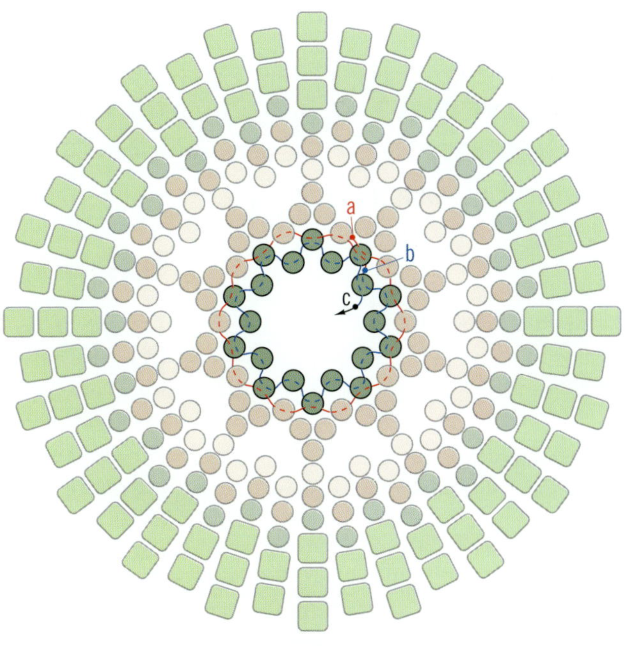

FIGURE 2

PEYOTE STITCH / BEAD WEAVING

Enchanted garden ring

Wrap your finger with an everlasting flower blossom.

designed by
Un-Roen Manarata

Use crystals, pearls, and seed beads to create a stunning flower ring that will catch everyone's attention. Handmade metal clay leaves are a sweet touch but can be replaced with charms trimmed from leaf chain if you prefer.

stepbystep

Large flower petals

[1] On 1 yd. (.9 m) of thread, pick up nine color A 11º seed beads. Sew back through the sixth bead, leaving a 6-in. (15 cm) tail **(figure 1, a–b)**.

[2] Work two flat peyote stitches (Basics) as follows: Pick up an A, skip the fifth A added in step 1, and sew through the fourth A **(b–c)**. Pick up an A, skip the third A added in step 1, and sew through the second A **(c–d)**.

[3] Pick up an A, and sew through the first A added in step 1 so the needle is pointing away from the tail **(d–e)**.

[4] Using As, work four peyote stitches on this side of the beadwork, exiting the end A for the last stitch **(e–f)**.

[5] Using As, work four peyote stitches on this side of the beadwork **(figure 2, a–b)**. Sew through the next two As to exit on the other side of the beadwork **(b–c)**.

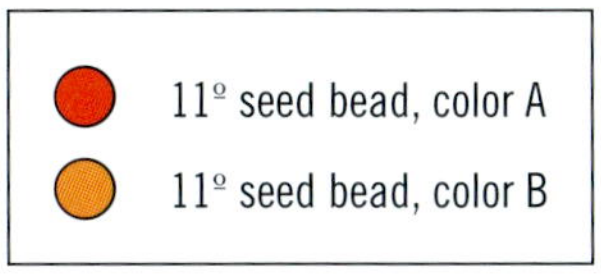

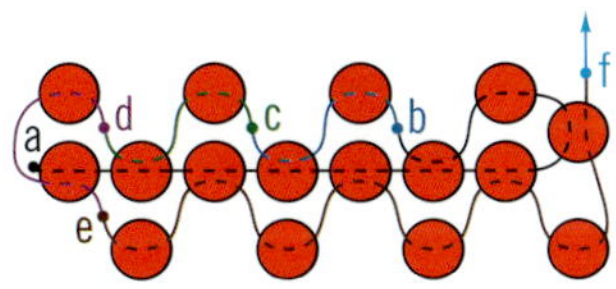

FIGURE 1

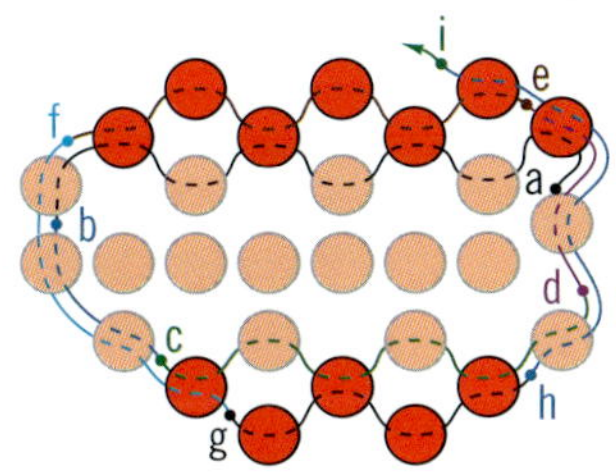

FIGURE 2

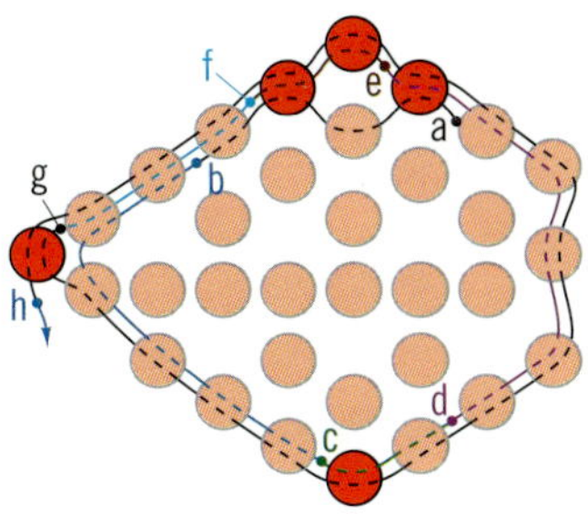

FIGURE 3

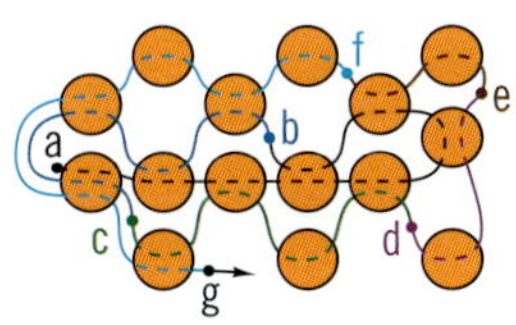

FIGURE 4

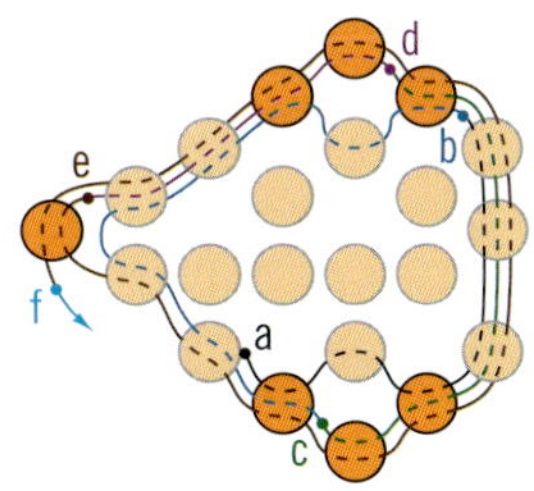

FIGURE 5

[6] Using As, work three peyote stitches on this side of the beadwork **(c–d)**. Sew through the end A and the first A added in the previous step **(d–e)**.

[7] Using As, work three peyote stitches on this side of the beadwork **(e–f)**. Sew through the next four As to exit the first A added in the previous step **(f–g)**.

[8] Using As, work two peyote stitches on this side of the beadwork **(g–h)**. Sew through the next four As to exit the first A added in the previous step **(h–i)**.

[9] Using As, work two peyote stitches on this side of the beadwork **(figure 3, a–b)**. Pull tight to give the beadwork a slight cup shape. Sew through the next six As to exit the first A added in the previous step **(b–c)**.

[10] Work one peyote stitch, and pull tight **(c–d)**. Sew through the next six As to exit the first A added in the previous step **(d–e)**.

[11] Work one peyote stitch, and pull tight **(e–f)**. Sew through the next three As **(f–g)**.

[12] Pick up an A to form the tip of the petal, and sew through all the beads on the outside edge of the beadwork to tighten. Exit the A at the tip of the petal **(g–h)**. End the tail (Basics), but avoid knotting in the three As at the tip of the petal. Do not end the working thread.

[13] Make four more large flower petals, but in step 1 use 24 in. (61 cm) of thread, and in step 12 end the working thread and tail. Avoid knotting in the three As at the tip of the petal.

Small flower petals

Follow the same technique as in “Large flower petals” using color B 11º seed beads:

[1] On 1 yd. (.9 m) of thread, pick up seven Bs. Sew back through the fourth B added, leaving a 6-in. (15 cm) tail **(figure 4, a–b)**.

[2] Work one peyote stitch. Pick up a B, and sew through the first B so the needle is pointing away from the tail **(b–c)**.

[3] Work two peyote stitches **(c–d)**. Pick up a B, and sew through the end B **(d–e)**. Pick up a B, and sew through the next B **(e–f)**.

[4] Work two peyote stitches, and sew through the next two Bs **(f–g)**.

[5] Work two peyote stitches, and sew through the next two Bs **(figure 5, a–b)**.

[6] Work two peyote stitches, and sew through the next four Bs **(b–c)**.

[7] Work one peyote stitch, and sew through the next four Bs **(c–d)**.

MATERIALS

red ring 1¼ in. (3.2 cm)

- crystal pearls (Swarovski, coral)
  2–3 6 mm
  2–3 4 mm
  2–3 3 mm
- **10–14** 4 mm bicone crystals (Swarovski, fire opal AB 2X and fuchsia AB 2X)
- 11º seed beads
  3 g color A (Toho 2113, silver-lined milky pomegranate)
  1 g color B (Toho 365, color-lined raspberry/amber)
- 1 g 15º seed beads (Toho 222, dark copper)
- **3** 9 x 12 mm metal clay leaves
- Fireline 6 lb. test
- beading needles, #11 or #12

purple ring colors:

- 6 mm, 4 mm, and 3 mm crystal pearls (Swarovski, burgundy)
- 4 mm bicone crystals (Swarovski, cyclamen opal and cyclamen opal AB 2X) and 3 mm bicone crystals (Thunder Polish, purple light)
- 11º seed beads
  color A (Miyuki 2005, matte metallic dark raspberry iris)
  color B (Miyuki 2027, matte opaque dusty mauve)
- 15º seed beads (Toho 222, dark copper)
- metal clay leaves

olive ring (Editor’s Notes, p. 42) colors:

- crystal pearls (Swarovski)
  6 mm (vintage gold)
  4 mm and 3 mm (bright gold)
- 4 mm bicone crystals (Swarovski, Indian sapphire champagne) and 3 mm bicone crystals (Swarovski, crystal Verde)
- 11º seed beads
  color A (Miyuki F460R, matte light lime with copper and pink hues; www.beadhaven.com)
  color B (Toho 162C, transparent rainbow topaz; www.agrainofsand.com)
- 15º seed beads (Miyuki 313, cranberry gold luster)
- 3.5 x 9 mm leaf dangles from leaf chain (antique brass)

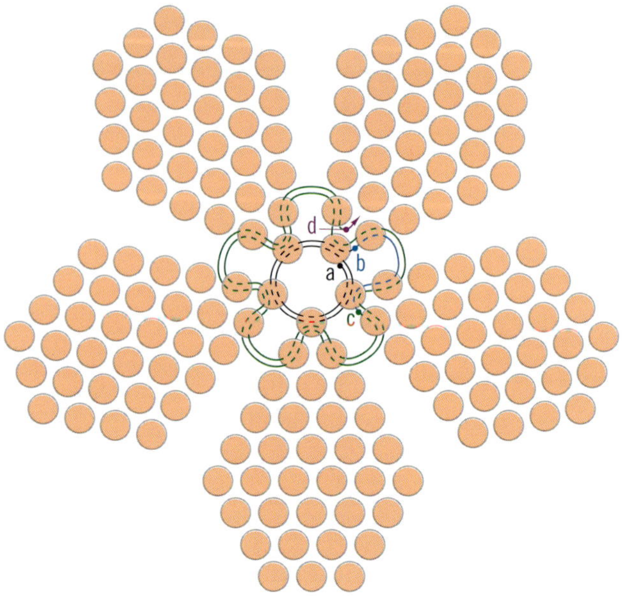

FIGURE 6

DESIGN NOTES:

- In step 3 of "Flower assembly," if the beads are too hard to sew through when retracing the thread path, you can skip this part of the step.
- You can substitute prefabricated metal leaves for the metal clay ones or omit them entirely. Dangles trimmed from a length of leaf chain were used in this olive-colored ring.

[8] Work one peyote stitch, and sew through the next two Bs **(d–e)**.
[9] Pick up a B to form the tip of the petal, and sew through all the outside edge beads to tighten. Exit the B at the tip of the petal **(e–f)**.
[10] End the tail, but avoid knotting in the three Bs at the tip of the petal. Do not end the working thread.
[11] Make four more small flower petals, but in step 1 use 24 in. (61 cm) of thread, and in step 10 end the working thread and tail. Avoid knotting in the three Bs at the tip of the petal.

Flower assembly

[1] Position the large petals as shown in **figure 6**, with the indentation of the petals facing up.
[2] With your working thread exiting the tip A on the first petal, sew through the tip A on each petal. Sew through them all again to pull them into a ring **(figure 6, a–b)**.
[3] Sew through the next A in the same petal, the corresponding A in the next petal, and the following tip A **(b–c)**. Repeat this stitch to complete the round, and retrace the thread path **(c–d)**. Do not end the working thread.
[4] Work as in steps 1–3 to assemble the small petals.

Ring band

[1] On 2 yd. (1.8 m) of thread, attach a stop bead (Basics), leaving a 6-in. (15 cm) tail.
[2] Pick up 12 As, and working in flat even-count peyote stitch (Basics), make a band to fit around your finger. Do not join the ends of the band yet.

Ring assembly

[1] Center the large flower on the ring band with the petals facing up. With the working thread from the flower exiting a tip A, sew straight down through the band, continue through the nearest A in the band, and sew back up through the band. Sew through the next tip A in the flower. Repeat this stitch to complete the round, and sew through to the back of the band. Do not end the working thread.
[2] Position the small flower face up on top of the large flower. Using the working thread from the small flower, secure it to the band as in the previous step, and then sew up through the band and the center of the flowers.
[3] Pick up three 15º seed beads, a 4 mm bicone crystal, and a 15º. Sew back through the 4 mm crystal and three 15ºs. Continue down through the center of the flowers and the band. Cross over a thread bridge in the band, and sew back up through the band and center of the flowers. Repeat this stitch to add five to seven crystals in the flower center.
[4] Add 4 mm bicone crystals, 6 mm pearls, 4 mm pearls, and 3 mm pearls under the large flower petals as desired, attaching them as in the previous step. Additional 15ºs can be added to vary the lengths.
[5] To add leaves: Pick up three or four 15ºs, a leaf, and three or four 15ºs. Sew down through the band to attach as before. If needed, end the working thread from the small flower, and switch to the working thread from the large flower to finish the embellishments. End both flower threads.
[6] Zip up (Basics) the ends of the ring band, and end the threads. ●

PEYOTE STITCH / BEAD EMBROIDERY

Beaded bangle trio

Make a coordinating set of bangles to stack or wear alone.

designed by **Marla Salezze**

MATERIALS

all bangles

- Fireline 6 lb. test
- beading needles, #12

three-bezel bangle

- large flat bezel bangle (gold)*
- **3** 12 mm rivolis (Swarovski, amethyst)
- 2 g 11º cylinder beads (Miyuki DB869, matte mauve AB)
- 1 g 15º seed beads (Toho 166B, transparent amethyst rainbow)
- E6000 adhesive

channel bangle

- channel bracelet bangle (gold)*
- 2 g 11º cylinder beads in each of **2** colors:
  A (Miyuki DB004, purple iris)
  B (Miyuki DB869, matte mauve AB)

aster charm bangle

- large flat bangle bracelet (gold)*
- large aster metal embellishment*
- **1** 12 mm rivoli (Swarovski, amethyst)
- **18** 3 x 4 mm faceted rondelles (Chinese, purple opal AB)
- 2 g 11º cylinder beads (Miyuki DB869, matte mauve AB)
- 1 g 15º seed beads (Toho 166B, transparent amethyst rainbow)
- Lacy's Stiff Stuff beading foundation
- Ultrasuede
- E6000 adhesive

PATTERN

Use a single color palette to unify three different pre-fab bangles while employing several stitching techniques. The result is a set of bracelets you can mix and match however you choose.

stepby**step**

Three-bezel bangle

[1] On 1 yd. (.9 m) of thread, pick up 32 11º cylinder beads. Tie them into a ring with a square knot (Basics), leaving a 12-in. (30 cm) tail, and sew through the first few beads in the ring.

[2] Working in tubular peyote stitch (Basics), work two rounds using cylinder beads. Step up at the end of each round.

[3] Work two rounds using 15º seed beads, pulling tight so the beadwork cups.

[4] Sew through to the other edge of the cup (the first round of cylinders). Place a 12 mm rivoli into the beadwork, and work two rounds using 15ºs on this edge. Pull tight to secure the rivoli in the bezel. End the working thread and tail (Basics).

[5] Repeat steps 1–4 to complete a total of three bezeled rivolis.

[6] Apply a dab of E6000 adhesive to a flat bezel indent on the bangle, and affix a bezeled rivoli. Repeat with the remaining rivolis, and let dry completely.

Channel bangle

[1] On a comfortable length of thread, pick up six color A 11º cylinder beads, leaving a 6-in. (15 cm) tail.

[2] Working in flat even-count peyote stitch (Basics) and using color A and B cylinders, follow the **pattern** to make a band long enough to wrap around the bangle. The band will not end with an even number of pattern repeats. End and add thread (Basics) as needed.

[3] Wrap the band around the bangle, and zip up the ends (Basics). End the working thread and tail.

Aster charm bangle

[1] Cut a 2 x 2-in. (5 x 5 cm) piece of Lacy's Stiff Stuff beading foundation. Fold the foundation in half, and cut a small (4 mm) slit in the middle, perpendicular to the fold. Unfold and refold the foundation in the other direction, and cut another small slit perpendicular to the fold, creating an X in the middle of the foundation. Apply a small dab of E6000 adhesive on the back side of the 12 mm rivoli, and press the rivoli into the X in the foundation, applying pressure so the rivoli lies flush. Allow to dry completely.

[2] At the end of 1 yd. (.9 m) of thread, tie an overhand knot (Basics), and sew up

The flip side of the dangle features a cute gold aster charm.

through the foundation from back to front next to the rivoli. Using 11º cylinder beads, work a round of beaded backstitch (Basics), picking up two beads per stitch and using an even number of cylinders. Sew through the first cylinder in the round.

[3] Using cylinders, work one round of tubular peyote stitch (Basics) on top of the round of backstitch. Step up through the first bead added in this round.

[4] Using 15º seed beads, work one more round of tubular peyote, pulling snug so the 15ºs begin to cover the edge of the rivoli. Sew through the beadwork and down through the foundation.

[5] Sew back up through the foundation, exiting next to the bezeled rivoli. Using 3 x 4 mm rondelles, work a round of beaded backstitch next to the round of cylinders. Sew down through the foundation.

[6] Sew up through the foundation to exit between two rondelles between the row of rondelles and cylinders. Pick up seven 15ºs, and sew through the foundation between the rondelles along the outer edge. Repeat this stitch between each pair of rondelles. End the thread.

[7] Trim the foundation close to the beadwork, being careful to avoid cutting any threads. Apply E6000 adhesive to the back of the foundation, and place it on the Ultrasuede, but don't get glue near the edge. Trim the Ultrasuede flush with the foundation.

[8] Tie an overhand knot at the end of 2 ft. (61 cm) of thread. Sew between the foundation and Ultrasuede, exiting the front surface next to the beadwork.

[9] Pick up two 15ºs, and sew down through the foundation and the Ultrasuede. Sew back up through both layers and the second 15º picked up.

[10] Pick up a 15º, and sew down through both layers. Sew back up through both layers and the 15º just added. Repeat this stitch around the perimeter. After adding the last bead, sew down through the first 15º in the round, the foundation, and the Ultrasuede. Sew back through the first 15º.

[11] Pick up 15 15ºs, loop around the bangle, and sew back through the 15º your thread exited at the start of this step. Retrace the thread path, and sew through an adjacent 15º in the edging.

[12] Repeat step 11 twice, and end the thread.

[13] Apply a dab of E6000 adhesive to the back of the aster embellishment, and adhere it to the center of the Ultrasuede. Allow to dry completely. ●

PEYOTE STITCH / FRINGE

Vintage blooms necklace

Use leftover beads to bring a channeled metal pendant into full blossom.

designed by **Amelia Brock**

stepbystep

Necklace

[1] On a comfortable length of thread, attach a stop bead (Basics), leaving a 6-in. (15 cm) tail.

[2] Pick up 16 11º cylinder beads, and work in flat even-count peyote stitch (Basics) to make a band that is long enough to wrap around the channel pendant and overlap by two rows (about 46–50 rows) (photo a). The band will shorten up later when you add the embellishments. As you stitch, make sure the band will fit properly within the channel. End and add thread (Basics) as needed.

[3] Embellish one surface of the peyote band as desired with the Lucite flowers, pressed glass leaves, crystals, pearls, and bead caps. Begin by attaching the largest Lucite flowers first: Exit the peyote band in the desired place. Pick up a Lucite flower, a 3 or 4 mm crystal or pearl, and a 15º seed bead. Skip the 15º, and sew back through the remaining beads and into the peyote band (photo b).

[4] Continue adding Lucite flowers, leaves, and bead caps, positioning them closer together than you normally would on a flat band (see "Embellishment tips" for design suggestions). As you work, wrap the band around the channel pendant on occasion to see how the embellishments will lie.

[5] After the flowers, leaves, and bead caps have all been attached, fill in between them with additional pearls and crystals: Pick up a pearl or crystal and a 15º, and sew back through the pearl or crystal and into the peyote band (photo c).

[6] When the band is fully embellished, wrap it around the channel pendant, and zip up (Basics) the end rows. End the working thread. Remove the stop bead, and end the tail.

[7] Open an 11 mm jump ring (Basics), and attach the pendant to the middle link of a 20-in. (51 cm) piece of chain.

[8] Open a 6 mm jump ring, and attach half of the clasp to an end chain link. Repeat at the other end of the chain.

[9] If desired, cut 24 in. (61 cm) of yarn, and tie it to an end jump ring. Weave the yarn through the chain, and tie it to the opposite end jump ring.

a

b

Earrings

[1] On a head pin, string a 4 mm bicone crystal, and make a plain loop (Basics). On an eye pin, string a 5 x 9 mm Lucite flower, and make a plain loop. On another eye pin, string a 7 x 12 mm Lucite flower, and make a plain loop **(photo d)**.

[2] Open the loop (Basics) above the crystal, and attach it to the loop below the 5 x 9 mm flower. Open the loop above the 5 x 9 mm flower, and attach it to the loop below the 7 x 12 mm flower. Open the loop above the 7 x 12 mm flower, and attach it to an earring finding **(photo e)**.

[3] Make another earring. ●

c

d

e

EMBELLISHMENT TIPS

Stack flowers for dimension.

Make longer stamen with several alternating cylinders and 15ºs.

Attach the metal bead caps the same way as the Lucite flowers.

• Attach the largest Lucite flowers first, and then go back and add the smaller ones.

• As you add the embellishments, the peyote band will curl. Don't worry, though – it will still fit around the channel pendant.

To add leaves, pick up a 15º, a leaf, and a 15º, and sew back into the peyote band.

Add loops of alternating seed and cylinder beads between flowers.

MATERIALS

pendant 1½ in. (3.8 cm)

- **1** 37 x 15 mm channel pendant (copper)*
- **5** 5 x 10 mm pressed glass leaf beads, top-drilled
- **11–15** 6–14 mm Lucite flowers, assorted shapes and colors
- **8–12** 3–6 mm bicone crystals, assorted colors
- **8–12** 2–6 mm crystal pearls, assorted colors
- 3–4 g 11º cylinder beads (Miyuki DB0380, opaque matte olive rose)
- 1–2 g 15º seed beads (Miyuki 364, color-lined dusty rose)
- **5** 8 mm etched daisy bead caps (copper)*
- 20 in. (51 cm) textured cable chain, 9 x 6 mm links (copper)*
- copper jump rings*
  1 11 mm large rope circle
  1 17 mm grande rope circle (to act as a toggle ring)
  2 6 mm textured circles
- twig toggle bar (copper)*
- nylon beading thread, size D, or Fireline 6 lb. test
- beading needles, #11 or #12
- **2** pairs of chainnose pliers
- textured yarn to coordinate with Lucite flowers

pair of earrings

- **2** 7 x 12 mm Lucite flowers
- **2** 5 x 9 mm Lucite flowers
- **2** 4 mm bicone crystals
- **2** 1½-in. (3.8 cm) head pins
- **4** 1½-in. (3.8 cm) eye pins
- pair of earring findings
- **2** pairs of chainnose pliers
- roundnose pliers
- wire cutters

TUBULAR BRICK STITCH / STRINGING / BEAD EMBROIDERY

Corkscrew bangle

Work up a spiraling bangle in tubular brick stitch, and finish with a decorative embroidered centerpiece or fancy clasp.

designed by **Marla Salezze**

stepbystep

Brick stitch tube

[1] On a comfortable length of thread, attach a stop bead (Basics), leaving a 6-in. (15 cm) tail.

[2] Work in ladder stitch (Basics) to make a four-bead ladder using a color A 8º seed bead, a color B 8º seed bead, an A, and a B. Form the ladder into a ring (Basics), and zigzag back through the beads to reinforce the ring. End with your thread exiting an A. This is the first round of the tube.

[3] Working in modified tubular brick stitch, pick up an A and a B, sew under the next thread bridge in the previous round from back to front, and continue up through the B just added (**figure 1, a–b**).

[4] Pick up an A, sew under the next thread bridge, and continue up through the same A (**b–c**).

[5] Pick up a B, sew under the next thread bridge, and continue up through the same B (**c–d**). Sew down through the first A added in this round and back up through the B just added (**d–e**) to complete round two.

[6] Pick up an A and a B, skip the next thread bridge between the first and last 8ºs added in the previous round, and sew under the following thread bridge. Continue back up through the B just added (**figure 2, a–b**).

[7] Repeat steps 4 and 5 (**b–c**) to complete round three.

[8] Repeat steps 6 and 7 until the beadwork is the desired length. If you're using an embroidered centerpiece, the beadwork should fit around the widest part of your hand minus 1¼ in. (3.2 cm) for the embroidered centerpiece. If you're using a clasp, the beadwork should be the desired bracelet length less the size of the clasp. End and add thread (Basics) as needed.

[9] Work a ladder stitch thread path through the last round, and end the working thread. Remove the stop bead, and end the tail.

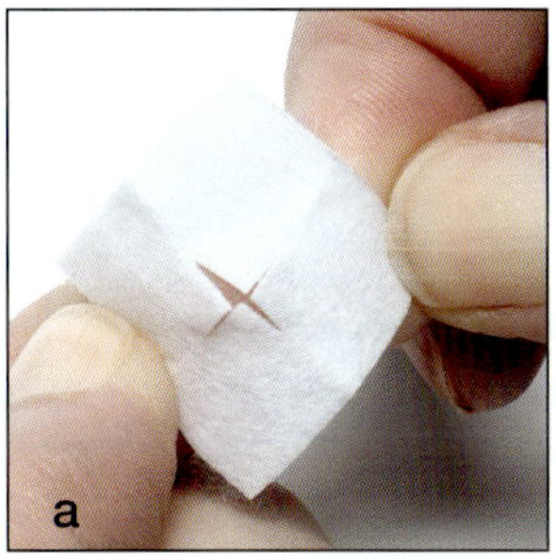

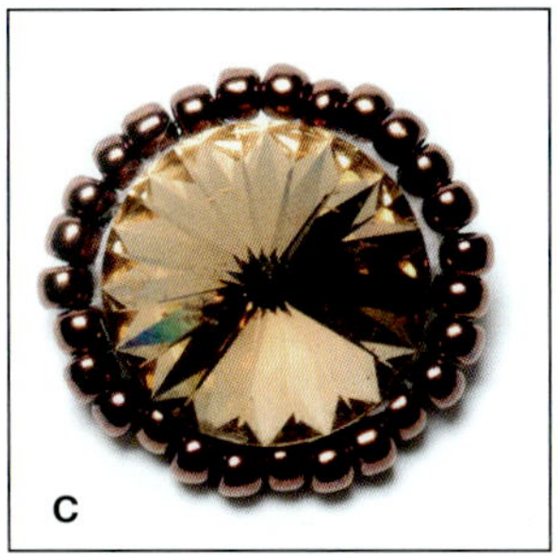

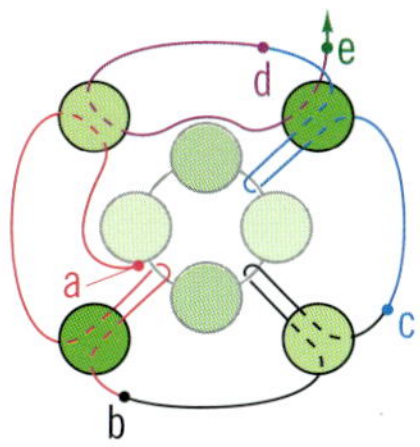

FIGURE 1

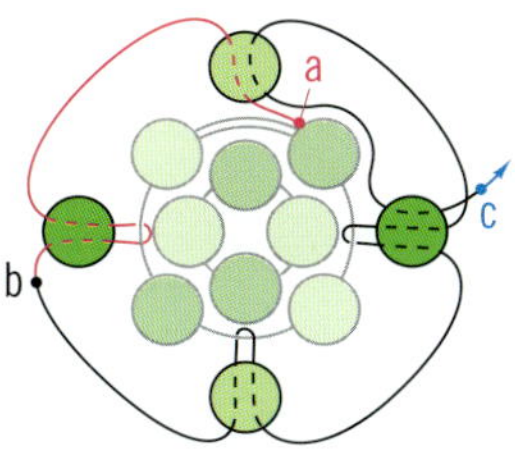

FIGURE 2

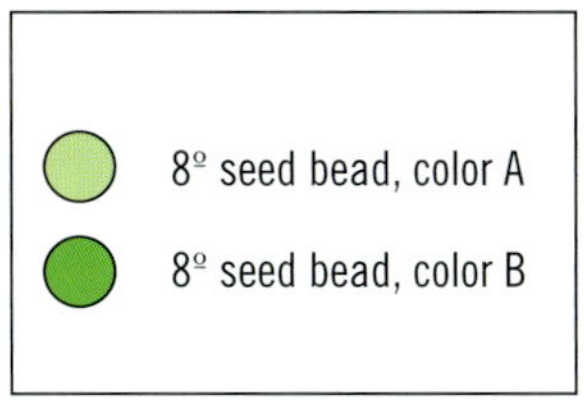

Embroidered centerpiece

[1] Cut an X in the center of a 1 x 1-in. (2.5 x 2.5 cm) square of beading foundation **(photo a)**. Apply glue to the back of the rivoli, and place the point into the X in the foundation. Allow the glue to dry, and then trim the foundation close to the edge of the rivoli **(photo b)**.

[2] Tie an overhand knot (Basics) at the end of 18 in. (46 cm) of thread. Sew through the foundation to exit near the edge of the rivoli. Using 11° seed beads, work a round of beaded backstitch (Basics), and end the thread by tying a knot on the back of the foundation **(photo c)**.

[3] Glue the embroidered component into the mini pendant finding, and set aside to dry.

Assembly

[1] Cut 10 in. (25 cm) of beading wire. On one end, string a crimp bead and a loop of the mini pendant finding or clasp. Go back through the crimp bead, leaving a short tail. With crimping pliers, crimp the crimp bead (Basics), and trim the tail short.

[2] String a bead cap, the brick stitch tube, a bead cap, a crimp bead, and the other loop of the mini pendant finding or clasp. Go back through the crimp bead, and crimp it as before.

[3] Using chainnose or crimping pliers, close a crimp cover over each crimp.

DESIGN NOTE:
To add a clasp to the bangle, replace the embroidered centerpiece with a decorative box clasp.

MATERIALS

green bangle 2½-in. (6.4 cm) inside diameter

- **1** 12 mm rivoli (Swarovski, olivine)
- 3 g 8° seed beads in each of **2** colors: A (Toho 952, rainbow light topaz/sea foam lined; www.beadaholique.com), B (Miyuki 459, metallic olive; www.auntiesbeads.com)
- 1 g 11° seed beads (Toho 952, rainbow light topaz/sea foam lined; www.beadaholique.com)
- **1** 25 x 20 mm ornate mini pendant circle double-loop finding by Nunn Design (PE2370, gold; www.fusionbeads.com)
- **2** 9 mm crown bead caps by Nunn Design (BM3309, gold; www.fusionbeads.com)
- **2** 2 mm crimp beads
- **2** 3 mm crimp covers (gold)
- Accu-Flex beading wire, .019 (Dijon gold)
- Nymo D thread (olive)
- beading needles, #10
- 1 x 1-in. (2.5 x 2.5 cm) square of Lacy's Stiff Stuff beading foundation
- E6000 adhesive
- crimping pliers
- chainnose pliers (optional)
- wire cutters

orange bangle colors:

- 8° seed beads in **2** colors: A (Miyuki 1003, silver-lined gold AB; www.auntiesbeads.com), B (Miyuki 329, gold-lustered African sunset; www.beadaholique.com)
- **1** 10 mm Corona clasp (gold with red magma chessboard crystal; www.alacarteclasps.com)
- Beadalon beading wire, .018 (gold)
- Fireline 6 lb. test

And the bead goes on

Cover plain wooden beads with beautiful patterns in right-angle weave and peyote stitch to create miniature works of art.

designed by **Pamela Jensen**

stepbystep

Center chain

[1] On 2 yd. (1.8 m) of thread, center four color A 11º seed beads, and sew through the first three As again to form a ring **(figure 1, a–b)**. This is the first right-angle weave stitch. Wrap the tail around a bobbin or piece of cardboard.

[2] Work stitches in right-angle weave (Basics) using the following beads:

Stitch 2: three color B 11º seed beads **(b–c)**.
Stitch 3: B, A, B **(c–d)**.
Stitch 4: three As **(d–e)**.
Stitch 5: three As **(e–f)**.

[3] Repeat step 2 four times **(f–g)**. You will have a total of 21 right-angle weave stitches.

[4] Work two more stitches using the following beads **(g–h)**:

Stitch 22: three Bs.
Stitch 23: B, A, B.

[5] To join: Making sure the chain is not twisted, pick up an A, sew through the first A on the other end of the chain, pick up an A, and sew through the A your thread exited at the start of this step **(h–i)**. Retrace the thread path through the join. You now have 24 right-angle weave stitches in the center chain.

Peyote band

[1] Work a round of peyote stitch (Basics) off of the edge beads in the center chain:
Round 1: Sew through the

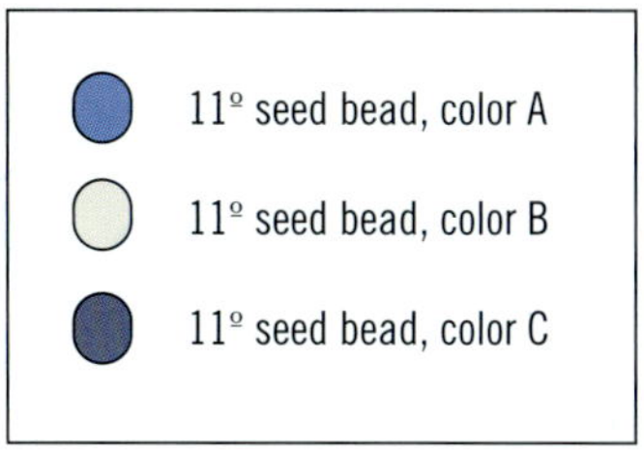

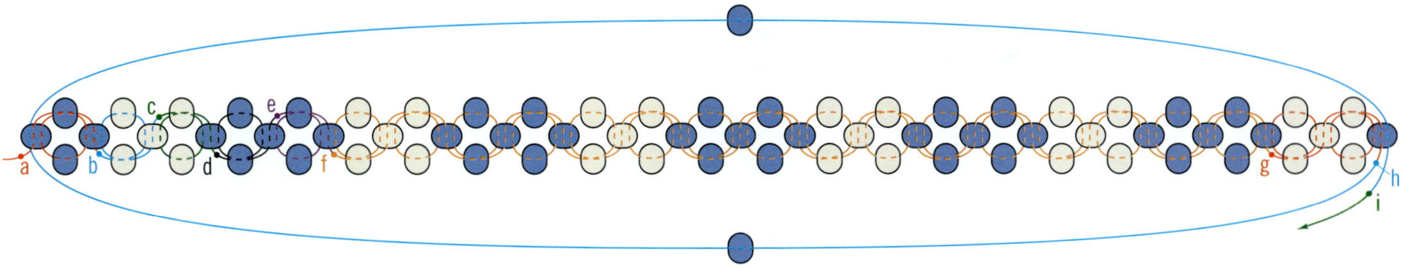

FIGURE 1

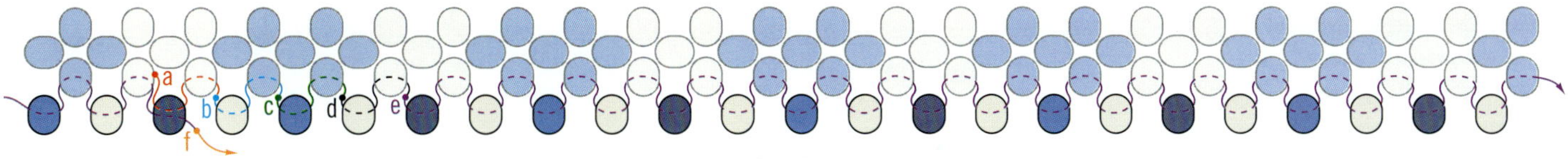

FIGURE 2

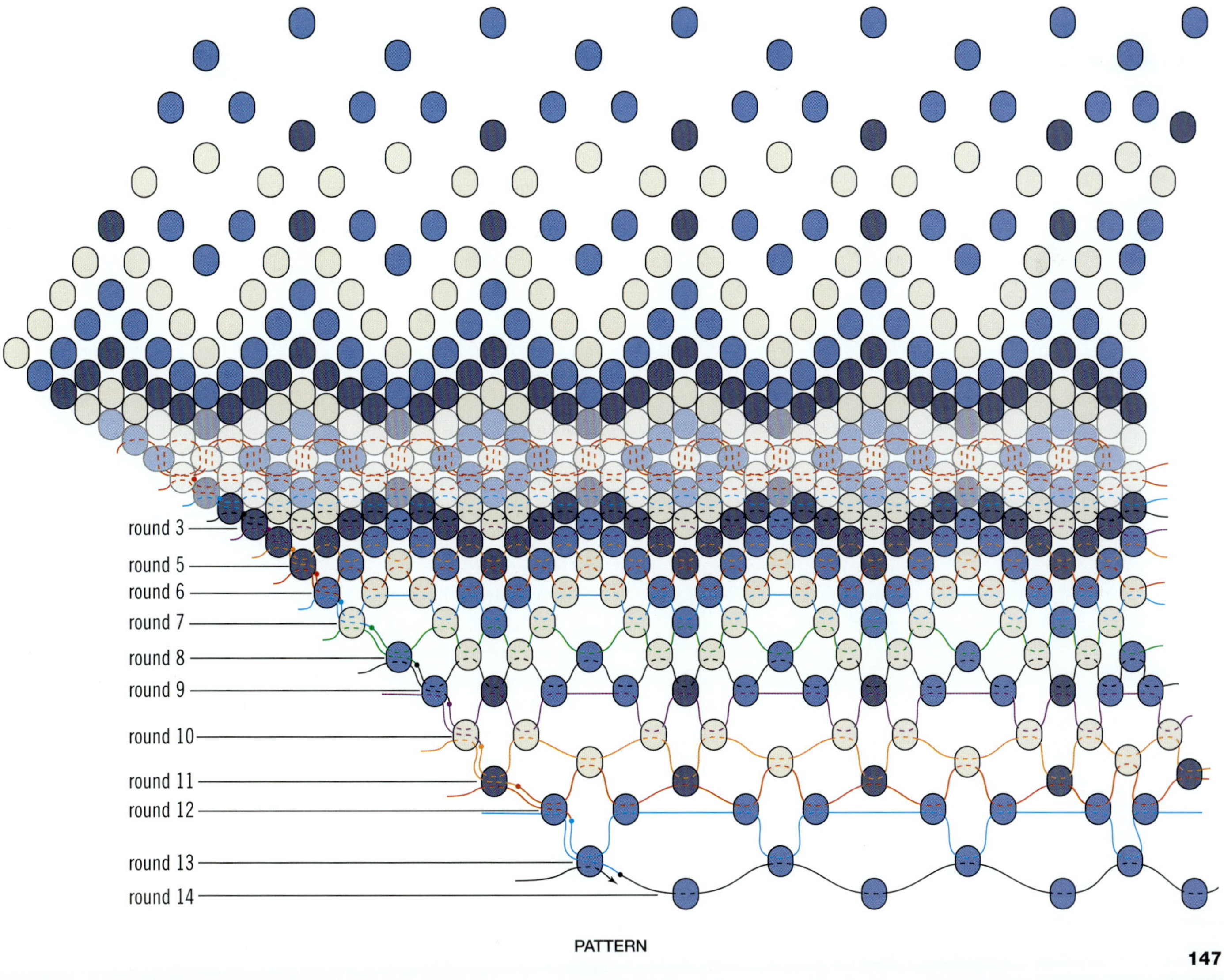

PATTERN

MATERIALS

22–24 mm beaded bead

- **1** 22 mm wooden bead
- 2–3 g 11º Czech seed beads in each of **3** colors: A, B, C
- Fireline 6 lb. test
- beading needles, #10 or #11
- bobbin or piece of cardboard

DESIGN NOTES:

- **By interchanging the As, Bs, and Cs, you can create a set of coordinating beads.**
- **Go online to www. BeadAndButton. com/freeprojects to download an additional pattern and a blank pattern you can color in to make your own design!**
- **Check your local craft store for inexpensive wooden beads, and then use small amounts of Czech seed beads from your stash to keep costs low.**

Download a blank pattern at www. BeadAndButton.com/ freeprojects to design your own patterned beaded beads!

beadwork to exit an edge B in the second right-angle weave stitch of the center chain. Work a stitch with a color C 11º seed bead **(figure 2, a–b)**, a B **(b–c)**, an A **(c–d)**, and a B **(d–e)**. Repeat these stitches five times to complete the round, and step up through the first C **(e–f)**.

[2] Unwind the tail from the bobbin. Thread a needle on the tail, and repeat step 1 along the other edge of the center chain.

[3] Center the beadwork on a wooden bead. For all subsequent rounds: Work peyote stitches with the indicated sequence of beads, repeating each sequence to complete the round and stepping up at the end of each round. Work each round with one needle, and then work the same round with the other needle along the other edge before moving on to the next round. Refer to the **pattern** on p. 147 as needed.

Round 2: C, B, B, C.

Round 3: C, B, C, A.

Round 4: C, C, A, A.

Round 5: C, A, B, A.

Round 6: A, B, B, A.

Round 7 is a decrease round, and the sequence is worked as follows: Work a stitch with a B, sewing through the next two Bs. Work a stitch with a B. Work a stitch with an A.

Round 8: A (over the decrease), B, B.

Round 9: A, C, A.

Round 10 is a decrease round, and the sequence is worked as follows: Pick up a B, and sew through the C in the previous round. Pick up a B, and sew through the next two As in the previous round. You will now have 12 beads per round.

Round 11: C, B (over the decrease).

Round 12: Work a round of peyote using As.

Round 13 is a decrease round, and is worked as follows: Pick up an A, and sew through the next two As. You will now have six As per round.

Round 14: Work a round of peyote using As. Retrace the thread path through the beads in this round, and end the threads (Basics). ●

NETTING / BEAD WEAVING

Timeless lace collar

Stitch a base of SuperDuos to support a uniquely shaped necklace of seed beads, crystals, and pearls.

designed by **Svetlana Chernitsky**

MATERIALS

necklace 16 in. (41 cm) plus extender chain

- **62** 6 mm crystal pearls (Swarovski, burgundy)
- **60** 4 mm fire-polished beads (amethyst luster; www.artbeads.com)
- **124** 3 mm bicone crystals (Swarovski, vintage rose)
- 19 g 2.5 x 5 mm SuperDuo beads (01640, silky gold iris; www.funkyhannahs.com)
- **2** 8º seed beads (Toho 705, matte raku blue/plum iris; www.artbeads.com)
- 11º seed beads
  2 g color A (Toho 31, silver-lined rosaline; www.beadaholique.com)
  11 g color B (Toho 222, dark bronze)
- lobster claw clasp
- 2–3-in. (5–7.6 cm) extender chain
- **2** 6 mm jump rings
- Fireline 6 lb. test
- beading needles, #11
- **2** pairs of chainnose, flatnose, and/or bentnose pliers

stepbystep

Base

[1] On 2½ yd. (2.2 m) of thread, attach a stop bead (Basics), leaving a 6-in. (15 cm) tail.

[2] Pick up four 2.5 x 5 mm SuperDuo beads, a 3 mm bicone crystal, a color A 11º seed bead, a crystal, and a SuperDuo, and sew through the available hole of the third SuperDuo added **(figure 1, a–b)**. Pick up a SuperDuo, and sew through the available hole of the first SuperDuo added **(b–c)**.

[3] Pick up an A and a SuperDuo, and sew through the available hole of the last SuperDuo added in the previous step **(c–d)**. Pick up a SuperDuo, and sew through the available hole of the next SuperDuo **(d–e)**.

[4] Pick up a crystal, an A, a crystal, and a SuperDuo, and sew through the available hole of the last SuperDuo added in the previous step **(e–f)**. Pick up a SuperDuo, and sew through the available hole of the next SuperDuo **(f–g)**.

[5] Repeat steps 3 and 4 using a tight tension for the desired length necklace, leaving ¾ in. (1.9 cm) for the clasp and ending with an even number of crystal picots. Our 16-in. (41 cm) base has 62 crystal picots.

[6] To complete this end, pick up an A, and sew through the available hole of the next SuperDuo **(figure 2, a–b)**.

[7] Pick up an 8º seed bead and five color B 11º seed beads, and sew through the 8º again to form a loop, snugging the beads close to the beadwork. Retrace the thread path through the loop, and sew through the available hole of the next SuperDuo **(b–c)**.

[8] Sew through the beads on the end of the base as shown **(c–d)**, and end the working thread and tail (Basics).

Pearl embellishment

[1] Add a comfortable length of thread to the end of the base with the loop of Bs, and exit the A at the center of the last crystal picot with the needle pointing toward the other end of the base **(figure 3, point a)**.

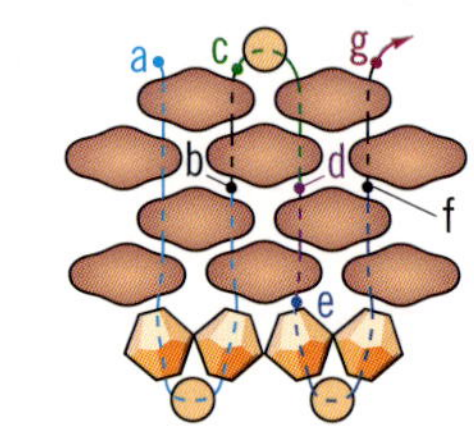

FIGURE 1

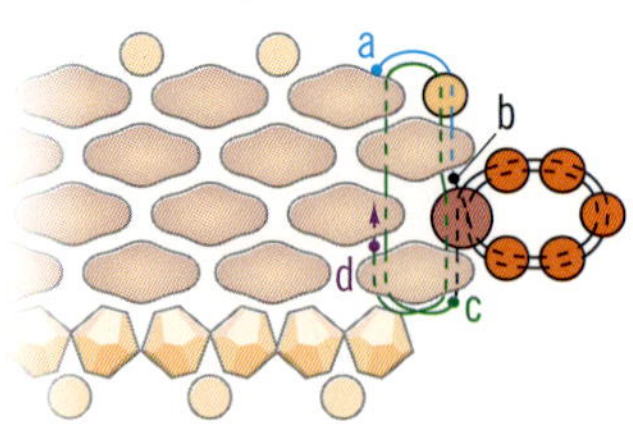

FIGURE 2

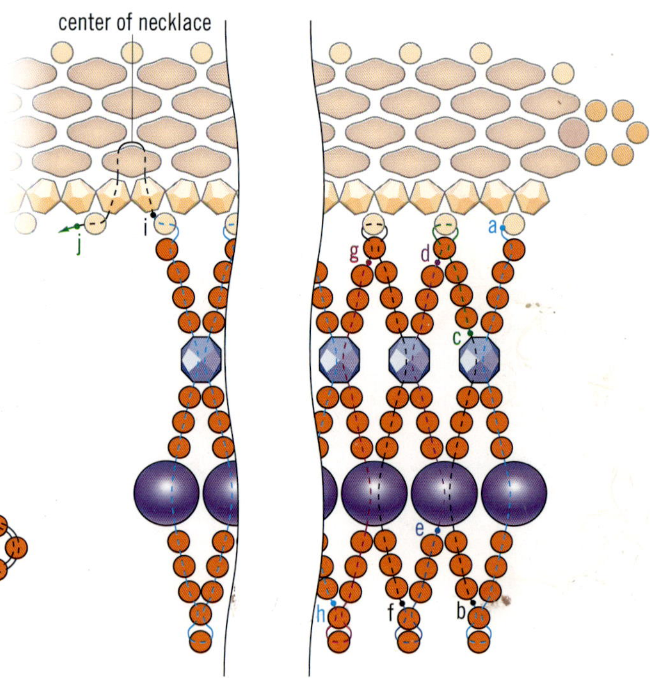

FIGURE 3

[2] Pick up four Bs, a 4 mm fire-polished bead, three Bs, a 6 mm pearl, and five Bs. Sew back through the second-to-last B just added **(a–b)**.
[3] Pick up three Bs, a pearl, and three Bs, and sew through the fire-polished bead added in the previous step **(b–c)**. Pick up four Bs, sew through the A at the center of the next crystal picot, and continue back through the last B added **(c–d)**.
[4] Pick up three Bs, a fire-polished bead, and three Bs, and sew through the last pearl added **(d–e)**. Pick up five Bs, and sew back through the second-to-last B just added **(e–f)**.
[5] Repeat steps 3 **(f–g)** and 4 **(g–h)** for half of the crystal picots in your base. We added the pearl embellishment to 31 crystal picots in our necklace. After sewing through the A at the center of the last picot on this half of the base, do not sew back through the last B added **(h–i)**.
[6] Sew up through the next crystal and the closest hole of the following SuperDuo. Continue down through the other hole of the same SuperDuo, the next crystal, and the following A **(i–j)**.
[7] Repeat steps 2–5 for the remainder of the necklace.
[8] Sew through the next crystal and the following four SuperDuos as shown **(figure 4, a–b)**.
[9] Repeat steps 6–8 of "Base" to complete this end **(b–c)**, and end the thread.
[10] Open a jump ring (Basics), and attach the lobster claw clasp to the loop on one end of the base. Open the other jump ring, and attach the extender chain to the loop on the other end of the base. ●

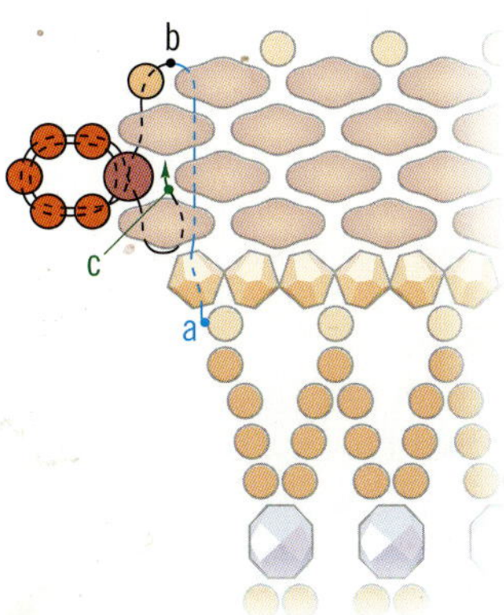

FIGURE 4

PEYOTE STITCH / NETTING

Rivoli rendezvous

designed by **Svetlana Chernitsky**

Crystal rivolis shine when surrounded by SuperDuos and bicones in these earrings and coordinating pendant.

stepbystep

Earrings

Bezel front

[1] Attach a stop bead (Basics) at the center of 2 yd. (1.8 m) of thread. With one end of the thread, pick up 36 11º cylinder beads, and sew through the first six beads again to form a ring **(figure 1, a–b)**. These beads will shift to form rounds 1 and 2 as the next round is added.

[2] Work rounds of tubular peyote stitch (Basics) as follows:

Round 3: Work a round using cylinders, and step up **(b–c)**.

Rounds 4 and 5: Work both rounds using 15º seed beads and a tight tension so the beadwork cups, stepping up at the end of each round **(figure 2)**.

Round 6: Pick up a 15º, and sew through the next 15º in round 5, the following 15º in round 4, and the next 15º in round 5. Repeat this stitch to complete the round **(figure 3)**. Tie a couple of half-hitch knots (Basics), but do not end the thread.

[3] Remove the stop bead, and thread a needle on the other end of the thread. Place the rivoli face down into the beadwork so the front of the rivoli is against the 15ºs.

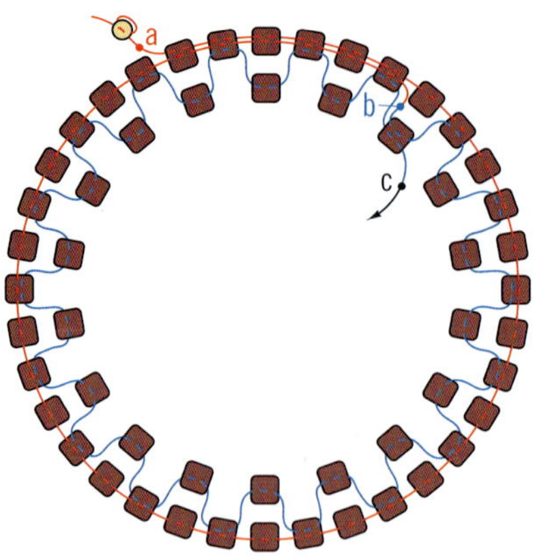

FIGURE 1

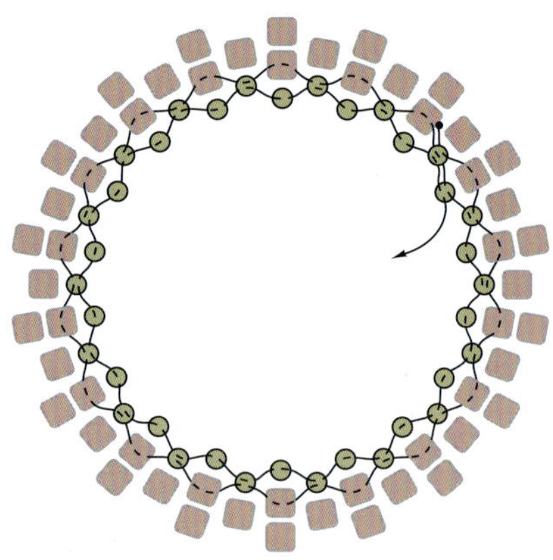

FIGURE 2

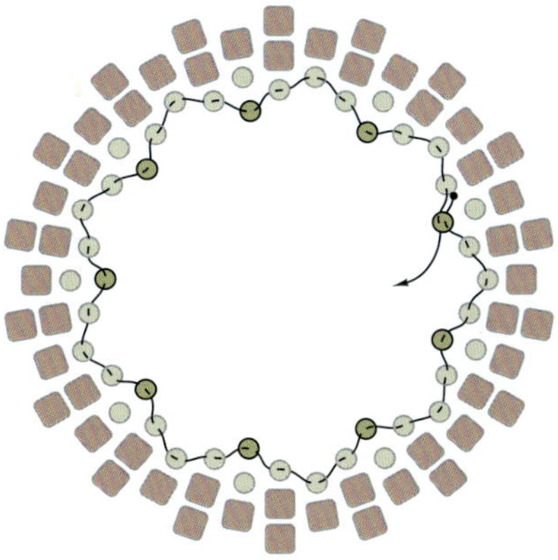

FIGURE 3

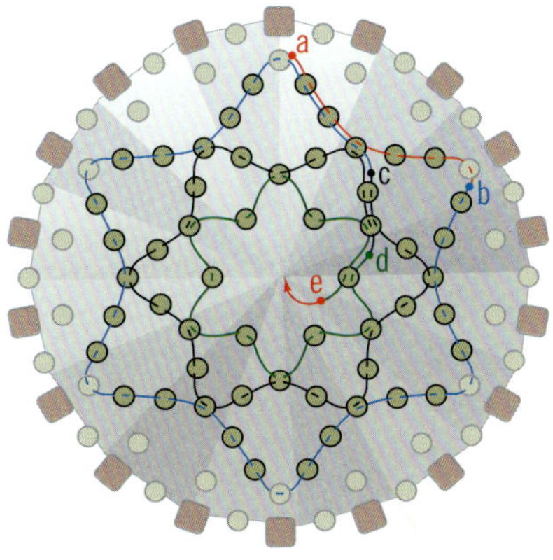

FIGURE 4

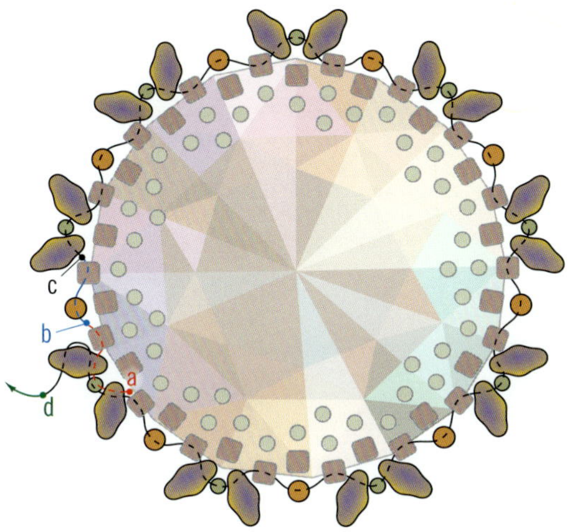

FIGURE 5

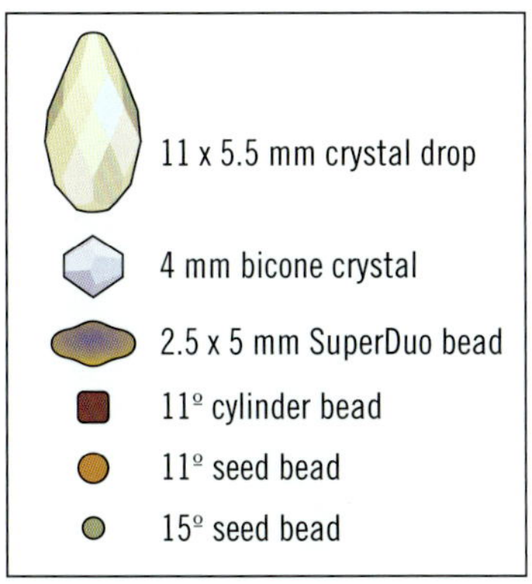

Bezel back

Work in rounds as follows:

Rounds 1 and 2: Work both rounds in peyote stitch using 15ºs and a firm tension so the beadwork cups around the back of the rivoli.

Round 3: Pick up five 15ºs, skip the next two up-beads in the previous round, and sew through the following up-bead **(figure 4, a–b)**. Repeat this stitch to complete the round, and step up through the first three beads picked up in this round **(b–c)**.

Round 4: Pick up three 15ºs, and sew through the center bead in the next five-bead set. Repeat this stitch to complete the round, and step up through the first two beads picked up in this round **(c–d)**.

Round 5: Pick up a 15º, and sew through the center bead in the next three-bead set. Repeat this stitch to complete the round, and step up **(d–e)**. Sew through the six beads picked up in this round, and end the thread (Basics).

Embellishments

[1] With the remaining thread, sew through the beadwork to exit a cylinder in round 2 of "Bezel front" **(figure 5, point a)**. Pick up a 2.5 x 5 mm SuperDuo bead, a 15º, and a SuperDuo, and sew through the next cylinder in the same round **(a–b)**. Pick up an 11º seed bead, and sew through the next cylinder in the round **(b–c)**. Repeat these two stitches to complete the round. Continue through the next SuperDuo, 15º, and SuperDuo set, and then sew through the available hole of the SuperDuo your thread is exiting **(c–d)**.

[2] Pick up a 15º, a 4 mm bicone crystal, and a 15º,

MATERIALS

pair of earrings 2 in. (5 cm)

- **2** 14 mm rivolis (Swarovski, crystal volcano; www.fusionbeads.com)
- **2** 11 x 5.5 mm crystal drops (Swarovski, light silk)
- **22** 4 mm bicone crystals (Swarovski, crystal purple haze)
- 3 g 2.5 x 5 mm SuperDuo beads (silky gold/violet iris)
- 2 g 11º cylinder beads (Miyuki DB0023, metallic gold iris hex-cut)
- 1 g 11º seed beads (Miyuki 457, metallic dark bronze)
- 1 g 15º seed beads (Toho 459, gold luster dark topaz)
- pair of earring findings (antique copper)
- Fireline 6 lb. test
- beading needles, #11

pendant (p. 26)

- **1** 14 mm rivoli (Preciosa, Bermuda blue; www.fusionbeads.com)
- **1** 11 x 5.5 mm crystal drop (Swarovski, lavender-chrysolite blend; www.fusionbeads.com)
- **11** 4 mm bicone crystals (Swarovski, crystal silver night)
- 2 g 2.5 x 5 mm SuperDuo beads (pastel petrol/teal; www.ariadesignstudio.com)
- 1 g 11º cylinder beads (Miyuki DB0111, transparent blue gray rainbow gold luster)
- 1 g 11º seed beads (Miyuki 1457, dyed emerald silver-lined dark sapphire)
- 1 g 15º Japanese seed beads (399H, amethyst/dark lined; www.beyondbeadery.com)
- 12 mm hammered ring (TierraCast, gunmetal)
- 36-in. (.9 m) dyed silk ribbon

and sew through the available hole of the next two SuperDuos. Repeat this stitch to complete the round. Continue through the first 15º, 4 mm, and 15º picked up in this round **(figure 6)**.

[3] Pick up three 15ºs, and sew through the next 15º and 4 mm. Pick up a 4 mm, a 15º, an 11 x 5.5 mm crystal drop, a 15º, and a 4 mm. Skip the next 15º and two SuperDuos, and sew through the following 15º with the needle pointing back toward the start of this stitch. Continue through the two SuperDuos you just skipped and the adjacent 15º **(figure 7, a–b)**. Sew through the beads picked up in this step, skip the next 15º, and sew through the following 4 mm and 15º along the outer edge **(b–c)**.

[4] Pick up three 15ºs, and sew through the next 15º, 4 mm, and 15º. Repeat this stitch two times. Pick up three 15ºs, and sew through the following 15º and 4 mm opposite the drop **(c–d)**.

[5] Pick up three 15ºs, an earring finding, and three 15ºs, and sew through the 4 mm again in the same direction **(d–e)**. Retrace the thread path through the loop, and exit the 15º after the 4 mm **(e–f)**.

[6] Work three more three-bead stitches **(f–g)**, and end the thread.

[7] Make a second earring.

Pendant

[1] Work as you would to make an earring, but in step 5 of "Embellishments," pick up 11 15ºs and a 12 mm hammered ring, and sew back through the 4 mm your thread exited at the start of this step in the opposite direction. Repeat this stitch to create a second 11-bead loop around the hammered ring. Retrace the thread path through both loops, and exit the 4 mm. Continue working three-bead stitches to complete the embellishment.

[2] Fold a 36-in. (.9 m) silk ribbon in half. String the fold through the hammered ring to form a loop, and then string the ends of the ribbon through the loop. Pull the ends to tighten the lark's head knot. ●

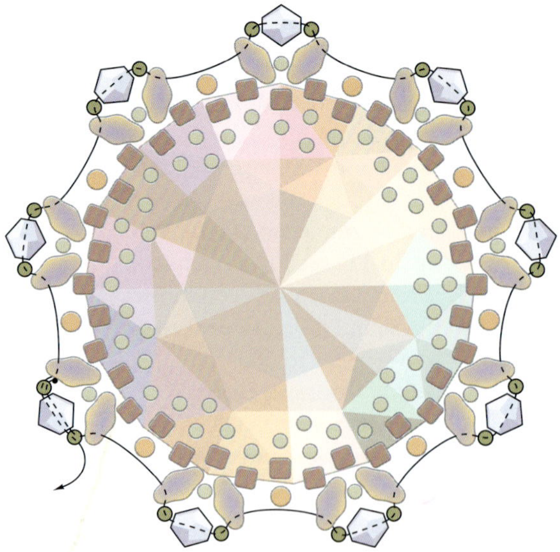

FIGURE 6

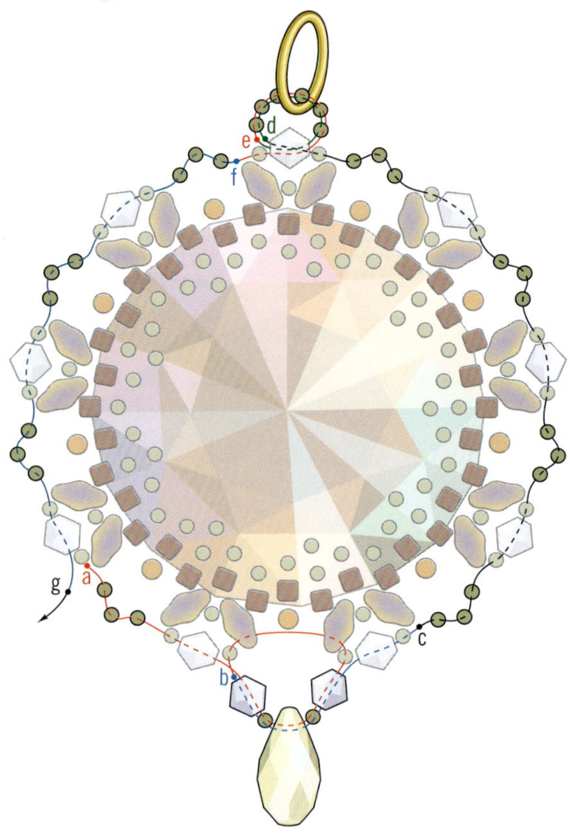

FIGURE 7

CUBIC RIGHT-ANGLE WEAVE /
PEYOTE STITCH

Do the BUMP

A raised peyote embellishment adds another dimension to cubic right-angle weave.

designed by **Kathleen Stauber**

a

b

c

d

e

f

g

h

stepby**step**

Bracelet

Square bases

[1] On 2 yd. (1.8 m) of thread, work the first CRAW unit (see "Cubic RAW how-to," p. 158) using color A 11° seed beads and leaving a 6-in. (15 cm) tail.

[2] Work four more CRAW units ("Cubic RAW how-to") off of the first one **(photo a)**. This completes the first leg of the square base. Sew through the beadwork to exit a top bead in the last unit so that your thread is exiting perpendicular to the last unit.

[3] Work four CRAW units in the new direction. This completes the second leg of the square base **(photo b)**. Sew through the beadwork to exit a top bead in the last unit so that your thread is exiting perpendicular to the last unit.

[4] Repeat step 3 to complete the third leg of the square base **(photo c)**.

[5] Work two CRAW units **(photo d)**, and then work a joining unit ("Cubic RAW how-to") to connect the fourth leg of the square base to the first leg **(photo e)**. End the tail (Basics) but not the working thread.

[6] Repeat steps 1–5 to make a total of six square bases.

Bump embellishments

[1] Add 2 yd. (1.8 m) of thread (Basics) to a square base, and exit the top bead in the middle unit of a leg, with your thread exiting the inside of the square.

[2] Pick up four As, and sew through the top bead in the middle unit of the next leg. Repeat this stitch to complete the round, and step up through the first A added in this step **(figure 1)**. This forms round 1 of the bump.

[3] Work the next seven rounds as follows:

Round 2: Pick up two As, skip two As in the previous round, and sew through the following A. Pick up two As, skip the corner bead, and sew through the first A in the next set of four **(figure 2, a–b)**. Repeat these two stitches to complete the round, and step up through the first two As added in this round **(b–c)**.

Round 3: Pick up a color B 11° seed bead, and sew through the next two As in the previous round **(c–d)**. Repeat this stitch to complete the round, and step up through the first B added in this round **(d–e)**.

Round 4: Pick up two Bs, and sew through the next B in the previous round **(figure 3, a–b)**. Repeat this stitch to complete the round, and step up through the first two Bs added in this round **(b–c)**.

Round 5: Pick up a B, and sew through the next two Bs. Repeat this stitch to complete the round, and step up **(c–d)**.

Round 6: Decrease by working a round of tubular peyote stitch (Basics) with one color C 11º seed bead per stitch, and step up **(d–e)**.

Round 7: Decrease again: Pick up a C, and sew through the next two Cs in the previous round **(figure 4, a–b)**. Repeat this stitch to complete the round, and step up through the first C in this round **(b–c)**.

Round 8: Work a round of tubular peyote stitch with one A per stitch, and then sew through the four beads added in this round **(c–d)**. End the thread.

[4] Embellish the remaining square bases.

Joining links

[1] Add 24 in. (61 cm) of thread to an embellished square, and exit a top edge bead in the second unit of a leg, with your thread exiting away from the square. Using color D 11º seed beads, work two CRAW units **(photo f)**. Using Ds, work a joining unit to connect the second D unit to the corresponding unit of another embellished square **(photo g)**.

[2] Sew through the second embellished square to exit the top bead in the fourth unit of the same leg. Work as in step 1 to create a second connection between the two squares **(photo h)**. End the thread.

[3] Repeat steps 1 and 2 to connect all the embellished squares in a row.

Clasp

[1] Working as in "Square bases," make a rectangle that is five units by six units. This is the toggle ring.

[2] Work as in "Joining links" to connect the toggle ring to an end embellished square.

[3] Add 1½ yd. (1.4 m) of thread to the embellished square at the other end. Work as in "Joining links," but make each link three units long. You are not connecting these links to another component, so after you complete the

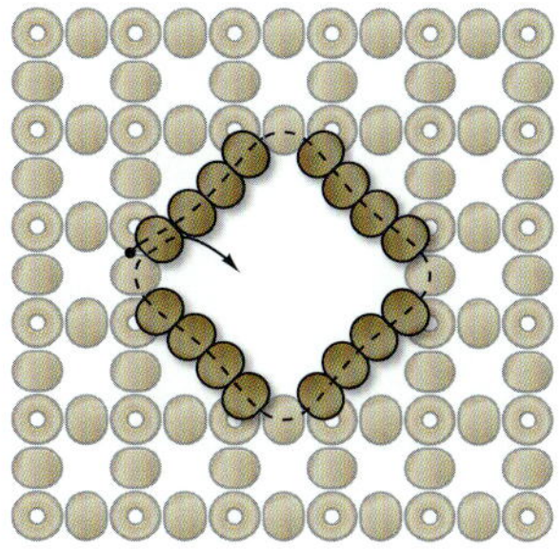

FIGURE 1

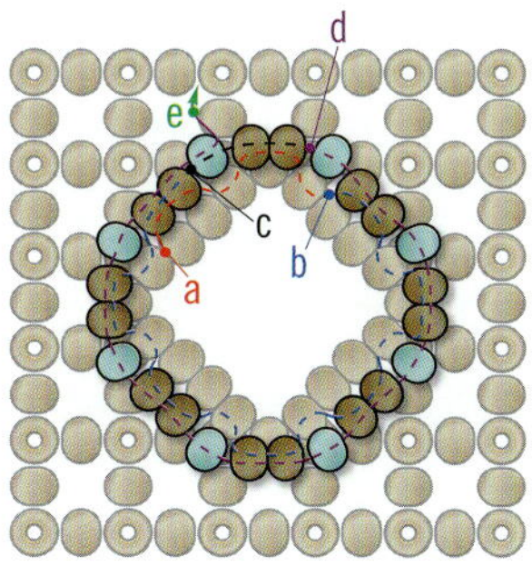

FIGURE 2

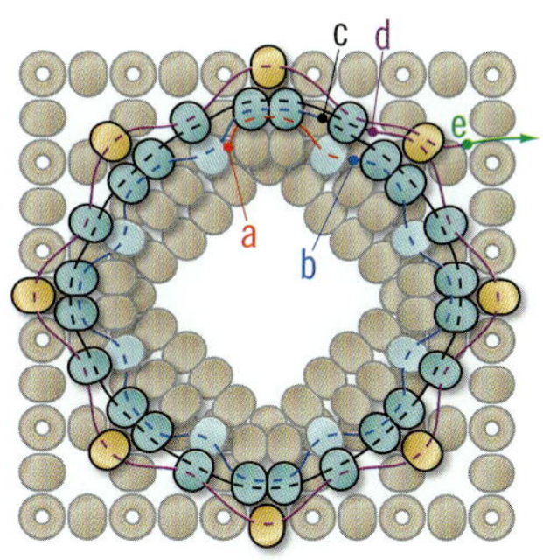

FIGURE 3

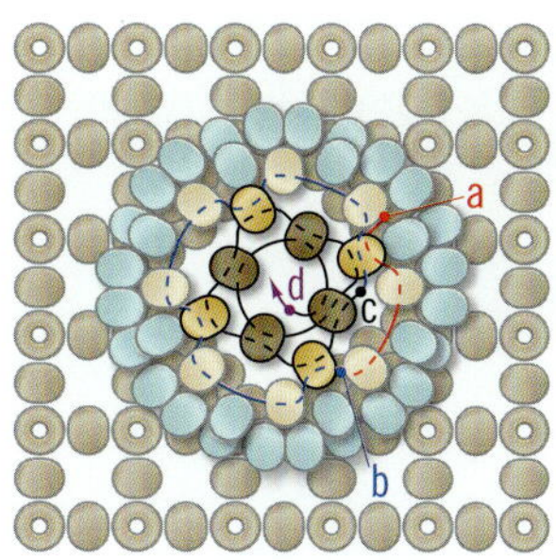

FIGURE 4

- 11º seed bead, color A
- 11º seed bead, color B
- 11º seed bead, color C

MATERIALS

bracelet 8 in. (20 cm)

- 11º Japanese seed beads (www.beyondbeadery.com)
  - 10 g color A (462Q, copper gold metallic iris)
  - 5 g color B (319N, lavender gray gold luster)
  - 2 g color C (P471, permanent galvanized gold)
  - 5 g color D (638, silver-lined ruby AB)
- Fireline 6 lb. test
- beading needles, #12

necklace 23 in. (58 cm)

- 11º Japanese seed beads (same colors as in bracelet)
  - 13 g color A
  - 6 g color B
  - 2 g color C
  - 20 g color D
- Fireline 6 lb. test
- beading needles, #12

first link, simply sew back to the end square, and add the second link.

[4] Work a joining unit to connect the links.

[5] Sew through the beadwork to exit the top bead in the joining unit so that your thread is pointing away from the joining unit. Work one unit using Ds, and exit the top bead opposite the connection with the links **(photo i)**.

[6] Pick up 19 As, and sew through the bead your thread exited at the start of this step to make a loop **(photo j)**. Sew through the first A again. This forms round 1 of the toggle button.

[7] Work as in step 3 of "Bump embellishments."

[8] Sew back through to a bead in round 1, and work step 3 of "Bump embellishments" on the other side. End the thread.

Necklace

Pendant and side squares

[1] Make eight embellished squares.

[2] Work as in "Bracelet: Joining links" to connect four squares at right angles to each other, forming the diamond-shaped pendant.

[3] Working off the remaining legs of one of the squares in the pendant, work as in "Joining links" to connect two more squares on each side.

Neck straps

[1] Add a comfortable length of thread to an end embellished square, and exit the top bead in the second unit of a leg, with your thread exiting opposite the previous connections.

[2] Work five units using Ds.

[3] Working off the inner edge of the last unit, work four units using Ds.

[4] Working off the outer edge of the last unit, work four units using Ds.

[5] Repeat steps 3 and 4 six times, ending and adding thread as needed, and then work step 3 again. This will result in a 23-in. (58 cm) necklace. To alter the length, work more or fewer repeats of steps 3 and 4.

[6] Add a comfortable length of thread to the same embellished square, and exit the top bead in the fourth unit of the same leg. Repeat steps 2–5 to make a neck strap on this side of the necklace.

[7] Repeat steps 1–6 on the other side of the pendant.

Clasp

[1] Working as in "Bracelet: Square bases," make a rectangle that is five units by six units. This is the toggle ring. Connect the toggle ring to one end of the necklace.

[2] Work as in steps 4–8 of "Bracelet: Clasp" to make a toggle button. ●

i

j

Cubic RAW how-to

Each cubic right-angle weave (or CRAW) unit has six surfaces — four sides, a top, and a bottom. Each surface is made up of four beads, but since the beads are shared, 12 beads are used to make the first unit, and only eight beads are used for each subsequent CRAW unit. For clarity, we used two colors of beads in the how-to photos.

Working the first CRAW unit

[1] On the specified length of thread, pick up four beads. Tie the beads into a ring with a square knot (Basics), leaving the specified length tail, and continue through the first two beads in the ring. This ring of beads will count as the first stitch of the unit.

[2] Work two right-angle weave stitches off of the bead your thread is exiting to create a flat strip of right-angle weave (Basics).

[3] To join the first and last stitches: Pick up a bead, sew through the end bead in the first stitch **(CRAW 1, a–b)**, pick up a bead, and sew through the end bead in the last stitch **(b–c)**. **CRAW 2** shows a three-dimensional view of the resulting cube-shaped unit.

[4] To make the unit more stable, sew through the four beads at the top of the unit **(CRAW 3)**. Sew through the beadwork to the bottom of the unit, and sew through the four remaining beads. This completes the first CRAW unit.

Working more CRAW units

[1] Each new CRAW unit is worked off of the top four beads of the previous unit. These beads are identified in **CRAW 4**. Sew through the beadwork to exit one of these top beads.

[2] *For the first stitch of the new unit:* Pick up three beads, and sew through the top bead your thread exited at the start of this step. Continue through the three beads just picked up **(CRAW 5)**. Sew through the next top bead in the previous unit.

[3] *For the second stitch of the new unit:* Pick up two beads, and sew through

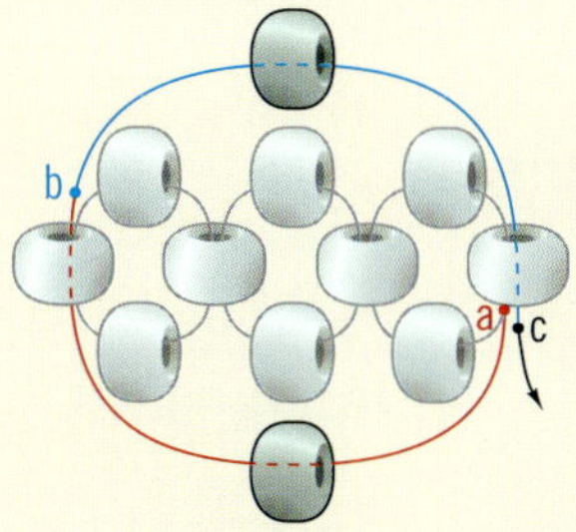

CRAW 1

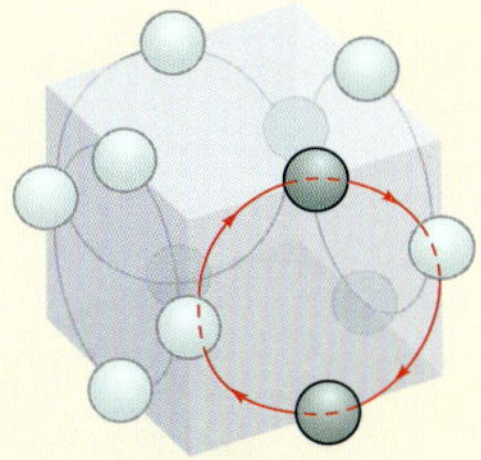

CRAW 2

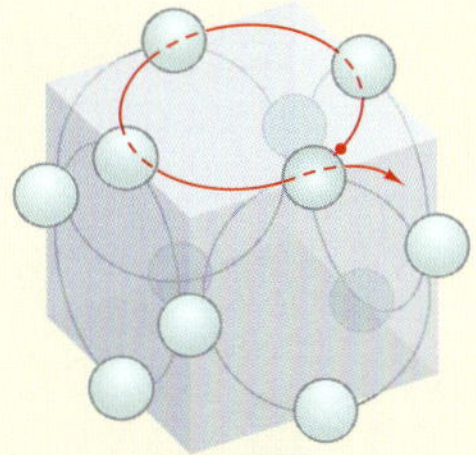

CRAW 3

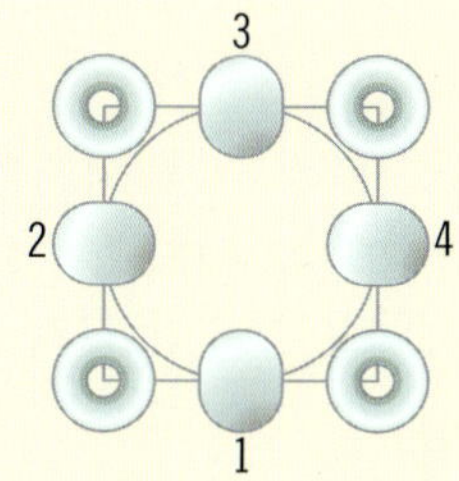

CRAW 4

the side bead in the previous stitch, the top bead your thread exited at the start of this stitch **(CRAW 6)**, and the next top bead in the previous unit.

[4] *For the third stitch of the new unit:* Repeat step 3 **(CRAW 7)**, and continue through the side bead in the first stitch of the new unit.

[5] *For the fourth stitch of the new unit:* Pick up a bead, and sew through the side bead in the previous stitch and the top bead in the previous unit **(CRAW 8)**.

[6] To make the unit more stable, sew through the beadwork to exit a top bead in the new unit, and sew through all four top beads **(CRAW 9)**. This completes the new CRAW unit.

[7] Repeat steps 2–6 for the desired number of CRAW units.

Working a joining unit

A joining unit is used to connect two completed CRAW units to each other. Units may be joined end to end or perpendicular to one another (as shown here).

[1] Sew through the beadwork to exit a top bead in one unit.

[2] *For the first stitch of the joining unit:* Pick up a bead, sew through the corresponding bead in the other unit, pick up a bead, and sew through the bead your thread exited at the start of this step **(CRAW 10)**. Sew through the first bead added and the adjacent bead in the next side. If you are joining pieces at an angle, try to do the stitches on the inside of the angle first.

[3] *For the second stitch of the joining unit:* Pick up a bead, and sew through the corresponding bead in the other unit, the previous joining bead, the bead your thread exited at the start of this stitch **(CRAW 11)**, and the bead just added. Sew through the adjacent bead in the next side.

[4] *For the third stitch of the joining unit:* Pick up a bead, and sew through the corresponding bead in the other unit, the previous joining bead, the bead your thread exited at the start of this stitch **(CRAW 12)**, and the bead just added. Sew through the adjacent bead in the next side.

[5] *For the fourth stitch of the joining unit:* All beads are already in place. Simply sew through the four beads that remain unconnected **(CRAW 13)**.

CRAW 5

CRAW 6

CRAW 7

CRAW 8

CRAW 9

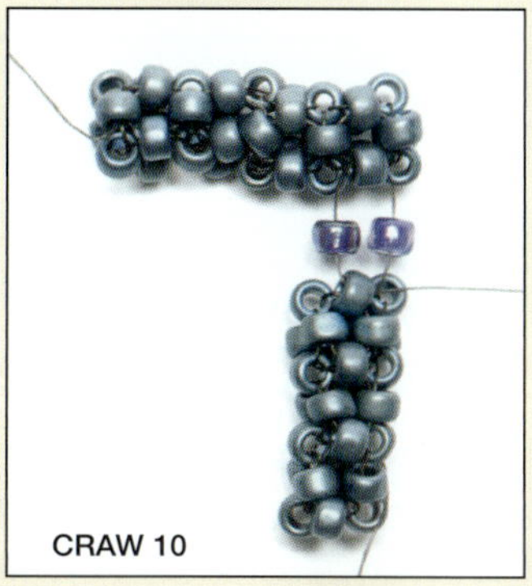

CRAW 10

CRAW 11

CRAW 12

CRAW 13

ST. PETERSBURG CHAIN / RIGHT-ANGLE WEAVE

Stacked St. Petersburg bracelet

designed by **Ruth Vickery**

Inspired by the beauty of St. Petersburg chain, this bracelet features strips of beadwork you can join two different ways.

The following instructions are for the black bracelet design. To make the blue bracelet, see "Alternate design" on p. 162.

stepbystep

Double layer strips

First layer

[1] On a comfortable length of thread, attach a stop bead (Basics), leaving a 6-in. (15 cm) tail. Pick up a color B 11º seed bead and six color A 11º seed beads. Sew through the third and fourth As in the same direction so the fifth and sixth As form a new column (**figure 1, a–b**). Pick up a B, and sew back through the next three As in the first column (**b–c**).

[2] Pick up a B, and sew through the two As in the next column (**c–d**).

[3] Pick up four As, sew through the first and second As just added in the same direction, and snug them up to the previous beads (**figure 2, a–b**). Pick up a B, and sew back through the next three As in the same column (**b–c**).

[4] Pick up a B, and sew through the two As in the next column (**c–d**).

[5] Repeat steps 3 and 4 for the desired length of the bracelet minus ½ in. (1.3 cm) for the clasp. End and add thread (Basics) as needed.

Second layer

[1] With the needle exiting the two As in the last column, pick up two As and a B. Skip the B, and sew back through the next four As and the following B (**figure 3, a–b**).

[2] Pick up six As, and sew through the third and fourth As in the same direction so the fifth and sixth As form a new column (**b–c**).

[3] Pick up a B, and sew back through the next three As in the same column (**figure 4, a–b**). Continue through the B and two As in the next column (**b–c**).

[4] Pick up four As, sew through the first and second As just added in the same direction, and snug them up to the previous beads.

[5] Repeat steps 3 and 4 for the remaining length of the strip.

[6] To complete the last column, pick up two As and a B, skip the B, and sew back through the next four As in the same column. Remove the stop bead, and end the working thread and tail.

[7] Make another double layer strip.

Joining the double strips

[1] Arrange the double layer strips as shown in **figure 5** so the two strips form a point. Add 1½ yd. (1.4 m) of thread to the beadwork, and exit the last inside edge B of the top strip, leaving a 1-ft. (30 cm) tail.

[2] Working in modified right-angle weave (Basics), pick up a 15º seed bead, a B, and a 15º, and sew through the corresponding B of the other strip (**figure 5, a–b**). Pick up a 15º, a B, and a 15º, and sew through the B your thread exited at the start of this step (**b–c**). Continue through the next six beads of this stitch (**c–d**).

[3] Pick up a 15º, and sew through the next B of the top strip (**d–e**). Pick up a 15º, a B, and a 15º, and sew through the corresponding B of the bottom strip (**e–f**). Pick up a 15º, and sew through the next B (**f–g**). Continue through the next four beads of this stitch (**g–h**).

[4] Pick up a 15º, and sew through the next B of the bottom strip (**h–i**). Pick up a 15º, a B, and a 15º, and sew through the corresponding B of the top strip. Pick up a 15º, and sew through the

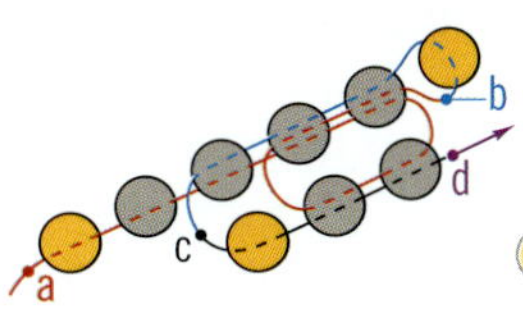

FIGURE 1

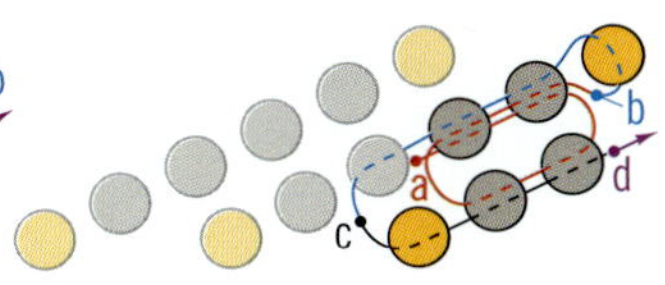

FIGURE 2

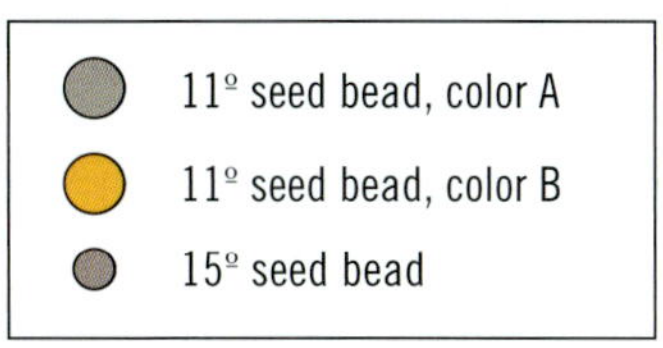

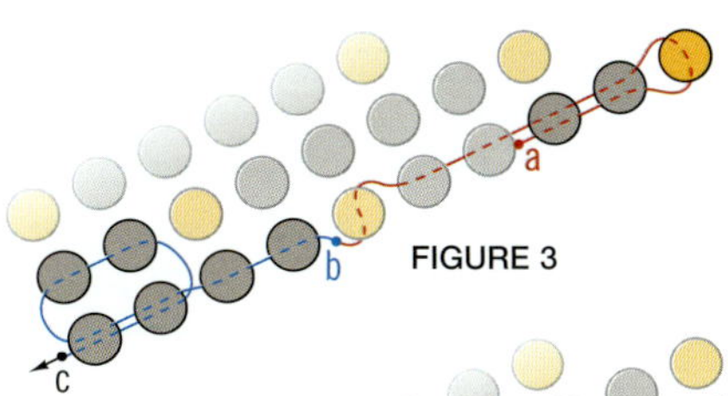

FIGURE 3

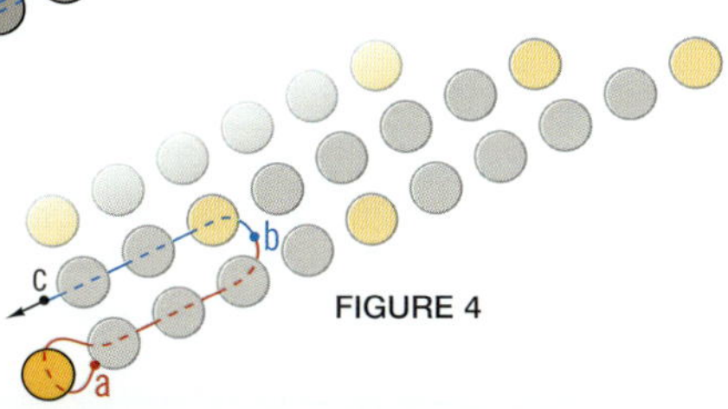

FIGURE 4

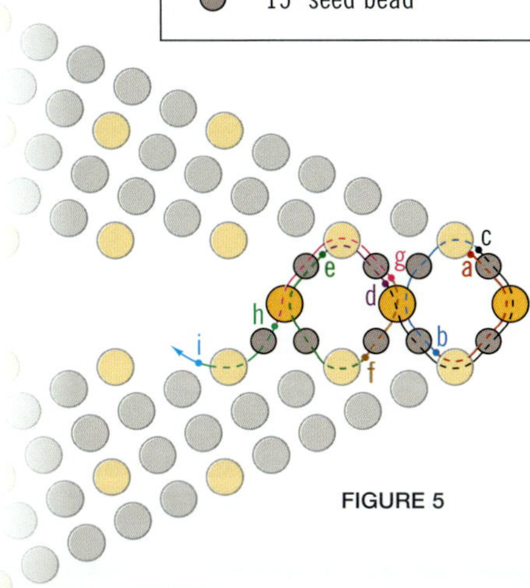

FIGURE 5

MATERIALS

black bracelet 6½ in. (16.5 cm)

- 11º seed beads
  8 g color A (Miyuki 401F, black opaque matte; www.bellomodo.com)
  3 g color B (Miyuki 462, gold metallic iris; www.bellomodo.com)
- 2 g 15º seed beads (Miyuki 401, black opaque; www.bellomodo.com)
- 1 ½-in. (1.3 cm) button
- KO beading thread
- beading needles, #11 or #12

blue bracelet colors:

- 11º seed beads
  color A (Miyuki 2038, matte opaque denim luster; www.auntiesbeads.com)
  color B (Miyuki 551, gilt light lined opal; www.auntiesbeads.com)
- 15º seed beads (Miyuki 150, transparent sapphire; www.auntiesbeads.com)
- 2 ⅜-in. (1 cm) buttons

DESIGN NOTE:

Fireline 6 lb. test may be used in place of KO thread.

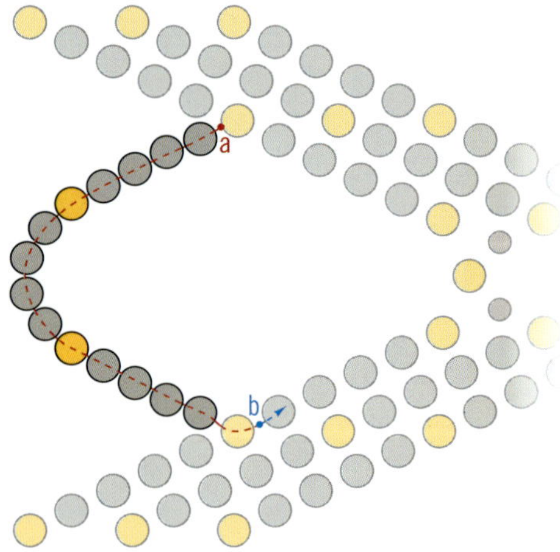

FIGURE 6

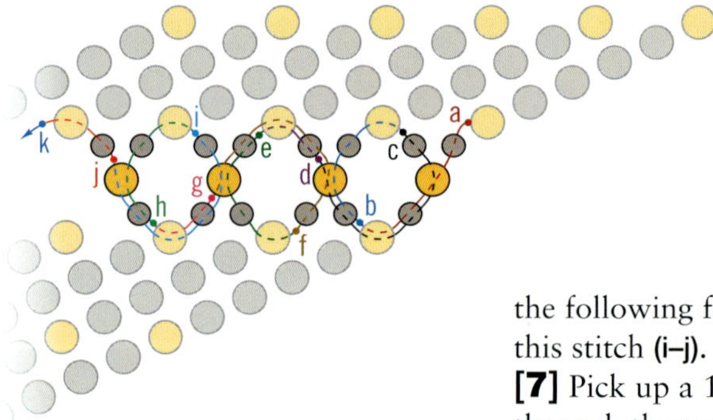

FIGURE 7

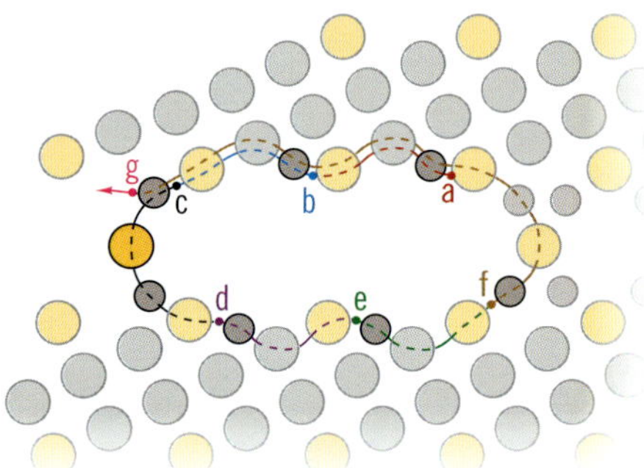

FIGURE 8

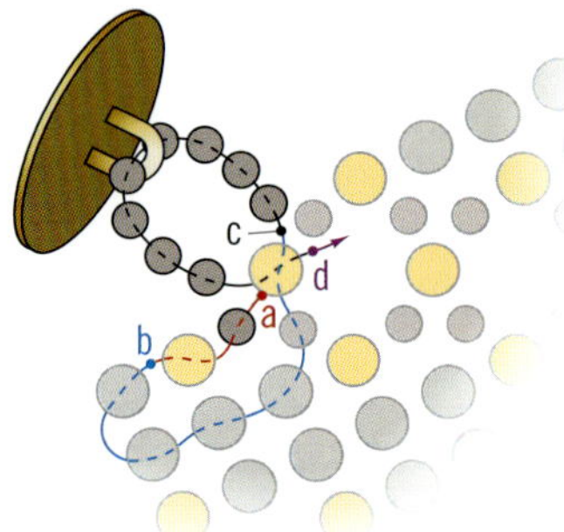

FIGURE 9

next B. Continue through the next four beads of this stitch.

[5] Repeat steps 3 and 4 for the remainder of the strips, but do not end the working thread.

Clasp

[1] With the 1-ft. (30 cm) tail, sew through the end 15º and B of the right-angle weave join. Pick up four 15ºs, the shank of a button, and four 15ºs, and sew through the B your thread is exiting. Retrace the thread path through the button and the first right-angle weave stitch, and end the tail.

[2] With the working thread, sew through the last column, and exit the center B **(figure 6, point a)**. Pick up four As, a B, four As, a B, and four As, and sew through the corresponding B on the opposite side **(a–b)**. Test the fit of the button, and add or remove beads if necessary. Retrace the thread path, and end the thread.

Alternate design

[1] Work steps 1–5 of "First layer" and step 1 of "Second layer" to make two strips 1 in. (2.5 cm) longer than the desired bracelet length. End the working threads and tails. Work steps 1–5 of "First layer" and steps 1–6 of "Second layer" to make a double layer strip 1 in. (2.5 cm) longer than the desired bracelet length. End the working thread and tail. Arrange the single strips on each side of the double strip so that the ends form a diagonal.

[2] Add 1½ yd. (1.4 m) of thread to the single top strip, and exit the last inside edge B with the needle pointing toward the other end **(figure 7, point a)**.

[3] Pick up a 15º, a B, and a 15º, and sew through the last inside edge B of the double strip **(a–b)**.

[4] Pick up a 15º, a B, and a 15º, and sew through the next B of the single strip, with the needle pointing toward this end of the beadwork **(b–c)**. Pick up a 15º, and sew through the next five beads of this stitch **(c–d)**.

[5] Pick up a 15º, and sew through the next B of the single strip **(d–e)**. Pick up a 15º, a B, and a 15º, and sew through the corresponding B of the double strip **(e–f)**. Pick up a 15º, and sew through the next B. Continue through the following four beads of this stitch **(f–g)**.

[6] Pick up a 15º, and sew through the next B of the double strip **(g–h)**. Pick up a 15º, a B, and a 15º, and sew through the corresponding B of the single strip **(h–i)**. Pick up a 15º, and sew through the next B. Continue through the following four beads of this stitch **(i–j)**.

[7] Pick up a 15º, and sew through the next B of the single strip **(j–k)**.

[8] To begin the button hole opening, pick up a 15º, and sew through the next A and B of the single strip **(figure 8, a–b)**. Repeat this stitch once more **(b–c)**.

[9] Pick up a 15º, a B, and a 15º, and sew through the corresponding B of the double strip **(c–d)**.

[10] Pick up a 15º, and sew through the next A and B of the double strip **(d–e)**. Repeat this stitch once more **(e–f)**.

[11] Pick up a 15º, and sew through the beadwork as shown to exit the first 15º picked up in step 9 **(f–g)**.

[12] Repeat steps 5 and 6 for the remainder of the strips.

[13] Pick up a 15º, and sew through the end B of the double strip **(figure 9, a–b)**. Sew through the beadwork to exit the B your thread exited at the start of this step **(b–c)**.

[14] Pick up four 15ºs, the shank of a button, and four 15ºs, and sew through the B your thread exited at the start of this step **(c–d)**. Retrace the thread path through the button and the last right-angle weave stitch. End the thread.

[15] Work as in steps 2–14 to attach the bottom single strip to the other side of the double strip, creating a second button hole opening at one end and attaching a second button to the other end. ●

RIGHT-ANGLE WEAVE / BEAD WEAVING

Ribbons of pearls ornament

Beaded ornaments make great gifts just in time for the holiday season.

designed by **Cathy Lampole**

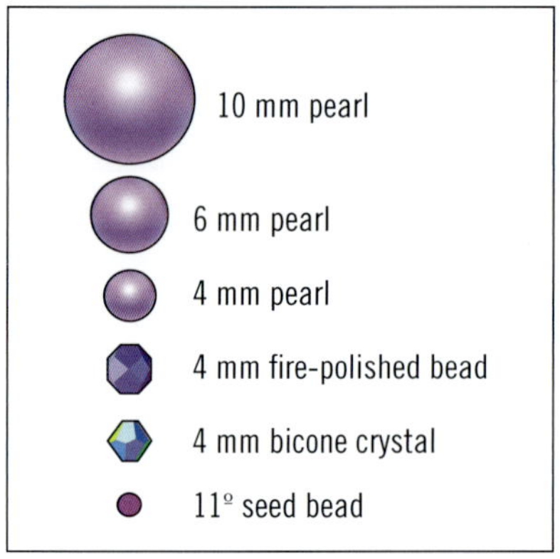

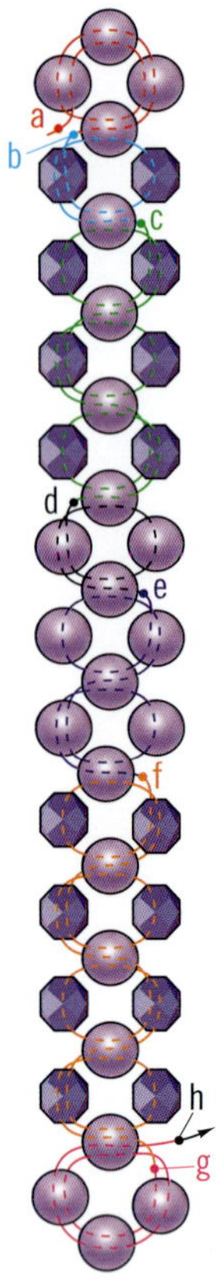
FIGURE 1

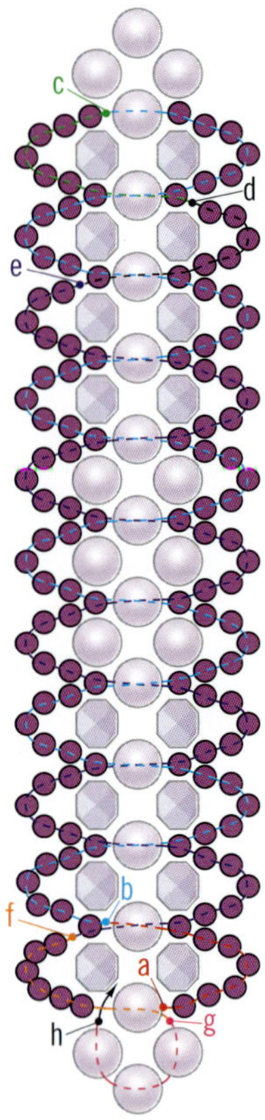
FIGURE 2

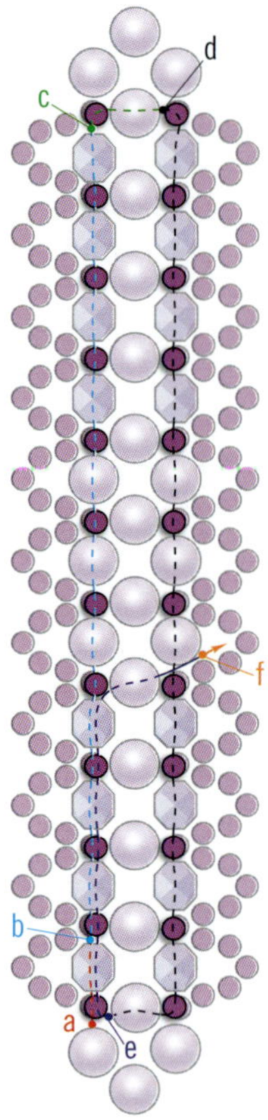
FIGURE 3

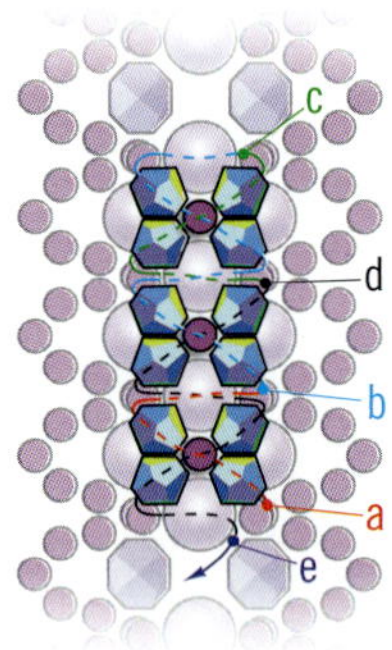
FIGURE 4

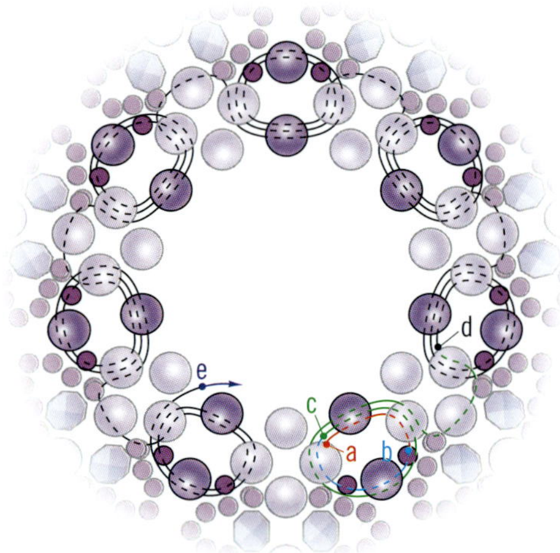
FIGURE 5

stepbystep

Embellished bands

[1] On 5 ft. (1.5 m) of thread, pick up four 4 mm pearls. Sew through all the beads again to form a ring, leaving a 6-in. (15 cm) tail **(figure 1, a–b)**.

[2] Working in right-angle weave (Basics), pick up a 4 mm fire-polished bead, a 4 mm pearl, and a fire-polished bead. Sew through the 4 mm pearl your thread is exiting, and continue through the next two beads **(b–c)**. Repeat this stitch three more times for a total of four fire-polished units **(c–d)**.

[3] Working in right-angle weave, pick up three 4 mm pearls. Sew through the 4 mm pearl your thread is exiting, and continue through the next two beads **(d–e)**. Repeat this stitch two more times for a total of three pearl units **(e–f)**.

[4] Repeat step 2 to work four fire-polished units **(f–g)**.

[5] Work one more pearl unit as in step 3. Sew through all the beads again, and exit the 4 mm pearl your thread exited at the start of this step **(g–h)**.

[6] Pick up seven 11º seed beads, skip the next edge bead, and sew through the following center 4 mm pearl in the band **(figure 2, a–b)**. Repeat this stitch 10 more times, alternating edges of the band **(b–c)**.

[7] Pick up six 11ºs, and sew through the 11º just before the next center 4 mm pearl. Continue through the 4 mm pearl and the following 11º **(c–d)**.

[8] Pick up five 11ºs, and sew through the 11º just before the next center 4 mm pearl. Continue through the pearl and the next 11º **(d–e)**. Repeat this stitch eight times, alternating edges of the band **(e–f)**. To complete the last stitch, pick up six 11ºs, and sew through the next center 4 mm pearl **(f–g)**. Continue through the next three 4 mm pearls **(g–h)**.

[9] Pick up an 11º, and sew through the next 4 mm edge bead **(figure 3, a–b)**. Repeat this stitch 10 more times, keeping an even tension **(b–c)**. For the last stitch, pick up an 11º, and sew through the next center 4 mm pearl **(c–d)**.

[10] Repeat step 9 on this edge of the band using an even tension, and exit the second center 4 mm pearl from the end **(d–e)**.

[11] Retrace the thread path from step 9 through the first four fire-polished units, and exit the next center 4 mm pearl **(e–f)**.

[12] Pick up a 4 mm bicone crystal, an 11º, and a bicone. Cross the pearl unit diagonally, and sew through the next center 4 mm pearl **(figure 4, a–b)**. Repeat the stitch two more times **(b–c)**.

[13] Pick up a bicone, and sew through the last 11º added in the previous step. Pick up a bicone, and sew through the next center 4 mm pearl **(c–d)**. Repeat these two stitches two more times **(d–e)**. End the working thread and tail (Basics).

[14] Repeat steps 1–13 to make a total of seven bands.

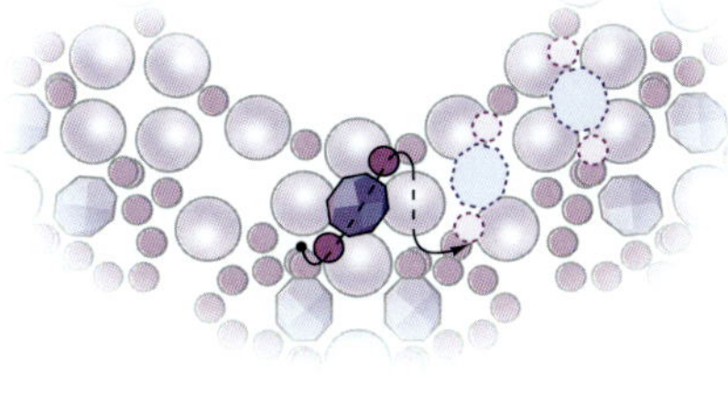

FIGURE 7

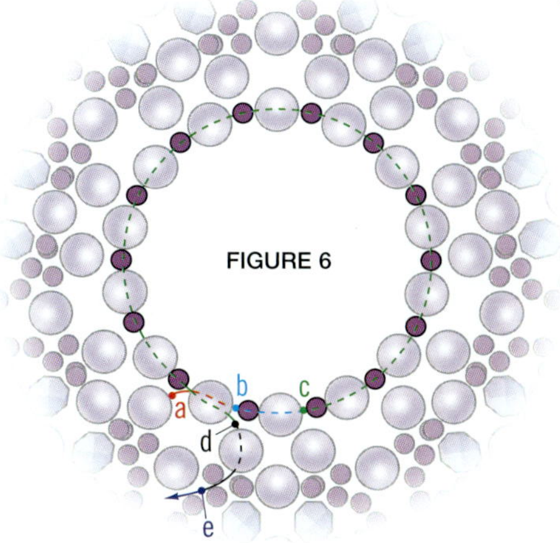

FIGURE 6

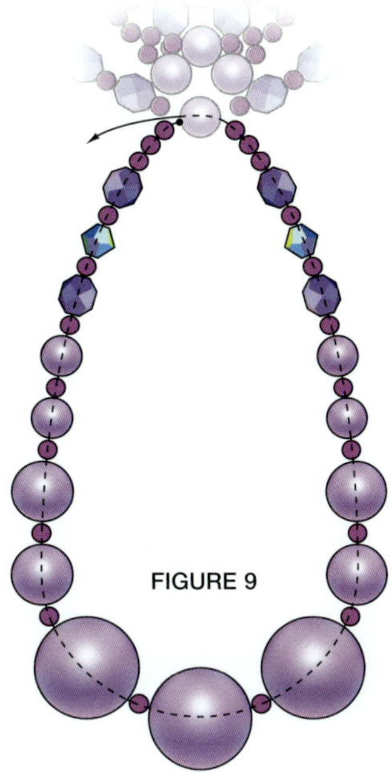

FIGURE 9

FIGURE 8

MATERIALS

purple ornament 2⅝ in. (6.7 cm)

- **1** 2⅝-in. (6.7 cm) diameter glass ball ornament (www.rabbithollowcreations.com)
- crystal pearls (Swarovski, mauve)
  21 10 mm
  28 6 mm
  210 4 mm
- **98** 4 mm bicone crystals (Swarovski, amethyst AB 2X)
- **168** 4 mm fire-polished beads (Czech, amethyst)
- 5 g 11º seed beads (Miyuki 1012, smoky amethyst AB)
- Fireline 6 lb. test
- beading needles, #11 or #12

white ornament colors:

- 10 mm, 6 mm, and 4 mm crystal pearls (Swarovski, light gray)
- 4 mm bicone crystals (Swarovski, crystal satin AB)
- 4 mm fire-polished beads (Czech, crystal AB)
- 11º seed beads (Miyuki 1001, silver-lined crystal AB)

Joining the bands

[1] Add 5 ft. (1.5 m) of thread to a band (Basics), exiting the first 4 mm edge pearl on the right side of the band with the needle pointing away from the beadwork.
[2] Pick up a 4 mm pearl, and sew down through the first 4 mm edge pearl on the left side of another band with the needle pointing toward the beadwork **(figure 5, a–b)**. Pick up an 11º, a 4 mm pearl, and an 11º, and sew up through the pearl your thread exited at the start of this step **(b–c)**. Retrace the thread path, and sew through the beadwork to exit the first 4 mm edge pearl on the right side of the band just added **(c–d)**.
[3] Work as in step 2 to join the remaining bands and to join the last band to the first band **(d–e)**. Place the beadwork on the ornament.
[4] Sew through the beadwork to exit an end 4 mm pearl on the top of the ornament **(figure 6, a–b)**. Pick up an 11º, and sew through the next 4 mm pearl **(b–c)**. Repeat this stitch to complete the round **(c–d)**, and sew through the next edge 4 mm pearl **(d–e)**.
[5] Pick up an 11º, a fire-polished bead, and an 11º, and cross diagonally to sew down through the next edge 4 mm pearl **(figure 7)**. Repeat this stitch to complete the round, and end the thread.
[6] Add 2½ yd. (2.2 m) of thread to the other end of a band, exiting the end 4 mm pearl. Pick up an 11º, a fire-polished bead, an 11º, a fire-polished bead, and an 11º, and sew through the end 4 mm pearl in the next band **(figure 8)**. Repeat this stitch to complete the round, and pull tight. The bands should fit snugly around the ornament. If they don't, increase or decrease the number of beads between the bands in this round for a proper fit. Retrace the thread path of the round again, exiting an end 4 mm pearl in a band.

Fringe loops

[1] Pick up three 11ºs, a fire-polished bead, an 11º, a bicone, an 11º, a fire-polished bead, an 11º, a 4 mm pearl, an 11º, a 4 mm pearl, an 11º, a 6 mm pearl, an 11º, a 6 mm pearl, an 11º, a 10 mm pearl, an 11º, a 10 mm pearl, an 11º, a 10 mm pearl, an 11º, a 6 mm pearl, an 11º, a 6 mm pearl, an 11º, a 4 mm pearl, an 11º, a 4 mm pearl, an 11º, a fire-polished bead, an 11º, a bicone, an 11º, a fire-polished bead, and three 11ºs. Sew through the end 4 mm pearl in the band in the same direction to form a loop **(figure 9)**. Retrace the thread path through the loop, and sew through the beadwork to exit the end 4 mm pearl in the next band.
[2] Repeat step 1 to add a loop to each band, and end the thread. ●

MODIFIED RIGHT-ANGLE WEAVE / BEAD WEAVING

Pathway of petals

This lovely bracelet has a uniform style that uses seed beads and round beads to accent its petals.

Petal beads take a bracelet from earthy to elegant.

designed by **Nichole Starman**

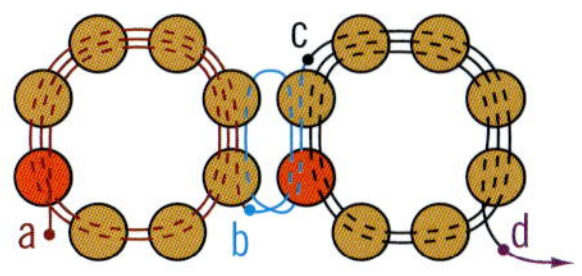

FIGURE 1

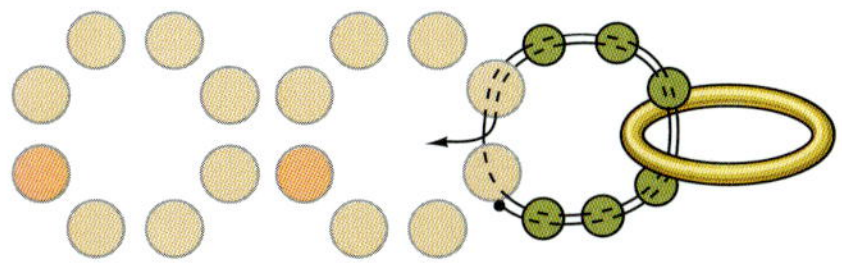

FIGURE 2

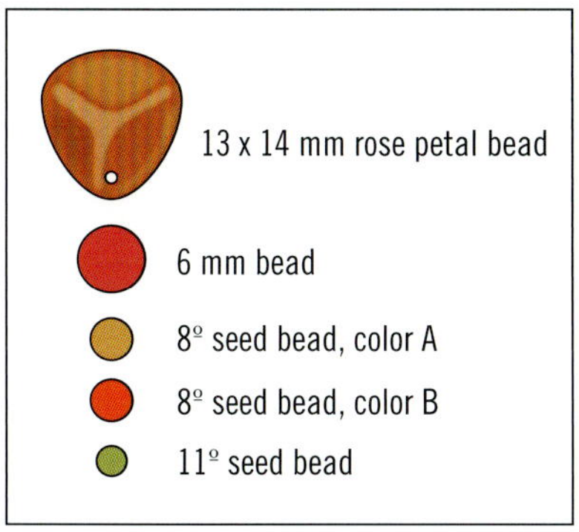

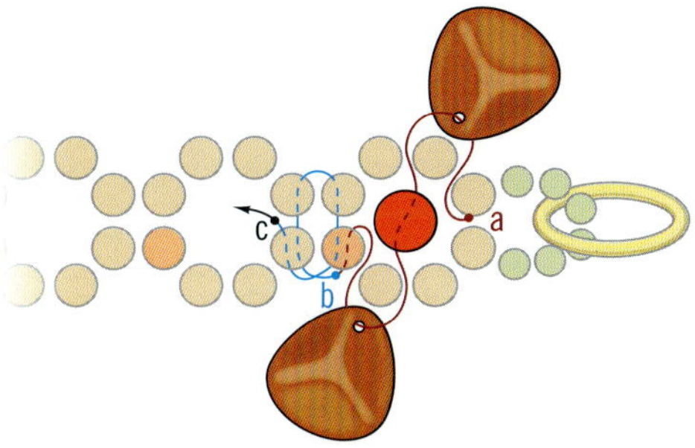

FIGURE 3

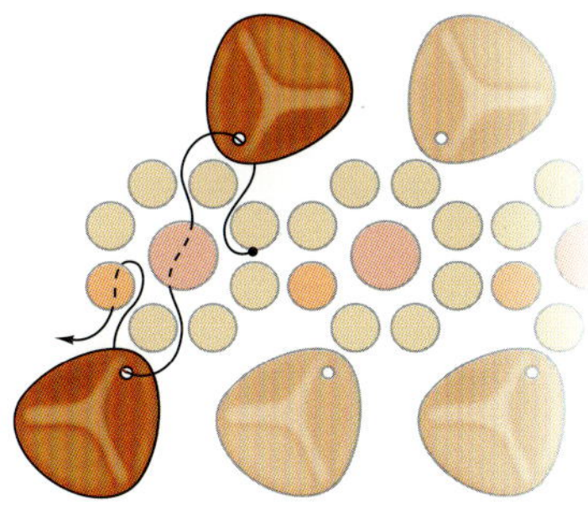

FIGURE 4

There is a front and a back to each petal bead. For the purposes of these instructions, the front has an indentation in the center, and the back has a slight peak.

stepbystep

Bracelet base

[1] On a comfortable length of thread, pick up a color B 8º seed bead and seven color A 8º seed beads. Sew through the beads again to form a ring, leaving a 6-in. (15 cm) tail, and continue through the next six beads **(figure 1, a–b)**.

[2] To work a four-bead join: Pick up a B and an A, and sew through the last two 8ºs your thread exited at the start of this step. Retrace the thread path, and continue through the new B and A **(b–c)**.

[3] To work the next base ring: Pick up six As, and sew through the B and the A your thread exited at the start of this step. Retrace the thread path, and continue through the next four As **(c–d)**.

[4] Repeat steps 2 and 3 for the desired length of the bracelet, ending on step 3.

This bracelet has 17 base rings, including the starting ring from step 1. End and add thread (Basics) as needed.

Clasp

Pick up three 11º seed beads, half of the clasp, and three 11ºs. Sew through the last two 8ºs your thread exited at the start of this step. Retrace the thread path, and exit between the two end 8ºs **(figure 2)**. If necessary, the number of 11ºs may be adjusted to accommodate your clasp.

Petals

[1] Pick up a 13 x 14 mm rose petal bead from back to front, a 6 mm round bead, and a petal from front to back. This forms a petal set. Sew down through the B in the next four-bead join **(figure 3, a–b)**.

[2] Sew through all four beads in the join to exit the A beside the B **(b–c)**.

[3] Repeat steps 1 and 2 for the length of the base except for the last base ring.

[4] To embellish the last base ring: Repeat step 1, exiting the first B added in the base **(figure 4)**. Sew through the

MATERIALS

brown bracelet 7½ in. (19.1 cm)

- **36** 13 x 14 mm rose petal beads (CT13010, opaque light beige/copper Picasso; www.bellomodo.com)
- **17** 6 mm round beads (gold/smoky topaz luster)
- 8º seed beads
  4 g color A (Toho 422, gold lustered dark chocolate bronze)
  17 color B (Toho 708, matte Casseopia)
- 2 g 11º seed beads (Toho 83, metallic iris brown)
- clasp
- Fireline or Wildfire 6 lb. test
- beading needles, #11 or #12

mauve bracelet colors:

- 13 x 14 mm rose petal beads (LS70001, stone topaz luster/mauve; www.bellomodo.com)
- 6 mm round beads (light rose glass pearl; www.fusionbeads.com)
- 8º seed beads (SB0799, sparkling rose-lined clear; www.fusionbeads.com)
- 11º seed beads (SB2077, sparkling raspberry-lined crystal clear; www.fusionbeads.com)

DESIGN NOTE:

The color B 8º seed beads are a guide for attaching the petals to the base. If you prefer, you can work the base in just one color of 8º.

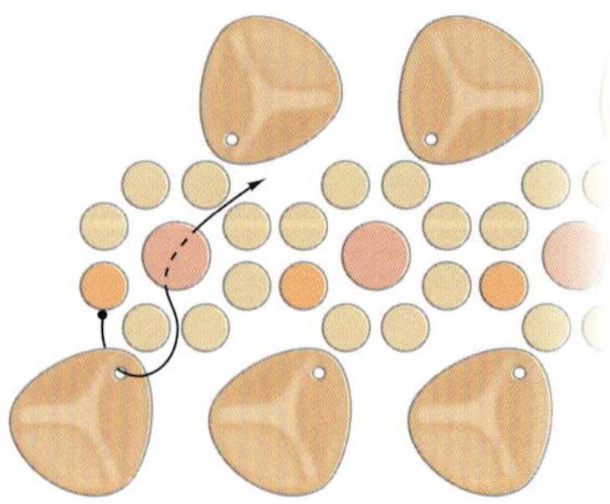
FIGURE 5

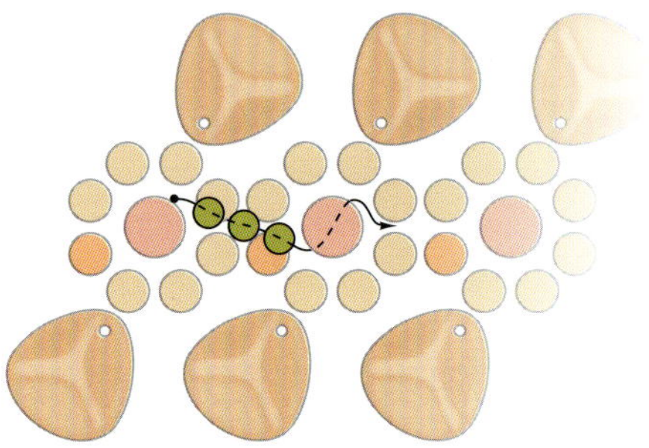
FIGURE 6

last petal from back to front, and continue through the 6 mm added in this step **(figure 5)**. Snug up the beads.

Top embellishment

[1] Position your bracelet horizontally on your work surface so that the edge of the bracelet closest to you has the color B 8ºs. This will be referred to as the bottom of the bracelet, and the edge farthest away from you will be called the top. Position the last petal to the bottom side of the base and the other petal in the same set to the top side of the base. Repeat for each petal set in the base.

[2] Pick up three 11ºs, and sew up through the 6 mm in the next petal set **(figure 6)**. Repeat this stitch for the length of the base.

[3] With the thread exiting the last 6 mm, pick up three 11ºs, and sew down through the 8º shown **(figure 7, a–b)**. Continue through the next three 8ºs, exiting the B in the next four-bead join **(b–c)**.

[4] Sew through the petal adjacent to the B, on the bottom side of the base, from back to front **(c–d)**.

[5] Pick up two 11ºs, and sew through the center 11º of the next three 11ºs added in step 2 **(figure 8, a–b)**.

[6] Pick up two 11ºs, and sew through the petal in the next set, on the top side of the base, from front to back **(b–c)**.

[7] Sew down through the two 8ºs shown in the next four-bead join **(figure 9, a–b)**. Continue through the following three 8ºs, exiting the B in the next four-bead join **(b–c)**.

[8] Sew through the petal adjacent to the B, on the bottom side of the base, from back to front **(c–d)**.

[9] Repeat steps 5–8 for the length of the base.

End petals and second clasp half

[1] With your thread exiting the last petal from back to front, pick up five 11ºs and a petal from front to back **(figure 10, a–b)**. Sew through the eight 8ºs in the last base ring **(b–c)**.

[2] Sew through the new petal from back to front **(c–d)** and the five 11ºs added in step 1 **(d–e)**.

[3] Sew through the next petal from front to back, and continue through the end B in the base **(e–f)**.

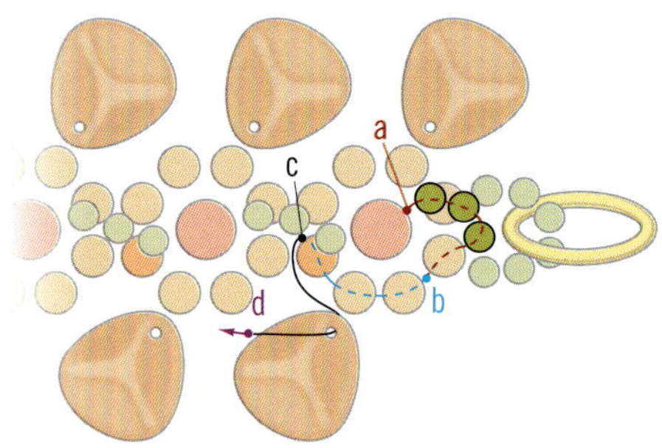

FIGURE 7

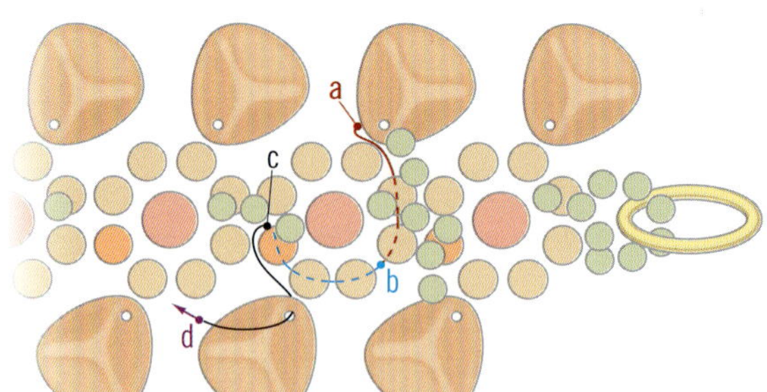

FIGURE 9

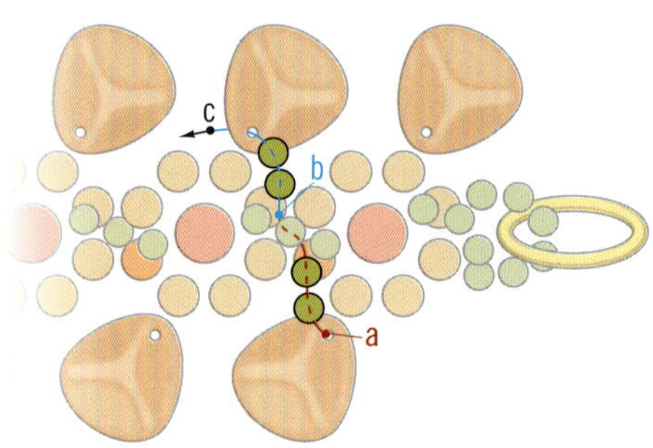

FIGURE 8

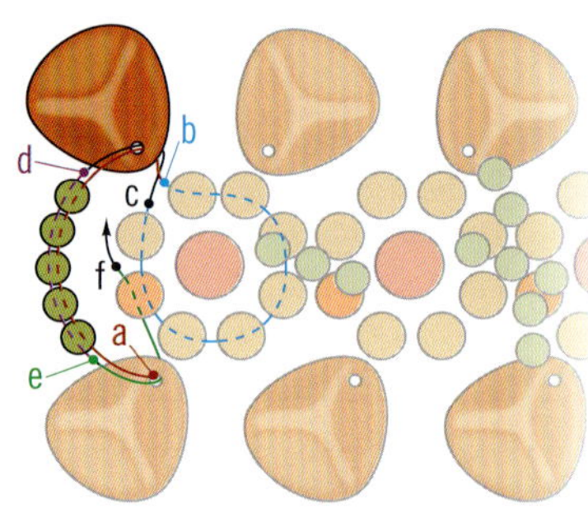

FIGURE 10

[4] Pick up an 11º, and sew through the third 11º added in step 1. Pick up an 11º, and sew through the end 6 mm **(figure 11)**.

[5] Sew through the beadwork to exit the end A and B, and repeat the instructions for "Clasp." End the working thread and tail.

[6] Add 24 in. (61 cm) of thread to the other end of the bracelet, exiting the last top-side petal from back to front. Pick up two 11ºs, and sew through the center 11º added in step 3 of the "Top embellishment" **(figure 12, a–b)**.

[7] Pick up two 11ºs and a petal from front to back, and sew through the 8º shown **(b–c)**. Sew through the new petal from back to front **(figure 13, a–b)**.

[8] Sew through the last two 11ºs added, the center 11º, the first two 11ºs added, and the following petal from front to back **(b–c)**. End the thread. ●

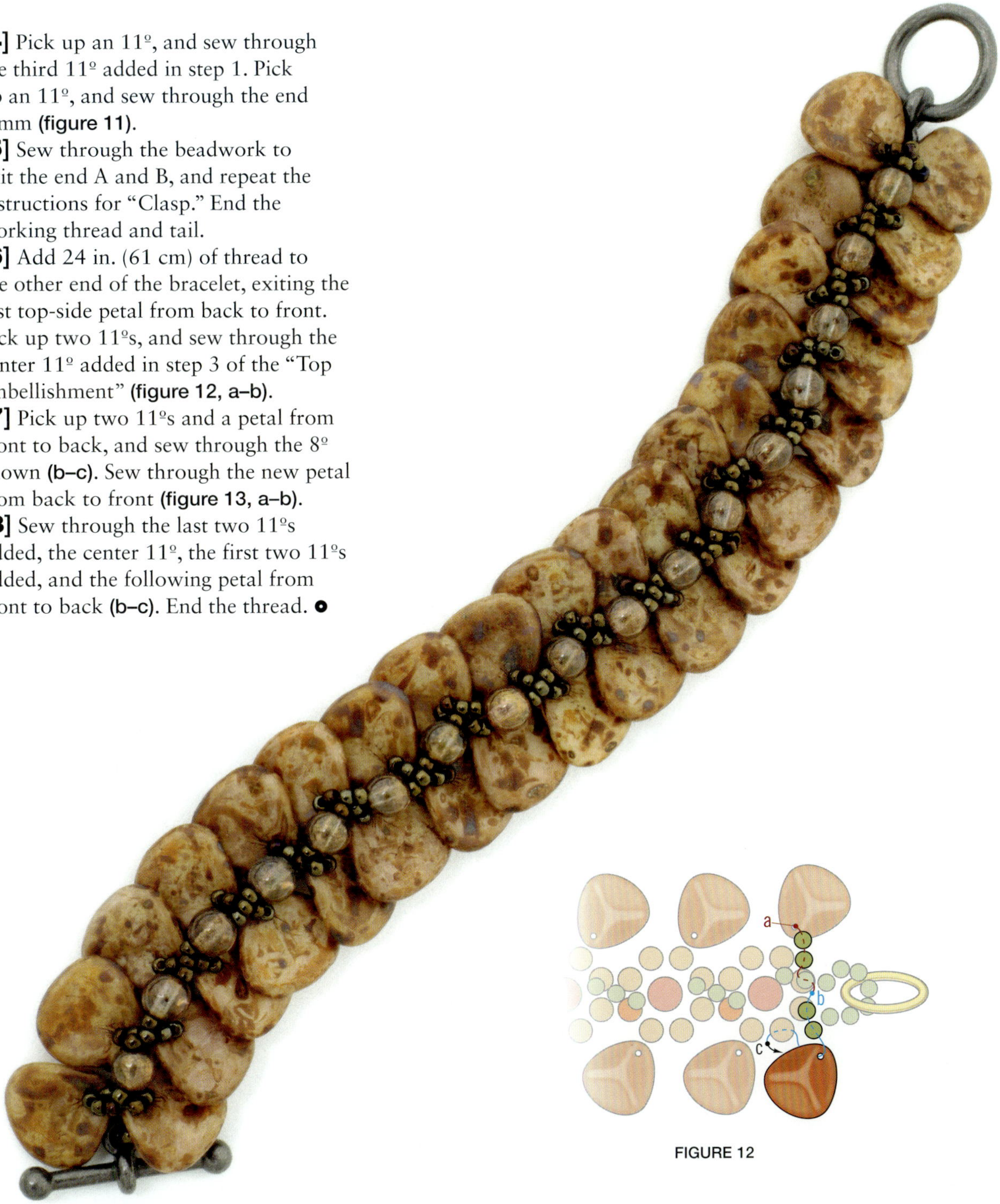

FIGURE 12

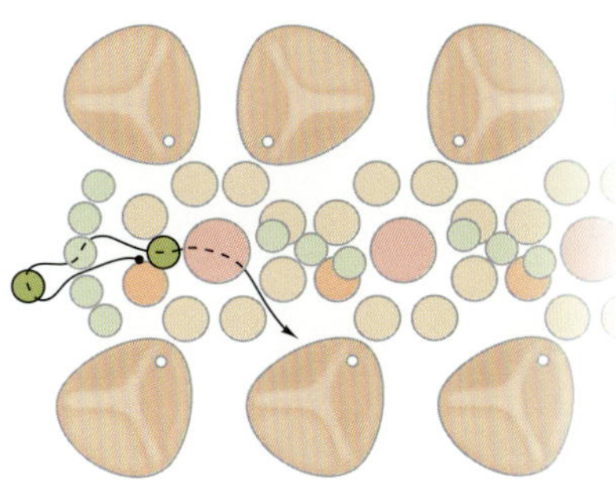

FIGURE 11

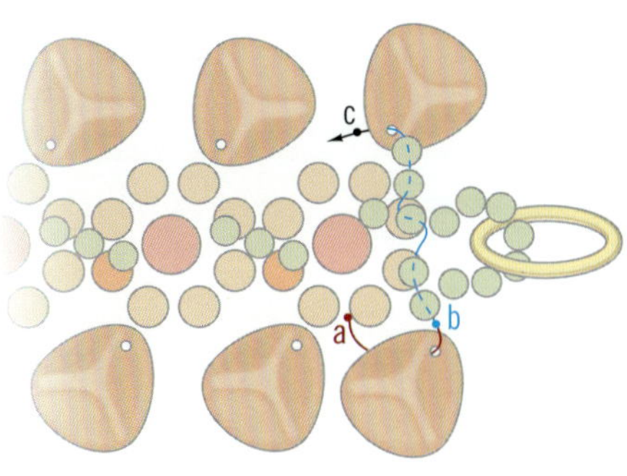

FIGURE 13

Studded bracelet

Stitch cubic right-angle weave tubes to string between two-hole bead studs for an easy-to-wear bracelet.

designed by **Dana Rudolph**

stepbystep

CRAW tubes

[1] On 18 in. (46 cm) of Fireline 6 lb. test, pick up four 11º seed beads, and sew through all the beads again to form a ring, leaving a 6-in. (15 cm) tail. Retrace the thread path of the ring, and then sew through the first three beads to exit opposite the tail. This is the first right-angle weave stitch.

[2] Make a flat strip of right-angle weave (Basics) that's three stitches long. Form the strip into a ring: Pick up an 11º, sew through the end 11º in the first stitch **(figure 1, a–b)**, pick up an 11º, and sew through the end 11º in the last stitch **(b–c)**. Sew through the four 11ºs on top of the cube, and then do the same on the bottom **(figure 2)**. This completes the first cubic right-angle weave (CRAW) unit.

[3] Subsequent CRAW units will be worked off of the four top 11ºs in the previous unit. For clarity, the next unit is worked in a different color bead in the photos. With your thread exiting one of the top 11ºs, work the

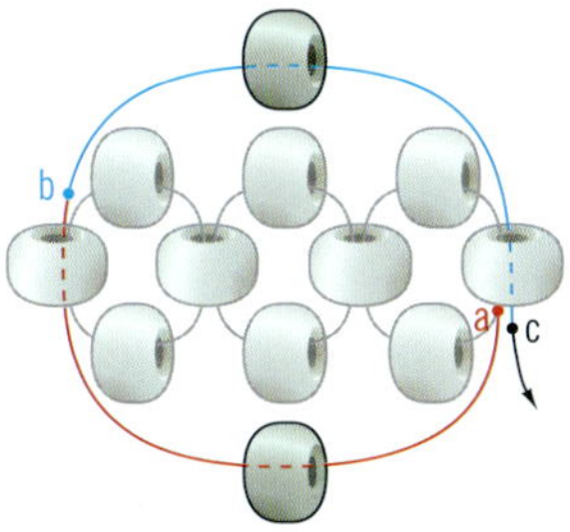

FIGURE 1

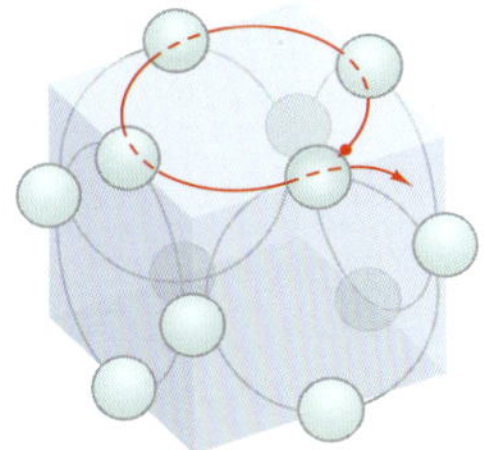

FIGURE 2

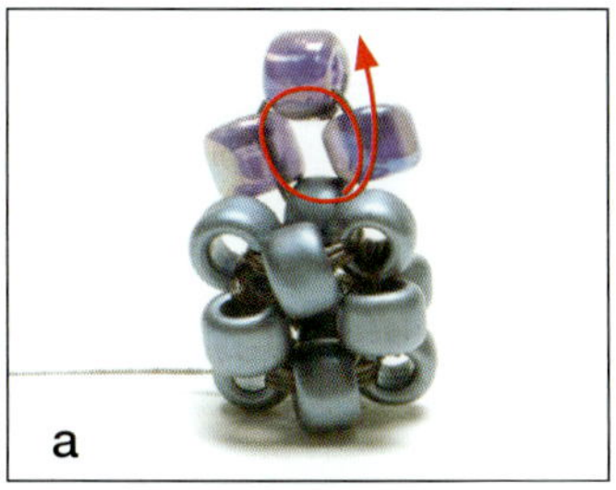
a

b

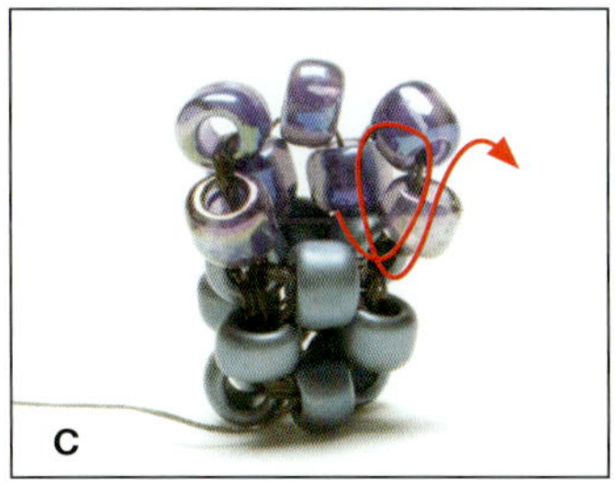
c

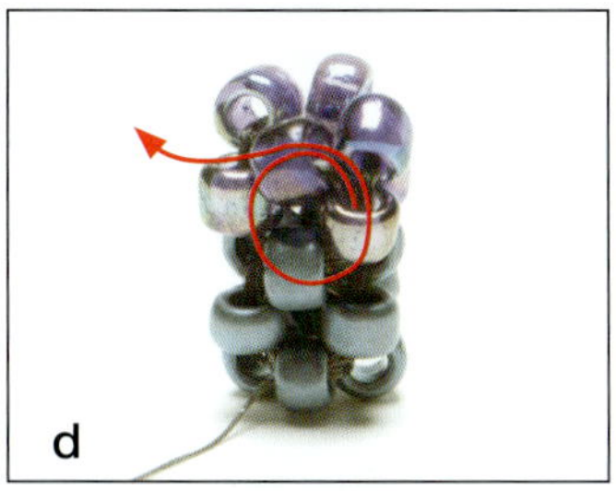
d

e

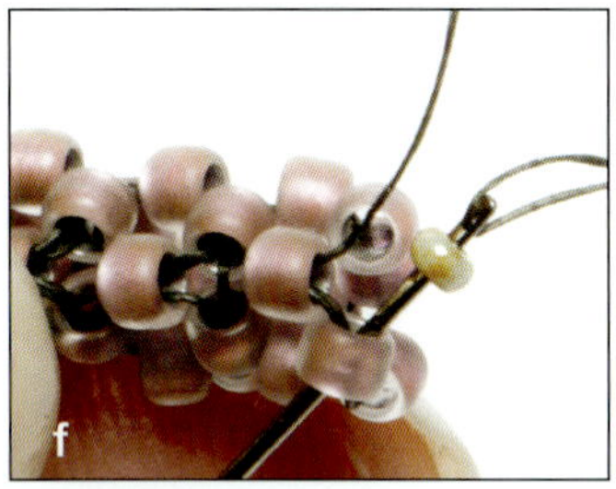
f

following stitches:
First stitch: Pick up three 11ºs, and sew through the top 11º your thread just exited and the first 11º just picked up **(photo a)**.
Second stitch: Pick up two 11ºs, sew through the next top 11º, the side 11º in the previous stitch, and the two 11ºs just picked up **(photo b)**.
Third stitch: Sew through the next top 11º, and pick up two 11ºs. Sew through the side 11º in the previous stitch, the third top 11º, and the first 11º just picked up **(photo c)**.
Fourth stitch: Pick up one 11º, and sew through the side 11º in the first stitch, the fourth top 11º, the side 11º in the previous stitch, and the 11º just picked up **(photo d)**. To complete the unit, sew through the four new top 11ºs **(photo e)**.

[4] Work step 3 again to make a tube that is three CRAW units long.

[5] With your thread exiting a top 11º in the last unit, pick up a 13º Charlotte, and sew through the next top 11º **(photo f)**. Repeat this stitch to add a 13º between all of the four top 11ºs.

Elasticize me!

For this fabulous stretchy stud bangle, use sturdy elastic — like Elastoma by BeadSmith — and string 8º seed beads between the CRAW tubes and the bead studs. Instead of a clasp, string another bead stud, tie overhand knots, and dot the knots with Super New Glue.

MATERIALS

cream/gold bracelet
6½ in. (16.5 cm)

- **6** 12 mm two-hole bead studs (opaque beige lumi)
- **4** 8º seed beads (Miyuki 196, 24kt yellow gold-lined opal)
- 5–6 g 11º seed beads (Miyuki 196, 24kt yellow gold-lined opal)
- 1 g 15º seed beads (Miyuki 196, 24kt yellow gold-lined opal)
- 2 g 13º Charlottes (24kt gold plate)
- 2-strand box clasp
- Fireline 6 lb. and 10 lb. test
- beading needles, #11

bronze/green bracelet colors:

- 12 mm two-hole bead studs (antique bronze)
- 8º seed beads (Miyuki 196, 24kt yellow gold-lined opal)
- 11º seed beads (Toho 457, gold-lustered green)
- 15º seed beads (Miyuki 91, 24kt gold plated)
- 13º Charlottes (24kt gold plate)

copper/green bracelet colors:

- 12 mm two-hole bead studs (copper matte; Eclectica, 262-641-0961)
- 8º seed beads (Miyuki 457L, metallic light bronze
- 11º seed beads (Miyuki 2008, matte/metallic patina iris)
- 15º seed beads, in place of the 13º Charlottes (Toho 721, galvanized blue gold)

Materials continued on p. 172

Materials continued from p. 171

green/orchid bangle 2¼-in. (5.7 cm) inner diameter

- **7** 12 mm two-hole bead studs (opaque green turquoise Picasso; Eclectica, 262-641-0961)
- **28** 8º seed beads (Miyuki 274, amethyst-lined crystal AB)
- 5–6 g 11º seed beads (Toho 267FM, frost crystal)
- 2 g 13º Charlottes (sage green)
- elastic cord, 1 mm diameter (clear)
- Super New Glue

g

[6] Sew through the next side 11º and the top 11º in the next CRAW unit. Work as in step 5 **(photo g)**. Repeat this step twice so that you have 13ºs at each corner of the three CRAW units that

h

make up the tube **(photo h)**. End the working thread and tail (Basics).

[7] Make a total of 14 tubes.

Assembly

[1] On 1 yd. (.9 m) of Fireline 10 lb. test, attach a stop bead (Basics), leaving a 6-in. (15 cm) tail.

[2] Pick up a repeating pattern of a CRAW tube and a 12 mm bead stud six times, and then pick up a tube, an 8º seed bead, three 15º seed beads, a loop of half of the clasp, and three 15ºs. Sew back through the 8º, and snug up the beads, but not too tight. Retrace the thread path through the tubes and studs.

[3] When you exit the first tube, pick up an 8º, three 15ºs, the corresponding loop of the other half of the clasp, and three 15ºs. Sew back through the 8º.

[4] Remove the stop bead from the tail, and tie the threads together with a square knot (Basics). End the threads.

[5] Repeat steps 1–4 by stringing the remaining tubes, going through the available holes of the studs, and attaching the available loops of the clasp. ●

MODIFIED RIGHT-ANGLE WEAVE / BEAD WEAVING

Pearls & bows

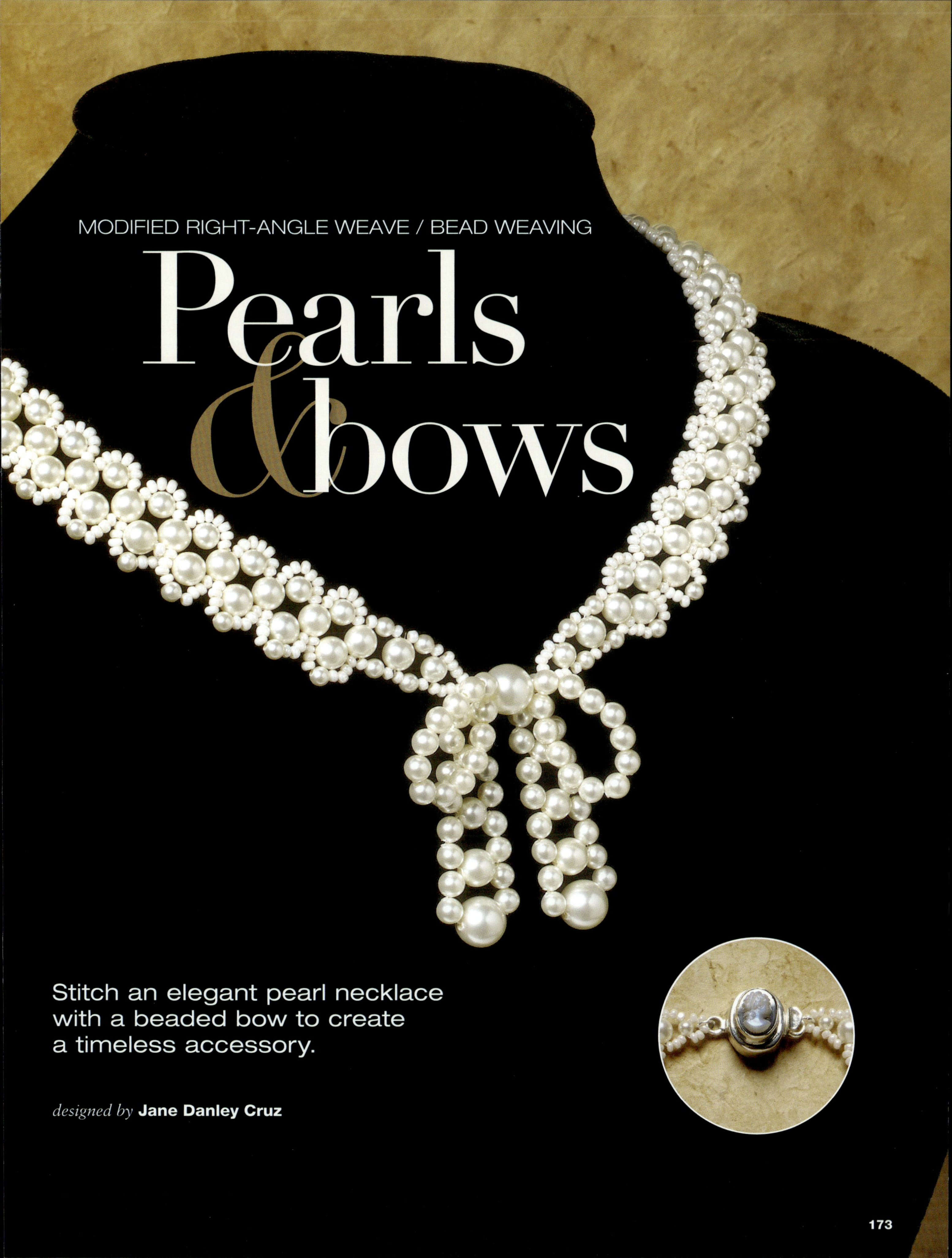

Stitch an elegant pearl necklace with a beaded bow to create a timeless accessory.

designed by **Jane Danley Cruz**

MATERIALS

necklace 16 in. (41 cm)

- crystal pearls (Swarovski, cream)
  - **3** 8 mm
  - **2** 6 mm
  - **86** 5 mm
  - **100** 4 mm
  - **52** 3 mm
- 3 g 13º Charlotte/true-cut seed beads (Czech, pearl eggshell; www.shipwreckbeads.com)
- clasp (www.agrainofsand.com)
- Fireline 6 lb. test (crystal)
- beading needles, #11

DESIGN NOTE:

To alter the length of your necklace, add or omit right-angle weave stitches from the neck straps, but make sure the straps are the same length. Each right-angle weave stitch adds about ⅜ in. (1 cm) to a strap.

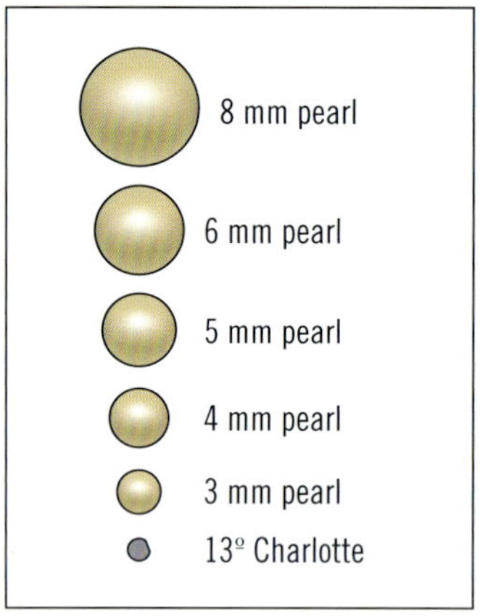

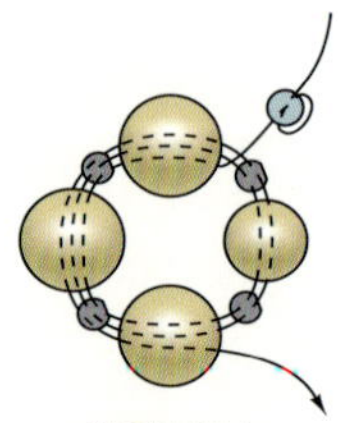

FIGURE 1

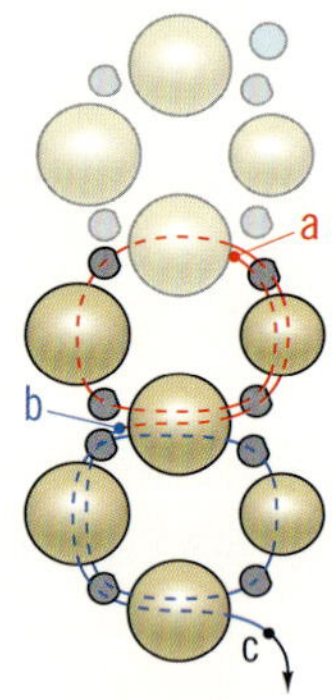

FIGURE 2

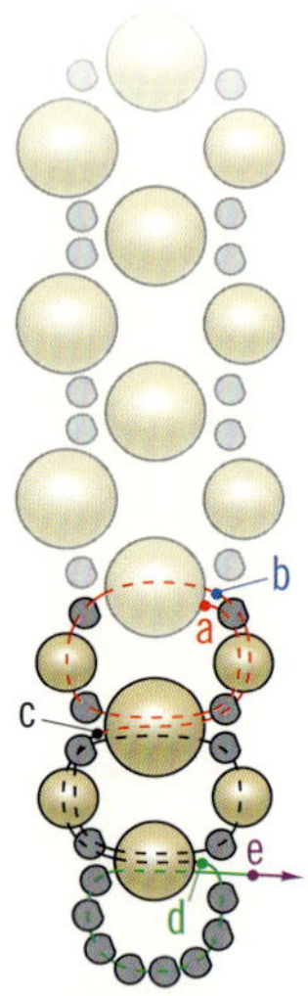

FIGURE 3

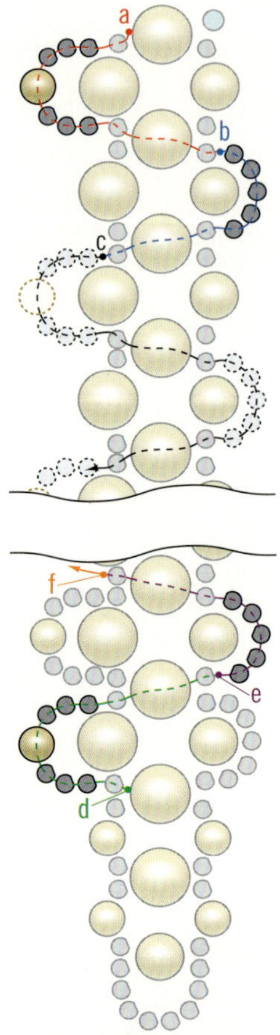

FIGURE 4

stepbystep

Neck straps

[1] On 1 yd. (.9 m) of thread, attach a stop bead (Basics), leaving an 8-in. (20 cm) tail. Pick up a 5 mm pearl, a 13º Charlotte seed bead, a 5 mm, a 13º, a 5 mm, a 13º, a 4 mm pearl, and a 13º, and sew through the beads again to form a ring. Continue through the first five beads to exit the 5 mm opposite the tail, and snug up the beads **(figure 1)**. You have completed the first right-angle weave stitch.

[2] To work the next stitch: Pick up a 13º, a 4 mm, a 13º, a 5 mm, a 13º, a 5 mm, and a 13º, and sew through the 5 mm your thread exited at the start of this step. Continue through the next four beads added in this step **(figure 2, a–b)**.

[3] To work the next stitch: Pick up a 13º, a 5 mm, a 13º, a 5 mm, a 13º, a 4 mm, and a 13º, and sew through the 5 mm your thread exited at the start of this step. Continue through the next four beads added in this step **(b–c)**.

[4] Repeat steps 2 and 3 using a firm tension until you have a total of 20 right-angle weave stitches. You will have 20 4 mm pearls along the inner edge and 20 5 mm pearls along the outer edge for a 16-in. (41 cm) finished necklace.

[5] Pick up a 13º, a 3 mm pearl, a 13º, a 5 mm, a 13º, a 3 mm, and a 13º, and sew through the 5 mm your thread exited at the start of this step **(figure 3, a–b)**. Continue through the next four beads added in this step **(b–c)**.

[6] Pick up a 13º, a 3 mm, a 13º, a 4 mm, a 13º, a 3 mm, and a 13º, and sew through the 5 mm your thread exited at the start of this step. Continue through the next four beads added in this step **(c–d)**. Pick up eight 13ºs, and sew through the 4 mm **(d–e)**. End the working thread (Basics) but not the tail.

[7] Make a second neck strap.

Embellishing the straps

[1] Add a comfortable length of thread (Basics) to the first right-angle weave stitch of a neck strap, exiting the end 5 mm with the needle pointing toward the outer edge **(figure 4, point a)**. Sew through the next 13º.

[2] Pick up three 13ºs, a 3 mm, and three 13ºs. Skip the next 5 mm, and sew through the following 13º, 5 mm, and 13º to exit the inner edge of the strap **(a–b)**.

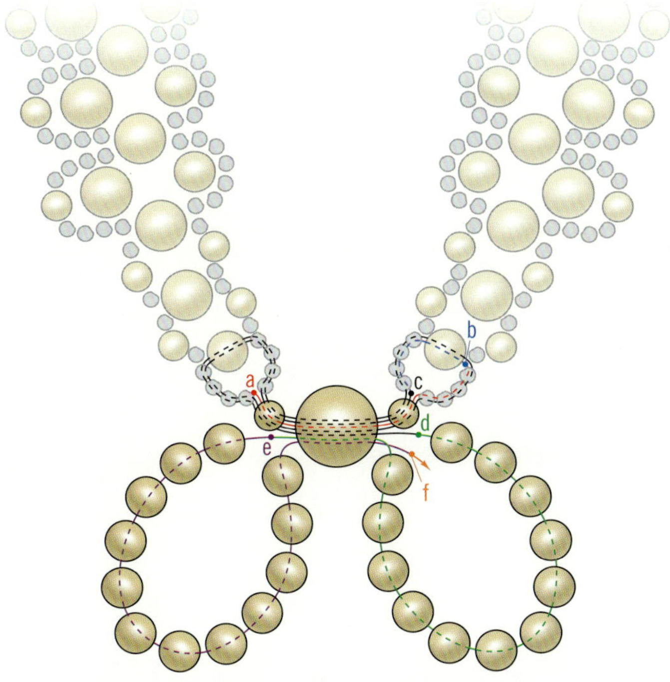

FIGURE 5

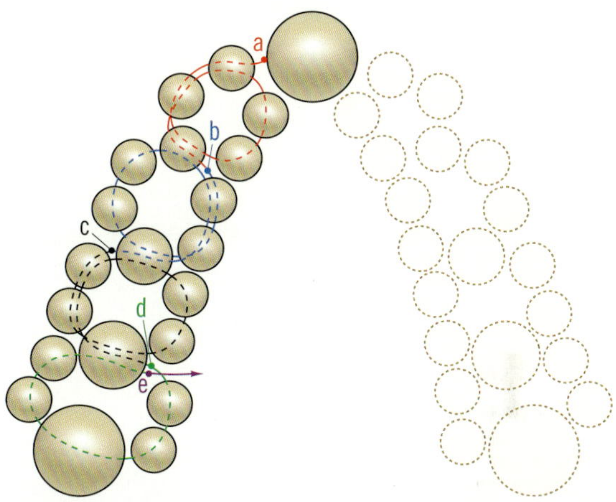

FIGURE 6

[3] Pick up five 13ºs, skip the next 4 mm, and sew through the following 13º, 5 mm, and 13º to exit the outer edge of the strap **(b–c)**.
[4] Work as in steps 2 and 3 for the next 18 right-angle weave stitches, ending and adding thread as needed.
[5] With your thread exiting the end 5 mm **(point d)**, sew through the next 13º. Work as in steps 2 **(d–e)** and 3 **(e–f)** to embellish the remaining stitches of this neck strap. End the thread.
[6] Repeat steps 1–5 for the other neck strap.

Joining the straps

[1] Add 2 ft. (61 cm) of thread to one neck strap, and exit the fourth 13º at the end opposite the stop bead **(figure 5, point a)**.
[2] Pick up a 3 mm, an 8 mm pearl, and a 3 mm, and sew through the corresponding four 13ºs at the end of the other neck strap **(a–b)**. Continue through the next 4 mm and four 13ºs **(b–c)**, sew back through the 3 mm, 8 mm, and 3 mm just added, and sew through the remaining four 13ºs on the first neck strap. Retrace the thread path through the join several times, and exit the 8 mm **(c–d)**.

Pearl bow

[1] Pick up 12 4 mms, and sew back through the center 8 mm in the opposite direction to form the first loop of the bow **(d–e)**. Pick up 12 4 mms, and sew back through the center 8 mm to form the second loop **(e–f)**. Retrace the thread path through the loops and the center 8 mm several times, and exit the center 8 mm behind one of the loops.
[2] Pick up five 4 mms, and sew through the beads again to form a ring. Continue through the first three beads, and snug the ring close to the center 8 mm **(figure 6, a–b)**.
[3] Pick up two 4 mms, a 5 mm, and two 4 mms, and sew through the 4 mm your thread exited at the start of this step. Continue through the next three beads added in this step **(b–c)**.
[4] Pick up two 4 mms, a 6 mm pearl, and two 4 mms, and sew through the 5 mm your thread exited at the start of this step. Continue through the next three beads added in this step **(c–d)**.
[5] Pick up two 4 mms, an 8 mm, and two 4 mms, and sew through the 6 mm your thread exited at the start of this step **(d–e)**.
[6] Retrace the thread path through the beads added in steps 2–5, and exit the center 8 mm behind the other loop.
[7] Repeat steps 2–6 on the other side of the center 8 mm. End the thread.

Clasp

[1] Remove the stop bead from the tail on one of the neck straps. Pick up three 13ºs, a 3 mm, and three 13ºs, and sew through the 5 mm your thread exited at the start of this step. Retrace the thread path, and exit the 3 mm.
[2] Pick up five 13ºs and half of the clasp, and sew through the 3 mm again. Retrace the thread path several times, and end the tail.
[3] Repeat steps 1 and 2 for the other neck strap. ●

CUBIC RIGHT-ANGLE WEAVE / BEAD WEAVING

Beaded bead parade

Stitch a procession of beaded beads outfitted in metallics and jewel tones.

designed by **Yvonne King**

Fire-polished beads look like rubies as they peek through these gold-tone rondelles stitched with round seed beads and triangles. One rondelle leads to the next as you work the bracelet as a continuous piece, and the end beads hide a magnetic clasp for easy wear.

stepbystep

First beaded bead

Cube-shaped frame

[1] On 3 yd. (2.7 m) of thread, pick up two 11º seed beads and an 11º triangle bead. Repeat this pattern three more times. Sew through all the beads again to form a ring, leaving a 1-yd. (.9 m) tail, and continue through the first two 11ºs, triangle, and 11º. Shape the ring into a square with an 11º, triangle, and 11º on each side **(photo a)**. This will be the base or bottom of the frame.

[2] Work in modified cubic right-angle weave as follows to create the sides of the frame:

Side 1: Pick up an 11º, a triangle, and an 11º. Repeat this pattern twice more, and sew through the three beads in the base your thread exited at the start of this step **(photo b)**.

Side 2: Sew through the next three beads in the base. Pick up an 11º, a triangle, and an 11º. Repeat this pattern once more, and sew through the nearest three beads from the previous side and the three beads in

Hidden magnets make for a perfectly integrated clasp.

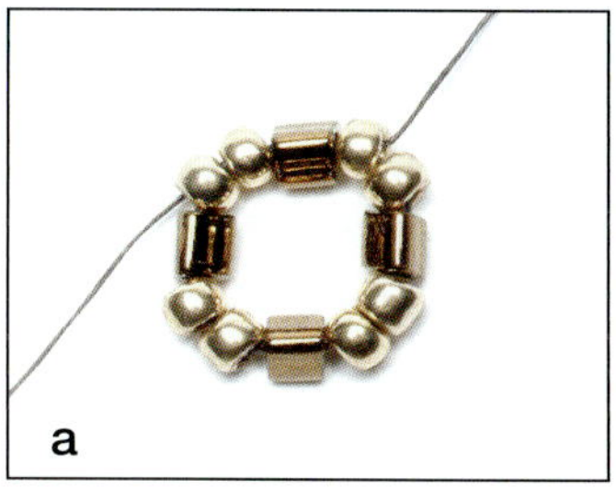
a

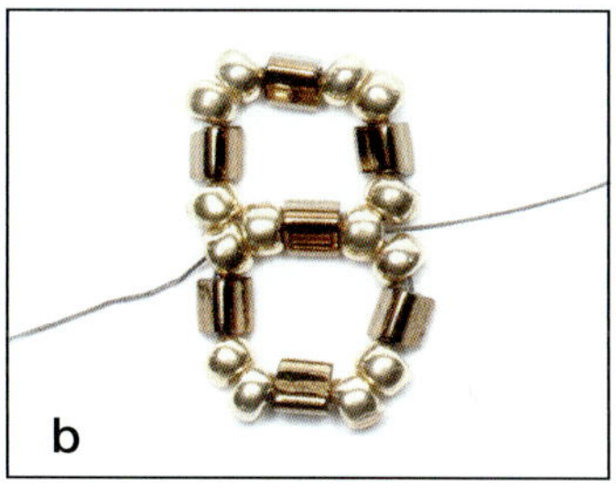
b

c

d

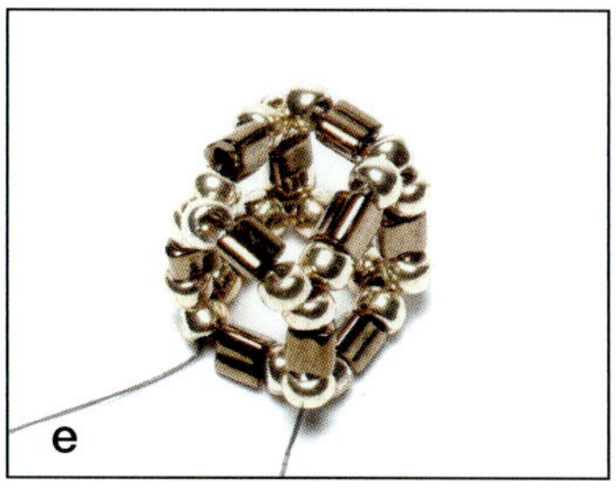
e

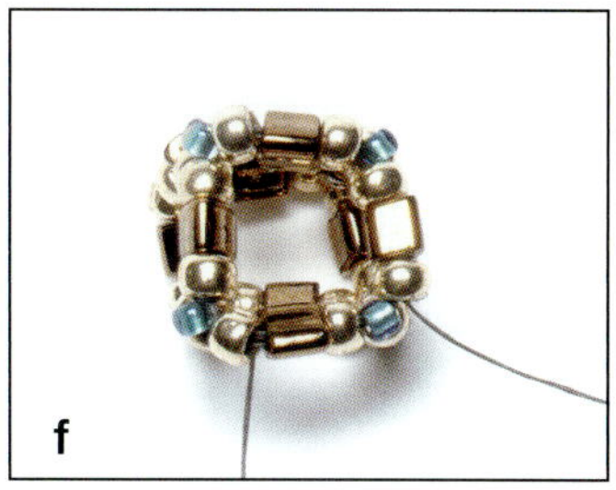
f

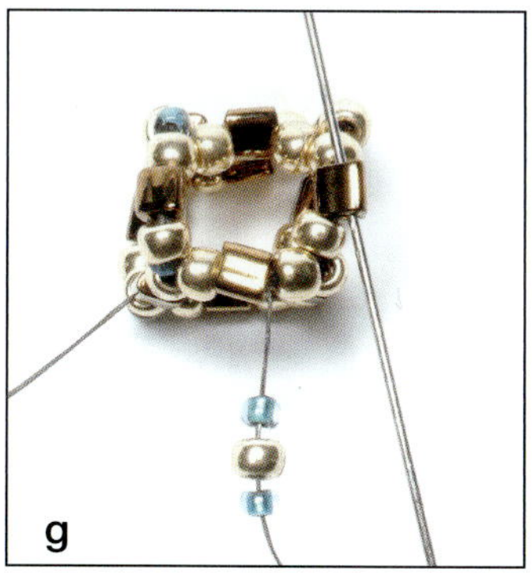
g

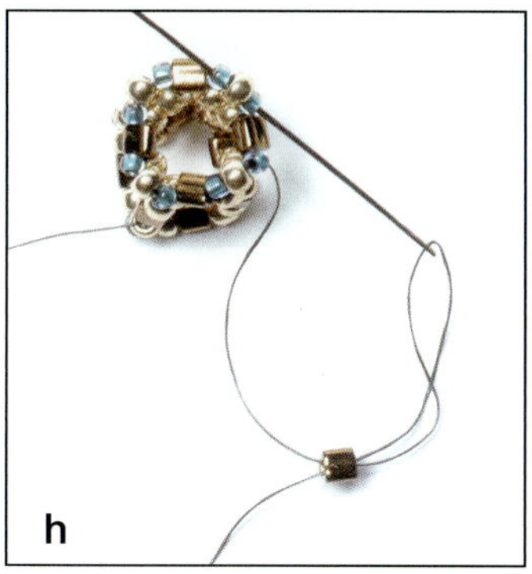
h

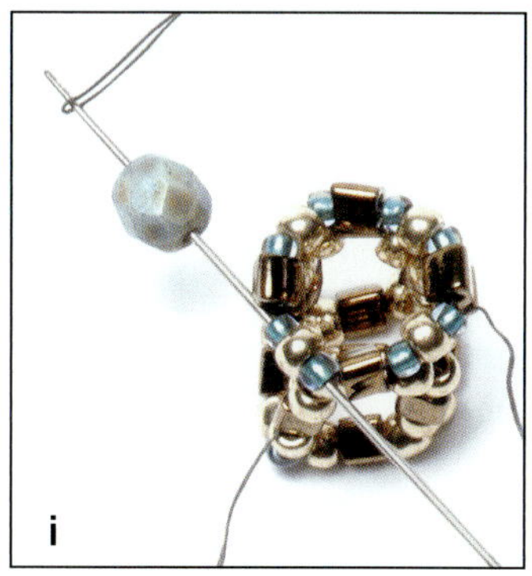
i

the base. Pull the thread tight to begin forming a three-dimensional form **(photo c)**.
Side 3: Repeat side 2 **(photo d)**.
Side 4: Sew through the last three beads in the base, and continue through the nearest three beads from side 1. Pick up an 11º, a triangle, and an 11º, and sew through the nearest three beads from side 3 **(photo e)**. Do not reinforce the base or any of the sides; your work should be floppy.

Embellishments

[1] Pick up a 15º seed bead, and sew through the next three beads of side 4. Repeat to add a 15º at each corner of side 4 **(photo f)**. Note: In the photo, side 4 is now facing up for clarity. This side of the cube will form the opening on one end of the beaded bead.
[2] Sew through the nearest 11º and triangle from side 3. In the following photos, side 3 will be facing up.
[3] Work two rounds of beadwork off this side as follows:
Round 1: Pick up a 15º, an 11º, and a 15º, and sew through the next triangle **(photo g)**. Repeat this stitch to complete the round, and step up through the first three beads added in this round.
Round 2: Pick up a triangle, and sew through the next three beads added in the previous round **(photo h)**. The triangles should stack to form a diamond shape. Repeat this stitch to complete the round, but do not step up.
[4] With your thread exiting the three beads at one corner, pick up a 4 mm fire-polished bead, and sew through the corresponding three beads in the previous corner, with your needle pointing toward the starting corner **(photo i)**.

MATERIALS

bracelet 6¾ in. (17.1 cm)

- **89** 4 mm fire-polished beads (Czech, garnet red; www.firemountaingems.com)
- 6–7 g 11º triangle beads (11-311-TRI, light topaz; www.cbbeads.com)
- 6–7 g 11º seed beads (Miyuki 457, metallic dark bronze; www.caravanbeads.com)
- 4–5 g 15º seed beads (Japanese 634, gold silver-lined AB; www.beyondbeadery.com)
- **2** 5/16 x 1/8-in. (8 x 3 mm) magnets for clasp (item #67488, www.harborfreight.com)
- Fireline 4 or 6 lb. test
- beading needles, #12

DESIGN NOTE:

Make separate beaded beads by omitting the connector, and string them on a Pandora-style bracelet. Use different colors of 4 mm fire-polished beads to mimic other gemstones.

Sew through the next 12 beads, and then work the same thread path through the remaining corners and the 4 mm. The 4 mm should be perpendicular to the side you embellished with 15ºs in step 1.

[5] Sew through the next triangle, and work a round of beadwork as follows:

Round 3: Pick up two 15ºs, and sew through the next triangle **(photo j)**. Repeat this stitch to complete the round, and retrace the thread path through the round. Exit a triangle.

[6] Sew through the adjacent triangle in the next side. Make sure this is not the side you embellished with 15ºs in step 1.

[7] Work as in steps 3–6 to embellish the remaining three sides. Note: Where the side you are working on meets a previously embellished side, you will have three stacked triangles as you work round 2. Also, in step 4, make sure the 4 mm is oriented parallel to the previous 4 mm(s). If it's not, sew through the beadwork to exit the three beads at the next corner before adding the 4 mm.

[8] Sew through the beadwork to exit an 11º, a triangle, and an 11º on the remaining, unembellished side. Repeat step 1. This is the opening on the other end of the beaded bead.

Connector

[1] With your thread exiting an 11º, a triangle, and an 11º on the side you just embellished, pick up a 15º, an 11º, a triangle, an 11º, and a 15º. Sew through the three beads your thread exited at the start of this step. Retrace the thread path, and exit the first 15º added in this step.

[2] Pick up an 11º, a 15º, an 11º, a 4 mm, an 11º, a 15º, and an 11º. Sew through the other 15º from the previous step, and sew back through all the beads just added. Sew through the first 15º from the previous step **(photo k)**. Your thread should exit both sides of the 15º, and the 4 mm in the loop of beads you just made should be next to the opening of the previous beaded bead. Sew through the beadwork to exit the 11º, triangle, and 11º added in the previous step.

Subsequent beaded beads

[1] Pick up an 11º, a triangle, and an 11º. Repeat this pattern two more times, and sew through the three beads your thread exited at the start of this step to form a ring. Shape the ring into a square with an 11º, triangle, and 11º on each side. This will be the base or bottom of the frame for the next beaded bead.

[2] Work step 2 of "Cube-shaped frame" and all the steps for "Embellishments" and "Connector." End and add thread (Basics) as needed. Being careful to attach the connectors to the same side each time, continue adding beaded beads until the bracelet is two beaded beads short of the desired length; the last two beads will be the clasp beads. For a 6¾-in. (17.1 cm) finished bracelet, work 16 beaded beads, not including the clasp beads.

Clasp beads

Work the first clasp bead just like the other beaded beads, but insert a 5⁄16 x 1⁄8-in. (8 x 3 mm) magnet into the cube-shaped frame before adding the embellishments. Make sure the correct (negative or positive) side is facing out and away from your bracelet. End the working thread. Work the second clasp bead with the tail, again making sure that the correct side is facing out. End the tail. ●

BEAD WEAVING / WIREWORK

Use three antiqued colors of SuperDuos to create a spiraling bangle and matching necklace and earrings with a vintage vibe.

designed by **Michelle McEnroe**

Super spiral set

MATERIALS

all projects

- Fireline 6 lb. test
- beading needles, #11 or #12
- for necklace and earrings only: **2** pairs of chainnose, flatnose, and/or bentnose pliers
- roundnose pliers
- wire cutters

bangle 2-in. (5 cm) inside diameter

- 6 g 2.5 x 5 mm SuperDuo beads in each of **3** colors:
  color A (14415, dark bronze)
  color B (T5342, olive Picasso opaque)
  color C (T6313, turquoise Picasso opaque)

necklace 23 in. (58 cm)

- **1** 1½–2-in. (35–50 mm) ceramic pendant (www.antelopebeads.com)
- **4** 6 mm beads (jasper)
- 1 g 2.5 x 5 mm SuperDuo beads in each of **3** colors (same colors as bangle)
- 22 mm toggle clasp (TierraCast CP2311, antique copper radiant square; www.fusionbeads.com)
- 19 in. (48 cm) chain (antique copper)
- **3** 8 mm jump rings (antique copper)
- **4** 4 mm jump rings (antique copper)
- **2** 2-in. (5 cm) eye pins (antique copper)

pair of earrings

- 1 g 2.5 x 5 mm SuperDuo beads in each of **3** colors (same colors as bangle)
- **4** 6 mm beads (jasper)
- **2** 11 x 16 mm filigree cones
- **2** 16 mm round links (antiqued copper notched link; www.etsy.com/shop/missficklemedia)
- **2** 2-in. (5 cm) eye pins (antique copper)
- **2** 2-in. (5 cm) head pins (antique copper)
- pair of earring findings (antiqued ball-tipped hammered copper; www.etsy.com/shop/missficklemedia)

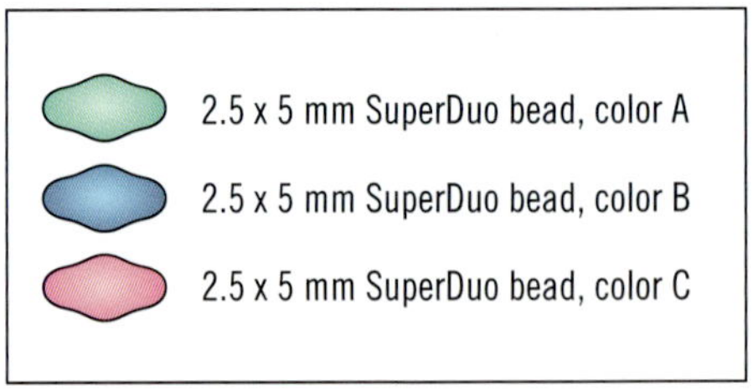

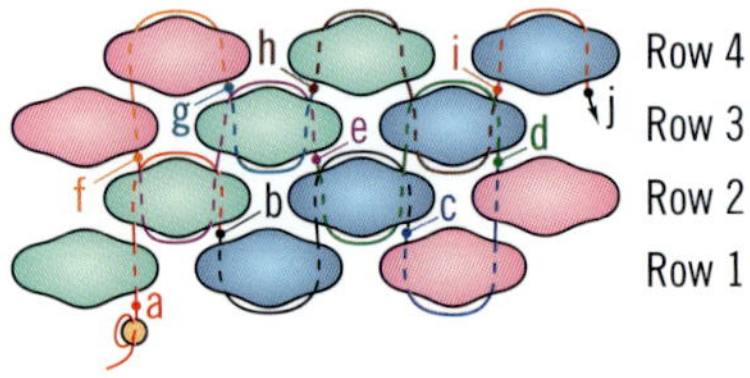

FIGURE

stepbystep

Bangle

[1] On a comfortable length of thread, attach a stop bead (Basics), leaving a 6-in. (15 cm) tail.

[2] Pick up two color A 2.5 x 5 mm SuperDuo beads, and sew down through the available hole of the last SuperDuo added **(figure, a–b)**.

[3] Pick up a color B 2.5 x 5 mm SuperDuo bead, and sew through the available hole of the same B. Repeat this stitch once more **(b–c)**.

[4] Pick up a color C 2.5 x 5 mm SuperDuo bead, sew up through the available hole of the same C, and pick up another C **(c–d)**. This completes rows 1 and 2.

[5] Work the next two rows as follows:

Row 3: Pick up a B, and sew down through the available hole of the same B. Continue down through the nearest hole of the B in the previous row, and sew up through the other hole of the same B **(d–e)**. Repeat these stitches to add an A, sewing through the A in the previous row **(e–f)**, and then pick up a C.

Row 4: Pick up a C, and sew down through the available hole of the same C **(f–g)**. Continue down through the nearest hole of the A in the previous row, and sew up through the other hole of the same A **(g–h)**. Repeat these stitches to add an A, sewing through the B in the previous row **(h–i)**. Pick up a B, and sew down through the available hole of the same B **(i–j)**.

[6] Pinch the ends of the beadwork to form a tube. If you pinch the beads to the front, the colors will spiral to the left. If you pinch them to the back, they will spiral to the right. For the purposes of these instructions, we will pinch them to the front.

[7] Sew down through the available holes of the next two Cs and A **(photo a)**. Continue up through the other hole of the same A, the following A, and the next C **(photo b)**.

[8] Sew through the beads as shown to exit the B in the last row **(photo c)**. Retrace the thread path. Remove the stop bead, and end the tail (Basics). Notice the thread is exiting the right-hand hole of the B. This means you will be working in a counterclockwise direction when adding the next round. Note: Since the rest of the bangle will be worked in rounds, they will now be referred to as such, rather than rows.

[9] Work the next two rounds as follows:

Round 5: Pick up an A, and sew down through the available hole of the same A. Continue down through the nearest hole of the A in the previous round, and sew up through the other hole of the same A **(photo d)**. Repeat this stitch to add a C and a B, and then continue up through the A added in this round. Your

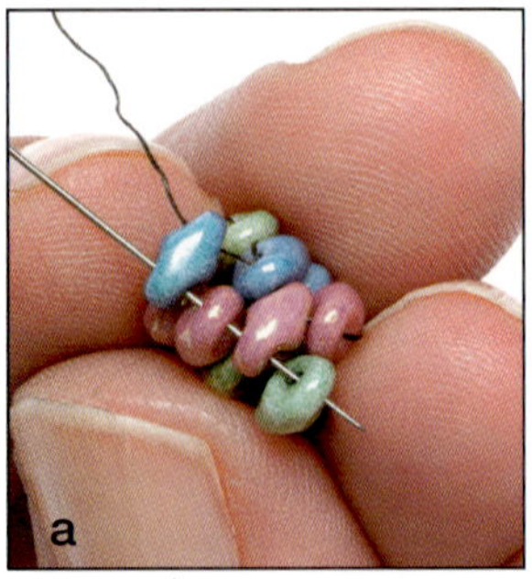
a

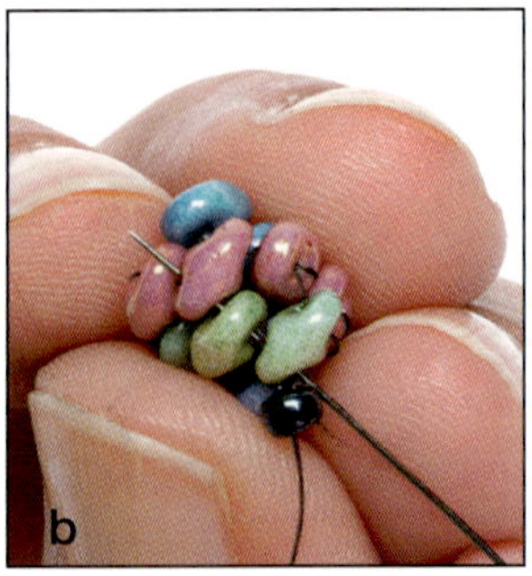
b

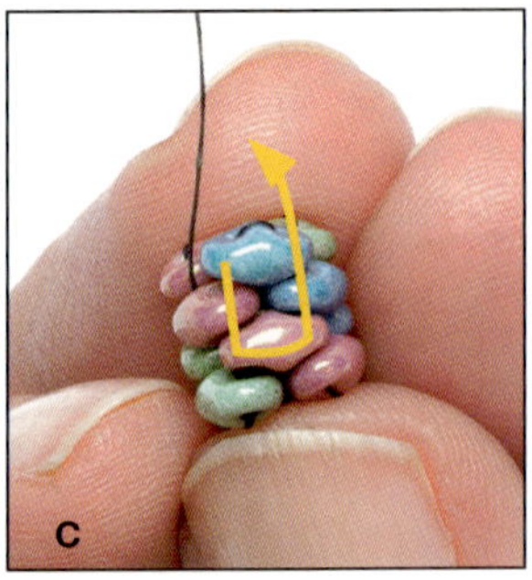
c

d

e

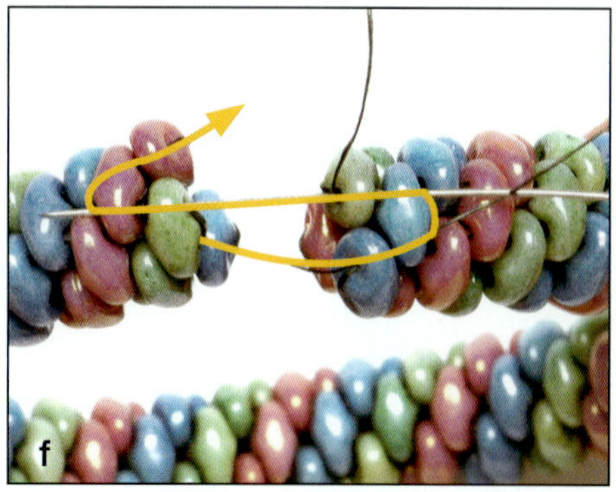
f

thread should be exiting the left-hand hole of the A **(photo e)**. This means you will be working in a clockwise direction when adding the next round.

Round 6: Pick up an A, and sew down through the available hole of the same A. Continue down through the nearest hole of the B in the previous round, and sew up through the other hole of the same B. Repeat this stitch to add a B and a C, and then continue up through the A added in this round. Your thread should be exiting the right-hand hole of the A. This means you will be working in a counterclockwise direction when adding the next round.

[10] Continue working the two rounds of step 9, alternating between clockwise and counterclockwise stitching and adding the correct colors to match the spiral. Keep going until the bangle just fits around the widest part of your hand, ending and adding thread (Basics) as needed. Do not end the working thread.

TIP: When starting a new round, remember this: If your thread is exiting the left hole, you'll bead to the left; if it's exiting the right hole, you'll bead to the right.

[11] Add 18 in. (46 cm) of thread to the tail end of the bangle, exiting an end SuperDuo. Align both ends of the bangle so that the pattern flows seamlessly, but do not twist the beadwork. The bangle should lie flat. If it does not, with the working thread (not the thread added in this step), add rounds until the colors follow the spiral pattern.

[12] With the thread on the tail end of the bangle, sew through the beadwork as shown **(photo f)** to join the end SuperDuos. Retrace the thread path of the join, and end the threads.

Necklace

Beaded bead links

[1] On 1 yd. (.9 m) of thread and leaving an 8-in. (20 cm) tail, work steps 1–10 of "Bangle" for a total of 10 rounds.

[2] Secure the SuperDuos in round 10 by sewing down through the other hole of the SuperDuo your thread is exiting, down through the nearest SuperDuo in the previous round, up through the other hole of the same SuperDuo, and up through the nearest hole of the next SuperDuo in round 10. Repeat until all the SuperDuos in round 10 have been secured. Using the tail, repeat this step for the SuperDuos in row 1, and end the working thread and tail.

[3] Make another beaded bead.

[4] On an eye pin, string a 6 mm bead, a beaded bead, and a 6 mm bead, and make a plain loop (Basics). Make a second beaded-bead link.

Necklace assembly

[1] Cut two 7¼-in. (18.4 cm) pieces of chain (long) and one 4¼-in. (10.8 cm) piece of chain (short).

[2] Open a 4 mm jump ring (Basics), and attach a beaded-bead link to one end of the short chain. Repeat on the other end of the chain with the other beaded bead.

[3] Open a 4 mm jump ring, and attach the other loop of a beaded bead to one end of a long chain. Repeat to attach the other beaded bead to the other long chain.

[4] Open an 8 mm jump ring, and attach half of the clasp to the other end of a long chain. Repeat to attach the other half of the clasp to the other long chain.

[5] Open an 8 mm jump ring, and attach the pendant to the center link of the short chain.

Earrings

[1] Work steps 1–3 of "Beaded bead links."

[2] On an eye pin, string a 6 mm bead, a beaded bead, and a filigree cone (wide end first), and make a plain loop (Basics).

[3] Open the loop (Basics) of an earring finding, and attach the top loop of the dangle.

[4] Open the bottom loop of the dangle, and attach a 16 mm link.

[5] On a head pin, string a 6 mm bead, and make a plain loop. Open the loop, and attach it to the 16 mm link.

[6] Assemble the other earring. •

DESIGN NOTES:

- Unfortunately, this pattern will not work with Twin beads.
- The size of the jump ring used to attach the pendant may have to be adjusted to accommodate the pendant's hole.
- To make the earrings a mirror image of each other, spiral one to the left and the other one to the right.

LADDER STITCH / BRICK STITCH / BEAD WEAVING

Metallic *lace* bracelet

Embellish a flexible knit-wire band with a cube bead edging and overlapping loops of round beads and seed beads.

designed by **Jimmie Boatright**

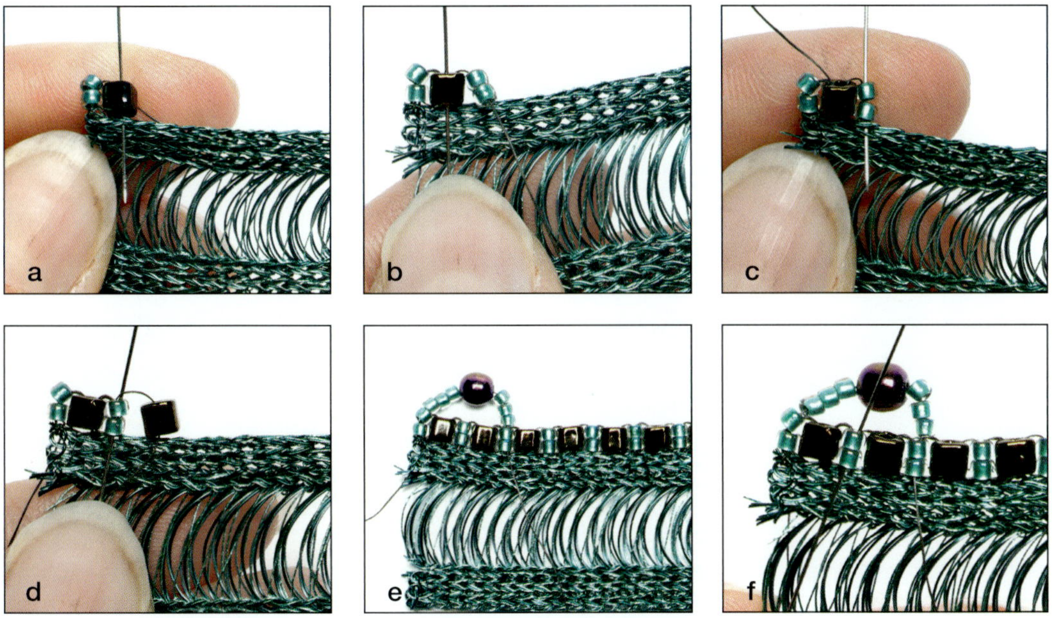

stepbystep

Measure your wrist, subtract about ½–1 in. (1.3–2.5 cm) for the clasp, and cut the knit wire to that length.

Edging row 1

[1] Add 1 yd. (.9 m) of thread (Basics) to one end of the knit-wire band as you would to add a thread to beadwork. Exit at the end of this edge.

[2] Pick up two 11º seed beads and a 3 mm cube bead. Working in modified ladder stitch, sew through all three beads just picked up. Snug up the beads so the cube sits next to the stack of two 11ºs, with the needle exiting the cube and pointing toward the band. Working in modified brick stitch, sew through the edge of the band **(photo a)** and back up through the cube.

[3] Pick up two 11ºs, and sew up through the last cube **(photo b)** and down through the new stack of two 11ºs. Sew through the edge of the band **(photo c)** and back up through the last 11º stack.

[4] Pick up a cube, and sew up through the last 11º stack **(photo d)** and down through the new cube. Sew through the edge of the band and back up through the cube.

[5] Repeat steps 3 and 4 for the length of this edge of the band, ending with step 3. End the thread (Basics).

[6] Work steps 1–5 along the other edge of the band.

Edging row 2

[1] Add 1 yd. (.9 m) of thread to one end of the band, exiting the first 11º stack in row 1.

[2] Pick up three 11ºs, a 4 mm round bead, and three 11ºs. Skip the next cube, 11º stack, and cube, and sew down through the following 11º stack to create a loop **(photo e)**.

[3] Skip the previous cube, and sew up through the next 11º stack **(photo f)**. Make sure your needle is in front of the loop created in step 2.

[4] Repeat steps 2 and 3 for the length of the band. End the thread.

[5] Work steps 1–4 along the other edge of the band.

Clasp

[1] Slide one end of the band into the jaws of a ribbon crimp end. Make sure the crimp is centered on the band and that there are no beads in the crimp.

[2] With chainnose pliers, crimp the ribbon crimp securely onto the band.

[3] Work steps 1 and 2 for the other end of the band.

[4] Open a jump ring (Basics), and attach the loop of a ribbon crimp to half of the clasp. Repeat this step on the other end. Note: If you use a toggle clasp, you may have to add two more jump rings to the toggle bar so it slides easily through the toggle ring. •

MATERIALS

copper bracelet 8 in. (20 cm)

- 9 in. (23 cm) WireLuxe knit wire (meadow; www.limabeads.com)
- **62–70** 4 mm round beads (Czech, luster opaque green; www.limabeads.com)
- **62–70** 3 mm cube beads (Toho 134, matte metallic teal/gold luster)
- 6–7 g 11º seed beads (Miyuki 457, metallic dark bronze)
- clasp
- **2** 20 mm ribbon crimp ends (antique copper)
- **2–4** 6 mm oval jump rings (antique copper)
- Fireline 6 lb. test
- beading needles, #10 or #11
- **2** pairs of chainnose pliers

green bracelet colors:

- WireLuxe knit wire (laguna; www.limabeads.com)
- 4 mm round beads (Czech, purple iris)
- 3 mm cube beads (Toho 458, metallic iris brown)
- 11º seed beads (Toho 264, inside-color rainbow crystal teal)

DESIGN NOTES:
Use the beads in your stash for a budget-friendly bracelet. Substitute 6º seed beads for the cube beads, or mix and match any 4 mm beads you have on hand.

LADDER STITCH / BEAD WEAVING

Triangular appeal

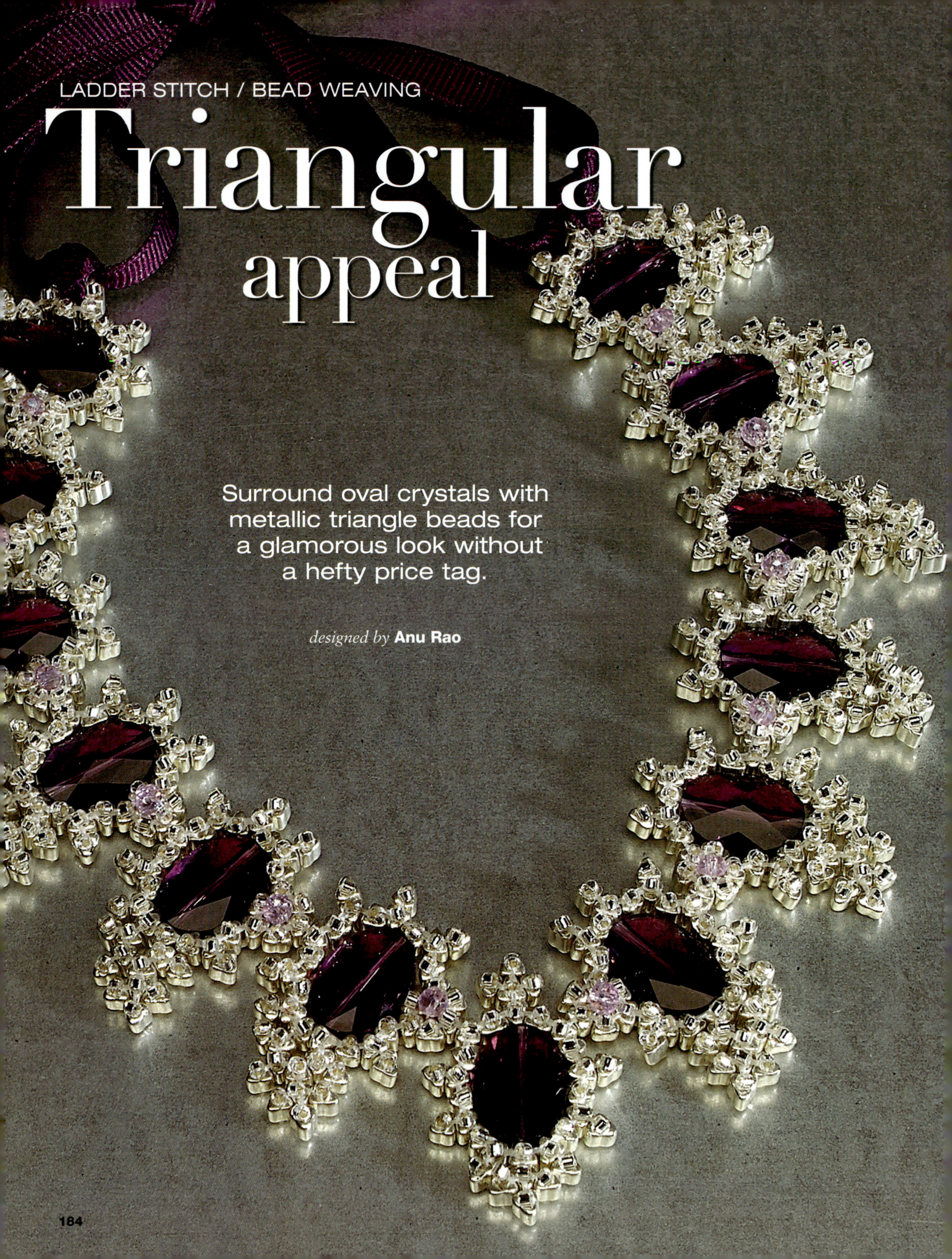

Surround oval crystals with metallic triangle beads for a glamorous look without a hefty price tag.

designed by **Anu Rao**

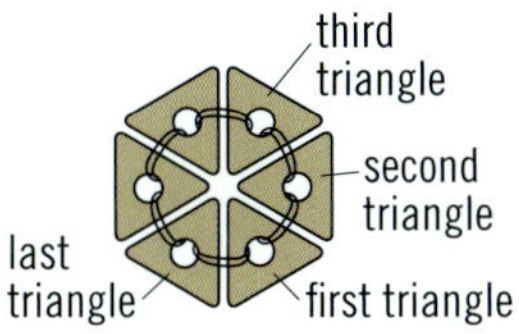

FIGURE 1

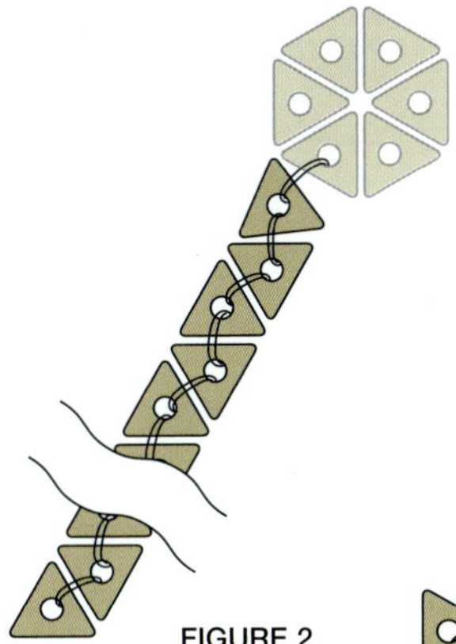

FIGURE 2

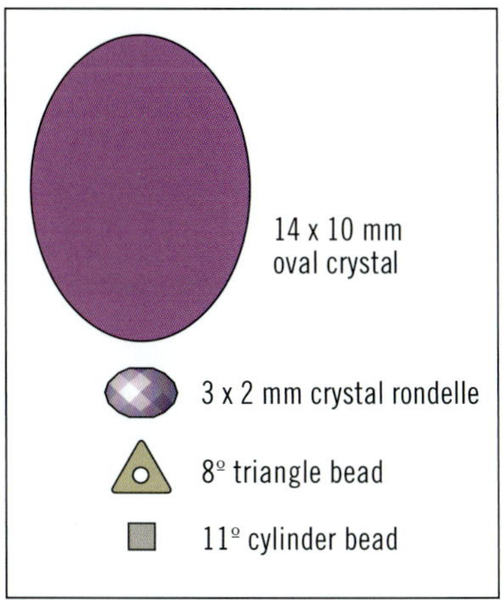

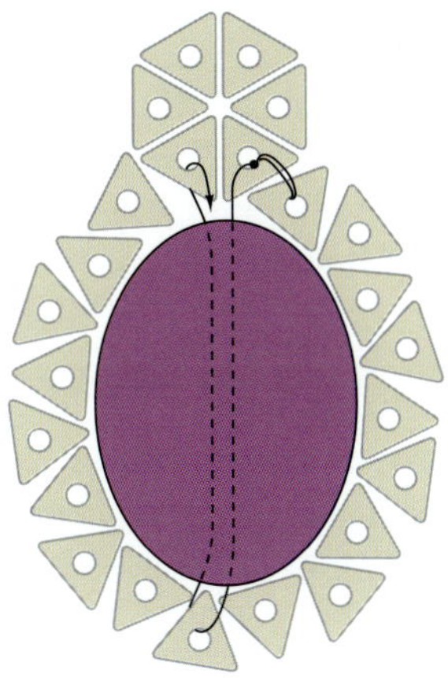

FIGURE 3

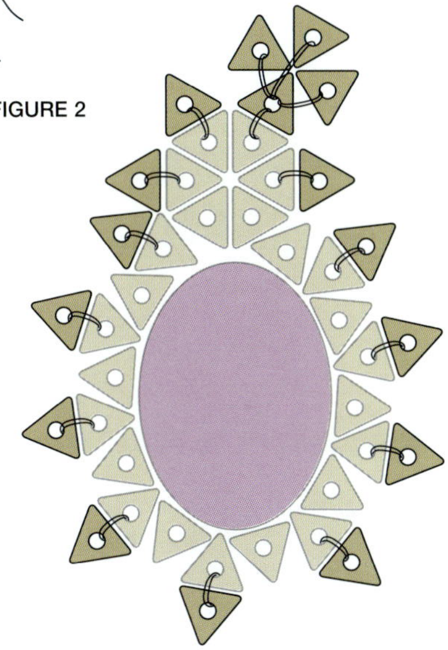

FIGURE 4

stepby**step**

Crystal components

[1] On 5 ft. (1.5 m) of thread, pick up two 8º triangle beads, leaving a 6-in. (15 cm) tail. Working in ladder stitch (Basics), sew through both beads again, positioning the beads side by side so that their holes are parallel. Retrace the thread path twice using a tight tension. You will work this reinforced ladder stitch to add all the other triangles in the necklace.

[2] Pick up a triangle, and stitch it to the previous triangle as in step 1, positioning the triangle as shown in **figure 1**. Exit the triangle just added.

[3] Repeat step 2 until you have a total of six triangles, positioning them as shown in **figure 1**. Work a ladder stitch through the first and last triangles to form a circular unit. Sew through the beadwork to exit the last triangle added.

[4] Pick up a triangle, and stitch it to the triangle your thread is exiting. Repeat to add 17 more triangles, forming a straight row of 18 triangles as shown in **figure 2**. Use a medium tension, making sure the triangles don't rotate out of position.

[5] Hold the 14 x 10 mm oval crystal in place, bending the row of triangles around the crystal. Stitch the last triangle in the row to the first triangle in the circular unit, forming a loop, and exit the first triangle in the circular unit (refer to **figure 3**).

[6] Sew through the crystal and the ninth triangle in the loop. The ninth triangle should have a flat side facing outward. Continue back through the crystal and through the last triangle in the circular unit **(figure 3)**. Retrace the thread path, exiting the first triangle in the circular unit. If the triangle loop is a little loose around the crystal, retrace the thread path through the triangles in the loop to tighten them.

[7] Sew through the beadwork to exit the second triangle in the circular unit, and stitch a triangle to it (refer to **figure 4**).

[8] Sew through the beadwork to exit the third triangle in the circular unit, and stitch a triangle to it. With your thread exiting the new triangle, stitch a triangle to one side of it. Repeat twice to add a triangle to the opposite side of the same triangle and a triangle between the two triangles just added.

[9] Sew through the beadwork to exit the next triangle in the circular unit. Work as in step 7 to add triangles to the next two triangles in the

MATERIALS
necklace 11 in. (28 cm) plus ribbons

- **13** 14 x 10 mm oval crystals (Swarovski #5050, amethyst)
- **12** 3 x 2 mm crystal rondelles (Thunder Polish 18AB, light purple)
- 18 g 8º triangle beads (Toho SB0438, metallic silver; www.fusionbeads.com)
- 3 g 11º cylinder beads (Miyuki DB041, crystal silver lined)
- **2** 34-in. (86 cm) satin ribbons
- Fireline 6 lb. test (crystal)
- beading needles, #11 or #12

DESIGN NOTES:

- **Use a thread color that best matches your triangle beads.**
- **You can substitute .010 clear monofilament for the thread, but note that monofilament can be hard to get through the triangles after a few passes.**
- **Use Toho triangles for this project. Miyuki triangles won't work.**

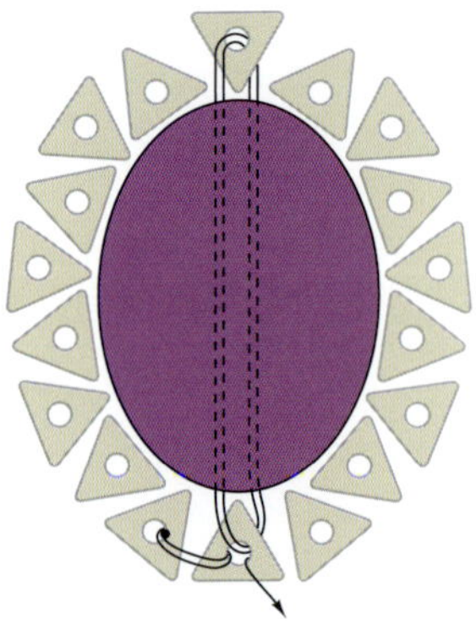

FIGURE 5

FIGURE 6

FIGURE 7

circular unit. Sew through the beadwork to exit the first triangle in the loop.

[10] Stitch a triangle to the first triangle in the loop. Sew through the next two triangles so your thread is exiting the next triangle with a flat side facing outward. Stitch a triangle to this triangle in the loop. Repeat around the loop to add a total of nine triangles (refer to **figure 4**). End the working thread and tail (Basics).

[11] Repeat steps 1–10 to make a total of 12 crystal components.

Center component

[1] Work as in steps 1 and 4 of "Crystal components" to make a straight row of 18 triangles. Form the triangles around a crystal, and join the first and last triangles at the bottom of the crystal. The triangles will fit tightly around the crystal, and the three triangles at the bottom will each have a flat side facing outward. Your thread should be exiting the center triangle of these three (refer to **figure 5**).

[2] Sew through the crystal, and continue through the ninth triangle in the loop. The ninth triangle should have a flat side facing outward. Sew back through the crystal and the triangle your thread exited at the start of this step. Retrace the thread path, exiting the center triangle of the three at the bottom **(figure 5)**.

[3] Referring to **figure 6**, embellish all the triangles with a flat side facing outward, adding a group of four triangles at both the top and the bottom. End the working thread and tail.

Connecting the components

Right side of necklace

You will connect the crystal components for the right side of the necklace first.

[1] Position the components so that the beaded "tail" is at the bottom of each component and is curving to the left (refer to **figure 7**).

[2] Add a comfortable length of thread (Basics) to a component, exiting the triangle shown **(figure 7, point a)**, and add a triangle. Stitch the triangle just added to the next triangle on this edge to form a circular unit. Leave the center of this circle open for attaching the ribbon later.

[3] With your thread exiting up out of a triangle, pick up an 11° cylinder bead, and sew back down through the same triangle. Sew up through an adjacent triangle, and repeat this stitch for the remainder of the triangles in this component. Exit the triangle shown **(point b)**.

[4] Stitch the triangle your thread is exiting to the triangle shown in the next component **(point c)**, exiting the triangle in the new component. Stitch this triangle to the following triangle in the previous component **(point d)** to form a circular unit.

[5] Sew up through the center of the circle. Pick up a 3 x 2 mm crystal rondelle, and sew back down through the center of the circle. Sew up through an adjacent triangle.

[6] Continue adding cylinders to all the triangles in the new component, exiting the triangle shown **(point e)**.

[7] Repeat steps 4–6 to connect a total of six components, ending and adding thread as needed.

Center component

[1] Position the center component as shown in **figure 8**, with the larger cluster of triangles at the bottom and your thread exiting the triangle shown **(point a)**. Stitch the triangle your thread is exiting to the triangle shown in the center component **(point b)**, exiting the triangle in the center component. Stitch this triangle to the following triangle in the previous component **(point c)** to form a circular unit.

[2] Sew up through the center of the circle. Pick up a rondelle, and sew back down through the center of the circle. Sew up through an adjacent triangle.

[3] Add cylinders to the center component as before, exiting the triangle shown **(point d)**.

Left side of necklace

[1] Position the remaining crystal components for the left side of the necklace so that the beaded "tail" is at the bottom of each component and is curving to the right (refer to **figure 8**).

[2] Stitch the triangle your thread is exiting to the triangle shown in the next component

(point e), exiting the triangle from the center component. Stitch this triangle to the following triangle in the next component (point f) to form a circular unit.

[3] Add a rondelle to the circle as before, and then add cylinders to the component, exiting the triangle shown (point g).

[4] Continue to connect and embellish the remaining components, ending and adding thread as needed. When you finish, your thread should be exiting the last component as in point g.

[5] Add one triangle to form a circular unit, embellish it, but do not add a rondelle. End the thread.

Finishing

Center a 34-in. (86 cm) ribbon through an end circular unit. Tie the ribbon to secure it to the beadwork. Tie an overhand knot (Basics) on each end of the ribbon if needed to keep it from fraying. Repeat this step to add the other ribbon on the other end of the beadwork.

FIGURE 8

KUMIHIMO /
BRICK STITCH /
PEYOTE STITCH

Fresh as a daisy necklace

Stitch a stunning focal piece to feature on a kumihimo necklace studded with floral accents.

designed by **Wendy Speare**

stepbystep

Kumihimo rope

[1] Cut eight 48-in. (1.2 m) pieces of Super-lon cord (or three times the desired finished length of the rope). Line up the ends, and tie them together with an overhand knot (Basics). Drop the knot through the hole in the kumihimo disk, and attach a 30 g weight to the knot. I use a rubber band to attach a plastic bag containing six nickels to the knot.

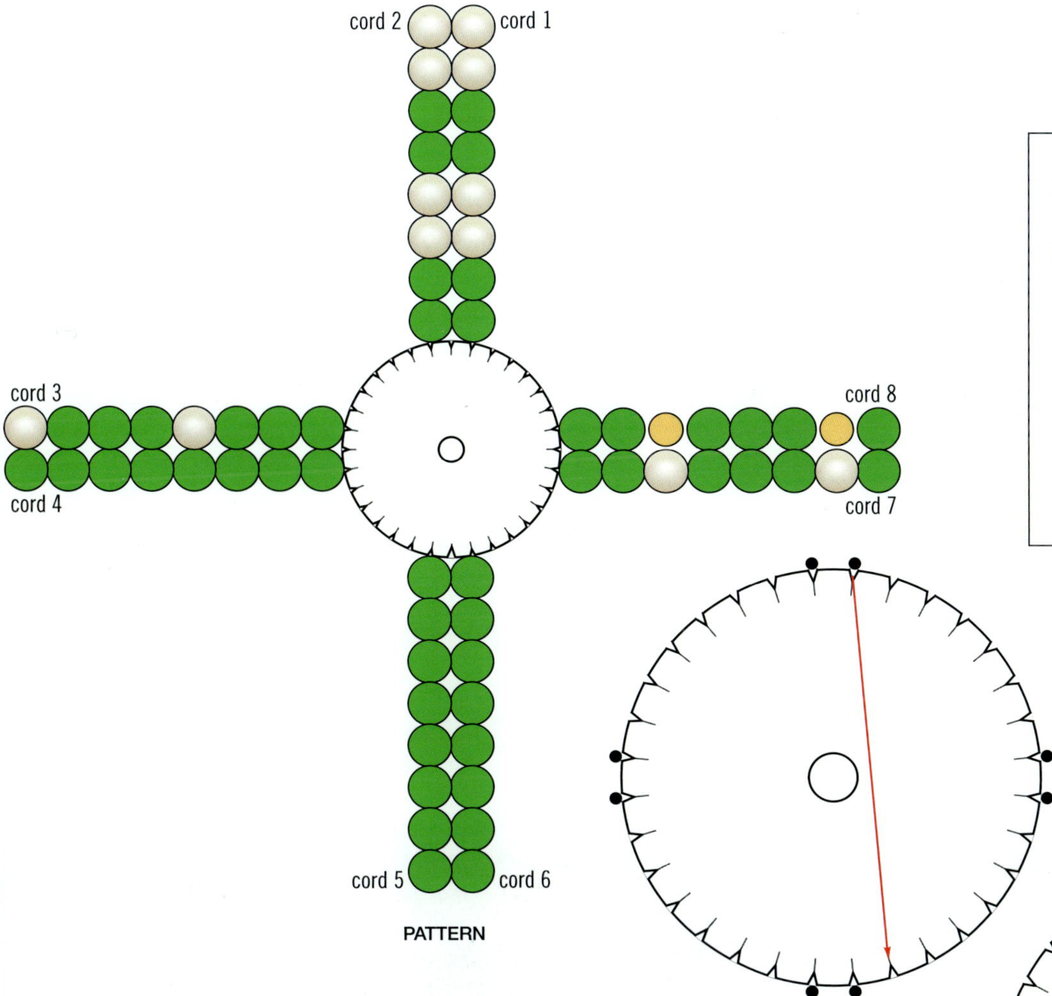

PATTERN

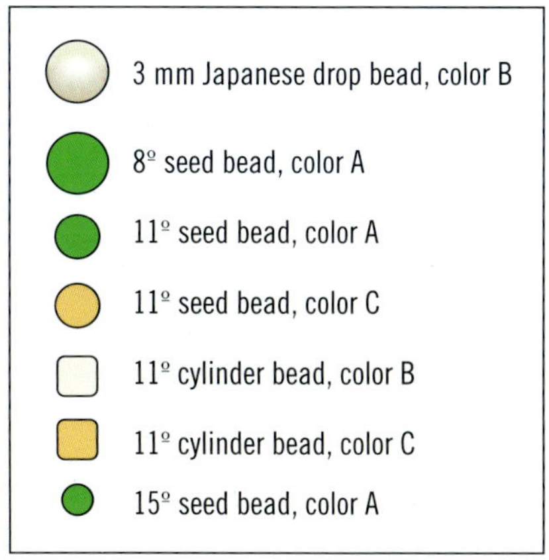

FIGURE 1

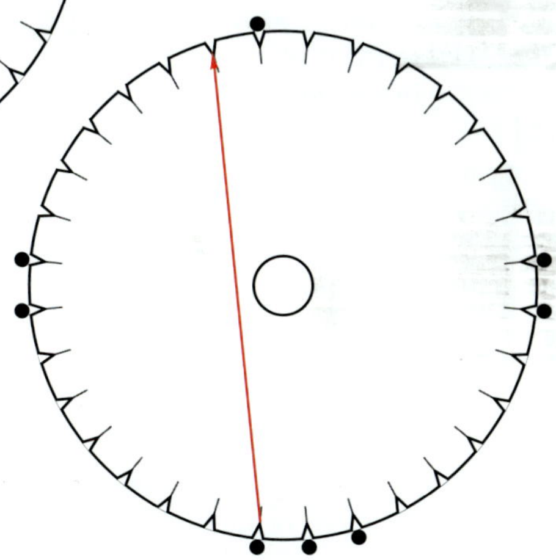

FIGURE 2

Bead stringing order

Referring to the **pattern** above, string the beads starting with those shown at the center of the diagram.

Cords 1 and 2: String a repeating pattern of two color A 8º seed beads, two 3 mm drops, two A 8ºs, and two drops.

Cord 3: String a repeating pattern of three A 8ºs, a drop, three A 8ºs, and a drop.

Cords 4–6: String all A 8ºs.

Cord 7: String a repeating pattern of two A 8ºs, a drop, three A 8ºs, a drop, and an A 8º.

Cord 8: String a repeating pattern of two A 8ºs, a color C 11º seed bead, three A 8ºs, a C 11º, and an A 8º.

[2] String 128 beads on each cord according to the **pattern** and **bead stringing order.** This will make about a 16-in. (41 cm) rope. String more or fewer beads in the established pattern to adjust the length. After you load a cord, push the beads up to within 3 in. (7.6 cm) of the disk, and wrap the beaded cord around a bobbin, leaving about 4 in. (10 cm) of cord hanging from the edge of the disk. Label the bobbin with the appropriate cord number, and slip the cord into the appropriate slit in the disk, as shown in **photo a.**

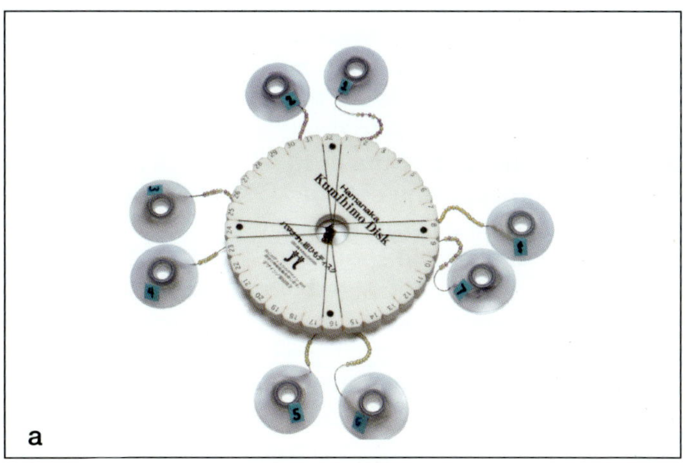

a

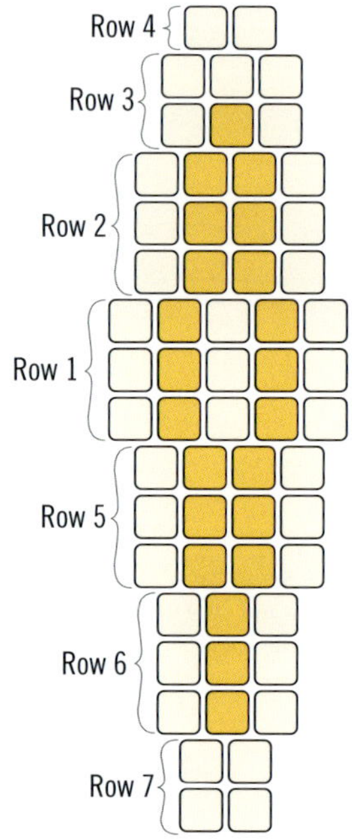

FIGURE 3

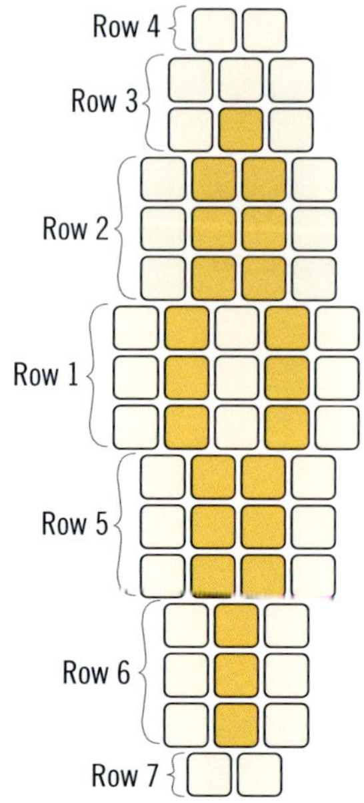

FIGURE 4

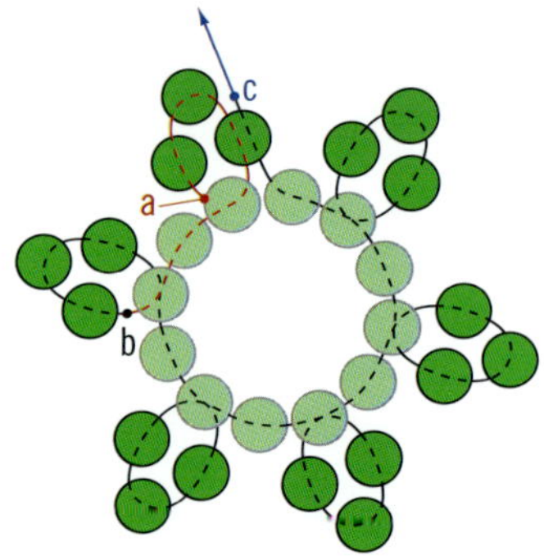

FIGURE 5

[3] Work a section of braid without beads: Pick up the top-right cord, and slide it into the slit to the right of the bottom two cords **(figure 1)**. Pick up the bottom-left cord, and slide it into the slit to the left of the top cord **(figure 2)**. Rotate the disk clockwise one-quarter turn. Repeat this step until you have about ½ in. (1.3 cm) of plain braid. Make sure you end with cords 1 and 2 at the top of the disk and all the cords in the original order.

[4] Continue braiding with the same motions as in step 3, but add beads: Pick up a cord, slide the next bead up to the point of the braid, and tuck the bead under the cord that crosses over it. Complete the move by sliding the cord into the appropriate slit. As you work, make sure the beads don't pop out from under the crossed cord. If they do, carefully unbraid the cords to the loose bead (being sure to maintain the correct cord order), tuck the bead under the crossing cord, and resume braiding.

TIP: Braiding is most successful when the cords are stretched taut across the hole in the disk. If the point of the braid begins to drop down below the face of the disk, gently pull the opposing sets of cords tight so the point of the braid raises up to the desired spot.

[5] When you have braided all the beads, or when the cord is the desired length, work ½ in. (1.3 cm) of braid without beads.

[6] Cut 6 in. (15 cm) of Super-lon cord, and tie it tightly with a square knot (Basics) around the unbeaded braid at the starting end of the rope **(photo b)**. Apply a drop of E6000 to the knot. Repeat this step at the other end of the rope. Allow the glue to dry.

[7] Cut through the braid between the knot you made in step 6 and the disk. Cut through the braid at the other end between the overhand knot and the beaded braid.

[8] Glue one end cap to each end of the rope **(photo c)**.

[9] Open a jump ring (Basics), and attach half of the clasp to one end of the rope. Repeat at the other end of the rope. Set the rope aside.

Daisy focal components

Bezeled rivoli

[1] On 1 yd. (.9 m) of thread, pick up 36 color C 11º cylinder beads, and tie them into a ring with a square knot, leaving a 6-in. (15 cm) tail.

[2] Work rounds of tubular peyote stitch (Basics), stepping up after each round:

Round 1: Work one round with C cylinders.

Round 2: Work one round with color C 15º seed beads.

Round 3: Work one round with color D 15º one-cuts.

[3] Pull the beadwork snug, and then sew through to exit a C cylinder in the first round. Insert the rivoli face up in the beadwork, and repeat rounds 2 and 3 on this side of the bezel. Tie a half-hitch knot (Basics). End the tail (Basics) but not the working thread.

Lower petals

[1] On 2 ft. (61 cm) of thread, pick up three color B 11º cylinder beads and three C cylinders, leaving a 6-in. (15 cm) tail. Sew through all the beads again to make two stacks of three beads. Working in ladder stitch (Basics) with three beads per stitch, add a stack of Bs, a stack of Cs, and a stack of Bs, as shown in row 1 of **figure 3**.

[2] In modified brick stitch (Basics), work half of the petal as follows:

Row 2: Work the first stitch with three Bs and three Cs, and then add a stack of three Cs and a stack of three Bs.

Row 3: Work the first stitch with three Bs and a C, and add a stack of two Bs.

Row 4: Work a stitch with two Bs.

[3] Sew through the edge beads to exit an edge B at the end of row 1. Work the rest of the petal in rows:

Row 5: Work the first stitch with three Bs and three Cs, and then add a stack of three Cs and a stack of three Bs.

Row 6: Work the first stitch with three Bs and three Cs, and then add a stack of three Bs.

Row 7: Work a stitch with four Bs.

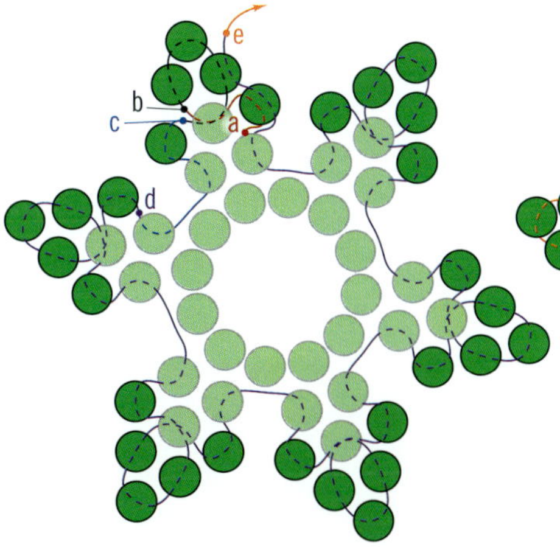

FIGURE 6

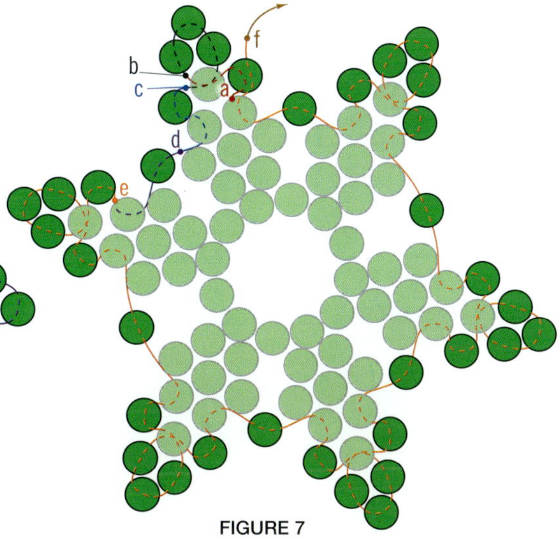

FIGURE 7

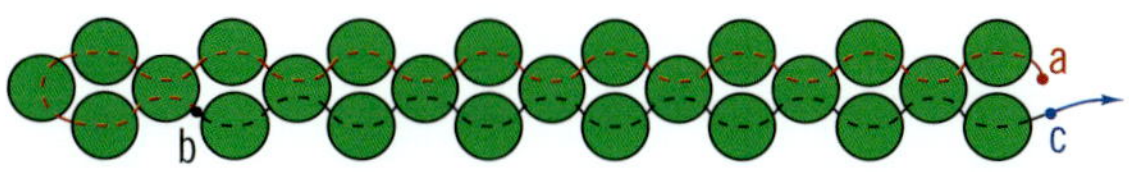

FIGURE 8

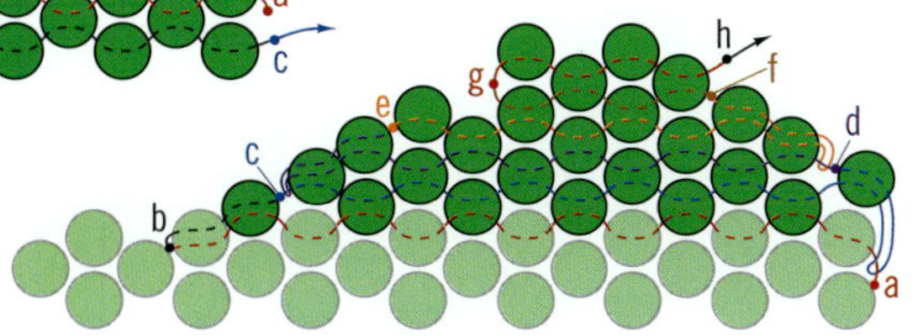

FIGURE 9

[4] End the tail but not the working thread.
[5] Make a total of 12 lower petals.

Upper petals

Work as in "Lower petals," but follow the pattern in **figure 4**. Note that the only difference is that row 7 is shorter in the upper petals than in the lower petals. Make a total of 13 upper petals.

Calyx

[1] On 1 yd. (.9 m) of thread, pick up 12 color A 11º seed beads. Tie the beads into a ring with a square knot, leaving a 6-in. (15 cm) tail, and sew through the next few beads.
[2] Work in rounds as follows:
Round 1: Pick up three A 11ºs, sew through the bead your thread exited in the same direction (making a picot), and continue through the next two beads in the ring **(figure 5, a–b)**. Repeat this stitch around to make a total of six picots, and step up through the nearest A 11º in the first picot **(b–c)**.
Round 2: Pick up an A 11º, and sew through the next bead in the picot **(figure 6, a–b)**. Pick up three A 11ºs, and make a picot **(b–c)**. Pick up an A 11º, and sew through the next bead in the round 1 picot and the first bead in the next picot **(c–d)**. Repeat these three stitches around, and step up through the nearest two beads from the start of this round **(d–e)**.
Round 3: Pick up an A 11º, and sew through the next bead in the picot **(figure 7, a–b)**. Pick up three A 11ºs, and make a picot **(b–c)**. Pick up an A 11º, and sew through the next bead in the round 2 picot **(c–d)**. Pick up an A 11º, and sew through the nearest bead in the next round 2 picot **(d–e)**. Repeat these four stitches around **(e–f)**. End the working thread and tail.

Leaves

[1] On 1 yd. (.9 m) of thread, pick up 17 A 11ºs. Leaving an 18-in. (46 cm) tail, skip the last three beads, and sew back through the previous one **(figure 8, a–b)**. Work six peyote stitches with A 11ºs, and end the row by picking up an A 11º **(b–c)**.
[2] Sew through the adjacent end bead, and work six peyote stitches **(figure 9, a–b)**. Sew under the adjacent thread

MATERIALS

green/white necklace 17 in. (43 cm)

- **1** 14 mm rivoli (Swarovski, crystal golden shadow)
- **5** g color B 3 mm Japanese drop beads (Miyuki 92021, opaque cream)
- **15** g color A 8º seed beads (Miyuki F463T, matte metallic green iris)
- 11º seed beads
  10 g color A (Miyuki F463T, matte metallic green iris)
  5 g color C (Miyuki 4202, Duracoat gold)
- 11º Miyuki Delica cylinder beads
  6 g color B (DB0052, white AB)
  4 g color C (DB0034, gold)
- 1 g color D 15º one-cuts (matte copper)
- 1 g 15º seed beads in each of **2** colors: A (Miyuki F463T, matte metallic green iris), C (Miyuki 4202, Duracoat gold)
- clasp
- **2** 4 mm end caps with loops
- **2** 4 mm jump rings
- nylon beading thread
- beading needles, #12
- **2** pairs of chainnose, flatnose, and/or bentnose pliers
- E6000 adhesive
- kumihimo disk with **8** bobbins and 30 g weight
- Super-lon beading cord, #18

DESIGN NOTES:

This is a great stash-busting project because most beaders have the majority of these supplies on hand. Here are tips to make it even more budget friendly:

- **Consider using color C 15ºs instead of color D 15º one-cuts.**
- **Dig through your supplies to find varied hues for colors A, B, and C. Don't worry if they don't match perfectly — the variation will make your final project even more interesting.**
- **Kumihimo disks aren't expensive, but if you don't have one, you can make your own! Glue together a stack of small foam dinner plates, and then cut a hole in the middle and 32 slits around the perimeter.**

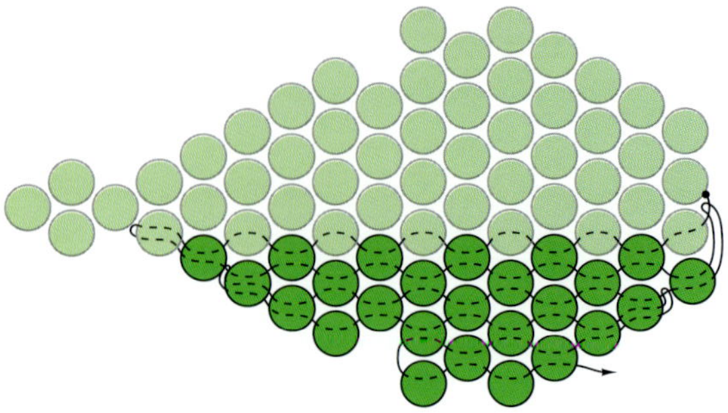

FIGURE 10

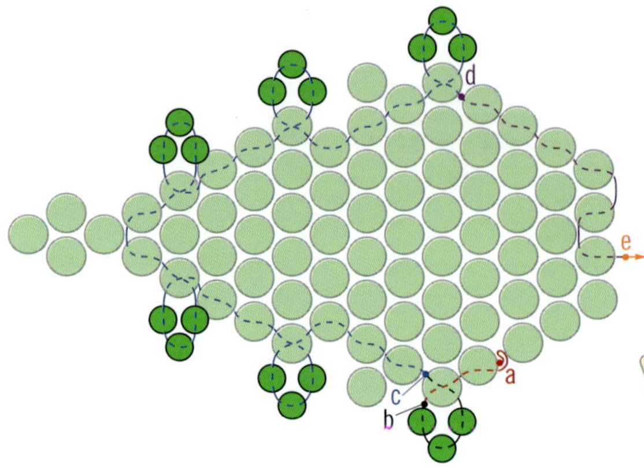

FIGURE 11

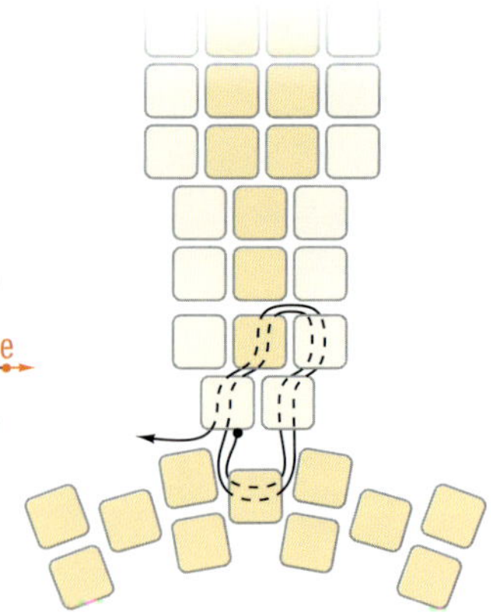

FIGURE 12

bridge, and sew back through the last two beads **(b–c)**.

[3] Work five peyote stitches. Pick up an A 11º, sew under the adjacent edge thread bridge, and sew back through the last bead added **(c–d)**.

[4] Work five peyote stitches, sew under the adjacent thread bridge, and sew back through the last two beads **(d–e)**.

[5] Work four peyote stitches, sew under the adjacent thread bridge, and sew back through the last two beads **(e–f)**.

[6] Work two peyote stitches **(f–g)**.

[7] Turn, and work two peyote stitches **(g–h)**. End the working thread.

[8] With the tail, repeat steps 2–7 **(figure 10)**.

[9] Sew under the adjacent thread bridge and back through the last two beads **(figure 11, a–b)**. Pick up three color A 15º seed beads, and make a picot **(b–c)**. Add five more picots as shown in **c–d**, and then sew through the beadwork to exit at **point e**. Don't end the thread.

[10] Make two more leaves, varying the size and shape if desired.

Bails

[1] On 1 yd. (.9 m) of thread, pick up four A 11ºs. Leaving a 6-in. (15 cm) tail, work in flat even-count peyote stitch (Basics) to make a strip that is 2⅛ in. (5.4 cm) long and four beads wide. End with an even number of rows **(photo d)**.

[2] Zip up (Basics) the ends to form the strip into a ring. End the tail but not the working thread.

[3] Make a second bail.

Daisy focal assembly

Attaching upper petals to the bezel

[1] Using the thread from an upper petal, sew through a C cylinder in the center round of peyote on the bezel, and sew back through the adjacent bead at the end of the petal and a bead in the next row. Retrace the thread path through the connection **(figure 12)**, and end the thread.

[2] Repeat step 1 with the remaining petals, spacing them evenly around the bezel. There is not a petal for every bead in the center round of the bezel, so begin by adding a petal to every other bead in the round, and then fill in the remaining petals as desired **(photo e)**.

[3] Sew through the beadwork to exit a cylinder in the round nearest the face of the rivoli. Using D one-cuts, work a round of picots: Pick up three D one-cuts, and sew through the next C cylinder in the round. Repeat around the ring **(photo f)**, and end the thread.

Attaching lower petals to the calyx

[1] Using the thread from a lower petal, sew through a side picot bead in round 1 of the calyx and the adjacent bead in the petal **(photo g)**. Retrace the thread path, and end the thread.

d

e

f

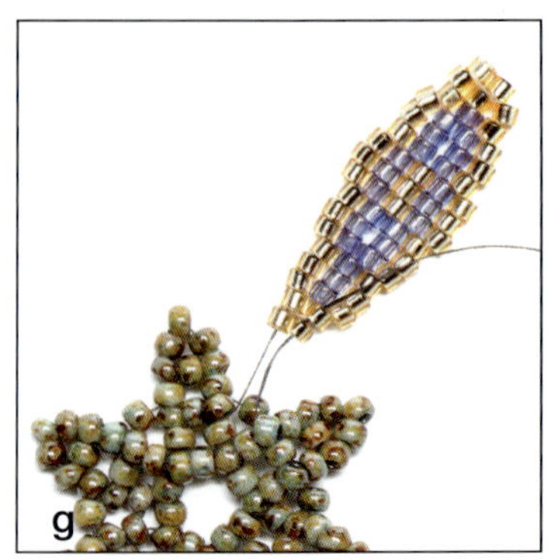
g

[**2**] Repeat with the remaining lower petals, spacing them evenly around the calyx.

Attaching the layers of petals

[**1**] With the petal side of the calyx facing up, place the bezel with the attached petals onto the calyx.
[**2**] Add 1 yd. (.9 m) of thread (Basics) to the calyx, and exit a center bead in a round 2 picot. Zigzag between the calyx and an adjacent bead in the bezel **(photo h)** until the layers are securely attached.
[**3**] Sewing through the petals, randomly tack the layers of petals together to prevent them from flopping forward when the pendant is worn. End the thread.

Attaching the leaves and bail to the calyx

[**1**] Position a leaf as desired under the calyx. With the thread exiting the leaf, pick up three to five A 11ºs, and

h

sew through the A 11º at the tip of a round 3 picot on the calyx. Working in square stitch (Basics), add another row of A 11ºs between the leaf and the calyx **(photo i)**. End the thread.
[**2**] Repeat step 1 with the remaining leaves, positioning them as desired.
[**3**] Position the flower as you would like it to hang. Using the thread from a bail, sew through a tip A 11º on the appropriate calyx picot. Retrace the thread path a few times, and end the thread. Repeat with the other bail **(photo j)**.

i

j

KUMIHIMO / HERRINGBONE STITCH / SPIRAL ROPE

Fanciful flowercup braid

designed by **Kerrie Slade**

Create a necklace or bracelet of cascading blossoms using Flowercup beads and seed beads in a kumihimo braid.

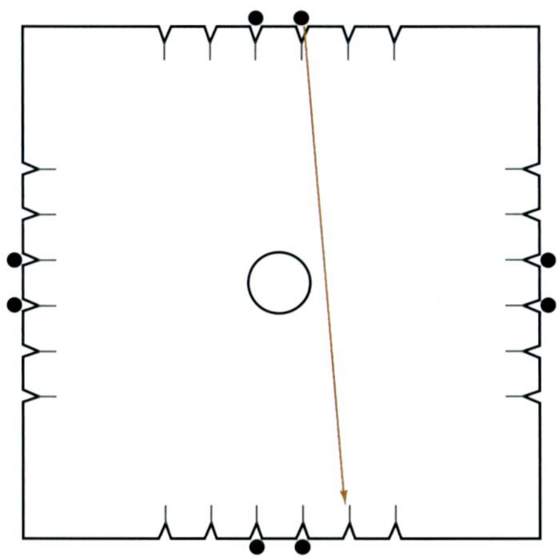

FIGURE 1

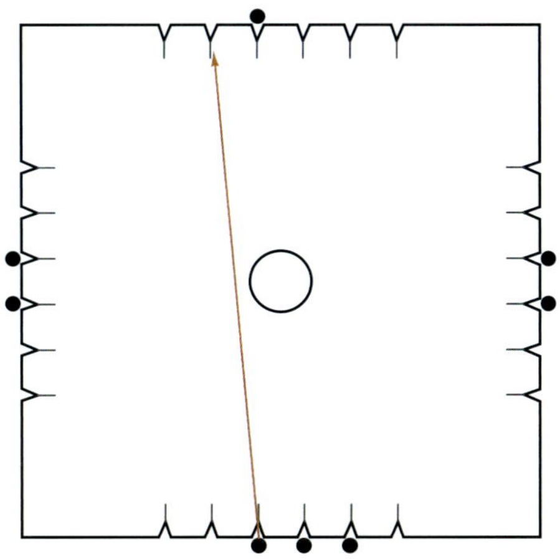

FIGURE 2

stepbystep

Setup

[1] Cut eight 30-in. (76 cm) lengths of S-Lon cord.

[2] Tie an overhand knot (Basics) at one end of a cord, and pick up 32 8º seed beads. Starting at the end with the knot, wrap the cord and the strung beads around a bobbin and secure, leaving 10 in. (25 cm) of cord to work with. Repeat this step three times for a total of four cords with 8ºs. These cords will be called 8º cords.

[3] For each of the remaining four cords, work as in step 2, but pick up the following beads: an 8º; a repeating pattern of a 7 x 5 mm Flowercup bead (narrow end to wide end) and two 8ºs 30 times; an 8º. These cords will be called Flowercup cords.

[4] Gather the ends of the cords, and tie them together with an overhand knot, leaving approximately 4 in. (10 cm) of cord free between the knot and the beads. Feed the knot through the center hole of the kumihimo disk from front to back, and attach a weight or binder clip.

[5] Position an 8º cord in the slit just to the left of the top-center or 12 o'clock position of the disk. Position a Flowercup cord in the slit just to the right of the top-center position. Turn the disk a quarter turn clockwise so a new set of slits is available. Repeat this step to position the remaining cords.

Kumihimo braid

[1] Without moving any beads, pick up the top right-hand cord, and bring it straight down to the right of the two cords in the 6 o'clock position **(figure 1)**. There will now be three cords in the 6 o'clock position.

[2] Pick up the bottom left-hand cord, and bring it straight up to the left of the single cord in the 12 o'clock position **(figure 2)**.

[3] Turn the disk a quarter turn clockwise so the cords in the 9 o'clock position are now in the 12 o'clock position. This completes the first quarter of one kumihimo sequence.

[4] Repeat steps 1 and 2 three times, and then turn the disk a quarter turn.

[5] Repeat steps 1–4 four times for a total of five complete kumihimo sequences.

[6] Making sure you begin with a Flowercup cord, work as in steps 1–4, but slide down a single 8º from each cord when you move it so that the 8º rests under the horizontal cord in the center hole.

[7] For the next 30 sequences, work as follows:

- On each Flowercup cord, slide down two 8ºs and a Flowercup bead as a unit.
- On each 8º cord, slide down a single 8º. Keep a consistent but not tight tension, and make sure each bead (or group of beads) sits under the horizontal cord and does not drop to the center of the braid, but rather is positioned along the outside of the braid.

[8] Work the last kumihimo sequence by sliding down the remaining 8º on each cord, and then work five complete sequences without beads.

[9] Pinch the braid below the center hole, unwind the bobbins from the cords, and remove the cords from the

MATERIALS

both projects

- S-Lon cord
- Fireline 6 lb. test
- beading needles, #10
- **2** pairs of chainnose, flatnose, and/or bentnose pliers
- **8** bobbins
- crochet hook (optional)
- E6000 or other adhesive
- kumihimo disk with weight or binder clip

necklace 23 in. (58 cm)

- **300** 7 x 5 mm glass Flowercup beads (Czech, silver; www.kandrasbeads.com)
- 24 g 8º seed beads (Toho 176B, transparent rainbow soft gray)
- 5 g 11º seed beads (Toho 176B, transparent rainbow soft gray)
- clasp (www.agrainofsand.com)
- **2** 6 mm jump rings

bracelet 8 in. (20 cm)

- **72** 7 x 5 mm glass Flowercup beads (Czech, silver; www.kandrasbeads.com)
- 5 g 8º seed beads (Toho 176B, transparent rainbow soft gray)
- 1 g 11º seed beads (Toho 176B, transparent rainbow soft gray)
- clasp (www.agrainofsand.com)
- **2** 6 mm jump rings

DESIGN NOTE:

To use a purchased pendant, work steps 1–3 of "End cap and clasp assembly" for all four end caps, but do not end the thread on one of the end caps that will be at the center of the necklace. With the thread exiting the 8º at the top of the end cap, pick up the pendant, and sew through the 8º at the top of the other end cap at the center of the necklace. Retrace the thread path through the join three or four times, and end the thread.

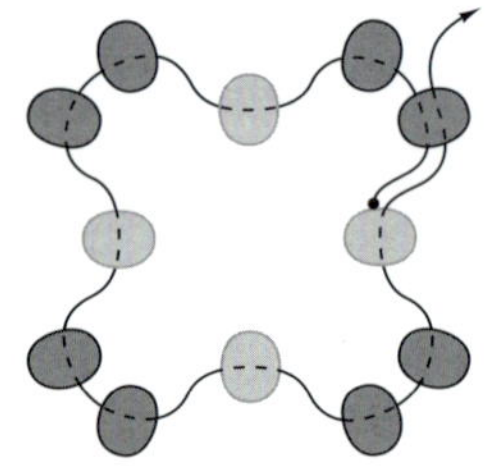

FIGURE 3

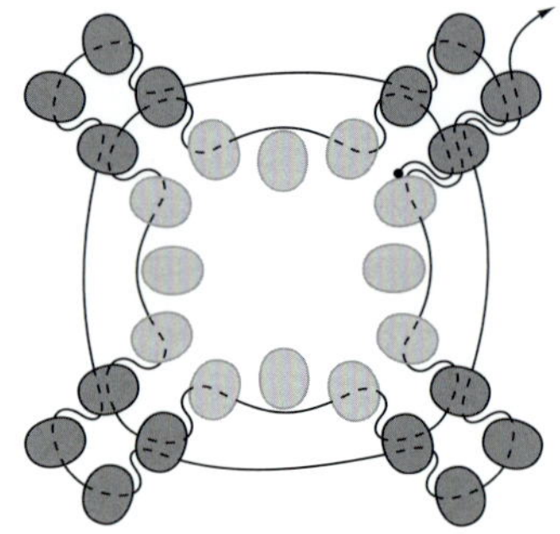

FIGURE 4

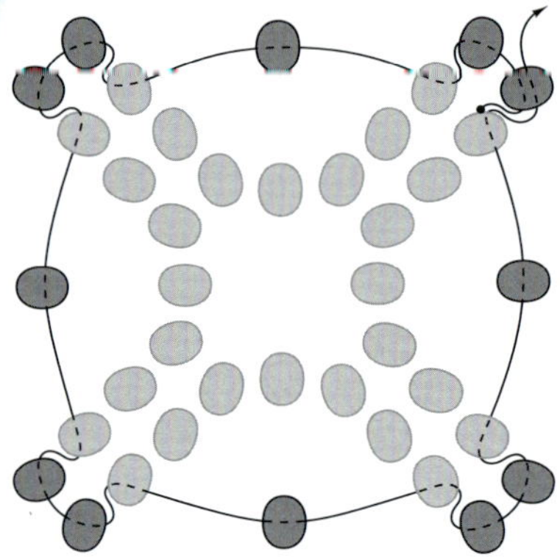

FIGURE 5

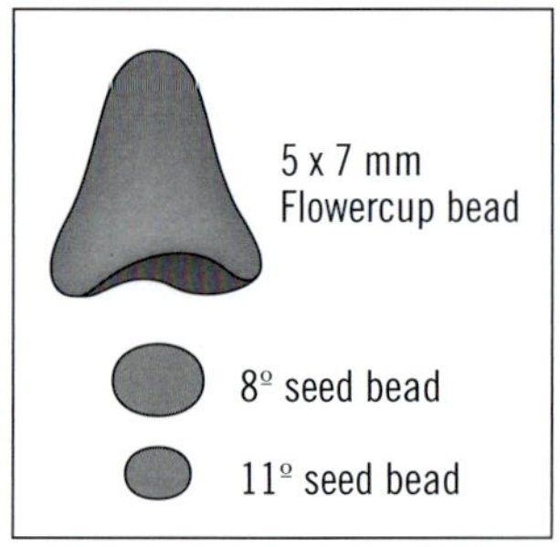

disk. Tie an overhand knot with the cords at the end of the braid. Remove the weight from the other end, and gently stretch out the cord to adjust the tension. Check the braid for any Flowercup units that may have dropped inside the braid. Use a pair of pliers or a crochet hook to bring them to the outside of the braid.

[10] Cut a 12-in. (30 cm) piece of thread, and wrap it tightly around the end of the braid just below the knot, about ¼ in. (6 mm) away from the beaded section, tying several knots as you wrap. Trim the thread, and cut off the knot at the end of the braid. Dab the end of the braid with E6000 or other adhesive to prevent fraying. Repeat this step on the other end of the braid.

[11] Make a second braid.

End caps

[1] On 1 yd. (.9 m) of thread, pick up four 11º seed beads, and sew through the beads again to form a ring, leaving a 12-in. (30 cm) tail.

[2] Work in rounds as follows:

Round 1: Pick up two 11ºs, and sew through the next 11º in the ring. Repeat this stitch to complete the round, and step up through the first 11º picked up in this round **(figure 3)**.

Rounds 2 and 3: Work two rounds of tubular herringbone stitch (Basics) **(figure 4)**.

Round 4: Work an increase round: Pick up two 11ºs, and sew down through the next 11º in the previous round. Pick up an 11º, and sew up through the following 11º in the previous round. Repeat these two stitches to complete the round, and step up **(figure 5)**.

Round 5: Work another increase round as in round 4.

Round 6: Work a round of tubular herringbone with no increase **(figure 6)**.

Round 7: Work an increase round.

Round 8: Pick up an 11º, and sew down through the next two 11ºs in the herringbone stack. Sew through the increase 11º picked up in the previous round, and then sew up through the first two 11ºs in the following stack. Repeat this stitch to complete the round, and step up **(figure 7)**. Do not end the working thread or tail.

[3] Make a total of four end caps.

End cap and clasp assembly

[1] With the working thread from one of the end caps, sew through the beads in round 8 to exit an increase 11º. Place the end cap on one end of the braid so that the wide end of the Flowercup beads points away from the end cap.

[2] Sew down through an 8º in the last kumihimo sequence in the braid, sew up through the next 8º in the braid, and continue through the next increase 11º in the end cap. Repeat this stitch to connect the end cap to the braid. Retrace the thread path several times, and end the working thread (Basics).

[3] With the tail exiting an 11º in the original ring of the end cap, pick up an 8º, and sew through the 11º on the opposite side of the ring. Sew back through the 8º just added and the 11º your thread exited at the start of this step in the same direction. Retrace the thread path, and end the tail.

[4] Open a jump ring (Basics), and attach the 8º at the top of the end cap to half of the clasp.

[5] Repeat steps 1–4 for the other braid.

[6] For the remaining end caps, work as in steps 1 and 2, but note that the Flowercup beads will be pointing toward the end caps.

[7] With the tail from one of the end caps, pick up an 11º, and sew through the next 11º in the original ring. Repeat

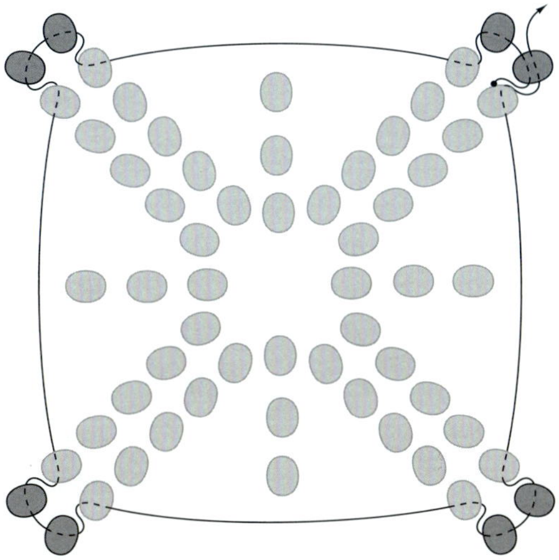

FIGURE 6

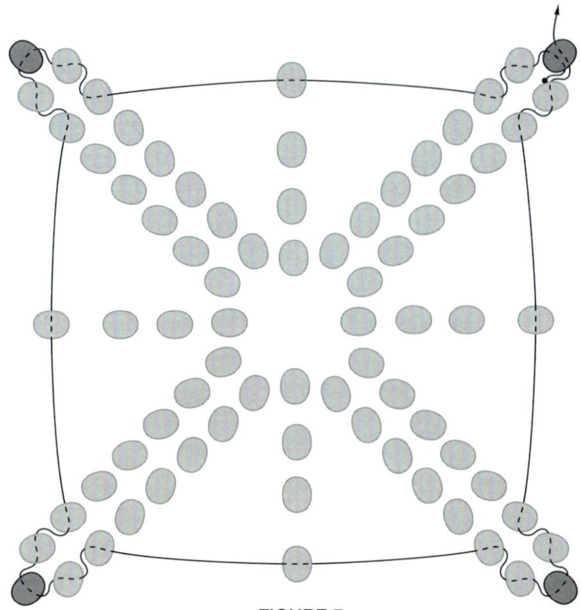

FIGURE 7

this stitch to complete the round, and step up through the first 11º picked up in this round.

[8] To join the two end caps: Sew through an 11º in the original ring on the other end cap, and sew through the next 11º added in the previous step. Continue to zigzag back and forth between the end caps to join. Retrace the thread path, and end the tails.

Spiral rope pendant

[1] On 2 yd. (1.8 m) of thread, pick up three 8ºs, a Flowercup bead (narrow end to wide end), an 11º, an 8º, and an 11º, leaving a 12-in. (30 cm) tail. Sew through the first three 8ºs again to form a loop around the 8ºs. Move the loop to the left of the core 8ºs.

[2] Working in spiral rope, pick up a Flowercup bead, an 11º, an 8º, and an 11º, and sew through the previous three core 8ºs. Move this loop to the left of the core. Repeat this stitch two more times for a total of four Flowercup loops around these three 8ºs in the core.

[3] Pick up two 8ºs, a Flowercup bead, an 11º, an 8º, and an 11º. Sew through the last 8º in the core and the first two 8ºs picked up in this step. Move this loop to the left of the core.

[4] Pick up a Flowercup bead, an 11º, an 8º, and an 11º, and sew through the last three 8ºs in the core. Repeat this stitch three times for a total of four loops.

[5] Repeat steps 3 and 4 until your pendant is the desired length.

[6] Pick up two 11ºs, and sew through the last 8º in the core and the first 11º just added (**figure 8, a–b**).

[7] Pick up two 11ºs, sew through the two previous 11ºs, and continue through the first 11º added in this step (**b–c**). Continue working in this manner to create a strip that is 22 rows long and two beads wide.

[8] Work in square stitch (Basics) to add a column of 11ºs along one edge of the strip (**figure 9**).

[9] Fold the strip over the join between the two end caps at the center of the necklace, and stitch this end of the strip to the two loops on this side of the pendant. End the working thread.

[10] With the tail, secure the end 11ºs on the remaining side of the strip to the two loops on this side of the pendant. End the tail.

Bracelet

[1] Work as in steps 1–5 of "Setup," but use 22-in. (56 cm) lengths of cord and string only 18 sets of Flowercup units on each of the four Flowercup cords.

[2] Work as in steps 1–10 of "Kumihimo braid."

[3] Work as in steps 1 and 2 of "End caps" to make two end caps.

[4] Work as in steps 1–4 of "End cap and clasp assembly" for both ends of the braid, noting that the Flowercup beads will be pointing toward one of the end caps. ●

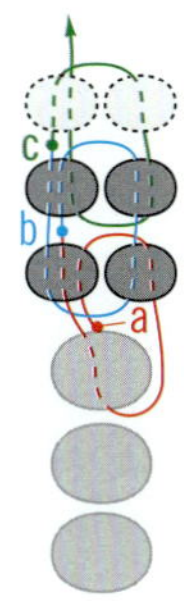

FIGURE 8

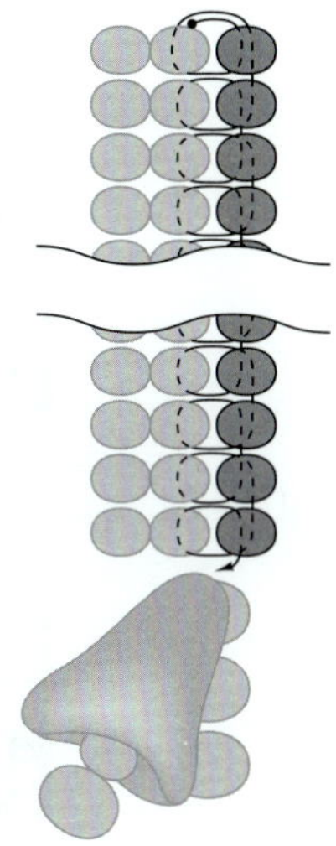

FIGURE 9

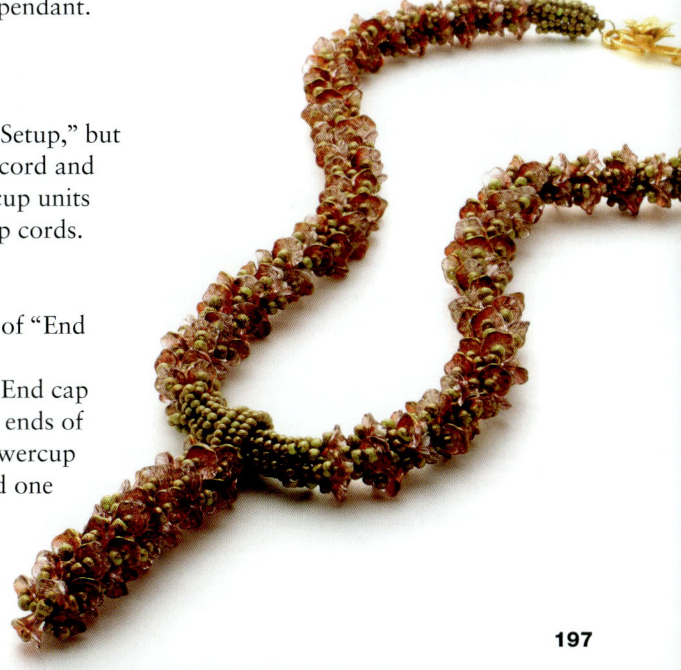

Bella bijoux

designed by **Jimmie Boatright**

Surround an art bead with crystals, and accent it with a trio of bezeled pearls and a delicate beaded chain.

stepbystep

Bezeled pearls

End and add thread (Basics) as needed as you stitch each bezeled pearl.

[1] On a comfortable length of thread, pick up a 10 mm pearl and 11 11º cylinder beads. Sew through the pearl again in the same direction, leaving a 6-in. (15 cm) tail. The cylinders will form a loop around one side of the pearl (**figure 1, a–b**). Pick up 11 cylinders, and sew through the pearl, positioning the new loop around the other side of the pearl (**b–c**).

[2] Sew through all the beads in the first loop, pick up a cylinder, and sew through all the beads in the second loop (**c–d**). Pick up a cylinder, and sew through the next three or four cylinders in the first loop (**d–e**). These beads will shift to form rounds 1 and 2 as round 3 of the peyote bezel is added.

[3] Work in rounds as follows:

Rounds 3–4: Work two rounds of tubular peyote stitch (Basics) using cylinders, and step up at the end of each round.

Round 5: Work a round of peyote using 15º seed beads, and then sew through the beadwork to exit a cylinder in round 1.

Rounds 6–8: Work three rounds of peyote using cylinders, stepping up at the end of each round.

Round 9: Work a round of peyote using 15ºs.

[4] Sew through the beadwork to exit a cylinder in round 7 (**figure 2, point a**). Using 15ºs, work a round of peyote off of the cylinders in this round. The 15ºs will sit on top of the cylinders in the ditch between rounds 6 and 8. Do not step up at the end of the round. Sew through the beadwork as shown in **figure 3** to exit a cylinder in round 3 (two rounds below the 15ºs along the other edge of the bezel).

[5] Pick up two cylinders,

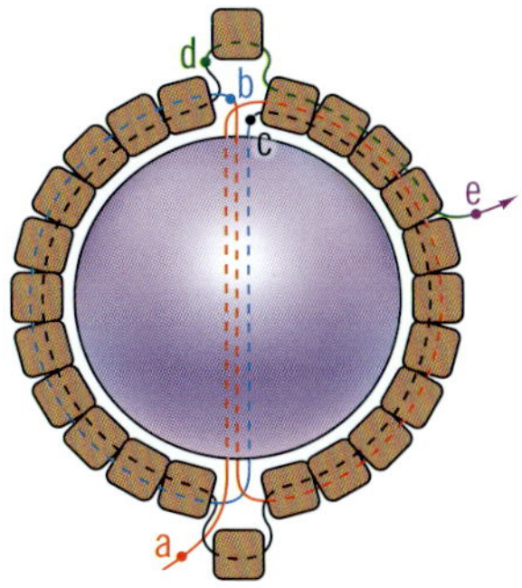

FIGURE 1

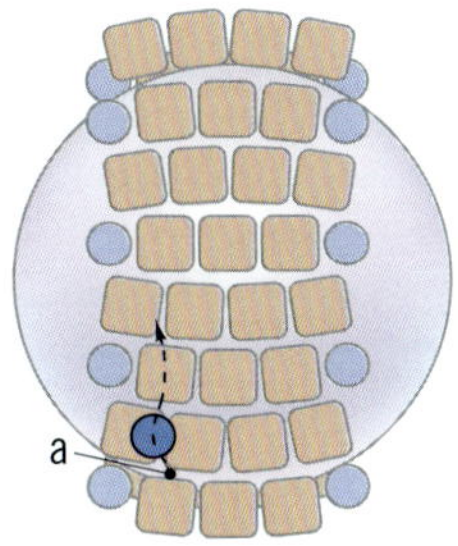

FIGURE 2

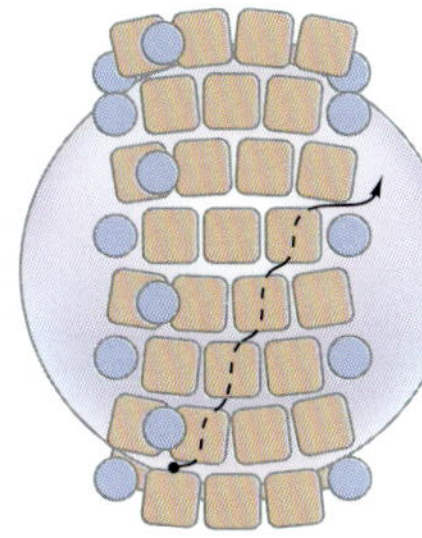

FIGURE 3

a 15º, a cylinder, a 15º, and two cylinders, and sew through the next cylinder in the round to create a loop **(photo a)**. Sew back through the last two cylinders just picked up **(photo b)**.

[6] Pick up a 15º, a cylinder, a 15º, and two cylinders, and sew through the next cylinder in the round **(photo c)**. Sew back through the last two cylinders picked up.

[7] Repeat step 6 to complete the round, but for the last stitch, pick up a 15º, a cylinder, and a 15º, and sew down through the first two cylinders in the first stitch **(photo d)**.

[8] Sew through the beadwork to exit a 15º added in step 4. Pick up a 4 mm bicone crystal and a 15º, and sew through the center cylinder in the opposite loop of beads **(photo e)**. Sew back through the 15º and bicone just added, and sew through the 15º your thread exited at the start of this step, sewing in the same direction as before (there should be a thread coming out of each side of the 15º). Sew through the beadwork to exit the next 15º added in step 4.

[9] Repeat step 8 to add a total of 12 bicones around the pearl. Sew through the beadwork to exit the 15º, cylinder, and 15º in a loop of beads.

[10] Pick up an 11º seed bead, and sew through the 15º, cylinder, and 15º in the next loop **(photo f)**. Repeat this stitch to complete the round, and step up through the first 11º.

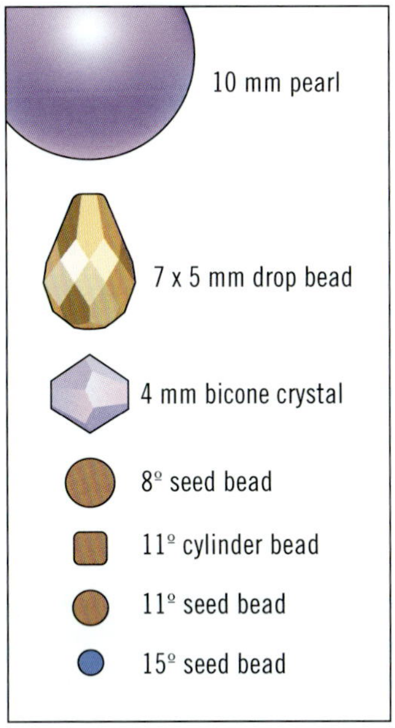

[11] To make a picot: Pick up three 11ºs, sew through the 11º your thread exited at the start of this step to form a ring, and continue through

a

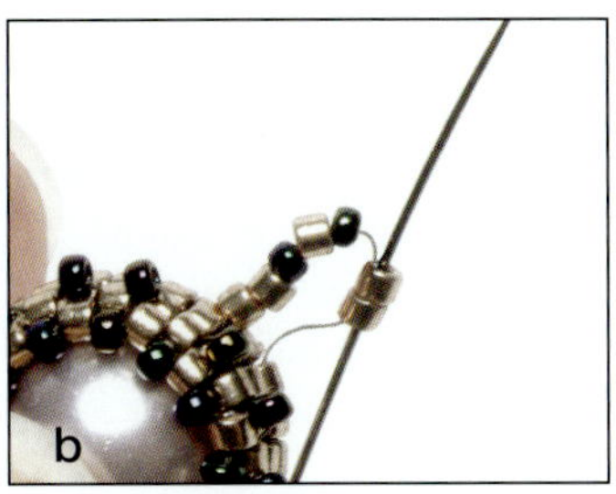

b

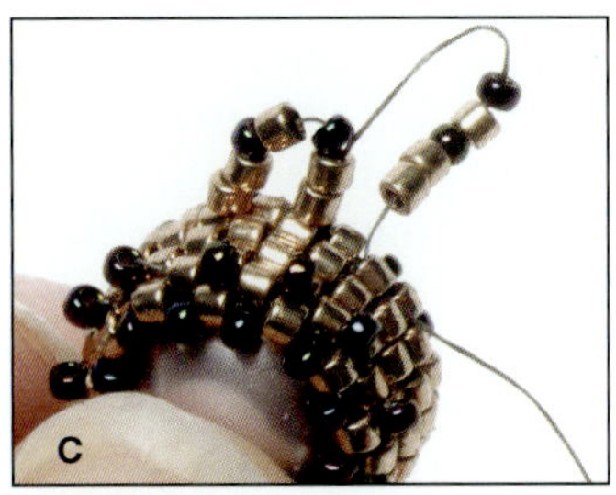

c

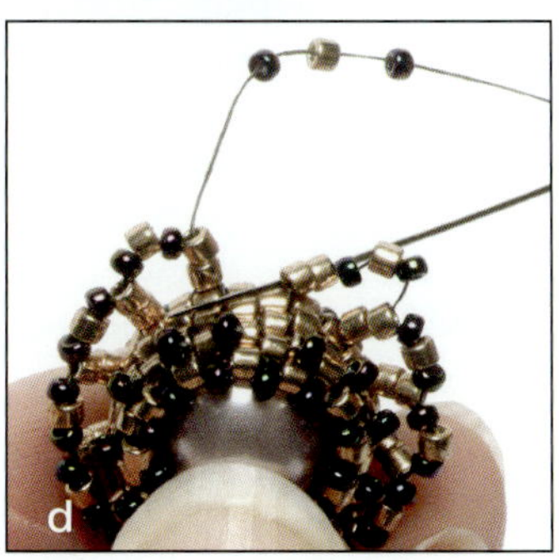

d

e

f

MATERIALS

necklace 20 in. (51 cm)

- **1** 30 mm *Bead&Button* 20th anniversary bead (www.BeadAndButton.com/anniversarybead)
- **3** 10 mm glass pearls (purple)
- **31** 7 x 5 mm glass drop beads (Czech, transparent gold)
- **66** 4 mm bicone crystals (Swarovski, sand opal AB2X)
- 1–2 g 8º seed beads (Miyuki 457, metallic dark bronze)
- 5 g 11º cylinder beads (Miyuki DB0115, transparent luster gold rose)
- 3 g 11º seed beads (Miyuki 457, metallic dark bronze)
- 4–5 g 15º seed beads (Miyuki 151, transparent cobalt)
- Fireline 6 lb. test
- beading needles, #11 or #12
- E6000 adhesive
- 2 x 2-in. (5 x 5 cm) square of beading foundation
- 2 x 2-in. (5 x 5 cm) square of Ultrasuede

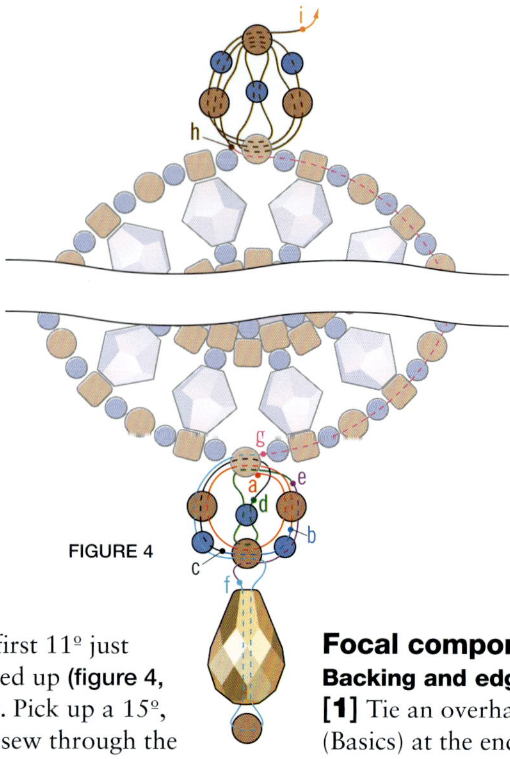

FIGURE 4

the first 11º just picked up **(figure 4, a–b)**. Pick up a 15º, and sew through the next 11º in the ring **(b–c)**. Repeat this stitch once, and then sew through the 11º your thread exited at the start of this step **(c–d)**. Pick up a 15º, and sew through the 11º on the opposite side of the ring. Sew back through the 15º just picked up, and continue through the 11º your thread exited at the start of this step **(d–e)**. Sew through the following 11º, 15º, and 11º in the ring **(e–f)**.

[12] To add a drop bead: Pick up a 7 x 5 mm drop bead (narrow end to wide end) and an 11º. Sew back through the drop bead, and continue through the 11º your thread exited at the start of this step and the following 15º and two 11ºs **(f–g)**.

[13] Sew through the beadwork to exit the 11º opposite the drop bead **(g–h)**. Work as in step 11 to create another picot **(h–i)**. End the working thread and tail.

[14] Make two more bezeled pearls. Each should have a picot and a drop on one end and a single picot on the other.

Focal component

Backing and edging

[1] Tie an overhand knot (Basics) at the end of 1 yd. (.9 m) of thread. Holding the anniversary bead in the center of a 2 x 2-in. (5 x 5 cm) square of beading foundation, sew up through the foundation from back to front, exiting near the hole at one end of the bead. Sew through the bead and down through the foundation on the other end of the bead **(photo g)**. Retrace the thread path four or five times to secure the bead.

[2] Sew up through the foundation close to the edge of the bead. Using cylinders, work a round of beaded backstitch (Basics) around the outer edge of the anniversary bead. Make sure you have an even number of cylinders in this round. Retrace the thread path through the cylinders several times to reinforce. Do not end the working thread; you will use it again in the steps for "Bezel," below.

[3] Trim the foundation close to the beadwork, making sure you don't cut any of the threads.

[4] Place your work on

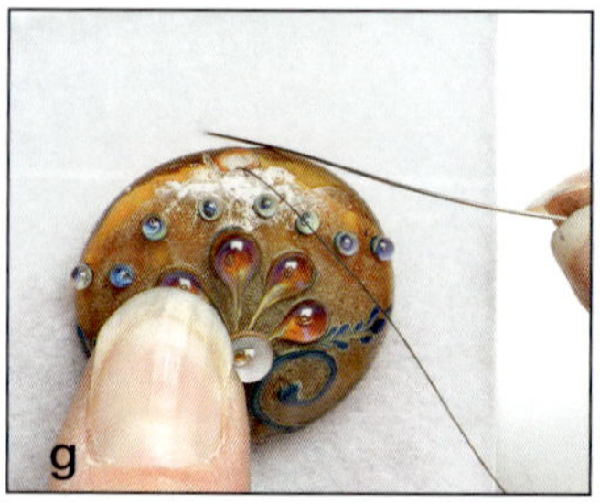
g

a piece of Ultrasuede, trace around the work, and cut out the shape.

[5] Glue the wrong side of the Ultrasuede shape to the back of your work, and allow the glue to dry.

[6] Tie an overhand knot at the end of a comfortable length of thread. Sew between the layers of Ultrasuede and foundation at the edge of the beadwork, and exit the front of your work, hiding the knot between the two layers.

[7] Pick up two 11ºs, sew down through both layers about one bead's width away, and then sew up through the last 11º.

[8] Pick up an 11º, sew down through both layers, and then sew up through the 11º again. Repeat this stitch to complete the round, but in the last stitch, pick up an 11º, sew down through the first 11º at the start of the round, continue through both layers, and then sew up through the last 11º. End this thread in the beadwork.

Bezel

[1] With the working thread from the focal component, work a round of peyote stitch off of the ring of beaded backstitch, and step up through the first cylinder picked up in this step. This is round 1 of the peyote bezel.

[2] Work in rounds as follows, ending and adding thread as needed:

Rounds 2–5: Work four rounds of peyote using cylinders, stepping up at the end of each round.

Round 6: Work a round of peyote using 15ºs.

[3] Sew through the beadwork to exit a cylinder in round 4. Using 15ºs, work a round of peyote off of the cylinders in this round. The 15ºs will sit on top of the cylinders. Sew through the beadwork to exit a cylinder in the first round of peyote added in step 1.

[4] Work as in steps 5, 6, and 7 of "Bezeled pearls" to create loops of beads as before.

[5] Sew through the beadwork to exit a 15º added in step 3. Pick up a 4 mm and a 15º, and sew through the center cylinder in the opposite loop of beads. Sew back through the 15º and bicone just picked up, and continue through the 15º your thread exited at the start of this step, sewing in the same direction as before. Sew through the beadwork to exit the next 15º in the round.

[6] Pick up four 15ºs, sew through the center cylinder in the next loop of beads, sew back through the four 15ºs just picked up, and sew through the 15º your thread exited at the start of this step in the same direction as before.

[7] Repeat steps 5 and 6 to complete the round.

[8] Sew through the beadwork to exit a center cylinder in a loop of beads. Pick up an 8º seed bead, and sew through the center cylinder in the next loop. Repeat this stitch to complete the round. Tie a couple of half-hitch knots (Basics), but do not end the working thread.

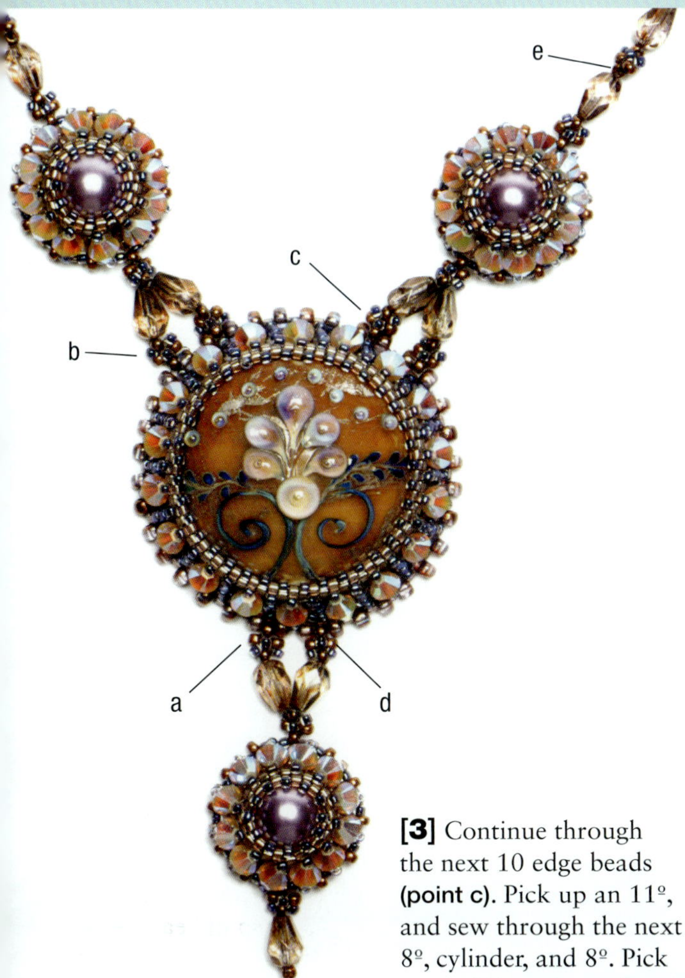

Assembly

[1] With the working thread from the bezel, refer to the **photo** above to sew through the beads along the bottom edge, exiting an 8º to one side of the center point with the needle pointing away from the center **(point a)**. Pick up an 11º, and sew through the next edge 8º. This is the first of two connection points for the bottom bezeled pearl.

[2] Continue through the next 22 edge beads **(point b)**, working toward the top of the anniversary bead. Pick up an 11º, and sew through the next 8º, cylinder, and 8º. Pick up an 11º, and sew through the next 8º. These will be the two connection points for the left bezeled pearl.

[3] Continue through the next 10 edge beads **(point c)**. Pick up an 11º, and sew through the next 8º, cylinder, and 8º. Pick up an 11º, and sew through the next 8º. These will be the two connection points for the right bezeled pearl.

[4] Continue through the next 22 edge beads, working toward the bottom of the anniversary bead **(point d)**. Pick up an 11º, and sew through the next 8º, cylinder, and 8º. This is the second of the two connection points for the bottom bezeled pearl. Continue through the first 11º picked up in step 1.

[5] Create a picot as in step 11 of "Bezeled pearls."

[6] Pick up a drop bead (wide end to narrow end), and sew through the tip 11º in the picot opposite the drop bead on a bezeled pearl. Sew back through the drop bead and the ring of the picot, and retrace the thread path. Sew through the beadwork to exit the next 11º connection point.

[7] For each of the remaining connection points, work as in step 11 of "Bezeled pearls" to create a picot, and then work as in step 6 of "Assembly," referring to the **photo** for placement. Note: Each tip 11º in a picot of a bezeled pearl will be used as a connection point twice. End and add thread as needed, and end the working thread when you finish.

Clasp

Toggle ring

[1] On 2 ft. (61 cm) of thread, pick up 30 15ºs, and sew through all the beads again to form a ring, leaving a 6-in. (15 cm) tail.

[2] Work a round of tubular peyote using 15ºs.

[3] Work a round of tubular peyote using 11ºs.

[4] Sew through the beadwork to exit a 15º in the initial ring, and then repeat steps 2 and 3 on this side of the ring.

[5] Zip up (Basics) the first and last rounds to form a ring. End the working thread and tail.

Toggle bar

[1] On 2 ft. (61 cm) of thread, attach a stop bead (Basics), leaving a 6-in. (15 cm) tail. Pick up eight cylinders, and work in flat even-count peyote stitch (Basics) to make a strip that is eight cylinders wide and 12 rows long. Remove the stop bead, roll the strip into a tube, and zip up the first and last rows.

[2] Sew through the center of the tube to exit one end. Pick up a 4 mm and a 15º, and sew back through the 4 mm and the tube. Pick up a 4 mm and a 15º, and sew back through the 4 mm and the tube. End the working thread and tail.

Neck straps

[1] Add 1 yd. (.9 m) of thread to the right bezeled pearl. Sew through the beadwork to exit the tip 11º above the drop bead **(point e)**. Work as in step 11 of "Bezeled pearls" to add a picot at the end of the drop.

[2] Attach a drop bead (wide end to narrow end) and an 11º as in step 12 of "Bezeled pearls," but instead of sewing through a 15º and two 11ºs, exit the new 11º. Add a picot at the end of the drop.

[3] Attach a 4 mm and an 11º the same way you attached the drop, and then add a picot at the end of the 4 mm.

[4] Attach a drop bead (narrow end to wide end) and an 11º as before, and then add a picot at the end of the drop.

[5] Repeat steps 2–4 for the desired length neck strap, ending and adding thread as needed. End with a picot.

[6] Pick up a 15º, sew through two center cylinders in the toggle bar, pick up a 15º, and sew through the 11º your thread exited at the start of this step. Retrace the thread path of the join.

[7] Retrace the thread path through the neck strap, sewing through the beads along an edge of each picot to reinforce. End the thread.

[8] Repeat steps 1–5 for the other neck strap.

[9] Pick up a 15º, sew through two adjacent 11ºs in the toggle ring, pick up a 15º, and sew through the 11º your thread exited at the start of this step. Retrace the thread path of the join.

[10] Repeat step 7 for this neck strap. ●

BEAD EMBROIDERY / FRINGE

Maharani
ring/pendant

It's a ring!
It's a pendant!
It's interchangeable!

designed by **Maggie Roschyk**

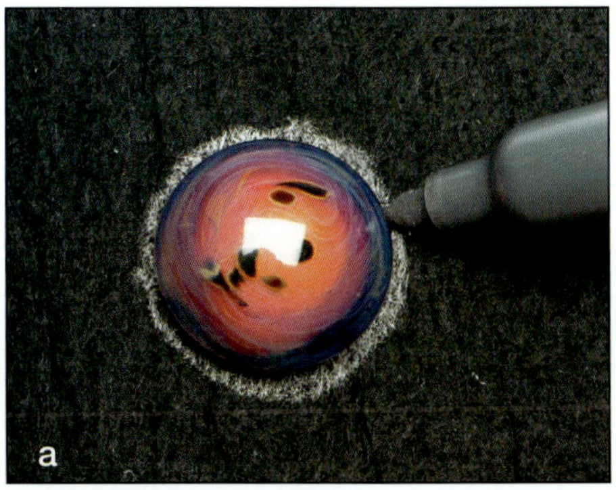

a

b

stepbystep

This project features Tammy Rae's ring-top cabochons. They have a stainless steel screw thread embedded in the back, which makes them interchangeable with ring and pendant findings. Whether you choose to make a ring or a pendant, the steps are the same. Once you've completed the bead embroidery, simply select the appropriate finding, and screw it into the back of the beadwork.

Foundation

[1] Cut a 2–3 mm hole at the center of a 3 x 3-in. (7.6 x 7.6 cm) piece of beading foundation.
[2] Place the foundation on top of the threaded stem of a stainless steel screw-on ring or pendant component. Screw the cabochon onto the component, sandwiching the foundation between the cab and the component.
[3] Using a permanent marker, trace an outline onto the foundation **(photo a)**. Remove the cab and the foundation from the ring or pendant component.

Bead-embroidered cabochon

[1] Tie an overhand knot (Basics) at the end of 1 yd. (.9 m) of thread, and sew up through the foundation from back to front, exiting along the outline of the cabochon.

c

[2] Using color A 1.8 mm cube beads, work a round of beaded backstitch (Basics) along the outside edge of the outline. Place the cabochon in the center of the As to check the fit **(photo b)**. A little bit of wiggle room is better than too tight.
[3] Sew through all the As in the ring to align the beads, but do not pull too tight. Sew down through the foundation between two As, and sew back up approximately ⅛ in. (3 mm) away from the ring of As.
[4] Pick up a 6–7 mm pearl, slide it to the foundation, and sew down through the foundation after the 6 mm. Retrace the thread path through the 6 mm several times to secure. The 6 mm should sit close to the ring of As **(photo c)**.

MATERIALS

ring or pendant 2½ in. (6.4 cm)

- **1** 20 mm round borosilicate glass ring topper cabochon by Tammy Rae (www.etsy.com/shop/glassbytammyrae)
- **1** stainless steel screw-on ring or pendant component (www.etsy.com/shop/glassbytammyrae)
- **1** 8 mm pearl (burgundy)
- **1** 6–7 mm pearl (blue)
- **2** 5 mm pearls (olive)
- **10–12** 3–4 mm pearls and bicone crystals (assorted colors)
- **4** 2.8 mm drop beads (Miyuki 457, dark bronze)
- 2 g 1.8 mm cube beads in each of **2** colors: A (Miyuki 462, metallic gold iris), B (Miyuki F463K, rainbow matte metallic)
- 1 g 11º seed beads (Miyuki 462, metallic gold iris)
- 1 g 15º seed beads (Miyuki 462, metallic gold iris)
- 4 in. (10 cm) rhinestone cup chain (Swarovski PP24, sand opal on gunmetal; www.agrainofsand.com)
- nylon beading thread, such as Nymo, size D (black)
- beading needles, #10 or #11
- wire cutters
- 3 x 3 in. (7.6 x 7.6 cm) beading foundation, such as Nicole's BeadBacking (www.nicolecampanella.com)
- 2½ x 2½ in. (6.4 x 6.4 cm) kidskin leather or Ultrasuede
- permanent marker (silver)
- white tacky adhesive

d

e

[5] Sew up through the foundation on one side of the 6 mm, exiting the point where the 6 mm meets the ring of As. Using 11º seed beads, work a semicircle of beaded backstitch around the 6 mm.
[6] Cut a 4-in. (10 cm) piece of cup chain. Position one end of the cup chain at the point where the 11ºs meet the ring of As, and wrap the cup chain around the ring of As.
[7] Sew up through the foundation between the As and the cup chain, exiting a point between the first and second cups. Sew across the metal tab between the cups and down through the foundation on the other side **(photo d)**. Sew up through the foundation between the As and the cup chain, exiting a point between the next two cups. Sew across the metal tab between the cups and down through the foundation on the other side. Continue to work in this manner, tacking the cup chain to the foundation around the ring of As. Make sure the cups are evenly distributed along the chain, and keep a consistent but not tight tension.
[8] Carefully trim the cup chain where it meets the ring of 11ºs on the other side of the 6 mm. Retrace the thread path across the metal tab between the last two cups on this end of the chain.
[9] Sew through to the back of the foundation, and end the thread by tying an overhand knot on the back of the foundation and trimming the tail.
[10] Tie an overhand knot at the end of 1 yd. (.9 m) of thread, and sew up through the foundation from back to front, exiting along the outside edge of the cup chain directly opposite the 6 mm. Work as in step 4 to add an 8 mm pearl **(photo e)**.
[11] Using 11ºs, work as in step 5 to stitch a semicircle around the 8 mm.
[12] Sew up through the foundation on one side of the 8 mm, exiting the point where the ring of 11ºs meets the cup chain. Pick up a 5 mm pearl, and sew it to the foundation as with the other pearls. Bring the thread across the back of the foundation to exit the corresponding point on the other side of the 8 mm, and add a 5 mm pearl to this side.
[13] Using color B 1.8 mm cube beads, work a round of beaded backstitch along the outside edge of the beadwork. Sew back through the Bs added in this step, and sew down through the foundation between two Bs. End the thread on the back of the foundation.

Leather backing

[1] Trim the foundation close to the beadwork, making sure you don't cut any of the threads and leaving approximately 1/16 in. (2 mm) of foundation showing around the outside edge of the beadwork.
[2] Cut a 2–3 mm hole at the center of a 2½ x 2½-in. (6.4 x 6.4 cm) piece of leather backing.
[3] Glue the foundation to the backing, making sure the center holes are aligned and no glue seeps into the hole. Allow the glue to dry completely.
[4] Carefully trim the backing around the perimeter of the beadwork, using the edge of the foundation as a guide.

Edging

[1] Tie an overhand knot at the end of 2 ft. (61 cm) of thread. Sew between the foundation and the backing at the

News flash Maggie is the proud new owner of the wholesale side of Heidi Kummli's Free Spirit Collection jewelry company. The line is sold at museum gift shops, airport gift shops, and high-end boutiques across the western United States.

f

edge of the beadwork, and exit the front of the foundation, hiding the knot between the two layers.

[2] To work the first stitch: Pick up two 11ºs, sew down through the foundation and the backing, and sew back up through the backing, the foundation, and the last 11º.

[3] To work subsequent stitches: Pick up an 11º, sew down through the foundation and the backing, and sew back up through the 11º just added. Repeat this stitch around the perimeter of the beadwork.

[4] After adding the last stitch, sew down through the first 11º picked up in the first stitch, the foundation, and the backing, and then sew back up through the backing, the foundation, and the first 11º. End the thread in the beadwork (Basics).

Fringe

The fringe can be worked using a variety of 15º seed beads, 11ºs, cube beads, 2.8 mm drop beads, 3 mm pearls, 3 mm bicone crystals, and 4 mm pearls. Start with the longest center fringe, and decrease the number of 15ºs in each fringe by one as you work away from the center, as shown in **photo f**. Keep your tension relatively loose so the fringe is not stiff.

[1] Add 2 ft. (61 cm) of thread to the beadwork (Basics), exiting the center 11º edge bead on the end nearest the 8 mm pearl. Pick up seven 15ºs, a B, a 3–4 mm bead, and a 15º. Skip the 15º, and sew back through the remaining beads added in this step and the edge 11º your thread exited at the start of this step. Sew through the next edge 11º on one side to be in position to add the next fringe.

[2] Pick up six 15ºs, a B, a 3–4 mm bead, and a 15º. Skip the 15º, and sew back through the remaining beads added in this step and the edge 11º your thread exited at the start of this step. Sew through the next edge 11º to be in position to add the next fringe.

[3] Work as in step 2 for the remaining four or five fringes on this side, decreasing the number of 15ºs in each fringe as you work away from the center.

[4] Pick up a 15º, a 2.8 mm drop bead, and a 15º, sew through the next edge 11º, and continue through the following edge 11º.

[5] Pick up a drop bead, and sew through the next edge 11º.

[6] Sew through the beadwork to exit the edge 11º on the other side of the center fringe, and work as in steps 2–5 to add the remaining fringe on this side. End the thread in the beadwork.

Assembly

Push the threaded portion of the ring or pendant component through the opening in the center of the bead embroidery. Place the cabochon on the threaded stem, and carefully screw the cab to the ring or pendant. •

Notice the screw thread embedded in the cab.

SHIBORI RIBBON /
BEAD EMBROIDERY / PEYOTE STITCH

Shibori roses

Use bead-embroidery techniques to turn shibori silk ribbon into a necklace of roses encrusted with all your favorite beads. Then add earrings (or a pin!) to match.

designed by **Jane Danley Cruz**

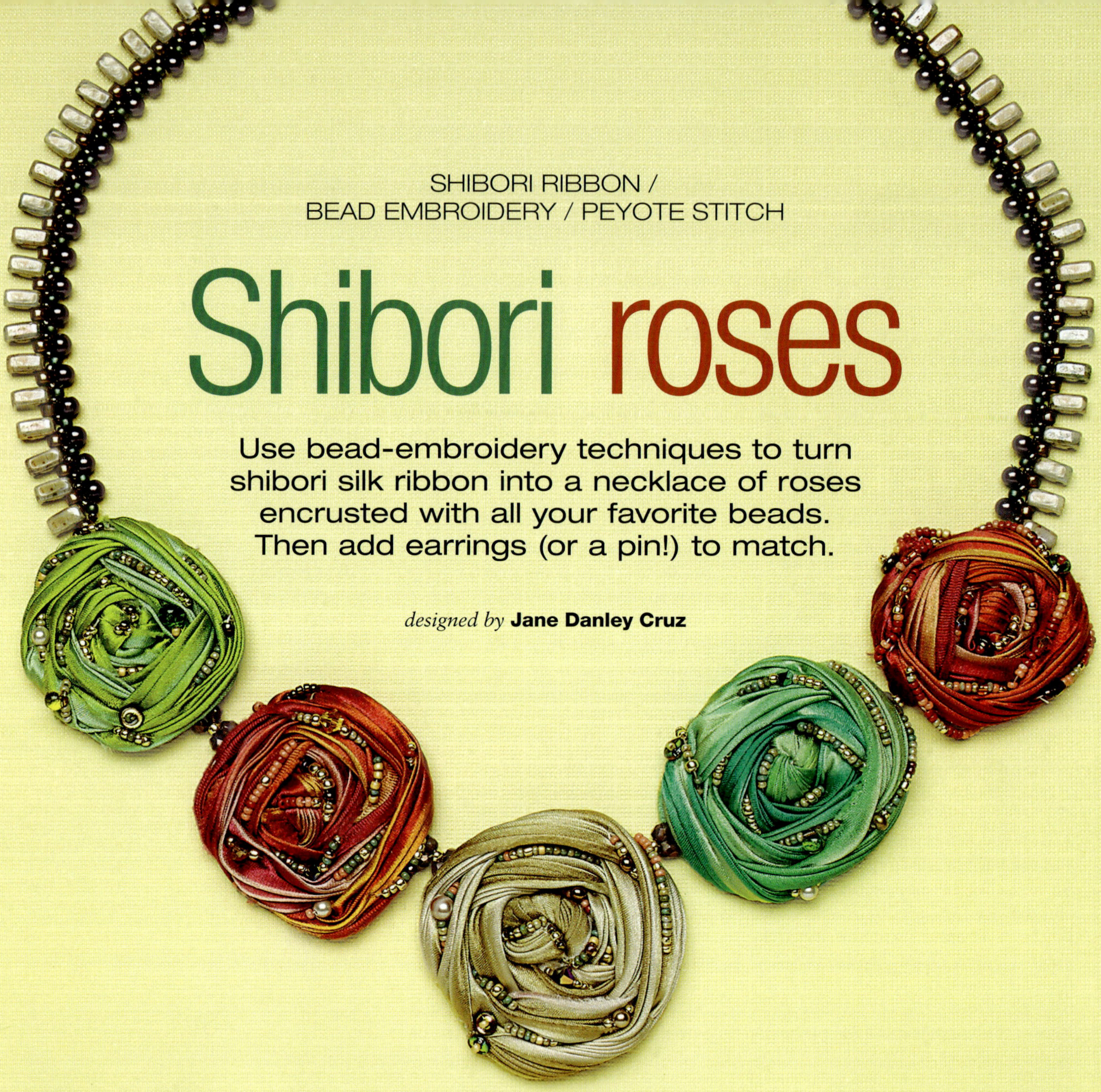

stepbystep

Shibori ribbon roses

[1] Cut a 2 x 2-in. (5 x 5 cm) square of beading foundation. Tie an overhand knot (Basics) at one end of 2 ft. (61 cm) of thread.

[2] Tie an overhand knot at one end of a 12-in. (30 cm) shibori silk ribbon, making sure the knot is very close to the end of the ribbon. Place the knot in the middle of the foundation square, with the long tail of the ribbon to the right. Hold the knot in place while you sew from back to front through the foundation and the knot, and then sew back down through the knot and the foundation about 3 mm away from where your thread exited **(photo a)**. Make a couple more stitches to tack the knot to the foundation, stitching in a crease of the knot.

[3] Fold the long tail of the ribbon in half so the wrong sides are together inside the fold. Make a small (6 mm) vertical stitch about 4 mm away from the knot near the top edge of the ribbon as shown in **photo b**. You should be sewing through both layers of the ribbon.

[4] Fold the ribbon straight down along the line of the last stitch **(photo c)**, overlapping the edge of the knot slightly. Turn the square one quarter turn counterclockwise so the tail of the ribbon is again on the right.

[5] Make a small vertical stitch in the center of the ribbon. This stitch should be lined up with the right-hand edge of the knot **(photo d)**.

[6] Continue working as in steps 4 and 5 **(photos e, f, and g)** until the rose is approximately 1½–1¾ in. (3.8–4.4 cm) in diameter and you have at least a ½-in. (1.3 cm) tail. Keep a firm tension on the ribbon, and overlap the edges of the rose slightly with each fold so there are no gaps where the foundation shows through.

[7] Work as in step 4, but twist the tail of the ribbon, and tuck it under the adjacent fold (photo h). Make two or three small stitches to secure the tail, and sew through the foundation so your needle is exiting the back of your work. Tie a couple of overhand knots, and trim the thread.
[8] Make a total of five shibori ribbon roses.

Embellishment and backing

[1] Tie an overhand knot at one end of 2 ft. (61 cm) of thread. Sew up through the foundation and the knot at the center of the rose. Pick up a mixture of five to seven 13º Charlottes and 15º seed beads as desired, push the beads down to the rose, and sew down through the knot a short distance away so the beads follow a crease in the knot and lie snug along the surface of the rose (photo i). Retrace the thread path through the beads to secure.
[2] Continue to embellish the rose as in step 1, using a variety of beads. Begin and end each stitch in a fold. When you are satisfied with your embellishment, tie an overhand knot on the back of your work, and trim the thread.
[3] Trim the foundation

j

around the rose, being careful not to cut any threads. Apply a thin layer of glue on the back of the rose, and place it on the wrong side of a 2 x 2-in. (5 x 5 cm) square of Ultrasuede (photo j). Allow the glue to dry completely, and then trim the Ultrasuede

MATERIALS

both projects

- nylon beading thread, such as Nymo, size D (colors to match shibori silk)
- beading needles, #11
- white tacky adhesive

necklace 19 in. (48 cm)

- **5** 12-in. (30 cm) shibori silk ribbons in the desired colors
- **56** 3 x 6 mm CzechMates two-hole brick beads (opaque green ultra luster)
- **54** 4 mm glass pearls (dark purple)
- **16** 3 mm fire-polished beads (stone amethyst luster)
- 1–2 g 8º seed beads (Miyuki 457, metallic dark bronze)
- 1 g 11º seed beads (Miyuki 2008, matte metallic patina iris)
- 4–6 g assorted beads, such as: 13º Charlottes, 15º seed beads, 3–4 mm drop beads, 3–4 mm pearls and bicone crystals, 4 mm O-beads
- clasp
- **2** 6 mm jump rings
- **5** 2 x 2-in. (5 x 5 cm) squares of beading foundation, such as Lacy's Stiff Stuff
- **5** 2 x 2-in. (5 x 5 cm) squares of Ultrasuede
- **2** pairs of chainnose, flatnose, and/or bentnose pliers

pair of earrings 1 in. (2.5 cm)

- **1** 12-in. (30 cm) shibori silk ribbon, cut into two 6-in. (15 cm) pieces
- 2–3 g assorted beads, such as: 13º Charlottes, 11º and 15º seed beads, 3 mm bicone crystals, 4 mm O-beads
- 2 g 15º seed beads for edging (Miyuki 457L, metallic light bronze)
- pair of earring findings
- **2** 2 x 2-in. (5 x 5 cm) squares of beading foundation, such as Lacy's Stiff Stuff
- **2** 2 x 2-in. (5 x 5 cm) squares of Ultrasuede

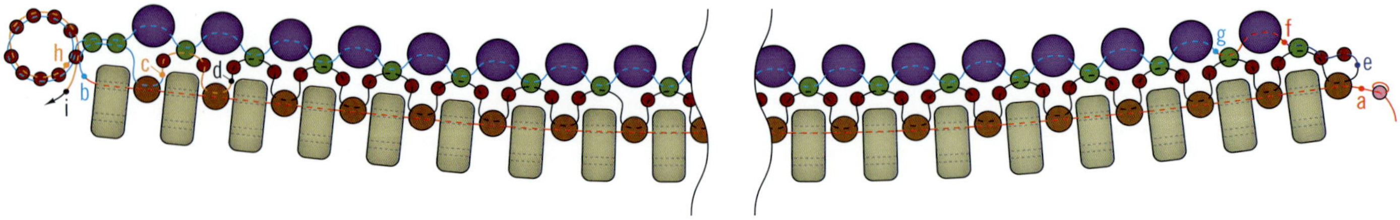

FIGURE

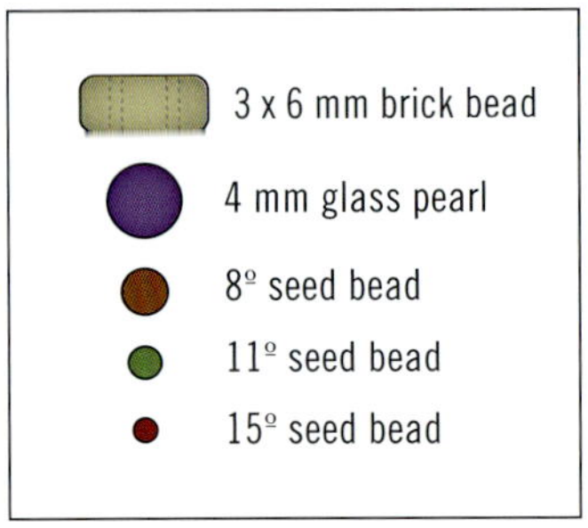

so it is the same size and shape as the foundation.

[4] Tie an overhand knot at one end of 2 ft. (61 cm) of thread. Sew between the layers of foundation and Ultrasuede at the edge of the rose, and exit the front of the foundation, hiding the knot between the layers. Do not sew through the ribbon.

[5] Sew up through the Ultrasuede and the foundation (again, without sewing through the ribbon) 3–4 mm from where you anchored the thread. Continue to whip stitch (Basics) the edges of the Ultrasuede and foundation around the rose.

[6] With the thread exiting the foundation, tie an overhand knot, and then sew through both layers to exit about ½ in. (1.3 cm) away from the edge. Trim the thread.

[7] Repeat steps 1–6 to complete the remaining roses.

Centerpiece

[1] Lay the roses on your work surface, and determine the connection points. Mark each point on the back of each rose with temporary thread.

[2] Tie an overhand knot at one end of an 8-in. (20 cm) length of thread. Beginning with the center rose, sew up through the Ultrasuede and foundation at the connection point marked in step 1, with the needle pointing away from the center rose.

[3] Pick up a 3 mm fire-polished bead, an 11º seed bead, and a 3 mm, and sew through the corresponding connection point on the next rose. Retrace the thread path, and then sew through the center rose about 2 mm away, with the needle pointing away from the center rose.

[4] Pick up a 3 mm, and sew through the 11º picked up in the previous step. Pick up a 3 mm, and sew through the second rose about 2 mm away from the previous connection point. Retrace the thread path through the connection several times, and then end the thread as in step 6 of "Embellishment and backing."

[5] Work as in steps 2–4 to connect the remaining roses.

Neck straps

[1] On 1 yd. (.9 m) of thread, attach a stop bead (Basics), leaving an 8-in. (20 cm) tail. Pick up a repeating pattern of an 8º seed bead and a 3 x 6 mm two-hole brick bead 28 times **(figure, a–b)**.

[2] To make the turn: Pick up a 15º and two 11ºs, skip the last brick, and sew back through the previous 8º **(b–c)**.

[3] Working in modified peyote stitch (Basics), pick up a 15º, an 11º, and a 15º,

Pin a rose on me!

[1] Make a single rose, and add beads as in steps 1 and 2 of "Embellishment and backing."

[2] Trim the foundation around the rose, and sew a pin-back finding to the back of the foundation.

[3] Cut a slit in the Ultrasuede to accommodate the pin-back finding, apply a thin layer of glue to the foundation, and position the Ultrasuede over it.

[4] Finish the beaded edge as in steps 3–5 of "Earrings," but pick up three beads in the first stitch and two beads for each subsequent stitch to create a picot edge. In our sample, we used a pendant/pin finding, which gives you even more options!

skip the next brick, and sew through the following 8º **(c–d)**. Repeat this stitch for the length of the band **(d–e)**.

[4] To make the turn: Pick up a 15º, and sew back through the previous 15º and 11º **(e–f)**.

[5] Working in modified peyote stitch, pick up a 4 mm pearl, and sew through the next 11º in the previous row **(f–g)**. Repeat this stitch for the length of the band, and then sew through the next 11º and 15º **(g–h)**. Adjust your tension so the band curves inward along the pearl edge.

[6] Pick up eight 15ºs, and sew through the 15º your thread exited at the start of this step. Retrace the thread path through the loop several times **(h–i)**. End the working thread in the beadwork (Basics) but not the tail.

[7] Make a second neck strap.

Assembly

[1] Position the neck straps and the centerpiece on your work surface so the pearl edge of each neck strap is to the inside. Determine the connection points, and make a mark on the back of the centerpiece at each point.

[2] Remove the stop bead from the tail of a neck strap, and sew up through the centerpiece at the corresponding mark, making sure not to sew through the ribbon. Sew back down through the centerpiece, and continue through the end 15º in the neck strap. Sew through the adjacent 8º, and retrace the thread path through the connection several times. End the tail.

[3] Open a 6 mm jump ring (Basics), and attach the loop at the end of the neck strap to half of the clasp.

[4] Repeat steps 2 and 3 for the remaining neck strap.

Earrings

[1] Using a 6-in. (15 cm) piece of shibori silk ribbon, work as in "Shibori ribbon roses" to make a rose that measures approximately 1 in. (2.5 cm) in diameter.

[2] Work as in steps 1–4 of "Embellishment and backing."

[3] To work the first edge stitch: Pick up two 15ºs, sew down through the foundation and the Ultrasuede about one bead's width away, and sew back up through the last 15º.

[4] To work subsequent edge stitches: Pick up a 15º, sew down through the foundation and the Ultrasuede, and sew back up through the 15º just added. Repeat this stitch around the perimeter of the beadwork.

[5] After adding the last stitch, sew down through the first 15º in the first stitch, and continue through the foundation and the Ultrasuede. Sew back up through the Ultrasuede, the foundation, and the first 15º.

[6] Pick up five 15ºs and the loop of an earring finding. Skip two 15ºs in the edging, and sew down through the next 15º. Retrace the thread path, and end the thread as in step 6 of "Embellishment and backing."

[7] Make a second earring. ⚬

BEAD EMBROIDERY / PEYOTE STITCH / RUSSIAN SPIRAL ROPE

Vintage vogue

In the Victorian era, lockets, watches, and coin purses were displayed on long chains. Recreate this vintage look with an art bead.

designed by **Jane Danley Cruz**

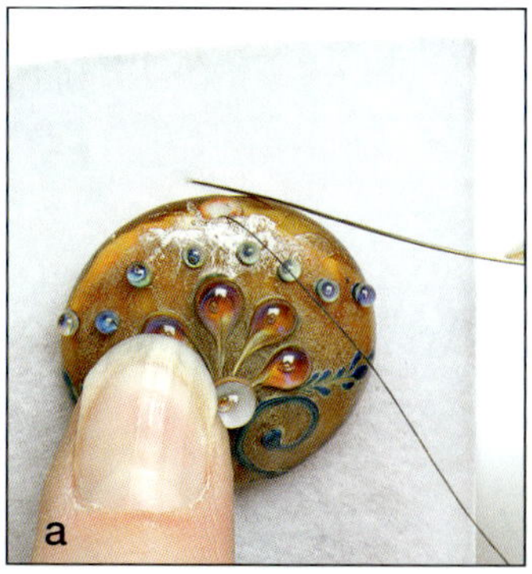
a

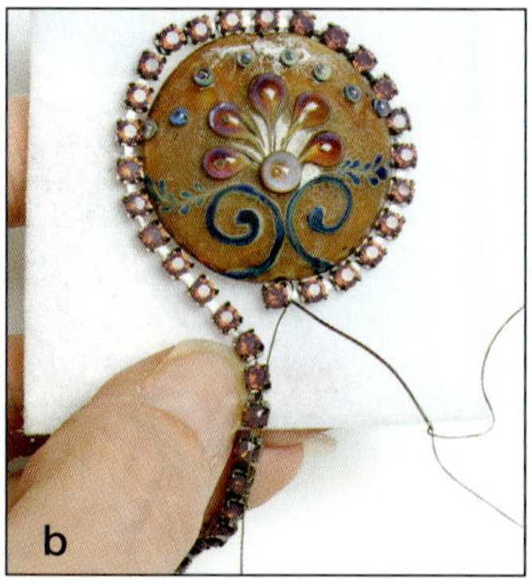
b

c

stepbystep

Pendant

Bead embroidery

[1] Tie an overhand knot (Basics) at the end of 1 yd. (.9 m) of thread. Holding the anniversary bead in the center of a 2 x 2-in. (5 x 5 cm) square of beading foundation, sew up through the foundation from back to front, exiting near the hole at one end of the bead. Sew through the bead and down through the foundation on the other end of the bead **(photo a)**. Retrace the thread path four or five times to secure the bead.

[2] Cut a 5¼-in. (13.3 cm) piece of cup chain, and position it along the outer edge of the anniversary bead. Sew up through the foundation between the bead and the cup chain, exiting a point between the first and second cups. Sew across the metal tab between the cups and down through the foundation on the other side **(photo b)**. Sew up through the foundation between the bead and the cup chain, exiting a point between the next two cups. Sew across the metal tab between the cups and down through the foundation on the other side. Continue to work in this manner, tacking the cup chain to the foundation around the bead. Trim the cup chain if necessary.

[3] Sew up through the foundation along the outer edge of the cup chain. Using color A 11º seed beads, work a round of beaded backstitch (Basics) around the outer edge of the cup chain. Make sure you have an even number of As in this round. Retrace the thread path through the As several times to reinforce. End the thread by tying a knot on the back of the foundation.

[4] Trim the foundation close to the beadwork, making sure you don't cut any of the threads and leaving approximately ⅛ in. (3 mm) of foundation showing around the outside edge.

[5] Place your work on another piece of beading foundation, trace around the work, and cut out the shape. Repeat to cut out the same shape from a piece of Ultrasuede **(photo c)**.

[6] Glue the wrong side of the Ultrasuede shape to the new foundation shape, and then glue the new foundation shape to the back of your work. The new foundation shape will be sandwiched between the Ultrasuede and the beadwork.

Peyote bezel

[1] Tie an overhand knot at the end of a comfortable length of thread. Sew between the layers of foundation at the edge of the beadwork, and exit the front of your work between the cup chain and the round of beaded backstitch, hiding the knot between the two layers of foundation.

d

[2] Sew through an A in the round of beaded backstitch. Working in tubular peyote stitch (Basics), pick up an A, skip the next A in the round, and sew through the following A **(photo d)**. Repeat this stitch to complete the round, and step up through the first A added in this step.

[3] Work four more rounds of tubular peyote stitch using As, allowing the beadwork to curve over the back of the pendant, and end and add thread (Basics) as needed. Keep your tension even but not tight. If your tension is tight, you will pull the round of beaded backstitch away from the cup chain, and the foundation will show.

[4] Work two rounds of peyote using 15º seed beads. Retrace the thread path through the last round, and tack down every fifth or sixth

MATERIALS

necklace 24 in. (61 cm)

- **1** 30 mm *Bead&Button* 20th anniversary commemorative bead (www.BeadAndButton.com/AnniversaryBead)
- **16** 3 mm bicone crystals (Swarovski, cyclamen opal)
- **8** 3 mm drop beads (Toho 221, bronze)
- **36–38** 2 mm glass pearls (Czech, light purple)
- 11º seed beads
  16 g color A (Miyuki 457, metallic dark bronze)
  6 g color B (Miyuki 379, mauve-lined light topaz luster)
- 15º seed beads (Miyuki 457L, metallic light bronze)
- clasp
- 5¼ in. (13.3 cm) cup chain (Swarovski PP24, cyclamen opal in gunmetal setting; www.agrainofsand.com)
- Fireline 6 lb. test
- beading needles, #11
- wire cutters
- E6000 adhesive
- **2** 2 x 2-in. (5 x 5 cm) pieces of Lacy's Stiff Stuff beading foundation
- 2 x 2 in. (5 x 5 cm) Ultrasuede

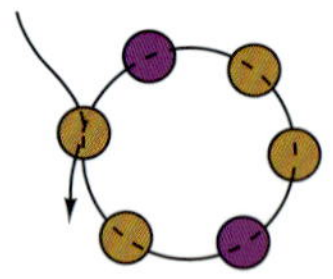

FIGURE 1

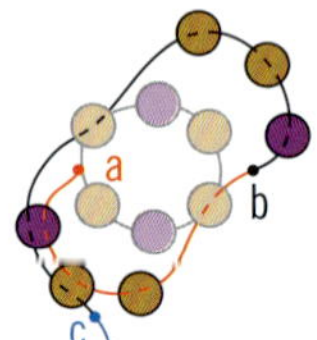

FIGURE 2

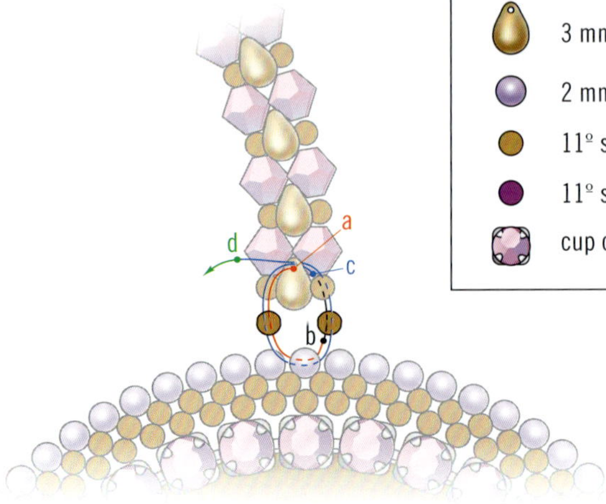

FIGURE 3

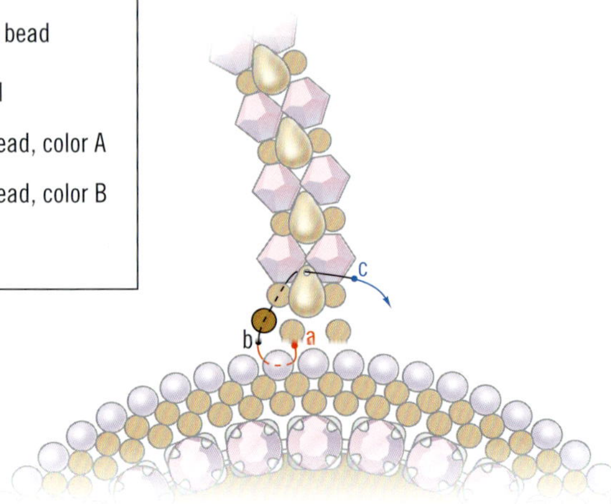

FIGURE 4

up-bead as follows: Exit the up-bead, sew through the Ultrasuede and both layers of foundation to the front of the piece, and sew back down to the back of the piece. Continue reinforcing the round and tacking down up-beads until the bezel and pendant layers are secure.

[5] Sew through the beadwork to exit an A in the first round of peyote stitch. Pick up a 2 mm pearl, and sew through the next A in the round. Repeat this stitch to complete the round, and end the thread in the beadwork.

Bail

[1] On 2 ft. (61 cm) of thread, pick up a repeating pattern of an A and a 3 mm bicone crystal eight times. Sew through all the beads again to form a ring, leaving a 12-in. (30 cm) tail, and continue through the first A and 3 mm crystal.

[2] Pick up a 3 mm drop bead, and sew through the next 3 mm crystal in the previous round. Repeat this stitch to complete the round, and step up through the first drop bead.

[3] Work a round of tubular peyote using 3 mm crystals.

[4] Work three rounds of tubular peyote using As. Retrace the thread path through the last round. Do not end the working thread.

[5] With the tail, work two rounds of tubular peyote using As. Retrace the thread path through the last round, and end the tail.

Russian spiral rope

[1] On a comfortable length of thread, pick up two As, a color B 11º seed bead, two As, and a B. Sew through the first A again to form a ring, leaving an 8-in. (20 cm) tail **(figure 1)**.

[2] Pick up a B and two As, and sew through the A following the next B in the previous round **(figure 2, a–b)**. Repeat this stitch, and step up through the first B and A added in this round **(b–c)**.

[3] Repeat step 2 for the desired length rope.

[4] Pick up an A, and sew through the A following the next B in the previous round. Repeat this stitch once, and then retrace the thread path.

[5] Pick up an A, and sew through the other A added in step 4. Sew back through the A picked up in this step, and sew through the A your thread exited at the start of this step in the same direction. Retrace the thread path, and exit the A picked up in this step. Do not end the working thread.

[6] With the tail, repeat steps 4 and 5. Do not end the tail.

Assembly

[1] With the thread from the bail, sew through the beadwork to exit a drop bead **(figure 3, point a)**. Pick up an A, and sew through a 2 mm pearl along the top edge of the bezel to one side of the center point **(a–b)**. Pick up an A, and sew through the A to one side of the drop bead **(b–c)**. Continue through the drop bead, and retrace the thread path through the join **(c–d)**.

[2] Sew through the beadwork to exit the first A added in the previous step. Sew through the 2 mm pearl on the other side of the center point of the bezel **(figure 4, a–b)**, pick up an A, sew through the A to the other side of the drop bead, and continue through the drop bead **(b–c)**. Retrace the thread path through the join. End the thread.

[3] Center the bail on the rope.

[4] With the working thread from the rope, pick up three As, half of the clasp, and three As, and sew through the A your thread exited at the start of this step. Retrace the thread path through the clasp connection several times, and end the thread.

[5] With the tail, work as in step 4 to attach the other half of the clasp to this end of the rope. ●

MULTIPLE STITCHES

Organic *twist* bracelet and necklace

designed by **Kerrie Slade**

Stitch a garland of leaves and flowers for your wrist using Czech striped seed beads. A matching necklace completes the set.

MATERIALS

all projects

- Fireline 6 lb. test
- beading needles, #10 or #11

blue/green bracelet 8½ in. (21.6 cm)

- Preciosa traditional Czech beads
  26 g 8º striped seed beads, color A (522, green/yellow)
  11 g 8º striped seed beads, color B (538, blue/white matte rainbow)

red/green bracelet (p. 217) colors:

- Preciosa traditional Czech beads
  26 g 8º striped seed beads, color A (522, green/yellow)
  11 g 8º striped seed beads, color B (03910, white with wide red stripe)

necklace 21 in. (53 cm)

- Preciosa traditional Czech beads
  36 g 8º striped seed beads, color A (522, green/yellow)
  6 g 8º striped seed beads, color B (538, blue/white matte rainbow)

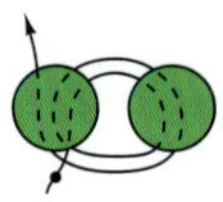

FIGURE 1

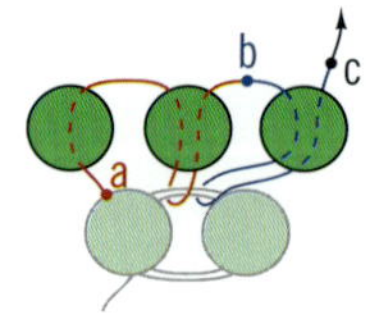

FIGURE 2

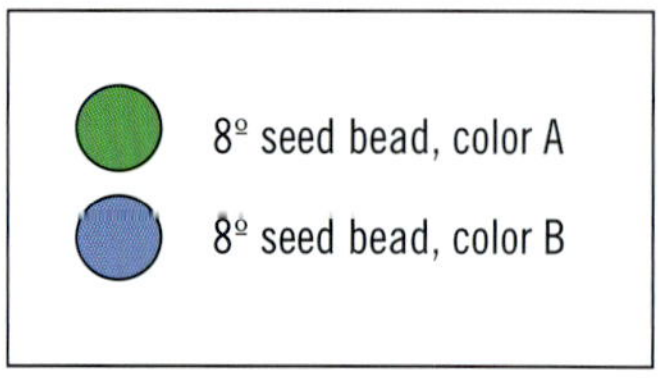

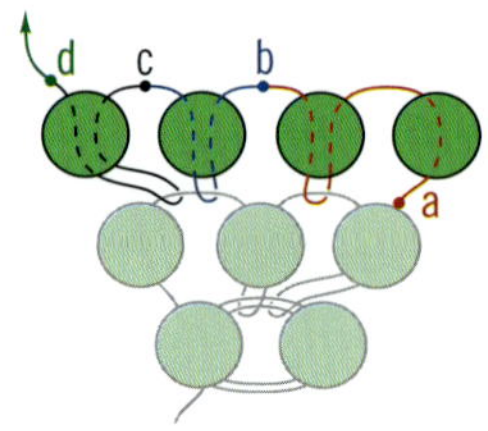

FIGURE 3

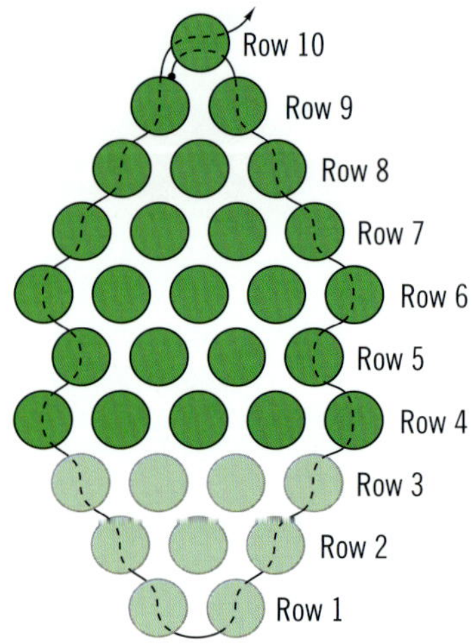

FIGURE 4

stepbystep

Bracelet

Rope

[1] On a comfortable length of thread and leaving a 24-in. (61 cm) tail, work in ladder stitch (Basics) to make a four-bead ladder with color A 8º seed beads. Form the ladder into a ring (Basics) to create round 1.

[2] Work in modified twisted tubular herringbone as follows:

Rounds 2–4:

- Pick up two As, sew down through the next A in the previous round, and sew up through the following A. Pick up two As, sew down through the next A in the previous round, and step up through the following two As.

Round 5: Pick up two As, sew down through the next A in the previous round, and sew up through three As in the following stack. Pick up two As, sew down through the next A in the previous round, and sew up through four As in the following stack. Pull tight.

[3] Repeat round 5 for the desired length bracelet, leaving ¾ in. (1.9 cm) for the clasp. Set the rope aside, and do not end the working thread or tail.

Leaves

[1] On 1 yd. (.9 m) of thread, pick up two As, and sew through both beads again, leaving a 12-in. (30 cm) tail. Position the beads so they sit side by side. This is row 1 of the leaf. Exit the first A so that your working thread is exiting opposite the tail **(figure 1)**.

[2] Work row 2 of the leaf in brick stitch (Basics) as follows:

- Pick up two As, sew under the thread bridge between the two beads in row 1, and sew back up through the second A just added **(figure 2, a–b)**.
- Pick up an A, sew under the thread bridge between the two beads in row 1, and sew back up through the A just added **(b–c)**.

[3] Work row 3 of the petal in brick stitch as follows, noting the different terms for each kind of stitch:

- Increase start stitch: Pick up two As, sew under the last thread bridge in the previous row, and sew back up through the second A just added **(figure 3, a–b)**.
- Regular stitch: Pick up an A, sew under the next thread bridge in the previous row, and sew back up through the A just added **(b–c)**.
- Increase end stitch: Pick up an A, sew under the same thread bridge as in the previous stitch, and sew back up through the A just added **(c–d)**.

[4] Continue to work in rows as follows using As. Refer to **figure 4** as needed.

Row 4:

- Increase start stitch
- Two regular stitches
- Increase end stitch

Row 5:

- Decrease start stitch: Pick up two As, sew under the second-to-last thread bridge in the previous row, and sew back up through the second A just added. Circle through both beads to align them, and exit the second A.
- Two regular stitches

Row 6:

- Increase start stitch
- Two regular stitches
- Increase end stitch

Row 7:

- Decrease start stitch
- Two regular stitches

Row 8:

- Decrease start stitch
- Regular stitch

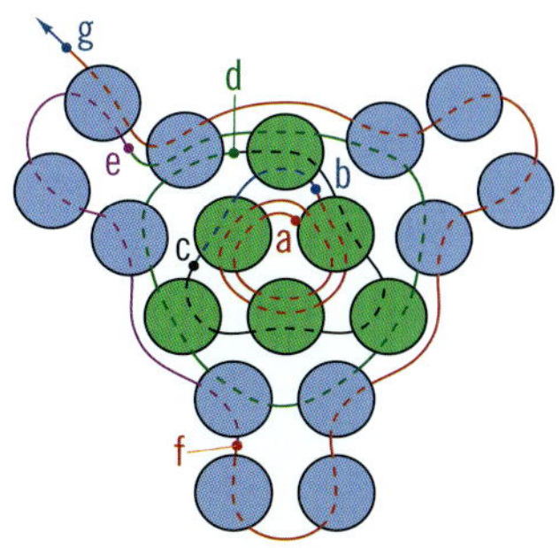

FIGURE 5

Row 9:
• Decrease start stitch
Row 10:
• Pick up an A, and sew through all the edge As, pulling the thread tight so the leaf cups slightly, and exit the A just added **(figure 4)**. End the working thread (Basics).

[5] With the tail, pick up two As, sew through the two As in row 1, and continue through the first new A. This forms a stem. If desired, add one or two more pairs of As in the same manner, making the stem longer. Set the leaf aside, but do not end the tail.

[6] Repeat steps 1–5 to make a total of 10 leaves. Vary the length of the stems in step 5.

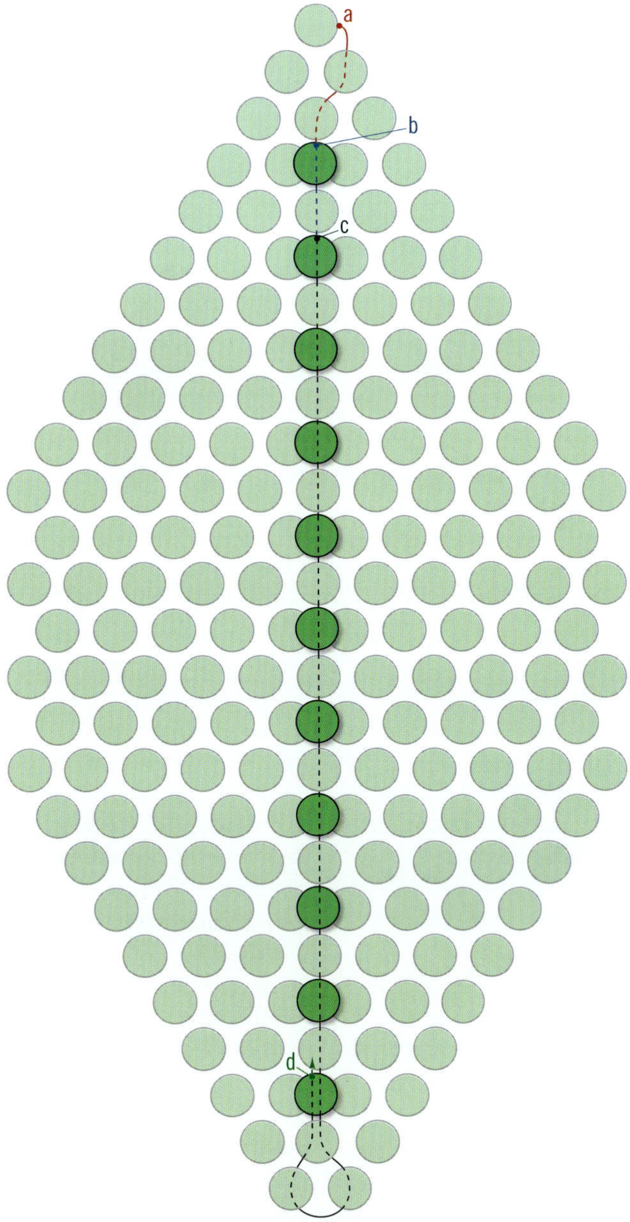

FIGURE 6

Small flower

[1] On 4 ft. (1.2 m) of thread, pick up three As, and sew through the beads again to form a ring, leaving a 12-in. (30 cm) tail **(figure 5, a–b)**.

[2] Pick up an A, and sew through the next A in the previous round **(b–c)**. Repeat this stitch two more times, and step up through the first A added in this step **(c–d)**.

[3] Work round 1 of the flower as follows: Pick up two color B 8º seed beads, and sew through the next A in the previous round. Repeat this stitch to complete the round, and step up through the first B added **(d–e)**. Pull tight so the beadwork begins to cup.

[4] Work round 2 of the flower in herringbone stitch as follows: Pick up two Bs, sew down through the next B in the previous round, and sew up through the following B **(e–f)**. Repeat this stitch twice, stepping up through two Bs in the first stack **(f–g)**.

[5] Work in modified twisted tubular herringbone as follows:

Round 3: Pick up two Bs, sew down through the next B in the previous round, and sew up through the following two Bs. Repeat this stitch once more. To complete the round: Pick up two Bs, sew down through the next B in the previous round, and sew up through the next three Bs. Pull tight.

Round 4: Pick up two Bs, sew down through the next B in the previous round, and sew up through the following three Bs. Repeat this stitch once. To complete the round: Pick up two Bs, sew down through the next B in the previous round, and sew up through the next four Bs. Pull tight.

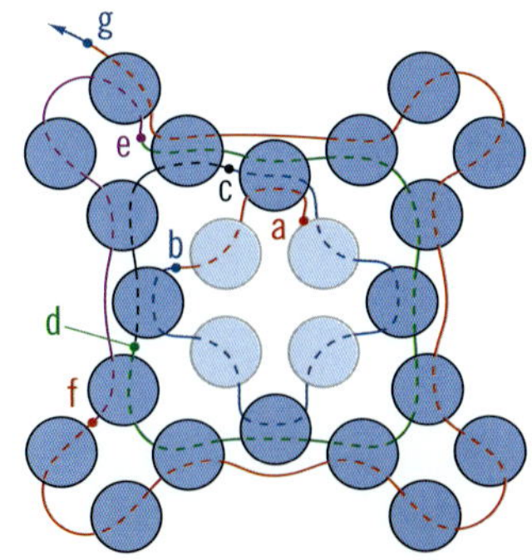

FIGURE 7

[6] Repeat round 4 eight more times for a total of 12 rounds.

[7] Pick up a B, sew down through the next two Bs, and sew up through the following four Bs. Repeat this stitch once more. To complete the round: Pick up a B, sew down through the next two Bs, and sew up through the following five Bs. End the working thread but not the tail.

[8] Using the tail, work as in step 5 of "Leaves" to add two pairs of As to two of the As in the starting ring **(photo a)**. Set the flower aside, but do not end the tail.

[9] Repeat steps 1–8 to make a total of six flowers with some of the following variations:
• Vary the length of the flower by increasing or decreasing the number of rounds added in step 6.
• Vary the stem length in step 8.
• Vary the length of the tips of the petals by making the following changes:

For the last round of Bs added to the petals: Pick up two Bs, sew down through the next two Bs, and sew up through the following four Bs. Repeat this stitch once. To complete the round, pick up two Bs, sew down through the next two Bs, and sew up

a

b

through the following five Bs. **In step 7:** Pick up a B, sew down through the next three Bs, and sew up through the following five Bs. Repeat this stitch once. To complete the round, pick up a B, sew down through the next three Bs, and sew up through the following six Bs.

Attaching the leaves and flowers

[1] Position the leaves and flowers as desired on the bracelet rope with all the components pointing in the same direction. Reserve one flower and one leaf for the clasp.
[2] With the tail of a component, sew through an A in the desired position on the rope, an adjacent A in the rope, and the remaining A in the stem **(photo b)**. Retrace the thread path of the connection several times, and end the tail.
[3] Repeat step 2 for the remaining components.
[4] Work as in step 2 to attach the two clasp components to the As on one end of the rope **(photo c)**. End all threads on this end.
[5] On the other end of the rope, and building off one set of end As, work as in step 5 of "Leaves" to add 16 pairs of As. Sew through the remaining set of end As to form a loop **(photo d)**. Make sure the flower from the opposite end fits through the loop, and add or remove pairs of As if necessary. Retrace the thread path of the connection several times, and end the thread.

Necklace

Rope

Repeat steps 1–3 of "Bracelet: Rope" for the desired length necklace, leaving 1 in. (2.5 cm) for the clasp.

Large leaf

[1] On 7 ft. (2.1 m) of thread, work as in steps 1–4 of "Bracelet: Leaves" to make a larger leaf following the pattern in **figure 6**.
[2] Sew through all the edge As, pulling the thread tight so the leaf cups slightly. Continue through the two As shown **(figure 6, a–b)**.
[3] Pick up an A (try to use one of the smaller As),

DESIGN NOTES:
- **On the spine of the large leaf, you can substitute 10° or 11° seed beads instead of the smaller of the 8° striped seed beads.**
- **Solid-color 8° seed beads can be substituted for the 8° striped beads.**

c

d

skip a row of As, and continue through the corresponding A in the next row **(b–c)**. Repeat this stitch for the remainder of the leaf to form a spine, and sew through the last four As as shown **(c–d)**.
[4] Pick up two smaller As, and sew through the next A in the spine. Repeat this stitch for the remainder of the leaf.
[5] Sew through the beadwork to exit the first A added in step 3. Sew through all the As in the spine, and end the working thread.
[6] Using the tail, work as in step 5 of "Bracelet: Leaves" to add a pair of As to the two As in row 1.
[7] Sew through a set of As on the end of the rope, and sew back through the two stem As added in the previous step. Reinforce the join by retracing the thread path and sewing through the surrounding As (not end As) several times. Exit an A in the other pair of As on this end of the rope.
[8] Pick up an A, and sew through the corresponding stem A. Continue through the adjacent stem A, pick up an A, and sew through the other A on the end of the rope. End all threads on this end of the rope.
[9] On the other end of the rope, make a loop as in step 5 of "Attaching the leaves and flowers," but work 26 pairs of As instead of 16. Be sure the large leaf fits through the loop, and adjust the number of rows if necessary. End the thread.

Large flower

[1] On 2 yd. (1.8 m) of thread, pick up four Bs, and sew through the beads again to form a ring, leaving an 8-in. (20 cm) tail. Continue through the next B.
[2] Work in rounds as follows:
Round 1: Pick up a B, and sew through the next B in the previous round **(figure 7, a–b)**. Repeat this stitch to complete the round, and step up through the first B added in this round **(b–c)**.
Round 2: Pick up two Bs, and sew through the next B in the previous round **(c–d)**. Repeat this stitch to complete the round, and step up through the first B added in this round **(d–e)**. Pull tight so the beadwork begins to cup.
Round 3: Working in herringbone stitch, pick up two Bs, sew down through the next B in the previous round, and sew up through the following B **(e–f)**. Repeat this stitch to complete the round, and step up through two Bs **(f–g)**. The

beadwork will begin to form a tubular shape.

[3] Work in modified twisted tubular herringbone as follows:

Round 4: Pick up two Bs, sew down through the next B in the previous round, and sew up through the following two Bs. Repeat this stitch twice. To complete the round: Pick up two Bs, sew down through the next B in the previous round, and sew up through the next three Bs. Pull tight.

Rounds 5–19: Pick up two Bs, sew down through the next B in the previous round, and sew up through the following three Bs. Repeat this stitch twice. To complete the round: Pick up two Bs, sew down through the next B in the previous round, and sew up through the next four Bs. Pull tight.

Round 20: Pick up two Bs, sew down through the next two Bs, and sew up through the following four Bs. Repeat this stitch twice. To complete the round: Pick up two Bs, sew down through the next two Bs, and sew up through the following five Bs.

Round 21: Pick up two Bs, sew down through the next three Bs, and sew up through the following five Bs. Repeat this stitch twice. To complete the round: Pick up two Bs, sew down through the next three Bs, and sew up through the following six Bs.

Round 22: Pick up two Bs, sew down through the next four Bs, and sew up through the following six Bs. Repeat this stitch twice. To complete the round: Pick up two Bs, sew down through the next four Bs, and sew up through the following seven Bs.

Round 23: Pick up a B, sew down through the next five Bs, and sew up through the following seven Bs. Repeat this stitch twice. To complete the round: Pick up a B, sew down through the next five Bs, and sew up through the following eight Bs. End the working thread and tail.

Calyx and bail

[1] Add 2 yd. (1.8 m) of thread (Basics) to the flower, exiting a B from step 1 of "Large flower."

[2] Pick up an A, and sew through the next B in the previous round. Repeat this stitch three more times to complete the round, and step up through the first A added in this step.

e

f

[3] Pick up two As, and sew through the next A in the previous round. Repeat this stitch to complete the round, and step up through the first A added.

[4] With your thread exiting an A in one of the sets just added, work as in rows 2, 3, 4, 7, 8, and 9 of "Bracelet: Leaves" to build a leaf off of the pair of As.

[5] Pick up an A, sew down through the next A in the last row, and continue through the A your thread exited at the start of this step.

[6] Sew through the nearest pair of Bs in the flower, and continue through the next A in the same row of the leaf to secure it to the flower. Sew through the beadwork to exit the first A in the next set added in step 3 **(photo e)**.

[7] Repeat steps 4–6 to add three more leaves to the base of the flower.

[8] Sew through the beadwork to exit an A in a pair of As added in step 3 at the base of a leaf. Pick up two As, sew through the previous two As, and continue through the first new A **(photo f)**. Building off these two As, work as in step 5 of "Attaching the leaves and flowers" to make a loop with 16 pairs of As. Make sure the loop will slide over the large leaf at the other end of the rope. Add or remove pairs of As if necessary, and retrace the thread path of the connection several times. End the thread.

[9] Slide the large flower onto the rope. ●

Componentry

Add bits of beadwork to metal components for a lively, linked bracelet.

designed by **Marla Salezze**

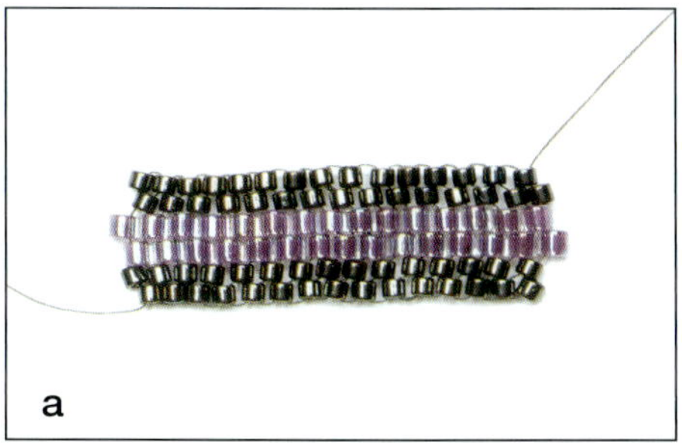
a

b

c

d

e

f

stepby**step**

Components

Peyote stitch channel bead

[1] On 1 yd. (.9 m) of Fireline, attach a stop bead (Basics), leaving a 6-in. (15 cm) tail. Pick up two 11º cylinder beads, two 10º cylinder beads, and two 11º cylinders.

[2] Work in flat even-count peyote stitch (Basics) as follows: Pick up an 11º cylinder, skip the last 11º picked up in the previous step, and sew through the following 11º. Pick up a 10º, skip the next 10º, and sew through the following 10º. Pick up an 11º, skip the next 11º, and sew through the following 11º. Continue working rows of peyote with an 11º, a 10º, and an 11º until you have a total of 30 rows **(photo a)**.

[3] Remove the stop bead. Wrap the strip around the 11 x 13 mm channel bead, and zip up (Basics) the end rows **(photo b)**. End the working thread and tail (Basics).

Ladder stitch channel bead

On 18 in. (46 cm) of Fireline and leaving a 6-in. (15 cm) tail, make a ladder (Basics) using nine or 10 6º seed beads. Wrap the ladder around the 11 x 6 mm channel bead, form the ladder into a ring (Basics), and end the working thread and tail **(photo c)**.

Netted pearl component

[1] On 2 ft. (61 cm) of Fireline, pick up a repeating pattern of a 6 mm pearl and a color B 15º seed bead five times. Tie the beads into a ring with a square knot (Basics), leaving a 6-in. (15 cm) tail, and sew through the first two beads to exit a B.

[2] Pick up nine Bs, and sew through the next B in the ring **(photo d)**. Repeat this stitch to complete the round, and step up through the first five Bs added in this round **(photo e)**.

[3] Pick up a 6 mm pearl, and sew through the middle (fifth) B in the loop around the next pearl **(photo f)**. Repeat this stitch to complete the round.

MATERIALS

copper bracelet 8 in. (20 cm)

- **1** 19 x 28 mm square link with two loops (copper)*
- **1** 11 x 13 mm channel bead (copper)*
- **1** 11 x 6 mm channel bead (copper)*
- **2** 10 mm sea hive bead caps (copper)*
- **2** 9 mm urchin bead caps (copper)*
- **3** 8 x 12 mm lampworked beads
- **18** 6 mm crystal pearls (Swarovski, light gold)
- **6** 5 mm freshwater pearls (brown)
- **1** 4 x 6 mm pressed glass bellflower bead (topaz)
- **6** 3 x 4 mm faceted glass rondelles (topaz AB)
- **10** 6º seed beads (Toho 2034, silver-lined topaz AB)
- 1 g 10º cylinder beads (Miyuki DBM0907, light bronze-lined crystal)
- 2 g 11º cylinder beads (Miyuki 0254, bronze luster)
- **6** 11º seed beads (Toho 459, gold luster topaz)
- 1 g 15º seed beads in each of **2** colors: A (Toho 989, bronze-lined crystal) B (Toho 459, gold luster topaz)
- **1** 2-in. (5 cm) eye pin (copper)
- **2** 9 mm 16-gauge textured jump rings (copper)*
- **2** 6 mm 16-gauge textured jump rings (copper)*
- nylon beading thread, size D
- Fireline 6 lb. test
- beading needles, #12
- **2** pairs of chainnose pliers
- roundnose pliers
- wire cutters
- Lacy's Stiff Stuff beading foundation
- E6000 adhesive

Materials list continued on p. 220

Materials list continued from p. 219

turquoise/fuchsia bracelet colors:

- metal components (same as on p. 219 but in silver)*
- 8 x 12 mm lampworked beads (Czech, fuchsia; www.fusionbeads.com)
- 6 mm crystal pearls (Swarovski, jade)
- 5 mm freshwater pearls (dark blue)
- 6 mm crystal margarita, in place of 4 x 6 mm bellflower (Swarovski, Bermuda)
- 3 x 4 mm faceted glass rondelles (Czech, turquoise)
- 6º seed beads (Japanese 356C, blue lavender-lined AB)
- 10º cylinder beads (Miyuki DBM0056, transparent rainbow light magenta)
- 11º cylinder beads (Miyuki DB0026, metallic dark steel)
- 11º seed beads (Toho 81, metallic hematite)
- 15º seed beads color A (Miyuki 352, fuchsia-lined aqua luster) color B (Miyuki 456, gunmetal iris)

Retrace the thread path through the beaded bead, and end the working thread and tail **(photo g)**.

[4] On an eye pin, string an 8 x 12 mm lampworked bead, a sea hive bead cap (wide end first), the netted pearl beaded bead, a sea hive bead cap (narrow end first), and a lampworked bead, and make a plain loop (Basics).

[5] Open a 6 mm jump ring (Basics), attach a plain loop, and close the jump ring. Repeat with another 6 mm jump ring at the other end **(photo h)**.

Bead-embroidered link

[1] Cut a 16 x 16 mm piece of Lacy's Stiff Stuff beading foundation. Cut 2 ft. (61 cm) of nylon thread, tie an overhand knot (Basics) at one end, and thread a needle on the other end. Sew up through the center of the beading foundation.

[2] Pick up a 4 x 6 mm bellflower bead and a B, sew back through the bellflower and the foundation, and sew up through the foundation next to the flower (**photo i** — here we substituted a 6º seed bead and a 6 mm crystal margarita for the bellflower).

[3] Pick up a 5 mm pearl. Align the pearl next to the flower, and sew down through the foundation. Retrace the thread path up through the foundation, and exit the pearl **(photo j)**.

[4] Pick up a 5 mm pearl, align it next to the flower, and sew down through the foundation. Retrace the thread path up through the foundation, and exit the new pearl. Repeat this step four times to add a total of six pearls around the flower **(photo k)**, and sew down through the foundation.

[5] Sew up through the foundation right next to the bellflower and between two pearls. Pick up eight color A 15º seed beads, and sew down through the foundation between the pearls along the outer edge **(photo l)**. Repeat this step between each pair of pearls.

[6] Working in beaded backstitch (Basics), fill in the remaining beading foundation with B 15ºs. Knot your thread on the back of the foundation, and trim. Using E6000, adhere the foundation to the inside of a 19 x 28 mm square link, and let dry.

[7] Open a 9 mm jump ring, and attach it to a loop on the link. Repeat to attach a 9 mm jump ring to the other loop **(photo m)**.

Toggle ring

[1] On 1 yd. (.9 m) of Fireline, pick up 42 As, and tie them into a ring with a square knot, leaving a 6-in. (15 cm) tail.

[2] Work in tubular peyote stitch (Basics)

g

h

i

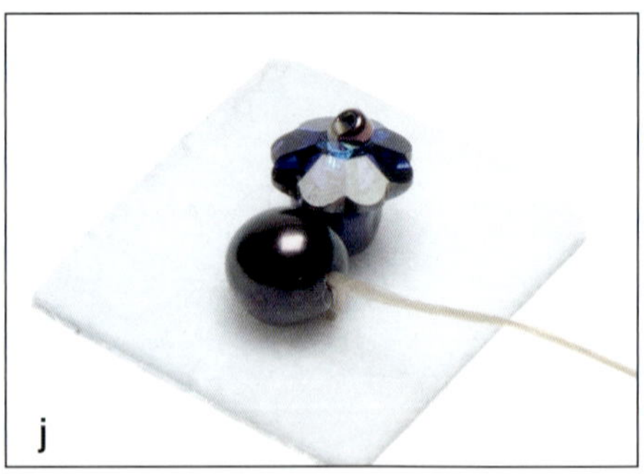
j

k

l

for a total of five rounds of As. Work five more rounds with 11º cylinders, and then zip up the last round of cylinders to the first round of As **(photo n)**. Sew through the beadwork to exit a cylinder in the middle round of cylinders. End the tail but not the working thread.

Toggle bar

[1] On 1 yd. (.9 m) of Fireline, attach a stop bead, leaving a 6-in. (15 cm) tail. Pick up 15 11º cylinders, and work in flat odd-count peyote stitch (Basics) using 11º cylinders until you have a total of 12 rows. Remove the stop bead, and zip up the end rows to form a tube. Sew through the beadwork to exit an end cylinder.

[2] Pick up three Bs, a 6 mm pearl, and three Bs, and sew through the opposite end cylinder. Sew up through the adjacent end cylinder.

[3] Pick up three Bs, sew back through the pearl, pick up three Bs, and sew through the cylinder opposite the one your thread exited at the start of this step **(photo o)**. There will be two sets of Bs attaching the pearl to the tube on each side. Retrace the thread path through the pearl.

[4] Sew through the beadwork to exit an end cylinder at the other end of the tube, and repeat steps 2 and 3 to add another pearl. Sew through the beadwork to exit the seventh cylinder from one end. End the tail but not the working thread.

Assembly

[1] Using the thread from the toggle bar, pick up three Bs, an 11º seed bead, a 3 x 4 mm rondelle, a 6 mm pearl, the peyote channel bead, a 6 mm pearl, a rondelle, an 11º seed bead, and seven Bs. Sew through a jump ring attached to the netted pearl component, and sew back through the 11º seed bead, rondelle, pearl, channel bead, pearl, rondelle, and 11º. Pick up three Bs, and sew through the seventh bead from the opposite end of the toggle bar. Retrace the thread path through all the beads added in this step a few times, and end the thread **(photo p)**.

[2] Using the thread from the toggle ring, pick up three Bs, an 11º seed bead, a 3 x 4 mm rondelle, a 6 mm pearl, an urchin bead cap, a lampworked bead, an urchin bead cap, a 6 mm pearl, a rondelle, an 11º seed bead, and seven Bs. Sew through a jump ring attached to the bead-embroidered link, and sew back through the 11º seed bead, rondelle, pearl, bead cap, lampworked bead, bead cap, pearl, rondelle, and 11º. Pick up three Bs, and sew through the next bead in the middle round of the toggle ring. Retrace the thread path through all the beads added in this step a few times, and end the thread **(photo q)**.

[3] On 18 in. (46 cm) of Fireline, attach a stop bead, leaving a 6-in. (15 cm) tail. Pick up three Bs, an 11º seed bead, a 3 x 4 mm rondelle, a 6 mm pearl, the ladder stitch channel bead, a 6 mm pearl, a rondelle, an 11º seed bead, and seven Bs. Sew through the remaining jump ring attached to the netted pearl component, and sew back through the beads to exit the first 11º picked up in this step.

[4] Pick up four Bs and the remaining jump ring on the bead-embroidered link, and sew through all the beads picked up in step 3 again. Retrace the thread path a few times, and end the working thread. Remove the stop bead, and end the tail **(photo r)**. ●

m

n

o

p

q

r

MULTIPLE STITCHES

Shining star
necklace

Dress up any outfit with this made-for-the-holidays necklace featuring a stunning crystal focal.

designed by **Agnieszka Watts**

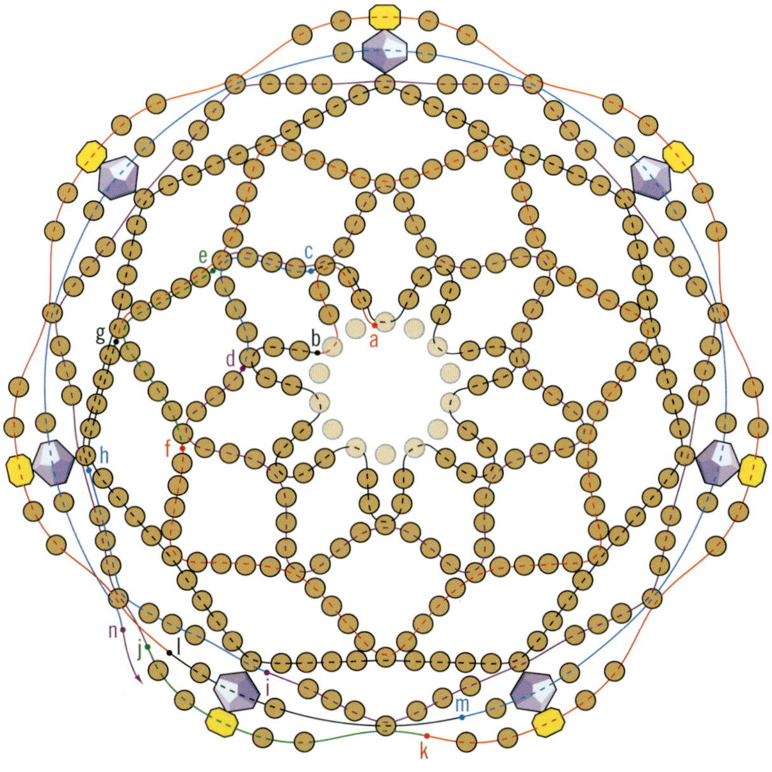

FIGURE 1

stepbystep

Pendant

[1] On 4 ft. (1.2 m) of thread, pick up 14 color F 15º seed beads. Sew through all the beads again to form a ring, leaving a 6-in. (15 cm) tail. Tie the working thread and tail together with a square knot (Basics).

[2] Work four rounds of netting:

Round 1: Pick up five Fs, skip the next F in the ring, and sew through the following F (**figure 1, a–b**). Repeat this stitch to complete the round, and step up through the next three beads to exit the center F in the first stitch of this round (**b–c**).

Round 2: Pick up seven Fs, and sew through the center F in the next stitch of the previous round (**c–d**). Repeat this stitch to complete the round, and step up through the next four beads to exit the center F in the first stitch of this round (**d–e**).

Round 3: Pick up nine Fs, and sew through the center F in the next stitch of the previous round (**e–f**). Repeat this stitch to complete the round, and step up through the next five beads to exit the center F in the first stitch of this round (**f–g**).

Round 4: Work as in round 3 (**g–h**).

[3] Place the 21 mm crystal drop in the center of the beadwork so the back of the drop is against the beadwork. For clarity, the crystal is not shown in **figure 1**.

[4] Work two more rounds of netting as follows:

Round 5: Pick up seven Fs, and sew through the center F in the next stitch of the previous round (**h–i**). Repeat this stitch to complete the round, and step up through the next four beads to exit the center F in the first stitch of this round (**i–j**).

Round 6: Pick up two Fs, an 11º hex-cut seed bead, and two Fs, and sew through the center F in the next stitch of the previous round (**j–k**). Repeat this stitch to complete the round using a tight tension,

MATERIALS

purple/gold necklace 19 in. (48 cm)

- **1** 21 mm crystal drop, double-sided faceted modified round (purple; www.firemountaingems.com)
- **1** 11 x 8 mm pear-shaped pearl (Swarovski, gold)
- crystal pearls (Swarovski)
  7 4 mm (gold)
  7 3 mm (dark purple)
- 3 mm bicone crystals (Swarovski)
  7 color A (amethyst AB)
  8 color B (gold aurum)
- 3 g 11º metal hex-cut seed beads (gold)
- 11º seed beads
  4 g color C (Toho 85, metallic iris purple)
  2 g color D (Toho 221, bronze)
- 15º seed beads
  1 g color E (Toho 85, metallic iris purple)
  2 g color F (Toho 221, bronze)
  5 g color G (Miyuki 462, metallic rainbow bronze; www.firemountaingems.com)
- toggle clasp
- **2** 8–9 mm bead caps
- Nymo D beading thread
- beading needles, #12

gray/silver necklace (p. 85) colors:

- 21 mm crystal drop, double-sided faceted modified round (gray with silver foil back; www.firemountaingems.com)
- 11 x 8 mm pear-shaped pearl (Swarovski, light gray)
- 4 mm crystal pearls (Swarovski, light gray)
- **1** 3 x 6 mm rhinestone rondelle (clear; www.firemountaingems.com)
- **14** 3 mm bicone crystals, colors A and B (Swarovski, silver night)
- 8º metal seed beads, in place of 3 mm crystal pearls (zinc; www.knotjustbeads.com)
- 11º seed beads
  color C (Miyuki 451, metallic hematite)
  color D (Toho P470, silver permanent galvanized)
- 15º seed beads
  colors E and G (Toho P470, silver permanent galvanized)
  color F (Miyuki 451, metallic hematite)

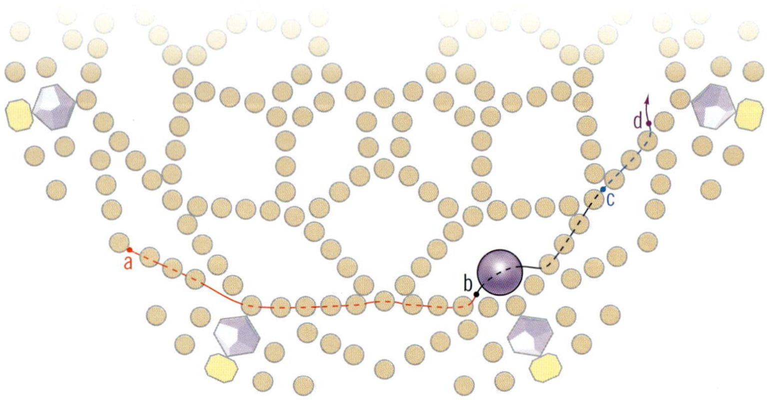

FIGURE 2

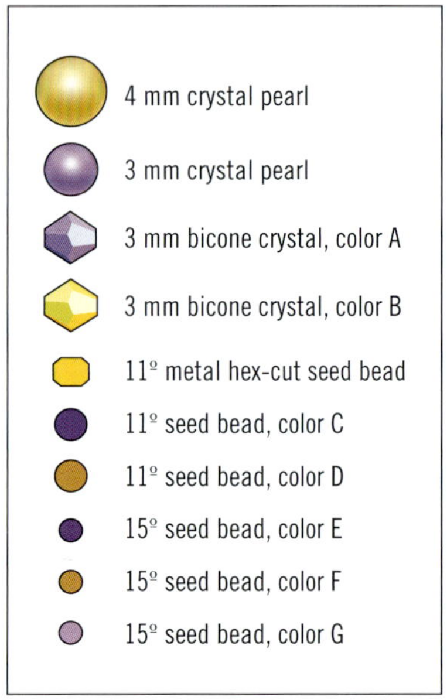

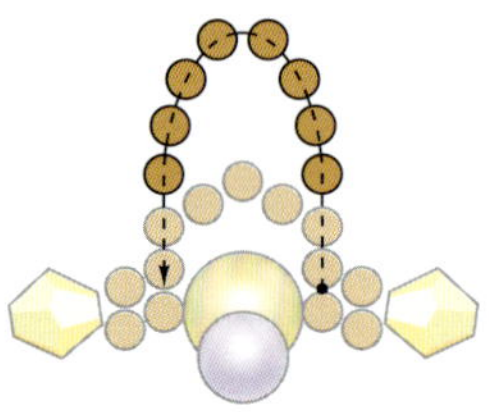

FIGURE 3

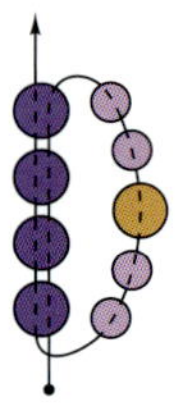

FIGURE 4

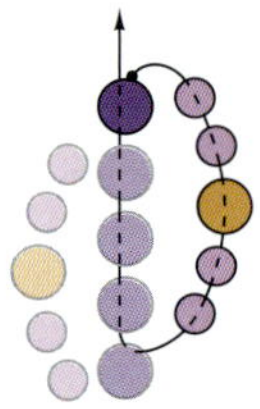

FIGURE 5

FIGURE 6

but do not step up **(k–l)**. Retrace the thread path of the round to tighten.

[5] Pick up an F, a color A 3 mm bicone crystal, and an F, and sew through the center F in the next stitch of round 5 **(l–m)**. Repeat this stitch to complete the round using a tight tension **(m–n)**. The As added in this step will sit between rounds 5 and 6.

[6] Sew through the next nine Fs toward the outside edge of the beadwork to exit the center F in a stitch from round 3. Sew through the following three Fs in round 4 **(figure 2, a–b)**.

[7] Pick up a 3 mm pearl, skip the next three Fs, and sew through the following four Fs to exit the center F in the next stitch of round 3 **(b–c)**. Continue through the following three Fs in round 4 **(c–d)**.

[8] Repeat step 7 to complete the round, but in the last repeat, do not sew through the last three Fs. Your thread should be exiting the center F in a stitch from round 3. Notice that the 3 mm pearls in this round sit near the front of the netted openings, just below the As added previously.

[9] Pick up two Fs, a 4 mm pearl, and two Fs, and sew through the center F in the next stitch of round 3 **(photo a)**. Repeat this stitch to complete the round. Notice that the 4 mm and 3 mm pearls occupy the same netted openings, but that the 4 mms sit toward the back. Continue through the first two Fs, 4 mm pearl, and F added in this step.

[10] Pick up an F, a color B 3 mm bicone crystal, and an F. Sew through the F right before the next 4 mm pearl, and continue through the 4 mm pearl **(photo b)**.

[11] Pick up seven Fs, and sew through the same pearl your thread is exiting in the same direction to form a loop. Continue through the next F **(photo c)**.

[12] Repeat steps 10 and 11 to complete the round, and continue through the first F, B, and F added in step 10.

[13] Sew through the first four Fs in the loop around the next pearl to exit the center F in the loop. Pick up three Fs, and sew through the same F your thread is exiting in the same direction to form a picot **(photo d)**. Continue through the next three Fs, and then sew through the beadwork to exit the center F in the next loop. Repeat this stitch five times, leaving one loop without a picot.

[14] Sew through the beadwork to exit the second F in the unembellished loop. Pick up eight Fs, skip three Fs in the loop, and sew through the next two Fs **(figure 3)**. End the working thread and tail (Basics).

[15] Add 16 in. (41 cm) of thread (Basics) to the beadwork, and exit the B opposite the loop added in the previous step. Pick up two Fs, a color C 11º seed bead, a B, an 11 x 8 mm pear-shaped pearl, and three Fs. Sew back through the pear-shaped pearl, B, C, and two Fs. Continue through the B your thread exited at the start of this step in the same direction. Retrace the thread path through the pearl dangle, and end the thread.

Spiral rope

[1] On a comfortable length of thread, pick up four Cs, two color G 15º seed beads, a color D 11º seed bead, and two

DESIGN NOTES:

- Nymo D is recommended for the pendant portion of this project; Fireline may not produce the same results. If desired, you can switch to Fireline for the spiral rope and bail.
- Don't have all the right beads in your stash? You can substitute 11º seed beads for the hex-cuts in round 6 of the pendant. You can also substitute 8º seed beads for the 3 mm pearls and hex-cuts in the spiral rope.
- The 21 mm crystal drop has a hole in it that will be covered up by the beadwork.

The back of this pendant is as pretty as the front.

Gs. Sew through the four Cs again to form a loop, leaving an 8-in. (20 cm) tail **(figure 4)**. Move the loop to the left of the Cs.

[2] Pick up a C, two Gs, a D, and two Gs, and sew through the previous three Cs and the new C added in this step **(figure 5)**. Move the loop to the left; each new loop will rest on top of the previous loop.

[3] Repeat step 2 for 5½ in. (14 cm), ending and adding thread as needed. For the next 7 in. (18 cm), substitute an 11º hex-cut for each D. Work the last 5½ in. (14 cm) as before. Leave approximately 1–1½ in. (2.5–3.8 cm) for the clasp, and decrease or increase the 7-in. (18 cm) section to make the necklace shorter or longer.

[4] Pick up a bead cap, 8–10 color E 15º seed beads, and half of the clasp. Sew back through the bead cap and into the beadwork of the rope. Retrace the thread path of the clasp connection, and end the working thread. Repeat this step with the tail at the other end of the necklace.

Bail

[1] On 40 in. (1 m) of thread, attach a stop bead (Basics), leaving a 6-in. (15 cm) tail. Pick up 10 Es, and work in flat even-count peyote stitch (Basics) until you have a total of 28 rows. The peyote strip should fit snugly around the center section of your necklace. Add or remove rows if necessary. Center the strip on the necklace, remove the stop bead, and zip up (Basics) the end rows to form a tube. End the tail but not the working thread.

[2] Sew through the peyote tube to exit the second E from the edge on the bottom side of the tube. Pick up four Es, and sew through the center two Fs in the eight-bead loop at the top of the pendant. Pick up four Es, skip two Es in the same row of the peyote strip, and sew through the next E **(figure 6)**. Retrace the thread path of the pendant connection, and end the thread. ●

Victorian swagger

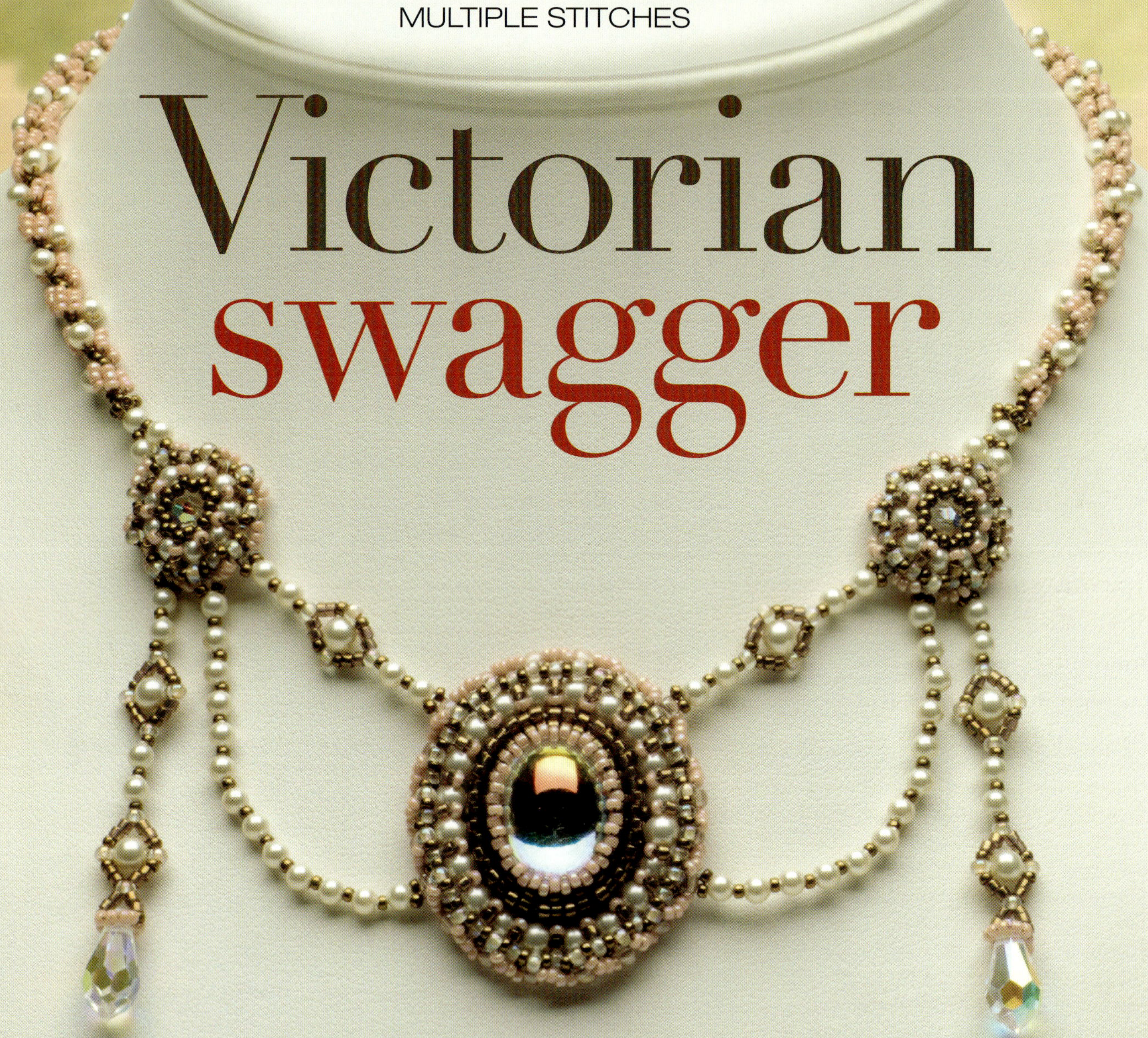

Suspend a bezeled cabochon from pearly swags for a demure and elegant necklace.

designed by **Sandra Lamoureux**

A toggle-style clasp mimics the small medallions.

a

b

c

d

Use basic bead weaving plus three classic techniques (peyote stitch, crossweave, and spiral rope) to showcase a favorite cabochon with a unique two-part bezel. Mirror the design with smaller medallions and a matching clasp.

stepby**step**

Large medallion

Bezeled cabochon

[1] On 1½ yd. (1.4 m) of thread, pick up 40 11º cylinder beads. Sew through all the beads again to form a ring, leaving a 12-in. (30 cm) tail. These beads will shift to form rounds 1 and 2 as the next round is added.

[2] Work the next rounds as follows. Step up after each round unless directed otherwise:

Rounds 3 and 4: Work two rounds of tubular peyote stitch (Basics) using cylinders and an even tension.

Rounds 5 and 6: Work two rounds of peyote using color B 15º seed beads and a firm tension so the beadwork cups.

Round 7: Sew through the beadwork to exit a cylinder in round 2 **(photo a)**. Using cylinders, work a round of peyote off of the beads in round 2. The new beads will sit on top of the beads in round 1. Do not step up at the end of the round **(photo b)**.

Round 8: Sew through the adjacent cylinder in round 3 **(photo c)**. Using cylinders, work a round of peyote off of the beads in round 3 **(photo d)**.

Rounds 9 and 10: Place the cabochon face down in the bezel, and sew through

DESIGN NOTE:
When you make the second spiral rope, push the loops of Bs to the right of the As to make a mirror image of the first rope.

MATERIALS

pink/white necklace
17 in. (43 cm)

- **1** 13 x 18 mm cabochon (crystal glass; www.dreamtimecreations.com)
- **2** 5.5 x 13 mm top-drilled drops (Swarovski, crystal AB)
- **1** 6 mm round crystal (Swarovski, crystal AB)
- **2** 4 mm round crystals (Swarovski, crystal AB)
- **26** 4 mm glass pearls (white)
- **128** 3 mm glass pearls (white)
- 1 g 8º seed beads (Toho 169, transparent rainbow rosaline)
- 2 g 11º cylinder beads (Miyuki DB0022, metallic bronze)
- 1 g 11º seed beads in each of **2** colors: C (Miyuki 457L, light metallic bronze), D (Toho 169, transparent rainbow rosaline)
- 5–6 g 15º seed beads in each of **2** colors: A (Miyuki 457L, light metallic bronze), B (Miyuki 596, opaque tea rose luster)
- Fireline 4 lb. test
- beading needles, #12

purple/gold necklace (p. 230)
colors:

- 13 x 18 mm glass cabochon (amethyst opal; www.artbeads.com)
- 5.5 x 13 mm top-drilled drops (Swarovski, tanzanite)
- 6 mm round crystal (Swarovski, light smoked topaz)
- 4 mm round crystals (Swarovski, light smoked topaz)
- 4 mm glass pearls (antique gold)
- 3 mm glass pearls (antique gold)
- 8º seed beads (Toho 26, silver-lined amethyst)
- 11º cylinder beads (Miyuki DB0023, metallic light bronze iris)
- 11º seed beads
  color C (Miyuki 457L, metallic light bronze)
  color D (Toho 26C, silver-lined amethyst)
- 15º seed beads
  color A (Miyuki 457L, metallic light bronze)
  color B (Toho 26C, silver-lined amethyst)

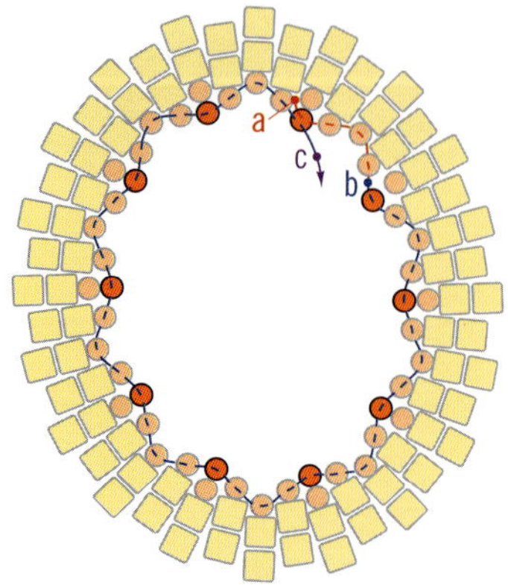

FIGURE 1

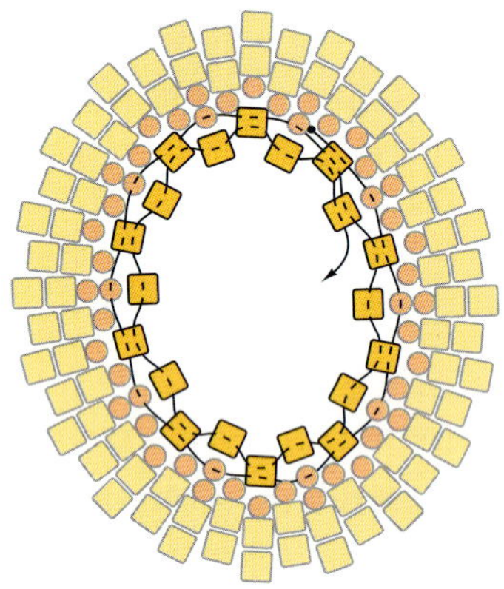

FIGURE 2

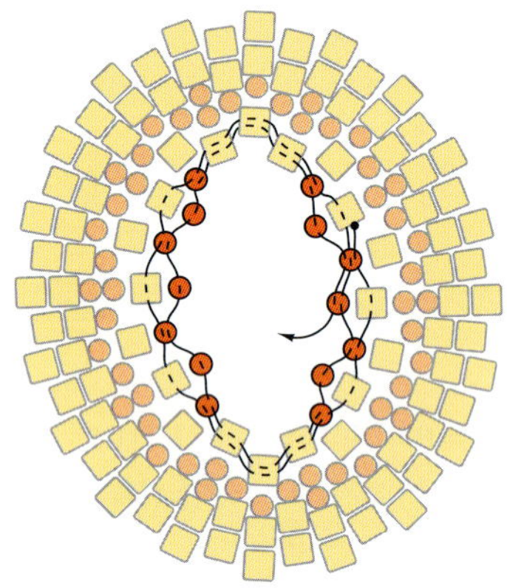

FIGURE 3

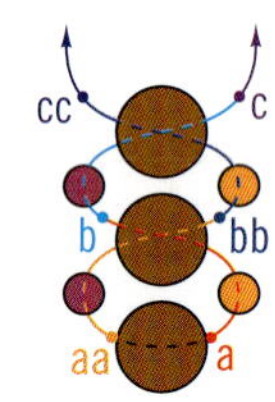

FIGURE 4

the beadwork to exit a cylinder in round 1 **(photo e)**. Work two rounds of peyote using color A 15º seed beads and a tight tension **(photo f)**.

[3] Rotate the beadwork so that there is an A in round 9 centered at each end of the cabochon. Sew through the beadwork to exit the A in round 10 that is just to the right of the top center A in round 9 **(figure 1, point a)**.

[4] Work the next rounds as follows. Step up after each round unless directed otherwise:

Round 11: Pick up an A, and sew through the next three As **(a–b)**. Repeat this stitch to complete the round **(b–c)**.

Rounds 12 and 13: Using cylinders and a tight tension, work two rounds of peyote off of the As picked up in the previous round **(figure 2)**.

Rounds 14 and 15: Referring to **figure 3**, work two rounds of peyote using As, but do not add an A between the cylinders at the ends of the cabochon. End the working thread (Basics).

[5] With the tail, sew through the beadwork to exit a cylinder in round 8. Using cylinders, work a round of peyote off of the beads in round 8. Retrace the thread path twice, keeping a very tight tension, and end the tail.

Embellishment ring

[1] Thread a needle on each end of 1½ yd. (1.4 m) of thread. With one needle, pick up a 4 mm pearl, and center the bead on the thread.

[2] With the right-hand needle, pick up a color C 11º seed bead and a 4 mm. With the left-hand needle, pick up a color D 11º seed bead, and cross through the last 4 mm picked up with the other needle **(figure 4, a–b** and **aa–bb)**. Repeat this stitch **(b–c** and **bb–cc)** until you have a total of 20 4 mms including the 4 mm from step 1.

[3] With the right-hand needle, pick up a C. With the left-hand needle, pick up a D. Cross both needles through the first 4 mm picked up in step 1 to form a ring.

[4] Place the bezeled cabochon face down on your work surface, and position the embellishment ring around the bezel so the Cs are nearest to the outside edge of the bezel. With the right-hand needle, sew through the adjacent C in the ring, and then sew through a cylinder in the outer round of the bezel. Repeat this stitch to attach the ring to the bezel, using a tight tension **(figure 5)**. Flip the bezeled cabochon face up, and sew through the next C.

[5] Pick up a B and a cylinder, and sew through the corresponding D along the outside edge of the ring **(figure 6, a–b)**. Sew back through the cylinder and the

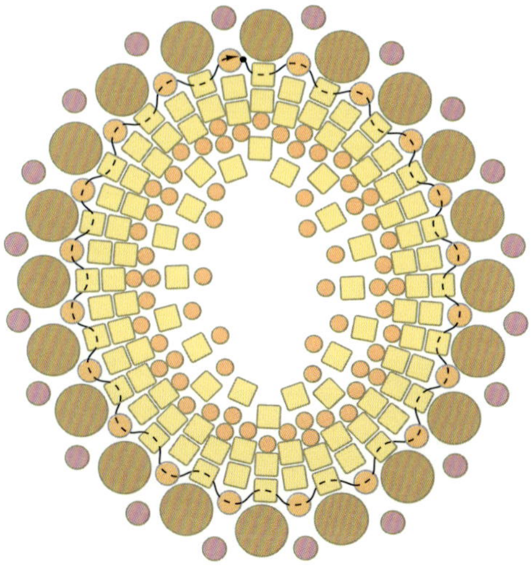

FIGURE 5

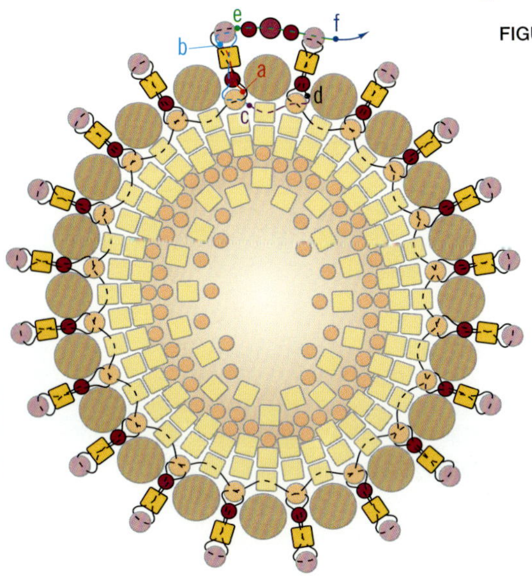

FIGURE 6

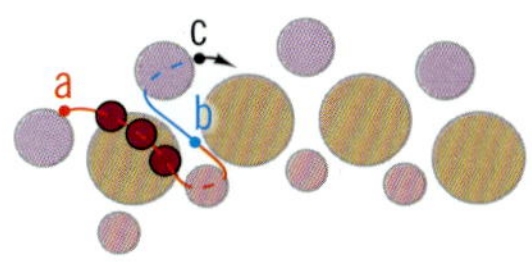

FIGURE 7

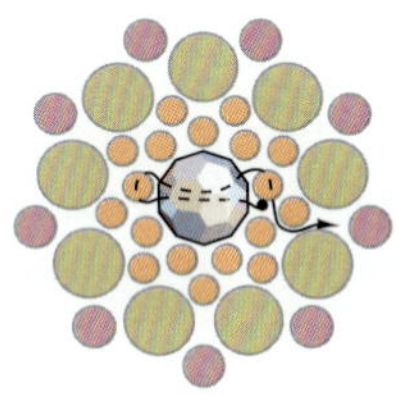

FIGURE 8

B, and continue through the C your thread exited at the start of this step **(b–c)**, the adjacent cylinder, and the following C **(c–d)**. Repeat this stitch to complete the round, and step up through the first B, cylinder, and D **(d–e)**.

[6] Pick up a B, a D, and a B, and sew through the next D along the outside edge of the medallion **(e–f)**. Repeat this stitch to complete the round. Retrace the thread path with a tight tension, and end this thread.

[7] Place the bezeled cabochon face down on your work surface. With the other needle exiting a 4 mm, sew through the nearest D. Pick up an A, an 8º seed bead, and an A, and sew through the next D. Repeat this stitch to complete the round, keeping a tight tension. Retrace the thread path.

[8] Flip the bezeled cabochon face up. Your needle should be exiting an 8º along the outer edge **(figure 7, point a)**. Pick up three Bs, and sew through the next D added in step 6 **(a–b)** and the nearest 8º **(b–c)**. Snug up the beads. Repeat this stitch to complete the round. Retrace the thread path if necessary to snug up the beads, and end the thread.

Small medallions

[1] Thread a needle on each end of 1 yd. (.9 m) of thread, and center a 3 mm pearl on the thread.

[2] With the right-hand needle, pick up an A and a 3 mm. With the left-hand needle, pick up a D, and cross through the 3 mm picked up with the other needle. Repeat this stitch until you have a total of nine 3 mms, including the 3 mm from step 1.

[3] With the right-hand needle, pick up an A. With the left-hand needle, pick up a D. Cross both needles through the first 3 mm picked up in step 1 to form a ring. With the right-hand needle, step up through the first A. With the left-hand needle, step up through the first D. Note that these Ds sit between the pearls.

[4] With the right-hand needle, pick up an A, and sew through the next A. Repeat this stitch to complete the round, and exit an A that sits between two 3 mms.

[5] Pick up a 4 mm round crystal, and sew through the corresponding A on the opposite side of the ring. Sew back through the crystal and the A your thread exited at the start of this step **(figure 8)**. Retrace the thread path with a firm tension.

[6] Sew through the beadwork to exit the next A between two 3 mms.

[7] Pick up a B and a cylinder, and sew through the nearest D along the outside edge of the ring. Sew back through the cylinder and the B, and continue through the A your thread exited at the start of this step and the next two As. Repeat this stitch to complete the round using a firm tension. Step up through the first B, cylinder, and D.

[8] Pick up an A, a D, and an A, and sew through the next D. Repeat this stitch to complete the round, and end the thread. Note that the Ds added in this step are adjacent to the pearls.

[9] Place the medallion face down on your work surface. With the remaining thread exiting a D along the outside edge of the ring, pick up an A, a D, and an A, and sew through the next D that sits between the pearls. Repeat this stitch to complete the round using a firm tension. Step up through the first A and D picked up in this step. The Ds added in this step are adjacent to the Ds added in step 8.

[10] Pick up three Bs, and sew through the next D picked up in step 8. Continue through the adjacent D picked up in step 9. Snug up the beads so the thread slides between the Ds. Repeat this stitch to complete the round, and end the thread.

[11] Make another small medallion.

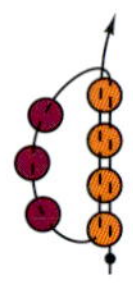

FIGURE 9

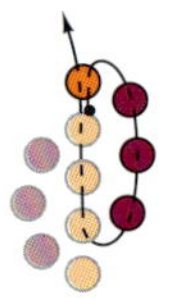

FIGURE 10

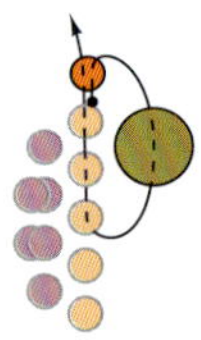

FIGURE 11

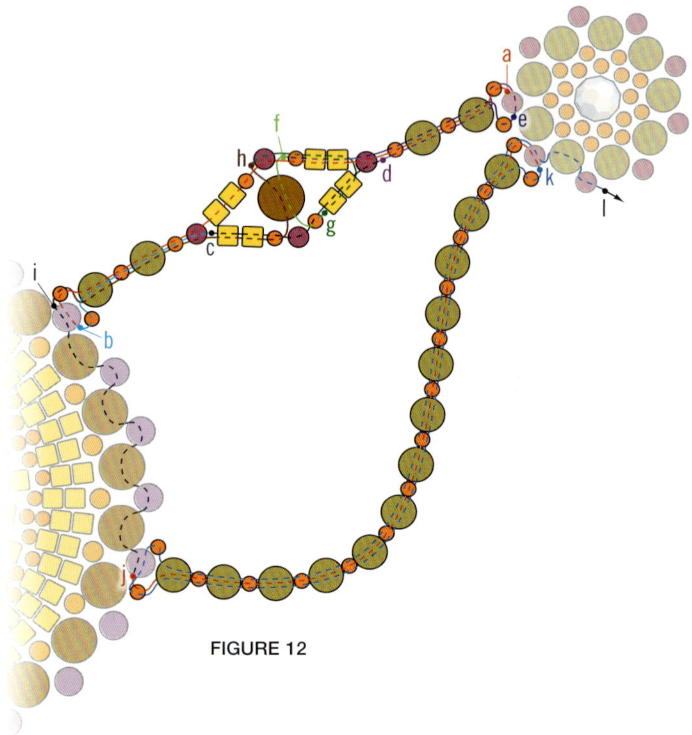

FIGURE 12

Clasp loop

Work as in steps 1–10 of "Small medallions" with the following changes:

- In step 2, work the repeat until you have a total of 11 pearls.
- Skip step 5.

Spiral ropes

[1] On a comfortable length of thread, pick up four As and three Bs, leaving a 6-in. (15 cm) tail. Sew through the As again, forming a loop of Bs around the As. Move the loop to the left of the As **(figure 9)**.

[2] Pick up an A and three Bs, and sew through the previous three As and the new A added in this stitch **(figure 10)**. Move the loop to the left; each new loop will rest on top of the previous loop. Repeat this step once more.

[3] Pick up an A and a 3 mm, and sew through the previous three As and the new A added in this stitch **(figure 11)**. Move the loop to the left.

[4] Ending and adding thread (Basics) as needed, continue in spiral rope working three stitches with an A and three Bs followed by one stitch with an A and a 3 mm until you have a total of 31 3 mms. Work three more stitches with an A and three Bs.

[5] With the thread exiting the last A, pick up an A, a 3 mm, and two As. Sew through a D along the edge of the clasp loop. Pick up an A, skip the previous A, and sew back through the next A, 3 mm, and a few As in the end of the rope. Retrace the thread path through the join several times, and end the working thread and tail.

[6] Make a second rope, but instead of attaching the clasp loop, pick up an A, a 3 mm, 10 As, a 6 mm round crystal, and three As. Sew back through the 6 mm and the next A, pick up nine As, and sew through the first A picked up in this step. Retrace the thread path through the join, and end the working thread and tail.

Swag #1

[1] On 4 yd. (3.7 m) of thread, attach a stop bead (Basics), leaving a 6-in. (15 cm) tail. Sew through a D along the outside edge of a small medallion.

[2] Pick up an A, a 3 mm, an A, a 3 mm, an A, a D, two cylinders, an A, a D, an A, two cylinders, a D, an A, a 3 mm, an A, a 3 mm, and an A.

[3] Place the large medallion face down on your work surface, and rotate it so that the long axis is in the vertical position. Sew through the third 8º from the top center with the needle pointing toward the bottom of the medallion **(figure 12, a–b)**.

[4] Pick up an A, skip the last A picked up in step 2, and sew through the next five beads **(b–c)**.

[5] Pick up two cylinders, an A, a D, an A, and two cylinders. Skip the next seven beads, and sew through the following D to make a diamond shape **(c–d)**. Continue through the next six beads to exit the D your thread exited at the start of step 2 **(d–e)**.

[6] Pick up an A, and sew through the first 3 mm picked up in step 2 and the next seven beads to exit an A **(e–f)**.

[7] Pick up a 4 mm pearl, and sew through the corresponding A on the other side of the diamond **(f–g)**. Continue through the next two cylinders on this side of the diamond and the two cylinders, the A, and the D on the other side of the diamond **(g–h)**. Sew through the 4 mm again, and

continue through the A and two cylinders on the other side of the diamond. Sew through the remaining beads leading up to the large medallion **(h–i)**.

Swag #2

[1] Sew through the beadwork to exit the seventh 8º from the top center of the large medallion **(point j)**. Pick up an alternating pattern of an A and a 3 mm 13 times, and then pick up an A. Sew through the D along the outside edge of the small medallion that is directly below the D to which swag #1 is attached **(j–k)**.
[2] Pick up an A, skip the last A picked up in the previous step, and retrace the thread path through the next 25 beads. Pick up an A, and sew through the 8º in the large medallion.
[3] Retrace the thread path of the swag, and exit the D along the outside edge of the small medallion that is directly below the D to which swag #2 is attached **(k–l)**.

Dangle

[1] Pick up an A, a 3 mm, an A, a 3 mm, an A, a D, two cylinders, an A, a D, an A, two cylinders, a D, an A, a 3 mm, an A, a 3 mm, an A, a D, two cylinders, an A, a D, an A, two cylinders, a D, two cylinders, an A, and a 5.5 x 13 mm drop.
[2] Pick up three Bs, and sew through the drop in the same direction to form a loop of beads around one side of the drop. Repeat this stitch to form a loop of beads around the other side.
[3] With your thread exiting the drop, pick up an A and two cylinders, and sew through the last D picked up in step 1. Pick up two cylinders, an A, a D, an A, and two cylinders. Skip the next seven beads, and sew through the following D to form a diamond shape. Continue through the next six beads to exit the next D.
[4] Pick up two cylinders, an A, a D, an A, and two cylinders. Skip the next seven beads, and sew through the following D to form a diamond shape. Continue through the next four beads. Pick up an A, and sew through the D in the small medallion.
[5] Add a 4 mm pearl to each of the diamond shapes as in step 7 of "Swag #1."
[6] Sew through the beadwork to exit the D in the small medallion. Continue through the edge beads to exit the third edge D from the D to which the dangle is attached.

Pearl connector

[1] Pick up an A, a 3 mm, an A, a 3 mm, and an A, and sew back through the last 3 mm. Pick up an A, a 3 mm, and an A, and sew through the D in the small medallion. Retrace the thread path, and then sew through the first five beads again.
[2] Sew through an end A in one of the ropes, pick up three As, and sew back through the end A to form a picot. Pick up three As, and sew back through the end A again to form another picot.
[3] Retrace the thread path through the connection several times. End the working thread, remove the stop bead, and end the tail.
[4] Work the steps for "Swag #1," "Swag #2," "Dangle," and "Pearl connector" to make a mirror image on the other side of the large medallion. •

Other Technique Projects

SHAPING / WRAPPING WIRE

Pomegranate pendant

Sink your teeth into wirework with this juicy accessory seeded with a handful of beads.

designed by **Irina Miech**

MATERIALS

pendant 1¾ in. (4.4 cm)

- **8** 4 mm round gemstone beads (garnet)
- 18 in. (46 cm) 18-gauge wire (silver)
- 22 in. (56 cm) 26-gauge wire (silver)
- silk ribbon (optional)
- bench block or anvil
- hammer
- chainnose pliers
- bail-making pliers or dowel
- roundnose pliers
- wire cutters

stepbystep

[1] Cut an 18-in. (46 cm) piece of 18-gauge wire. Using roundnose pliers and your fingers, shape the wire into a spiral that's 1¼ in. (3.2 cm) in diameter. Using chainnose pliers, create three zigzags for the "crown" of the pomegranate, which will be the bottom of the pendant. Continue spiraling the wire, stopping ½ in. (1.3 cm) from the top of the pendant. Refer to the **template** as needed.

[2] To make the bail: Wrap the wire around the outer arm of the spiral until you reach the top. Place a pair of bail-making pliers or a dowel at the top of the pendant, and wrap twice around it and the outer arm of the spiral. Wrap twice around just the outer arm of the spiral, and trim the excess wire **(photo a)**.

[3] Place the piece on a bench block or anvil. Hammer the spiral, but do not hammer the bail or wraps. Reshape the wire if necessary.

[4] Cut a 22-in. (56 cm) piece of 26-gauge wire. Leaving a short tail, begin wrapping the wire around the outer arm of the spiral next to the last two wraps from the bail. Continue wrapping around the spiral for ¾ in. (1.9 cm), leaving small gaps between the wraps **(photo b)**.

[5] String a 4 mm round bead, and wrap three times around the nearest inner arm of the spiral, leaving small gaps between the wraps as before. String a 4 mm bead, and wrap three times around the outer arm of the spiral **(photo c)**.

TEMPLATE

[6] Repeat step 5. Add one more bead, but this time wrap around the inner arm of the spiral for ⅜ in. (1 cm). Bring the wire to the next inner arm of the spiral, and wrap twice **(photo d)**.

[7] Add three more beads as before, but position them between the two inner arms of the spiral **(photo e)**. Continue wrapping around the inner arm of the spiral that eventually crosses the outer arm of the spiral. When you reach the crossing point, wrap around both arms until you reach the wraps from the bail. Trim both ends of the 26-gauge wire.

[8] String the pendant on a silk ribbon or as desired. ●

CURVE STITCHING WITH WIRE

Spiro playground

Create an elegant look with a technique inspired by a favorite children's toy — the Spirograph!

designed by **Lisa Niven Kelly**

As a kid, I loved playing with the Spirograph. Curve stitching (also known as string art when done with fiber) creates a similar look. Learn this complex-looking method using wire with my easy-to-create Spiro pendant, and then try your hand at creating something all your own.

stepbystep

Curve stitching technique

To avoid wasting supplies, practice this technique first with string instead of wire.

[1] Cut 4 ft. (1.2 m) of string. Hold a 2-in. (5 cm) tail against the back of the notched washer, and guide the string through the first notch to the left of the top hole. Bring the string clockwise across the top of the washer, skip the next eight notches, and guide the string into the next notch **(photo a)**.

[2] Bring the string behind the washer and up through the next notch to the right of the one where your string started at the top **(photo b)**.

[3] Continue wrapping the string around the washer in this manner, shifting one notch clockwise from the one used in the previous pass **(photos c and d)**. Shift the washer as needed, but be sure to continue holding the tail in place.

DESIGN OPTIONS

Make a Spiro pendant without the rivoli. This sample was done exactly as in the instructions but without the rivoli. When it was done, I realized the back was more interesting than the front, so I pulled the tail to the front and finished it on the other side.

Add a second layer of wraps! After finishing off the wire for the first layer, start another one, but skip only six notches instead of eight. This will position the second layer closer to the outer edge.

Use colored craft wire.

For an antiqued look, oxidize your washer and wire before wrapping, or submerge the entire piece in liver of sulfur after you're done. Do not tumble-polish finished pieces that contain rivolis (the tumbler ruins the coating). Instead, polish it with a Pro Polish Pad, or buff it with steel wool and a polishing cloth.

Try skipping a notch instead of going through every one. Or use two colors of wire together, as shown here. Make sure you try this with string first!

Mix wire and fiber for added color or texture.

Use a gold-filled washer and wire for a different color palette.

Punch another hole (before wrapping) if you want your pendant to hang from two jump rings or to add dangles.

MATERIALS

pendant 1 in. (2.5 cm)

- 1-in. (2.5 cm) sterling silver notched washer (www.beaducation.com)
- 18 mm rivoli
- 4½ ft. (1.3 m) 28-gauge sterling silver wire, dead soft
- 5 mm inside-diameter (ID) jump ring, 18-gauge
- **2** pairs of chainnose pliers
- nylon-jaw pliers (optional)
- wire cutters
- awl or embroidery needle (optional)
- 1.5 mm hole-punch pliers (optional)
- liver of sulfur (optional)
- Pro Polish Pad, or #0000 steel wool and a polishing cloth (optional)
- nail polish
- string (for practice)

TIPS

- To prevent the back coating on a rivoli from wearing off over time, apply a thick coat of nail polish to the back, either before or after wrapping.
- Make sure you pull tight on the wire as you wrap. This will keep the wire straight and give it the right amount of tension. If you need to undo any wraps, pull the wire off with a lot of tension to minimize kinks. Before resuming the wrapping process, straighten the wire by running it through nylon-jaw pliers.
- If you complete the circle of wraps and find that the top notch has only one wrap but the corresponding bottom notch has two, then you skipped a notch somewhere along the way and will need to undo your work and correct it.

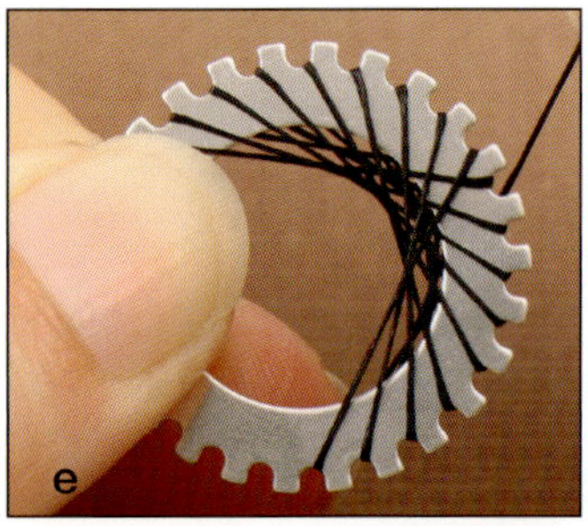
e

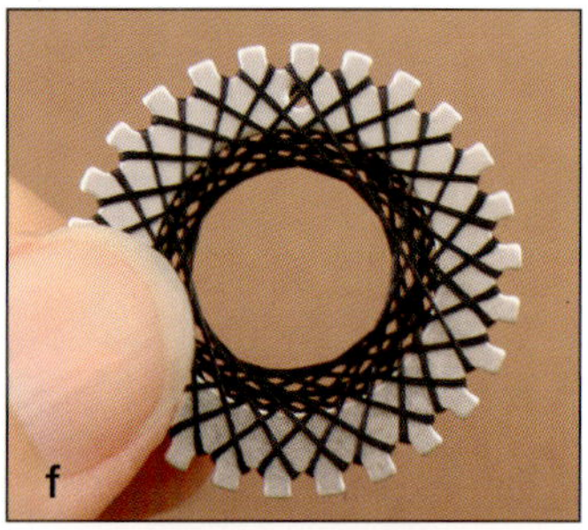
f

g

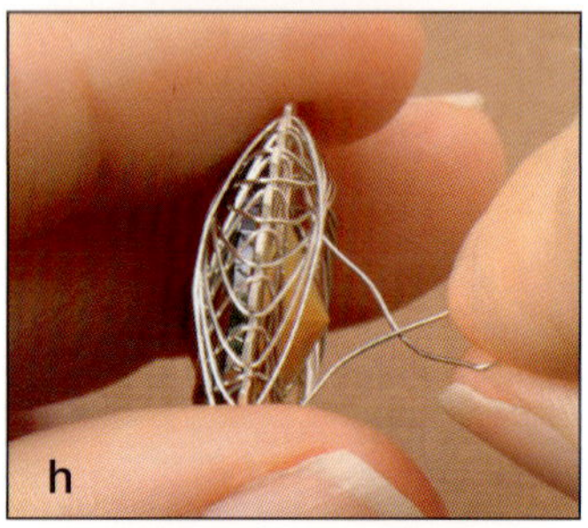
h

i

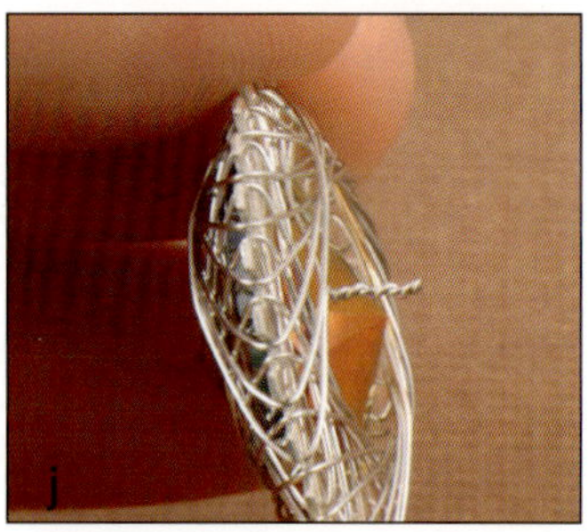
j

After the first nine passes, you'll see that the notch that the string comes up through already has another pass of string in it **(photo e)**. Don't worry — this is not a mistake. Just continue around clockwise until all the notches have two strings **(photo f)**. After the final pass, guide the working end across the back of the washer to meet up with the tail.

Spiro pendant

[1] Cut 4½ ft. (1.3 m) of 28-gauge wire. With your thumb, hold an 18 mm rivoli on the front of the notched washer; hold a 2-in. (5 cm) tail of wire against the back with your pointer finger.

[2] Pulling the wire taut to keep it straight, wrap it around the washer as in "Curve stitching technique" **(photo g)**. Pay attention to the position of the rivoli as you work to make sure it doesn't shift out of place.

[3] Cross the working wire and tail into an X shape on the back of the washer **(photo h)**. Holding the wires still, rotate the washer until the twisted wires tighten down to the back of the washer **(photo i)**.

[4] Trim the twisted wires to ¼ in. (6 mm) **(photo j)**. Grasp the tip of the twist with chainnose pliers, and make a simple loop **(photo k)**. Pinch the loop shut, and tuck it under the wraps **(photo l)**.

[5] Look at the front of your pendant, and if needed, adjust the wire wraps slightly with an awl or a thick needle. Or use your thumbnail to adjust the shape of the opening around the stone **(photo m)**.

[6] Open a 5 mm jump ring (Basics), and attach it to the hole in the washer. If the wire wraps cover the hole, push them aside a bit with the jump ring. String your pendant as desired.

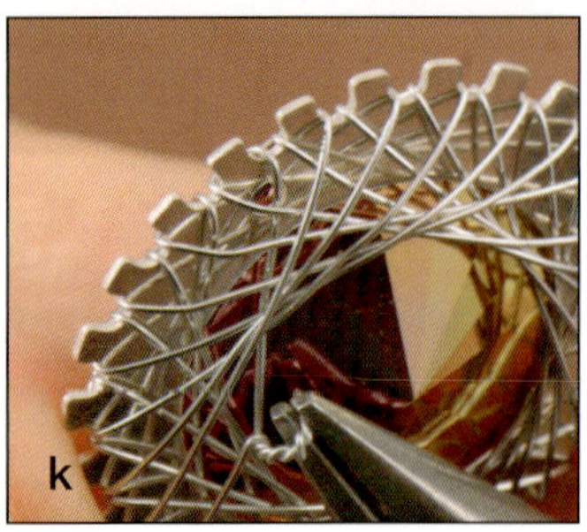
k

l

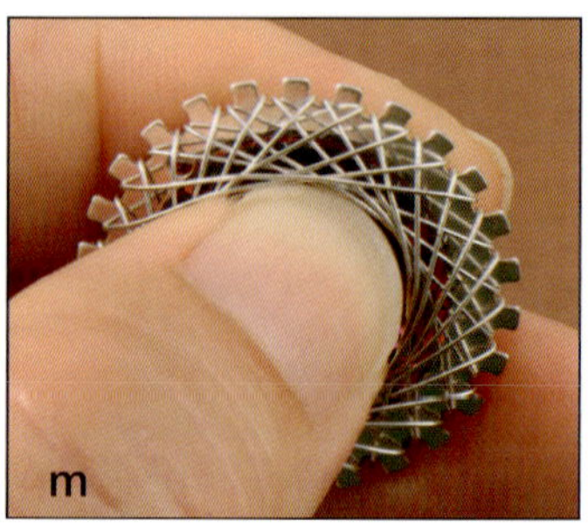
m

4-in-1 necklace

MATERIALS

necklace 23–42 in. (58 cm–1.1 m)

- **12** 4 x 8 mm rice-shaped mother-of-pearl beads
- **6** 6 mm crystal pearls (Swarovski, creamrose)
- **5** 6 mm round crystals (Preciosa, honey)
- **24** 4 mm fire-polished beads (Czech, antique rose luster; www.czechbeadsplus.com)
- pair of MultiStrand connectors (gold plate; http://mcleesjewelrydesign.com/connectors)
- 12 ft. (3.7 m) 24- or 26-gauge wire (bronze)
- 12 in. (30 cm) chain
- **6** 4 mm inside-diameter (ID) jump rings (brass)
- **42** 3⁄32-in. ID jump rings (brass)
- **2** pairs of chainnose, flatnose, and/or bentnose pliers
- roundnose pliers
- wire cutters

DESIGN NOTE:
For a look reminiscent of *Downton Abbey*, use only pearls for the bead units.

Use MultiStrand connectors to make a necklace that converts from one, two, three, or four strands with ease!

designed by **Julia Gerlach**

stepbystep

[1] Cut a 3-in. (7.6 cm) piece of 24- or 26-gauge wire, and make a wrapped loop (Basics) at one end. String a 4 mm fire-polished bead, and make another wrapped loop. Set this bead unit aside.

[2] Repeat step 1 with all of the 4 mms, 6 mm pearls, 6 mm crystals, and 4 x 8 mm mother-of pearl (MOP) beads. You should have a total of 47 bead units.

[3] Open all the jump rings (Basics).

[4] Connect all the bead units in the following order using small (3⁄32 in.) jump rings:

Strand 1: 4 mm; 6 mm crystal; 4 mm; MOP; 4 mm; 6 mm pearl; 4 mm; MOP; 4 mm

Strand 2: MOP; 4 mm; 6 mm crystal; 4 mm; MOP; 4 mm; 6 mm pearl; 4 mm; MOP; 4 mm

Strand 3: MOP; 4 mm; 6 mm pearl; 4 mm; MOP

Strand 4: 4 mm; 6 mm crystal; 4 mm; MOP; 4 mm; 6 mm pearl; 4 mm

Strand 5: MOP; 4 mm; 6 mm crystal; 4 mm; MOP; 4 mm; 6 mm pearl; 4 mm; MOP; 4 mm; 6 mm crystal; 4 mm; MOP; 4 mm; 6 mm pearl; 4 mm

[5] Connect the individual strands (in order) into one long strand using large (4 mm) jump rings. The last bead unit attached on each strand should be linked to the first bead unit of the next strand. Attach a large jump ring to each end of the completed strand.

[6] Cut a 12-in. (30 cm) piece of chain. Using small jump rings, attach each end of the chain to a MultiStrand connector.

[7] Slide the large jump rings onto the connector hooks to make the desired necklace arrangement:

1-strand necklace: Attach one end of the strand to each connector.

2-strand necklace: Attach rings 1 and 6 to one connector, and ring 4 to the other.

3-strand necklace: Attach rings 1 and 4 to one connector, and rings 2 and 6 to the other.

4-strand necklace: Attach rings 1, 3, and 6 to one connector, and rings 2 and 5 to the other. ●

WRAPPED LOOPS

Charmed **by the sea** necklace

Combine a pastel palette of crystals and pearls with chain and charms for the perfect summer accessory.

designed by **Alison Jayne Layton**

DESIGN NOTES

- **Use a Chain Sta during "Assembly" to make it easier to attach the clusters and dangles to the shell chain.**
- **If desired, finish each end of the necklace with strung beads instead of the oval chain.**
- **If the chain you use for your chain clusters has links smaller than 4 mm, consider leaving an empty link between dangles.**

Dangles

Make dangles: On a head pin, string a 1.5 mm bead and a 4, 6, or 8 mm crystal or pearl. Make the first half of a wrapped loop (Basics). Repeat with the remaining crystals and pearls. Select three color A 6 mm pearls and six 8 mm round crystals. Complete the wraps on the pearls but not the crystals, and set these nine dangles aside to use in "Assembly."

Chain clusters

With the remaining dangles, make three identical chain clusters as follows:

- Cut a 2-in. (5 cm) piece of curb chain. Open a 6 mm jump ring (Basics), and attach it to an end link. Attach a color A 4 mm pearl dangle to the other end, and complete the wraps.
- Attach dangles to the 2-in. (5 cm) chain as follows, completing the wraps as you go. Work from the top of the chain to the bottom of the chain:
- 2nd link: Attach a color F 6 mm crystal to one side of the link and a color E 6 mm pearl to the other side.
- 3rd link: Attach a color K 8 mm rondelle to one side of the link and a color G 6 mm crystal to the other side.
- 4th link: Attach a color B 6 mm pearl and an 8 mm round to one side of the link and a color B 4 mm pearl and a color H 6 mm crystal to the other side.
- 5th link: Attach a color I 6 mm crystal to one side of the link.
- 6th link: Attach a color C 4 mm pearl and a color D 4 mm pearl to one side of the link and an 8 mm round to the other side.
- 7th link: Attach a color A 6 mm pearl to one side of the link and a color J 6 mm crystal to the other side.
- 8th link: Attach a color K 6 mm crystal to one side of the link and a color H 8 mm rondelle to the other side.
- The lower 1 in. (2.5 cm) of chain should be free of dangles, except for the 4 mm pearl attached to the bottom link.

Assembly

Open the jump ring at the top of a chain cluster, and string a color A pearl dangle that you set aside in "Dangles" on one side of the chain cluster and the starfish charm on the other side. Attach the jump ring to the center link of the shell chain. Attach an 8 mm crystal dangle to the next link on each side of the chain cluster. Working away from the center link, attach the following to each side of the shell chain:

- 5th link: Attach a chain cluster.
- 6th link: Attach an 8 mm crystal dangle.
- 7th link: Using a jump ring, attach a shell charm and a color A 6 mm pearl dangle.
- 8th link: Attach an 8 mm crystal dangle.
- Cut two 5-in. (13 cm) pieces of oval chain, making sure there is a large link at each end. Use a jump ring to attach an oval chain to each end of the shell chain. Use a jump ring to attach the lobster claw clasp to one end of the necklace. ●

MATERIALS

necklace 19 in. (48 cm)

- pewter shell charms (TierraCast)
  - **2** 24 mm spindle shells
  - **1** 18 mm starfish
- Swarovski crystals
  - **12** 8 mm rounds (crystal)
  - **3** 8 mm rondelles in each of **2** colors: H (golden shadow), K (chrysolite opal)
  - **3** 6 mm bicones in each of **6** colors: F (tanzanite), G (white opal), H (golden shadow), I (light amethyst), J (white opal Titan), K (chrysolite opal)
- Swarovski crystal pearls
  - **6** 6 mm, color A (white)
  - **3** 6 mm in each of **2** colors: B (bronze), E (gold)
  - **3** 4 mm in each of **4** colors: A (white), B (bronze), C (powder rose), D (light blue)
- **60** 1.5 mm silver-plated beads
- 10 mm lobster claw clasp
- **60** 1½-in. (3.8 cm) 24-gauge head pins
- **8** 6 mm outside-diameter jump rings
- chain (matte gold finish)
  - 7½ in. (19.1 cm) shell-fringe chain
  - 11 in. (28 cm) oval-link chain, 5 x 9 mm links
  - 6 in. (15 cm) curb chain, 4 mm links
- **2** pairs of chainnose, flatnose, and/or bentnose pliers
- roundnose pliers
- wire cutters

KNOTTING

Pearl vine bracelet

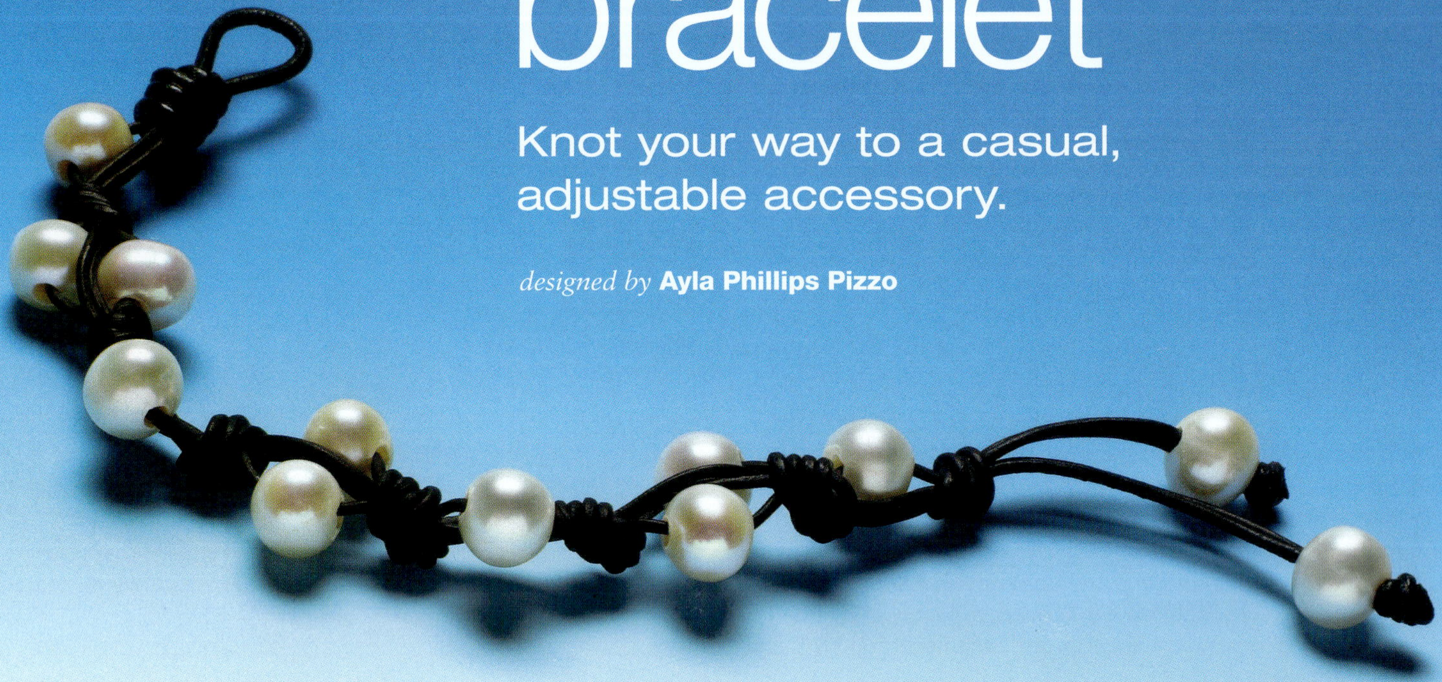

Knot your way to a casual, adjustable accessory.

designed by **Ayla Phillips Pizzo**

stepbystep

Toggle loop

[1] Cut four 18-in. (46 cm) pieces of 1 mm leather cord, and keep them nearby.

[2] Cut a 10-in. (25 cm) piece of 1.5 mm leather cord, and make a bend 7 in. (18 cm) from one end. Pinch the doubled cord to form a loop **(photo a)**.

[3] Loosely coil the longer end around the doubled cord three or four times, coiling toward the loop **(photo b)**. Feed the long end back through the coil. Insert the ends of the four 1 mm cords into the coil so that they are parallel with the long end of the 1.5 mm cord. Tighten the coil by pulling on the loop and the long end **(photo c)**.

[4] Test the size of the loop with an 8 mm pearl, which will serve as a toggle pearl. The pearl and a small knot must be able to pass snugly through the loop. To make the loop bigger, pull on the loop. To make the loop smaller, pull on the long end of the 1.5 mm cord.

[5] Trim both ends of the 1.5 mm cord and the short ends of the 1 mm cords close to the coil. You should now have four cords exiting the coil **(photo d)**. Apply glue to the coil, and let dry for two to three minutes.

Center pearls

[1] On your work surface, arrange the four cords so they are parallel. On an outer cord, string a pearl, and slide it close to the coil. Bring the four cords together after the pearl, and tie an overhand knot (Basics) with all of the cords, keeping them parallel and in order **(photo e)**. Aim to tie the knot no more than ¾ in. (1.9 cm) from the coil.

[2] On each outer cord, string a pearl, and slide them close to the previous knot. Bring the four cords together after the pearls, and tie another overhand knot about ¾ in. (1.9 cm) from the previous knot **(photo f)**.

[3] Repeat steps 1 and 2 until you have seven pearl sections. For the repeats of step 1, string the pearl on alternating outer cords.

Toggle pearls

[1] On two cords, string a pearl, and tie an overhand knot after the pearl at the desired "first length" for your adjustable bracelet **(photo g)**. On the remaining two cords, string a pearl, and tie an overhand knot at the desired second length. Trim the ends close to both knots. Apply glue to the knots, and let dry.

[2] Slide the toggle pearls away from the end knots, apply glue to the cords where the pearls were previously, and slide the pearls back over the glue. Let dry.

MATERIALS

bracelet 6½–8 in. (16.5–20 cm)

- **12** 8 mm large-hole pearls (cream)
- 10 in. (25 cm) 1.5 mm leather cord (black)
- 2 yd. (1.8 m) 1 mm leather cord (black)
- Super New Glue
- wire cutters

CLASP OPTIONS:

This double-toggle closure allows you to wear your bracelet at two different lengths! Slide both toggle pearls into the loop for the shorter version, or single out the longest pearl for more length.

Knot your average pearl necklace

Use two styles of knots to accent large-hole pearls strung on leather cord.

designed by **Ayla Phillips Pizzo**

You'll be surprised at how easy it is to tie beautiful (and intentional!) knots with 1.5 mm round leather cord. Coiled knots take on the look of accent beads while simple overhand knots are the perfect stoppers for pretty pearls.

stepbystep

Toggle loop

[1] Cut a 21-in. (53 cm) piece of leather cord, and make a bend 6½ in. (16.5 cm) from one end. Pinch the doubled cord to form a loop **(photo a)**.

[2] Loosely coil the short end around the doubled cord three or four times, coiling toward the loop **(photo b)**. Feed the short end back through the coil, and tighten the coil by pulling on the loop and the short end **(photo c)**.

[3] Test the size of the loop with a 10 mm pearl, which will serve as the toggle bead. The pearl and a small knot must be able to pass snugly through the loop. To make the loop bigger, pull on the loop. To make the loop smaller, pull on the short end.

[4] Trim the short end close to the coil, and apply glue to the coil. Let dry for two to three minutes.

Center pearl

[1] Make a bend in the cord 7½ in. (19.1 cm) from the other end, and pinch the doubled cord to form a very small (4–6 mm) loop.

[2] Loosely coil the short end around the long end three or four times, coiling away from the loop **(photo d)**. Feed the short end back through the coil, but do not tighten the coil.

[3] Cut a 3-in. (7.6 cm) piece of cord, and feed one end into the coil. Tighten the coil by pulling on the short end, causing the loop to disappear and become part of the coil **(photo e)**. Make sure that there is about 7½ in. (19.1 cm) of cord between the toggle loop coil and the coil just made. String a pearl on the 3-in. (7.6 cm) cord.

[4] Cut a 21-in. (53 cm) piece of cord, and make a bend 6½ in. (16.5 cm) from one end. Work as in step 2 to create a loose coil. Holding the pearl in place, feed the other end of the 3-in. (7.6 cm) cord into the coil. Tighten the coil. Trim the 3-in. (7.6 cm) cord close to the coils **(photo f)**, apply glue to both coils, and let dry.

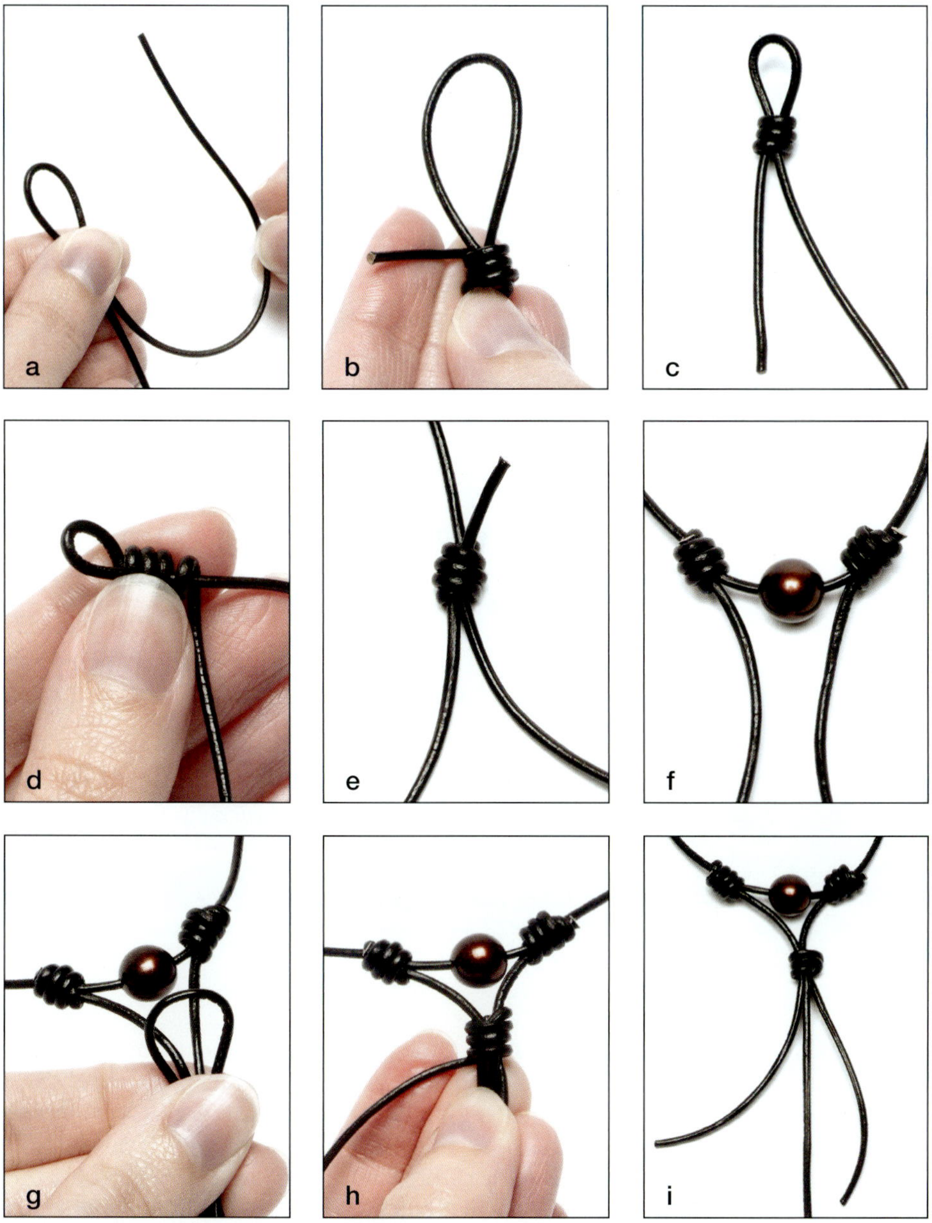

Pearl dangles

[1] Cut a 9-in. (23 cm) piece of cord, fold it in half, and hold it against the two cords that extend below the center pearl **(photo g)**.

[2] With one half of the 9-in. (23 cm) cord, loosely coil around the other three cords three or four times, coiling away from the fold **(photo h)**. Feed the short end back through the coil, and tighten the coil. Trim the short end close to the coil **(photo i)**, apply glue to the coil, and let dry.

[3] You should now have three cords that extend below the center pearl. On one cord, string a pearl, and tie an overhand knot (Basics) below it. Repeat with the remaining cords, adjusting the knots so that the pearls hang at the desired lengths. Trim any excess cord below the knots, apply glue to the knots, and let dry.

Toggle bead

[1] On the remaining cord opposite the toggle loop, string a pearl. Tie an overhand knot above the pearl so that the pearl will line up with the toggle loop. Trim any excess cord.

[2] Slide the pearl down the cord, and apply glue to where the pearl was positioned previously. Slide the pearl back in place. Apply glue to the knot as well, and let dry. ●

MATERIALS

necklace 17–18 in. (43–46 cm)*

- **5** 10 mm large-hole pearls (maroon)
- 1½ yd. (1.4 m) 1.5 mm leather cord (black)
- Super New Glue
- wire cutters

CHAIN MAIL

Lorelei links

Learn this designer's new Lorelei chain mail weave to make a two-tone, bead-studded bracelet.

designed by **Amy Leggett**

stepbystep

Getting started

[1] Close two 3⁄16-in. jump rings, and open all the remaining jump rings for the project (Basics).

[2] Slide an open 3⁄16-in. jump ring through the two closed jump rings **(photo a)**, and close this jump ring. Repeat this step to "double" the new jump ring so that you have two pairs of 3⁄16-in. jump rings.

[3] Secure a twist tie to the first pair of 3⁄16-in. jump rings to help stabilize your weave. Flatten the jump rings so that the two pairs lean in opposite directions, as in **photo b**. In each pair, notice that one jump ring lies on top of the other. This will be called the "top ring" in the pair. Also, wherever you have two adjacent pairs of 3⁄16-in. jump rings in this project, the pair on the left will be called the "first pair," and the pair on the right will be called the "second pair."

First pattern

[1] Slide a ¼-in. jump ring up through both rings in the second pair of 3⁄16-in. jump rings, and continue through the top ring in the first pair of 3⁄16-in. jump rings, exiting between the top and bottom rings **(photo c)**. String a 3º seed bead on the ¼-in. jump ring so that the bead is positioned along the bottom edge of your work, and close the new jump ring.

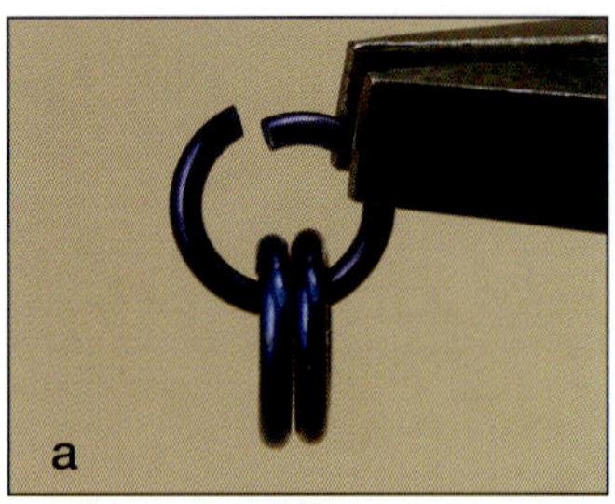
a

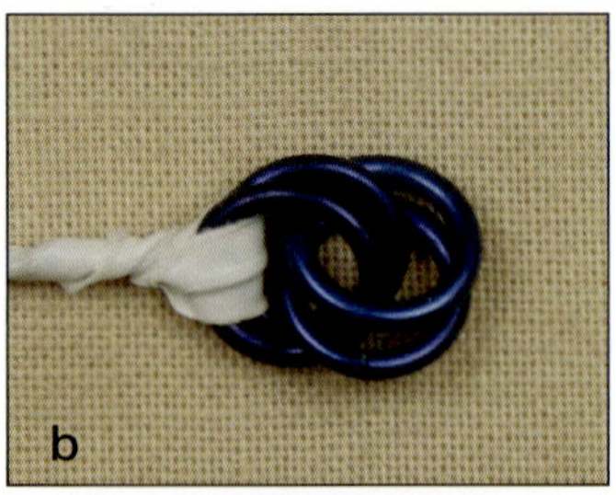
b

c

d

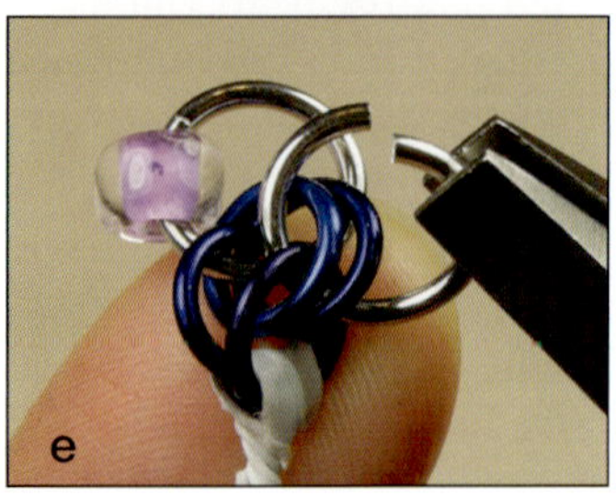
e

f

[2] Flip your work so that the bead is now positioned along the top edge. Do not let the lean of the 3/16-in. jump rings change **(photo d)**.
[3] Repeat step 1 to add another 1/4-in. jump ring **(photo e)** and seed bead **(photo f)**. You now have a pair of 1/4-in. jump rings. Once again notice that one 1/4-in. jump ring lies on top of the other. This will be called the "top ring" in the pair.
[4] Attach a 3/16-in. jump ring to the last two 1/4-in. jump rings, and double the new jump ring **(photo g)**. The new pair of 3/16-in. jump rings should lean in the same direction as the previous pair of 3/16-in. jump rings.
[5] Slide a 3/16-in. jump ring up through the top ring in the 1/4-in. jump ring pair, and continue through both rings in the last pair of 3/16-in. jump rings **(photo h)**. Close the new jump ring **(photo i)**.
[6] Flip your work, but do not let the lean of the 3/16-in. jump rings change.
[7] Repeat step 5 to add another 3/16-in. jump ring **(photo j)**. The new pair of 3/16-in. jump rings should lean in the opposite direction as the previous pair.

Second pattern

[1] Slide a 1/4-in. jump ring through the top ring in the first 3/16-in. jump ring pair, and continue through both rings in the second pair. String a seed bead on the 1/4-in. jump ring so that the bead is positioned along the top edge of your work, and close this jump ring **(photo k)**.
[2] Flip your work so that the seed bead is now positioned along the bottom edge. Do not let the lean of the 3/16-in. jump rings change **(photo l)**.
[3] Repeat step 1 to add another 1/4-in. jump ring and seed bead **(photo m)**.
[4] Attach a 3/16-in. jump ring to the last two 1/4-in. jump rings, and double the new jump ring **(photo n)**. The new pair of 3/16-in. jump rings should lean in the same direction as the previous pair of 3/16-in. jump rings.
[5] Slide a 3/16-in. jump ring through the top ring in the 1/4-in. jump ring pair, and continue through both rings in the 3/16-in. jump ring pair. Close the new jump ring **(photo o)**.
[6] Flip your work, but do not let the lean of the 3/16-in. jump rings change.

g

h

i

j

k

l

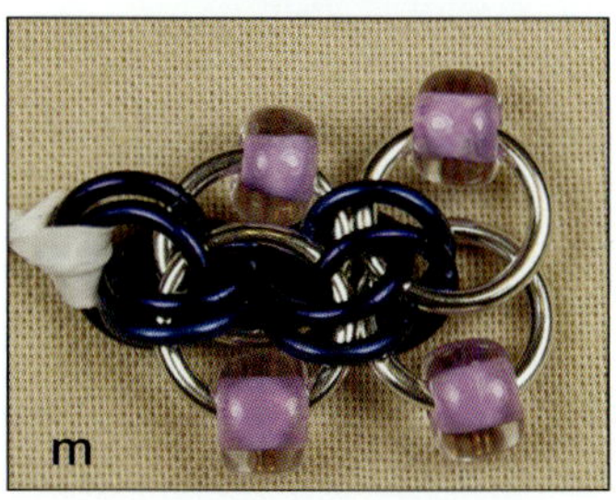
m

n

o

MATERIALS

Don't let chain mail lingo scare you! In the materials below, ID simply stands for inner diameter and SWG refers to Standard Wire Gauge (as opposed to AWG, or American Wire Gauge).

bracelet 8¼ in. (21 cm)

- **30** 3º seed beads (SB3759, lilac-lined crystal clear; www.fusionbeads.com)
- **30** 1/4-in. ID 18-gauge SWG jump rings (bright aluminum; ring L18 at www.bluebuddha boutique.com)
- **64** 3/16-in. ID 18-gauge SWG jump rings (anodized aluminum, blue; ring H18 at www.bluebuddhaboutique.com)
- **4** 1/8-in. ID 18-gauge SWG jump rings (bright aluminum; ring D18 at www.bluebuddha boutique.com), or any other small jump rings for attaching a clasp
- clasp
- **2** pairs of chainnose, flatnose, and/or bentnose pliers
- twist tie

DESIGN NOTES:

- The chain mail for this bracelet measures 6¾ in. (17.1 cm). Choose a clasp that adds the right amount of length for your wrist size. My clasp measures 1½ in. (3.8 cm) for a finished bracelet of 8¼ in. (21 cm).
- Avoid silver-lined seed beads for this project. The friction of the jump rings going through the beads will wear away the silver foil.
- Try this weave without the beads, with two colors of 3/16-in. jump rings (above, right), or with all bright aluminum rings (above, left)!

p

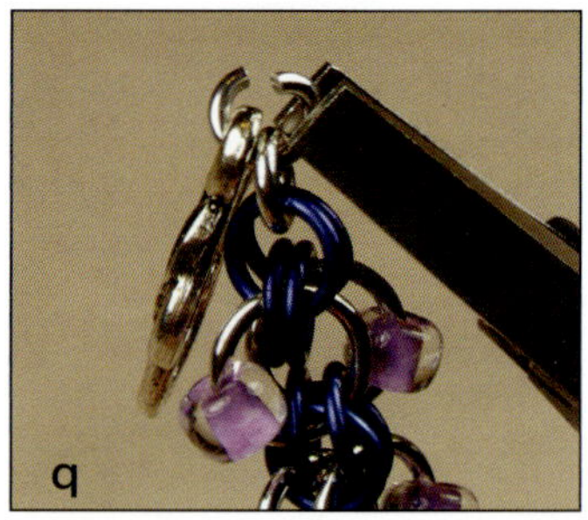

q

[7] Repeat step 5 to add another 3/16-in. jump ring **(photo p)**. The new pair of 3/16-in. jump rings should lean in the opposite direction as the previous pair.

Keep going!

Repeat the steps for "First pattern" and "Second pattern" until you have a total of 15 seed beads along each edge.

Clasp

[1] Slide a 1/8-in. jump ring through the last two 3/16-in. jump rings, and close the new jump ring. Slide another 1/8-in. jump ring through the previous 1/8-in. jump ring, string half of the clasp **(photo q)**, and close the new jump ring.

[2] Remove the twist tie, and repeat step 1 on the other end of the bracelet.

LEATHER / CHAIN

Plain chain no more!

The leather and chain craze has taken over! This adorable bracelet gets you started with leather and chain.

designed by **Becky Guzman** *with* **Jane Danley Cruz**

MATERIALS

bracelet 7 in. (18 cm)

- 15 in. (38 cm) 5.7 mm rolo chain
- 7 in. (18 cm) decorative chain
- 4 ft. (1.2 m) 1.5–2 mm leather cord
- 14 mm 2-strand slide clasp
- **4** 6 mm 16-gauge jump rings
- **2** 4 x 3 mm leather end caps (Vintaj)
- glue, such as Gorilla Super Glue Gel
- **2** pairs of chainnose, flatnose, and/or bentnose pliers
- wire cutters

Combining leather and chain is not only fashionable, it's fun! And don't stop at plain ol' chain — incorporate cup chain, decorative chain, charms, large-hole beads, metal beads, and focals for a trendy accessory with lots of curb appeal. It can be as easy as threading your shoelaces once you know the tricks of the trade. Read the following tips, and then try out your newfound knowledge with Becky's "Kinesis bracelet." P.S. These make great gifts!

Truths about leather

• Size matters. Because leather is a natural product, the diameter of leather cord can range in size by up to 0.3 mm. When you purchase a length of cord labeled 1.5 mm, be aware that it may range in actual diameter from 1.2 to 1.8 mm. This significant variation means that an unusually thick cord labeled 1.5 mm may be the same size (or larger) than an unusually thin cord labeled 2 mm. If you're planning to combine leather and chain, "try before you buy" is the motto for success: Make sure the cord can easily pass twice through the links in the chain.

• Measure twice, cut once. Once you've cut the leather cord, there's no way to make it longer. It's better to have too much cord than too little. Too much, and you can trim it to the correct size once you've woven your project. Too little, and you have to start over with a longer cord.

• Check to make sure the cord you're using doesn't have splices or isn't noticeably thicker or thinner in places. Remember, quality is queen!

• Ask the shop to cut the cord on an angle when they remove it from the spool (or do it yourself when you get home). This will make the leather much easier to string through the chain or beads.

Truths about chain

• There may be a 1–2 mm variation in chain link measurements, but however slight, this can make a huge difference if the leather cord you choose does not fit through the chain.

• When pairing decorative chain with rolo chain, make sure the links on each chain are similar in size. This rule also applies to using cup chain with rolo chain: Make sure the size of each cup is similar to the size of the links in the rolo chain, or choose a smaller cup chain and incorporate two cups per rolo link. Keep in mind you'll need about twice as much of the smaller cup chain since you'll be pushing the cups in the chain closer together.

• Rolo chain is available in a variety of sizes, which vary depending on the manufacturer. One manufacturer produces a 5.7 mm rolo chain, while another's comparable rolo chain measures 6 mm. Before you make a purchase, it's a good idea to place your decorative chain or cup chain side by side with the rolo chain and make sure your cord will pass through the links twice.

• Thoroughly examine the decorative chain or cup chain to make sure there are no obvious dangles or crystals missing or broken, and make sure the length you're purchasing is a continuous length rather than smaller pieces "patched" together.

Truths about combining leather and chain

Here's a chart to use as a rule of thumb when combining leather and chain. (Of course, keep in mind the size variables discussed above.)

CHAIN LINKS	LEATHER CORD DIAMETER
7 mm	2–2.5 mm
5.7 mm	1.5–2 mm
4.8 mm	1.5 mm (or a thicker 1 mm)
3.8 mm	1 mm (the thinner the better)

If you are struggling to get the cord through the links in the chain, here are five tips to try:

• Check to make sure the end of the cord is cut on an angle.

• Pull the cord through your hands to straighten it out. You can narrow the stringing end by stretching it slightly.

• Shake out the chain to loosen the links.

• Make sure your leather is properly positioned as you weave through the chain.

stepbystep

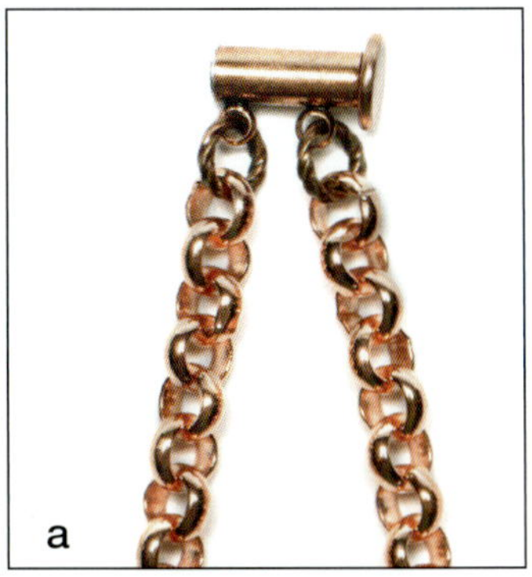
a

b

c

d

e

f

g

h

• Use chainnose, flatnose, or bentnose pliers to pull and nudge the leather through a particularly snug spot, being careful not to mar the surface of the cord.

Kinesis bracelet

[1] Cut two 7-in. (18 cm) pieces of rolo chain and one 7-in. (18 cm) piece of decorative chain.

[2] Open a 6 mm jump ring (Basics), and attach a loop of the clasp to the end link of a rolo chain. Repeat for the other loop of the clasp and chain (**photo a**).

[3] Cut 4 ft. (1.2 m) of 1.5–2 mm leather cord, and string it through a jump ring from step 2 so the cord exits between the two chains. Pick up an end link of the decorative chain, and string the other jump ring. The decorative chain will lie between the two rolo chains (**photo b**). Center the chains on the cord.

[4] With the right-hand cord, skip the next link in the nearest rolo chain, and push the cord through the following link, the nearest link in the decorative chain, and the corresponding link in the other rolo chain (**photo c**).

[5] Flip your work over, and pick up the cord that is now on the right-hand side. Work as in step 4, but do not go through the link in the decorative chain. This cord will lie behind the cord from the previous step (**photo d**). Flip your work back to the first side. This will be the front of your bracelet.

[6] Repeat steps 4 and 5, skipping every other link in each rolo chain for the desired length, ending with one link remaining on each of the rolo chains. Trim the chain if necessary. Adjust the decorative chain as you work so all the dangles are on the front, and snug up the cords so the edges of the skipped links in the rolo chain just touch each other on the back of your work (**photo e**). Keep a consistent tension so the cord fits snugly around the rolo chain and the edges of the bracelet are even.

[7] Open a jump ring, and attach the final link on one of the rolo chains to the corresponding loop of the clasp. Repeat for the remaining rolo chain and loop of the clasp (**photo f**). Test the fit, and remove links if necessary.

[8] Thread the right-hand cord through the nearest jump ring, the final link in the decorative chain, and the following jump ring. Flip the bracelet over, and repeat this step on the back, skipping the decorative chain (**photo g**).

[9] Trim one cord to within ¼ in. (6 mm) of the last jump ring. Apply a dab of glue to the end of the cord, and place a leather end cap over it (**photo h**). Repeat for the remaining cord. Allow the glue to dry completely. ●

Contributors

Sandie Bachand began beading five years ago under the care of gifted teachers in her area. She lives in north Georgia with her husband, who is a constant source of encouragement, and two kittens who are currently enamored with SuperDuos. Contact Sandie through Kalmbach Books.

Virginia Blakelock is a pioneer in modern beadwork and is part-owner of the online store Beadcats. Her book, *Those Bad, Bad Beads*, inspired many to take up beading. Visit www.beadcats.com, or contact her at funkyskunk@beadcats.com.

Jimmie Boatright is a retired public school educator who teaches her original designs at Beadjoux Bead Shop in Braselton, Ga. Visit www.beadjoux.com to see more of her designs or to purchase patterns. Contact her at dboatri931@aol.com.

Amelia Brock became a jewelry artist three years ago after meandering through a local bead store. She started Blue Magnolia Jewelry with her sister, Kim Myers, in Chandler, Ariz. Contact Amelia at bluemagnolia jewelry@gmail.com.

Carolyn Cave lives in Lacombe, Alberta, Canada, and loves creating and experimenting with new designs, bead colors, and textures. Her book, *Beautiful Designs with SuperDuos and Twin Beads*, is available from Kalmbach Books. Contact her via email, ladybeadledesigns@nucleus.com, or through her Facebook page, Lady Beadle Designs.

Svetlana Chernitsky has been beading for eight years and loves working with two-hole beads. Email her at lirigal@gmail.com, or visit www.lirigal.com and www.etsy.com/shop/lirigal.

Lorraine Coetzee of Cape Town, South Africa, has been beading since 2006. To see more of her work, visit artfire.com/ext/shop/studio/Trinity DesignerJewellery. Email her at trinitydj@tiscali.co.za.

Jane Danley Cruz is a former associate editor for *Bead&Button* magazine. She is currently working on her first book with co-author, Connie Whittaker. Contact Jane at jmdcruz262@gmail.com.

Phyllis Dintenfass designs, publishes, and teaches off-loom beadwork. Her finished jewelry has been exhibited in juried shows in this country and abroad. Visit her website, phylart.com, or contact her via e-mail at phylart@new.rr.com.

Anna Elizabeth Draeger is a well-known jewelry designer and the author of *Crystal Brilliance, Crystal Play,* and *Great Designs for Shaped Beads*. Visit originaldesignsbyanna.squarespace.com.

Abigail Engelking has been making jewelry for 17 years, starting with wirework and gemstones and expanding into silversmithing. Her work has also been featured in fashion shows. Contact her at abigail33@telus.net, or visit www.craftsy.com/user/2141178/pattern-store, www.abigailsbeaddesign.etsy.com, and www.facebook.com/abigail.engelking to see her work.

Josie Fabre has been beading for more than 10 years. She became hooked on peyote stitch and designing patterns after she made several squares for the 2012 Bead-It-Forward project. She is a full-time scientist and mother, but beads every chance she gets. She is inspired by nature, art, and architecture. Contact her at jpfabre@bellsouth.net or www.josie.etsy.com.

Diane Fitzgerald is the author of 12 beading books, the most recent being *Shaped Beadwork and Beyond*. She teaches internationally and sells kits and instructions online at www.dianefitzgerald.com.

Julia Gerlach is the editor of *Bead&Button* magazine. Contact her at jgerlach@beadandbutton.com.

Graehound is a mixed-media studio artist working toward her MFA who enjoys creating intricate beadwork when not illustrating. Contact her at autobot@graehound.com or visit her website, www.graehound.com.

Becky Guzman, along with her family, runs Diakonos Designs, a fun and creative bead store that features oodles of leather, chain, and unique beads. She lives in Stoughton, Wis., and she also creates clay beads. Contact Becky at becky@diakonosdesigns.com or via www.diakonosdesigns.com.

Judy Henegar teaches her original designs at My Bead Gallery in Englewood, Fla. She is a charter member and VP of the Gulf Coast Bead Society. Contact Judy at djh2934@aol.com.

Pamela Jensen is a bead artist from Portland, Oregon. Contact Pamela at pamladynw@yahoo.com.

Rose Kasallis has been beading for more than three years. She enjoys the colors and shapes of beads and the puzzle of how to make them fit together. Email her at embellishedbyrose@yahoo.com, or visit www.etsy.com/people/embellishedbyrose.

Lisa Niven Kelly is the founder and CEO of Beaducation.com. Lisa was named one of the country's Top 10 Teachers as voted by the readers and editors of *Bead&Button* magazine. Email her at lisa@beaducation.com.

Alice Kharon has been beading for 11 years and is an instructor at the Chicago Jewelry School, specializing in in designing contemporary modern wearable jewelry. Contact her at alice.kharon@yahoo.com.

Yvonne King started her bead addiction in 2011 along with her sister-in-law, and the following year she began designing bead-weaving patterns. She especially loves right-angle weave and working with seed beads. To see more of her work, visit http://my-amari.com.

Isabella Lam owns a bead store in Israel with her husband. Email her at scarlet@actcom.co.il, or visit www.etsy.com/shop/bead4me, www.etsy.com/shop/isabellalam, or www.isabellalam.com.

Sandra Lamoureux has been beading since 2009 and has been designing since 2010. Her designs are featured at Beadiful in Cumming, Ga., where she also teaches classes. Contact her via email at sjlamoureux@mindspring.com.

Cathy Lampole owns the bead shop That Bead Lady in Newmarket, Ontario, Canada. For store information, visit www.thatbeadlady.com.

Alison Jayne Layton has been designing and making jewelry for over three decades, working primarily with Swarovski crystals. She frequently draws her inspiration from the shorelines of her beloved Scotland. Connect with her via email at stonescapesjewellery@rogers.com, via Facebook (Stonescapes Studio), or check her out on Pinterest.

Amy Leggett is a self-taught bead weaver and chain mailler who has been creating jewelry for more than 20 years. She has her own business, themetalmark.com. You can also find her at facebook.com/themetalmark or email her at amy@themetalmark.com.

Un-Roen Manarata of Belgium is a Swarovski Elements Ambassador, designer, teacher, writer, author, illustrator, and metal clay instructor. Contact her at un-roen@elfen.be or via her website, www.elfen.be.

Michelle McEnroe has been beading for more than five years and finds it the most fulfilling of all her crafts. Contact her at glasscat@optionline.net, or visit www.etsy.com/shop/mcenroemoments.

Lesha McPhearson is a bead designer specializing in ethnic, geometric, abstract, tessellated, and repeat designs for loom and peyote bead patterns. You may contact her at beadholden@msn.com or see her patterns at www.artfire.com/ext/shop/studio/beadholdendesigns.

Sarah Meadows is a writer and jewelry maker living in the Midwest. Email her at SarahSequins@yahoo.com or visit her website, SaturdaySequins.com.

Irina Miech owns Eclectica, a bead store in Brookfield, Wis., and is the author of several books, including *Beautiful Wire Jewelry for Beaders*. Contact her at 262-641-0910 or info@eclecticabeads.com. You can also visit her store website, www.eclecticabeads.com.

Sonoko Nozue started bead weaving in 1993. She was the first teacher from Japan to teach at the Bead&Button Show. Contact her in care of Kalmbach Books.

Ayla Phillips Pizzo fell in love with beads after randomly picking up a beading kit to break the boredom of an Illinois winter. She now owns her own store, Ayla's Originals in Evanston, Illinois, and her Ayla's Own Jewelry line has received national attention. Contact her at info@aylasoriginals.com, or visit www.aylasoriginals.com.

Nina Raizel has been beading since she was 14 years old and enjoys learning new techniques. She also works in metals, and has a jewelry studio in Seattle, Wash. Email her at nina.raizel@gmail.com, or visit www.nina-raizel.com.

Anu Rao is a dentist and mother of three girls and has been beading for a few years. Contact her at anu7rao@yahoo.com.

Maggie Roschyk is a frequent contributor to *Bead&Button* and the author of *Artistic Seed Bead Jewelry* from Kalmbach Books. Contact Maggie at blueroses@wi.rr.com.

Dana Rudolph is a designer and the owner of My Bead Gallery in Englewood, Fla. Contact her at mybeadgallery@gmail.com, or visit www.mybeadgallery.com to see more of Dana's work.

Marla Salezze is a jewelry designer and teacher of bead weaving. She is on the 2015 Nunn Design Innovations Team and a member of the Bead Society of Eastern Pennsylvania. Contact her and purchase kits for her projects at www.beadedbymarla.com.

Kerrie Slade is a beadwork designer living in Mansfield, England. She has had her work published in numerous books and magazines around the world. Kerrie now teaches internationally and sells patterns through her website, www.kerrieslade.co.uk.

Lynne Soto teaches bead jewelry making to individuals and groups through her business "Lessons with Lynne." She also teaches her original designs at the Bead&Button Show. Contact her via email at mscalto2@att.net.

When **Wendy Speare** isn't working on her own designs, she is sharing her expertise and love of beading with the customers at Poppyfield Bead Company. She can be reached at beadfingers3@gmail.com.

Nichole Starman has been designing Czech glass bead shapes and colors since 2000. Her insight and knowledge of the glass bead market has led to some of the biggest revolutions in the beading world, including the CzechMates 2-Hole Beading System. Nichole's designs show the textural and sculptural possibilities of the CzechMates, particularly in combination with TOHO seed beads. Contact Nichole at nichole@starmanbeads.com.

Kathleen Stauber is a science teacher by day and a beader by night. Her inspiration for her featured design was Rachel Nelson-Smith's "Sea star bangle," which she saw in Rachel's book, *Seed Bead Fusion*. Contact Kathleen via email at klstauber@yahoo.com.

Amee K. Sweet-McNamara is a fiber artist and the author of *Soutache & Bead Embroidery*, available from Kalmbach Books. To contact Amee or to see more of her work, visit www.ameerunswithscissors.com.

Alexandra Sydorenko has been beading since her childhood in Ukraine. Currently living in New Jersey, she teaches classes for the local bead stores and bead society, while getting published in multiple magazines internationally. Contact her at oleksandrasydorenko@gmail.com.

Ruth Vickery started beading more than 10 years ago and recently began designing her own beadwork. Her favorite stitch is St. Petersburg chain, and she loves vintage beads and recycling jewelry. Contact her at vickery.ruth@gmail.com.

Sharon Wagner is a beadwork designer and instructor in Sterling Heights, Mich. Sharon is known for her designs using Crystaletts buttons. Contact her at sharonwagner@comcast.net or via www.yadasibeads.com, or visit Yadasibeads on Etsy.

Agnieszka Watts is a beadwork artist, instructor, and Illinois artisan. She loves seed beads because of the versality of this medium. Agnieszka is a member of the Starman Trendsetters designer team for 2014–2015 and helped organize one of the first professional seed bead workshops in Poland in the Fall of 2015. Contact her at me7asia@yahoo.pl and visit her website, Agnesse Artistry by Agnieszka Watts.

Connie Whittaker is an associate editor for *Bead&Button* magazine. Contact her at cwhittaker@kalmbach.com.

Eleanna Zegkinoglou lives in Athens, Greece, with her husband and young daughter, and works as a pianist and music educator. She started beading more than seven years ago and loves the endless possibilities of bead weaving. She was the winner of the Grand Prize Bronze Medal for 2012 of the Fire Mountain Gems and Beads Contest for Swarovski Elements. Contact her at eleannazegkinoglou@yahoo.com.

Index